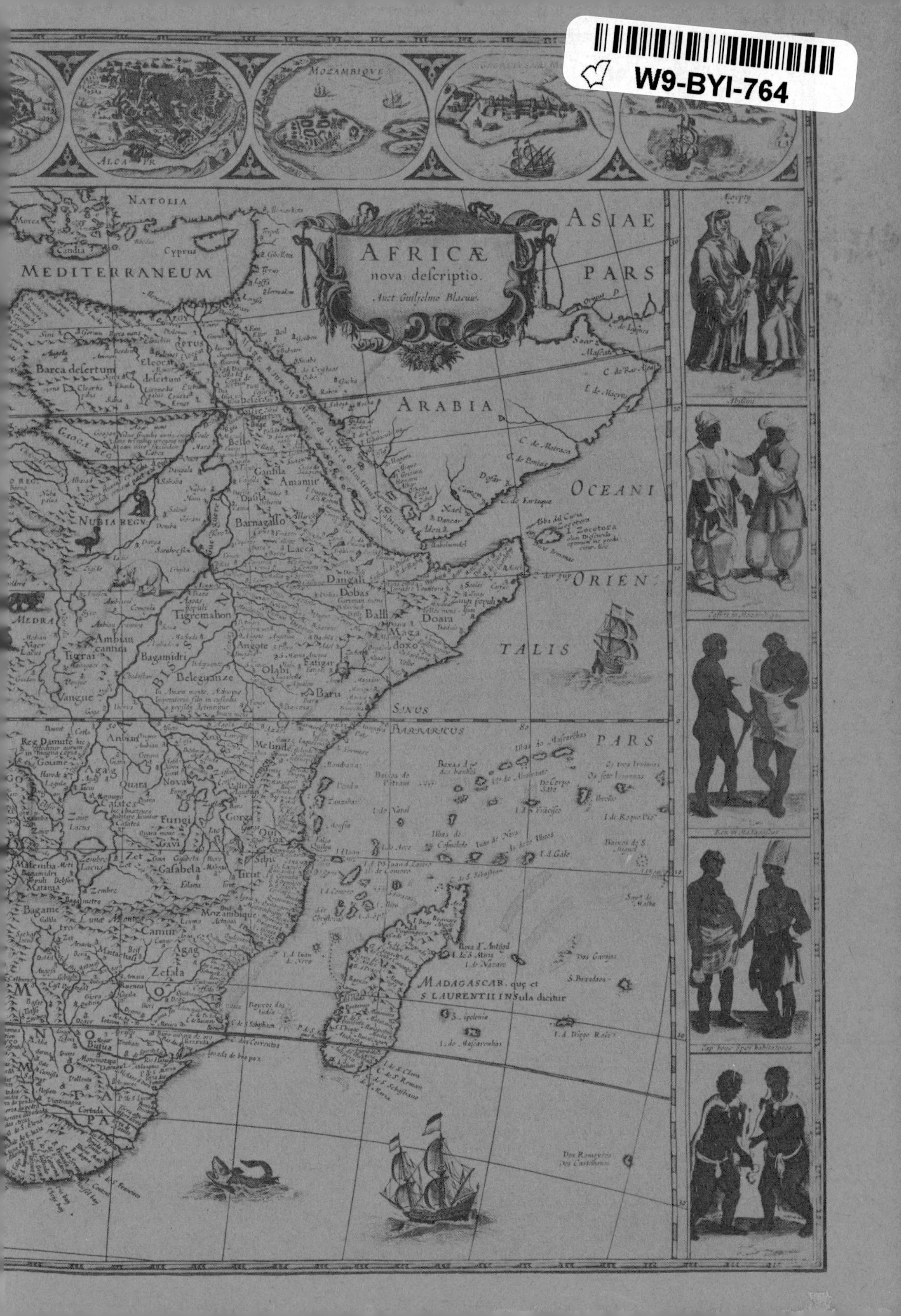

MOZAMBIQUE
AFRICÆ
nova descriptio.
Auct. Guiljelmo Blaeuw.
NATOLIA
Cyprus
MEDITERRANEUM
ASIAE
PARS
Barca desertum
ARABIA
OCEANI
ORIEN
TALIS
NUBIA REGN
Barnagasso
Dangali
Dobas
Balli
Maga doxo
Tigremahon
Bagamidri
Beleguanze
Baru
SINUS
BARBARICUS
PARS
Melinde
MADAGASCAR, quæ et
S. LAURENTII INSula dicitur
Zanzibar
Mozambique
Zefala
Gasabela
Fungi
Quara
Nova
Gavi
Camur
Agag
Tirut
Sibut
Anbian
Goiame
Zaire Lacus
Zembre Lacus
Zocotora
Aden
Maſcate
I. de Natal

A Political History of TROPICAL AFRICA

A Political History of TROPICAL AFRICA

ROBERT I. ROTBERG HARVARD UNIVERSITY

Harcourt, Brace & World, Inc.

NEW YORK / CHICAGO / SAN FRANCISCO / ATLANTA

MAPS BY Vaughn Gray

Library of Congress Catalog Card Number: 65-21072

Printed in the United States of America

La anthu a ku Africa, ngati lingayenere

and

in memory of Merida.

PREFACE

The existence of African history has in recent years achieved widespread recognition. Many universities in America and Europe now offer general and specialized courses in the subject at several levels; news media are similarly aware of its respectability. No longer can otherwise distinguished educators and journalists call Africa the continent without a past, or imply that the peoples of tropical Africa had no history before the coming of the white man. The activities of a few stalwart academic pioneers, the publications of a growing army of research-minded followers, and the efforts of several energetic evangelists have helped to encourage a profound change in public attitudes. Due to their efforts, enlightenment has in large part ousted prejudice.

Although the acceptance of African history as a discipline worthy in its own right of serious scholarly attention is recent, it differs from the histories of other continents only insofar as its sources, or lack of sources, pose new problems. The historians of Africa and the historians of Europe or America all ask the same basic questions of their source materials. Essentially, they seek by a number of means to establish veracity. Since the writing of history depends largely upon the availability of documentation, this becomes a labor of authentication. In tropical Africa, however, written records remain comparatively scarce. For the transitional zones, where contact with outsiders was more common, narratives exist in Arabic and in several European languages from about the tenth century. Yet in the main, these accounts—particularly the earliest ones—are derivative. Later, for the period when Europeans began to trade regularly with Africans, detailed, often heavily embroidered reports are available. With colonial enterprise and settlement comes a further, more abundant variety of documentation. Yet before the late nineteenth century, few Africans wrote in any language, and the Europeans maintained their ignorance of the vast interior of the African continent. They knew only of its extremities, and accordingly their records often contain half-truth and speculation rather than information that can be verified by the use of conventional historical methods.

Since written records alone were seen to be insufficient, the historians of Africa, perforce, made bold, imaginative use of hitherto neglected sources. In some parts of Africa, they successfully supplemented their sparse written evidence with information derived from oral accounts that had been handed down from generation to generation. Orally derived evidence can corroborate or shed doubt upon written inferences; it has also been used to suggest sites where archaeologists later found that it profited them to dig. Although the acidity of the African soil, the extremes of its climate, and the ravages of termites have over the years destroyed much that might elsewhere have been preserved, the efforts of archaeologists have already contributed substantially—particularly along the eastern coast—to the recovery of Africa's past. Some have uncovered ruined cities and hoards of coins that have been examined by numismatists. Others have drawn inferences from rock drawings and the comparatively few extant epigraphs.

Depending upon the period or the area of their particular concern, the historians of Africa naturally rely upon a judicious mixture of these three primary kinds of evidence. The discipline of linguistics, particularly the branches that concern themselves with the history of languages, examine linguistic borrowings, analyze common innovations, and scrutinize the shifts over time in basic, or presumed basic, vocabularies, provide further data for those who would write Africa's history. Ethnobotanists examine the diffusion and distribution of cultivated plants. Modern ethnographic reports offer some explanations for cultural survivals; in this regard, extrapolation can often prove useful.

These traditional and innovational tools have together provided historians with the variety of new evidence that has already begun to revolutionize the study of all preliterate society, especially of tropical Africa. Today we stand on the threshold of exciting new discoveries that will no doubt be made by those historians who can adapt a combination of new techniques to their individual research needs. Hopefully soon, they will provide answers to, or at least hypotheses to explain, the many remaining riddles of Africa's past. Certain conundrums may never be resolved satisfactorily, but within a decade or two, we shall probably be in a position to write knowledgeably, and at length, of the history of the many peoples of tropical Africa who—for want of detailed evidence—hardly figure in the pages of this book. Then, too, we may be able to demonstrate continuity greater than can be shown now. Before long, the theory of the diffusion of divine kingship—which now gives so much apparent strength to interpretations of African history—and other theories that similarly provide unifying themes, may receive the substantiation that they now lack. Or, alternatively, the historical revolution may produce new, less racially grounded theories of cultural influence.

It is in many respects premature to write a political, much more a general history of what, on epistemological and practical grounds, has been limited to tropical Africa. Perhaps after many persons have completed much more research, we can begin to write histories that may claim to be definitive. For those who prefer not to wait, however, the present book attempts to provide an introduction and a guide—often necessarily oversimplified—to the political past of tropical Africa that is based upon a variety of published materials and original investigations. It is a history not only of the African people, but also of the aliens who influenced the course of that history. The book attempts to synthesize our present knowledge and to take account of informed speculation; it does not seek balance in presentation simply for the sake of balance. Although cultural and economic trends find a place, its narrative—because of the nature of the available evidence—focuses primarily upon politics and political change. In this way it seeks to provide a core around which others will hopefully, and before long, wrap additions, qualifications, revisions, and new interpretations. If so, then the labor of several years will be rewarded.

No book of this breadth could have been written without the generous moral and physical assistance of a number of individuals, from all of whom I profited much. With characteristic kindness and insight, Professor J. D. Fage read and criticized a considerably different original draft. Professors Graham Irwin and Leonard M. Thompson suggested important improvements to the final version. When he could ill afford the time, Professor John D. Hargreaves read and commented perceptively upon the three chapters of the present book that refer to events in the nineteenth century. Mr. H. Neville Chittick examined the first three chapters in the light of his own recent research in East Africa; his detailed suggestions forestalled the too ready acceptance of speculation as established fact and saved me from some of the sins of solecism. Professor David Owen read a part of the original typescript and, throughout the long period during which this book was in embryo, provided encouragement and moral support at crucial intervals. Professor Sir Hamilton Gibb allowed me to benefit from his own unparalleled knowledge of the Arabic sources. Professor Francis Rogers kindly guided me through a mass of Portuguese material and criticized my third chapter with his usual careful attention to detail. Professor L. Carl Brown translated several Arabic passages and read two of the earlier chapters. Dr. Erich Gruen brought the best traditions of classical scholarship to the assistance and criticism of various drafts of the first chapter; like Professor Philip Dawson, who read and suggested a number of significant changes in the final draft of the fifth chapter, he responded willingly to innumerable requests for advice. Other colleagues, particularly Dr. Martin Kilson and Dr. Joseph Nye, discussed the raw material at length and later read and commented upon the chapters that deal with the events of the colonial and nationalist periods. Professor Elliot Berg also criticized the original drafts—now largely telescoped—of the chapters that refer to the twentieth century. Others, especially Mr. J. W. T. Allen, Dr. A. J. Arkell, Dr. Kwamena Bentsi-Enchill, Dr. Asa Davis, and Dr. Louis Leakey, took the time to discuss their own work and to read portions of mine.

A number of participants in the modern history of Africa allowed me to consult them in person or by letter. I am particularly grateful to Mr. Kofi Baako, the late Dr. Joseph Danquah, Chief H. Oladipo Davies, Sir Stewart Gore-Browne, President Dr. Kenneth D. Kaunda, Mr. Oscar Kambona, Vice-President Rashidi Kawawa, Prime Minister Jomo Kenyatta, Mr. Abu Mayanja, Mr. Eridadi M. K. Mulira, Prime Minister A. Milton Obote, Mr. Nsilo Swai, and Mr. Harry Thuku.

Mr. George W. Baer spent long hours reading and suggesting improvements in the original draft of this book; he later materially facilitated my research at a time when an intervening ocean limited access to important printed materials. Mr. David Kinsey gave generously of his knowledge of Arabic and helped me with recurring problems of translation and transliteration. Mr. Edmund Collins kindly translated a difficult text from the mediaeval Latin. Miss Matilde Zimmermann helped me with the Italian sources. (Unless stated otherwise, translations contained in the text that follows are my own. For economy of printing, I omit diacritical marks from words in non-European languages; in accord with modern style, most Bantu proper names will be found shorn of pronominal concords.)

Over the years, my students without overt complaint have forborne experiments in the teaching of African history. Of their number, Mr. Edward Alpers, Mrs. Nancy L. Bowles, Miss Pamela O'Neill, Miss Lucy Quimby, and Mrs. Marilyn Robinson Waldman in various ways each contributed significantly to the final form of this book.

The bibliography that follows the text herein is intended to provide a working guide to the great mass of relevant literature. Over several years, a number of persons have helped me either to compile or to verify the entries. Miss Yen-Tsai Feng cheerfully provided regular advice and material assistance from her base in Widener Library. I am also deeply indebted to Miss Nancy Barber, and to the Misses Carolyn Clement and Linda Harsh.

With her usual efficiency, Mrs. Claudia Lawrence Rogers typed the original, very much longer, draft and much of the present version. Mrs. Mary Hodgdon continued and Mrs. Jane F. Tatlock undertook not only to complete the text but with great industry to make of a collection of cards and scraps of paper the draft and final versions of the bibliography. My wife Joanna provided the original sketches of many of the present maps. She helped to accumulate the data on which the book draws, materially facilitated its preparation, substantially improved the various drafts of the chapters that follow, and encouraged me throughout. No form of words can convey the extent of my debt.

R. I. R.

Harvard University
December 22, 1964

CONTENTS

LIST OF MAPS

A Political History of TROPICAL AFRICA

Africke hath euer beene the least knowen and haunted parte in the world, chiefly by reason of the situation thereof under the torride Zone; which the ancients thought to be unhabitable. Whose opinion, although in verie deede it is not true, bicause we knowe that betweene the two Tropickes there are most fruitefull countries.

—John Pory, 1600

AFRICA IN ANCIENT TIMES

1

Man began in Africa. About 750,000 to one million years ago, near man—a hominid—learned to make tools and thereby transformed himself gradually into truc man. This process of evolution took place, probably not exclusively, near the shores of Victoria Nyanza and on the plateaux of what is now East Africa. Hitherto, near man had subsisted largely upon a herbivorous diet, occasionally supplemented by the meat of small animals. He had developed a liking for flesh, but neither with his teeth nor with his fingernails could he penetrate the skin of large animals. With stone tools, however, this first man was able to indulge his carnivorous tastes and, by so doing, to begin his own domestication. The use of tools accelerated the speed of this evolutionary adaptation, and for about 600,000 years he slowly improved his stone-working skills. He "invented" the first offensive weapons—stone bolas and, later, stone-tipped spearheads—and by using them he managed to slaughter increasingly large animals, such as the giant wart hog and the antlered giraffe.

After many years of isolation, early man betook himself and his new skills to Europe and to Asia Minor, perhaps because parts of Africa were becoming progressively dry or because Europe and Asia were becoming increasingly warm. Whatever the reason, it seems likely that the first true European and the first true Asian were African immigrants who had been impelled to seek a more hospitable homeland for themselves. On all three continents there is evidence that, during this period, man began to fashion stone hand-axes for the first time. Thereafter, human progress was more rapid in Europe and Asia than in Africa and, relative to its earliest development, Africa lost its initial pre-eminence in world history. Conceivably, human life required less effort in tropical Africa than in Europe or Asia, where man found that survival demanded considerable adaptation. In any event, the deserts grew drier and, because of overgrazing on their margins, expanded, cutting off Africa from cultural developments in Asia and Europe.[1]

To some extent, Africa became a cultural backwater. Nevertheless, its peoples increased their understanding of the universe, adapted fire for their own purposes, and taught themselves to fashion better tools of stone, bone, and ivory. There was a gradual growth in technological expertise and a progressive sophistication in the handling of environmental problems. But not until changing ecological conditions or the spread of new, revolutionary techniques made possible the emergence of neolithic cultures were the peoples of tropical Africa able to attempt to regain their previous equality with the peoples of Europe and Asia.

This breakthrough or neolithic revolution, whether predominantly technical or organizational, probably reached its culmination during the millennia before Christ in northeastern Africa, in the Niger basin, and in parts of the Western Sudan. In these areas, the indigenous inhabitants successfully made the necessary transition from the stage of food-collecting to that of food-producing. For the first time, man grew his own grain and domesticated cattle, sheep, and goats. He had more leisure than before, made elaborate pottery and polished axes, and fashioned implements with which to dry skins and cook meat and porridge. Gradually, almost imperceptibly, many Africans shifted from hunting and gathering to an initially tentative dependence upon carefully nurtured crops and animals. Indeed, throughout most of Africa the neolithic revolution may not have occurred until after the death of Christ. Before that revolution, many Africans lived, it is thought, in small bands of collectors. Their settlement patterns probably were conditioned by the need to follow game and to be near available water supplies. They alternated between wet- and dry-season dwelling areas. Their food was predominantly vegetable, gathered laboriously by hand, but they probably also knew how to trap small animals and to poison (with arrows or bait) animals that were too large to be met in direct combat. Among these pre-neolithic peoples there doubtless were specialists who traded salt and implements; likewise, wandering bands might well have had some loose mutual ties of a governmental kind.

From rock paintings we learn that in many places a strict division of labor existed between the sexes: men hunted and women collected and cooked the food and cared for the children. The making of baskets and the manufacture of grinders, bracelets, necklaces, and awls were women's work, while the men made their own stone implements. The women fashioned pottery from clay and sand by the coil method, and decorated their pots by the application of fiber or by incisions made with bone and stone instruments. They painted their bodies and wore ornaments of all kinds. They made fragments of the shells of

---

[1] On the newest discoveries, see L. S. B. Leakey, P. V. Tobias, and J. R. Napier, "A New Species of the Genus *Homo* from Olduvai Gorge," *Nature* (April 4, 1964), pp. 7–9. On climatic variances, see Étienne A. Bernard, "Interprétation astronomique des pluviaux et interpluviaux du Quaternaire africain," *Actes du IVe Congrès panafricain de préhistoire et de l'étude du Quaternaire* (Tervuren, 1962), I, pp. 67–95.

ostrich eggs into necklaces, bracelets, or hair rings, and they (the East Africans at least) wore amazon stones—a bright green variety of feldspar worn as amulets—and chalcedony obtained from what is now the Tibesti region of Chad or, conceivably, from what is now India or Indonesia.

Unfortunately, we know little more. Bantu-speaking Africans were in the process of peopling eastern and southern Africa during the first few centuries after Christ, possibly as a result of a dispersion from an area south of the Zambezi-Congo watershed, but we do not yet understand why or how they came to the vast areas of Africa that they now inhabit.[2] It is unlikely that any large portions of Africa were unpopulated—we have impressive archaeological evidence of reasonably widespread habitation—but for the most part we simply do not yet know who occupied most of tropical Africa during the period before about A.D. 500. For the present, our detailed knowledge is limited to two, perhaps analogous, classical cultures of tropical Africa and to what has been preserved of the early relations of Africa with the peoples of the Mediterranean basin.

I. The Rise and Fall of Kush

A neolithic transformation apparently took place in northeastern Africa, in what is now the Sudan, during the fourth millennium before Christ. Toward the end of that millennium, the peoples of the Middle Nile began to trade with the peoples of Lower Egypt, exchanging oils, foodstuffs, and other goods for manufactured articles. Commerce led to war, and in the period of about 3100 to 3000 B.C., King Jer of the first Egyptian dynasty conquered the people of Nubia.[3] For the next three thousand years, the peoples of Egypt and the Sudan—bound as they were by the course of the Nile River—warred frequently and traded almost continuously. About 2700 B.C., for instance, the armies of King Senefru of the fourth Egyptian dynasty—the father of the king who built the Giza pyramids near Cairo—returned from an invasion of Nubia with 7,000 prisoners and 200,000 cattle and sheep. From about 2600 B.C., there appear to have been permanent Egyptian settlements in Nubia, and a regular traffic in the usual forms of tribute existed between Nubia and Lower Egypt.[4]

The Sudan became increasingly important to Egypt during its Sixth Dynasty (*c.* 2423–2242 B.C.). Egyptian ships were built of wood from the south, and Nubians were conscripted into the Egyptian army in order to battle the Asiatic

[2] The early theories of Bantu origin and dispersion are now discredited on linguistic grounds. Most of the peoples who inhabit the parts of Africa that lie south of a line drawn from the confluence of the Niger and Benue rivers (Nigeria) to the mouth of the Tana River (Kenya) share serological factors and speak morphologically related languages. In the plural, they generally term themselves Bantu. See Malcolm Guthrie, "Bantu Origins: A Tentative New Hypothesis," *The Journal of African Languages*, I (1962), p. 16; Joseph Greenberg, *Studies in African Linguistic Classification* (New Haven, 1955), p. 40.

[3] See Anthony John Arkell, *A History of the Sudan from the Earliest Times to 1821* (London, 1961), pp. 39–40. The Nok culture is discussed *infra*, p. 106.

[4] Walter B. Emery, "Preliminary Report on the Excavations at Buhen, 1962," *Kush*, XI (1963), p. 120.

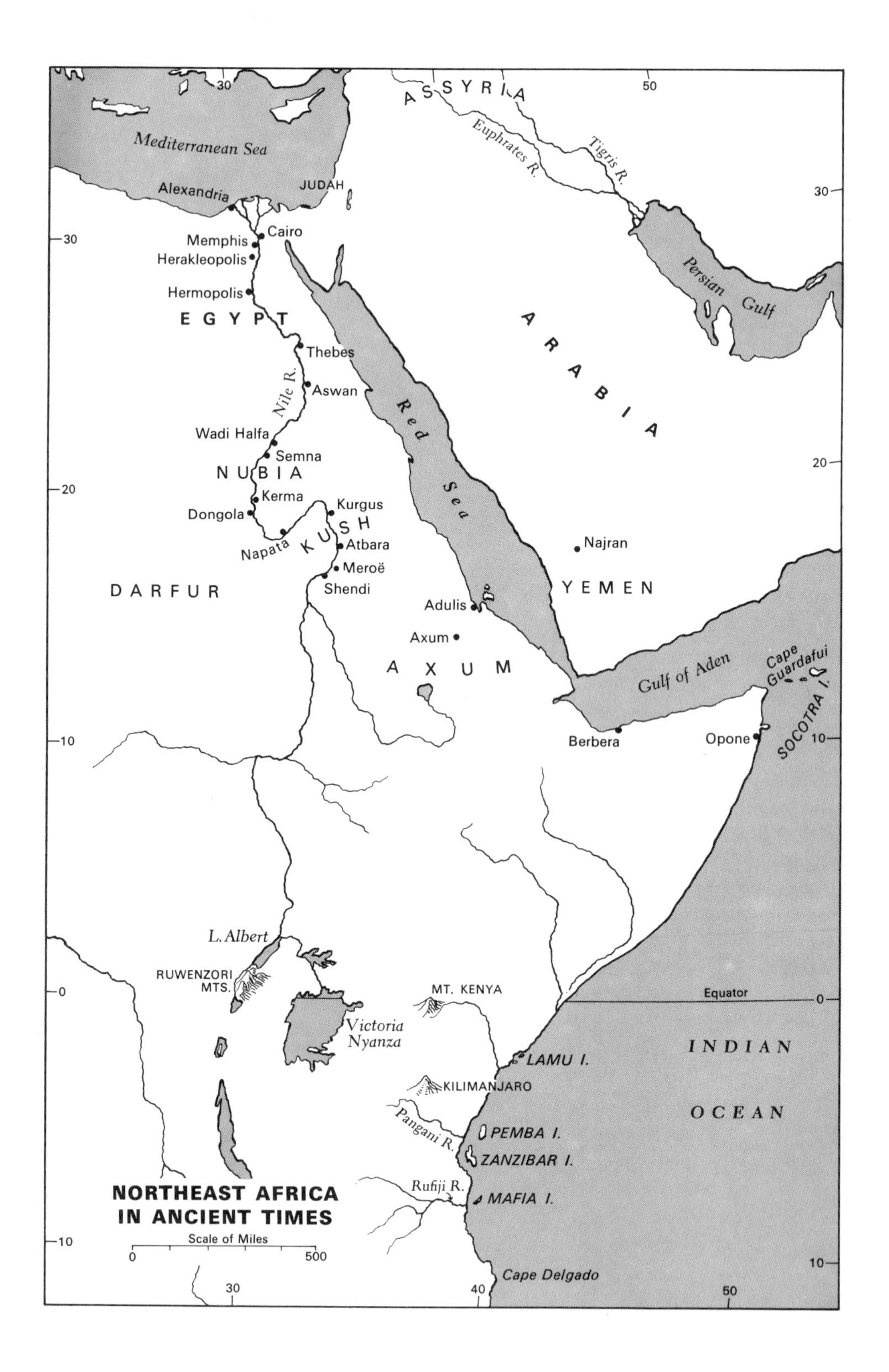
NORTHEAST AFRICA
IN ANCIENT TIMES
Scale of Miles
0
500
Mediterranean Sea
ASSYRIA
Euphrates R.
Tigris R.
JUDAH
Alexandria
Cairo
Memphis
Herakleopolis
Hermopolis
EGYPT
Thebes
Aswan
Nile R.
Wadi Halfa
Semna
NUBIA
Kerma
Dongola
Kurgus
KUSH
Napata
Atbara
Meroë
Shendi
DARFUR
Red Sea
ARABIA
Persian Gulf
Najran
YEMEN
Adulis
Axum
AXUM
Gulf of Aden
Cape Guardafui
SOCOTRA I.
Berbera
Opone
L. Albert
RUWENZORI MTS.
Victoria Nyanza
MT. KENYA
Equator
LAMU I.
KILIMANJARO
Pangani R.
PEMBA I.
ZANZIBAR I.
Rufiji R.
MAFIA I.
Cape Delgado
INDIAN
OCEAN
30
40
50

Bedouin. From Thebes, caravans frequently ventured into the little explored "elephant lands" beyond Nubia, and Harkhuf, the most intrepid of the early traders, recorded how he had opened up the "Land of Yam"—conceivably the Darfur region of the modern Sudan—after four long journeys there in the last years of the Sixth Dynasty. On one occasion Harkhuf returned to Aswan after about seven months with a heavily loaded caravan of three hundred asses bearing frankincense, ebony, ivory, and leopard skins. Another time he returned from the "Land of Yam" with a "dancing dwarf" who delighted the court of King Pepi II (*c.* 2235 B.C.).[5] Despite Harkhuf's apparent success, these were dangerous expeditions; the caravans penetrated areas in which the indigenous population was actively hostile to Egypt. As a result, King Pepi II sent the "keeper of the door to the south"—a prominent Egyptian nobleman—to "hack up" the unruly people of the Sudan. Two forays into the south were necessary, but the "keeper" eventually succeeded in pacifying the people of "Wawat and Irtet" and in bringing their recalcitrant kings before the Egyptian court.

The people of the Sudan preyed upon Egypt for the first time after the Egyptian central government collapsed in about 2242 B.C. Normal trade ceased temporarily, and the so-labeled C people, perhaps driven from their homes in the southwest by conditions of increasing desiccation, settled in lower Nubia, bringing with them their long-horned cattle, goats, and garments of animal skin. These "C" people superimposed their own culture upon the previous inhabitants and, in turn, a new Egyptian kingdom reasserted its hegemony over Nubia. By 2000 B.C., the armies of the Egyptian Middle Kingdom (*c.* 2150–1580 B.C.) had built a number of massive mud-brick forts along the Nile, presumably in order to secure their southern frontier. During the reign of King Senusret I of the Twelfth Dynasty (*c.* 1970–1936 B.C.), the armies of Egypt completed the pacification of the Sudan, occupying it as far south as the site of modern Semna, where there would have been alluvial soil sufficient to support a large garrison town. To commemorate his victories, King Senusret I erected a stele at Buhen, across the Nile River from Wadi Halfa. On the stele, the king of Thebes faces the god Montu, lord of Thebes, who says: "I have put all the countries in [Nubia] under thy feet." The king is presented with a long line of captives each of whom represents a subject province. One of the captives is "Kush," which seems to be the earliest mention of the name.[6]

Egypt wanted the wealth of Kush. From Kush Egypt took raw materials and manufactured articles, indigenous graves testifying to the opulence of the people of Kerma, the capital or leading commercial town of Kush. Here the Egyptians of the Twelfth Dynasty maintained a large entrepôt as the center of a trading network that stretched south to the Atbara River and west to Darfur and Lake Chad. And when conditions of peace prevailed, the Egyptians

---

[5] James Henry Breasted, *Ancient Records of Egypt* (Chicago, 1906), I, pp. 152–153 [333–335], p. 161 [353]. See also Herodotus, iv, 181–185. In the following classical references, Loeb edition notations are followed throughout.

[6] Arkell, *History*, pp. 59–60. See also Georges Posener, "Pour une localisation du pays Koush au Moyen Empire," *Kush*, VI (1958), pp. 43–45.

exported impressive quantities of gold and ivory from Kerma to Thebes. The local products included highly polished red beakers, wooden beds inlaid with ivory figures, mica representations of animal and bird life, leather headgear, alabaster and antimony pots, copper daggers with ivory handles, and copper copies of Egyptian black-topped beakers. The industries of Kerma also converted blue-glazed faience into tiles, beads, drinking vessels, amulets, bracelets, ear studs, and figurines. But toward the end of the Middle Kingdom, the people of Kush rebelled against their colonial rulers, destroyed the trading posts, and ousted the Egyptians from the Sudan. At about the same time, the Asiatic Hyksos dynasty thrust the armies of Thebes from Lower Egypt.

For about a century, from about 1700 to 1600 B.C., Kush asserted its independence and traded on an equal footing with the people of Egypt. But its independence was short-lived. At the beginning of the New Kingdom (*c.* 1580–1050 B.C.) King Ahmes eliminated the power of the Hyksos dynasty in the Egyptian Delta, and thereafter conquered all of Nubia. King Tuthmosis I (*c.* 1530–1520 B.C.) carried the attack farther south into the heartland of Kush. Once beyond the Third Cataract, his armies swept over the easily navigated Dongola Reach, invested Kerma, and continued past Napata (the modern Kareima) and the Fourth Cataract as far as Kurgus, south of the modern Abu Hamed, where they erected a fort. His warriors beheaded the kings of Kush and occupied most of the area within the big bends of the Nile. Tuthmosis

Nubians offer tribute to their Egyptian rulers. From a tempera reproduction of a wall painting in the tomb of Huy, viceroy of Nubia, *c.* 1355 B.C. The Metropolitan Museum of Art, New York.

Men with giraffe, presumably tribute being borne from the land of Kush. From a tempera reproduction of a wall painting in the tomb of Rekhmare, vizier of Tuthmosis III, *c.* 1480 B.C. The Metropolitan Museum of Art, New York.

rightly boasted that he had "penetrated valleys which the royal ancestors knew not" and that his name had, perforce, "penetrated the whole earth."[7] Egyptian soldiers may have even ventured beyond the Fifth and Sixth Cataracts to the site of modern Omdurman—where tropical Africa began—for the first representations of Negroid Africans in the art of the New Kingdom date from this time.

Kush and Nubia were soon integrated into the greatest of Egypt's empires. A series of Egyptian viceroys ruled the two provinces with the assistance of both civil and military bureaucrats.[8] The Egyptians controlled the farms, fisheries, apiaries, and shipyards of Kush; only priests were permitted to wash gold, and those who dared to interfere with the prerogatives or the property of the church incurred heavy penalties. From the peoples of Kush, the colonial government extracted a regular tribute in gold and slaves. Kush supplied Egypt during the period from about 1525 to 1100 B.C. with ebony, ivory, ostrich feathers and eggs, copper, carnelian (a reddish chalcedony much valued for seal wax), red ochre, amazon stone, cattle, leopards and leopard skins, giraffe and fly whisks made from their tail hairs, baboons, and dogs. The viceroys also conscripted the citizens of Kush and Nubia into the armies of the New Kingdom. These "foreign" soldiers helped to suppress a number of uprisings against Pharaonic rule and, in time, to overthrow their Egyptian leaders.

Kush broke away from Egypt in about 950 B.C., when Solomon reigned in Israel. While the Libyans of Herakleopolis fought the high priests of Thebes

---

[7] Arkell, *History,* p. 84.

[8] Labib Habachi, "The First Two Viceroys of Kush and Their Family," *Kush,* VII (1959), pp. 55–62; George A. Reisner, "The Viceroys of Ethiopia," *The Journal of Egyptian Archaeology,* VI (1920), pp. 28–55, 73–88.

for the throne of Egypt, the kings of Kush and their Sudanese soldiers conquered Nubia and Upper Egypt and, during the first years of the eighth century B.C., struggled to wrest control of the Delta from the Libyans. Piankhy (751–716 B.C.), Kush's greatest king, commanded a large army and navy that swept north into the Delta, taking Herakleopolis, Hermopolis, and Memphis in a series of tactically brilliant campaigns in about 732 B.C.[9]

In the years of King Shabako (*c.* 707–696 B.C.) and his immediate successors, Kush became for a time an international power of some significance. After Egyptian princes of the Delta had rebelled, Shabako forcibly reimposed the rule of Kush over all of Lower Egypt and transferred his capital from distant Napata to Thebes. But the presence of the Kushites in Egypt soon brought their army into conflict with that of Assyria, then the most powerful state in western Asia. Assyria had conquered Samaria and, by the reign of Shabako, had driven the people of Israel into exile. Both Kush and Assyria vied for control of the small, intervening kingdom of Judah and, in 701 B.C., King Sennacherib led his Assyrian armies into Judah.[10] The warriors of Kush went to the assistance of the people of Judah but, even before the battle could be joined, an outbreak of plague forced the Assyrians to retreat.[11] Soon, however, Kush and Assyria were once again at war. In 671 B.C., King Esarhaddon led the Assyrian camel trains to the borders of Egypt. There the arms of Kush proved no match for the iron spears and swords of Assyria. Again, in 666 B.C., after a short period during which Kush had reasserted its control over Lower Egypt, the Assyrians conquered the Delta and planted their flags in the court of Thebes. A few years later, the Assyrian army sacked Thebes and permanently ended the power of Kush in Egypt.[12] Thenceforth, Kush paid tribute to the kings of Lower Egypt.

The dynasty that had been defeated by Assyria in Egypt continued to rule in Kush for one thousand years. At first, the rulers of Kush visibly retained their Egyptian way of life and, aside from their growing difficulty in controlling the nomadic Beja who lived east of the Nile, their kingdom maintained itself gloriously. The royal sarcophagi of this period are massive and richly inscribed with traditional texts; the funerary objects are as grand as those of earlier epochs. Even territorially, Kush remained important. The writ of the kings of Kush extended perhaps as far south as the site of modern Malakal on the White Nile and, for some years at least, the kings of Kush continued to meddle in the affairs of Upper and Lower Egypt. In the seventh and sixth centuries B.C., however, the pretensions of Kush in Egypt were opposed vigorously by the Saite kings of the Delta. In a decisive battle near the Third Cataract, King Psammetik II of the Delta and his army of Egyptian conscripts and Greek and Carian mer-

[9] Piankhy's exploits are inscribed on the granite stele at Jebel Barkal. See Breasted, *Ancient Records*, IV, pp. 406–444 [796–883].
[10] II Kings 17–19.
[11] II Kings 19:35–36. Herodotus, ii, 141, indicates that field mice (a classical symbol for plague) ate the Assyrian quivers and bowstrings and forced the Assyrians to retreat.
[12] See Nahum 3:8–10.

Detail of the statue of Aspelta, king of Kush (593–568 B.C.), found in the temple at Jebel Barkal in Kush. Museum of Fine Arts, Boston.

cenaries routed the men of Kush. Overrunning the Dongola Reach, they sacked Napata, the capital of Kush, in 591 B.C., plundered the court and the villages of the central Sudan and, as they withdrew, installed a garrison at the Second Cataract.[13] Kush no longer threatened the people of Egypt; its rulers thereafter looked south and confined their energies to the expansion of Kush within the Sudan.

Aspelta, king of Kush from 593 to 568 B.C., reorganized his empire and transferred its capital to Meroë, near Shendi above the Sixth Cataract. Gradually, Meroë became the center of a culture that was fast losing its pure Egyptian overlay and was tending more and more to assert a uniquely Sudanese syncretism, combining much that was Mediterranean with more that was indigenous. Indeed, the ruins of Meroë are an impressive reminder of that synthesis: the town stretched north and south along the east bank of the Nile and contained walled palaces and the great temple devoted to the god 'Amen. To the east were the cemeteries with their many tombs and pyramids, and to the southeast

[13] Serge Sauneron and Jean Yoyotte, "La Campagne nubienne de Psammétique II et sa signification historique," *Bulletin de l'Institut Français d'Archéologie Orientale*, L (1952), pp. 157–207. See also Herodotus, ii, 161.

was the so-called Sun Temple with its Meroitic hieroglyphs.[14] The people of Meroë evidently were pastoralists who depended for food upon grain obtained from better-watered agricultural land upstream. They also worked iron, and Meroë evidently was the first, if not the most important, industrial town of tropical Africa. Sandstone hills east of the city contained iron ore, wood for fuel was available nearby, and iron slag heaps over which the Sudanese railway later ran testify convincingly to a site of intensive metallurgical activity. The Assyrian military successes had been to some extent a result of their iron equipment; lessons learned by the generals of Kush on the plains of Egypt, and later at the sack of Napata, would certainly have encouraged the expansion of what conceivably could have been by that time a traditional Meroitic industry. Whatever the cause, knowledge of the skills necessary to smelt and forge iron successfully probably spread in subsequent centuries from Meroë to the rest of tropical Africa.[15]

During the four centuries from the sack of Napata to the Roman invasion, Kush cast off more and more of its Egyptian accoutrements. Meroitic hieroglyphs replaced Egyptian as the literary language of Kush and, during the third or second centuries B.C., the still undeciphered cursive script of Meroë in turn succeeded these local hieroglyphs. Cultural riches declined—the burial chambers of the period reflect a marked impoverishment except during the reign of King Ergamenes (225–200 B.C.)—but, militarily, the state remained sufficiently strong to include within its borders the peoples living at the junction of the two Niles. During the first century B.C., the armies of Kush even raided Nubia, but Petronius, the Roman prefect of Egypt, took offence and, in 23 B.C., razed Napata.[16] By then Kush was probably in commercial contact with India, Arabia, and Axum as well as with the Mediterranean world. A variety of impressive statues and reservoirs, dating from the first years of the Christian era, show Indian influence; there is also evidence that at this time the cultivation of cotton was introduced from Asia. Ruins of baths at Meroë point to Roman influence, and Pliny tells us that the Roman Emperor Nero on one occasion sent two centurions to determine whether or not Kush was worth the trouble of conquest. After exploring much of what is now the southern Sudan—perhaps even venturing as far as Lake Albert—they decided that Kush should not, in fact, be invaded.[17] By the day of the geographer Ptolemy, Kush seemed relatively unimportant, and its apparent demise can be ascribed to the rise of the Noba of ʻAlwa and, during the fourth century A.D., of neighboring Axum.[18]

---

[14] John Garstang, Alexander Henry Sayce, and F. Lloyd Griffith, *Meroë, the City of the Ethiopians* (Oxford, 1911), pp. 25–27. Herodotus, iii, 18, may refer to this temple.

[15] See G. A. Wainwright, "Iron in Napatan and Meroitic Ages," *Sudan Notes and Records,* XXVI (1945), pp. 5–36.

[16] Pliny, *Natural History,* vi, 35, 181–182; Strabo, XVII, i, 49–54; Dio Cassius, liv, 5, 4–6; F. Lloyd Griffith, "Meroitic Studies IV," *The Journal of Egyptian Archaeology,* IV (1917), pp. 159–170. But see Mikhail I. Rostovtzeff (rev. by P. M. Fraser), *The Social and Economic History of the Roman Empire* (Oxford, 1957), II, p. 679, n. 56.

[17] Pliny, *NH,* vi, 35, 180.

[18] See L. P. Kirwan, "The Decline and Fall of Meroë," *Kush,* VIII (1960), pp. 170–172; P. L. Shinnie, "The Fall of Meroë," *Kush,* III (1955), pp. 84–85. See also *infra,* pp. 30–31.

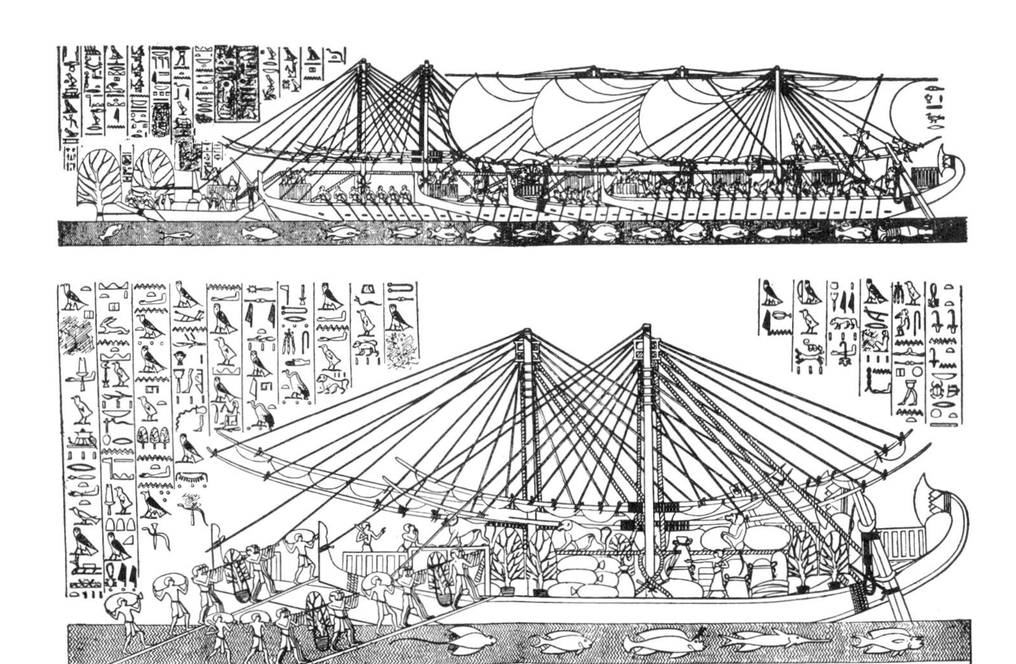

Queen Hatshepsut's expeditions to Punt are depicted in a series of reliefs in her temple of Der el-Bahri at Thebes. Here, in the upper panel, her fleet departs. Below, in Punt, the vessels are being loaded, as the surrounding hieroglyphs describe: "[1]The loading of the ships very heavily with marvels of [2]the country of Punt; all goodly fragrant woods of God's-Land, heaps of [3]myrrh-resin, with fresh myrrh trees, [4]with ebony and pure ivory, with green gold [5]of Emu, with cinnamon wood, [6]khesyt wood, with ihmut-incense, [7]sonter-incense, eye-cosmetic, [8]with apes, [9]monkeys, [10]dogs, [11]and [12]with skins [13]of the southern panther, [14]with natives and [15]their children. Never was brought [16]the like of this for any king who has been since the beginning." (From J. H. Breasted, *A History of Egypt*, New York, 1905)

II. Tropical Africa and the Mediterranean World During the First Age of Exploration

Despite the somewhat intimate relations between Kush and Egypt and despite the efforts of a number of ancient seafarers, the peoples of tropical Africa had remained fundamentally ignorant of life in the Mediterranean basin throughout the millennia before Christ. The inhabitants of eastern Africa probably had welcomed voyagers from Indonesia, India, and Arabia much earlier, but the Egyptians were the first visitors to leave understandable records of mutual contact. During their Eighteenth Dynasty (*c.* 1580–1322 B.C.), the Egyptians seem to have traded frequently with the so-called land of Punt—probably what is now Somalia west of Cape Guardafui—and with the island now known as Socotra, their ships returning home laden with incense and myrrh.[19] In the

[19] Breasted, *Ancient Records*, I, pp. 70, 160, 163–164, II, pp. 102–121 [I, 161, 351, 360–361, II, 246–295].

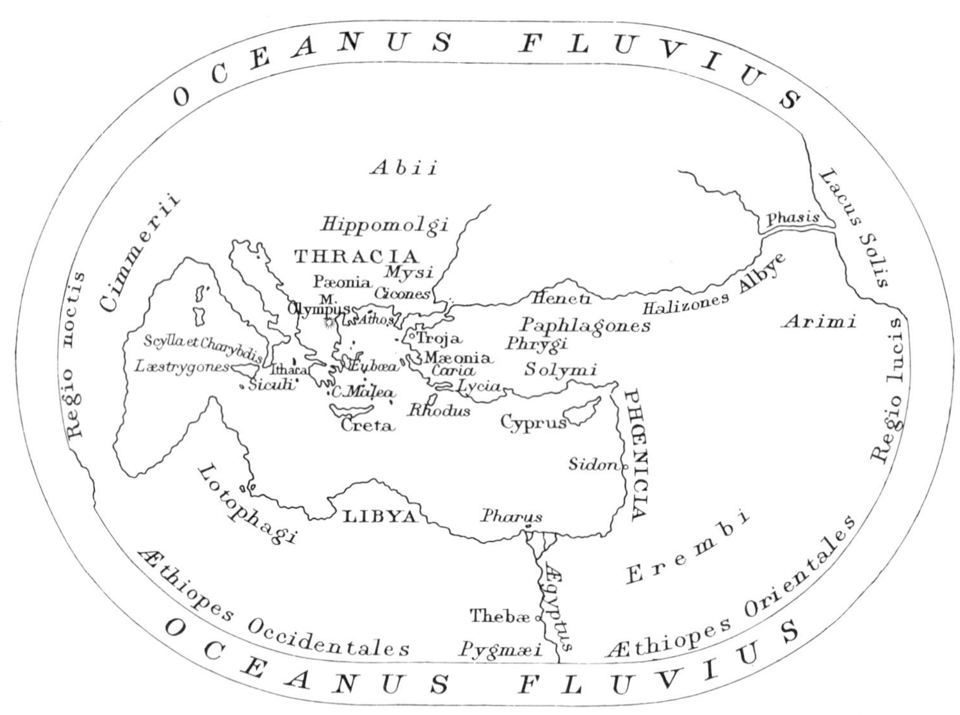

The world according to Homer, 1000 B.C. (John Bartholomew & Son Ltd.)

time of Queen Hatshepsut (*c.* 1346–1322 B.C.), the Egyptian merchant navy was very active, and one or more captains may have even sailed with the monsoon winds as far as Sofala in what is now Moçambique. But if they did so, they left no known record of their voyages. Furthermore, the inscriptions of Queen Hatshepsut that detail the various voyages to the land of Punt show leafy incense trees and humpless cattle more characteristic of southern Arabia and Socotra than of eastern Africa.[20]

If Homer is a reliable guide, the peoples of tropical Africa and the Mediterranean failed to build upon these initial contacts. For him and his contemporaries, the world was flat, with an oceanic rim. He connected eastern Africa to Phoenicia and joined Phoenicia to Armenia and the Crimea. In the west, he linked Morocco to Spain, making the Mediterranean a self-contained sea. Hesiod similarly portrayed Africa as a narrow band of land separating the Mediterranean lake from the ever-flowing river that encircled the earth.[21]

Why did Homer and Hesiod, and why do we, know so little about tropical Africa at that time? Could ancient mariners not have sailed around Africa with ease? Could early merchants not have emulated Harkhuf and traded far up the Nile, returning with detailed information about the people and places of

---

[20] James Hornell, "Sea-Trade in Early Times," *Antiquity*, XV (1941), pp. 233–256.

[21] Homer, *Iliad*, xviii, 402–403, 607–608; Hesiod, fr. 64; Strabo, I, i, 3–5. Both Homer and Hesiod probably lived during the eighth century B.C. Homer wrote, however, about the Trojan War of *c.* 1184 B.C.

Africa? Moreover, could Africans not have made their way overland to Egypt or, at a later date, to Carthage? Alas, all we know of this period in the history of tropical Africa is derived from a few fragmentary and largely unsatisfactory Egyptian, Greek, and Roman reports. Men of the ancient world were, understandably, inhibited physically and psychologically from attempting to cross the vast, if then less arid, Saharan desert. They likewise feared to venture along a coastline that continued endlessly into the unknown. The peoples of the Mediterranean also believed that the climate of southern Africa was bound to be unbearably hot and pestilential. Moreover, the sailors of the day, however intrepid, feared to take too many risks in their frail ships.[22] Their nautical instruments were inadequate for measuring distance or time or for taking the necessary bearings (the mariner's compass was a much later invention). What was even more decisive, perhaps, was that they had little economic incentive to explore. The Mediterranean world easily obtained sufficient luxury goods from the Arabs—who in turn traded with the peoples of Persia, India, and, possibly, eastern Africa—or from the Berbers, who controlled the commerce of the Sahara.

The earliest coastal explorations

Phoenicians in the employ of King Solomon may have been among the first to overcome these obstacles and to continue the reconnaissance begun by the navies of Queen Hatshepsut. According to the Hebrew chronicles, in the period between 1000 and 900 B.C. the sailors of Solomon brought back gold, ivory, peacocks, and apes from Ophir, which lay between Sheba and Havilah.[23] They traded regularly with Ophir, usually returning every three years. But the precise location of this fabled entrepôt remains an open question. It has variously been placed in India, Ceylon, Australia, and New Zealand in the east, and in South America, Arabia, Ethiopia, and southern Africa in the west. Some earlier writers have equated Ophir with Sofala, and Havilah with the Zimbabwe complex of Southern Rhodesia, where the smelting of gold was practiced for at least nine hundred years. But in all likelihood, Ophir was either a way station, located perhaps in the land of Punt, where Arabs and Indians traded goods that they had obtained from ports possibly as distant as Sofala, or an accessible Ethiopian port on the Red Sea. In the last case, the factors of Ophir could have obtained gold from the interior mines, ivory from abundant elephants killed nearby, and spices and jewels from the Yemen or Punt.

During the following centuries, the peoples of Arabia, Phoenicia, and Egypt visited the shores of tropical Africa. The Greeks became interested in Africa after 800 B.C., when their city-states emerged from the chaos left by the Dorian invasions. They investigated the northern coastline of Africa and "discovered"

[22] See Eric H. Warmington, "Africa in Ancient and Medieval Times," *The Cambridge History of the British Empire* (Cambridge, Eng., 1936), VIII, p. 53; Charles Rathbone Low, *Maritime Discovery: A History of Nautical Exploration from the Earliest Times* (London, 1881), I, pp. 10–36.

[23] I Kings 9:27–28, 10:10–22; II Chronicles 9:1–21.

been evident; meanwhile the Moçambique and Agulhas currents would have swept them around the Cape of Good Hope and, after spending a number of months sowing and reaping their wheat north of the Cape, they would have sailed on into the Bight of Biafra. Thereafter, they might have found it necessary to row strenuously in order to make progress along the Gold Coast and around Cape Palmas. After another halt made in order to grow wheat somewhere in modern Mauritania or Morocco, they could have quickly reached the Pillars of Heracles and familiar waters.[30]

Whether or not the Phoenicians of King Necho were in fact the first to circumnavigate the African continent, later sailors of the sixth century B.C. directed their efforts toward western Africa. The traders of Phoenicia and Carthage were determined to prevent their Greek competitors fom venturing into the Atlantic Ocean lest they should discover the commercially profitable routes to Cornwall and Brittany. For a time, the Carthaginians managed to blockade the Pillars of Heracles against the Greeks and to establish entrepôts along the shores of the southern as well as the northern Atlantic. Indeed, by the end of the sixth century B.C., Carthaginian and other Mediterranean sailors were certainly trading on a regular basis with peoples who lived in Africa south of the Pillars of Heracles.[31] Among the traders was a Massilian named Euthymenes, who supposedly visited the West African coast, perhaps about the end of the sixth century. He claimed to have sailed as far as a river, possibly the Senegal, where the waters were blown back by the wind and where there was an abundance of crocodiles.[32] And in about 500 B.C., at least one seafarer was blown away from the coast of northwestern Africa to an offshore island that may have been Madeira.[33]

Carthage naturally would have wanted to widen its commercial contacts with Africans by establishing colonial outposts. Sometime between 500 and 470 B.C., the government of Carthage ordered Hanno, a Magonid suffete, to "sail past the Pillars of Heracles and to found cities of Libyphoenicia" in Africa.[34] Fortunately, Hanno's subsequent voyage at the head of a convoy of sixty ships containing thirty thousand persons is comparatively well documented. For upon his return, this nobleman, who may have been the same Hanno who kept tame lions in his courtyard and who also trained his pet parrot to recite "Hanno is God, Hanno is God," engraved a record of his expedition upon a stele in the Temple of Cronos at Carthage, a later Greek translation being preserved in

[30] This section is based primarily upon the reconstruction in J. Talboys Wheeler, *The Geography of Herodotus* (London, 1854), pp. 337–346. See also Willi Müller, *Die Umsegelung Afrikas durch phönizische Schiffer ums Jahr 600 v Chr. Geb.* (Rathenau, 1889), pp. 36, 45–48.

[31] Herodotus, iv, 196.

[32] See J. Oliver Thomson, *History of Ancient Geography* (Cambridge, Eng., 1948), p. 77, and the references cited therein.

[33] Diodorus, v, 19–20.

[34] "Cities of Libyphoenicia" meant cities whose inhabitants were Phoenicians residing in Africa. But see the critical discussion and commentary in Gabriel Germain, "Qu'est-ce que le *Périple* d'Hannon? Document, amplification littéraire ou faux intégral?" *Hesperis*, XLIV (1957), pp. 205–248.

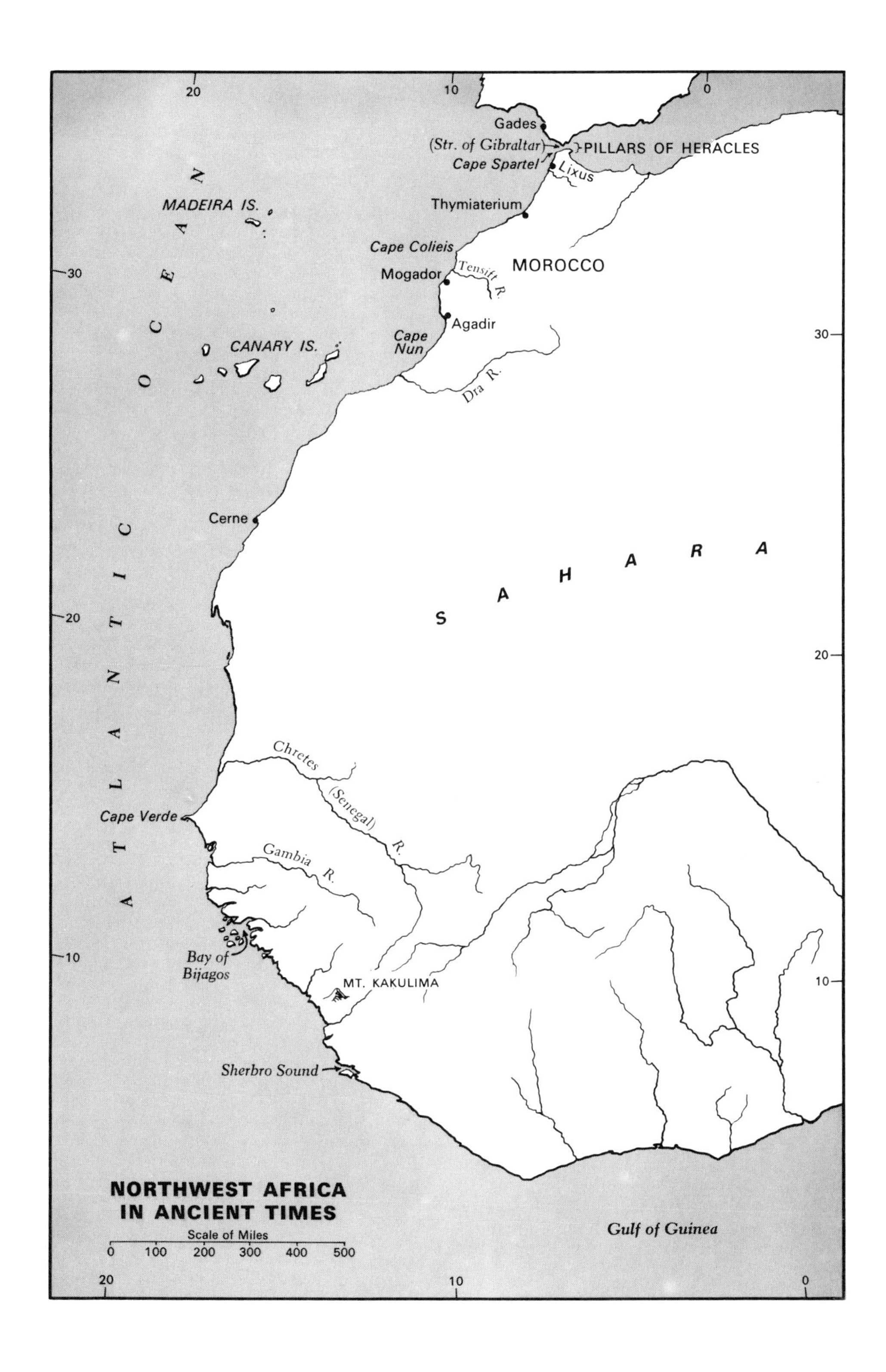
Gades
(Str. of Gibraltar)
PILLARS OF HERACLES
Cape Spartel
Lixus
Thymiaterium
MADEIRA IS.
Cape Colieis
MOROCCO
Mogador
Tensift R.
Agadir
Cape Nun
CANARY IS.
Dra R.
ATLANTIC OCEAN
Cerne
SAHARA
Chretes
(Senegal) R.
Cape Verde
Gambia R.
Bay of Bijagos
MT. KAKULIMA
Sherbro Sound
Gulf of Guinea
NORTHWEST AFRICA IN ANCIENT TIMES
Scale of Miles
0 100 200 300 400 500

Heidelberg.[35] Although this document is not altogether free from obscurities, it permits a partial reconstruction of the voyage.

Hanno established Thymiaterium (the modern Mehdia), the first Carthaginian city in Africa Atlantica, two days after passing the Pillars of Heracles. Sailing to the west, he reached Cape Colieis (Cape Cantin), where he erected a temple to Poseidon, god of the sea. After crossing the mouth of what is now the river Tensift, Hanno founded five coastal towns, including the modern Mogador and Agadir, passed the headland now known as Cape Nun, and then came to a large river called Lixus (the modern Dra), where nomads pastured their flocks. Here the Carthaginians, having befriended the Lixitae, stayed for some months. From the Lixitae Hanno learned that the regions beyond were inhabited by "inhospitable Ethiopians," or Africans, whose land was "infested with wild beasts," and in whose highlands lived "a freakish race of men, the Troglodytes," who, the Lixitae said, were "fleeter of foot than horses."

Hanno persuaded several men of Lixus to accompany him as interpreters, and together the expedition continued to sail south. Near the Tropic of Cancer, on a small island at the head of a gulf, Hanno established Cerne (its precise location is unknown), a post that was to become the most important Carthaginian colony in West Africa.[36] Some distance to the south, his convoy discovered the estuary of a large river, called Chretes, that is generally identified with the modern Senegal. The Carthaginian ships sailed through the delta of the river and came to a great lake containing three islands, above which towered mountains "peopled by savage men wearing skins of wild beasts," who showered stones down upon them in order to prevent the Carthaginians from landing. Forced back, Hanno's men "discovered" another branch of the Senegal replete with crocodiles and hippopotamuses, and then returned to Cerne, perhaps in order to obtain fresh supplies.

Once again Hanno led his ships southward. For twelve days they skirted a land peopled with "Ethiopians," whose language was unintelligible to the Lixitae, before halting in the lee of what doubtless was Cape Verde, with its "varied and fragrant trees." Two days after doubling the Cape, they came into an immense gulf, probably the mouth of the modern Gambia River. The surrounding land was low-lying, and at night they saw flames (grass fires are common to all of tropical Africa before the season for sowing) "leaping up on every side at intervals, now greater, now less." Five days later, after sailing along the coast, Hanno came to another gulf, called Horn of the West by the Lixitae, which may have been the Bay of Bijagós. Hanno reported:

> *In [the bay] there was a large island, and within the island a lake of the sea, in which there was another island. Landing [on the smaller island] during the day*

[35] See the text in C. Müller, *Geographici Graeci Minores* (Paris, 1855), I, pp. 1–14, which is based upon the Heidelberg ms.; Pliny, *NH*, ii, 67, viii, 21. See also Jérôme Carcopino, *Le Maroc antique* (Paris, 1943), pp. 73–163; Stéphane Gsell, *Histoire ancienne de l'Afrique du Nord* (Paris, 1921), I, pp. 472–476, II, p. 190.

[36] See Pliny, *NH*, vi, 36, 1–2, for Ephorus' and Polybius' mention of Cerne. But Raymond Mauny does not think that Hanno passed the river Dra. See his "Note sur le périple d'Hannon," *Comptes rendus: Première Conférence Internationale des Africanistes de l'Ouest* (Paris, 1951), II, p. 529.

we saw nothing but forests, but by night many burning fires, and we heard the sound of pipes and cymbals, and the noise of drums and a great uproar. Then fear possessed us, and the soothsayers commanded us to leave the island.[37]

The Carthaginians fled from the islands and sailed along a "burning country full of fragrance, from which great torrents of fire flowed down to the sea"—probably another extensive grass fire driven by the wind. Hanno continued:

And we sailed along with all speed, being stricken by fear. After a journey of four days, we saw the land at night covered with flames. And in the midst there was one lofty fire, greater than the rest, which seemed to touch the stars. By day this was seen to be a very high mountain, called Chariot of the Gods.[38]

Many writers have equated the Chariot of the Gods with Mount Cameroons, a volcano, perhaps active then, that dominates the Bight of Biafra from a height of 13,360 feet.[39] But it is unlikely that Hanno's timetable would have permitted such a long voyage from Cerne, particularly against the strong Guinea current. Instead, Hanno might have seen Mount Kakulima, which is only 2,910 feet high, but which rises out of the otherwise flat country of modern Sierra Leone. A spectacular grass fire on the flanks of Kakulima could have been described, with poetic license, as a lofty flame touching the stars.

In Hanno's eyes, a grass fire also could have set "the lake ablaze by night" as the Carthaginians sailed south beyond Kakulima to another bay, the so-called Horn of the South, or the modern Sherbro Sound. In the bay was an island, within which was a lake enclosing another island, and on the smaller island Hanno met a large number of men and women with "hairy bodies." His interpreters called them "gorillas," and after giving chase, the Carthaginians captured three females, "who bit and scratched their leaders, and would not follow us." Hanno's men killed these "gorillas" and took their hides to Carthage without ascertaining whether the "gorillas" were, in fact, humans or animals. It seems unlikely that they were what we now term gorillas, and it appears just as improbable that they were a race of small Africans. A more reasonable assumption is that they were chimpanzees. In any event, Hanno and the Carthaginians, in need of provisions, returned home to report upon the colonies—with which Carthage was to trade regularly until its conquest by Rome in 146 B.C.[40]—and to order the carving of the stele. Hanno's example gave rise to the subsequent belief that Africa was capable of circumnavigation. But, although he apparently possessed a knowledge of West Africa greater than any foreigner before A.D. 1436, his efforts did not immediately result in the tying of tropical Africa commercially to the Mediterranean world.

The first attempt to circumnavigate Africa from west to east dates from this

---

37 Hanno (trans. Wilfred H. Schoff), *The Periplus of Hanno* (Philadelphia, 1913), pp. 6–7.

38 *Ibid.*, p. 7.

39 Richard Hennig, "Hannos 'Götterwagen,'" *Geographische Zeitschrift*, XXXIII (1927), pp. 385–392. But see Germain, "Qu'est-ce que le *Périple* d'Hannon?" p. 220.

40 Trade probably continued overland, particularly after the introduction of the camel from Egypt. See the discussion in E. F. Gautier, *L'Afrique noire occidentale* (Paris, 1935), pp. 123–127, and an opposing view in Raymond Mauny, "Que faut-il appeler 'pierres' d'aigris?" *Notes Africaines*, 42 (April, 1949), pp. 33–34.

period. The Persian King Xerxes (485–465 B.C.), who evidently possessed some knowledge of the then prevalent geographical theories, ordered Sataspes, a young Achaemenid, to expiate a misdeed by sailing from the Pillars of Heracles around Africa to the Red Sea. Sataspes procured a vessel and a crew in Egypt and sailed into the Atlantic Ocean. He doubled the headland now known as Cape Spartel and continued in a southwesterly direction for many months, but "when he found that, far though he had sailed, there was always need to sail further yet, he put about and returned to Egypt." [41] When he reached the court of King Xerxes, he averred that at the point where he turned to come home, his crew had "found the coast occupied by small men, who wore clothes made from palm leaves." Wherever the sailors landed, the "pygmies" abandoned their "settlements" and escaped into the hills, while the Egyptians entered their villages and took their cattle, otherwise doing them "no harm." If we assume that Sataspes probably by-passed the Cathaginian outposts and that fairly large African cantonments were more common south of the Senegal River than they were north of it, Sataspes' ship might well have reached the Gulf of Guinea before being "brought to a standstill" by the doldrums.[42]

A geographical and commercial frontier

During the fifth and fourth centuries B.C., Carthage effectively controlled the trade routes between West Africa and the Mediterranean world. Its navy commanded the Pillars of Heracles, forcing the merchants of the Greek city-states to pay Carthaginian imposts when they sent Attic pottery to Cerne in exchange for ivory and gold. For the Aegean men of commerce, this situation was intolerable; they began to wonder whether they could not circumvent Carthage's economic hegemony by sailing directly to Cerne *via* the Red Sea. But informed opinion said no. Already, contemporaries of Aeschylus (*c.* 525–456 B.C.) had "demonstrated" the existence of a land link between tropical Africa and India. To them, the Arabian Sea was a lake and the Nile and Indus rivers were one.[43] Many thought that West Africa was similarly attached to another, unnamed land mass. With the historian Ephorus (*c.* 405–330 B.C.), Greeks also commonly believed that even if Africa were unattached, the heat to be found there would be too great to permit circumnavigation.[44] (Few paid attention to Aristotle [384–322 B.C.] when he postulated the existence of a temperate zone in the southern hemisphere of Africa that corresponded to the known northern temperate zone.) [45] Jealously guarding their commercial monopoly, the Cartha-

---

[41] Herodotus, iv, 43, to whom we are indebted for this information (which he probably obtained from a descendant of Zopyrus, the father of the girl involved), says that Sataspes had raped a girl of a prominent family and "was about to be impaled as punishment by Xerxes, when his mother, who was a sister of Darius, begged him off by promising to inflict upon him a punishment even more severe"—the circumnavigation of Africa.

[42] See the references, *pro* and *con*, in Thomson, *History*, p. 73. Xerxes, after hearing his account, exacted the original penalty, and Sataspes was impaled.

[43] Aeschylus, *The Suppliant Woman*, 384–386, 560.

[44] Pliny, *NH*, vi, 34–35. But cf. Herodotus, i, 203, iv, 42.

[45] Aristotle, *Meteorologica*, ii, 5.

ginians also rumored abroad that the Atlantic was a windless, muddy, shallow, seaweed-infested ocean unfit for human travel south or east of Cerne.[46]

Ptolemy I Soter (323–285 B.C.), who had served with Alexander the Great and had then founded a dynasty of Greek rulers of Egypt, was naturally desirous of furthering Egyptian trade with India.[47] The Arabs controlled the caravan routes, however, and prohibited any direct commercial connections between Egypt and India. In order that he might discover a new sea route to India, Soter sent a large flotilla of ships, commanded by Admiral Philo, to explore the farthest known limits of the Red Sea. Philo and his successors brought back elephants and ivory and quickly reopened the historically profitable commercial relations between Egypt and the peoples of the Cinnamon Coast (modern Somalia) and the Yemen. The Egyptians established new trading posts from which they conducted elephant-hunting expeditions, and many Greeks and Egyptians came to know intimately, for the first time, what is now coastal Arabia, Ethiopia, and Somalia. On their maps, they extended the coastline of Africa beyond the southern limits of the Red Sea to Cape Guardafui, where they bent the continent in a westerly direction toward Cerne.

Rome ended the sea power of Carthage in 242/41 B.C. It failed, however, to use its new freedom of the seas to investigate Africa, possibly because its leaders believed that the temperate zone of the northern hemisphere was the only inhabited part of the earth, and that the Mediterranean world was cut off from the south by a belt of impenetrable heat.[48] Eratosthenes (276–220 B.C.), the learned Alexandrian mathematician, astronomer, geographer, and historian, thought that Africa possessed a pronounced bulge, located south of the Arabian peninsula, that pointed toward India. At the horn of the bulge, Africa turned northwest in the direction of the Pillars of Heracles. Significantly, Eratosthenes also deduced that the tides of the Indian and the Atlantic oceans were sufficiently similar to permit a circumnavigation of the African continent. But his theory was disputed by Crates (d. 145 B.C.), who imagined a separate world south of Africa, and by Hipparchus (190–125 B.C.) and Polybius, who both reflected the view that the African land mass continued indefinitely into the south.[49] In about 146 to 140 B.C., Polybius may have even sailed as far as the Senegal River, but his careful researches appear to have been ignored by writers of later generations.[50] Of considerable contemporary importance, however, was a rumor that Phoenicians from Gades (now Cadiz) in Iberia had managed to circumvent the Ptolemaic commercial control of the Red Sea by sailing around

[46] Ps.-Scylax, "The Periplus," quoted in Bunbury, *Ancient Geography,* I, p. 386. See also Eric H. Warmington, *Greek Geography* (London, 1934), pp. 76–77, for Himilco's views as set down by Avienus.

[47] Alexander ended the usual association of the Nile with the Indus by sailing to the latter's mouth in 325 B.C. He did not, however, live to circumnavigate Africa as he had intended. See C. van Paassen, *The Classical Tradition of Geography* (Groningen, 1957), pp. 263–267.

[48] Strabo, II, v, 7–8.

[49] Polybius, iii, 37; F. W. Walbank, A *Historical Commentary on Polybius* (Oxford, 1957), I, pp. 369–370; Strabo, I, ii, 24–27; Bunbury, *Ancient Geography,* II, pp. 32–33; Cary and Warmington, *Ancient Explorers,* p. 98.

[50] Pliny, *NH,* v, 1.

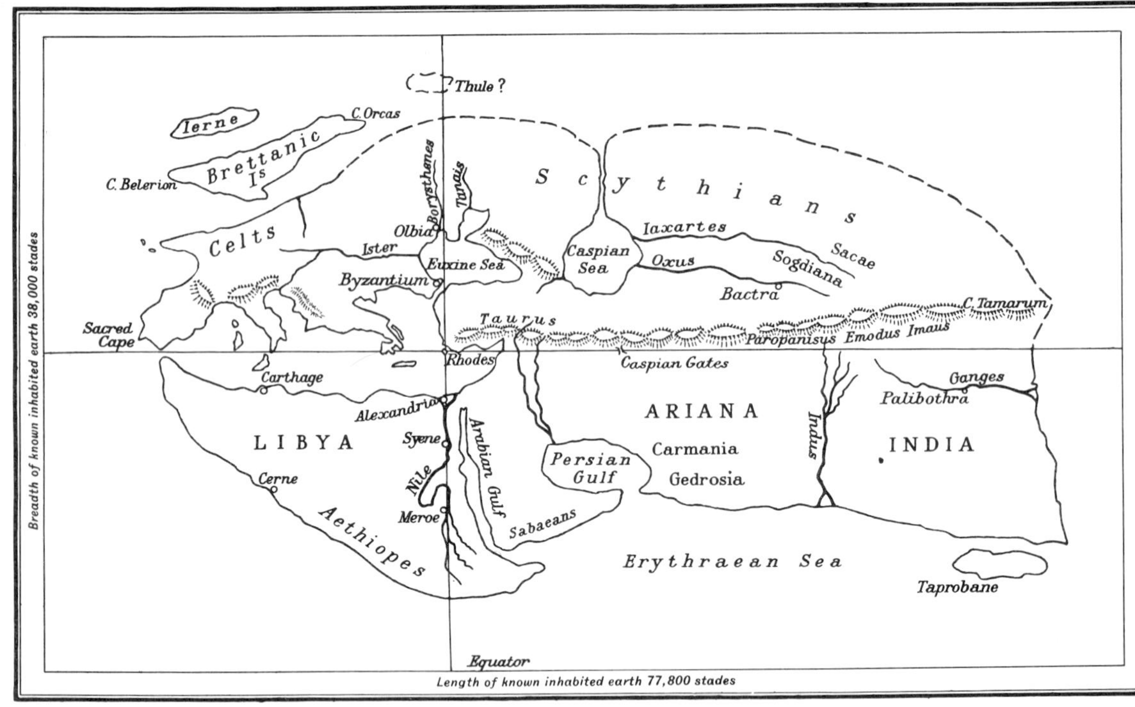

The world according to Eratosthenes, 220 B.C. (John Bartholomew & Son Ltd.)

Africa from west to east. Thereafter, they supposedly traded freely with the peoples of eastern Africa, Arabia, and India.[51]

Ptolemy VIII, Euergetes II or "Physcon" (*c.* 182–116 B.C.), naturally hoped that his captains could find a sea route to India that would enable Egypt both to counter the Phoenician economic threat and to evade the tolls levied by Arabs upon overland trade to the east. In the last years of his reign, he ordered Eudoxus, a wealthy merchant from Cyzicus, a port on the Propontis, to find his way to India. Eudoxus, accompanied by an Indian who earlier had been shipwrecked along the shores of the Red Sea, obeyed, and returned from a coastal voyage to India in about 120 B.C. with a cargo of precious stones and aromatic woods.[52] About five years later, Eudoxus again sailed to India, but on the return trip his ship "was driven out of [its] course by the winds to the south of Ethiopia" —probably the northeast monsoon—and eventually Eudoxus was shipwrecked along the eastern coast of Africa south of Cape Guardafui. Here he shared his bread, wine, and dried figs with persons to whom they had been unknown, thereby "winning their friendship"; Eudoxus may have also taught these people the use of fire.[53] In exchange, his new acquaintances offered Eudoxus fresh water

51 Pliny says that Coelius Antipater had "seen a person who sailed from Spain to Aethiopia for the purpose of trade," about 124 B.C. Pliny, *NH*, ii, 67.

52 Strabo, II, iii, 3–4.

53 On fire, see Cary and Warmington, *Ancient Explorers*, p. 99.

and guides, and helped him to compile a glossary of their language. They also gave him the end of a wooden prow with a horse carved upon it, which they said had come from a ship that had been wrecked upon their shores sometime before. The ship, they told him, had come from the west. Eudoxus eventually took his carved prow back to Egypt and showed it to the shipmasters of Alexandria, who said that the prow could only have come from a ship constructed in Gades. Strabo gives their reasons:

> *Whereas the merchants of Gades fit out large ships, the poor men fit out small ships which they call "horses" from the devices on the prows of their ships, and that they sail with these small ships on fishing voyages . . . as far as the river Lixus . . . some shipmasters, indeed, recognized the figure-head as having belonged to one of the ships that had sailed rather too far beyond the Lixus River and had not returned safely.*[54]

The mariners of Alexandria were so certain in their judgment that Eudoxus decided that he might also—and to some profit—sail from Egypt to India *via* the waters beyond Africa.

Eudoxus obtained a ship in Cyzicus and a crew and cargo in Dicaearchia, Massilia, and Gades. Everywhere, Strabo reports, he noisily proclaimed his scheme and raised money by dubious means:

> *. . . he built a great ship and also two tow-boats like those used by pirates; and he put music-girls on board, and physicians, and other artisans, and finally set sail on the high sea. . . .*[55]

Somewhere along the coast of what is now Morocco, however, Eudoxus ran aground. There he built a new vessel and sailed south for some leagues until (so Strabo says) he found Africans speaking the same language that he had recorded in eastern Africa. Then, presumably because he thought that by sailing from the west he had attained the coast on which he had originally been shipwrecked, Eudoxus abandoned his voyage to India and, turning north, beached his vessels along the northwestern shores of Africa. He failed to persuade the king of the interior kingdom of Bocchus to join him in the search for a safe route to India; he then crossed what later became Roman Numidia on foot and eventually reached Gades, where his tales circulated until they were finally recorded in a distorted form by Pomponius Mela during the first Christian century.[56] In Gades, Eudoxus filled two ships—a long-oared one in which to sail and a round one in which to explore the coasts—with grain and set off once again into the unknown. This, however, was his last voyage; of Eudoxus, the ancients heard no more. Although he had suggested that a route from Europe to India around Africa was feasible, his failures inhibited subsequent Western attempts to settle the question of Africa's circumnavigation.

By the first century B.C., Arab, Indian, Indonesian, and Chinese mariners

---

[54] Strabo, II, iii, 4.

[55] *Ibid.* The towns are now Puteoli, Italy; Marseille; and Cadiz.

[56] Mela, iii, 9:88–99.

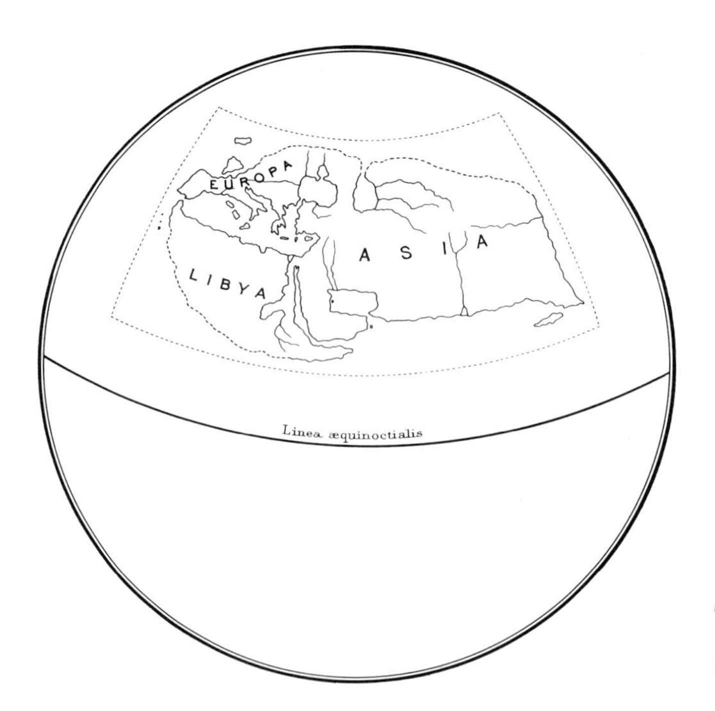

The world according to Strabo, A.D. 18. (John Bartholomew & Son Ltd.)

probably knew far more about tropical Africa than their counterparts in the West, from whom there is little further mention of the continent until the beginning of the Roman Empire. Once Rome ruled Egypt, however, the sea route to India, *via* the Cinnamon Coast, gained renewed importance. During the reign of Augustus (27 B.C.–A.D. 14), as many as 120 ships may have set sail in any given year for northeastern Africa and India. A few furtive sailors may have even doubled Cape Guardafui and continued south along the coasts of eastern Africa despite Strabo's dictum that Africa was cut off from Rome by a dangerous torrid zone.[57] Augustus' mariners failed to discover a useful sea road to India that would enable them to escape the clutches of the Arab sheikhs and the Persian and Parthian potentates who controlled the ports *en route*. Even during the early years of the reign of Emperor Tiberius (A.D. 14–37), Roman captains still paid tolls when they plied the Arabian and Persian coasts. At about this time or conceivably before, Hippalus, a Greek merchant, revolutionized the commerce of the Indian Ocean by demonstrating to the satisfaction of the Mediterranean world that the monsoon winds that blew steadily from May to October from the southwest, and from November to March from the northeast, would permit small ships to sail the open seas directly from the Cinnamon Coast to the Malabar Coast in India.[58] The ease with which he gathered his cargoes

[57] Strabo, XVII, iii, 1.

[58] *Periplus of the Erythraean Sea,* 57. The voyage from Aden to the Malabar Coast took about forty days. Pliny, *NH,* vi, 26. See also Mortimer Wheeler, *Rome Beyond the Imperial Frontiers* (London, 1954), pp. 128–129.

of pepper, gems, pearls, ebony, sandalwood, balm, and spices also excited the cupidity of Rome.

The periplus of the erythraean sea

Soon other merchants, utilizing the discovery of Hippalus, ventured onto the high seas and were carried, perhaps unexpectedly, down the coast of eastern Africa. In the bazaars of Socotra, Barbaricon, Broach, and Malabar, these merchants would, in any event, have learned of commercial possibilities beyond Cape Guardafui. By the reign of the Emperor Nero (A.D. 54–68), Rome was trading regularly with the people of eastern Africa. Greek and Egyptian entrepreneurs had penetrated to the court of the king of Axum and had even sailed as far as lands that lay athwart the equator.

The *Periplus of the Erythraean Sea*, an anonymous Egyptian merchant's guidebook of the second or third century A.D., carefully catalogues the products and the entrepôts important in the commerce of the Indian Ocean.[59] From Adulis, Axum's port on the Red Sea, to Berbera on the southern littoral of the Gulf of Aden, the indigenous products included ivory, tortoise shell suitable for inlaid furniture and woodwork, obsidian (a dark volcanic stone valued for statues and votive offerings), spices, and myrrh. Berbera supplied true frankincense, a hard cinnamon, Indian copal, macir (an aromatic bark), and, "but rarely," slaves. East of Berbera merchants could buy good cassia and frankincense, fragrant gums, spices, some tortoise shell, ivory, and myrrh.[60]

Beyond Cape Guardafui, the so-called Cape of Spices, Opone (probably near the modern Ras Hafun) was the first major port. Here the local merchants offered large quantities of cinnamon, tortoise shell, and "slaves of the better sort," who were sent to Egypt. The *Periplus* next alludes to the paucity of harbors along the Somali coast, describes some stretches of desert, and refers to islands that may have been Lamu, Pate, and Manda. After about fifteen days, its author came to what he called the island of Menuthias. This island, which may be Mafia, Zanzibar, or Pemba, was, by his reckoning, about three hundred stadia (thirty-four miles) from the mainland; it appeared low and wooded, with "rivers and many kinds of birds and mountain-dwelling tortoises." On Menuthias

> [There were] *no wild animals except the crocodiles; but there they do no harm to men. In this place there are boats which are sewn together, and* [canoes] *hollowed from single pieces of wood, which they use for fishing and catching tortoises. In this island they catch them in a peculiar manner, in wicker baskets instead of fish-nets, which they place across the edges of the breakers.*[61]

---

59 On new South Arabian and Indian evidence, Jacqueline Pirenne and others think that the true date may be between A.D. 210 and 220. Heretofore most scholars accepted a first century date. See Jacqueline Pirenne, "Un Problème-clef pour la chronologie de l'Orient: la date du 'Périple de la mer Erythrée,' " *Journal Asiatique*, CCXLIX (1961), pp. 441–459. But Gervase Mathew dates the *Periplus* in A.D. 110. Roland Oliver and Gervase Mathew (eds.), *History of East Africa* (Oxford, 1963), I, p. 94.

60 *Periplus*, 8.

61 *Ibid.*, 15. Sewn boats may imply the presence or the influence of Indonesians. The passage is also corrupt and possibly an amalgam. It is unlikely that the author personally visited Menuthias. I am indebted to Dr. Gruen for translations from the *Periplus*.

Rhapta, which the author of the *Periplus* affirms to be the "very last market-town of Azania," lay a sail of two days from Menuthias. At Rhapta, conceivably a site in the Rufiji delta, Muhembo near the modern Pangani, or Chogwe, upstream on the Pangani River, visitors purchased soft ivory, rhinoceros horn, tortoise shell, and palm oil.[62]

Regarding the people of Rhapta, and therefore those of eastern Africa, the *Periplus* says only:

> *Men of piratical habits, and of very great size, live all about this land, having similar types of rulers in each place. The Mopharitic ruler governs it in accord with some ancient right that subjects it to the sovereignty of the state that is become first in Arabia. The people of Muza now hold it subject to tribute from the king, and send thither many small boats, employing Arab helmsmen and servants who live together with the people of Rhapta and intermarry with them, and who know the area and understand their language.*[63]

At this time, it seems, the inhabitants of "great size" were probably Africans ruled by indigenous or Arab (even Indonesian) subjects of the sheikhs of Mopharitis and Muza, two principalities of southern Arabia. These people of Rhapta were relatively prosperous, importing lances especially made for the trade, hatchets, daggers, awls, various kinds of glass, wine, and wheat—useful "for getting the good-will of the savages"—into a region where the local population probably still subsisted upon sorghum and millet, if they cultivated at all, and depended upon visiting merchants for their supply of metal implements.

Greeks and occasional Romans continued to compete with Arabs and Indians for the wealth of Africa, at least until the economic decline of Rome in the third century A.D. Their reports, and the tales of the bazaars on the shores of the Indian Ocean, gave to Africa the distorted configuration that it retained, in some detail, until the nineteenth century. One early seafarer, a certain Diogenes, may, however, have visited the interior of East Africa. As recorded by Marinus of Tyre and, later, by Ptolemy, the second-century A.D. Egyptian astronomer and geographer, Diogenes was blown off course when passing Cape Guardafui. He sailed south for twenty-five days, landed north of Rhapta, and either traveled inland or collected information about the interior. Upon his return, he described two large inland lakes and a range of snowy mountains in the region where the Nile River rose. He (or possibly his later interpreters) also reported a snow-capped southern African range, called the Mountains of the Moon, that stretched east and west for five hundred miles. The snow melted and fed two lakes to the north, and from each lake flowed two rivers that later joined to form the Nile.[64] Did Diogenes or his African and Arab informants visit Mount Kenya and Kilimanjaro, both of which are snow-topped? Or did he reach Ruwenzori, which has glacial moraines resembling the visible surface of

---

[62] See J. W. T. Allen, "Rhapta," *Tanganyika Notes and Records*, 27 (1949), pp. 55–58; Oliver and Mathew, *History*, p. 97.
[63] *Periplus*, 16.
[64] Ptolemy, i, 9.

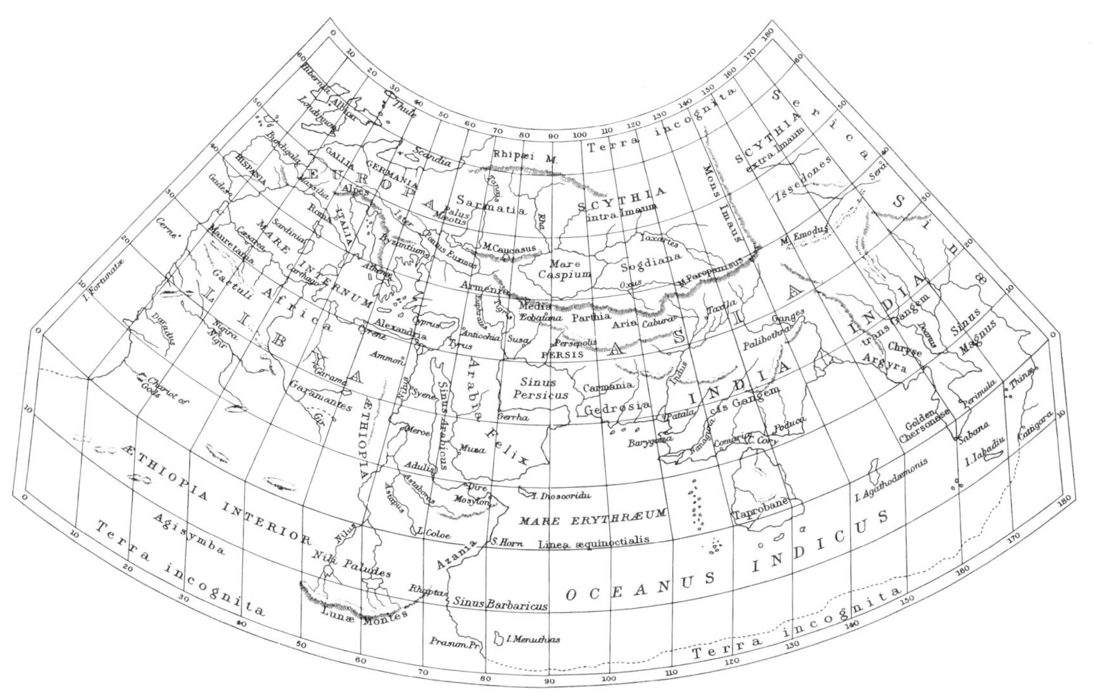

The world according to Ptolemy, A.D. 150. (John Bartholomew & Son Ltd.)

the moon? Did he then assume, or did he somehow learn, that the snows fed the lakes and the lakes the rivers? Might Diogenes in fact have espied Victoria Nyanza, the lake that does feed the White Nile?

Ptolemy compiled his *Geography* between A.D. 125 and 155. He duly determined the size, shape, and features of the earth by carefully comparing and extracting details from copious peripli, accounts, and tales supplied by, or handed down from, explorers and the friends of explorers. Ptolemy's version (which may have been revised in Alexandria in the fifth century, or later) summarizes the Mediterranean world's knowledge of Africa during the second century.[65] His view of Africa influenced Western ideas about the continent in many respects until the Portuguese voyages and, with regard to much of the interior, until the nineteenth century. Ptolemy's Africa is rectangular—he seems to have known little about the west coast, which he shows as almost straight, and his Niger River flows from lakes to swamps without any outlet to the sea (probably following the tale of the Nasamonians). In the east, he postulated Prason, or Cape Delgado, as the southernmost limit of the continent. There he joined Africa to Chinese Asia by a long foot of land. Menuthias (which in his account may be one of the Comoro Islands or even Madagascar) is a small island to the east of Prason and southeast of Rhapta. The eastern interior, fol-

[65] Ptolemy, iv, 1–8.

lowing Diogenes, contains Mounts Pylae and Maste (Kenya and Kilimanjaro?), the Mountains of the Moon, two lakes, and rivers that wind their way to the Nile. White elephants, rhinoceros, and leopards abound. The indigenous inhabitants are divided into western and eastern groups, cannibals and fish-eaters. In the far south of Ptolemy's Africa is the mysterious land of the Agisymba, which the geographer probably placed much farther south than the Agisymban region (probably Chad) that a Roman officer named Julius Maternus had visited during the early part of the second century A.D.[66]

III. The Kingdom of Axum

Even as Ptolemy wrote, the Ethiopian people of Axum began to emerge from centuries of relative obscurity. About 350 B.C., numerous immigrants from the fertile Yemeni plateaux established colonies in the highlands west of the Red Sea.[67] From the flourishing Arabian kingdoms of Ma'in, Qataban, Saba, and Hadramawt, where they had already ingeniously developed the countryside by building dikes, terraces, and irrigation systems with which to capture and utilize the monsoon rains, they brought important cultural contributions: a highly developed sense of social and religious organization, knowledge of the cultivation of incense trees and spices and of the domestication of cattle and camels, an urban architecture, codified laws of property and, of primary importance, a system of writing. It is only from engraved examples of this written language—originally Sabaean (a southern Arabian language related to Hebrew and Phoenician) and later the distinctive Ge'ez—and the Greek used by the royal court from the first through the fourth centuries A.D., that we can begin to appreciate the early history of these peoples.[68]

Sometime during the second century B.C., after distance and time had eroded their filial ties to Arabia, the Yemeni immigrants established the city and the kingdom of Axum in the highlands of modern Tigre. They continued to trade with the mother country and, by the middle of the first century A.D., the kings of Axum also supplied Greece and Rome with African raw materials. They controlled much of what is now Eritrea and northeastern Ethiopia, and from Kush their caravan leaders obtained ivory, gold, and rhinoceros horns. Local farmers grew spices and gum arabic, and the inhabitants of the Red Sea littoral collected tortoise shell from nearby islands. The *Periplus* tells us that Axum's main port was Adulis, significantly "established by law." There the merchants of Axum offered their own products in exchange for undressed cloth made in Egypt, dyed cloaks of poor quality, linen mantles, articles of flint glass, brass, sheets of soft copper, iron ingots, small axes, wine, a little olive oil, and gold

---

[66] Ptolemy, i, 8.

[67] Although the ruling dynasty of modern Ethiopia traces its line of descent from the liaison between King Solomon and the Queen of Sheba (I Kings 10:1–13; II Chronicles 9:1–12), the Queen of Sheba (Saba?) seems not to have come from what is now modern Ethiopia.

[68] See Carlo Conti Rossini, *Storia d'Etiopia* (Milano, 1928), I, pp. 113–114; Edward Ullendorff, *The Semitic Languages of Ethiopia* (London, 1955), pp. 8–17.

and silver—"made after the fashion of the country"—for King Zoscales, whose court was in Axum. The *Periplus* describes him as being "miserly in his ways and always striving for more, but otherwise upright, and acquainted with Greek literature." [69]

The powerful Ethiopian armies increased the international importance of Axum during the second and third centuries A.D. They made conquests along the Red Sea and the Blue Nile, and they claim to have humbled a people "who lived beyond the Nile on mountains difficult of access and covered with snow, where the year is all winter with hailstorms, frosts and snows into which a man sinks knee-deep." [70] In the latter part of the third century, Axum also appears to have assisted Queen Zenobia of Palmyra in her campaign against Egypt and Rome, but the extent of this assistance is not known. During this period, the imperial interests of Axum were more sharply focused upon Arabia, where King Afilas of Axum transformed his control of a number of provinces into an attack upon King Shammar Yuhar'ish and a conquest of the Yemen.

The civilization of Axum reached its fullest flower during the fourth century A.D. 'Ezana, the most influential ruler of the period, unified Ethiopian Axum and integrated the Yemen into the empire, vanquished the nomadic Beja, and finally invaded Kush, which earlier had been subdued by his father. In A.D. 330, because the people of Meroë had broken solemn oaths, "had killed their neighbours without mercy," had failed to heed 'Ezana's warnings, and "had [betaken] themselves to flight," he "made war on them." The armies of Meroë

> *fled without making a stand, and I pursued them for twenty-three days, killing some and capturing others. . . . I burnt their towns, both those built of bricks and those built of reeds, and my army carried off their food and copper and iron . . . and destroyed the statues in their temples, their granaries, and cotton trees and cast them into the [Nile].* [71]

'Ezana's army swept into Kush as far as the confluence of the Atbara and Nile rivers, thereafter probably razing Meroë and villages along the Dongola Reach.

These victories were of epic proportions; however, the conversion of 'Ezana to Christianity proved an even more decisive event in the history of what was to become the world's oldest continuing Christian kingdom. In about A.D. 333, Frumentius, a Syrian Christian who earlier had become the young prince's tutor after being shipwrecked along the Red Sea coast, persuaded the mature 'Ezana—who conceivably wanted to cement an alliance with the emperor at Constantinople—to accept the Christian faith. Frumentius, during a visit to Alexandria, was made ethnarch of Ethiopia by St. Athanasius. In Axum, Monophysite Christianity became the state religion, the coins and inscriptions

---

[69] *Periplus*, 5.

[70] J. W. McCrindle (trans.), *The Christian Topography of Cosmas, an Egyptian Monk* (London, 1897), pp. 61–62. Were the conquered people Falasha? Was the river really the Takkage, not the Nile? And were the mountains those of Semien?

[71] Translated in L. P. Kirwan, "A Survey of Nubian Origins," *Sudan Notes and Records*, XX (1937), pp. 49–51; E. A. Wallis Budge, *A History of Ethiopia, Nubia and Abyssinia* (London, 1928), I, pp. 252–258.

of 'Ezana henceforth carrying such Christian invocations as "By might of the Lord of Heaven who in Heaven and on Earth has power of all." [72] The mint stamped the coins of Axum with crosses where previously they had been marked with a crescent and a disk. Slowly Monophysite Christianity spread throughout the empire of Axum, perhaps assisting in the integration of what otherwise must have been a disparate congerie of tribes and ethnic groups.[73]

The monasteries became the cultural centers of the kingdom. During the fifth century, the clerical ranks were swelled significantly by the addition of monks forced to flee from Syria after the Council of Chalcedon, in A.D. 451, had declared the Monophysite persuasion heretical. (Essentially, Monophysites believed that the human and the divine in Christ constituted only one nature.) These foreign monks founded numerous new churches, constructed a series of impregnable retreats, introduced new conceptions of austerity, and in general tried to wean Axumites away from traditional religious practices. They began a ceaseless struggle against Judaism, which was then being vigorously promoted in southern Arabia, and against all of the other enemies of the young Christian religion. During this period, they also wrote down a version of the New Testament and translated it into Ge'ez according to the Lucianic recension, composed a number of liturgical chants, and introduced religious dances that have remained important in the celebrations of their Church.

Axum was in regular contact with Byzantium, Persia, India, and Ceylon during the fifth and sixth centuries. Her markets, with their supplies of emeralds, gold, incense, cassia, and spices, attracted merchants from all corners of the globe. Among them were the Greeks and Egyptians who told the merchant Cosmas Indicopleustes of the town of Axum's gracious architecture and the beauty of its statues. The palace of the king of Axum, Cosmas reported, had four corners set with towers, mounted on which were four statues in the form of unicorns; on the grounds of the palace tame giraffes and elephants strolled.[74] A traveler of the late sixth century, Emperor Justinian's ambassador Julian, said that the king of Axum wore "a linen cloth interlaced with gold wrapped about his loins."

> *A short tunic hung floating from his shoulders, ornamented with pearls and precious stones arranged in rosettes; upon his head he wore a cloth of linen, interwoven with gold, in the form of a turban, with four gold ornaments suspended from each side; while a golden chain served as a necklace. The monarch was seated upon a high four-wheeled chariot drawn by a team of elephants, and in his hands he held two javelins and a buckler of gold. . . .*[75]

---

[72] Previous rulers offered their thanks to the "mighty God, Arês, who begat me," and sacrificed to Zeus, Ares, and Poseidon. See McCrindle, *Cosmas*, pp. 65–66. See also A. Kammerer, *Essai sur l'histoire antique d'Abyssinie* (Paris, 1926), pp. 99–103.

[73] See J. Spencer Trimingham, *Islam in Ethiopia* (London, 1952), pp. 38–39.

[74] McCrindle, *Cosmas*, p. 359. See also E. O. Winstedt (ed.), *The Christian Topography of Cosmas Indicopleustes* (Cambridge, Eng., 1909), pp. 335–346.

[75] A. H. M. Jones and Elizabeth Monroe, *A History of Ethiopia* (Oxford, 1955), pp. 32–33. See also Procopius, *History of the Wars*, I, xx, 9–10. But see Jean Doresse, *Ethiopia* (New York, 1959), p. 85, where the same quotation is erroneously attributed to Joannus Malalas.

Cosmas visited Adulis at a time when its ruler Ella Atsbeha was engaged in a bloody religious war with the Yemen. The evangelical zeal of the Christian communities of southern Arabia conflicted with the religious fervor of King Yusef-As'a (Dhu Nuwas) of Yemeni Himyar, who had been converted to a fanatical Jewish sect. He began to persecute the Christians of southern Arabia, who in turn appealed to the king of Axum and Emperor Justin I. The latter supposedly encouraged the king of Axum, as the nearest Christian ruler, to aid his oppressed co-religionists in Arabia. Whether or not the reported communication is apocryphal, the Ethiopian expeditions of A.D. 523 brought a temporary halt to the persecutions. The Himyarites later massacred large numbers of Christians at Najran, but in A.D. 525 the armies of Axum, with assistance from the Roman and Persian navies, subdued the Yemen and killed Yusef-As'a.[76]

Axum soon lost its effective hegemony in the Yemen and, with it, her influence as a Christian protector. The Ethiopian troops in the conquered territory successfully rebelled and detached the Yemen from Axum. Then, in the last years of the sixth century A.D., the Persians overran all of Arabia and eliminated the last vestiges of Axum's influence in its former homeland. Their navy also raided the western shores of the Red Sea and deprived Axum of some of its coastal holdings and commercial outlets. Later, the depredations of the nomadic Beja, who threatened Axum from the north, and the power of Islam in the Hejaz and in Egypt, increased the extent of Axum's isolation from the centers of the Byzantine world. Despite the Prophet Muhammad's partiality for the rulers of Axum, his followers fought the Axumites during the latter years of the seventh century and finally devastated Adulis in about A.D. 710.[77] Their actions conclusively turned the highland kingdom in upon itself. We can therefore date the decline of Axum and, after an appropriate interlude, the rise of modern Ethiopia, from the nascence of Islam.

---

[76] Jacques Ryckmans, *La Persécution des chrétiens Himyarites au sixième siècle* (Istanbul, 1956); Kammerer, *Essai*, pp. 107–114.

[77] But see Budge, *Ethiopia*, p. 274.

[The peoples of Mali in the Western Sudan] possess some admirable qualities. They are seldom unjust, and have a greater abhorrence of injustice than any other people. Their sultan shows no mercy to anyone who is guilty of the least act of it. There is complete security in their country.

—Ibn Battuta, 1355

2 *THE ERA OF EMPIRES AND CITY-STATES, 800–1500*

For the period between A.D. 800 and 1500, we cannot begin to demonstrate a continuum relevant for all of tropical Africa and must therefore be content, for the moment, with a selection of episodes physically and temporally separated. Such a treatment follows the accounts of those peripatetic merchants and explorers who journeyed to East and West Africa at a time when Islam was in the ascendant and the wealthy of Europe and Asia were clamoring for the exotic commodities of *bilad-es-Sudan*—the land of the blacks. We must rely upon armchair geographic compilations gathered from travelers or the men of the marts, upon the more complete descriptions of those who actually visited Africa south of the Sahara, upon oral tradition collected after the fact, and upon a growing collection of archaeological evidence. What results is an outline of events in the savannah belt south of the Sahara and north of the forest, along the eastern coast, and in the central interior. We also gain some perspective upon Africa's relations with the remainder of the known world.

I. The Western and Central Sudan

Tradition dates the founding of Ghana, the first West African kingdom of which we possess any detailed knowledge, as early as the third century A.D. In the territories of Awkar and Hawd, in what is now southeastern Mauritania, twenty-two Ghanaian kings supposedly ruled before the time of the *Hijra* (A.D. 622), another twenty-two reigning until the First Dynasty was overthrown during the eighth century.[1] Several writers assume that the original ruling elite included descendants of a group of Judaic or Syrian farmers, merchants, and professionals who had fled from Cyrenaica after abortive risings against Rome in the first

[1] 'Abd al-Rahman bin 'Amir as-Sa'di (trans. Octave Houdas), *Tarikh es-Soudan* (Paris, 1900), p. 18; Mahmud al-Kati (trans. Octave Houdas and Maurice Delafosse), *Tarikh el-Fettach* (Paris, 1913), p. 76.

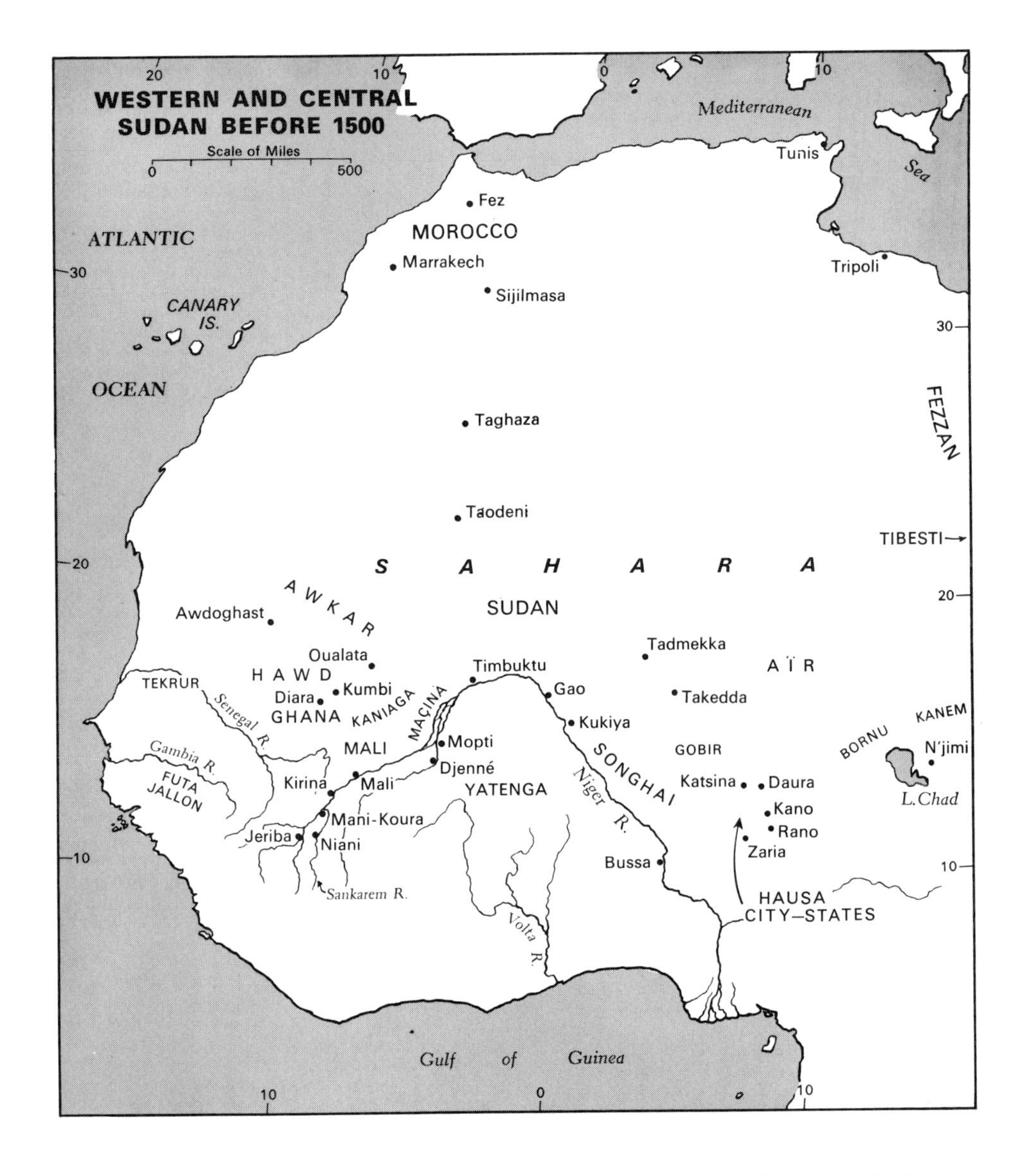

and second centuries A.D. According to this view, now widely regarded with suspicion, the exiles intermarried with Berbers living west of Cyrenaica and eventually established themselves, together with their cattle, among the Mande-speaking Soninke population of Ghana. They constituted an elite that gradually helped the Soninke to take advantage of their economically unparalleled position athwart the main trade routes between the markets of the Niger River basin and the trade centers of the Mediterranean littoral.[2] But outside influence need

[2] Maurice Delafosse, *Haut-Sénégal-Niger* (Paris, 1912), II, pp. 24–27; Raymond Mauny, "Le Judaïsme, les Juifs et l'Afrique occidentale," *Bulletin de l'Institut Français d'Afrique Noire*, XI (1949), pp. 354–378.

not have been responsible for the formation and construction of a Ghanaian state. Indigenous aptitude, firmly rooted in traditional modes of social organization and coupled with an expanding economy, could easily have proved sufficient.

The rise of ghana

Muhammad bin Ibrahim al-Fazari, an eighth-century Arab astronomer, provides the first written mention of Ghana—what he calls the land of gold.[3] The ninth-century Persian mathematician and geographer Muhammad Khwarizmi placed Ghana upon the first important Islamic map of the world and assigned to it a longitude and a latitude; the Egyptian historian Ibn 'Abd al-Hakam, who lived at about the same time, alluded generally to the existence of the gold of Ghana.[4] But only 'Ahmad ibn Wadih al-Ya'qubi, a geographer who wrote toward the end of the ninth century, clothed the Ghanaian skeleton with substantial flesh. He based his survey of the Western Sudan upon information perhaps obtained in Cairo. "Finally," he concluded, "there is the kingdom of Ghana. Its king is mighty, and in his land are gold mines. Under his authority are various other kingdoms . . . and in all of this region there is gold." [5]

In the eyes of the early medieval writers, Ghana's renown remained exclusively commercial. She and her successor states dominated the southern entrepôts of a caravan route that wound its way north *via* Awdoghast across the Sahara to Taodeni and Taghaza, where there were salt mines, to Sijilmasa, a prosperous Sanhajan market town whose merchants had engrossed the salt trade, and thence to Fez in Morocco.[6] In the bazaars of Ghana, local entrepreneurs bartered gold, ivory, and slaves for the salt of the Sahara—which supposedly was worth its weight in gold—and for the horses, cloth, swords, and books of North Africa and Europe. The Ghanaians controlled the major sources of gold, one of which was the "Wangara" region referred to by medieval writers and perhaps located along the upper reaches of the Senegal River. According to 'Abdul Hasan 'Ali al-Mas'udi, a tenth-century geographer from Baghdad who spent two decades exploring the Islamic world and countries as distant as China and Madagascar, the Ghanaians obtained the gold of Wangara by trading for it "silently."

> *The kingdom of Ghana is one of great importance, and it adjoins the land of the gold mines. Great peoples of the Sudan live there. They have traced a boundary*

---

[3] Text in Yusuf Kamal, *Monumenta cartographica Africae et Aegypti* (Cairo, 1926–1938), III, i, p. 510.

[4] Ibn 'Abd al-Hakam (trans. Albert Gateau), *Conquête de l'Afrique du Nord et de l'Espagne* (Alger, 1947), p. 123.

[5] 'Ahmad ibn Wadih al-Katib al-'Abbasi al-Ya'qubi (ed. Th. Houtsma), *Historiae* (Leiden, 1883), I, p. 220. I am grateful to Prof. L. Carl Brown for new translations from the Arabic of al-Ya'qubi. See also H. Richmond Palmer (ed.), *Sudanese Memoirs* (Lagos, 1928), II, p. 20.

[6] On Sijilmasa and trade routes, see 'Abd Allah Muhammad ibn 'Ahmad al-Muqadassi (trans. Charles Pellat), *Description de l'occident musulman* (Alger, 1950), p. 29; Benjamin E. Thomas, *Trade Routes of Algeria and the Sahara* (Berkeley, 1957), pp. 165–166, 173; E. W. Bovill, *Caravans of the Old Sahara* (London, 1933), pp. 43–44; Daniel McCall, "The Traditions of the Founding of Sijilmassa and Ghana," *Transactions of the Historical Society of Ghana*, V (1961), pp. 3–32.

which no one who sets out to them ever crosses. When the merchants reach this boundary, they place their wares and cloth on it and then depart, and so the people of the Sudan come, bearing gold, which they leave beside the merchandise and then [themselves] depart. The owners of the merchandise then return, and if they are satisfied with what they have found, they take it. If not, they go away again, and the people of the Sudan return and add to the price until the bargain is concluded.[7]

During the middle of the tenth century, Ibn Hawqal, who also came from Baghdad, took two months to go from Sijilmasa to Awdoghast and Ghana. He confirmed the earlier economic reports: in Awdoghast in 951 he saw eloquent testimony—a promissory note for the sum of 42,000 *dinars* issued by a local merchant to his factor in Sijilmasa [8]—to the value of commercial intercourse between the Western Sudan and the Mediterranean. He also indicated that the wealth of Awdoghast and the riches of Sijilmasa were all ultimately derived from Ghana, whose king "was the richest in the world because of his gold." [9]

Ghana reached its imperial zenith during the tenth and eleventh centuries. In 990, its cavalry regiments conquered Awdoghast, then the center of a Sanhajan state, and subjected peoples living between the middle reaches of the Senegal River and the great bend in the Niger River to the rule of the kings of Ghana.[10] At the center of this large empire was a capital city that al-Kati called Kumbi [11] and that 'Abu 'Ubayd al-Bakri, the eleventh-century Arab geographer of Cordoba, described from documentary evidence:

Ghana consists of two towns lying in a plain. One of these towns is inhabited by Muslims. It is large and possesses twelve mosques in one of which the people assemble for the Friday prayer. There are imams, muazzins, and salaried reciters of the Koran as well as jurists and learned men. Around the town are wells of sweet water from which they drink and near which they grow vegetables.

The town in which the king lives is six miles from the Muslim one and bears the name Al Ghaba. The land between the two towns is covered with houses. The

---

[7] 'Abdul Hasan 'Ali al-Mas'udi (trans. G. Barbier Meynard and Pavet de Courteille), *Les Prairies d'or* (Paris, 1845), IV, p. 93. The English translation is from J. D. Fage, "Ancient Ghana: A Review of the Evidence," *Transactions of the Historical Society of Ghana,* III (1957), p. 79. Mas'udi's description of "dumb barter" is reminiscent of classical accounts. See Herodotus, iv, 195–197; J. W. McCrindle (trans.), *The Christian Topography of Cosmas* (London, 1897), pp. 52–53; J. Oliver Thomson, *History of Ancient Geography* (Cambridge, Eng., 1948), pp. 307, 367. The description was later echoed by Duarte Pacheco Pereira (trans. George H. T. Kimble), *Esmeraldo de Situ Orbis* (London, 1937), p. 89 [i, 29]; George Francis Lyon, *A Narrative of Travels in Northern Africa* (London, 1821), p. 149.

[8] One *dinar* equaled the weight of seventy-two grains of barley. At current prices, 42,000 *dinars* would approximate $300,000.

[9] Ibn Hawqal (trans. MacGuckin de Slane), "Description de l'Afrique," *Journal Asiatique,* XIII (1842), p. 253. The author explained that he had not discussed the Western Sudan at length because "naturally loving wisdom, ingenuity, religion, justice, and regular government, how could I notice such people as these, or magnify them by inserting an account of their countries?"

[10] On Awdoghast, see the summary in J. Spencer Trimingham, *A History of Islam in West Africa* (London, 1962), p. 21n; Raymond Mauny, *Tableau géographique de l'Ouest africain au Moyen Âge* (Dakar, 1961), pp. 71–72.

[11] Al-Kati, *Tarikh,* p. 76.

houses of the inhabitants are made of stone and acacia wood. The king has a palace and a number of dome-shaped dwellings, the whole surrounded by an enclosure like the defensive wall of a city. In the town where the king lives, and not far from the hall in which he holds his court of justice, is a mosque where pray the Muslims who come on visiting diplomatic missions. Around the king's town are domed buildings, woods, and copses where live the sorcerers of these people, the men in charge of the religious cult.[12]

Archaeologists have tentatively located the remains of the Muslim town at Kumbi Salih about two hundred miles north of modern Bamako. Its stone ruins cover approximately one square mile, within which are a mosque, several large tombs, and well-built houses of stone, a material uncommon in the Western Sudan. The houses are decorated with triangular niches and Qur'anic inscriptions. Surrounding the city are two square miles of ancient cemeteries, stark testimony to the longevity of Kumbi Salih. Although its royal twin has not yet been unearthed—perhaps because its dwellings were built of materials less durable than those of Kumbi Salih—a site ten miles distant, now called Ghanata, may eventually prove to be the indigenous center of Al Ghaba.[13]

From his capital a powerful monarch ruled the far-flung empire of Ghana with the assistance of a number of viceroys, each of whom exercised a subordinate command in the provinces. Councilors, some of whom may have possessed supposed oracular powers, advised the king and his viceroys in accordance with what al-Bakri calls their religion of paganism and their cult of idols.[14] The elaborate protocol of the king's court expressed the religious and secular veneration accorded to the king of Ghana by his subjects. Al-Bakri wrote:

The king adorns himself like a woman, wearing necklaces and bracelets, and when he sits before the people he puts on a high cap decorated with gold and wrapped in turbans or fine cotton. The court of appeal is held in a domed pavilion around which stand ten horses with gold embroidered trappings. Behind the king stand ten pages holding shields and swords decorated with gold, and on his right are the sons of the subordinate kings . . . all wearing splendid garments and with their hair mixed with gold. On the ground around him are seated his ministers, whilst the governor of the city sits before him. On guard at the door are dogs of fine pedigree, wearing collars of gold and silver adorned with knobs. . . . The royal audience is announced by the beating of a drum . . . made out of a long piece of hollowed-out wood. When the people have gathered, his co-religionists draw near upon their knees sprinkling dust upon their heads as a sign of respect, whilst the Muslims clap hands as their form of greeting.[15]

---

[12] 'Abu 'Ubayd al-Bakri (trans. MacGuckin de Slane), *Description de l'Afrique septentrionale* (Alger, 1913), pp. 328–329. The English translation is from Fage, "Ancient Ghana," p. 81.

[13] See Paul Thomassey and Raymond Mauny, "Campagne de fouilles à Koumbi Saleh," *Bulletin de l'Institut Français d'Afrique Noire,* XIII (1951), pp. 438–462; Thomassey and Mauny, "Campagne de fouilles de 1950 à Koumbi Saleh (Ghana?)," *ibid.,* XVIII (1956), pp. 117–140; Fage, "Ancient Ghana," pp. 91–92.

[14] Al-Bakri, *Description,* p. 328.

[15] *Ibid.,* pp. 329–330.

The king derived the revenues with which to support such ostentation by taxing all exports and imports. He prevented depressions in the local price of gold by imposing artificial controls upon the accumulation of gold. Within his markets, merchants also traded kola nuts, honey, and slaves for copper, dried fruit, cowrie shells, and the ever-precious salt.

Although the armies of Ghana had conquered the Sanhajan stronghold of Awdoghast in 990, both contenders continued to struggle for control of the profitable commerce of the Western Sudan. Until the middle of the tenth century, the divided Sanhajan tribes were too weak to defy Ghana. In time, however, economic pressures attendant upon a decline in caravan profits, the commercial and military power of Ghana, and—if traditional accounts are credible—the efforts of a religious revivalist, who preached a doctrine of purity and the annihilation of the unfaithful, unified the Lamtuna, Masufa, and Godala branches of the Sanhajan people. Earlier in the tenth century, a Godala chief, Yahia ibn Ibrahim, supposedly returned from a pilgrimage to Mecca, *via* Fez and Sijilmasa, with a new understanding of the essentials of the Islamic faith. In order to increase his people's appreciation of the true meaning of the word of the Prophet Muhammad, he persuaded 'Abdullah ibn Yasin, a priest resident in Sijilmasa, to spread the reformist gospel among the Godala. But when Ibn Yasin preached, his message offended them. Together with Yahia ibn 'Umar and 'Abu Bakr, two descendants of an important Sanhajan chief, 'Abdullah ibn Yasin fled to the Atlantic littoral after the death of Yahia ibn Ibrahim. They supposedly secreted themselves upon a small island in the mouth of the Senegal River and subjected one another, and a growing group of followers, to a severe regimen of religious and military instruction.[16] By 1042, according to tradition, 'Abdullah ibn Yasin and his supporters were sufficiently strong to unite the Lamtuna, Masufa, and Godala, by force, under an Almoravid [17] banner and to pose a severe challenge to the might of Ghana.

'Abdullah ibn Yasin proclaimed a *jihad* or holy war. In 1054, his followers reconquered Awdoghast, a large city of markets, palm groves, and "henna trees as large as olive trees," [18] and massacred the Ghanaian garrison. The Almoravid army, which included about thirty thousand foot soldiers and several regiments of camel-mounted cavalry, then continued north under the leadership of 'Abdullah ibn Yasin (who died in 1057) and Yusuf ibn Tashfin. It occupied Fez in 1062, parts of southern Spain in 1086, and all of Islamic Iberia by 1102.[19] Meanwhile, a group of Almoravids had, after the conquest of Fez, detached themselves from the main current of the movement and had chosen instead to follow 'Abu Bakr. Revolts within this branch of the army threatened to destroy its unity; 'Abu Bakr therefore launched a southern campaign along the traditional caravan route. Ghana, which still controlled access to the riches of

---

[16] *Ibid.*, p. 316; Delafosse, *Sénégal*, II, p. 34.

[17] From *al-murabitun,* meaning "people of the hermitage."

[18] Al-Bakri, *Description*, p. 317.

[19] 'Abd al-Rahman ibn Khaldun (trans. MacGuckin de Slane), *Histoire des Berbères et des dynasties musulmanes de l'Afrique septentrionale* (Alger, 1854), II, pp. 67–105.

the Western Sudan, seemed an obvious target. In 1076/77, ten years after the Battle of Hastings, the Almoravids razed the capital city of Ghana after a prolonged and bloody struggle.[20]

Although the state of Ghana continued to exist, its imperial power was beyond repair. Its rulers may have hoped to resurrect the glory of Ghana by transferring the capital of their kingdom to the banks of the Niger River,[21] but the nomadic Almoravids laid waste to the land and pillaged the old empire of Ghana to such an extent that the delicate balance of nature on which the local agriculturalists depended was permanently disrupted. Islam made numerous converts in Ghana, thereby sundering the traditional social fabric, in some ways irreparably. Furthermore, decades of warfare naturally interfered with the trans-Saharan trade and brought economic hardship to the peoples of the Western Sudan. The commercial ties that had linked the provinces to the capital of imperial Ghana, and that had joined Ghana to North Africa, were cut. Oualata, to the north, replaced Kumbi as the most important of the southern market towns.

By the thirteenth century, Ghana was too weak to maintain its independence. The Sussu and Malian armies attacked the Ghanaian capital. Ibn Battuta, who traveled extensively within the Western Sudan during the fourteenth century, failed to mention Ghana, and the Andalusian historian 'Abd al-Rahman ibn Khaldun, a contemporary of Ibn Battuta, considered Ghana tributary to the young empire of Mali.[22]

Mali and songhai

Mali, with its center in the comparatively fertile plateau region between the upper reaches of the Senegal and Niger rivers, replaced Ghana as the most important kingdom of the Western Sudan. Both al-Bakri and al-Idrisi (who wrote in the twelfth century) referred to an African province or city-state—named Malel—which conceivably might have been the area from which the empire of Mali later expanded. Al-Bakri said that the king of Malel was a Muslim who had joined the faith after prayers for rain had brought relief from a lengthy drought. Al-Idrisi reported that the kings of Malel attacked "entirely naked" people in order to sell them into slavery in North Africa.[23] Either or both of these accounts, as well as a number of later versions, may be corrupt. The oral tradition is often contradictory as well, but during the twelfth century there appear to have been kings of Mali (perhaps then styled Kangaba) who were sufficiently important or wealthy to have made the *hajj* or pilgrimage to Mecca.[24] Fortunately, written evidence and traditional reports of Mali converge during the thirteenth century in the person of Sundiata. Between 1230 and 1234,

[20] *Ibid.*, p. 110.
[21] 'Abu 'Abdullah Muhammad al-Idrisi (trans. P. Amédée Jaubert), *Géographie* (Paris, 1886), I, p. 11.
[22] Ibn Khaldun, *Histoire,* p. 110. Cf. Ibn Fadl 'Allah al-'Umari (trans. Maurice Gaudefroy-Demombynes), *L'Afrique, moins l'Égypte* (Paris, 1927), p. 54.
[23] Al-Bakri, *Description,* p. 333; al-Idrisi, *Géographie,* p. 13.
[24] Charles Monteil, "Les Empires du Mali," *Bulletin du Comité d'Études Historiques et*

he transformed an age-group or clan organization into the nucleus of a powerful army and began to extend the borders of Mali in many directions. His soldiers conquered the petty neighboring kingdom of Sangaran, defeated the warriors of Labé, in the Futa Jallon, and ravaged villages on both banks of the upper Niger and Sankarani rivers. Everywhere Sundiata installed faithful viceroys and ordered them to send tribute regularly to his capital—which may then have been Jeriba on the upper Niger, Mani-Koura farther downstream, or Niani on the Sankarem River.[25]

Sundiata's successes challenged the might of Sumanguru, ruler of the Sussu kingdom of Kaniaga. Sumanguru's royal predecessors, some of whom may have been emigrants from Tekrur, had established the kingdom of Kaniaga during the twelfth century. From a capital in the upper Niger region, its armies had absorbed the young nearby city-state of Diara and had accelerated the transfer of Muslim merchants from the markets of Awdoghast and Ghana to the new oasis town of Oualata.[26] Sumanguru, who ruled Kaniaga after 1200, added new provinces to the empire and then, in about 1234, attempted to subdue the rising power of Mali. Finally, at Kirina near the modern Kulikoro, the soldiers of Sundiata killed Sumanguru and vanquished the armies of Kaniaga during the first months of 1235. Between 1235 and 1240, Sundiata forcefully incorporated the Sussu provinces into Mali and, in 1240, destroyed the market-capital of Ghana for the last time.[27]

Sundiata, who ruled until about 1255, developed Mali economically and made his capital an important entrepôt of the main trade route across the Sahara. He monopolized the sale of gold from the regions formerly controlled by Ghana, imported salt from Taghaza and Taodeni, and systematically organized an imperial government. Meanwhile, his generals were adding new lands—each with its vassal governor—to the empire. By the middle years of the thirteenth century, the *mansas* of Mali reigned supreme from Tekrur in the west to the great bend of the Niger in the east, and from the Voltaic regions in the south to Oualata in the north. Following Sundiata's death, *mansa* Wali evidently conquered Songhai, a small kingdom of the middle Niger.[28] Thereafter, the military leaders of Mali overawed their kings until Sakura, a freed slave attached to the royal family, seized power for himself in about 1285. Battling at the head of his army, he captured the copper mines of the Sahara, invaded Tekrur—which was showing signs of independence—and attacked Songhai, which may have already revolted against its Malian overlords. In about 1300, however,

---

Scientifiques de l'Afrique Occidentale Française, XII (1929), pp. 343–356; Delafosse, *Sénégal*, II, pp. 173–176.

[25] For Sundiata, see Djibril Tamsir Niane, *Soundjata, ou l'épopée Mandingue* (Paris, 1960). On the capital site, see Mauny, *Tableau*, pp. 122–124; J. D. Fage, *An Atlas of African History* (London, 1958), p. 18.

[26] G. Boyer, *Un Peuple de l'Ouest soudanais, les Diawara* (Dakar, 1953), pp. 22–23.

[27] Delafosse, *Sénégal*, II, pp. 56, 180; Mamby Sidibé, "Soundiata Keita: héros historique et légendaire, empereur du Manding," *Notes Africaines*, 82 (April, 1959), pp. 44–45.

[28] Monteil, "Mali," p. 365; Jean Rouch, *Contribution à l'histoire des Songhay* (Dakar, 1953), p. 175.

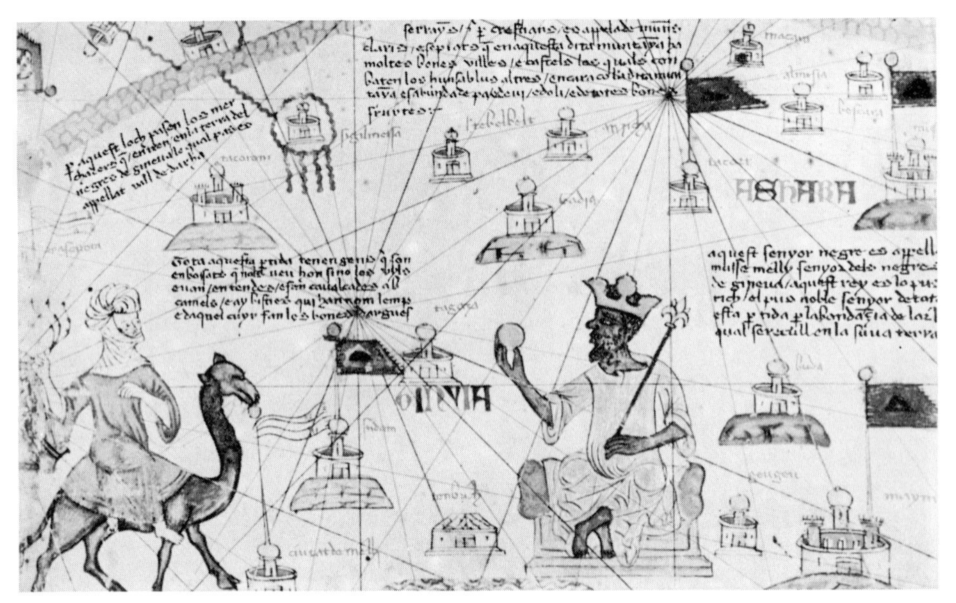

Detail of the Catalan Atlas of 1375, showing Musa, the *mansa* of Mali, awaiting a Muslim merchant. Pictures of Musa appeared on maps from the fourteenth to the eighteenth century. Bibliothèque Nationale, Paris.

while crossing the desert on his return from a pilgrimage to Mecca, he was mysteriously assassinated on the coast of what is now Tripolitania.[29]

The most illustrious of Mali's ruling *mansas* was Musa, who reigned from 1312 to 1337. His fame was such that from 1339 to about 1750 the cartographers of Europe replaced the *terra incognita* neatly inscribed upon their maps of Africa with *Rex Melli* or *Musa Mali.* They put aside their "elephants, for want of towns," and instead substituted Musa on a throne, scepter in hand.[30] During the fifteenth century, the sailors of Portugal dutifully searched for the land of Musa and they even may have traded with its representatives.[31] *Mansa* Musa conquered new territories and integrated the older provinces into his empire, but he achieved lasting international fame primarily because of the lavish *hajj* that he undertook in 1324/25.

In 1324, Musa started for Cairo preceded by five hundred slaves, each carrying a six-pound staff of gold. A caravan followed consisting of one hundred camels individually laden with three hundred pounds of gold. Other camels

[29] Charles F. Beckingham, "The Pilgrimage and Death of Sakura, King of Mali," *Bulletin of the School of Oriental and African Studies,* XV (1953), pp. 391–392; al-Maqrizi, "Pèlerinages des sultans du Tekrur," in al-'Umari, *L'Afrique,* p. 89; Ibn Khaldun, *Histoire,* p. 111; Heinrich Barth, *Travels and Discoveries in North and Central Africa* (London, 1858), IV, p. 587.

[30] The first cartographical representation was the *Mappa Mundi* of Angelino Dulcert in 1339. See Charles de la Roncière, *La Découverte de l'Afrique au Moyen Âge* (Cairo, 1924), I, pp. 56–57. Trimingham, *Islam,* p. 67, thinks that Musa's significance in the history of Mali has been seriously exaggerated.

[31] See *infra,* p. 71.

carried the provisions and the clothes necessary for a journey of such remarkable pretension. In Cairo, Musa's wealth, piety, generosity, and fine clothes all made a favorable impression. Twelve years later, in the time of Ibn Fadl 'Allah al-'Umari, the writer and administrative official, the citizens of Cairo recalled how Musa had freely given gold to petty officials, and how his retainers had cheerfully paid inflated prices to the shopkeepers and bazaar traders of the city. And after Musa had visited the Holy Cities, the poor were reputedly richer and the charities oversubscribed. Moreover, Musa evidently distributed his golden largesse without any thought of political reward. His advisors persuaded him—but only with difficulty—to pay the expected protocol visit to the Mamluk emir of Egypt.[32]

Word of an energetic Malian military campaign against Songhai, the riverain kingdom that during the fourteenth century occupied both banks of the Niger from Gao to what is now Bussa, accelerated Musa's return home. In the traditional accounts, Songhai is the name of a people who originally lived along the right bank of the middle Niger in the first centuries after Christ. Two hostile clans, the Sorko fishermen and the Gabibi agriculturalists, both acquired new territories upstream as far as the big bend in the river, the Sorko dominating the Gabibi until late in the seventh century. At this point in time, veiled Lamtuna warriors—the feared *mulaththamun*—supposedly swept out of the desert at the behest of the Gabibi. The Lamtuna thereafter ruled along the Niger and established the first Songhaian dynasty with its capital at Kukiya. But the Sorko, who had fled upstream to Gao, continued to war against the Lamtuna. Finally, in the late seventh, eighth, or early ninth century, the armies of Songhai invaded Gao and forced the Sorko to flee farther upstream to Mopti and Djenné.[33]

By the end of the ninth century, Songhai may have even become "the greatest and most glorious of the kingdoms of the Western Sudan, and the one to which all the other kingdoms of the Western Sudan give obedience."[34] Toward the end of the tenth century, al-Muhallabi said of this same kingdom that flocks and herds provided its wealth and that its people drew salt from the extensive storehouses of the *za*, or king. Significantly, the capital contained a mosque, to which the reigning *za* repaired to offer his prayers.[35] Both these passages refer to Kawkaw, a name that has been equated only etymologically with Gao, and therefore with the kingdom of Songhai. If correct, the second report may, despite the slight temporal discrepancy, support the traditional acceptance of Islam by *za* Kossoi in 1009/10.[36] Certainly by 1100, according to marble stelae found near modern Gao, the rulers of Songhai were Muslim and, if al-Idrisi's later account also refers to Songhai, Gao or the author's "Kukia"

[32] Al-'Umari, *L'Afrique*, pp. 72–79.
[33] Barth, *Travels*, p. 579, places the invasion of Gao in 679/80; Delafosse, *Sénégal*, I, p. 241, gives *c.* 690; Trimingham, *Islam*, p. 85, offers *c.* 850. None of the authors justifies his date.
[34] Al-Ya'qubi, *Historiae*, p. 220.
[35] Yaqut ibn 'Abdullah, quoted in Trimingham, *Islam*, p. 86.
[36] As-Sa'di, *Tarikh*, p. 5; but cf. al-Kati, *Tarikh*, pp. 332–333. See also al-Bakri, *Description*, pp. 342–343.

was one of the most renowned towns "in the land of the Negroes." Its king was an independent monarch who possessed a large bodyguard, a considerable retinue of generals, and soldiers who rode horses and camels and "are brave and overawe the neighboring tribes." The common people wore skins, but merchants dressed in tunics and gowns, with turbans around their heads, and ornaments of gold.[37]

Until its conquest by Mali in the thirteenth or fourteenth century, Songhai was an important, probably powerful kingdom of the middle Niger. From Gao, which because of its favorable location was the commercial capital of Songhai, caravan routes radiated across the intervening savannah and Sahara *via* Tadmekka and Takedda to the markets of Ghana, Almoravid Iberia, Tunis, Cyrenaica, and Egypt. In the bazaars of Gao, merchants traded copper, salt, and products of the Mediterranean world possibly for gold, animal skins, and the dyed cloaks of the Hausa city-states. For Mali, at any rate, the acquisition of Songhai—whether or not it occurred before or during the reign of *mansa* Musa—was doubtless an event of great commercial and strategic importance.

In about 1325, after returning from Cairo, Musa ruled dominions that evidently stretched from the middle reaches of the Gambia River to Aïr and the cataracts of Bussa on the Niger River. All the gold of Mali was his by right. From its sale in Fez, and perhaps from the sale of copper, tribute from dependent states, and the spoils of war, Musa paid his servants and maintained his elaborate court.[38] He also taxed the sale of crops and livestock and imposed tolls upon all import and export transactions. For these proceedings, the ordinary medium of exchange was the cowrie shell, the import of which brought the merchants of Musa's day a handsome profit.[39] This apparent prosperity was reflected by Musa's ostentatious *hajj* as well as by his embassy to the sultan of Fez (with whom he would, in any case, have wanted to keep on good terms), his patronage of the Granadan poet and architect 'Abu Ishaq Ibrahim as-Sahili, and by his sponsorship of new mosques. Traditionally, Musa is supposed to have celebrated his successful *hajj* by ordering as-Sahili to erect great mosques and other buildings in Gao and Timbuktu. Whether as-Sahili designed new mosques or merely redesigned or added to the old, his cultural efforts, and the economic expansion of Mali, may have played a part in the subsequent growth of Timbuktu, a crossroads town the founding of which may be dated from the last years of the eleventh century.[40]

After a short period of weak rule by the improvident *mansa* Maghan I, *mansa* Sulaiman (*c.* 1341–1360) reasserted the rule of Mali throughout the savannah and semi-desert reaches of the Western Sudan. During Maghan's day, Musa's vast, sprawling empire had tended to disintegrate and the Mossi armies had

[37] J. Sauvaget, "Les Épitaphes royales de Gao," *Bulletin de l'Institut Français d'Afrique Noire*, XII (1950), pp. 418–440; al-Idrisi, *Géographie*, pp. 21–23; Palmer, *Memoirs*, II, pp. 9–11.

[38] For each particularly valient exploit, Musa supposedly gave his warriors a large, prized pair of trousers. This was the highest honor that he could confer. Al-'Umari, *L'Afrique*, p. 66.

[39] *Ibid.*, p. 76.

[40] As-Sa'di, *Tarikh*, p. 35; Monteil, "Mali," pp. 407–408. But cf. Leo Africanus (trans. John Pory), *The History and Description of Africa* (London, 1896), III, p. 824.

even plundered Timbuktu and Maçina. Sulaiman restored peace and order, built many mosques, and thereafter governed impressively in a region renowned for its fissiparous tendencies.[41] The Tangerian traveler Ibn Battuta, who visited Mali in 1352/53, remarked upon the safety of the roads throughout the kingdom. He also said that wherever he had gone, he had easily exchanged salt or glass ornaments for millet, rice, chickens, beans, and drink.

Ibn Battuta reserved his warmest praise for the security of the country and the qualities of the people, whom he compared most favorably to others whom he had encountered in the course of his long and varied peregrinations throughout the world.

> *They are seldom unjust, and have a greater abhorrence of injustice than any other people. Their sultan shows no mercy to anyone who is guilty of the least act of it. There is complete security in their country. Neither traveller nor inhabitant in it has anything to fear from robbers or men of violence. They do not confiscate the property of any white man who dies in their country, even if it be uncounted wealth. On the contrary, they give it to the charge of some trustworthy person among the whites, until the rightful heir takes possession of it. They are careful to observe the hours of prayer, and assiduous in attending them in congregations, and in bringing up their children to them. On Fridays, if a man does not go early to mosque, he cannot find a corner to pray in, on account of the crowd.*[42]

He praised the peoples of Mali for the zeal with which they learned the Qur'an by heart: "They put their children in chains if they show any backwardness in memorizing it, and they are not set free until they have it by heart." On the other hand, he complained that women went about naked, and many Malians ate carrion, dogs, and asses. Customarily, Ibn Battuta said, these people also followed the, in his eyes, reprehensible practice of putting dust and ashes upon their heads as a gesture of respect.[43]

The pageant of the court of Mali, and the obsequiousness with which the people regarded their *mansa,* impressed Ibn Battuta. He described a routine proceeding:

> *On certain days the sultan holds audiences in the palace yard, where there is a platform under a tree. . . . It is carpeted with silk and has cushions placed on it.* [*Over it*] *is raised the umbrella, which is a sort of pavilion made of silk, surmounted by a bird in gold, about the size of a falcon. The sultan comes out of a door in a corner of the palace, carrying a bow in his hand and a quiver on his back. On his head he has a golden skull-cap, bound with a gold band which has narrow ends shaped like knives, more than a span in length. His usual dress is a velvety red tunic, made of . . . European fabrics. . . . The sultan is preceded by his musicians, who carry gold and silver* [guitars] *and behind him come three hundred*

---

[41] Al-'Umari, *L'Afrique*, p. 53.

[42] H. A. R. Gibb (trans. and ed.), *Ibn Battuta: Travels in Asia and Africa* (London, 1929), pp. 329–330.

[43] *Ibid.*, pp. 330–331. For a discussion of the African, non-Islamic character of Sudanic institutions and customs, see Joseph Greenberg, "The Negro Kingdoms of the Sudan," *Transactions of the New York Academy of Sciences*, XI (1949), pp. 130–131. See also *supra*, p. 38.

armed slaves. He walks in a leisurely fashion, affecting a very slow movement, and even stops from time to time. . . . As he takes his seat the drums, trumpets, and bugles are sounded. Three slaves go out at a run to summon the sovereign's deputy and the military commanders, who enter and sit down. Two saddled and bridled horses are brought, along with two goats, which they hold to serve as a protection against the evil eye. [The interpreter] stands at the gate and the rest of the people remain in the street, under the trees.[44]

At festivals, Sulaiman held an even more elaborate court. Armor-bearers brought in "quivers of gold and silver, swords ornamented with gold, and with golden scabbards, gold and silver lances, and crystal maces." Four servants were posted to drive away the flies, and the king's hundred wives and slave girls all attended in beautiful robes. On their heads they wore "gold and silver fillets, with gold and silver balls attached." Thirty boys in red woolen tunics and white skullcaps played the drums while others turned cartwheels in the air.[45]

The death of *mansa* Sulaiman in about 1360 marked the beginning of the depression in Mali's imperial fortunes. After a prolonged period of civil war, Mari Jata II, the son of *mansa* Maghan, finally wrested control from Kasa, Sulaiman's son, and despatched a triumphant embassy to the sultan of Morocco bearing, among other gifts, a giraffe, which it somehow managed to keep alive across the Sahara. The giraffe naturally created a sensation in Fez.[46] In keeping with this display, Mari Jata II was, supposedly, a spendthrift who plunged the kingdom into debt and oppressed his subjects. He died of sleeping sickness in 1373/74 and was succeeded by his brother Musa II, who in turn was really the puppet of Mari Diata—a chief of the royal slave garrison.

Mari Diata recaptured the copper mines of Tadmekka, re-established the domination of the *mansa* of Mali over peoples living near Gao and, in general, arrested Mali's decline. Indeed, under the successful pretender Maghan III, who ruled after about 1390, Mali received tribute from Tekrur and from the Sanhaja chiefs of the Western Sudan. But, by about 1433, Timbuktu, Oualata, and several other major trading towns had passed out of Mali's imperial orbit. Maçina broke away in about 1450, the Mossi armies returned in about 1477/78 to ravage the central part of the empire and, in about 1485, the Wolof ended the vassalage of Tekrur. During these desperate days, Mali even appealed unsuccessfully to Portugal for assistance.[47] Even so, for young Leo Africanus, who toured the Western Sudan in the early years of the sixteenth century, Mali was a kingdom of rich inhabitants, bounteous wares, and abundant supplies of millet, meat, and cotton. In Mali, he wrote, there were a "great store of temples, priests, and professours, which professours read their lectures onely in temples, bicause they haue no colleges at all." The people of this region, Leo Africanus continued, excelled "all other Negros in witte, ciuilitie, and industry."

[44] Gibb, *Battuta*, p. 326. The "interpreter" makes little sense. *Griot*, or court chronicler, should perhaps be substituted.

[45] *Ibid.*, p. 328.

[46] Ibn Khaldun, *Histoire*, p. 114.

[47] João de Barros, in G. R. Crone (trans. and ed.), *The Voyages of Cadamosto* (London, 1937), p. 144.

Their capital, where the *mansa* had his residence, was an "ample village" containing six thousand or more families.[48] Although Leo Africanus was clearly impressed by the capital and the people of Mali, it was already prey to the warriors of Songhai, who overran its northern dependencies between 1499 and 1507. Thereafter, in a somewhat shrunken state, Mali remained a petty, if occasionally notable, principality until its final demise in the last years of the seventeenth century.

The star of Songhai meanwhile ascended. In Ibn Battuta's day, although it probably still paid tribute to Mali, Gao was "one of the finest towns in the Negrolands."

> *It is also one of their biggest and best-provisioned towns, with rice in plenty, milk, and fish, and there is a species of cucumber there . . . which has no equal. The buying and selling of its inhabitants is done with cowry-shells. . . .*[49]

Sometime thereafter, Songhai won its freedom, incorporated parts of Mali—including the Bambara city-states and Maçina—into its own territory, and crowded hesitantly upon the threshold of greatness until the heyday of Sonni Ali. This first great king ruled Songhai from about 1464 to 1492. Riding at the head of the powerful Songhaian cavalry, he took Timbuktu from its Tuareg governors in 1468 (thereby driving its resident scholars to Oualata), subdued the villagers living along the banks of the bend of the Niger River, conquered the market town of Djenné in 1473 after a long siege, and attacked and ruled parts of Mossi Yatenga. As the sixteenth-century scribe Mahmud Kati bin al-Kati recorded, Sonni Ali

> *Was always victorious and sacked all the countries that he chose to attack. With him present, none of his armies were ever put to rout: always he conquered, never was he conquered. He left no region, no town, no village, from the country of Kanta to Sibiridougou, without attacking it at the head of his cavalry, warring against its inhabitants, and ravaging their territory.*[50]

By 1490 Songhai stretched from the semi-desert regions ruled earlier by Ghana to the borders of Aïr, and from northern Yatenga and Borgu to Oualata. Surrounding the state were Sonni Ali's enemies—the Fulani of Maçina, the Tuareg, and the Mossi—all of whom threatened at any moment to cut its tenuous riverain communications. These rivals he forestalled with a powerful army of conscripts and an ably commanded flotilla of canoes. Traditionally, he was also a master magician who could temporarily transform himself, his horses, and his soldiers into other creatures, or make them invisible at will. Whether or not he was a Muslim, he terrorized foreign followers of Islam and obeyed its call only when to do so usefully served his imperial strategy.[51] For him, the

[48] Leo Africanus, *History*, p. 823.
[49] Gibb, *Battuta*, p. 334.
[50] Al-Kati, *Tarikh*, p. 82. For a summary of the conquests of Sonni Ali, see Rouch, *Contribution*, p. 182.
[51] *Ibid.*, p. 185; Mervyn Hiskett, "An Islamic Tradition of Reform in the Western Sudan from the 16th to the 18th Century," *Bulletin of the School of Oriental and African Studies*, XXV (1962), pp. 578–579. But cf. Trimingham, *Islam*, p. 94.

shells, glass beads, broken pieces of copper, and paper each had its fixed value in cotton. Both writers, the second perhaps drawing upon the first, also reported that the *mai* refrained from ever showing his face in public; he talked to his subjects from behind a curtain.[61]

In Bornu the new rulers overcame serious internecine quarrels during the fifteenth century and grew sufficiently powerful to subdue the "So" and to collect tribute from peoples as far distant as Kano. Under Ali Ghazi ibn Dunama (*c.* 1476–1503), their cavalry harried many of the Hausa city-states as well as Jukun Kwararafa, and exchanged captured slaves for the horses of Barbary. Perhaps to symbolize the kingdom's prosperity, they established another capital—Ngazargamu—on the Yo River in Bornu, which became the center of a sophisticated administrative system. Subsequently, Ali Ghazi's successors used his administrative and military machine to redress old scores in Kanem: between about 1503 and 1526, *mai* Idris ibn Ali Katagarmabe assembled a great army and twice marched into his people's former homeland. After winning an initial victory, wrote 'Ahmed ibn Fartua, *mai* Idris Katagarmabe, with God's assistance, defeated Emir Adam ibn Salma, compelled Adam to swear an oath of fealty, and returned to Bornu with "his wrath appeased." [62]

The city-states of hausaland

In the traditional histories of the many Hausa towns, one story recurs which may mark the shift from matrilineal to patrilineal succession. It recounts the tale of a stranger from the east who settled in Bornu (or Kanem) and then fled west to escape the ire of the reigning *mai*. Together with his pregnant concubine, he arrived in Daura, where he asked for water, but before his request was granted he had to slay a snake, with a head like that of a horse, who guarded a well. As his reward, this stranger from the east claimed the hand of the queen of Daura in marriage. Their descendants ruled the six most important Hausa towns—Daura, Kano, Zazzau (later Zaria), Gobir, Katsina, and Rano—and thereafter followed the patrilineal, rather than the matrilineal, line of succession.[63] From the eighth through the thirteenth or fourteenth centuries, an alien ruling class gradually assumed control of the different towns—first in Gobir, later in Zazzau and Kano. During the fourteenth century, Zazzau became the leading Hausa polity. But none of the city-states was ever sufficiently powerful to control any of the others for long; there never was a Hausa empire and, although smaller villages sometimes paid tribute to the rulers of a nearby town, a hundred or more towns could, at various times, justify their claims of independence. Each was a separate community surrounded by fields of cotton

---

[61] Gibb, *Battuta*, p. 336; al-Maqrizi, extracts in Thomas Hodgkin (ed.), *Nigerian Perspectives* (London, 1960), p. 77. See also Dixon Denham, Hugh Clapperton, and Walter Oudney, *Travels and Discoveries in Northern and Central Africa* (London, 1831 [first edition, 1826]), I, p. 267.

[62] "Kanem Wars," in Palmer, *Memoirs*, I, p. 17.

[63] *Ibid.*, II, pp. 133–134.

and grain. Katsina was the leading commercial center, although northerly Gobir was also important.

Leo Africanus visited the Hausa city-states at the beginning of the sixteenth century. Gobir, he wrote, contained many villages inhabited by shepherds and other herdsmen. They tended abundant cattle.

> *Heere are also great store of artificers and linnen weauers: and heere are such [leather] shooes made as the ancient Romans were woont to weare, the greatest part whereof be carried to [Timbuktu] and [Gao]. Likewise heere is abundance of rice, and of certaine other grains and pulse, the like whereof I neuer saw in Italie. . . .*[64]

In the province of Kano, Leo saw local grain, rice, cotton, and wild citrons and lemons which differed "not much in taste from the best of all."

> *In the midst of this prouince standeth a towne called by the same name, the walles and houses whereof are built for the most part of a kinde of chalke. The inhabitants are rich merchants and most ciuill people.*[65]

The people of Katsina—who were "extremely black, hauing great noses and blabber lips"—produced barley and millseed. Their houses, however, were base and mean. They remained prey to their more powerful neighbors—the rulers of Songhai and Bornu—who coveted the wealth that they had amassed by exporting dyed cotton goods, woven garments, leather articles, and metal manufactures *via* Aïr and Ghadames to Tunis. Small, divided among themselves, and militarily weak, these states built protective mud walls and battled fiercely, both before and after the sixteenth century, to avoid being absorbed by their neighbors.

II. The Coast and the Interior of Eastern Africa

Very little more emerges from the shadows that shroud the history of the greatest part of tropical Africa before about 1500. An understandable dearth of material hinders any attempt to describe the early social, economic, and political environment during these years of the peoples who lived between the Niger River and the Indian Ocean. The oral traditions are obscure, the linguistic evidence is sparse, and literate persons seem not to have ventured into the interior. Our *present* knowledge of the affairs of early eastern Africa is thus confined almost totally to the activities of the Arabs and to the coastal island-states that they administered. Even the written records of Ethiopia contain little that is not bare chronicle. The history of southern Africa, despite the presence there of interesting ruins and other signs of an early advanced civilization, is still more speculative than certain. Any reconstruction must consequently lean heavily upon the relatively little evidence available, while con-

---

[64] Leo Africanus, *History*, p. 828.
[65] *Ibid.*, p. 830.

tinuing to introduce those surmises and conjectures which may ultimately achieve sufficient substantiation to become the stuff of history.

The Bantu-speaking peoples hold many of the keys to the history of tropical Africa. What areas did they inhabit and what were their movements during the period of about 700 to 1500? Did they establish sedentary civilizations during this period, and/or did they migrate long distances in search of new homes and new ways of life? Did they construct centralized, hierarchically governed states, or did they prefer more egalitarian arrangements similar to the political formulae of the modern Tonga of Northern Rhodesia? We know of the Bantu kingdoms of Kongo, Rwanda, and Cwezi, all of which may have been established by 1400, but we do not know how they were formed, how their leaders ruled, or why or how they fell. What were the relations of these states to one another and to the rest of the world? How widespread was trade between these and similar kingdoms, other Bantu-speaking peoples, and the inhabitants of Arabia, India, Sumatra, Java, Borneo, and China? To what extent was tropical Africa before 1500 in a state of such internal turmoil that its inhabitants looked inward, avoiding external commitments? Our information, unfortunately, relates primarily to the peoples of the coast and, only secondarily, to those of the interior.[66]

The founding of the coastal states

From about 200 B.C., the coast of eastern Africa occupied an important place in the economic life of the Indian Ocean peoples. Utilizing trade winds and strong currents, sailors of many eastern principalities probably traded upon its shores even before the third century A.D., when an anonymous merchant compiled the *Periplus of the Erythraean Sea.*[67] Indian beads and Chinese porcelain and coins testify mutely to the extent and frequency of this commercial intercourse, whether they were carried to eastern Africa in Chinese, Indian, or, more probably, Arab vessels. The export of soft ivory, timber, tortoise shell, rhinoceros horn, spices, and, to a lesser extent, gold, silver, and ambergris, was important.

After about A.D. 600, the inhabitants of southern Arabia appear to have become the masters of the commerce of the Indian Ocean basin. Perhaps also encouraged by political and religious changes at home, these Arabs and Debuli from Sindh in India began to settle in greater numbers than before in the harbors of eastern Africa and upon islands adjacent to its shores. The traditional, somewhat uncritical accounts of the coast date the earliest permanent Arab influence from pre-Islamic times. Some say that followers of Islam first arrived in the late seventh century, particularly after al-Hajjaj, governor of Arabia, overran Oman at the behest of the Umayyad caliph of Damascus. With different emphasis, others claim that followers of the caliph—not those who

[66] For a discussion of the use of different kinds of evidence, see the papers read at the Third Conference on African History and Archaeology, 1961, in *The Journal of African History,* III (1962), pp. 175–306.

[67] See *supra,* pp. 27–28.

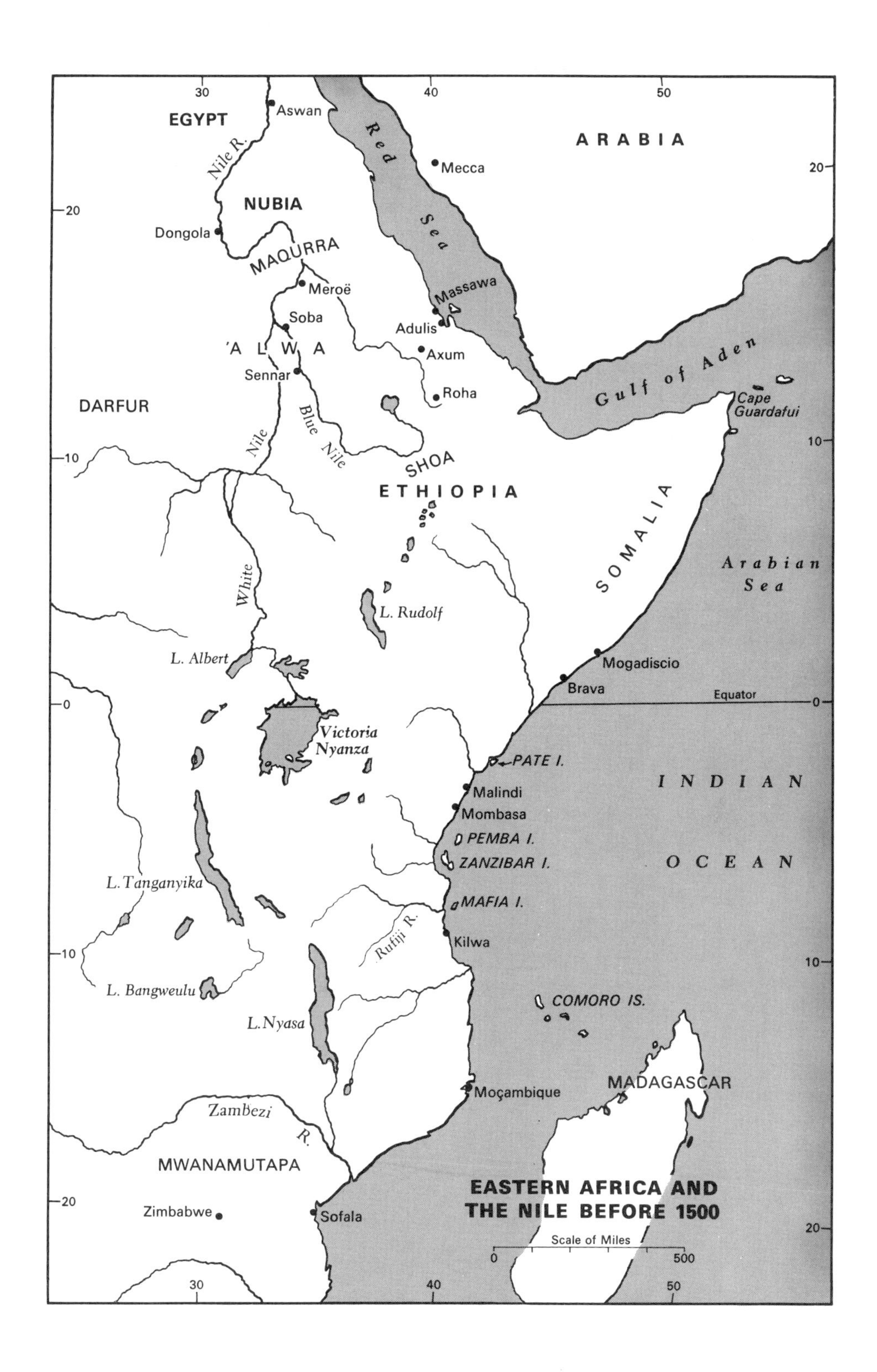
EGYPT
Aswan
Nile R.
NUBIA
Dongola
MAQURRA
Meroë
Soba
'A L W A
Sennar
DARFUR
Blue Nile
Nile
White
Red Sea
ARABIA
Mecca
Massawa
Adulis
Axum
Roha
SHOA
ETHIOPIA
Gulf of Aden
Cape Guardafui
SOMALIA
Arabian Sea
L. Rudolf
L. Albert
Victoria Nyanza
Mogadiscio
Brava
Equator
PATE I.
Malindi
Mombasa
PEMBA I.
ZANZIBAR I.
MAFIA I.
INDIAN OCEAN
Rufiji R.
Kilwa
L. Tanganyika
L. Bangweulu
L. Nyasa
COMORO IS.
MADAGASCAR
Moçambique
Zambezi R.
MWANAMUTAPA
Zimbabwe
Sofala
EASTERN AFRICA AND THE NILE BEFORE 1500
Scale of Miles
0
500
30
40
50
20
10
0
10
20

had opposed his rule—established trading posts in eastern Africa during the same period. According to another version, the members of a schismatic Shi'ite sect fled to eastern Africa during the eighth century. Persians, that is Shirazis (or men of Sirâf?), supposedly settled in eastern Africa—particularly in Mogadiscio, Brava, Zanzibar, and Kilwa—during the ninth and tenth centuries. In the traditional chronicles of the coast, none of which were written down until centuries after the events described, these immigrants either established or thereafter ruled the small, separate, coastal trading centers.[68]

None of these versions overlap sufficiently to authenticate either the chronological references or the myths of origin as such, but together they imply a gradual process of Arab and Muslim Indian settlement along the coast from the seventh through the tenth and eleventh centuries. Furthermore, the Shirazi story need not refer to the Persian city or the province of Fars in which it is located, but to the Shirazis who had lived in Arabia, Persians who had for long lived on the Somali coast, or simply to Persian cultural influences transmitted by the early Arab immigrants. Architectural traces, pottery, some Swahili words, the various chronicles, Chinese references, and oral reports all indicate that the peoples of the Persian Gulf littoral contributed, but not necessarily directly, to the civilization of eastern Africa.[69] These sources, in varying degrees, also support the accounts of Arab immigration. The recent excavation of two buildings on Kilwa, one of which contains an octagonal bathing pool, provided the first strikingly new architectural evidence of Umayyad and 'Abbasid inspiration.[70] The buildings themselves date, however, from the thirteenth or the fourteenth century.

Unhappily, these early accounts do not indicate whether the Arab or Persian intruders took over older African entrepôts or whether they lived apart from the indigenous inhabitants. Only one reports the disappearance of an immigrant group through intermarriage. At the same time, Arab dealers exported black slaves to the Persian Gulf during the early years at least of the ninth century. In Basra, these slaves revolted in 869, slew their rulers, mercilessly attacked the local population, and were sufficiently numerous to remain unsubdued until 883.[71]

---

[68] Salil ibn Raziq (trans. and ed. George Percy Badger), *History of the Imâms and Seyyids of 'Oman* (London, 1871), p. 5; João de Barros, "Da Asia," in G. S. P. Freeman-Grenville, *The Medieval History of the Coast of Tanganyika* (London, 1962), pp. 31–32; C. H. Stigand, *The Land of Zinj* (London, 1913), p. 29; "Libro degli Zengi," in Enrico Cerulli (trans. and ed.), *Somalia: Scritti Vari Editi ed Inediti* (Roma, 1959), II, pp. 258–261, 266–268.

[69] Freeman-Grenville, *Medieval History*, p. 29; Gervase Mathew, "Recent Discoveries in East African Archaeology," *Antiquity*, XXVII (1953), pp. 212–214; James S. Kirkman, "The Excavations at Ras Mkumbuu on the Island of Pemba," *Tanganyika Notes and Records*, 53 (1959), pp. 173–174; Arthur E. Robinson, "The Shirazi Colonization of East Africa," *ibid.*, 7 (1939), pp. 92–112; A. H. J. Prins, "Uncertainties in Coastal Cultural History: The 'Ngalawa' and the 'Mtepe,' " *ibid.*, 53 (1959), p. 212; Gervase Mathew, "The East African Coast Until the Coming of the Portuguese," in Roland Oliver and Gervase Mathew (eds.), *History of East Africa* (Oxford, 1963), I, pp. 102–104.

[70] Neville Chittick, "Kilwa and the Arab Settlement of the East African Coast," *The Journal of African History*, IV (1963), pp. 183–188.

[71] The slaves of Basra first revolted in 696. See Arnold T. Wilson, *The Persian Gulf* (Oxford, 1928), p. 66; Stigand, *Zinj*, p. 6.

The Arab writers whose accounts are so helpful with respect to the Western and Central Sudan contribute little to our understanding of eastern Africa before the fourteenth century. In the ninth century, al-Ya'qubi mentioned the amber of eastern Africa, and 'Abu Zaid, who lived on the Persian Gulf, wrote of eastern Africa's millet and sugar cane and of its kings who constantly sent their slave battalions into battle with one another.[72] Al-Mas'udi, who visited Madagascar (or Zanzibar) and the countries of Asia during the tenth century, decried the unintelligence of the "cheerful" local people of eastern Africa. They lived among elephants, rhinoceros, and giraffe and used tame oxen as beasts of burden. They ate bananas, millet, coconuts, meat, and honey. They were governed by custom, as they knew no religious law. From them, Arabs obtained amber, gold, saffron, leopard skins, tortoise shell, and ivory.[73]

The merchants of China increased their trade with Africa during the years of the T'ang dynasty (A.D. 618–907). In the ninth century, the scholar Tuan Ch'eng-shih reported upon the country of Po-pa-li in the "southwestern sea." There, he said, the people ate only meat. In what may have been a description of the Masai, he wrote:

> *They often stick a needle into the veins of cattle and draw blood which they drink raw, mixed with milk. They wear no clothes except that they cover (the parts) below their loins with sheepskins. Their women are clean and [chaste]. The inhabitants themselves kidnap them, and if they sell them to foreign merchants, they fetch several times their price. The country produces only ivory and ambergris.*[74]

But this is probably a second-hand account, derived perhaps from the Malayan, Sumatran, Sinhalese, South Indian, or Arab traders from whom the Chinese obtained their African ivory and ambergris.

From about the late eleventh or early twelfth century, the coast and the islands of eastern Africa contained a number of small towns. Each of the entrepôts traded with its neighbors and with those foreigners who sailed with the monsoon from Malabar or Arabia. Between 1053 and 1175, for example, the merchants of these towns increased their trade tenfold with distant China, where they exported primarily elephant tusks, rhinoceros horn, tortoise shell, pearls, aromatic woods, incense, and myrrh.[75] Most of the East African cities may have contained occasional buildings of coral rag and lime mortar that

---

[72] Freeman-Grenville, *Medieval History,* p. 39; 'Ahmad ibn Wadih al-Ya'qubi (trans. Gaston Wiet), *Les Pays* (Cairo, 1937), pp. 237–238.

[73] Al-Mas'udi, *Les Prairies d'or,* I, p. 334, III, pp. 7, 11, 29.

[74] Jan Julius L. Duyvendak, *China's Discovery of Africa* (London, 1959), pp. 13–14. See also Friedrich Hirth, "Early Chinese Notices of East African Territories," *Journal of the American Oriental Society,* XXX (1909), pp. 47–48.

[75] Friedrich Hirth and William Woodville Rockhill (trans. and ed.) *Chao Ju-Kua* (St. Petersburg, 1911), pp. 17–21; W. W. Rockhill, "Notes on the Relations and Trade of China with the Eastern Archipelago and the Coast of the Indian Ocean During the Fourteenth Century," *T'oung Pao,* XV (1914), pp. 419–431; G. S. P. Freeman-Grenville, "East African Coin Finds and Their Historical Significance," *The Journal of African History,* I (1960), pp. 34–35.

were richly embossed in metal; much of the housing, however, was of wood or mud. Of the many trading centers, Mogadiscio, Mafia, and Kilwa, the last of which was settled, according to archaeological evidence, in the ninth century, achieved pre-eminence earliest. The Kilwans probably gained prominence after they had conquered the people of nearby Sanje ya Kati in the eleventh century. The Kufic inscriptions on a mosque on Zanzibar Island date from the early twelfth century.[76] In the twelfth century, Malindi may have been the center of the iron trade described by al-Idrisi. He also mentions Brava, the iron works of Mombasa (by which he may mean Pangani), and Sofala, which exports gold.[77] A Chinese book of the same period spoke of the country of Pi-pa-lo, which may or may not be the same as Po-pa-li. There the inhabitants sold myrrh, tortoise shell, ambergris, and ivory. They possessed camels, "camel-birds," a quadruped "striped like a camel and in shape like an ox," and a mule with "red, black, and white stripes wound as girdles around the body"—references to ostriches, giraffe, and zebras respectively.[78] Sinologists surmise that these passages describe the country of Somalia, but they as well as the earlier discussion of Po-pa-li may be a composite rather than a precise account.

During the Sung dynasty (1127–1279), "barbarian" invasions from the north encouraged the Chinese to look favorably for the first time upon overseas trade. The Sung sailors extended Chinese sea contacts to southern Asia and the western reaches of the Indian Ocean. They imported vast quantities of tropical products and naturally exported similar amounts of gold, silver, copper, silk, and porcelain. As a result, there was a disastrous drain of specie to places as distant as Japan and Arabia—Sung coins have also been found in Mogadiscio and in Zanzibar, where they mix with those of Mongol Tabriz. In the middle of the twelfth century, the Chinese government consequently forbade merchants to export excessive sums of money. In the early years of the thirteenth century, the government further enjoined its merchants to ship manufactured items instead of coins. Many of the Chinese objects found as far afield as Zimbabwe and the coast of modern Tanzania presumably date from this period, as do geographical notices of territories that may have been Somalia, Zanzibar, and Madagascar. References also abound to *k'un lun*—slaves as "black as ink." [79] But none of this evidence implies that Chinese traders ever personally visited eastern Africa before the fourteenth century. Although they were capable of sailing across the Indian Ocean in their large, maneuverable ships (they were using the mariner's compass by 1100, at least a century before the compass was

---

[76] James S. Kirkman, "Historical Archaeology in Kenya, 1948–1956," *Antiquaries' Journal*, XXXVII (1957), p. 23.

[77] Al-Idrisi does not mention Kilwa, which was already in existence. Al-Idrisi, *Géographie*, pp. 56–57. See also G. S. P. Freeman-Grenville (ed.), *The East African Coast* (Oxford, 1962), pp. 19–20.

[78] Chao Ju-Kua, *Chu-Fan-Chih* [*Gazetteer of Foreigners*] (1226), was derived from Chou Ch'u-fei, *Ling-Wai-Tai-Ta* [*Information on What Lies Beyond the Passes*] (1178). See Hirth and Rockhill, *Chao Ju-Kua*, pp. 128–129.

[79] *Ibid.*, pp. 48, 50n; Duyvendak, *Discovery*, p. 24; G. A. Wainwright, "Early Foreign Trade in East Africa," *Man*, LXVII (1947), pp. 116, 143–148.

The ruins at Kilwa, showing a section of the bathing pool inside Husuni Kubwa. (From "Kilwa" by Neville Chittick, *Journal of African History*, IV (1963), Cambridge University Press.)

known in Europe),[80] the Chinese evidently were content to continue trading with tropical Africa *via* the marts and the middlemen of southeastern Asia and Arabia.

The rise of kilwa and zimbabwe

Kilwa established its importance as the leading commercial town of eastern Africa during the twelfth and thirteenth centuries. In the time of Sultan Ali bin al-Hasan (*c.* 1150–1225), its first ruler, the seamen of Kilwa may have ousted the representatives of Mogadiscio (or Madagascar?) from Sofala and thereafter engrossed its sale of gold. According to a traditional account that may refer to this period, some of the inhabitants of Kilwa settled in Sofala, married into the local clans, erected a factory for merchandise, and "became absolute masters of the gold trade." [81] Perhaps for reasons connected with this trade, Ali bin al-Hasan minted the oldest coins thus far demonstrated to be of an unmistakably East African origin. They were of copper, with inscribed rhymes, and they antedate all of the known rhymed coinage of India and Persia. The rhymed couplets of these coins and the possibly later dome of the Kilwa mosque are strikingly similar in certain ways to those of later Muslim India. And the

[80] See Joseph Needham, *Science and Civilization in China* (Cambridge, Eng., 1959), III, pp. 552, 559–560; Frederic C. Lane, "The Economic Meaning of the Invention of the Compass," *The American Historical Review*, LXVIII (1963), pp. 605–617.

[81] João de Barros, "Chronica doȿ reyes de Quiloa," in Freeman-Grenville, *Medieval History*, p. 89. The chronology presented herein, which differs materially from that set out by Freeman-Grenville, *ibid.*, is based on important new work by Neville Chittick, to be published in *The Journal of African History* (1965).

thirteenth-century geographer Ibn Sa'id al-Maghribi wrote that the inhabitants of Kilwa were "brothers" to India and Sindh.[82] In any event, with an economy based firmly upon the raw materials of the interior, Kilwa conquered a part of the East African coast and the islands of Pemba and Zanzibar. Its rulers beautified Kilwa and erected a fortress of stone and lime in place of the usual wooden houses.[83]

Kilwa and Sofala clearly owed a part of their early prosperity to the gold of the interior. There Africans collected alluvial gold, smelted it, and sent it overland along well-trodden paths *via* Lake Nyasa to Kilwa.[84] Although Arab, Greek, Chinese, and Indian bottoms ultimately carried golden ingots to Asia and to Europe—where in thirteenth-century London they were minted into the first gold coins [85]—we know embarrassingly little about the interior peoples or governments from whom the precious metal was obtained. Together with the mines of Penhalonga, Zimbabwe—possibly the capital of one of the early kingdoms of the interior—may have been a chief source.

Unlike the similar, if smaller, edifices of eastern and southern Africa, the impressive Zimbabwe ruins comprise a so-called acropolis—a massive defensive fortification with intricate passageways, numerous rooms, and evidence of gold smelting—and, in the valley below the "acropolis," an elliptical "temple" or "great enclosure" and the footings of many stone houses. The vast "temple" is thickly walled in large, undressed stone blocks. Inside there are more stone embankments and a peculiar, conical tower that dominates the valley's stillness. The foundations of stone rondavels stretch for several thousand yards at right angles to the "temple," and there are ruins of other, less easily identifiable structures throughout the remainder of the valley. All of the high stonework in both the "acropolis" and the "temple" was fitted without mortar; the original workmen used wooden or stone lintels and also constructed what appears to be an extensive drainage system.[86]

The oldest parts of the Zimbabwe ruins appear to date from about the eighth century and seem to have served as the spiritual, if not the commercial, center of the early Guruuswa kingdom. The rulers of Guruuswa were the Karanga who had previously come from "the north"—at a time when "there was no longer sufficient room for all of us" [87]—and had subsequently moved across

---

[82] In Gabriel Ferrand (trans. and ed.), *Relations de voyages et textes géographiques: Arabes, Persans et Turks relatifs à l'Extrême-Orient* (Paris, 1914), II, pp. 336–337.

[83] Although the excavated outline of the magnificent Kilwan palace of Husuni Kubwa does not tally with the description given in the chronicle, it and the fortress could conceivably be the same. Chittick, "Kilwa and the Arab Settlement," p. 187.

[84] Roger Summers, *Inyanga: Prehistoric Settlements in Southern Rhodesia* (Cambridge, Eng., 1958), pp. 263, 312.

[85] Oliver and Mathew, *History*, p. 112.

[86] See Gertrude Caton-Thompson, *The Zimbabwe Culture: Ruins and Reactions* (Oxford, 1931), pp. 15–18; Roger Summers, *Zimbabwe: A Rhodesian Mystery* (Johannesburg, 1963), pp. 85–94. See also the bibliography in H. A. Wieschhoff, *The Zimbabwe-Monomotapa Culture in Southeast Africa* (Menasha, Wisc., 1941).

[87] Quoted in D. P. Abraham, "The Monomotapa Dynasty," *Nada*, XXXVI (1959), p. 62. See also Caton-Thompson, *The Zimbabwe Culture*, pp. 188, 197.

The Temple or Great Enclosure of Zimbabwe from the air. The conical tower is to the upper right in the ellipse, obscured by trees. Beyond the walls are the foundations of stone rondavels. (R. D. K. Hadden, The Office of the Commissioner for Rhodesia)

the Zambezi River onto the great cis-Zambezian plateau. There, according to the traditional accounts, the Karanga formed clans and built the *dzimbahwes* ("big stone houses") by which they were later known. They created an empire and made the autochthonous inhabitants of the region pay tribute. In the twelfth and thirteenth centuries, the Karanga rulers of Guruuswa may have traded with Kilwa, consequently amassing the vast hoard of glass beads, Chinese porcelain, and copper coins that was discovered among the ruins of Zimbabwe in the nineteenth century. The people of Zimbabwe may have also carved the attractive soapstone birds that were found in the ruins and that were subsequently offered by Europeans as evidence of Phoenician, Solomonic, or Asian influence.[88]

Whatever its origin and role in the economic, political, and religious life of the time, the Zimbabwe complex remained in use at least until the beginning of the seventeenth century. But at least by 1450, Mwanamutapa (Monomotapa) had become the most important Karanga kingdom of southern Africa. Its rulers probably built or added to the "acropolis" during the fifteenth and sixteenth centuries. During the Portuguese period, however, the capital of the Mwanamutapa empire was located about 250 miles north of the Zimbabwe ruins. The connection between Mwanamutapa and Zimbabwe remains obscure.

Political developments in the northeast

Along the middle reaches of the Nile River, the Christian kingdoms of Maqurra (Mukuria) and 'Alwa (Alodia) probably flourished during, if not

[88] See Carl Mauch, *Reisen im Innern von Süd-Afrika* (Gotha, 1874), p. 51; J. Theodore Bent, *The Ruined Cities of Mashonaland* (London, 1892), p. 188; Richard N. Hall and W. G. Neal, *The Ancient Ruins of Rhodesia* (London, 1902), pp. 111–112. See also João dos

before, the period of Kilwa's pre-eminence on the distant shores of eastern Africa. Both kingdoms—with their respective capitals at Dongola, between the Third and Fourth Cataracts of the Nile, and at Soba, near the confluence of the White and Blue Niles—and the northern Sudanese state of Nubia (Nobatia) had adopted Monophysite Christianity in the sixth century A.D., after the Byzantine Emperor Justinian I and his consort Empress Theodora had separately despatched thither missionary delegations representing the Monophysite and the Orthodox persuasions.[89] During the seventh century, the forces of the king of Maqurra (of which Nubia was now a part) had proved sufficiently strong to prevent Egypt's Arab army from overrunning their homeland. Consequently, the emir of Egypt and the king of Maqurra had concluded a treaty of peace that helped to free Maqurra from the fears of an Arab invasion for six hundred years.[90]

The subsequent histories of these kingdoms are obscure. The kings of Maqurra and 'Alwa governed theocracies which may have perpetuated for several centuries the influence of eastern Christianity in their writings, speech, architecture, and religious ritual. In the tenth century, Ibn Salim of Aswan wrote favorably of the thirty cities of northern Maqurra that contained many "good buildings, with churches and monasteries." But in his day, when the kings of Maqurra may have even ruled Darfur, 'Alwa evidently was the more important Sudanese kingdom:

> *Souba is the residence of the chief of Aloa* ['*Alwa*]; *it lies . . . between the White and the Green* [*Nile*] *rivers, near their confluence. . . . The city contains handsome edifices and extensive dwellings, and churches full of gold, and gardens, and inns where Moslims live. The chief of Aloa is a greater person than the chief of Mokra* [*Maqurra*]; *he has a stronger army than the latter, and his country is more extensive and more fertile.*[91]

Maqurra and 'Alwa both may have reached their cultural and material zenith by the beginning of the twelfth century. Early in the next century, 'Abu Salih, an Armenian resident in Egypt, praised the sights of these kingdoms: in his day, Dongola, "a large city on the banks of the blessed Nile," contained many churches and large houses and wide streets. The lofty house of the king possessed several domes of red brick and resembled the buildings of Iraq. 'Alwa contained four hundred churches, monasteries, and, in its capital, "a very large and spacious church, skilfully planned and constructed."[92] But in the latter part of the

---

Santos, *Ethiopia Oriental*, in Samuel Purchas (trans. and ed.), *Hakluytus Posthumus, or Purchas His Pilgrimes* (Glasgow, 1905), IX, p. 235.

[89] Joannus, Bishop of Ephesus (trans. and ed. Robert Payne Smith), *The Third Part of the Ecclesiastical History* (Oxford, 1860), pp. 253–257, 316–327.

[90] Ibn 'Abd al-Hakam (trans. Charles Cutler Torrey), "The Mohammedan Conquest of Egypt and North Africa," in *Biblical and Semitic Studies . . . of Yale University* (New York, 1902), pp. 308–309. See also al-Ya'qubi, *Historiae*, p. 217.

[91] In an extract from al-Maqrizi, in Burckhardt, *Travels*, pp. 454–455. See also U. Bouriant (trans.), *Description topographique et historique de l'Égypte* (Paris, 1900), II, p. 557.

[92] 'Abu Salih (trans. and ed. Basil Thomas Alfred Evetts), *The Churches and Monasteries of Egypt and Some Neighbouring Countries* (Oxford, 1895), pp. 263–265. See also Peter L. Shinnie, *Excavations at Soba* (Khartoum, 1955), p. 77.

thirteenth century, Maqurra, weakened by internecine conflict, became increasingly prey to the armies of Mamluk Egypt. For a number of years, the kings of Maqurra successfully managed to resist the invaders. But internal divisions, Mamluk military successes, and the peaceful settlement of Arabs within the kingdom encouraged the growth of Islam in Maqurra and helped to bring about its demise as an independent polity during the fourteenth century.[93] 'Alwa evidently was overrun by the Arabs, or was extensively Arabicized, during the succeeding century.

To the east of 'Alwa, the rulers of Axum had meanwhile reasserted their traditional control over parts of the Red Sea littoral during the ninth and tenth centuries. They had also begun forcibly to include new peoples of the central Ethiopian interior—among whom were the supposedly Jewish Agau—within the confines of their Christian kingdom. But toward the end of the tenth century, Queen Gudit of the Agau successfully challenged the kings of Axum: her followers persecuted Christians, razed churches, sacked the ancient capital, and forced the court of the reigning monarch to flee to Shoa.[94] Of her own reign and those of her immediate successors, little information of substance survives. Sometime early in the twelfth century, however, an Agau commoner known as Tekla Haymanot usurped the throne and declared himself the first Zagwe ruler of Axum. From their capitals in Lasta, the Agau homeland, later Zagwe kings—devout Christians who claimed descent from Moses—governed the nucleus of what was to become an empire. To the heritage of modern Ethiopia, they contributed the ten impressive rock-hewn monolithic churches built near Roha during the reign of Lalibela (*c.* 1190–1225). They also reopened channels of communication to Cairo and Jerusalem and tried unsuccessfully to contain the newly formed Muslim sultanates by which the Christian kingdom was soon almost encircled.[95]

In about 1270, Yekuno Amlak regained the throne of Axum for the putative Solomonid dynasty. He moved the capital of the kingdom to Shoa, encouraged a literary revival, introduced Amharic as the language of the court, and fought bitterly against the Muslims of Ifat. During the reign of 'Amda Seyon (1314–1344), Christian soldiers engaged the main Muslim armies in battle almost continually, finally overwhelming them in about 1328/29.[96] By do doing, 'Amda Seyon became in effect the first emperor or "king of kings" of all of Ethiopia. His conquests were eventually consolidated during the reign of Zar'a Ya'qob (1434–1468), a ruler who sponsored the construction of a number of churches and monasteries and patronized the arts. In order to strengthen Ethiopia in the face of renewed Islamic subversion, he sought to foster a spirit of religious

[93] Harold A. MacMichael (ed.), *A History of the Arabs in the Sudan* (Cambridge, Eng., 1922), I, pp. 138–139, 179–186.

[94] Eusèbe Renaudot (ed.), *Historia Patriarcharum Alexandrinorum Jacobitarum* (Paris, 1713), p. 381; E. A. Wallis Budge (trans.), *Mashafa Sĕnekĕsâr: The Book of the Saints of the Ethiopian Church* (Cambridge, Eng., 1928), I, pp. 233–234; Ibn Hawqal, in J. Spencer Trimingham, *Islam in Ethiopia* (London, 1952), p. 52.

[95] *Ibid.*, pp. 58–65.

[96] Jules Perruchon (trans.), "Histoire des guerres d'Amda Syon," *Journal Asiatique*, XIV (1889), pp. 327–363, 441–483.

King Yekuno Amlak (1270–1285), the first sovereign of the restored Solomonid line in Ethiopia. From a late eighteenth-century illuminated manuscript. The British Museum, London.

evangelism within the empire while waging war against Adal, the strongest of the hostile sultanates.[97]

By the end of the fifteenth century, Ethiopia had by and large assumed its modern shape. It extended from Massawa to Lake Shala and encompassed the four most important former Muslim principalities as well as two "pagan" states. But the political organization of the expanded empire proved unable to cope with the governmental problems of such vast reaches and, in consequence, the largely unresolved conflicts of the fourteenth and fifteenth centuries were dramatically re-enacted during the sixteenth century. After the Danakil and Somali chiefs had proclaimed their holy wars, Christian Ethiopia used every military and political stratagem at her disposal to counter threatening Islamic attacks. Her appeals for Portuguese assistance, her involvement with the Ottoman Empire, and her subsequent wars of liberation must be viewed in this context.

The heyday of the coastal states

Kilwa retained its position of commercial prominence at least until the middle of the fourteenth century. Sultan Abu'l Mawahib al-Hasan ibn Sulaiman

[97] Jules Perruchon (trans.), *Les Chroniques de Zar'a Yâ'eqôb et de Ba'eda Mâryâm* (Paris, 1893), pp. 3–103.

(*c.* 1310–1333) made a pilgrimage to Mecca and conquered Kisimani Mafia, a rich, rival entrepôt located on an island that commanded the delta and trade routes of the Rufiji River; he was reigning when Ibn Battuta visited Kilwa.[98] In 1329/30, Ibn Battuta was on his way from Mecca to Oman and, ultimately, to India. First he paused in Mogadiscio, then Kilwa's most significant competitor to the north. In Ibn Battuta's eyes, Mogadiscio was an "enormous" town inhabited by wealthy merchants who exported locally woven wool or cotton fabrics and possessed large numbers of camels and sheep. For food these merchants of Mogadiscio customarily slaughtered hundreds of camels daily.

> *Their [staple] food is rice cooked with ghee, which they put into a large wooden platter, and on top of this they set platters of* kūshān. *This is the seasoning, made of chickens, flesh meat, fish and vegetables. They cook unripe bananas in fresh milk and put this in one dish, and in another dish they put curdled milk, on which they place . . . pickled lemon, bunches of pickled pepper steeped in vinegar and salted, green ginger, and mangoes. When they take a mouthful of rice, they eat some of these salted and vinegar conserves after it. A single person of the people of Magdashaw [Mogadiscio] eats as much as a whole company of us would eat, as a matter of habit, and they are corpulent and fat in the extreme.*[99]

The sheikh and the Egyptian *qadi* of Mogadiscio treated Ibn Battuta, a man of learning, with due hospitality. They gave him some leaves of betel and areca nuts, sprinkled him with rose water of Damascus in the Arab manner, and lodged him in a luxuriously furnished hostel otherwise occupied by students of the Qur'an. One Friday the sheikh sent Ibn Battuta a set of robes, consisting of a fairly typical Swahili loin cloth made of silk, an embroidered tunic of Egyptian linen, a furred mantle of Jerusalem stuff, and an Egyptian turban. The sheikh displayed a similar, if more elegant costume, and walked away from the mosque beneath four canopies or ceremonial parasols of colored silk, each festooned with the figure of a bird in gold.[100] In front of him, Ibn Battuta reported, the sheikh's retainers sounded drums, trumpets, and fifes. The sheikh usually ate separately from his councilors and dispensed justice only when his advisors felt unable to decide the cases themselves. He was, it seems, a local man. While he spoke to Ibn Battuta in Arabic, he normally conversed in a local language that may, by this time, have been Swahili.

The island town of Mombasa was then less important than it was to become. Although Ibn Battuta only stayed there overnight, he noticed that the people grew bananas, lemons, citrons, and a type of apple. Otherwise they ate fish and imported grain from the mainland. They possessed "admirably constructed" wooden mosques, around which were wells and what he described as paved areas of beaten earth.[101]

Finally Ibn Battuta arrived in Kilwa, the obvious object of this part of his

---

[98] "The Laws and Traditions of Kilwa," in Freeman-Grenville, *Medieval History*, p. 96.
[99] H. A. R. Gibb (trans.), *The Travels of Ibn Battuta* (Cambridge, Eng., 1962), II, p. 376.
[100] *Ibid.*, p. 377.
[101] *Ibid.*, p. 379.

travels. This large, substantially built city contained "jet-black" inhabitants who adorned their faces with cicatrices. They warred against the heathen peoples of the mainland, perhaps for slaves. The local ruler, al-Hasan ibn Sulaiman, directed these expeditions and, from his abundant sources of wealth, gave generously to the poor (a practice that Ibn Battuta pointedly indicates was not that of his successors). Perhaps because the learned traveler related his adventures only many years after his visit, in the manner of a modern writer of memoirs, he unfortunately says nothing of importance about the mosque, the citadel, or any of the other stone buildings of Kilwa which, from all other evidence, we should expect him to have noted.[102]

In his concluding remarks, however, Ibn Battuta hints at Kilwa's subsequent decline. When he reports that Da'ud ibn Sulaiman (*c.* 1333–1356) was less generous than his predecessor, he implies a sudden impoverishment of the royal treasury. Furthermore, neither Da'ud nor any of his fourteenth-century successors, according to the traditional accounts, had the funds with which to rebuild Kilwa's mosque after its collapse in about 1332.

During the fourteenth century, the rise of the northern island-state of Pate may have eclipsed the importance of Kilwa. According to the Pate chronicle, which unfortunately is an eighteenth- or nineteenth-century redaction, the Nabhani family from Muscat established the island-state in 1204. In the middle years of the fourteenth century, its navy, perhaps somehow supported by Egypt, conquered towns located to the north as well as to the south. After taking Malindi and Mombasa, the victorious men of Pate assaulted Kilwa from a temporary outpost on nearby Songo Mnara.[103] Everywhere they installed *jumbes*, or administrative officials, as part of what must have been a conquest of short duration. Later, conceivably as a part of the same process, the rulers of Kilwa employed men from Malindi (or from farther afield?) as palace bureaucrats.

By the end of the fifteenth century, eastern Africa contained thirty-seven distinct, separately governed market towns, and a number of small village settlements that had been influenced architecturally and politically by the larger settlements. These were sizable towns containing numerous houses of coral rag and lime mortar. The houses possessed elaborate sanitary arrangements and their inhabitants used and decorated their walls with Chinese porcelain.[104] At

---

[102] Ibn Battuta wrote that all the buildings of Kilwa were "of wood." But the great mosque and the citadel, both of which had already been constructed of coral rag and lime mortar, must have been standing during his visit. The resolution of this apparent divergence may simply lie with Ibn Battuta: he wrote down or dictated his *Travels* long after his visit to East Africa; his memory was never faultless. Freeman-Grenville, *Medieval History,* p. 107, by translating "of wood"—*min al-khashb*—as "with elegance"—*min al-hasb*—seeks to make Ibn Battuta read true. Professor Gibb does not, however, accept the suggested change.

[103] Gervase Mathew, "Songo Mnara," *Tanganyika Notes and Records,* 53 (1959), p. 158; Freeman-Grenville, *Medieval History,* pp. 113–115. In the light of Neville Chittick's recent re-formulations, these earlier arguments must be treated as highly speculative.

[104] J. S. Kirkman, *The Arab City of Gedi* (London, 1954), pp. 2–8; Gervase Mathew, "Chinese Porcelain in East Africa and on the Coast of South Arabia," *Oriental Art,* II (Summer, 1956), pp. 50–55.

The Great Mosque at Kilwa, which has been dated from the thirteenth through the fifteenth century, viewed from the north. Beyond the Mosque a large residence is being excavated. (H. Neville Chittick, Director, The British Institute of History and Archaeology in East Africa)

this time, Pate may have still possessed imperial ambitions, but Mombasa, Zanzibar, and Malindi were its equals. Sofala, still nominally governed by Kilwa, was virtually independent. All of the towns were comparatively prosperous, presumably because of their commercial connections with the traders of contemporary Malacca, Gujerat, Decca, Annam, and Burmese Martaban. In recent years, archaeologists digging along the coast of eastern Africa have unearthed glazed pottery from Persia and Egypt, stoneware from Burma and Siam, carnelian, amber, crystal, topaz, and porcelain of the Sung and Ming dynasties.

From about 1417 to 1431, the navies of Ming China may have even traded directly and exchanged embassies with the island-states of eastern Africa. The Ming dynasty (1368–1662) was interested in giraffe, which Malindi, or a port in what is now Somalia, apparently supplied. Had the Chinese not equated an African name for giraffe with the Chinese word for unicorn, had the presence of unicorns not been valued in China as a particularly propitious sign of heaven's approval and as a proof of the virtue of the reigning emperor, and had a real giraffe not resembled the mythical unicorn, China's trade with Africa might have remained exiguous. But when an African giraffe arrived in China during the early years of the fifteenth century, the emperor's satisfaction and delight knew no bounds. Africa, in his eyes, had contributed an emblem of perfect virtue, government, and harmony to the lasting satisfaction of Ming China.

Amazing is this gentle animal, of strange shape and wonderful form. . . . Truly the Emperor has received from Heaven a great Mandate which is widely manifested. May the sacred Age be ten thousand years.[105]

The Portuguese, who marveled at the beauty and the prosperity of these eastern African entrepôts, brought an era of independence and free trade to a close. They overran the cities of eastern Africa and transformed its economic life. Their intervention marked an important and unexpected departure for the peoples of the African continent.

---

[105] Jan Julius L. Duyvendak, "The True Dates of the Chinese Maritime Expeditions in the Early Fifteenth Century," *T'oung Pao*, XXXIV (1939), pp. 409–410; James S. Kirkman, "China and Africa in the Middle Ages," *The Journal of African History*, IV (1963), p. 297. See also Paul Pelliot, "Les Grands Voyages maritimes chinois au début du XVe siècle," *T'oung Pao*, XXX (1933), p. 315.

All the great ocean have we sayl'd, and crost,
To the Antartick *from the* Artick *strand*
Gone all the Round *of Affrick's spacious* Coast;
We have felt many a Clyme, *seen many a* Land.
We serve a potent King, *who hath ingrost*
His Peoples' *loves so, that, at his command,*
With cheerful faces, not vast Seas *alone,*
But we would pass the Lake of Acheron.

And 'tis by that command *we travel now*
To seek the Eastern Land *which Indies laves;*
By that *this distant* Ocean-Sea *we plough,*
Where none but Monsters *sayl'd the horrid Waves,*
But now 'tis reason, we *should likewise know*
(In Truth *have found a Harbour in your Caves)*
Who you *are? What this* Land *in which you dwell?*
Or, if of India you can tydings tell?

—Camões, 1572

AFRICA AND THE FIRST WAVE OF EUROPEAN EXPANSION, 1400–1700

3

Portugal looked toward Africa from the beginning of the fifteenth century. Supported by the merchants and shipowners of Lisbon and Oporto, King João I had shortly before ended Castile's attempt to dominate Portugal. Under his rule, local businessmen flourished. But they continued to compete with the merchants of Castile and Venice for the spices, precious stones, and gold of Africa and Asia. Like their competitors, they sought to circumvent the new Ottoman control of the traditional overland routes to the East and to prevent the continuance of what had already been a serious drain of European specie to the Levant and the East. Desirous of obtaining direct access to the fabled gold and cereals of tropical Africa, the mercantile interests of Portugal thus turned toward nearby Morocco, whose economic ties to the Western Sudan were well known and of long standing.

In 1415, Portugal conquered Ceuta, an important Moroccan port. Thereafter, in response both to the initial commercial influence that had led King

João to take Ceuta and to the new information that had been obtained in the Moroccan bazaars, the leaders of Portugal sought a sea route that would enable their sailors to tap the riches of tropical Africa and distant Asia. In these exploits, the Portuguese also drew upon the experiences of their own deep-sea fishermen and those of the Genoese merchants and mariners who had already reached the Canary Islands and had, perhaps, even visited West Africa and doubled the Cape of Good Hope.[1] The Portuguese probably also availed themselves of the knowledge displayed by fourteenth- and fifteenth-century cartographers and speculated, together with the intuitive thinkers of the Mediterranean world, about the unknown lands that lay beyond the Sahara.

I. The Second Age of Exploration

Prince Henrique, who was subsequently to become famous as Henry the Navigator, grew up with a consuming interest in Africa and in exploration. After winning his knighthood at Ceuta, he planned and backed a continuous program of exploration in order to discover a sea route to the Indies. According to his panegyric chronicler, Prince Henrique wanted to know—for practical purposes—what lay beyond the Canaries and Cape Bojador, in order to develop trade, outflank the Muslims of North Africa by allying Portugal to an African or Asian Christian king, evangelize the "heathen," and engage in noble adventures.[2] Most of all, Henrique and his sea captains wanted to find and obtain African gold and Asian spices. Theirs was a systematic quest of unprecedented dimensions and persistence: for eighty-three years, sailors sailed small ships into the unknown from Lisbon, Lagos, Oporto, and the other ports of Portugal. For good or evil, their efforts exposed tropical Africa to the avaricious gaze of Europe.

Only with great difficulty did Henrique persuade Portuguese sea captains to venture onto uncharted seas. They reached Porto Santo in 1418, Madeira in 1419, attempted unsuccessfully to conquer the Canaries in 1425,[3] but repeatedly failed or refused to double Cape Bojador. Finally in 1434, Gil Eanes sailed past the Cape and landed a short distance north of modern Aauinat Tartar. Eanes found no evidence of human habitation, but the sprig of rosemary that he car-

---

[1] Armando Cortesão and Avelino Teixeira da Mota, *Portugaliae monumenta cartographica,* (Lisboa, 1960), I, pp. 28–29, VI, p. 39, and the references cited therein; Charles Raymond Beazley, *The Dawn of Modern Geography* (Oxford, 1906), III, pp. 411–418. During the fourteenth century, French sailors conceivably may have visited the coast of western Africa. See Jules Hardy, "Les Dieppois en Guinée en 1364," *Revue de la Normandie* (1864), pp. 7–14; Raymond Mauny, "Les Prétendues Navigations dieppoises à la côte occidentale d'Afrique au XIVe siècle," *Bulletin de l'Institut Français d'Afrique Noire,* XII (1950), pp. 122–132.

[2] Gomes Eanes de Zurara (trans. Charles Raymond Beazley and Edgar Prestage), *The Chronicle of the Discovery and Conquest of Guinea* (London, 1896), I, pp. 27–30 [chap. 7]. See also a new translation by Léon Bourdon and Robert Ricard, *Chronique de Guinée* (Dakar, 1960); Francis M. Rogers, *The Quest for Eastern Christians* (Minneapolis, 1962), p. 63.

[3] Francis M. Rogers, *The Travels of the Infante Dom Pedro of Portugal* (Cambridge, Mass., 1961), pp. 313–314.

Prince Henrique of Portugal in 1453, from a section of an illuminated manuscript. MS. Portugais 41, Bibliothèque Nationale, Paris.

ried to Henrique symbolized the successful beginning of the first wave of European expansion into tropical Africa.[4]

Henrique wanted his sea captains to continue their explorations of the unknown, to obtain human captives who might provide information about the African continent, and to purchase the products of the coast. A succession of sailors fetched skins and oils and began to trade and transport slaves. In 1441, Antão Gonçalves and Nuno Tristão captured twelve Africans after a fierce struggle north of Cape Blanc and returned home to receive the praise of Prince Henrique. They explained their motives:

> *By carrying off these . . . captives . . . the* Infante *[Henrique] may come to know something about this folk, yet that doth not prevent what is still better, namely, for us to carry off many more; for, besides the knowledge which the Lord* Infante *will gain by their means, profit will also accrue to him by their service or ransom.*[5]

During the next few years, Portuguese sailors captured other Africans. They collected gold dust, animal hides, and ostrich eggs. In 1443, Tristão reached

[4] Zurara, *Chronicle*, pp. 33–34 [chap. 9]. See also Duarte Pacheco Pereira (trans. and ed. George H. T. Kimble), *Esmeraldo de Situ Orbis* (London, 1937), p. 66 [i, 22].

[5] Zurara, *Chronicle*, p. 46 [chap. 13].

Cape Blanc and the island of Arguin—soon to become Portugal's main base in West Africa. In 1444, Tristão approached the verdant shores and rustling palms of tropical Africa. In 1445, Dinis Dias landed near the mouth of the Senegal River, which he naturally assumed to be a branch of the Nile, and doubled Cape Verde. By 1448, other Portuguese sailors had ventured a further three hundred miles into the unknown, adding new luster to Henrique's grand design. In the same year, Pope Eugènius IV granted plenary indulgences to those sailors who might die while taking Christianity to the infidels, and Pedro, then regent of Portugal, gave Henrique a complete monopoly over all trade and discovery beyond Bojador.[6]

[6] The papal bull of Eugènius IV was dated January 5, 1443, the grant of monopoly, October 22, 1443. The bulls of 1455 and 1456 further granted Prince Henrique and the Order of Christ the sole right and duty of converting the Africans of Guinea. Pope Sixtus IV, in a

Trade with the "newly discovered" coast of Africa began in earnest. The ease with which they could obtain slaves, gold, and other commodities naturally excited the cupidity of the Portuguese. Furthermore, if exploration could be made to pay its way, it could be prosecuted with renewed vigor. From 1443, slave-raiding took precedence. In the next year, for example, six caravels flying the Cross of the Order of Christ reached Arguin and captured 235 Africans after a series of pitched battles.[7] In 1445, the Portuguese purchased Africans for the first time. Thereafter, they regularly carried small groups of enslaved Africans to Lagos and Lisbon. Wars with Castile and Morocco had depleted the available supply of urban labor, and the people of Portugal understandably welcomed the importation of a cheap substitute. No matter how honestly they excused the traffic in slaves as a means of saving souls for Christ, their economy came more and more, particularly after 1450, to rely upon it.

During the decade that ended with the death of Prince Henrique in 1460, sailors in the employ of Portugal extended their exploratory operations as far as the Sherbro Sound. Alvise da Cadamosto, a Venetian, Antoniotto Usodimare and Antonio da Noli, two Genoese, and Diogo Gomes, a Portuguese, visited the Senegal and the Gambia rivers, "discovered" the Cape Verde Islands, and were among the first explorers to value the friendship of peoples who lived along the shores of West Africa. More frequently than their predecessors, they sought to demonstrate to skeptical Africans that white men were not in fact cannibals. They also appreciated the wisdom of making commercial contact with slave traders; indeed, inland from Arguin was Ouadane, where Sanhajan raiders eagerly exchanged slaves and gold for Portuguese wheat, cloth, and silk. Along the Senegal River, Cadamosto bartered horses for the slaves of Cayor. Gomes reached the Gambia, where he exchanged Portuguese cloth and glass necklaces for great quantities of gold. Upstream, at Cantor, he learned of a trade route that ran east to what he was told were the fabulously rich kingdoms of Mali and Songhai.[8]

João II acceded to the throne of Portugal in 1481 and immediately encouraged new ventures in Africa. In 1482, Diogo Cão crossed the equator, passed Cape Ste. Catherine, and sailed into the unknown. After passing the mouth of the Niari River, he came unexpectedly upon a stretch of ocean where the water was both fresh and discolored about twenty miles offshore.[9] Bemused by the size and power of the river that was later called the Zaïre or the Congo, Cão landed on its southern bank and erected a seven-foot limestone pillar, or *padrão*, in the name of St. George.[10] Upstream Cão found that he could com-

bull of June 21, 1481, confirmed the sense of these earlier bulls. See Charles-Martial de Witte, "Les Bulles pontificales et l'expansion portugaise," *Revue d'histoire ecclésiastique*, XLIV (1954), pp. 443, 458–460; *ibid.*, LI (1956), pp. 426–453; *ibid.*, LIII (1958), p. 35.

[7] The Africans feared that they would be eaten. Zurara, *Chronicle*, pp. 63–78 [chaps. 19–23].

[8] G. R. Crone (trans. and ed.), *The Voyages of Cadamosto* (London, 1937), pp. 13, 29–31, 33, 35–44, 48, 60–61, 92–95 [chaps. viii, xv, xviii, xx–xxvii, xxxi, xxxviii].

[9] Ernst Georg Ravenstein, "The Voyages of Diogo Cão and Bartholomeu Dias, 1482–88," *The Geographical Journal*, VII (1900), pp. 628–629.

[10] A *padrão* consisted of a cube mounted upon a shaft. The cube was surmounted by a cross. Upon its face were the royal arms of Portugal. Upon its other sides were inscriptions, usually

municate with the local inhabitants by the use of signs. He therefore landed four assimilated Guineans and instructed them to proceed to the court of the *manikongo*, king of the Kongo.[11] Cão confidently expected his emissaries to negotiate an alliance with the supposedly powerful monarch that would enlist the Kongo in Portugal's religious and commercial struggle with Islam.

Cão sailed away south as far as Cape Santa Maria. Upon returning to the Congo, he learned that the *manikongo* had detained the four Guineans. Cão retaliated by capturing four Kongolese hostages, all of whom he publicly promised to exchange for his own emissaries on the occasion of a subsequent visit to the Congo. Cão then sailed home, perhaps unaware of how significant his actions were to be.

Diplomatically, it proved a masterful maneuver. In Portugal, the four Kongolese learned the language of their captors, acquainted themselves with a new form of material prosperity, and awaited the day when they could describe this strange Lusitanian civilization to their friends and families at home. João II, who hoped both that the Kongo kingdom would prove to be a gateway to the riches of the interior and that the *manikongo* would divulge the secrets of a route to the mysterious lands of Prester John, treated the Kongolese with deference. He housed and clothed them and saw that they were everywhere regarded as honored guests. In time, his attentions transformed the Kongolese into messengers of goodwill.

The "discovery" of the Congo hastened Portugal's search for a sea road to the Indies. In the summer of 1487, Bartolomeu Dias doubled the Cape of Good Hope—what Sir Francis Drake later called "a most stately thing, and the fairest cape we saw in the whole circumference of the earth." [12] Dias had at last discovered the elusive sea passage to the East. But it may have been another ten years before Portugal took advantage of his pioneer exploits. By then Columbus, who annotated a report of Dias' triumph, had discovered America.[13]

The quest for prester john

Portugal simultaneously pursued its quest for the legendary Prester John. A spurious, derivative twelfth-century letter reported that Prester John possessed large hoards of gold and gems, massive armies, and numerous bishops with whom he periodically dined. "I . . . surpass," he supposedly wrote, "in virtue, riches and power all creatures under heaven."

---

in Latin and Portuguese, recording the dates of the discovery and the names of the king and explorer responsible. Previously the Portuguese explorers marked their "discoveries" with wooden crosses that evidently have not stood the test of time.

[11] *Kongo* herein refers to the people of that name and to their country, *Congo* only to the area of the later country.

[12] Sir Francis Drake, in Richard Hakluyt (ed.), *The Principal Navigations, Voyages, Traffiques and Discoveries of the English Nation* (Glasgow, 1904), XI, p. 132. Dias, according to João de Barros, is supposed to have named the promontory Cape of Storms. Later, Barros avers, King João changed the name to Cape of Good Hope because the doubling of the promontory promised to provide a sea route to the Indies.

[13] The Treaty of Tordesillas, concluded with Spain in 1494, gave Portugal rights to what became Brazil and also to the eastern route to India.

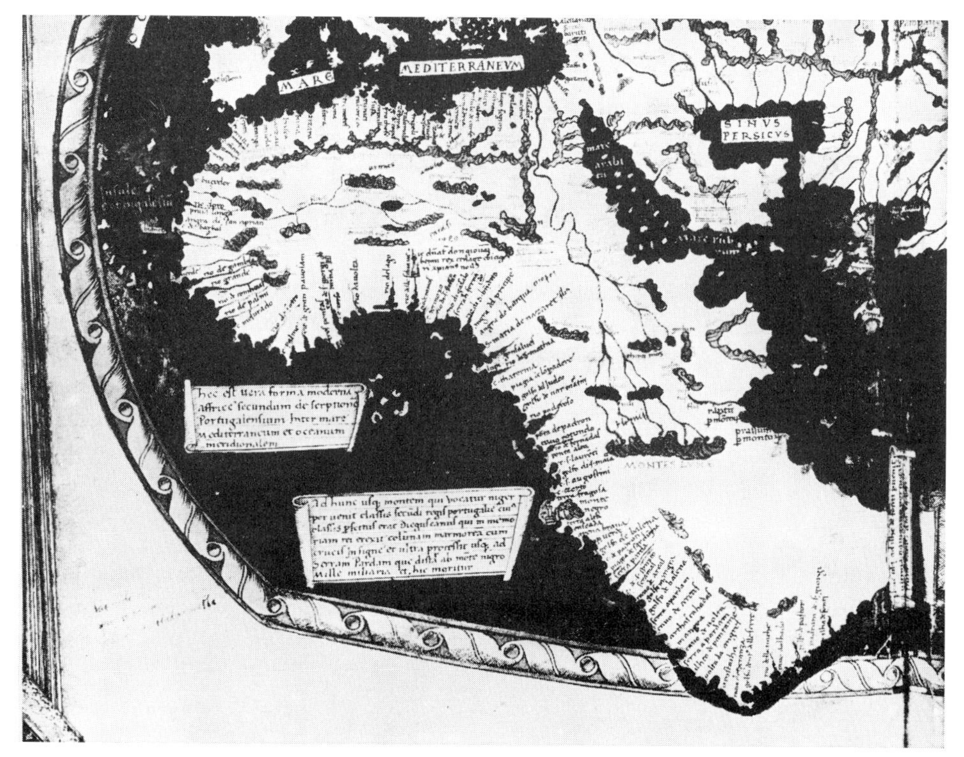

"The Discovery of the Cape of Good Hope," a map drawn by the German cartographer Heinricus Martellus in 1489, two years after the successful doubling of that cape by Bartolomeu Dias. The map includes many West African details, although few physical features are marked in the interior and the names on the eastern coast are almost entirely copied from Ptolemy. The British Museum, London.

> *Seventy kings are our tributaries. I am a zealous Christian and universally protect the Christians of our empire. . . . Honey flows in our land, and milk everywhere abounds. . . . For gold, silver, precious stones, animals of every kind and the number of our people, we believe there is not our equal under heaven. . . . The palace in which our sublimity dwells . . .* [has a] *roof . . . of ebony. . . . At the extremities over the gables, are two golden apples in each of which are two carbuncles, that the gold may shine by day, and the carbuncles sparkle by night. . . . The windows are of crystal. The tables on which our courtiers eat are of gold and some of amethyst. . . . At our table, thirty thousand men . . . are daily entertained. . . . Every month we are served in rotation by seven kings, sixty-two dukes, and two hundred and sixty-five counts and marquises. . . . Twelve archbishops sit on our right at table . . . every day, and twenty bishops on our left. . . .*[14]

[14] Quoted in E. Denison Ross, "Prester John and the Empire of Ethiopia," in Arthur Percival Newton (ed.), *Travel and Travellers of the Middle Ages* (London, 1926), pp. 176–177. For a discussion of the source of the legend and the origins of the name (which conceivably might merely have meant "priest John"), see Vsevolod Slessarev, *Prester John: The Letter*

Encouraged by the letter during an era when Christian Europe anxiously besought allies in order to counter the threat posed by Islamic and Mongolian armies, the potentates of Byzantium naturally sent ambassadors to consult Prester John. William of Rubruck, Marco Polo, and Odoric of Pordenone all failed to find Prester John in Asia but, after the visits of Ethiopian churchmen to Lisbon and to other Western capitals during the fourteenth and fifteenth centuries, the *cognoscenti* generally assumed that Prester John and the emperor of Ethiopia were one and the same.[15] As early as 1442, Henrique had instructed his captains to seek information about, and the definite location of, the kingdom of Prester John. The extent and configuration of Ethiopia were then unknown, however, and the sages of Europe regularly confused Ethiopia with all of continental Africa—which bore the same name—and, at times, with India. To add to their confusion, at Benin the Portuguese mariners learned of a monarch called Ogane who resembled the mythical Prester John—he lived in the interior, he was powerful, and he reputedly was a Christian.[16]

In 1487, King João II ordered Dias, who went by sea, and Pêro da Covilhã and Afonso de Paiva, who went overland, to find Prester John.[17] Covilhã spoke Arabic and had previously spied for both Portugal and Castile; Paiva was from the Canary Islands. From Lisbon they traveled *via* Rhodes to Cairo and Aden, which they reached in 1488. Covilhã sailed on to Calicut and returned *via* Goa, Ormuz, and perhaps Sofala to Cairo.[18] There he heard that Paiva had died *en route* to Ethiopia. Covilhã thereupon visited Mecca and Medina in a pilgrim's disguise and sailed across the Red Sea to the port of Zeila. In 1493, after many adventures, he finally arrived at the court of Emperor Alexander (Iskender) of Ethiopia—the fifteenth-century Prester John. Covilhã remained in the king's court for thirty-three years; it proved no doubt an enforced but unobjectionable stay. Other Portuguese ambassadors, including the priest Fran-

---

and the Legend (Minneapolis, 1959), pp. 25–27, 32–54, 91–92; Rogers, *Pedro*, pp. 101-103; Constantin Marinescu, "Le Prêtre Jean: son pays; explication de son nom," *Académie Roumaine: Bulletin de la Section Historique*, X (1923), pp. 93–112; Charles E. Nowell, "The Historical Prester John," *Speculum*, XXVIII (1953), pp. 436–440, 444–445.

[15] Certain Genoese associated Prester John with Ethiopia as early as 1306. Osbert G. S. Crawford (ed.), *Ethiopian Itineraries* (Cambridge, Eng., 1958), pp. 213–214. See also Charles de la Roncière, *La Découverte de l'Afrique au Moyen Âge* (Cairo, 1924), I, p. 60; William Woodville Rockhill (trans. and ed.), *The Journey of William of Rubruck to the Eastern Parts of the World* (London, 1900), pp. 150, 162–163; Henry Yule and Henri Cordier (trans. and eds.), *Cathay and the Way Thither* (London, 1913), II, pp. 244–245 (London, 1914), III, pp. 15–28; Thomas Wright, *The Travels of Marco Polo* (London, 1880), pp. 121, 147 [chaps. 44, 54].

[16] Was he the *oni* of Ife? See Barros, in Crone, *Cadamosto*, pp. 126–127.

[17] Previously King João II had sent two emissaries to Jerusalem, but they were unable or unwilling to venture to the land of Prester John without a knowledge of Arabic.

[18] Francisco Álvares (trans. and eds. Charles F. Beckingham and G. W. B. Huntingford), *The Prester John of the Indies* (Cambridge, Eng., 1961), II, p. 374, indicates that Covilhã definitely visited Sofala. See also John Milner Gray, "Early Portuguese Visitors to Kilwa," *Tanganyika Notes and Records*, 52 (1959), pp. 117–118; W. G. L. Randles, "South East Africa and the Empire of Monomotapa as Shown on Selected Printed Maps of the 16th Century," *Studia*, I (1958), p. 113. Did Covilhã inform King João of the city-states of eastern Africa? If so, did the king receive Covilhã's information in time to inform Gama?

cisco Álvares, visited Ethiopia during the sixteenth century, and from their day Ethiopia was again intertwined with Europe.

The culmination of the reconnaissance

Manuel I, who became king of Portugal in 1495, pursued an active Indian policy. As his ambassador he sent Vasco da Gama—Camões' "stalwart Aeneas"—to the entrepôts and princely capitals that Covilhã had perhaps described in a letter to Lisbon.

In 1498, when he finally reached eastern Africa, Gama was astounded to see a succession of prosperous, long-established ports.[19] In Moçambique harbor, four Arab ships loaded pearls, silver, rubies, cloves, pepper, and ginger. At Mombasa, where he found many Arab dhows, Gama rebuffed the hospitality of the local sheikh and sailed on to Malindi. There the Portuguese recalled scenes along their native Tagus: splendid whitewashed houses lined a great bay within which Indian-Arab and Indian vessels rode calmly at anchor. Wearing a robe of damask trimmed with green satin, the local sheikh came to visit Gama. He sat "on two cushioned chairs of bronze, beneath a round sunshade of crimson satin attached to a pole." [20] He gave Gama six sheep and spices in abundance, and welcomed the Portuguese sailors despite Gama's niggardly reciprocal present; it consisted of only two strings of coral beads, two pieces of striped cotton, a hat, some small bells, and three wash basins. Perhaps Gama had at last become a diplomat, but it seems more probable that the sheikh desired an alliance that would free Malindi from the yoke of Mombasa.

Before long Malindi became inextricably tied to Portugal, and East Africa to Europe. Similarly, by 1498, Portugal had bestirred Africans of the east and the west. It had involved tropical Africa with Europe in ways that were bound to be of a significantly different order from that continent's earlier contacts with the Arab or Asian worlds.

II. Trade and Influence Along the Western Coasts

During the fifteenth century, Portugal exercised a limited commercial and political influence over the peoples of western Africa from a few strategically sited, heavily fortified, coastal entrepôts. At Arguin Portuguese merchants exchanged European horses, cloth, linen, wheat, bowls, pots, combs, looking glasses, and needles for civet cats, the coarse *malagueta* pepper (chillies), gum arabic, salt, small quantities of gold, and many slaves.[21] They successfully tapped and diverted a part of the trade that had formerly gone overland from Ouadane to Fez, thereby helping to refocus the traditional trans-Saharan economic ties

[19] Other Portuguese sailors, perhaps following the instructions of Covilhã, may well have anticipated Gama's visit to eastern Africa. See Ahmad ibn Majid (trans. T. A. Shumouskii), *Tri Neizvestnye Lozii* (Moskva, 1957), p. 31 [l. 94r]. Mrs. Lucy Behrman kindly translated the relevant passages from the Russian.

[20] Vasco da Gama (trans. and ed. Ernst Georg Ravenstein), *A Journal of the First Voyage of Vasco da Gama* (London, 1898), p. 42.

[21] Crone, *Cadamosto*, pp. 14–25 [chaps. ix, xi]; Pacheco, *Esmeraldo*, pp. 72–73 [i, 10].

The bronze figure of a Portuguese *arquebusier*, cast in Benin *c.* 1600. This is one example of the way in which foreigners became enshrined in the art of Benin. The figure's spiral stance contrasts strikingly with the foursquare posture of most other Benin figures. The British Museum, London.

of the Western Sudan. But by the 1470's, Portugal's primary interest had naturally shifted to the commercially more rewarding regions of Africa south of the Senegal River. From São Tiago, in the Cape Verde Islands, Portuguese traders brought European goods to peoples living along the banks of the upper Senegal and the upper Gambia rivers. Later some of these traders settled in African villages and exercised a unique kind of local influence. Lusitanian missionaries also spread the Portuguese language and culture along the coast from the Senegal River to Sherbro Sound. The peoples of the Grain and Ivory Coasts, however, were at first given a wide berth because their harbors were few and their coasts difficult of access.

Throughout these areas, the traders, the settlers, and the missionaries each attempted—usually unsuccessfully—to interfere directly in African politics,[22] but they cared more for commerce, and assiduously acquired slaves and gold. They cultivated the local rulers and, in deference to their own economic self-interest, played a limited and transient political and social role in the affairs of West Africa.

In the western half of the Gulf of Guinea, the Portuguese initially anchored their caravels in the offshore roads and purchased gold dust and slaves from Africans who swam or paddled to meet them. But in order to organize the trade

---

[22] On at least one occasion, a Wolof chief became a Portuguese vassal. John William Blake (trans. and ed.), *Europeans in West Africa, 1450–1560* (London, 1942), I, pp. 32–33, 35–36, 80–86.

more efficiently, King João II ordered a fortress to be built on the Gold Coast. Africans protested its erection, but Diogo de Azambuja intervened vigorously and contrived, in 1482, to construct a citadel at Elmina that remained Portugal's most important West African outpost for 150 years.[23] During that long period, each of Elmina's governors had occasion to emulate the forceful policies enunciated by Azambuja. Cannon and muskets preserved Portugal's commercial hegemony, and three new forts later added a further dimension to this foreign control.

Politically, Portugal's power was extended only to Africans living in the environs of the Gold Coast forts. Portuguese governors weaned villagers residing in the shadow of these forts away from their traditional ways of life and transformed them into faithful vassals. Portugal employed them in local trade wars and eventually governed their villages directly.[24] Beyond this coastal frontier, however, Portugal made few friends. Portuguese merchants confined their extensive trade with the Denkyera people—who exchanged gold for cloth and slaves from Benin—to the coastal markets. Thus, both because the paths leading inland were guarded jealously and the Portuguese garrisons were small, the bulk of the commerce of the Gold Coast remained in African hands.

Along the Slave Coast, Portuguese merchants and missionaries were particularly active in São Tomé and Benin. After "discovering" it in 1473, the Portuguese converted São Tomé into a very profitable colonial outpost. Soon after they settled there, they began to trade with the peoples of nearby Africa. From them they easily obtained slaves to tend the sugar that grew well in the island's fertile, well-watered soil. The Portuguese also obtained pungent pepper, palm oil, leopard skins, and ivory. Benin supplied the best pepper, and Portugal established a permanent trading post in Ughoton (Gwato), Benin's port, where factors and missionaries resided at least until 1520. (Missionaries remained continuously at nearby Warri until the end of the seventeenth century.[25]) The Portuguese interlopers introduced their language and their religion into Benin. They treated the indigenous rulers as allies and welcomed them with full honors when Benin sent embassies to Lisbon.[26] In some ways, too, Portugal's activity in Benin foreshadowed the idealized and unrealized aspects of her involvement in the Kongo.

The kingdom of the kongo

Relations between Portugal and the kindom of the Kongo began auspiciously. In 1484/85, Diogo Cão returned the four hostages to the banks of the

[23] *Ibid.*, I, pp. 70–78; Pacheco, *Esmeraldo*, pp. 119–121 [ii, 5]; Roncière, *La Découverte* (1925), II, pp. 64–65.

[24] Blake, *Europeans*, I, pp. 133–135; John Barbot, *A Description of the Coasts of North and South Guinea*, in Awnsham and John Churchill, *A Collection of Voyages and Travels* (London, 1732), V, p. 155.

[25] A. F. C. Ryder, "Missionary Activity in the Kingdom of Warri to the Early Nineteenth Century," *Journal of the Historical Society of Nigeria*, II (1960), pp. 2–17.

[26] Blake, *Europeans*, I, pp. 78–79, II, p. 318; Jacob Egharevba, *A Short History of Benin* (Ibadan, 1960), pp. 22–31.

Congo River. They made their way to Mbanza, the large Kongo capital, and presumably amused and astounded their countrymen with elaborate descriptions of Europe and the bizarre affectations of its citizens. Their tales evidently impressed the reigning *manikongo* Nzinga Nkuwu and his royal council. Together they decided to welcome Portugal's initiative: the Kongolese agreed to send a few of their inhabitants to obtain technical and religious training in Lisbon and to receive Portuguese builders, farmers, and missionaries in exchange.

At this time, the kingdom of the Kongo was probably little more than a loose confederation of six states located roughly within what is now the northern third of Angola. Its inhabitants domesticated swine, sheep, and chickens and wove mats and cloth of raffia or palm fronds.[27] Like other agricultural Bantu, they cultivated millet and sorghum, hunted, and fished. But the Portuguese, perhaps drawing upon outdated local opinions (the *manikongo's* sovereignty earlier may have extended to peoples living between the Congo, Cuanza, and Cuango rivers [28]), tended to overestimate the importance of the Kongo.

In 1490/91, three ships took Portuguese priests, artisans, and soldiers to the Congo River. It was primarily a peaceful expedition: both the priests and the artisans gave gifts to the *manikongo*. The priests began to proselytize in Mbanza. Soon they had baptized the *manikongo*, giving him the name João. The German lay brothers, who had accompanied the priests, set up a printing press, and the military commanders helped the Kongolese to defeat a rebellious vassal. But we know little more about internal developments in the Kongo until Portuguese São Toméans began to raid it early in the sixteenth century. Meanwhile, the voyages of Gama occupied Portugal overseas.

Afonso (1505–1543), the first trained Christian *manikongo*, tried to ally himself to Portugal both economically and politically. He wanted Portugal to help him introduce the people of the Kongo to Western ways. But now that they had found the sea road to the Indies, the Portuguese were no longer particularly interested in Afonso and his people. Instead, the merchant and plantation oligarchs of São Tomé raided the Kongo and in time established themselves in Mbanza, where they trafficked openly in slaves and other contraband. Afonso appealed vainly to Lisbon for help. In 1508, a fresh group of Portuguese priests arrived in Mbanza with ambitious ideas of an educational and evangelical kind. They proved persons of no better repute, however, than the slavers. Many of them sold the household servants that had been given to them by Afonso; they possessed private residences, mistresses, and illegitimate children.[29]

---

[27] Filippo Pigafetta (trans. Margarite Hutchinson), *A Report of the Kingdom of Congo and of the Surrounding Countries* (London, 1881 [original Italian edition, 1591]), pp. 30–31, 43, 59, 69, 108–109.

[28] Jean Cuvelier, *L'Ancien Royaume de Congo* (Bruges, 1946), pp. 17–18; Jan Vansina, "Notes sur l'origine du royaume de Kongo," *The Journal of African History*, IV (1963), pp. 37–38.

[29] James Duffy, *Portuguese Africa* (Cambridge, Mass., 1959), pp. 13–14. For much of the following, Duffy provides the best treatment in English.

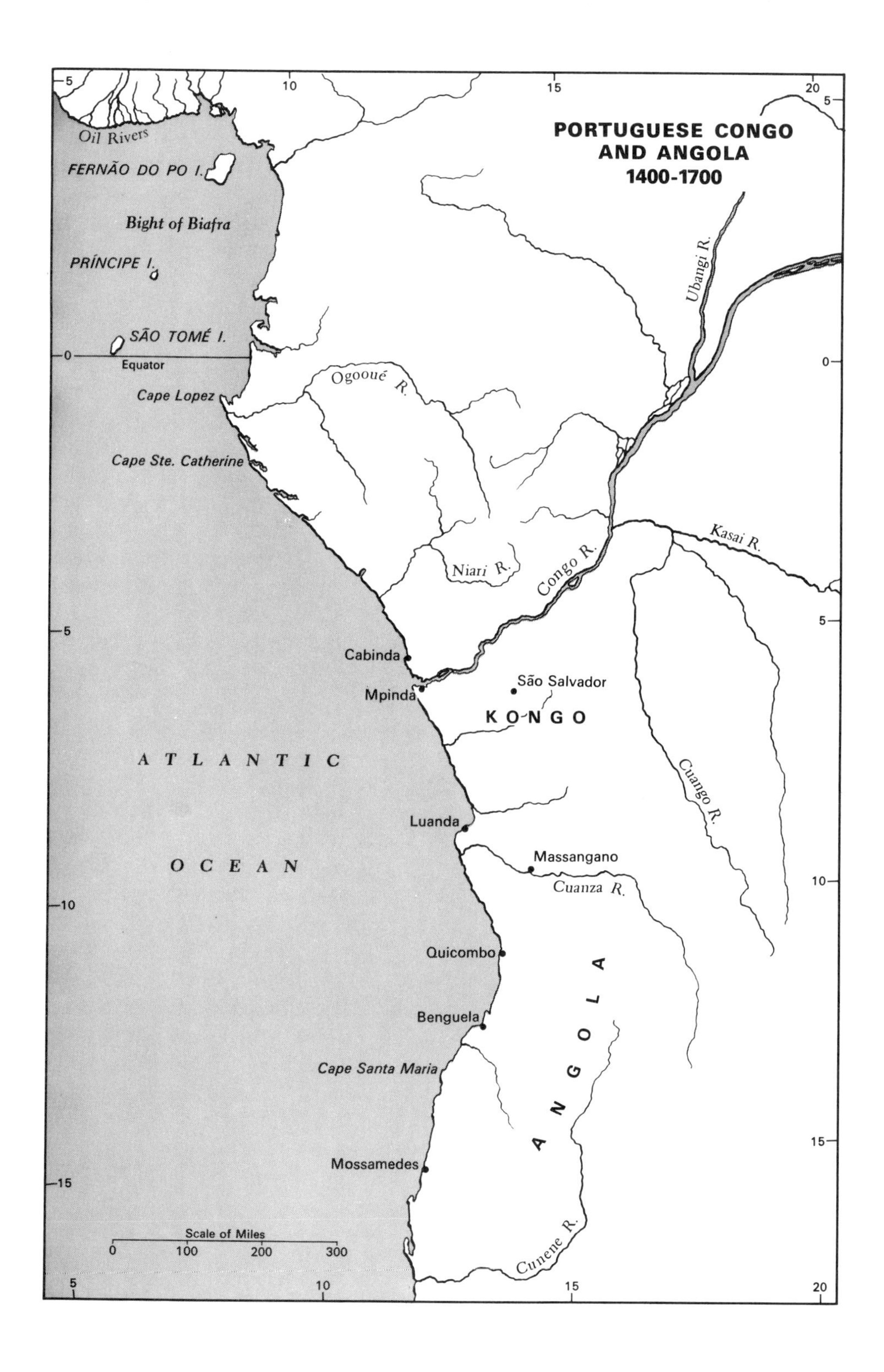
PORTUGUESE CONGO
AND ANGOLA
1400-1700
Oil Rivers
FERNÃO DO PO I.
Bight of Biafra
PRÍNCIPE I.
SÃO TOMÉ I.
Equator
Cape Lopez
Cape Ste. Catherine
Ogooué R.
Ubangi R.
Niari R.
Congo R.
Kasai R.
Cabinda
Mpinda
São Salvador
KONGO
ATLANTIC
OCEAN
Cuango R.
Luanda
Massangano
Cuanza R.
Quicombo
Benguela
ANGOLA
Cape Santa Maria
Mossamedes
Cunene R.
Scale of Miles
0
100
200
300

Afonso only rarely obtained the relief that he requested in plaintive petitions to Lisbon. But in 1512, King Manuel of Portugal—at last aware of the problems in Mbanza—sought to reverse the prevalent trend of events by despatching a special representative to the *manikongo's* court. He gave Simão da Silva detailed instructions in a *regimento*, or royal ordinance. It contained no suggestion of a colonial dominion. Manuel bade Silva to teach Portuguese military and legal procedures to the people of the Kongo. He urged Silva to tell the Kongolese how to conduct themselves in the presence of royalty and he gave him permission to assist Afonso in local wars. The *regimento* also indicated that Silva was to build churches, control the local Portuguese community, and repatriate those priests and traders who had been misbehaving. He was not, however, to interfere with the practice of indigenous customs. In sum, Manuel enjoined Silva to create, if he could, a new Lusitanian civilization in an African context. In return, Manuel anticipated that Portugal would derive considerable commercial benefit from its connection with the Kongo. "It would be a pity," read the *regimento*, "for Portuguese ships carrying expensive cargo and personnel to depart from the Congo with empty holds." Manuel wanted his ships to return home "loaded with slaves, copper, and ivory to defray the expenses [that] he had voluntarily shouldered." [30]

The *regimento* had little practical effect. Silva, who might have been sufficiently strong to implement Manuel's proposed reforms, died of fever on his way to meet Afonso. His successor, the trader Álvaro Lopes, was too weak to prevent the São Toméans from strengthening their rapacious hold upon the commerce of the Kongo. Despite the protests of Afonso, São Toméans and Portuguese priests continued to trade in slaves and keep local mistresses. After an abortive revolt by the local slaves, Afonso once again appealed forlornly to Lisbon for assistance. He asked for a fresh supply of priests and teachers and for control over the slave raiders.[31] But Lisbon complacently left the Kongo and its problems to the oligarchy of São Tomé, then its richest African province. The vicar apostolic of São Tomé investigated the complaints, excused the activities of the São Toméans in Mbanza, and at last compelled Afonso to cope with the local conditions of chaos alone.

Until his death in 1543, Afonso tried unsuccessfully to deal with the problems of the Kongo. He attempted to curb the slave trade—it had already fractured the links that had previously bound the kingdom together—but commissions and regulations accomplished little. Uninterrupted slaving since the beginning of his reign had corrupted his authority. The capital had consequently become an artificial entity isolated from the ordinary life of the country and populated by a collection of freebooters, lax and demoralized clergy, students returned from Europe, concubines, and mulatto functionaries.[32] All of

---

[30] See António da Silva Rego, *Portuguese Colonization in the Sixteenth Century: A Study of the Royal Ordinances* (Johannesburg, 1959), pp. 45–50.

[31] See Afonso to Manuel, October 5, 1514, in Visconde de Paiva Manso, *Historia do Congo* (Lisboa, 1877), pp. 13–31; Duffy, *Portuguese*, p. 16.

[32] Ernst Georg Ravenstein (ed.), *The Strange Adventures of Andrew Battell of Leigh* (London, 1901), p. 114; Jean Cuvelier and L. Jadin, *L'Ancien Congo d'après les archives romaines (1518–1640)* (Bruxelles, 1954), pp. 86–90.

these factors contributed to Afonso's increasingly bitter disillusionment with the Kongo's European connection. In his eyes, Portugal had conferred only humiliation upon the people of the Kongo.

After the death of Afonso, the Kongo aroused progressively less interest abroad. Three Jesuit and Carmelite missions met with a hostile response when they attempted to revitalize the Christian witness. Bloody civil wars were the rule in 1543/44 and again in 1561, when the reigning *manikongo* was murdered during Mass.[33] Afonso's successors imitated their local European examples: they captured, purchased, and sold slaves and lived with concubines. In 1570, when Portuguese marines helped to drive the marauding Ayaka people from Mbanza, the reigning *manikongo* promised to acknowledge the suzerainty of Portugal by sending to its king cowrie shells worth about 20 percent of the revenues of the Kongo.[34] But Portugal cared little for its one-time ally. The white traders left Mbanza, and the interests of Lisbon—insofar as they were directed to Africa—tended more and more to be centered upon the kingdom of Ngola. Mbanza, with its twelve empty churches, soon stood deserted.

The ndongo kingdom of ngola

Diogo Cão had found little to excite his interest when he coasted along the shores of what is now Angola. Later the slavers of São Tomé extended their traffic from the Kongo south to the Ndongo kingdom that the Portuguese called Ngola, after the title of its ruler. During this period, the *ngola* of Ndongo was a vassal of the *manikongo* of the Kongo. Envious perhaps of the Kongo's association with Portugal, the *ngola* in 1519 requested Portuguese traders and priests from King Manuel. And together with their message, the Ndongo sent samples of silver that naturally were of interest to the Portuguese king.[35] He promptly despatched an exploratory embassy consisting of Manuel Pacheco and Baltasar de Castro. But these ambassadors were unable to obtain from São Tomé the required priests. The *ngola* therefore rebuffed Pacheco and imprisoned Castro for seven years. But, despite the failure of its first mission, Portugal remembered that the Ndongo kingdom contained the promise of silver.

During the second half of the sixteenth century, four powerful groups—the Kongolese, the Jesuits, the São Toméans, and the Portuguese Crown—competed for economic hegemony in Ngola. With assistance from the slavers of São Tomé, the people of Ndongo proclaimed their independence and defeated the Kongolese armies in the battle of Caxito in 1556. The Society of Jesus wanted to succeed in Angola after it had failed in the Kongo,[36] but the Jesuit expedition of 1560 met only with hostility from a new, unsympathetic *ngola*. Indeed, the reigning *ngola* held Paulo Dias de Novais (a grandson of

---

[33] Pigafetta, *Congo*, p. 93.

[34] For a discussion of the Ayaka, see Gladwyn Murray Childs, *Umbundu Kinship and Character* (London, 1949), pp. 181–188; Ravenstein, *Battell*, pp. 20–35, 83–87; Pigafetta, *Congo*, pp. 96–99. The government of Portugal did not acknowledge the *manikongo's* submission of vassalage until 1883.

[35] See Silva Rego, *Colonization*, pp. 50–53.

[36] See Childs, *Kinship*, p. 193. *Angola* refers to the area of the modern colony, *Ngola* to the kingdom of that name.

Bartolomeu Dias), Father Francisco de Gouveia, and two companions hostage. Gouveia died in detention, but after his release in 1565, Dias carried slaves, ivory, and copper to Lisbon.

The rulers of Portugal were unwilling to see the possibilities of more slaves, gold, and silver slip from their grasp. To both them and the Jesuits, the evident enmity of the people of Ndongo was a further incentive. In 1571, the Portuguese Crown therefore gave Paulo Dias, who had presumably painted a tempting picture of the potential riches of Ngola, the proprietorship of what he called Angola. Like the Crown's earlier concession to Fernão Gomes, the grant to Dias was an inexpensive device that theoretically ensured the speedy conquest, colonization, and evangelization of a large part of southern Africa. Upon Dias the Crown conferred the geographically significant (but really meaningless) title of "Governor and Captain General of the Kingdom of Sebaste in the Conquest of Ethiopia." Dias received "forever" about 140 miles of coastline south of Luanda and all of the territories inland from that coast. In return Dias was to cultivate and settle his lands and to garrison "Sebaste" with technicians and soldiers. He was expected to build three fortresses and a church and to explore the shores of Africa as far south as the Cape of Good Hope. The grant specifically enjoined Dias to construct a colonial empire upon the Brazilian model, which had already demonstrated its value. The success of the proprietorship depended, however, more upon the reactions of the indigenous inhabitants of Angola than upon the decrees of Portugal.[37]

Dias' much-heralded army of conquest landed at Luanda in 1575. There it stayed for three years while Dias erected a fortress, a church, and a hospital in the town to which he added the name São Paulo. Meanwhile, the Jesuits who had accompanied his expedition fanned the fires of war, and the São Toméans previously resident in Luanda clamored incessantly for a conflict that would increase their traffic in slaves. In 1579, Dias therefore advanced up the Cuanza River toward Cabaza, the distant capital of Ngola. The battle was joined: for ten years the people of Ngola fought a number of bitter actions in an initially successful attempt to preserve their freedom.[38] Turmoil filled the kingdom of Ngola. Innumerable Africans and at least two thousand Portuguese soldiers lost their lives. As a result of their resistance, the Ndongo rulers were able to confine the political influence of Portugal to a narrow strip of land that extended for seventy miles along both banks of the Cuanza River from Luanda to Massangano. The proprietorship of Dias was a failure, for he neither colonized the lands that he had been granted nor discovered the sources of silver and gold. He had, however, provided the exporters of Luanda with a steady supply of slaves and the Portuguese Crown with the dubious notion of conquest.

During the following three centuries, Portugal strove to transform the people of Angola into docile colonial subjects. After the death of Dias in 1589, one

[37] For the text, see Alfredo de Albuquerque Felner, *Angola* (Coimbra, 1933), pp. 407–412.
[38] See Baltasar Almeida de Sousa to Philip II, May 21, 1591, in Hakluyt, *Navigations*, VI, pp. 468–469.

Portuguese governor after another tried unsuccessfully to extend the imperial frontier in Angola. In this regard their efforts were opposed by the Jesuits—who wanted to maintain theocratic rule in the provinces that had been given to them by Dias—by the São Toméan slavers—who wanted to perpetuate their own brand of free enterprise—and by the local inhabitants. Nevertheless, in the early seventeenth century, Portuguese governors taxed harshly and firmly administered a wedge of territory that extended for 150 miles inland from Luanda. They enslaved some, forced other Africans to work on local plantations, and eventually transformed the colony of Angola into a labor reservoir for Brazil.

III. Paramountcy in Eastern Africa

The coastal markets of eastern Africa occupied a permanent place in Europe's plans for commercial expansion from the beginning of the sixteenth century, when Portuguese mariners began to capitalize upon Vasco da Gama's "discovery" of a sea route to Calicut. The Portuguese navy attacked and invested many of the prominent coastal towns, established the beginnings of a commercial empire, and finally embroiled East Africa in the wars that the nations of Europe waged for hegemony in the Indian Ocean. Commercial strategies helped to shape the history of eastern Africa and, to a lesser extent, the history of the interior.

The conquest of the city-states

During the early years of the sixteenth century, Portugal sought to build a new commercial empire upon the foundations laid by Gama. Pedro Álvares Cabral sailed to East Africa and India in 1500; after accidently sighting Brazil, he doubled the Cape of Good Hope and landed at Moçambique Island—where the local inhabitants were friendly—and at Kilwa, where his fleet met with hostility. Sancho de Tovar, a captain of one of the ships in Cabral's fleet, later visited Sofala in order to discover the sources of its reputed wealth.[39]

At about this time, Portuguese visitors lavished praise upon the island towns of East Africa. In their eyes, Kilwa was "a Moorish town with many fair houses of stone and mortar, with many windows after our fashion, very well arranged in streets, with many flat roofs. The doors are of wood, well carved, with excellent joinery. Around it are streams and orchards and fruit-gardens with many channels of sweet water."

> *And in this town was great plenty of gold, as no ships passed towards Çofala without first coming to this island. Of the Moors there are some fair and some black, they are finely clad in many rich garments of gold and silk and cotton, and the women as well; also with much gold and silver in chains and bracelets, which they wear on their legs and arms, and many jewelled earrings in their ears.*

---

[39] See William Brooks Greenlee (trans.), *The Voyage of Pedro Álvares Cabral to Brazil and India* (London, 1938), pp. 61–68, 89–90. Diogo Dias may have "discovered" Madagascar in 1500 after being separated from Cabral's main fleet.

Sugar cane grew on Mafia, Zanzibar, and Pemba, but the inhabitants supposedly did not know how to make sugar. They were "feeble folk" who possessed few weapons. But the kings of these islands lived in great luxury. They wore fine cotton and silk garments and their women, like those of Kilwa, displayed jewels of silver and Sofala gold, earrings, necklaces, bangles, and bracelets.

Mombasa and Malindi were very fair places, again with lofty stone and mortar houses and streets that were well aligned. The men of Mombasa were either tawny, black, or white in color, and their women wore "fine garments of silk and gold in abundance."

> *This is a place of great traffic, and has a good harbour, in which are always moored craft of many kinds and also great ships, both of which come from Çofala and those which go thither, and others which come from the great kingdom of Cambaya [in India] and from Melynde; others which sail to the Isles of Zinzibar. . . .*

The Portuguese found Mombasa and Malindi "full of food." The administrator Duarte Barbosa, who visited East Africa in 1501, mentioned fat-tailed sheep, cattle, fowls, much millet and rice, sweet and bitter oranges, lemons, pomegranates, Indian figs, various vegetables, and much sweet water. The people of Mombasa fought and traded with the people of the mainland, from whom they obtained honey, wax, and ivory. Pate and Lamu, island towns to the north, were often at war with the "heathen" of the mainland. Their towns were thus well walled with stone and mortar. Beyond was Brava, which had no king and was ruled by a merchant oligarchy, and Mogadiscio, where the Portuguese found flesh meat, wheat, barley, horses, and fruit in abundance.[40]

In 1502, King Manuel of Portugal sent Gama back to the scene of his earlier exploits to teach these prosperous and hostile East Africans to respect the might of Lisbon's navy. Gama was to compel them to open up their markets to Portuguese traders, to assist the Portuguese search for precious minerals, and to provide food and shelter when requested. In Sofala and Moçambique strong-arm tactics proved unnecessary. But Gama extorted large sums of "protection" money from the sheikh of Kilwa and burned every Arab ship that he found in African waters. Ruy Ravasco, another Portuguese sea captain, similarly subdued Zanzibar and Brava in 1503, compelling them thereafter to pay tribute.[41]

At this time, Venice still controlled the overland trade in Indian spices. With each report of a Portuguese success, the merchants of Venice naturally feared for their own commercial prospects. They therefore obtained the help of the sultans of Egypt and the sheikhs of Arabia and sought unsuccessfully to harass the Portuguese in the Indian Ocean. King Manuel in turn intensified his country's efforts in the Indian Ocean arena. To Dom Francisco de Almeida,

---

[40] Mansel Longworth Dames (trans. and ed.), *The Book of Duarte Barbosa* (London, 1918), I, pp. 17–31 [10–17]. Barbosa probably wrote his history between 1516 and 1518. See also the brief references to the trading relations of eastern Africa in Tomé Pires (trans. and ed. Armando Cortesão), *The Suma Oriental of Tomé Pires* (London, 1944), I, pp. 43, 46–47.

[41] Dames, *Barbosa,* p. 30 [16].

A caravel, *c.* 1511, similar to the kind used by Vasco da Gama and other Portuguese sailors. Biblioteca e Museu de Marinha, Lisbon.

a ranking nobleman, he gave the task of securing Portugal's hegemony there. In 1505, at the command of twenty-two ships and 2,500 soldiers and sailors, Almeida sailed swiftly to Moçambique, where he forced the ruling sheikh to accept the domination of Portugal. When the sultan of Kilwa proved less amenable to the new dispensation than the sheikh of Moçambique, Almeida's men invested the town and took its slaves and stocks of gold, silver, and ambergris as booty. Almeida installed a puppet ruler and erected a fortress on the foreshore.[42] Next Almeida's soldiers and sailors sacked Mombasa and butchered about 1,500 inhabitants after the local sheikh had refused to acknowledge the suzerainty of Portugal. The invaders bombarded the sheikh's palace, fired the flimsy African houses, and captured the town after hand-to-hand combat in the streets and on the rooftops. They captured abundant treasures of gold, silver, silk, sandalwood, camphor, Persian carpets, ivory, copper, brass, and slaves, before sailing on to India.[43] After the Portuguese had departed, the sheikh of Mombasa wrote of his calamity to the sheikh of Malindi:

> *May God protect you Sayyid Ali. I have to inform you that we have been visited by a mighty ruler who has brought fire and destruction amongst us. He raged in*

---

[42] *Ibid.*, p. 18 [10]; S. Arthur Strong (ed.), "The History of Kilwa," *The Journal of the Royal Asiatic Society*, XX (1895), p. 404.

[43] Dames, *Barbosa*, p. 21 [11]. Almeida also sacked Mafia. See D. W. I. Piggot, "History of Mafia," *Tanganyika Notes and Records*, 11 (1941), p. 37.

our town with such might and terror that no one, neither man nor woman, neither the old nor the young, nor even the children, however small, was spared to live. His wrath was to be escaped only by flight. Not only people, but even the birds in the heavens were killed and burnt. The stench from the corpses is so overpowering that I dare not enter the town, and I cannot begin to give you an idea of the immense amount of booty which they took from the town. Pray hearken to the news of these sad events, that you may yourself be preserved.[44]

Tristão da Cunha and Afonso de Albuquerque continued Almeida's mission of conquest. In 1506, they razed and looted Oja, whose sheikh had claimed the protection of the caliph of Cairo, and went on to deal with the rulers of the other northern coastal communities. After being blockaded, Lamu promised to pay Portugal an annual tribute, the first installment of which was tendered in Venetian silver coins. Brava proved unwilling to follow Lamu's example, so Cunha and Albuquerque invaded, bombarded, and at last, after a fierce fight, captured the town. They sailed to Mogadiscio, but the lateness of the monsoon season and the determination of the town's defenders caused prudence to prevail. Cunha and Albuquerque set sail for Socotra and southern Arabia.[45]

Pedro de Anhaia had meanwhile reached Sofala after suffering a savage buffeting in the Antarctic Ocean. In Sofala the elderly sheikh permitted the Portuguese intruders—perhaps because he assumed that they would swiftly be destroyed by fever—to construct a fortress of mud and straw. But Anhaia soon controlled a part of Sofala's gold trade. The local people naturally greeted this unexpected turn of events with hostility and turned upon the Portuguese. In the subsequent conflict, Portuguese cannon and muskets killed about one thousand Arabs and Africans. The invaders installed a sheikh responsive to their wishes, and successfully engrossed the gold that had formerly gone to Kilwa and overseas. They soon found, however, that by upsetting Sofala's traditional economic arrangements they had unwittingly cut themselves off from the indigenous suppliers of its wealth.

From 1510 to 1600, Portugal was sovereign from Sofala to Mogadiscio. With advanced weapons and an unwillingness to give any quarter to the Arabs and the Mamluk Egyptians, it established itself as the major power of the Indian Ocean. Refusing to cooperate with others, its navy drove Arab ships away from the East African coast—although they later returned. For a time, Portugal also monopolized East Africa's trade with the Orient. Its commanders quelled frequent rebellions and installed a number of puppet sheikhs. They even tried to replace Arabic-speaking middlemen with local Portuguese, and to trade with Africans of the interior from the fortified coastal bazaars.[46] But theirs was a naive approach that contributed to a period of economic stagnation in the coastal marts.

---

[44] Quoted in Justus Strandes (trans. Jean F. Wallwork), *The Portuguese Period in East Africa* (Nairobi, 1961), p. 73.

[45] Walter de Gray Birch (trans. and ed.), *The Commentaries of the Great Afonso d'Albo-querque* (London, 1875), pp. 35–45.

[46] But see John Milner Gray, "Portuguese Records Relating to the Wasegeju," *Tanganyika Notes and Records,* 29 (1950), pp. 92–93.

North of the town of Moçambique, the influence of Portugal rarely extended beyond the narrow confines of those states that had been attacked by Almeida or Cunha. On the coast, Portuguese-speaking visitors introduced new words into indigenous languages and were responsible for a certain amount of miscegenation. Otherwise, Portugal asserted itself primarily by force of arms. In 1522 and 1529, its soldiers pillaged and ravaged Mombasa. Subsequently, they forcibly repressed one Arab-inspired revolt after another. And in 1589, after the Ottoman Turks had befriended the rightful ruling families of the coastal city-states, the Portuguese navy punished rebellious Pemba, Pate, and Lamu, destroyed Manda, captured an Ottoman fleet in the harbor of Mombasa, and again burned Mombasa itself.[47] In this last endeavor, the Portuguese unexpectedly received help from an African warrior group named Zimba. These people, about whom we know little, followed the Portuguese into Mombasa and completed the destruction of the town. The Zimba earlier may have threatened Tete and Sena, on the Zambezi River, and the port of Moçambique. In 1587, they had attacked Kilwa. After ravaging Mombasa, they tried unsuccessfully to storm Malindi, but met defeat at the hands of the Segeju.[48]

After 1590, the viceroy in Goa ruled the region from Kilwa to Mogadiscio only nominally. And as a result of the Turkish depredations and the Zimban devastation of Mombasa, Portugal built Fort Jesus on a promontory overlooking the harbor of Mombasa.[49] Thereafter, the viceroy placed the so-called Swahili coast under the jurisdiction of the "Captain of the Coast of Malindi and the Fortress of Mombasa." The captain, from his headquarters in Fort Jesus, tried—with only occasional success—to assert his rule over the East African coast. His factors resident in Kilwa, Mafia, Pemba, Zanzibar, Lamu, and Pate exchanged cotton textiles, iron goods, and Indian wares for ivory, ambergris, tortoise shell, wax, millet, and rice. They also taxed imports and exports.[50]

During the last half of the sixteenth century, soldiers, traders, and missionaries maintained the presence of the Portuguese in East Africa north of the Rovuma River. Each of the larger coastal entrepôts had its small military garrison. Lusitanians of pure or mixed blood traded in the garrison towns as well as in the thirty or forty other marts of importance. Jesuits, from 1560, and Augustinians, from 1597, swelled the Portuguese establishment. The Augustinian

---

[47] Charles R. Boxer, "The Portuguese on the Swahili Coast, 1593–1729," in Charles R. Boxer and Carlos de Azevedo, *Fort Jesus and the Portuguese in Mombasa* (London, 1960), p. 17. Cf. G. S. P. Freeman-Grenville, "Historiography of the East African Coast," *Tanganyika Notes and Records*, 55 (1960), p. 285.

[48] For a discussion of the Zimba, see René Avelot, "Les Grands Mouvements de peuples en Afrique: Jaga et Zimba," *Bulletin de Géographie Historique et Descriptive*, I (1912), pp. 115–135, 188–191; João dos Santos (trans. Gaëtan Charpy), *Histoire de l'Éthiopie orientale* (Paris, 1688), pp. 149–157; E. C. Baker, "Notes on the History of the Wasegeju," *Tanganyika Notes and Records*, 27 (1949), pp. 24–26; John Milner Gray, "A Journey by Land from Tete to Kilwa in 1616," *ibid.*, 25 (1948), pp. 46–47; Roger Summers, *Inyanga* (Cambridge, Eng., 1958), p. 255. Cf. Ptolemy, i, 9, iv, 1–8.

[49] See Carlos de Azevedo, "Fort Jesus," in Boxer and Azevedo, *Fort Jesus*, pp. 89–117.

[50] John Milner Gray, "Rezende's Description of East Africa in 1634," *Tanganyika Notes and Records*, 23 (1947), pp. 10–11, 16–18.

A view of the entrance gate at Fort Jesus, Mombasa. The fort dates from the 1590's, although the gate area could not have been constructed before the early seventeenth century. (James S. Kirkman, Warden, Coastal Historical Sites of Kenya)

friars built a monastery at Mombasa and staffed churches at Zanzibar, Malindi, and Faza.

Despite these varied activities, and the manner in which the Portuguese navy cowed the sheikhs of East Africa, Portugal never controlled or settled the coast. During this period, the number of Portuguese resident in East Africa rarely exceeded one thousand.[51] And perhaps because they were so few in number, none seem ever to have ventured inland, or to have tried, like their compatriots south of the Rovuma River, to exert an influence upon the peoples of the interior.

In East Africa, as in Asia—where Europeans, Persians, and Arabs successfully challenged the hegemony of Portugal during the seventeenth century—the Portuguese captains faced rebellion and invasion. Mombasa revolted after Yusuf bin Hasan, the ruling sheikh and the son of a previous sheikh whom the Portuguese had assassinated, had exchanged the faith of Europe for that of his forbears. Before returning to Mombasa in 1630, Yusuf had spent about eighteen years under Augustinian tutelage in Goa. But he was less assimilated than the Portuguese had thought. In 1631, during the celebration of the Feast of the Assumption, Yusuf fatally stabbed the captain of Fort Jesus and proclaimed Mombasa's independence. His supporters killed other members of the Portuguese community and drove the Augustinian fathers to flight. Yusuf supposedly sought to justify his actions in a letter to Goa:

> *I have to remind the Government that I was born in the royal lineage, and that my father and mother were unjustly executed by the Portuguese, and this in spite of the fact that my father was a brother-in-arms of His Majesty and had always been loyal to him. . . . Since my accession I have frequently had cause to complain of the gratuitous insults offered me by the* [Portuguese] *captain. . . . Never had I had redress. No respect was paid to my person, and my treatment*

[51] *Ibid.*, pp. 17, 20.

did not accord with my station. A royal heart is greatly affected by insults and affronts, and by injustice.[52]

Yusuf tried to rally other city-states to his banner, but only Mtangata and Tanga backed him without qualification. Within Mombasa Yusuf occupied Fort Jesus and withstood the Portuguese assaults of 1631/32. Despite these victories, Yusuf mysteriously evacuated Fort Jesus and Mombasa during the last months of 1632. For the next five years, he led a privateering existence in the waters of the Indian Ocean. He preyed briefly upon Portuguese shipping and probably died at Jiddah in 1637. However brief, his tragic, colorful saga symbolized the failure of Portugal to contribute in any positive manner to the fortunes of seventeenth-century East Africa.

Despite frequent rebellions, Portugal continued to rule Lamu, Manda, and Pate with a firm hand until 1650, when the harshness of the exactions to which they were subjected by the captains of Fort Jesus turned these islanders from reluctant subjects into determined foes. In order to increase their chances of success, they requested help from the Omani Arabs, who had but recently ousted the Portuguese from Muscat. The struggle escalated, and by the middle of 1651 nearly all of the sheikhs of coastal East Africa were bearing arms against Portugal. Only Mombasa remained within the empire.

By 1660, Oman ruled a part of the East African coast. Its army sacked and looted Mombasa, raided Bombay and Diu in India, and in 1670 even pillaged Moçambique, Portugal's leading outpost in southern Africa. Finally in 1698, after a long siege, Oman captured Fort Jesus, thereby erasing the last vestige of Portugal's presence in East Africa north of Moçambique.[53]

Portugal had involved East Africa with the Western world and had altered the direction and flow of coastal commerce. But its overall influence had been largely negative. It had been interested more in immediate exploitation than in long-term colonial development; the city-states of East Africa consequently ceased early to play a major part in its imperial considerations. Instead, India and the Orient attracted the bulk of its efforts. And Moçambique, because it provided a haven for the ships that returned from Goa to Lisbon, remained of importance to Portugal long after Kilwa, Zanzibar, Mombasa, and Malindi had all reclaimed their independence.

The captaincy of moçambique and the kingdom of mwanamutapa

In 1507, Portuguese troops deposed the puppet sheikh who had been installed by Almeida and began ruling Moçambique directly. Thereafter the island-state became both the center of Portuguese authority in southeastern Africa and a

---

[52] Quoted in Strandes, *Portuguese Period*, pp. 199–200. See also S. R. Welch, *Some Unpublished Mss. Relating to the History of South and East Africa* (Pretoria, 1930), pp. 11–15.

[53] See the "Chronicle of Mombasa," quoted in William Fitzwilliam Owen, *Narrative of Voyages to Explore the Shores of Africa, Arabia, and Madagascar* (New York, 1833), I, p. 249. Boxer, "Swahili Coast," pp. 59–72, used the "Historia de Mombaça" in the Biblioteca Naçional Lisboa. See also Salil ibn Raziq (trans. George Percy Badger), *History of the Imâms and Seyyids of 'Oman* (London, 1871), pp. 78–87, 92.

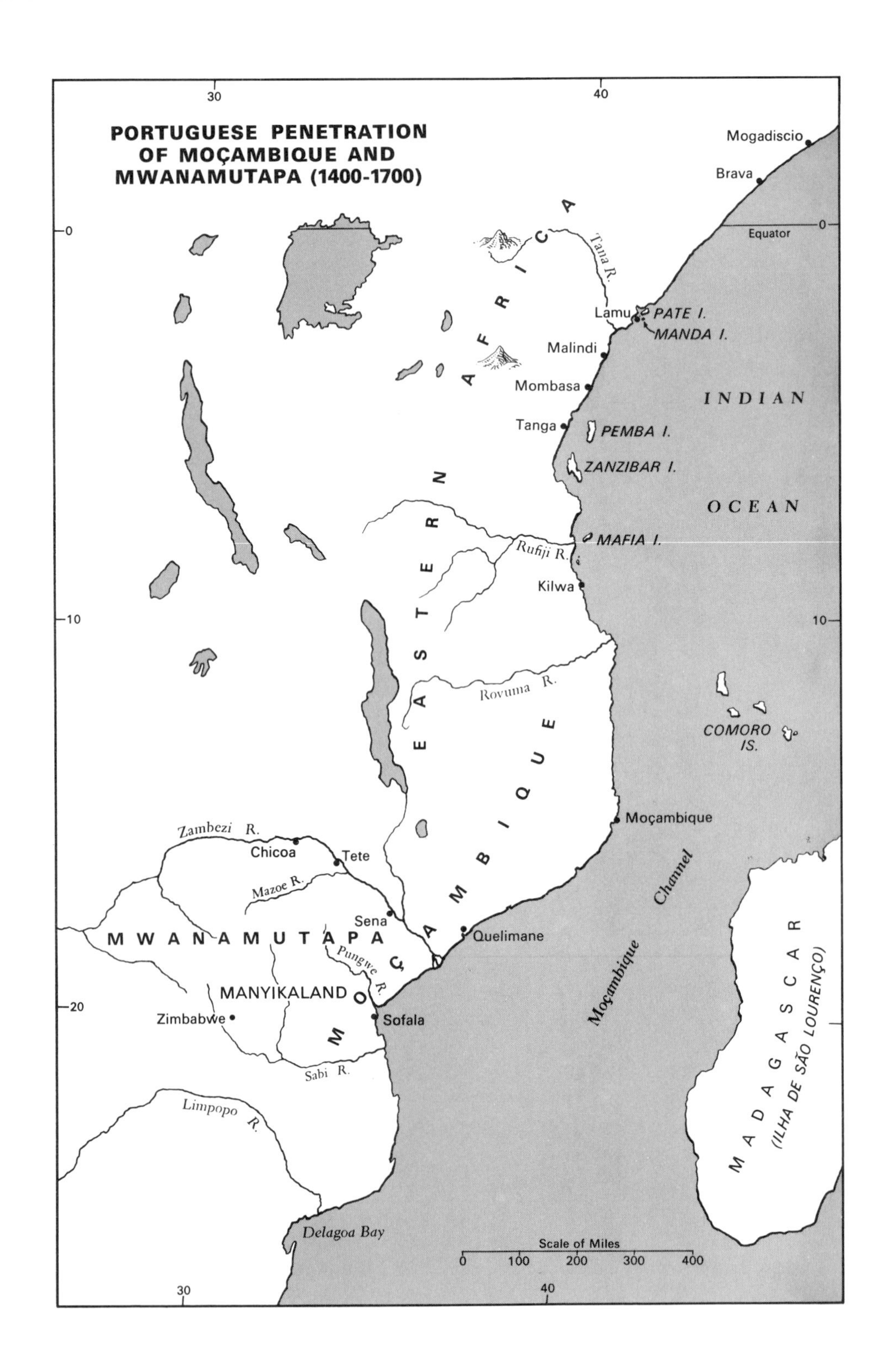
PORTUGUESE PENETRATION
OF MOÇAMBIQUE AND
MWANAMUTAPA (1400-1700)
30
40
0
10
20
Mogadiscio
Brava
Equator
Tana R.
EASTERN AFRICA
Lamu
PATE I.
MANDA I.
Malindi
Mombasa
Tanga
PEMBA I.
ZANZIBAR I.
INDIAN
OCEAN
MAFIA I.
Rufiji R.
Kilwa
Rovuma R.
COMORO
IS.
MOÇAMBIQUE
Moçambique
Zambezi R.
Chicoa
Tete
Mazoe R.
Sena
MWANAMUTAPA
Quelimane
Moçambique Channel
Pungwe R.
MANYIKALAND
Zimbabwe
Sofala
Sabi R.
Limpopo R.
MADAGASCAR
(ILHA DE SÃO LOURENÇO)
Delagoa Bay
Scale of Miles
0
100
200
300
400

bastion of Portugal's far-flung mercantile empire. In its harbor, ships of Europe and Asia rode at anchor on their way to and from the Orient. There they refueled and provisioned, removed the dead or dying, repaired their sails and hulls, and added to the wealth of the Portuguese community. But even after completing the construction of a fortress in 1560, the island's foreign population may not have numbered more than four hundred, all of whom owed their livelihood to the trade with India, and not to that with the African mainland. There was limited miscegenation and some fleeting contact with those Africans who came to trade but, at first, no conquest or settlement. Furthermore, the viceroy instructed the commandant of Moçambique to respect the rights of chiefs and to interfere in the interior only under exceptional circumstances. Initially, the official policy was "to live and let live"; Moçambique consequently had little association, let alone influence, with the peoples of Africa. The town of Moçambique, like nearby Quelimane, remained little more than a distant extension of Portuguese culture.

Sofala was the center from which Portuguese adventurers and traders set out for the interior. In 1505, Anhaia occupied it and, in 1506, Diego de Alcaçova reported that Sofala derived its wealth from the gold mines of an African kingdom of the interior whose ruler was known as Mwanamutapa—a name that fascinated Lisbon for decades after.[54]

António Fernandes, a *degredado*, probably knew southeastern Africa better than any other European of the early sixteenth century.[55] Although he personally left no known record of his journeys, his route and the places that he visited can be ascertained from reports written by a contemporary.[56] In about 1509, Fernandes set off from Sofala to the fabled country of the gold mines. Contriving to fend for himself in inhospitable surroundings and to learn one or more indigenous languages, he followed the Sabi or the Zambezi River west and north into Manyikaland. He walked for twenty days, traversed the lands of five chiefs, and arrived at Penhalonga—the probable source of the gold of Kilwa and Sofala. Fernandes then crossed the Pungwe River and walked toward

---

[54] Alcáçova to the King of Portugal, November 20, 1506, in *Documents on the Portuguese in Mozambique and Central Africa, 1497–1840* (Lisboa, 1962), I, p. 393. Mwanamutapa, or Monomotapa, was generally known. See Dames, *Barbosa*, pp. 9–13 [5–6]; Arthur Coke Burnell and P. A. Tiele (eds.), *The Voyage of John Huyghen van Linschoten to the East Indies* (London, 1884), I, pp. 30–33; Henry Yule and Arthur Coke Burnell (eds.), *Hobson-Jobson: Being a Glossary of Anglo-Indian Colloquial Words and Phrases and of Kindred Terms* (London, 1886), pp. 645–646.

[55] Portuguese ships frequently deposited *degredados*—reprieved criminals and political exiles—on the African coasts. These men were instructed to gather information about the country and the inhabitants. If they did so successfully, they were often pardoned and allowed to return to Portugal.

[56] See the ingenious reconstruction in Hugh Tracey (trans. Gaetano Montez), *António Fernandes: Descobridor do Monomotapa, 1514–15* (Lourenço Marques, 1940). But see W. A. Godlonton, "The Journeys of Antonio Fernandes: The First Known European to Find the Monomotapa and to Enter Southern Rhodesia," *Rhodesia Scientific Association: Proceedings and Transactions*, XL (April, 1945), pp. 98–102. See also D. P. Abraham, "The Early Political History of the Kingdoms of Mwene Mutapa, 850–1589," in *Historians in Tropical Africa* (Salisbury, S.R., 1962), p. 66.

the confluence of the Mazoe and Zambezi rivers, during which time he arrived in another rich region where he watched Africans extract gold from the ground.[57] After traversing a country that abounded in elephants, he reached the Zambezi River and thereafter made his way to the domain of Inhaperapera, a powerful chief. There, too, gold was abundant. Fernandes next turned west to the mines of modern Bindura and to Mbiri, the site of the capital of Mwanamutapa's kingdom. According to a reconstruction of this visit to Mbiri, Fernandes gave Chikuyo, the reigning king, a muzzle-loading gun and some powder and shot. Chikuyo was friendly and, by a combination of Cikaranga and hand signs, Fernandes conveyed to the king Portugal's plea for friendship and its desire to enter upon a trading relationship with the kingdom of Mwanamutapa.[58] Thereafter, Fernandes visited the copper mines of modern Sinoia and at last returned to Sofala with tales of the wealth and power of Chikuyo's kingdom.

The accounts of Fernandes' second and third journeys add little to our information of the interior.[59] Although he mentions pastoral Africans of light color, bad proportions, and "sheep-like tails," Fernandes tells us little about the people whom he meets.[60] It is evident, however, that perhaps because of some imperial "Pax Mwanamutapa" he traveled and explored without serious let or hindrance.

The expeditions of Fernandes were magnificent solos. But in official circles of the day, his reports apparently created little excitement. Although Sofala's factor advised the Crown to establish gold-trading stations in the interior, so long as gold continued to trickle to the coast Lisbon refused to devote its energies and finances to such adventures. Only after Arab traders managed to siphon this traffic away from Sofala did Portugal attempt to involve itself directly with its gold supply. In 1531, Portuguese troops occupied Sena, an Arab town on the Zambezi River. A few years later, another Portuguese detachment founded Tete, on the Zambezi River, closer to the resources of Mwanamutapa and Manyikaland. Indeed, after 1550, a Portuguese trader named António Caiado even installed himself as a free-lance advisor to the reigning *mwanamutapa*. As the self-styled "Captain of the Gates," royal factor, and envoy plenipotentiary, he was the first of many Europeans who found that it profited them to live among the Bantu-speaking peoples of Africa.

Christian missionaries turned their attention to the inhabitants of the interior during the second half of the sixteenth century. Roman Catholic priests accompanied the earliest Portuguese expeditions to Moçambique Island, but it was not until 1560 that the Society of Jesus proposed specifically to venture inland. Gonçalo da Silveira, one of Lisbon's more eloquent and successful priests, led the first expedition and, within a week of his arrival in Moçambique, he

---

[57] Africans told Fernandes that one could always recognize gold-bearing land because a clover-like plant grew over it.

[58] Abraham, "Political History," p. 66.

[59] There is no mention of the great Zimbabwe, located more than two hundred miles south of Mbiri. On the other hand, "Zimbabwe" is a generic, not a specific, name.

[60] Were these Bushmen? See also Godlonton, "Journeys," p. 90.

started for the "spiritually desolate" lands of Mwanamutapa. After spending seven weeks near Quelimane, where he converted a petty chief and many villagers, he journeyed alone up the Zambezi River to Sena and Tete, where he made arrangements to enter the kingdom of Mwanamutapa, then ruled by Nogomo Mupunzagato. With Caiado's assistance, he finally reached his destination in the last months of 1560.

Silveira set about his work with despatch. Within twenty-five days he had baptized the king, his queen and her sister, and a number of retainers and villagers. But Swahili-speaking traders also resided in Nogomo's court. Naturally jealous of their commercial prerogatives, they sowed doubt in the king's mind. The traders offered "evidence" that Silveira really was a spy possessed of a magic that would enable him and his Portuguese compatriots to seize control of the kingdom. Silveira was warned. But the priest dismissed those who feared for his life and, before long, he was strangled in his sleep by Nogomo's brother-in-law.[61] His martyrdom conveniently provided Portugal with a rationale for its subsequent attempt to conquer Central Africa.

When Sebastião began to rule Portugal in 1568, his advisors persuaded him to avenge Father Silveira's death and, incidentally, to acquire the mines of the interior by attacking Mwanamutapa. Sebastião charged Francisco Barreto, a former governor-general of Goa, with the command of one thousand soldiers and Jesuit missionaries.[62] For two years the army remained in Moçambique. In 1571, it moved to Sena, naturally taxing the capacities of the small settlement and creating innumerable logistical difficulties. The rains came, the heat remained, and disease descended upon the town. Barreto, perhaps by way of retribution, killed the members of the local Muslim trading community. Then he sent an envoy to the court of Nogomo; unbeknown to the impatient Barreto, however, the envoy drowned after visiting the king. Not until late 1572, by which time disease had claimed about eight hundred soldiers, did Barreto establish diplomatic contact with Mwanamutapa. But then Barreto himself succumbed to fever, and his remaining soldiers returned to the coast.

In 1574, Vasco Fernandes Homem tried again to impose Portuguese power in Central Africa. He organized a new army of four hundred soldiers and marched from Sofala to Penhalonga. There he regretfully concluded that the gold fields could be worked economically only with machinery. He thus directed his attentions to Chicoa on the Zambezi River, where a silver lode supposedly existed. But half of his army later died under African attack while searching unsuccessfully for the fabled silver of Chicoa.[63] Despite a few desultory expeditions in the seventeenth century, Portugal's search for the riches of Central Africa proved wholly unrewarding.

From the time of Homem to the nineteenth century, Portugal's concern

---

[61] Abraham, "Political History," p. 70.

[62] For a fuller account, see Santos, *Histoire*, pp. 109–117; Duffy, *Portuguese*, pp. 36–37.

[63] Eric Axelson, *Portuguese in South-East Africa, 1600–1700* (Johannesburg, 1960), pp. 34, 66, blames Estêvão de Ataíde for the failure of Portugal to exploit the silver mines of Chicoa. See also Abraham, "Political History," p. 73.

with the interior of Central Africa expressed itself hesitantly. Nonetheless, Dominicans and Jesuits competed for converts along the Zambezi as far as Tete. Small Luso-African trading colonies existed, and individuals appropriated large tracts of African land. Some Portuguese married Africans, were recognized as headmen and chiefs, and ultimately came to rule vast areas of the interior.[64] Rather than forfeit the allegiance of its erstwhile independent subjects, Portugal reluctantly recognized these holdings. The settlers remained absolute master of their estates, however, and during the seventeenth century missionaries and administrators frequently complained of the excessive ruthlessness of these Lusitanian colonists. The settlers coerced and exploited plantation labor and, from the middle of the seventeenth century, indulged in the undoubtedly profitable pursuit of slave-raiding. Thereafter, they shipped slaves regularly to Brazil.

Early in the seventeenth century, Mwanamutapa became more accessible to outsiders than before. Wars rent the peace of Central Africa: Portugal intervened on the side of the tribal groups opposed to Mwanamutapa and, in time, weakened the hold of Gatsi Rusere, its king. Portuguese entrepreneurs helped to depose his successor and, in 1630, to install the puppet king Mavura. During the twenty-two years of Mavura's reign, Portuguese priests and settlers entered Mwanamutapa in large numbers. After Mavura's death, succeeding kings struggled unavailingly to rid themselves of Dominican friars and the increasingly powerful Portuguese colonists. Periodically after 1656, and continuously from 1693 to 1700, Africans fought the settlers and their private armies for political and economic control of the kingdom. The then governor of Moçambique understood the problem.

> *It was the insolence of our people that caused these wars, because those who possess many Kafirs and have power are guilty of such excesses that the* [African] *Kings and Princes, offended, break out in these disorders. Everybody . . . wants to govern. And they say that if there cannot be somebody to tame and rule these* [Portuguese] *potentates, then everything will be lost.*[65]

By 1700, Portuguese intervention had helped to destroy Mwanamutapa. Thereafter, they began to turn their scattered trading areas into the nucleus of what later became the colony of Moçambique.

---

[64] See D. P. Abraham, "Maramuca: An Exercise in the Combined Use of Portuguese Records and Oral Tradition," *The Journal of African History*, II (1961), pp. 218–220; Axelson, *Portuguese*, p. 137.

[65] The governor of Moçambique to the king of Portugal, September 23, 1694, in *ibid.*, p. 184. See also Charles R. Boxer, *Race Relations in the Portuguese Colonial Empire* (Oxford, 1963), pp. 49–51.

The inhabitants of Great Benin *are generally good-natur'd and very civil, from whom it is easy to obtain whatever we desire by soft means. If we make them liberal* Presents, *they will endeavour to recompence them doubly; and if we want any thing, and ask it of them, they very seldom deny us, tho' they have occasion for it themselves. But they are so far in the right, to expect that their* Courtesy *should be repaid with* Civility, *and not with* Arrogance *or* Rudeness; *for to think of forcing any thing from them, is to dispute with the* Moon.

—David Van Nyendael, 1702

KINGDOMS OF THE SAVANNAH AND FOREST, 1500–1800

4 While Portuguese and other European adventurers were busily exploring the coasts of Africa and trading in its slaves, the inhabitants of the Western and Central Sudan continued to elaborate their traditional forms of statecraft without reference to the changes taking place along their southern and western marches. There, and in the forests of tropical Africa, the irruption of Europe had to some extent stimulated the creation and the growth of indigenous kingdoms that, until the nineteenth century, steadfastly managed to maintain their integrity in the face of European importunities.

I. The Western and Central Sudan

In 1493, Songhai's Muslim community helped Muhammad Ture, a Soninke-born general, to overthrow Abu Bakr Da'o, the "pagan" successor of Sonni Ali, on the battlefield of Anfao, near Gao.[1] With their support, Muhammad established the new dynasty of *askiyas* and proceeded to increase the authority of Songhai in the Western Sudan. He reorganized the army, consolidated and extended the conquests of Sonni Ali from Djenné to Say, and protected the

[1] Mahmud al-Kati (trans. Octave Houdas and Maurice Delafosse), *Tarikh el-Fettash* (Paris, 1913), p. 102; Jean Rouch, *Contribution à l'histoire des Songhay* (Dakar, 1953), pp. 186–187. But 'Abd al-Rahman bin 'Amir as-Sa'di (trans. Octave Houdas), *Tarikh es-Soudan* (Paris, 1900), p. 117, gives "Ankogho" as the battlefield.

Muslim traders and scholars who had been persecuted by his predecessors. Indeed, a contemporary chronicler ascribed the renaissance of Timbuktu to the generosity of Muhammad.[2] In his day, the learned imams, or priests, returned from Oualata to their favorite mosques in Timbuktu; Islam once again flourished on the Niger. Muhammad's motives were, however, political as well as religious. He combined them in 1497/98, when, in the manner of *mansa* Musa, he undertook a pilgrimage to Mecca. Escorted by about one thousand foot soldiers and five hundred cavalrymen, Muhammad proceeded across the Sahara to the Holy City, where he founded a hospice for the peoples of the Western Sudan and gave 100,000 *dinars* to charity. Afterwards, in Cairo, the 'Abbasid sharif confirmed Muhammad in his usurpation and invested him with the politically and religiously significant caliphate of the Sudan.[3]

Ebb and flow: the tides of later songhai

From 1498 to 1515, Muhammad endeavored by conquest to justify his new titles. During 1498/99, in what may have been his only campaign against the "infidel," he plundered the Mossi kingdom of Yatenga, then in an ascendant phase. Later he annexed the region of old Ghana, west of Maçina, and invaded the Diara province of Mali. In 1505, he pursued the dissident followers of Abu Bakr Da'o into Borgu, where he ultimately won a costly victory that was designed to prevent internecine strife. After another invasion of Mali, and a sortie perhaps as far west as the Futa Jallon, Muhammad's armies turned their attentions toward the east. In 1513/14, they raided the Hausa city-states, controlled the route to Aïr and, with the help of the *kanta* of Kebbi, took Agades from the Tuareg in 1515.[4] At this time, *askiya* Muhammad ruled an empire that encompassed a one thousand mile swath of river and savannah from Nioro in the northwest to the borders of Kebbi and Borgu in the southeast.

Although he himself often led the armies of Songhai into battle, Muhammad's genius was more political and administrative than military. He raised a standing army and became the first ruler of the Western Sudan to rely upon regular conscription. In Gao, which remained the center of the empire, he and his council of ministers organized a secretariat to provide the bureaucratic functions necessary in sixteenth-century Songhai. Of the councilors the most important were the *kalisi farma*, or keeper of the treasury, the *dyina koy*, or chief of the army, and the *hikoy*, or admiral of the fleet. Both the army and the navy depended upon the treasury for the collection of sufficient taxes and tribute to pay for their campaigns of conquest. The keeper of the treasury taxed both the profits of trade and the produce of the land and thus contributed

[2] Al-Kati, *Tarikh*, pp. 114–117.

[3] *Ibid.*, pp. 25–26, 126–132; as-Sa'di, *Tarikh*, pp. 119–120.

[4] For a summary of these campaigns, see Rouch, *Contribution*, p. 195. See also as-Sa'di, *Tarikh*, pp. 117–129; al-Kati, *Tarikh*, pp. 135–147; Lucien Marc, *Le Pays Mossi* (Paris, 1909), pp. 137–139; Leo Africanus (trans. John Pory), *The History and Description of Africa* (London, 1896), III, pp. 829–830. For Mossi dates, see J. D. Fage, "Reflections on the Early History of the Mossi-Dagomba Group of States," in Jan Vansina, Raymond Mauny, and L. V. Thomas (eds.), *The Historian in Tropical Africa* (London, 1964), pp. 177–187.

measurably to the stability of Muhammad's empire. Other councilors were responsible for justice, agriculture, forests, and the *askiya's* court.[5] Muhammad personally controlled the appointment of provincial governors, each of whom had hitherto possessed his own local sources of military and financial power. Muhammad, in sum, molded a number of Songhaian regions into an empire.

The times were prosperous. The merchants of Songhai obtained salt from Taghaza and exchanged it for the luxury goods of North Africa and the horses that contributed to the empire's military success. In about 1510, Leo Africanus visited "the great town of Gago" or Gao:

> *The houses . . . are but meane, except those wherein the king and his courtiers remaine. Here are exceeding rich merchants: and hither continually resort great store of Negros which buy cloth here brought out of Barbarie and Europe. This town aboundeth with corne and flesh, but is much destitute of wine, trees, and fruits. Howbeit here is plentie of melons, citrons, and rice: here are many welles also containing most sweete and holesome water. Here is likewise a certaine place where slaues are to be sold, especially vpon such daies as the merchants vse to assemble. . . . The king of this region hath a certaine priuate palace wherein he maintaineth a great number of concubines and slaues, which are kept by eunuches. . . . It is a woonder to see what plentie of Merchandize is dayly brought hither, and how costly and sumptuous all things be.*[6]

The *kanta* of Kebbi posed the first successful challenge to the might of Muhammad. After the victory at Agades, the *kanta* supposedly quarreled with Muhammad over the spoils. He fostered a revolt among Hausa conscripts and, with their support, defied Muhammad. Thereafter, he declared the independence of Kebbi and successfully ruled it from Al Surami, his capital east of the Niger. Kebbi contrived to maintain its independence throughout the sixteenth century despite the efforts of Muhammad and his successors.[7]

Within the Songhaian empire, the first *askiya* slowly lost control. As he aged and became blind, his sons grew more and more powerful. In 1528, three of his sons and their followers defeated the loyalist army gathered by Muhammad's brother.[8] Muhammad, then an octogenarian, abdicated and was later exiled to an island in the Niger. He died in 1538, supposedly at the age of ninety-five.

With the abdication of Muhammad, Songhai plunged itself into chaos. Musa, Muhammad's son by a concubine, succeeded his father but was in turn assassinated by his brothers. One brother, Muhammad Bengan Korei, a musically minded *askiya,* ruled from 1531 to 1537 and failed to conquer Kebbi before being ousted by his cousin Isma'il, who died a natural death in 1539. At this point, the fortunes of Songhai temporarily revived. During the reign of the cruel *askiya* Ishaq (1539–1549), the armies of Songhai again ranged far afield.

---

[5] See the list in Rouch, *Contribution,* p. 192.
[6] Leo Africanus, *History,* pp. 826–827.
[7] For a discussion of Kebbi, see Yves Urvoy, *Histoire des populations du Soudan central* (Paris, 1936), pp. 31, 33, 248–251; as-Sa'di, *Tarikh,* pp. 129–130, 146.
[8] *Ibid.,* pp. 132–134.

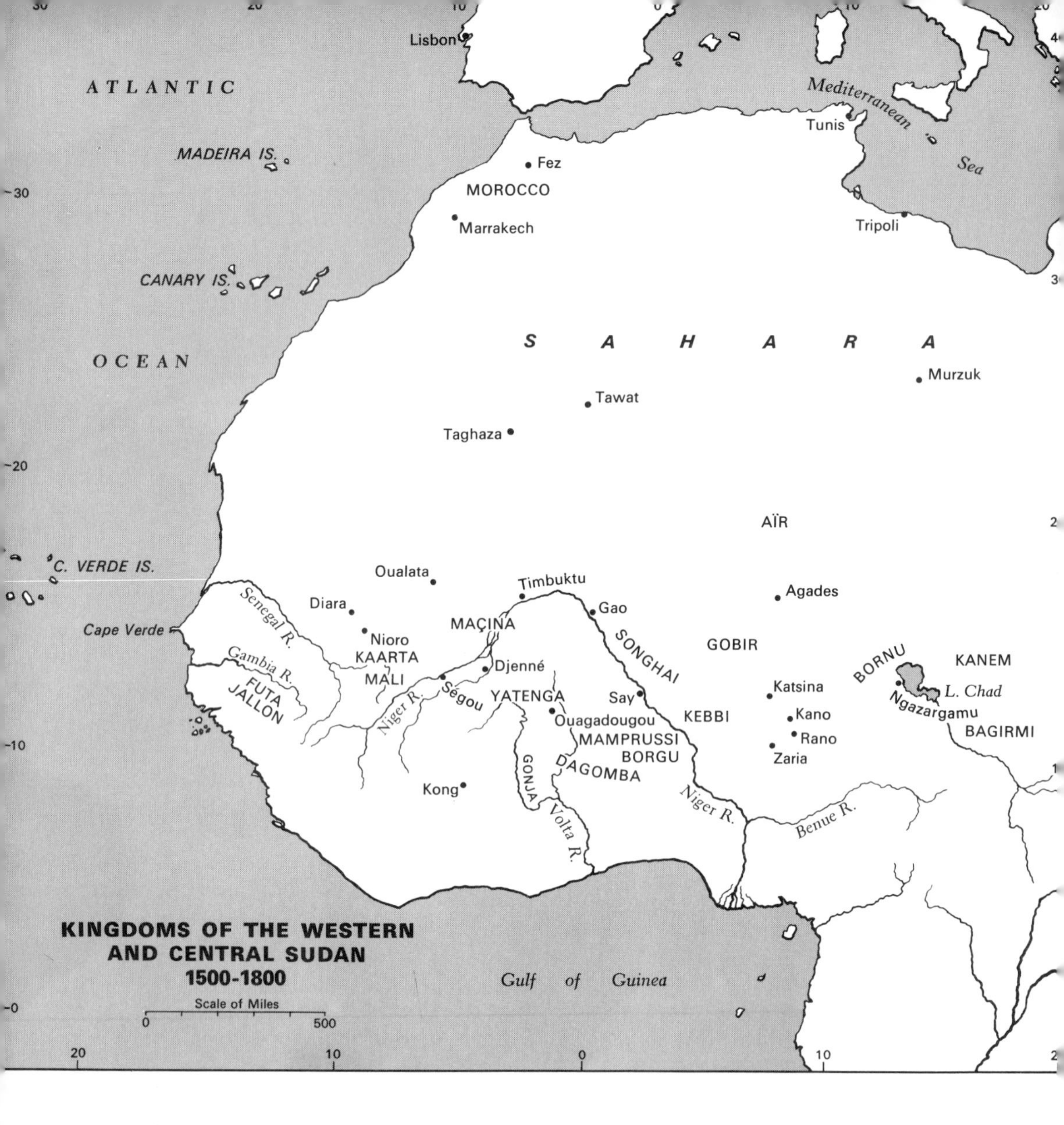

They invaded the capital of a no longer powerful Mali, attacked the people of Dendi, and raided the Saharan salt mines of Taghaza. Under Ismail's brother Da'ud (1549–1582), Songhai continued to reassert itself. The army invaded Yatenga, conquered Maçina, failed to humble Katsina, again pillaged Mali, contained the Tuareg, and reaffirmed Songhai's control of the trans-Saharan trade routes at the expense of Morocco. Da'ud also concluded a treaty of peace with Kebbi. He supposedly patronized the Islamic scholars of his kingdom and was himself a learned man.[9] The three sons of Da'ud were made of weaker

[9] Al-Kati, *Tarikh*, pp. 177–178.

stuff. They struggled among themselves, one deposing another, the third repressing his opponents unmercifully. During the short reign of this last brother, *askiya* Ishaq II (1588–1591), Songhai's long-standing struggle with Morocco reached a point of resolution.

Like Portugal, the sultans of Morocco coveted the wealth of tropical Africa. During the sixteenth century, Portuguese traders diverted a part of Africa's gold from the overland route to Fez. At the same time, Portugal's successful trade with the Orient deprived Moroccan middlemen of a market for Eastern goods. These external events intensified a balance of payments crisis that Morocco shared with the rest of North Africa and, to some extent, encouraged the rulers of Morocco to examine the trading potential of the Sahara and the Sudan.[10] In 1546, Moroccan troops therefore attacked Taghaza. Later, in 1581, 'Ahmad al-Mansur, sultan of Morocco, seized the important oases of Tawat and Tigurarin. Three years later, twenty thousand Moroccan soldiers perished in an abortive attempt to traverse the Sahara to Songhai and, in 1585, al-Mansur invaded Taghaza without conquering it. He nonetheless demanded that the *askiyas* of Songhai surrender the mines and, with them, their control over the Saharan trade. *Askiya* Ishaq II refused.

To make good his claim, al-Mansur in 1590 sent three thousand men, led by the Andalusian eunuch Judar Pasha, to Gao. Five months later, after a remarkable journey across the desert, Judar and the majority of his troops reached the Niger River. At this time, wrote a seventeenth-century chronicler, the people of Ishaq's Songhai had already fallen upon evil days. Faith had transformed itself into infidelity; the things "forbidden by God" were practiced overtly:

> *They drank wine; they gave themselves up to sodomy and, as to adultery, it had become so frequent that its practice had seemingly become legal . . . this was the point at which the sons of the* askiyas *committed adultery with their sisters.*[11]

It was, however, their lack of weapons, not their absence of moral fibre, that doomed the rulers of Songhai in 1591. North of Gao, at Tondibi, the Moroccan muskets and cannon easily overwhelmed the more numerous local bowmen and mounted spearmen. Ishaq II and his followers evacuated Gao, leaving no treasures for the disappointed Moroccans, and fled down the Niger. Judar thereafter conquered Timbuktu.[12]

Imperial Songhai disintegrated. Its component peoples each asserted their independence and raided each other. The Fulani of Maçina attacked the peoples of the upper Niger, Tuareg threatened the peasants who lived in the great

---

[10] See Raymond Mauny, "L'Expédition marocaine d'Ouadane (Mauritanie) vers 1543–44," *Bulletin de l'Institut Français d'Afrique Noire,* XI (1949), pp. 129–140; J. O. Hunwick, "Ahmad Baba and the Moroccan Invasion of the Sudan," *Journal of the Historical Society of Nigeria,* II (1962), pp. 317–318.

[11] As-Sa'di, *Tarikh,* p. 224.

[12] Al-Kati, *Tarikh,* pp. 279–281; as-Sa'di, *Tarikh,* pp. 226–230; Henri de Castries, "La Conquête du Soudan par el-Mansour (1591)," *Hespéris,* III (1923), p. 473; Maurice Delafosse, "Relations du Maroc avec le Soudan à travers les âges," *ibid.,* IV (1924), p. 171; Heinrich Barth, *Travels and Discoveries in North and Central Africa* (London, 1858), IV, pp. 249, 614–617.

A Tuareg on camelback crossing the Sahara. From a watercolor by George F. Lyon, c. 1818. (George F. Lyon, *Narrative of Travels in Northern Africa,* London, 1821)

bend of the river, and Bambara assaulted Djenné. Meanwhile, in 1591/92, the Moroccan army defeated the remaining warriors of Songhai and killed *askiya* Muhammad Gao, who had replaced Ishaq II at the behest of the cavalrymen of Songhai. Until 1599, Nuh, his legitimate successor, fought a guerilla war against the Moroccans. In what had earlier been southern Songhai, he harassed the Moroccans and led them a merry chase down the Niger into Dendi, where they and their horses were destroyed by fever.[13]

Songhai, although it merely encompassed a small number of loosely linked village-states, remained a kingdom of the Niger throughout the seventeenth century. One of its chroniclers summed up the disaster:

> *When the Moroccan army arrived in the Sudan they found one of God's most favored countries in richness and fertility. Peace and security reigned throughout all its provinces . . .* [but] *. . . now all that has changed: Danger has replaced security; misery has replaced opulence; tranquility has been succeeded by trouble, calamities, and violence. Throughout the land, men devoured one another . . . in all directions raiding and warfare spared neither life nor wealth nor the predicament of the inhabitants. Disorder was general; it spread all over, increasing itself until it reached the highest possible degree of intensity.*[14]

In Timbuktu and the northern provinces of old Songhai, the Moroccans at first ruled through puppet *askiyas.* Moroccan generals quelled revolts in the main towns and temporarily forestalled the Tuareg. But the generals quarreled among themselves and, early in the seventeenth century, they attempted to rule in Timbuktu without reference to the sultan of Morocco. After 1603, the colonels and soldiers elected their own generals and governors. Subject peoples and outlying provinces similarly asserted their independence of both Morocco and the troops of Timbuktu. In the eighteenth century, a collection of smaller

---

[13] See Maurice Delafosse, *Haut-Sénégal-Niger* (Paris, 1912), II, pp. 243–249.
[14] As-Sa'di, *Tarikh,* p. 223.

states occupied what had once been the heartland of the mighty empire of Songhai.

Of these smaller, but nevertheless significant, states, firm knowledge remains scarce. During the sixteenth, seventeenth, and eighteenth centuries, while the Fulani occupied and developed Maçina, the Mande-speaking merchants of Djenné, the neighboring entrepôt on a branch of the Niger River, strengthened their economic ties to the peoples of the Voltaic region. Fellow Mande, many of whom may have belonged to the Dyula trading class, channeled the traffic in gold through Begho, a market town located south of the big bend of the Black Volta River, to Kong and Bobo Dioulasso on its way to Djenné. To the north of the Volta River, the Muslim-influenced state of Gonja also contained important market centers. And beyond Gonja, along the White Volta River, the related Dagomba-Mamprussi-Mossi states asserted an individuality that had been nourished by centuries of contact with the governmental and commercial forces of the Western Sudan. At the same time, Dagomba and Mamprussi, like Gonja, eventually entered the orbit of Ashanti, while the two prominent Mossi kingdoms of Yatenga and Ouagadougou gradually grew farther apart. They preyed upon the peoples of Borgu and Bussa and occasionally fought the Dogon. Beyond Djenné, along the upper Niger, the Bambara similarly warred against their neighbors and, by the end of the eighteenth century, had established the kingdoms of Ségou and Kaarta.

Bornu and the wars of the central sudan

In the sixteenth century, the young kingdom of Bornu became the leading power of the Central Sudan. Of the immediate successors to *mai* Idris ibn Ali Katagarmabe—who subdued the Bulala of Kanem—we know little. But the chronicles of the reign of Idris Alawma (1570–1610), Bornu's greatest modern *mai*, are fortunately extant. These documents portray Idris as an intelligent, fearless servant of God and Bornu. He encouraged or imposed a revival of religious observance, built a number of brick mosques and a Bornuese hostel in Mecca, liberally supported the Islamic charities, and even interrupted a war against the Bulala in order to visit the tombs of his predecessors and to read the Qur'an thrice. He preached reform and attempted to compel his people to adopt new codes of personal behavior. In taking a firm stand against the practice of adultery and obscenity—heretofore offences committed openly—he "wiped away the disgrace, and the face of the age [became] blank with astonishment." He "cleared away," the chronicler reported, "and reformed as far as he could the known wrong doing." [15] Furthermore, *mai* Idris replaced customary with Islamic law: "To gain a strict observance of the Kura'an and the Sunna he turned over all disputes to the learned judges, and put off his own shoulders onto theirs all manner of judgments." [16] That is, as a part of his attempt to

---

[15] 'Ahmed ibn Fartua (trans. and ed. H. Richmond Palmer), *History of the First Twelve Years of the Reign of Mai Idris Alooma of Bornu (1571–1583)* (Lagos, 1926), p. 12.
[16] *Ibid.*, p. 20.

modernize Bornu, Idris established religious courts and deprived the chiefs of their traditional jural roles.

Idris was an innovator who recast and reorganized Bornu to meet the needs of his age. Early in his reign, after making a pilgrimage to Mecca, he discovered the value of firearms, and he imported muskets and Mamluk musketeers into Bornu, where he employed them against the less fortunate peoples of the Central Sudan. To enable his army to cross rivers and lakes with despatch, Idris also replaced the traditional narrow pirogues with larger, safer boats that could be paddled as well as poled. He introduced camels into the baggage corps and dispensed with the usual droves of oxen and mules. In the civil sphere, Idris paid particular attention to agriculture and, by introducing standard units of measure for grain, permitted his subjects to buy and sell their crops more easily. By imposing a new unity, he allowed the people of Bornu generally to indulge in peaceful production and trade. He eliminated brigandage and made the roads safe for travelers. Above all, Idris was a strong ruler, perhaps even the first authoritarian king of the Central Sudan. Whereas many of his predecessors had ruled as the representatives or leaders of an oligarchic council, he was among the first to appoint most of his own ministers and to control all of the functions of government. He was an intuitive centralizer who gave Bornu a stable, "national" government.

During his comparatively long reign, *mai* Idris consolidated the conquests of his predecessors and, in a series of hard-fought campaigns, made the peoples of the Central Sudan fear his soldiers and their guns. Against Kano, for example, the muskets of Bornu proved decisive. According to the chronicle, the people of Kano were in the habit of "treacherously" raiding Bornu from a number of walled towns:

> *They kept on raiding Bornu and then flying to their nearest stockades with what they had filched from the Muslims and concealed, before the pursuers from Bornu could reach them. They got back without being overtaken. Such was the kind of treachery they practised on all the borders of Islam, coming and going between the two countries continually.*[17]

Idris' army therefore began destroying the stockade of Majia, one of Kano's more important redoubts. But its inhabitants discharged a cloud of arrows, whereupon the soldiers of Bornu fired their guns. Immediately, the chronicler recorded, "the pagans turned their backs in flight and fled to the bush in the night." And when the warriors of Kano's other fortified outposts learned of the Bornuese guns, they "scattered pell mell" and became "downcast in the present and fearful for the future." Later, the N'gizim of Mawa boldly attacked the soldiers of Bornu with darts and arrows—being ignorant of Bornu's new strength "and badly deceived." The musketeers of Bornu retaliated, pouring "a hot fire into them" that killed the defenders instantaneously—"as if they had drunk poison."[18]

---

[17] *Ibid.*, p. 30. Nothing in the "Kano Chronicle" alludes to these wars.
[18] *Ibid.*, p. 40.

Idris spared none of his enemies. On a number of occasions he conquered Aïr after forcing the Tuareg to flee into the desert. He attacked the kingdoms of Bagirmi and Mandara, both of which lay southeast of Lake Chad, and made them pay tribute throughout his reign. But Idris directed his most strenuous campaigns against the Bulala of Kanem and the "So" people of Bornu. Although he subdued the Bulala—"their hearts turned and they fled incontinently without pause [their cavalry leaving] the infantry behind like a worn-out sandal" [19]—Bornu prudently, or perhaps as a tacit acknowledgment of the endurance of their opponents, agreed to delimit its mutual border with Kanem: "The big drum was beaten . . . and the boundary made so clear that there could be no dispute." [20] Against the "So," the armies of Bornu never won a total victory. Instead, Idris and his generals both attacked them continuously and settled Muslims near their walled towns "so as to allow [the "So"] little empty country" and no room in which to maneuver. By these means Idris and his successors eventually incorporated the "So" into the kingdom of Bornu.

We know little of the eleven *mais* who ruled Bornu between the death of Idris and the beginning of the nineteenth century. During the second half of the seventeenth century, both the Tuareg and the Jukun Kwararafa threatened the security of Bornu, establishing a pattern that was to hold true for the remainder of the century. The chronicles of this period indicate that the peoples of Bornu suffered both the depredations of their neighbors and recurring cycles of famine. They also suggest an unalleviated decline in the fortunes of what had previously been the most powerful state of the Central Sudan.[21] During the eighteenth century, the rulers of Bornu relinquished their control of the trade routes across the Sahara; within the empire, Fulani immigrants grew more numerous. The eighteenth-century *mais* supposedly were more pious than able and more enamored of luxury and ostentation than of their political responsibilities during an age of change. Ali ibn hajj Hamdun (1750–1791), a profligate who supposedly begat more than three hundred male children, led a disastrous expedition against Mandara.[22] His personal weaknesses and his military failures may well have plunged Bornu to its imperial nadir. The later Fulani invaders of the nineteenth century profited from these periods of indifferent rule.

Hausaland before the jihad

The walled cities of Hausaland remained centers of political and commercial importance during the sixteenth, seventeenth, and eighteenth centuries. Zaria raided her southern neighbors for slaves and sold them in the markets of Hausaland. Rano was a manufacturing center and Kano and Katsina remained

---

[19] 'Ahmed ibn Fartua, "The Kanem Wars," in H. Richmond Palmer (trans. and ed.), *Sudanese Memoirs* (Lagos, 1928), I, p. 24.

[20] *Ibid.*, p. 30.

[21] "The Diwan of the Sultans of Bornu," and the "List of Maghumi Mais and Kuburi Sheikhs," in H. Richmond Palmer (trans. and ed.), *The Bornu Sahara and Sudan* (London, 1936), pp. 94–95, 244–258.

[22] *Ibid.*, p. 255; Barth, *Travels*, II, p. 660; Simon Lucas, in *The Proceedings of the Association for Promoting the Discovery of the Interior Parts of Africa*, I (1810), p. 153.

important entrepôt towns. Many of these city-states accepted Islam during the first half of the sixteenth century. The citizens of Katsina, for example, made "praying places" during the reign of Ibrahim Maje (1494–1520), and during the same period the people of Kano cut down their sacred tree and erected a Friday mosque in its place.[23]

Throughout the sixteenth and seventeenth centuries, the Hausa cities fought among themselves and attacked or were attacked by the armies of Bornu, Kebbi, Kwararafa, Songhai, and Tuareg Aïr. In these battles the warriors of Hausaland fought on horseback and wore quilted armor, coats of mail, and iron headgear of a kind once widely used by the Crusaders of Europe.[24] As a result of these wars during the seventeenth century, Katsina and Kano both increased their power relative to the other city-states. Indeed, in the time of Bawa bin Muhamma Kukuna, its thirty-fifth *sarki* (1660–1670), Kano's strength proved sufficient to deter would-be antagonists. His was therefore a peaceful interlude during which Islamic learning, a Qur'anic school, and the activities of numerous holy men all flourished.

By the middle of the eighteenth century, Kano and Gobir were the strongest of the Hausa cities. During the reign of *sarki* Muhamma Kumbari bin Sharefa (1731–1743), Kano and Gobir fought almost continuously without resolving their differences. Kumbari's son, *sarki* Alhajji Kabe (1745–1753), tried to end these wars by challenging the *sarkin* Gobir to war. The *sarkin* Gobir offered to conclude a peace treaty, but Kabe refused. In the end, Kano and Gobir only perpetuated their earlier rivalry; each alternately humbled the other's army. As the chronicle records, "there was no peace in Kano, only trouble after trouble what with the war with Gobir and other wars." [25] Even if they failed to conquer Kano, Gobir's Fulani generals and "pagan" armies provided two sources of internal strength.[26] In 1764, they humbled neighboring Zamfara and posed a serious threat to the independence of the other cities of Hausaland. But the *sarkin* Gobir was unable to unify Hausaland, and only in the next century were the Fulani able to impose any overall rule throughout the area.

II. The Kingdoms of the Western Forest

The earliest history of each of the kingdoms of the West African forest is wrapped in obscurity. The apposite legends of origin are in some respects simi-

[23] "List of Kings of Katsina," and the "Kano Chronicle," in Palmer, *Memoirs*, III, pp. 81, 111; Mervyn Hiskett, "Material Relating to the State of Learning Among the Fulani Before Their *Jihad*," *Bulletin of the School of Oriental and African Studies*, XIX (1957), pp. 572–573.

[24] Quilted armor, mail, and iron helmets may have first been used in Hausaland by Kanajeji bin Yaji, *sarkin* Kano (1390–1410). Palmer, *Memoirs*, III, p. 107. J. Spencer Trimingham, *A History of Islam in West Africa* (London, 1962), p. 122n, believes that the Hausa warriors derived their quilted armor from Mamluk Egypt, and that "local armourers quickly learnt to make it, though it remained costly and was only worn by chiefs and their special retainers." It was widely used from the eighteenth century. The armor could also have come from Ethiopia.

[25] Palmer, *Memoirs*, III, p. 125. *Sarkin* is the genitival form of *sarki*, *sarkuna* the plural.

[26] See Urvoy, *Soudan central*, pp. 246–248.

lar, but they are all allegorical and difficult to interpret. A Yoruba story of creation explains:

> *In the beginning the earth was covered with water. Olorun, the supreme god, let his son Oduduwa down a chain carrying a handful of earth, a cockerel and a palm nut. Oduduwa scattered the earth over the water and the cockerel scratched it so that it became the land on which the palm tree grew.*[27]

The Yoruba, like many other West African peoples, also believe that their ancestors originally came from Mecca and that they slowly traveled westward until they arrived in what is now western Nigeria.[28] There these immigrants established Ife as the mother city of Yorubaland, and some of their number supposedly continued south to found Benin. The court historians of Benin say:

> *Many, many years ago, the Binis came all the way from Egypt to found a more secure shelter in this part of the world after a short stay in the Sudan and at Ile-Ife. . . . Before coming here, a band of hunters was sent from Ife to inspect this land and the report furnished was very favourable. Tradition says that they met some people who were in the land before their arrival. These people are said to have come from the Sudan originally.*[29]

Some of the peoples of modern Ghana likewise claim family ties with Egypt and the Orient, and European writers have frequently sought to associate the origins of the forest kingdoms of tropical Africa with the cultures of Phoenicia and India.[30]

These legends of origin are to some extent embellishments of tradition, invented in order to satisfy latter-day needs. They also may allude specifically or generally to the invasion of the forest kingdoms by alien elites. A tale of the twelfth century, for example, may refer to either the peaceful or the forceful arrival of a foreign governing class in Benin:

> *. . . the people* [of *Benin*] *. . . sent an ambassador to the Oni Odudua, the great and wisest ruler of Ife, asking him to send one of his sons to be their ruler. For things were getting from bad to worse and the people saw that there was need for a capable ruler.*
>
> *In order to test the ability of the Binis to look after his son, Odudua first of all sent seven lice to the Benin chiefs to be cared for and returned after three years. This condition was fulfilled and Odudua was greatly surprised to see the lice in increased sizes when they were sent back to him by the chiefs. He exclaimed that "the people who can take care of such minute pests as lice can undoubtedly take care of my son . . ." So Prince Oranmiyan . . . was sent. . . .*[31]

---

[27] Michael Crowder, *A Short History of Nigeria* (New York, 1962), p. 46. See also Peter C. Lloyd, "Yoruba Myths: A Sociologist's Interpretation," *Odù*, 2 (1956), p. 22; H. Ulli Beier, "Before Oduduwa," *ibid.*, 3 (1956), pp. 30–31.

[28] Samuel Johnson (ed. O. Johnson), *The History of the Yorubas* (Lagos, 1921), p. 3; Roger W. Westcott, "Did the Yoruba Come from Egypt?" *Odù*, 4 (1956), pp. 10–15. See also A. B. Mathews, "The Kisra Legend," *African Studies*, IX (1950), pp. 144–147.

[29] Quoted in Jacob Egharevba, *A Short History of Benin* (Ibadan, 1960), p. 1.

[30] See Eva L. Meyerowitz, "The Akan and Ghana," *Man*, LVII, 99 (1957), pp. 83–88; Flora Shaw, *A Tropical Dependency* (London, 1906), pp. 218–235.

[31] Quoted in Egharevba, *Benin*, pp. 6–7.

Two terra cotta heads excavated at Ife. They recall the sculpture of the Nok culture. The Ife Museum, Nigeria.

We know little of the peoples of the western forests before about A.D. 1000. Sometime between 1200 B.C. and A.D. 200, neolithic cultural concepts may have spread from the savannah, where they were most fully expressed by the agricultural peoples of Nok, to the nearby forest regions. There, particularly in Ife, these new ways of organizing human life gradually achieved widespread acceptance. The naturalistic terra cotta heads unearthed at Ife and dated from 900 B.C. to A.D. 200 or 300 stylistically resembled the heads and figurines found at Nok. The peoples of both cultures handled the eyes, limbs, and bodies of their figures similarly, clothing them with elaborate bead ornaments. Nok and Ife are the only African cultures known to have produced approximately life-size pottery representations. Moreover, the naturalistic bronze (really brass) heads of Ife seem to have continued this neolithic artistic tradition and to have in turn stimulated bronze-working in Benin. Perhaps sometime during the thirteenth or fourteenth century A.D., the artists of Ife transmitted their knowledge of the *cire-perdue* (lost-wax) technique of bronze-casting to Benin, where the inhabitants soon produced figures similar in style to those of Ife and Nok. The legend of the lice may indeed reflect the changes of this period.[32]

[32] Frank Willett, "Ife and Its Archaeology," *The Journal of African History,* I (1960), pp. 245–246. See also Frank Willett, "The Discovery of New Brass Figures at Ife," *Odù,* 6 (1958), pp. 29–34; William Fagg and Frank Willett, "Ancient Ife," *ibid.,* 8 (1960), pp. 21–34; Egharevba, *Benin,* p. 12; R. E. Bradbury, "Chronological Problems in the Study of Benin History," *Journal of the Historical Society of Nigeria,* I (1959), p. 286; Bernard E. B. Fagg, "The Nok Culture in Prehistory," *ibid.,* I (1959), pp. 288–293. By the *cire-perdue* method, a bronze mold was made by covering a rough clay core with wax to re-

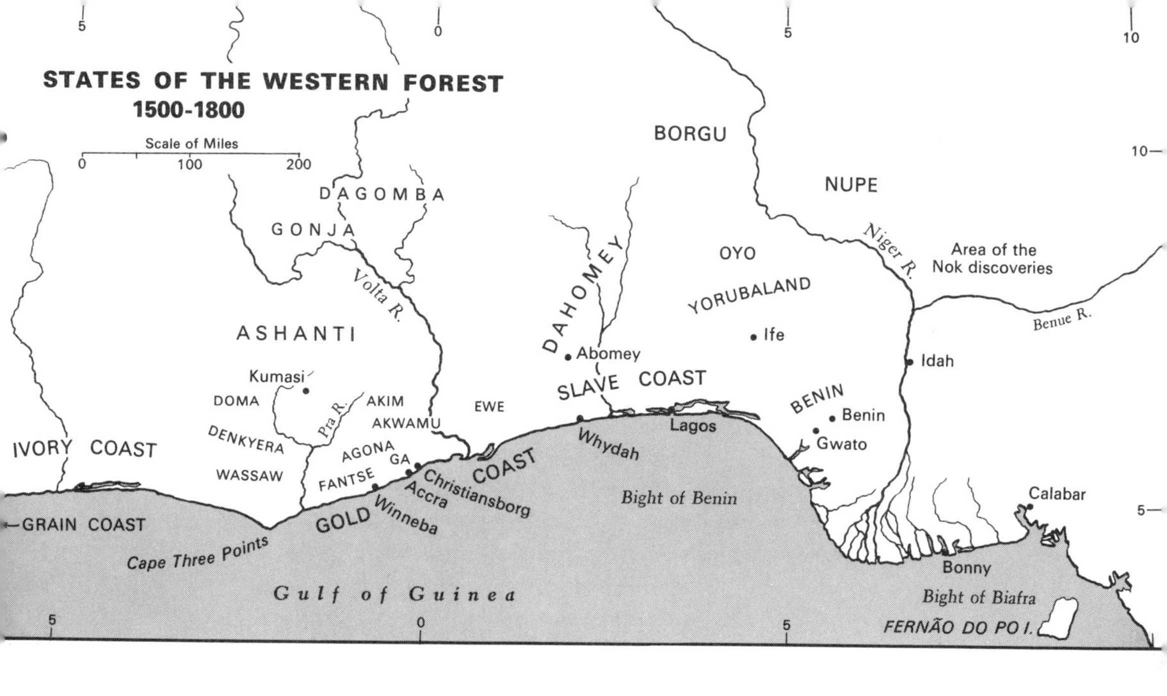

The kingdom of benin

Early in the fifteenth century, Benin reached its imperial apogee under Ewuare the Great (*c.* 1440–1473). This "great magician, physician, traveller and warrior"—a "powerful, courageous and sagacious" king—supposedly fought against and captured more than two hundred towns and villages west of the Niger River. He captured their rulers and compelled their people to pay tribute.[33] During the reign of Ewuare, Benin grew into an important town; his people made a number of good roads, dug wide defensive ditches, and built strong walls around the town. Under his protection, religious and secular arts flourished—numerous sacred carvings, household ornaments, and elaborately decorated doors all testify to the prosperity and stability of fifteenth-century Benin. Ewuare's second son, the generous *oba* Olua (1473–1480), supposedly founded Itsekiri Warri in order to give his cruel, unpopular son a kingdom over which he might rule. But Olua's action left the throne of Benin without a rightful heir, and after his death, Benin endured a short period of unstable republican government that, before long, approximated anarchy.[34] Because the rural people pillaged Benin, in about 1481/82 the leading citizens of the capital city rebelled and enstooled, or enthroned, Ozolua as their new *oba*. He returned rebellious subjects to the fold of Benin and "made himself respected at home and dreaded abroad"; "in fact," says the chronicler, Benin became "a terror to all other

semble the object to be cast. The wax was then covered with a shell of clay. And when the brass was cold, the artist chipped away the clay inside, leaving the object cast.

[33] Egharevba, *Benin*, p. 14. See also P. Amaury Talbot, *The Peoples of Southern Nigeria* (London, 1926), I, pp. 154–155.

[34] We know little about this "republican" government. Egharevba, *Benin*, p. 23, simply says that it lasted for three years, "for those placed in authority were unable to manage the affairs of the country rightly and were not obeyed."

tribes in this part of West Africa and the Empire became wonderfully enlarged."[35]

During the reign of Ozolua (1481/82–1504), Benin began to receive a steady flow of European visitors.[36] The farmers of Benin supplied *pimenta del rabo,* a pepper far superior to the *malagueta* or "grains of paradise" that grew along the Guinea coast of West Africa. In order to expedite what for a time was a flourishing trade, Portugal established a factory at Ughoton (Gwato), Benin's main port and, until 1506, purchased as much *pimenta del rabo* as they could persuade the people of Benin to sell.[37] From about 1485, Portuguese traders also exchanged slaves purchased in Benin for the gold of Elmina. Duarte Pacheco Pereira commented upon this practice after a visit to Benin in 1498/99:

> *The kingdom of Beny . . . is usually at war with its neighbours and takes many captives, whom we buy at twelve or fifteen brass bracelets which they prize more; from there the slaves are brought to the castle of S. Jorze da Mina where they are sold for gold.*[38]

Throughout the first third of the sixteenth century, Benin built upon this early relationship with Portugal and prospered from the sale of pepper, slaves, ivory, and Yoruba cloth. In turn the merchants and princes of Benin imported firearms—the first to be used in the forest region—copper, coral beads, and umbrellas.

During the early years of the reign of *oba* Esigie (*c.* 1504–1550), Benin attempted to further its connection with Europe. Esigie therefore sent an ambassador to Lisbon "because he desired to learn more about these lands, the arrival of people from [Portugal] in his country being regarded as an unusual novelty." A contemporary commented:

> *This ambassador was a man of good speech and natural wisdom. Great feasts were held in his honour, and he was shown many of the good things of these kingdoms. He returned to his land in a ship of the king's, who at his departure made him a gift of rich clothes for himself and his wife: and through him he also sent a rich present to the king [of Benin] of such things [a copper stool, coral beads, and a big umbrella] as he understood he would greatly prize.*[39]

---

[35] *Ibid.*, p. 26.

[36] The date usually accepted for the arrival of the Portuguese in Benin is 1483–1486, but John William Blake (trans. and ed.), *Europeans in West Africa, 1450–1560* (London, 1942), I, pp. 6, 8–12, following Antonio Galvão (trans. and ed. C. R. Drinkwater Bethune), *The Discoveries of the World* (London, 1862), p. 75, successfully argues that Fernão do Pó knew the Benin coast as early as 1472 to 1475, but that he probably did not venture to the capital city itself. Egharevba, *Benin*, p. 27, perhaps in default of local knowledge, says nothing about the discovery of the Benin coast, but indicates that the Portuguese first visited Benin City in 1485/86.

[37] After 1506, when pepper grown in India began to oust the pepper of Africa from the markets of Europe, the merchants of Portugal purchased progressively less from Benin. See Ruy de Pina, "The Discovery of the Kingdom of Benin," in Blake, *Europeans*, I, p. 78.

[38] Duarte Pacheco Pereira (trans. and ed. George H. T. Kimble), *Esmeraldo de Situ Orbis* (London, 1937), p. 126 [ii]. See also João de Barros, in G. R. Crone (trans. and ed.), *The Voyages of Cadamosto* (London, 1937), pp. 124–125. Pacheco said that the kingdom of Benin was eighty leagues long and forty leagues wide.

[39] Pina, extract in Blake, *Europeans*, I, pp. 78–79.

Bronze head from Benin, *c.* 1500, showing the plastic representational abilities that may have been derived from Ife and Nok. Museum of Primitive Art, New York.

The king of Portugal also despatched missionaries to Benin. They built churches, proselytized—in order "to administer a stern rebuke about the heresies and great idolatries and fetishes" [40]—and, in 1515/16, helped the warriors of Benin to conquer Idah. As a token of his gratitude, *oba* Esigie ordered his son and two of his noble councilors to become Christians. The son evidently acquired a Portuguese education from the priests and submitted to baptism. Indeed, when a British captain visited Benin in 1553, he found Esigie's son, who had become *oba* Orhogbua, speaking "the Portugall tongue, which he had learned of a child." [41] He and his successors used Portuguese muskets to conquer peoples living as far west as Eko (modern Lagos) and as far east as Bonny. The peoples of Benin also claim to have founded Onitsha on the Niger River.

In the seventeenth century, Benin was among the most prosperous and favored towns of tropical Africa. A Dutch visitor wrote:

> *[Benin] seems to be a very big town, for when one enters it, one first arrives in a big, broad street; unpaved; which seems to be seven or eight times as broad as the Warmoesstraad at Amsterdam. This street is straight, never curves and from where I was lodged . . . which was as much as a quarter of an hour from the gate, I still could not see an end to the street, but I did see a big, tall tree, as far away as I could distinguish anything and I talked with a Dutchman there, who said that he had been as far as that tree, but could see no end, although he did*

[40] *Ibid.*, p. 79.

[41] Quoted in Richard Eden, "Account of [Thomas] Windham's Voyage to Guinea," in Blake, *Europeans*, II, p. 318. The people of Benin also remembered Orhogbua for his introduction of cooking salt. See also Duarte Pires to King Manuel, October 20, 1516, quoted in *ibid.*, pp. 123–124.

Benin City in the seventeenth century, showing the *oba* and his army preceded by musicians and retainers, with the walls of the city in the background. This was probably drawn by an artist who had never visited Benin. (Olfert Dapper, *Description de l'Afrique,* Amsterdam, 1686)

> *see that the houses started to become smaller, some being dilapidated, so that one could presume on that basis that the end was not far.*

He described Benin's very tall bulwark, broad, dry moat, big, wooden gate, and its suburb beyond the gate, and then went on to marvel at its houses:

> *The houses in this town are arranged in an orderly fashion, standing side by side and being joined to each other as the houses in Holland are. One enters the houses in which important people live . . .* via *two or three steps. They have a porch in front, where one can sit dry, and the porch is swept every morning by their slaves.*

The visitor also liked the people of Benin, for they would "do each other no wrong, nor would they take anything from strangers; for if they did, they would be punished by death, for there they lightly put people to death if they harm strangers." [42]

Throughout the seventeenth century, Benin supplied Europe and America with slaves. Its army warred for slaves and other booty in order to maintain

---

[42] Attributed to Dierick Ruyters, in Pieter de Marees (ed. S. P. L'Honoré Naber), *Beschryvinghe ende historische Verhael van het gout Koninckrijck van Gunea* ('s-Gravenhage, 1912), pp. 232–240. The original was printed in 1602. I am indebted to my colleague Auke Th. Alkema for this new translation from the original Dutch. In Ruyters' own narrative (ed. S. P. L'Honoré Naber), *Toortse der Zee-Vaert* ('s-Gravenhage, 1913), which was written at least twenty-two years (in 1623) after his visit to West Africa, he said little about Benin (see pp. 79–80).

what had become an extensive, complicated economy. But as the century progressed, Benin found slaves increasingly difficult to obtain because of stiff competition from the raiders of Yorubaland and because of the conditions of turmoil in which all of the forest peoples found themselves embroiled. The bureaucracy of Benin, which comprised a number of ranks of nobility and "a particular Supervisor over every thing that can be thought of," grew more powerful and less responsive to changes in the nature and organization of the slave trade and to the wishes of their subjects.[43]

Benin suffered a steady decline in its imperial fortunes. External economic factors—the relatively high cost and poor quality of the slaves offered by Benin and the greater ease with which Europeans could trade with Calabar or Dahomey—an inner decay that came about as a result of more than a century of warfare, and the rise of the powerful Yoruba kingdom of Oyo sharply reduced the power and influence of the *obas* of Benin.[44] Thereafter, more and more vassal states revolted against Benin and obtained their freedom. By the end of the eighteenth century—its trade with Europe having become intermittent—the now militarily weak kingdom of Benin had shrunk considerably in size and apparent influence.

The yoruba kingdom of oyo

Oyo succeeded Benin as the most powerful of the Nigerian forest kingdoms. During the seventeenth century, between the reigns of Obalokun Agana Erin (*c.* 1600) and the great warrior Onisile (*c.* 1700), its cavalry forcibly subordinated the peoples of Yorubaland to a new rule by the *alafins* of Oyo.[45] In the north, the kings of Nupe—a polity founded in the fourteenth or fifteenth century[46]—and Borgu also paid tribute to the *alafin,* and in the south, the slave traders of Oyo gradually ousted the merchants of Benin from their positions of commercial prominence.

Throughout the eighteenth century, the cavalry of Oyo—its generals depended upon the breeders of the Central Sudan for their crucial supply of horses—securely established the suzerainty of the *alafins* over a vast empire that extended at its height from the borders of Benin to the lagoons of Togo. Oyo warred for booty and for slaves, which it then sold to the merchants of Europe and America. From 1738 to 1747, for example, the conscripts of Oyo successfully plundered Dahomey in order to obtain slaves for the overseas trade. Observers had already praised the *alafin's* army:

> [Oyo] *being all Horsed, and a warlike Nation, in a short time Mastered half the King of* Ardra's *Territories, and made such a Slaughter amongst his Subjects, that*

---

[43] David Van Nyendael, "A Description of *Rio Formosa,* or the River of *BENIN,*" in Willem Bosman, *A New and Accurate Description of the Coast of Guinea* (London, 1705), p. 435.

[44] Even so, *oba* Eresoyen (*c.* 1735–1750) supposedly displayed his wealth by paving a floor of his palace with cowrie shells—the currency of the time. Egharevba, *Benin,* p. 41.

[45] Old Oyo or Katunga was apparently founded in the fourteenth or fifteenth century. See Frank Willett, "Investigations at Old Oyo, 1956–1957: An Interim Report," *Journal of the Historical Society of Nigeria,* II (1960), p. 75; Johnson, *Yorubas,* pp. 168–177.

[46] For the traditional history of Nupe, see S. F. Nadel, *A Black Byzantium* (Oxford, 1942), p. 73. But see Palmer, *Memoirs,* III, pp. 79–80.

Bronze plaque showing the *oba* of Benin and his attendants, *c.* 1600–1700. Museum of Primitive Art, New York.

> *the Number of the Dead being innumerable, was commonly express'd by saying they were like the Grains of Corn in the Field. . . . This Nation strikes such a Terror into all the circumjacent* Negroes, *that they can scarce hear them mentioned without Trembling. . . .*[47]

Although some writers have tended to label it feudal, the political and social structure of the kingdom of Oyo seems to have been essentially traditional.[48] The *alafin* owed his election to provincial councilors and, theoretically at least, acknowledged the spiritual supremacy of the *oni* of Ife. Nevertheless, the *alafin* possessed absolutist powers, the secular and supernatural exercise of which was curtailed only in part by an aggregate of institutionalized checks. He ruled through a series of palace ministers, who were assisted in turn by military commanders, and devolved his authority in the provinces to locally elected *obas*. Councils expressed the opinions of the inhabitants of the Yoruba towns about matters of immediate as well as imperial importance. The *obas* were generally

---

[47] Bosman, *Description*, pp. 397–398. See also John Adams, *Remarks on the Country Extending from Cape Palmas to the River Congo* (London, 1823), pp. 79, 92–93; Robert Norris, *Memoirs of the Reign of Bossa Ahádee . . . and a Short Account of the African Slave Trade* (London, 1789), pp. 11–12.

[48] In general, it would be misleading to attribute feudality to the political systems of early Africa. They lacked "an extreme subdivision of the rights of real property: a graded system of rights over land created by this subdivision and corresponding in broad outline to the grades of personal dependence. . . ." They failed to exhibit "a development pushed to the extremes of the element of personal dependence in society." See the convenient definitions in F. L. Ganshof, *Feudalism* (New York, 1961), p. xix. See also Jack Goody, "Feudalism in Africa?" *The Journal of African History*, IV (1963), pp. 1-16.

reluctant to see any of their rulers exercise excessive personal power and, if the *obas* and the people of Oyo presented an *alafin* with symbols of rejection—an empty calabash or the eggs of parrots—he was supposedly then, in honor, to commit suicide. In the late seventeenth century, for example, the powers opposed to the reigning *alafin* Gberu marshalled the forces of communal sanction in order to rid themselves of him:

> *The chiefs . . . grew suspicious and apprehensive of their own safety should the King add the use of secret poison to his unlimited regal power. They soon found a pretext for rejecting him, and he had to put an end to his own life.*[49]

Earlier the chiefs and people of Oyo had rejected one *alafin* because of his "bad temper." Another tortured his subjects and was, in consequence, supposedly burned alive in the palace.

Nourished by the slave trade, Oyo grew prosperous during the course of the eighteenth century. The selling of slaves proved profitable, and the pottery and fabrics of Oyo achieved a wide distribution. According to a nineteenth-century ship captain, the cloth of Oyo was superior "both for variety of pattern, color, and dimensions, to any made in the neighbouring states; and some of the articles wrought by them in iron exhibited much skill and ingenuity." [50] But the very natural concentration upon the commodities which could be sold most profitably to visiting traders in coastal entrepôts helped slowly to bring about the end of Oyo. The southern provinces of the empire grew wealthier than those of the north, and competition for slaves intensified intra-Yoruban rivalry. Toward the end of the eighteenth century, a cruel chief minister usurped control and, by murdering successive *alafins*, destroyed the symbols of Oyo's spiritual legitimacy. Thereafter, the Fon and the Egba broke away, and, in the nineteenth century, Ilorin, with Fulani assistance, proclaimed its independence, prevented Sudanese horses and slaves from reaching the distribution centers of Oyo, and inaugurated the long period of war that absorbed the energies of the peoples of Yorubaland until the British occupation.

The fon kingdom of dahomey

Before the seventeenth century, the Fon, who later formed the nucleus of the kingdom of Dahomey, inhabited a transitional savannah zone north of the true forest. Only an allegorical version of their earlier history exists,[51] but by 1700 the Fon kings had invaded the forest and had readied their armies for an all-out attack upon the prosperous peoples of the western Slave Coast. There the kingdoms of Hueda (Savi and Whydah) and Adja (Allada) enjoyed the benefits of a thriving trade with Europe and America. Middlemen supplied visiting sea captains with slaves in exchange for guns, cloth, rum, and iron bars.[52]

---

[49] Johnson, *Yorubas*, p. 175. See also Archibald Dalzel, *The History of Dahomey* (London, 1793), pp. 12–13, 156–158.

[50] Adams, *Remarks*, p. 94.

[51] Édouard Dunglas, "Contribution à l'histoire du Moyen-Dahomey," *Études Dahoméennes*, XIX (1957), pp. 77–81; M. F. Sossouhounto, "Les Anciens Rois de la dynastie d'Abomey," *ibid.*, XIII (1955), pp. 25–30.

[52] For details, see Colin W. Newbury, *The Western Slave Coast and Its Rulers* (Oxford, 1961), pp. 22, 29, 40 ff; Adams, *Remarks*, pp. 235–265.

The early eighteenth-century Fon kings naturally looked with envy upon this lucrative commerce. Agadja (*c.* 1720–1735) fully realized the extent to which economic advantages would follow direct contact by Dahomeans with European merchants. A suitable opportunity appeared in 1724/25 when the king of Adja died, whereupon Agadja's warriors invaded and conquered Adja. They overran Hueda in 1727 and, although Dahomey briefly lost control from 1729 to 1731, Hueda never really regained its commercial independence.[53]

From the middle of the 1730's to the end of the eighteenth century, Dahomey was deeply absorbed in the slave trade. In the coastal centers, Fon merchants bargained with resident European factors and on occasion sold slaves directly to itinerant shipmasters. In short, Dahomey's leaders devoted all of their imperial energies to satisfying the voracious appetites of foreign buyers. Throughout the century therefore, they sought to entrench their control over the coast, to encompass more and more northern territories in order to ensure a steady supply of the most desirable kind of slave, and to command in exchange for their captives the highest possible prices that the Europeans would pay. The ruling class of Dahomey also began to farm its own plantations with the labor of some of the slaves captured in campaigns against neighboring states.

Dahomey engaged in a number of large-scale offensive and defensive actions in order to preserve its commercial and political pre-eminence. King Tegbessu, who succeeded Agadja, fought frequently to maintain his empire's hegemony on the western Slave Coast. At the same time, the armies of Oyo harassed the eastern reaches of his kingdom and, in 1738, even invaded Abomey, the capital of Dahomey. (The kings of Dahomey paid tribute to Oyo until about 1827.) Despite this disaster, Tegbessu continued to war and to live in the style of his predecessors.

After a stay in Abomey in 1772, Robert Norris, a slave trader, recorded the sights of the court:

> [*I*] *was received at the door by* Mayhou [*the king's second most important official*]; *on each side of it was a human head,* recently cut off, *lying on a flat stone, with the face down, and the bloody end of the neck towards the entrance. In the guard house were about forty women, armed with a musket and cutlass each; and twenty eunuchs, with bright iron rods in their hands; . . . we passed through a third door into the court, where the king was seated, on a handsome chair of crimson velvet, ornamented with gold fringe, placed on a carpet, in a spacious cool piazza, which occupied one side of the court. He was smoking tobacco* [*from* Bahia], *and had on a gold laced hat, with a plume of ostrich feathers; he wore a rich crimson damask robe, wrapped loosely round him; yellow slippers, and no stockings: several women were employed fanning him, and others with whisks, to chase away the flies: one woman, on her knees before him, held a gold cup, for him to spit in.*[54]

---

[53] Dunglas, "Contribution," p. 148; John Atkins, *A Voyage to Guinea, Brasil, and the West-Indies* (London, 1737), pp. 119–121; Norris, *Memoirs,* pp. x–xii; Dalzel, *Dahomey,* pp. 9–10; William Snelgrave, *A New Account of Some Parts of Guinea and the Slave Trade* (London, 1734), pp. 5–9, 123.

[54] Norris, *Memoirs,* pp. 94–95. For a mention of Dahomey's army and its monarch, see John M'Leod, *A Voyage to Africa* (London, 1820), pp. 37–38, 45.

The akwamu kingdom of the gold coast

To the west of Dahomey, the commercial interests of Europe likewise contributed considerably to the rise and development of new indigenous states. The first to emerge was Akwamu, a federation that brought together a number of small tribal groups living between the Volta and Pra rivers.[55] From a capital north of Winneba, its rulers—who may have been of Mande origin—forcibly extended its domain during the early seventeenth century to the banks of the Volta in the east and to the borders of the Akim and Fantse kingdoms in the west. Theirs was a response to the external economic stimulus; five European nations, particularly the Danes at Accra, competed along the eastern Gold Coast for African gold and slaves.

Considerations of commercial expediency influenced the actions of Akwamu throughout the last half of the seventeenth century. The ruling *akwamuhene* and his generals naturally sought to control the roads leading to the port of Accra and, ultimately, the trade itself. By the collection of "tolls" from travelers using these roads, Akwamu acquired sufficient capital with which to purchase guns and gunpowder at the European forts. Wars followed: In 1677, Akwamu conquered an aroused Ga kingdom and sacked Great Accra, its capital.[56] Four years later, after the Danes were no longer in a position to continue giving support to the Ga chiefs, Accra was finally "reduced to a province" of Akwamu.[57] Akwamu next subdued several small, seaboard states and thereafter successfully dominated the eastern Gold Coast.

Akwamu enjoyed the inherent economic advantages of its position of paramountcy. The rents from the forts, "tolls" on the interior traffic, duties on imports and exports, and the trading of slaves directly to European merchants gave Akwamu the funds with which to launch new ventures in aggrandizement. In 1689, for example, its armies overran Agona, located west of Accra, ostensibly because its queen refused to marry Ansa Sasraku, the great *akwamuhene*. A European visitor later wrote of Agona's sovereign:

> *Agonna . . . is . . . governed by a Woman, with as much Courage and Conduct as other Countries are ruled by Men. . . . This Governess is so wise, that to keep the Government entirely in her own hands, she lives unmarried. But that she may not remain a perfect stranger to the soft Passion, she generally buys a brisk jolly Slave, with whom she diverts herself; prohibiting him on forfeiture of his Head, to intrigue with any other Woman; And when the Youth hath lost his Charms, or her Passion palls, he is exchanged for another . . . she is so perfectly Mistress of her Favours, that she may confer them on whom she pleaseth without Fear or Scandal.*[58]

---

[55] Akwamu is treated authoritatively in Ivor Wilks, "The Rise of the Akwamu Empire, 1650–1710," *Transactions of the Historical Society of Ghana*, III (1957), pp. 99–136.

[56] Great Accra was located ten miles inland from the modern Accra, which was then known as Apreg, or Small Accra.

[57] See John Barbot, *A Description of the Coasts of North and South Guinea*, in Awnsham and John Churchill, *A Collection of Voyages and Travels* (London, 1732), V, p. 185.

[58] Bosman, *Description*, p. 63. See also W. Walton Claridge, *A History of the Gold Coast and Ashanti* (London, 1915), I, p. 145.

In order to secure his western border, Ansa Sasraku subsequently concluded a nonaggression pact with the Fantse peoples. It left his armies free to extend their conquests beyond the Volta River and to settle an old score with the Danes of Christiansborg Castle, near Small Accra.

In 1693, perhaps by way of repaying the Danes for their support of Accra between 1677 and 1679, the warriors of Akwamu slipped past the guards and captured Christiansborg Castle. Trusting the assurances of Asameni, a well-known Akwamuese broker, the Danish sentries permitted eighty soldiers disguised as "buyers" to enter their otherwise impregnable fortress in order to inspect guns then on sale. Unbeknown to the Danes, however, the men of Akwamu had secreted powder and shot in the folds of their garments. After some hand-to-hand combat, they readily disarmed the outmanned Danish garrison and commandeered the castle. The young Danish governor was then in his chamber. According to an English contemporary:

> *He came out of his chamber with his sword in his hand to see what was the matter, and was immediately assaulted by two blacks, against whom he made good his ground for some time, calling to his second and soldiers for assistance, but finding none come, but in their stead arm'd blacks, he betook him to a window, whence he flung himself out, and fled to the Dutch* [fortress].[59]

Asameni hoisted the flag of Akwamu—"a black painted in the middle brandishing a scymiter" on a white background—and thereafter governed Christiansborg with due ceremony. During the period of his tenure, an English sea captain anchored offshore:

> *This black general sent two of his servants to invite . . .* [us] *. . . to dine with him, which we accepted, and were carried there in hammocks he had sent to attend us. . . .*
>
> *We were treated at dinner with plenty of punch and victuals, and indeed pretty well dress'd, considering the swinish manner 'tis the custom of the negroes to eat. . . .* [The black general] *drank the king of England's, the African company's, and our own healths frequently, with vollies of cannon, of which he fired above 200 during our stay there. . . .*[60]

But after a year, the *akwamuhene*—who had perhaps suffered economically from the ouster—sold Christiansborg Castle back to the Danes, who in turn agreed to forego all reparations that might be due them because of the temporary loss of their headquarters.

During the first thirty years of the eighteenth century, Akwamu remained the most powerful kingdom on the northern shores of the Gulf of Guinea. Under Ado, the reigning *akwamuhene*, its armies conquered distant Whydah in 1702, the trans-Voltaic Ewe states of Peki, Ho, and Kpandu in 1707/8, and

---

[59] Thomas Phillips, *Journal of a Voyage from England to Africa . . . and So Forward to Barbadoes in the Years 1693 and 1694*, in Churchill, *Collection*, VI, p. 212. The unfortunate governor was later captured at sea by "Long Ben" Avery, the English pirate, who forced him to walk the plank near Príncipe.

[60] *Ibid.*

Kwahu, on the road to Ashanti, in 1710. Ado also concluded treaties with the Dutch and the Ashanti, which together provided Akwamu with unprecedented security. Indeed the Dutch, by the agreement of 1703, acknowledged the sovereignty of Akwamu over Accra and paid the *akwamuhene* one ounce of gold for every twenty pounds of gold traded there. In return, the *akwamuhene* promised to keep open the trade routes, to prevent his subjects from trafficking with white "interlopers," and to eschew warfare that might hinder the peaceful flow of commerce.

Until about 1725, Akwamu retained the territorial and economic advantages of its greatness. Yet in describing this greatness, a Dutch visitor had earlier noted the lone chink in the armor of Akwamu. "The Aquamboe [Akwamu] Negroes," he wrote, "are very Haughty, Arrogant and War-like; their Power is also very terrible to all their Neighbouring countries, except *Akim*." [61] In 1733, after internecine strife and a series of disastrous campaigns had weakened the military might of Akwamu, the armies of Akim—where the gold mines were rich—defeated the warriors of Akwamu and reduced the once proud empire to a petty principality. The very size of Akwamu had perhaps sapped its vitality, taxed the kingdom's administrators beyond their abilities, or proved an unexpectedly burdensome expense. Whatever the cause, the greatest indigenous power in the Gold Coast tended thereafter to be centered in the northwestern part of the forest, where the Ashanti kingdom slowly gathered strength.

The rise of the ashanti

The Ashanti people owed much to Akwamu. The Ashanti kingdom's secular architect, the renowned Osei Tutu, supposedly spent a considerable portion of his early life at the court of the rulers of Akwamu.[62] There he presumably observed the techniques of military and economic organization that had contributed to Akwamu's greatness, and he patiently bided his time. Finally, in about 1670, when the Ashanti people summoned him home to succeed his father as their ruler, Osei Tutu began to use his acquired knowledge in order to create a new military force in the forest. At this time, the Ashanti people of a number of small forest states—many of whom shared lineal and cultural ties—were simultaneously being hindered economically by the middlemen of coastal Denkyera and attacked by the people of western Doma. But Osei Tutu, by the exercise of skillful diplomacy and generalship, welded these relatively weak Ashanti states into an alliance that, in time, defeated Doma. He also founded Kumasi, in Tafo country, as his capital and gave to the Ashanti alliance, or proto-kingdom, spiritual bonds without which his own efforts might, in the long run, have been made nugatory. With or without the assistance of the priest Okomfo Anokye—who may conceivably have lived in a later era [63]—Osei

---

[61] Bosman, *Description*, p. 65. Original italics.
[62] See Claridge, *History*, pp. 192–194.
[63] Traditionally, Osei Tutu and Anokye were said to have been contemporaries. But Professor Ivor Wilks now has evidence that leads him to doubt the traditional details of the Anokye story. *In. litt.*, January 31, 1964.

Tutu attributed to his own royal stool (the symbolic representation of kingship) a spiritual supremacy over the stools of the other Ashanti states. At a gathering in Kumasi, a golden stool supposedly fell from the heavens onto the knees of Osei Tutu. The allied chiefs were then persuaded that the golden stool contained the *sunsum* (spirit) of the Ashanti nation and that they should acknowledge fealty to it and to the *asantehene* (Osei Tutu) as its custodian.[64]

The new Ashanti union obtained its economic independence in 1700/1701, when the Ashanti warriors conquered Denkyera. A contemporary wrote:

> *Thus you see the towring Pride of* Dinkira *in Ashes, they being forced to fly before those, whom they not long before thought no better than their Slaves, and themselves being now sold for Slaves.*[65]

By defeating Denkyera, Ashanti obtained access to salt deposits and its first direct connection to the European trading outposts of the western Gold Coast. Ashanti exchanged slaves and gold for European guns and consumer goods; it even collected rent from the Dutch occupants of Elmina castle and, in time, also became the ground landlord of the English fort at Accra.

After the death of Osei Tutu in 1712, and the military debacle of 1717, during which the reigning *asantehene* lost his life in a war against the Akim peoples, Opuku Ware (*c.* 1721–1750) emerged as the greatest of the early rulers of Ashanti.[66] He consolidated the unitary kingdom founded by Osei Tutu and successfully began the impressive series of conquests that transformed Ashanti into the most powerful of the nations of the Gold Coast. His armies defeated the peoples of Akim and Sefwi, added Banda, and temporarily Wassaw, Takyiman, and Gyaman, to the growing empire and, in 1744/45, even humbled distant Gonja and Dagomba, whose arrows and spears proved no match for Ashanti's Dutch muskets.

Despite these victories, and the growing might of Ashanti, the Wassaw, Akim, and Fantse kingdoms reasserted their control of the trading paths between Kumasi and the coastal forts during the troubled reign of the weak Kusi Obodum (*c.* 1750–1764). His young successor, the *asantehene* Osei Kojo, ruled vigorously—perhaps prodded by his mother—for thirteen years.[67] Consciously seeking to emulate the great Opuku Ware, Osei Kojo defeated the Akim armies, attacked Wassaw, and finally fought the first of a number of wars with the Fantse—the erstwhile allies of Ashanti. But even he failed to "clear the paths" for commerce. His merchants still suffered the depredations of a number of middlemen and collectors of "tolls."

Yet Ashanti responded fruitfully to the European economic stimulus.

[64] The stool was wooden with three supports and partly covered with gold. For an early mention of the stool, see Thomas Edward Bowdich, *Mission from Cape Coast Castle to Ashantee* (London, 1819), p. 39.

[65] Bosman, *Description*, p. 77. The first Dutch edition was published in 1704.

[66] For a discussion of these dates, see Margaret Priestley and Ivor Wilks, "The Ashanti Kings in the Eighteenth Century: A Revised Chronology," *The Journal of African History*, I (1960), pp. 83–92.

[67] *Ibid.*, p. 94. See also Margaret Priestley, "The Ashanti Question and the British: Eighteenth-Century Origins," *The Journal of African History*, II (1961), pp. 41–46.

Whether directly or *via* middlemen, its army secured the steady supply of guns and ammunition that encouraged the development of a strong, aggressive state. To obtain these armaments, Ashanti captured and traded slaves and, because other kingdoms were richer in easily accessible gold-bearing reefs, concentrated its efforts almost exclusively upon this commerce in humans. Indeed, in order to replenish the slave supplies that were so vital to its prosperity, Ashanti preyed incessantly upon its neighbors. Frequent punitive expeditions and recurrent periods of warfare thus provided the means, if not the cause, of Ashanti expansion.

By the end of the eighteenth century, Ashanti ruled much of the Gold Coast's western forest. The writ of the *asantehene* extended directly to peoples living within an area that stretched 150 miles from east to west and 90 miles from north to south. Beyond this nucleus, a number of vassal states owed at least nominal allegiance to the *asantehene*. Conquest, followed by a rapid assimilation of elites, gave cohesion to the peoples of central Ashanti. The outer ring of vassal states, however, possessed strikingly dissimilar backgrounds. Many were Muslim. The *asantehene*, therefore, was never able to govern them in a manner that could remove the sources of friction and possible disaffection. Unwilling to annex and to administer these states from Kumasi,[68] and unable to associate them in any meaningful way to the Ashanti heartland, the *asantehene* found, in the nineteenth century, that tribute was a poor substitute for ethnic or linguistic loyalty.

III. The Eastern Kingdoms

The present state of our knowledge permits us to write only of some of the peoples of the interior of eastern Africa before the nineteenth century. Although the traditions of this vast area are many, and often rich, the events to which they point are obscure, the chronological clues are uncertain, and even the general trends are, at times, vague. Yet wherever archaeologists have used these traditions to guide their exploratory excavations, they have unearthed evidence of a kind that has tended to corroborate the oral reports. Nevertheless, until the results of recent and continuing research are known, treatment in broad outline must suffice.[69]

The cwezi and their successors

In the fourteenth and fifteenth centuries, the Cwezi kings apparently governed a large part of the area between Victoria Nyanza and Lakes Edward and Albert.[70] Like the Hima who earlier may have overrun the area, they were cattle

[68] See Claridge, *History*, pp. 228. See also Ivor Wilks, *The Northern Factor in Ashanti History* (Legon, 1961), pp. 18–24; Bowdich, *Mission*, pp. 235–236.

[69] The best summary of the history of the interior of East Africa is Roland Oliver, "Discernible Developments in the Interior, *c.* 1500–1840," in Roland Oliver and Gervase Mathew (eds.), *History of East Africa* (Oxford, 1963), I, pp. 169–211.

[70] K. W. [Tito Winyi, *omukama* of Bunyoro], "The Kings of Bunyoro-Kitara," *The Uganda Journal,* III (1935), pp. 158–159; Julien Gorju, *Entre le Victoria l'Albert et l'Édouard*

owners whose activity gave rise to a large corpus of traditional lore. The Cwezi also are credited with the construction of a number of scattered and extensive earthworks. At Bigo bya Mugenyi, near the historic capital site of Ntusi, exists what might have been the last important redoubt of the Cwezi kingdom of Kitara. It consists of two concentric rings of trenches, the outer one of which is about three miles long. The inner ring, higher up on a central hill, contains a continuous series of ramparts. The trenches are about twelve feet deep and appear to have been used—possibly from the beginning—and later rebuilt as fortifications. Although the Cwezi may have penned their cattle between the two rings, the area within the inner circle of ramparts was, it seems, occupied by people who used iron and made tools, weapons, and pots of a kind familiar to later inhabitants of western Uganda.[71]

Sometime in the late fifteenth or early sixteenth century, the Cwezi kings of Kitara were overthrown by Lwo invaders from the north.[72] These Nilotic warriors reconsolidated the Kitara empire and founded the new Bito dynasties of Bunyoro and Buganda. Despite their prowess, they adopted the cultural and linguistic traits of their more sophisticated subjects and were, in time, absorbed into the Bantu milieu. Their armies ranged far afield—even into Rwanda—but they failed to conquer all of the peoples upon whom they preyed. Instead, the Lwo or Bito irruption stimulated the development of new interlacustrine states ruled by Hinda and Tutsi aristocrats who popularized the breeding of cattle, perhaps for its own sake, the cultivation of bananas, and particular concepts of statecraft. And in time these new organizational ideas spread south and east to influence many of the Bantu-speaking peoples of what became Tanganyika and northern Nyasaland.[73]

Contemporaneous with or somewhat subsequent to the invasions of Kitara were the Lwo migrations from the Bahr el Ghazal up the White Nile into what became northern Uganda. During the sixteenth and seventeenth centuries, the Lwo either ousted or submerged the Madi, Lugbara, and Didinga peoples living on either side of the Albert Nile and north of Lake Kyoga. Imposing their own speech and a cultural overlay, the Lwo established the tribal systems now known as Alur and Acholi.

Perhaps during the seventeenth century, new pressure from the "Itunga"

(Rennes, 1920), pp. 46–51. But see Christopher Wrigley, "Some Thoughts on the Bacwezi," *The Uganda Journal*, XXII (1958), p. 16.

[71] P. L. Shinnie, "Excavations at Bigo, 1957," *The Uganda Journal*, XXIV (1960), p. 27; E. J. Wayland, "Notes on the Biggo bya Mugenyi," *ibid.*, II (1934), pp. 21–32. See also Roland Oliver, "Ancient Capital Sites of Ankole," *ibid.*, XXIII (1959), pp. 51–63; E. C. Lanning, "Ancient Earthworks in Western Uganda," *ibid.*, XVII (1953), pp. 51–61; E. C. Lanning, "The Earthworks at Kibengo, Mubende District," *ibid.*, XXIV (1960), pp. 183–196.

[72] Roland Oliver, "The Traditional Histories of Buganda, Bunyoro, and Nkole," *The Journal of The Royal Anthropological Institute*, LXXXV (1955), p. 115. But see J. P. Crazzolara, *The Lwoo* (Verona, 1950), I, pp. 107–108; Christopher Wrigley, "Kimera," *The Uganda Journal*, XXIII (1959), pp. 38–43.

[73] Monica Wilson, *The Peoples of the Nyasa-Tanganyika Corridor* (Cape Town, 1958), pp. 22, 47–50.

pastoralists, who in turn began to move into trans-Kyoga, forced a number of Lwo clans to continue their migration to the Kavirondo Gulf, where they soon injected themselves into an area populated predominantly by peoples speaking Bantu languages. The Lango comprised the vanguard of this "Itunga" thrust; they adopted the linguistic ideas of the Lwo and eventually carved out an enclave for themselves in what may already have been a Lwo district. The Teso, migrating from Karamoja during the eighteenth century, followed the Lango into the Lake Salisbury region at a time when the Turkana may—then as now—have been intensifying their pressure upon the available grazing land west from Lake Rudolf toward what is now Karamoja. The Karamojong and the Jie and, indeed, the Masai, may also have been affected by this pressure of people and cattle. During the seventeenth century perhaps, the Masai passed through Suk and Nandi country into the Great Rift Valley, settling in the southern part. They penetrated into what became Tanganyika, and fought against and subtly influenced the Bantu-speaking peoples with whom they came into contact. Certainly in large parts of eastern Africa the seventeenth and eighteenth centuries were, in a very real sense, the centuries of movement, of dispersion, and of the influence and absorption of one clan or tribe by another.[74]

During these centuries, the rulers of the interlacustrine kingdoms strengthened their grip upon their subjects, increased their economic and political power, and repulsed the second and third waves of Lwo immigrants. Bunyoro was initially pre-eminent. Its army raided Kaaro-Karungi (Ankole), Rwanda, Karagwe, and Kiziba, ruled Buganda and Busoga, and even threatened the peoples living beyond Bukedi and Bugisu.[75] But in the late seventeenth century, perhaps after Bunyoro's army had suffered its first major reversals, the small kingdom of Buganda began to annex the contiguous province of Bunyoro. This process of expansion at the expense of Bunyoro continued throughout the eighteenth century, during which time Busoga probably also claimed its independence. Likewise, Kaaro-Karungi, the Hinda kingdom, conquered portions of Bunyoro and Mpororo, also during the eighteenth century, forestalled a Rwanda invasion, and gradually extended its rule to include a large segment of western Uganda. Meanwhile, Buganda occupied lands along the western bank of the Victoria Nile, absorbed southern Buddu and Koki and, by the end of the eighteenth century, governed the western shores of Victoria Nyanza from the Kagera River to Lake Kyoga. It also readied itself for the nineteenth-century

[74] J. C. D. Lawrance, *The Iteso* (London, 1957), pp. 10–12; Aidan W. Southall, "Alur Tradition and Its Historical Significance," *The Uganda Journal,* XVIII (1954), pp. 142–158; Crazzolara, *Lwoo* (1950), I, pp. 52, 55, 81–82 (1954), III, pp. 333–334, 349–350, 564–565; J. P. Crazzolara, "The Lwoo People," *The Uganda Journal,* V (1937), pp. 6–10, 21; A. Tarantino, "Lango Wars," *ibid.,* XIII (1949), pp. 145–153; Henry A. Fosbrooke, "An Administrative Survey of the Masai Social System," *Tanganyika Notes and Records,* 26 (1948), pp. 3–5.

[75] Ruth H. Fisher, *Twilight Tales of the Black Baganda* (London, 1911), pp. 128–144; K. W., "The Kings," IV (1936), pp. 78–79; Edmond Césard, "Le Muhaya," *Anthropos,* XXXII (1937), pp. 32–57; G. Pagès, *Un Royaume hamité au centre de l'Afrique* (Bruxelles, 1933), pp. 558–559; J. Ford and R. de Z. Hall, "The History of Karagwe," *Tanganyika Notes and Records,* 24 (1947), p. 6.

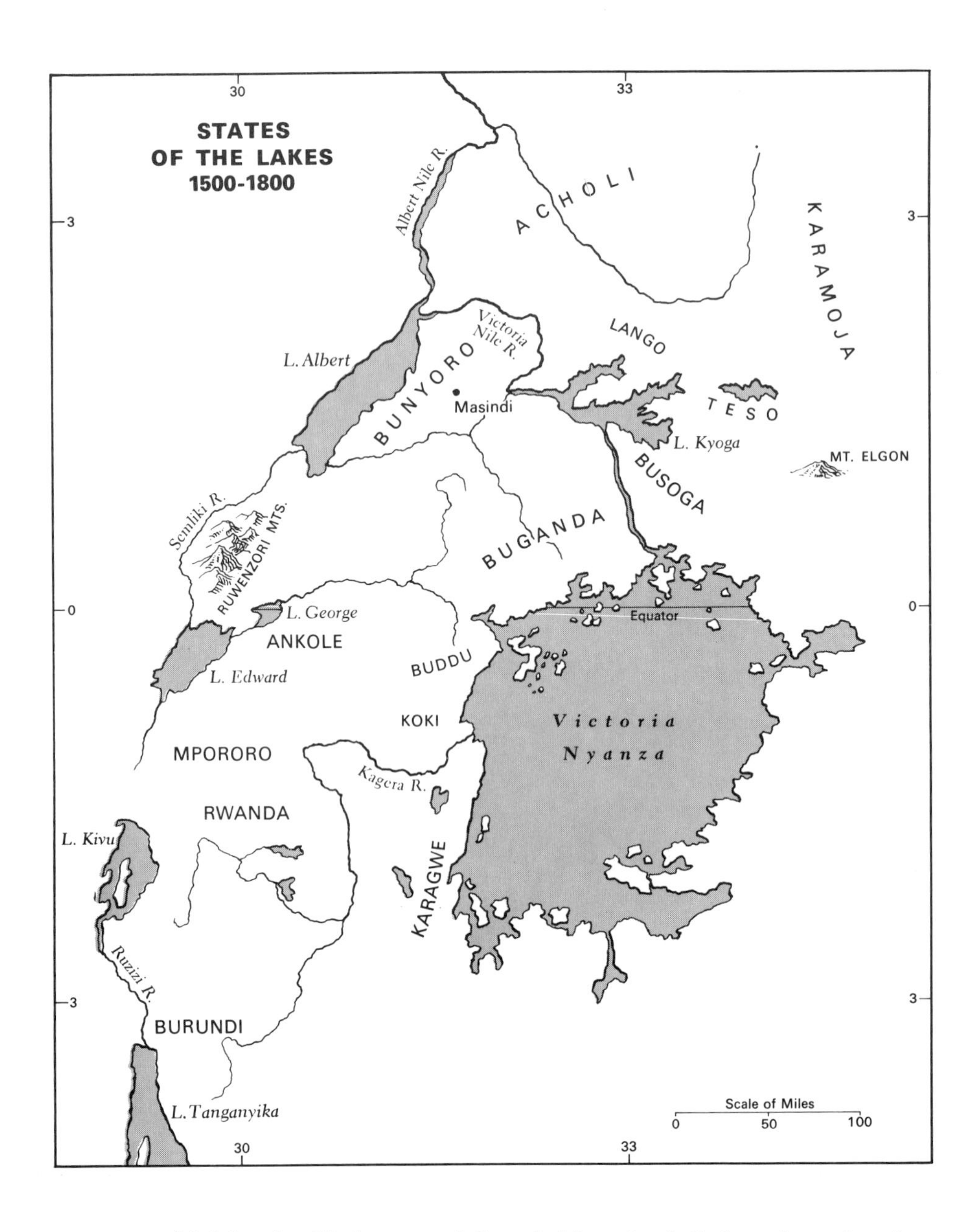

conquest of Mubende. Kyabugu and Semakokiro, the *kabakas* who reigned at the end of the eighteenth century, even exchanged ivory for plates, cups, saucers, glass, copper bracelets, cowries, and cotton goods imported into Karagwe by Arabic- and Swahili-speaking traders.[76] They thereby opened channels of communication with foreigners and, by so doing, began the long relationship with

[76] John Milner Gray, "Early History of Buganda," *The Uganda Journal,* II (1935), pp. 268–269; John Roscoe, *The Baganda* (London, 1911), p. 225.

non-African forces that was subsequently to engulf their successors and radically to alter the history of the kingdom.

To the south, many of the peoples of the Congo and Zambezi basins claim a previous relationship of some kind to the Lunda-Luban empire of *mwata yamvo*. Early in the sixteenth century—according to the traditional account—marriage joined the royal houses of the Lunda and Luba tribes.[77] Subsequently, the first *mwata yamvo*, whose eighteenth- and early nineteenth-century successors ruled a vast area that extended from the upper reaches of the Cuango and Zambezi rivers to the banks of the Luangwa River, created a capital between the Lulua and Bushimaie rivers in what later became western Katanga. Subsequent *mwata yamvos* traded with the Portuguese settlements in Angola and, in the eighteenth century, obtained guns and gunpowder from them. But dissatisfaction within the ruling class of the Lunda-Luban empire led at about this time, if not earlier, to a series of migrations—either of ruling elites or whole segments—westward, southward, and eastward. This process of fission appears to account for the settlement of the Bemba, the Bisa, and the Lunda of Kazembe between the Luapula and Luangwa rivers as well as the establishment along the upper reaches of the Zambezi and Kasai rivers of the Lunda of Kanongesha, Ikalenge, and Ishinde, the Luvale, the Luchazi, the Kaonde, and the Cokwe.[78]

A number of other peoples also profess to have migrated from Katanga into modern Zambia and Malawi, but their exact relationship, if any, to the empire of *mwata yamvo* remains uncertain. Only the various Lunda groups and the Luvale, it seems, consistently acknowledged the sovereignty of the *mwata yamvo*. And in the nineteenth century, the Lunda of Kazembe rivaled even the Lunda of *mwata yamvo* for hegemony in eastern Katanga.

The early history of Zambia and Malawi for the most part has remained obscure. Yet recent excavations by archaeologists have provided striking evidence of human activity in the middle Zambezi valley and on the adjacent Tonga plateau—the area where the oral accounts are shallowest, or virtually

---

[77] Jan Vansina, "The Foundation of the Kingdom of Kasanje," *The Journal of African History*, IV (1963), pp. 355–366; Edmond Verhulpen, *Baluba et Balubaïsés du Katanga* (Anvers, 1936), pp. 134–135; Ian G. Cunnison (trans. and ed.), *Central Bantu Historical Texts, II: Historical Traditions of the Eastern Lunda* (Lusaka, 1961), pp. 3–4; S. J. Chibanza, "Kaonde History," in *Central Bantu Historical Texts, I* (Lusaka, 1961), pp. 43–44. Of interest is the finding of Jacques Chileya Chiwale (trans. and ed.), *Central Bantu Historical Texts, III: Royal Praises and Praise Names of the Lunda Kazembe of Northern Rhodesia, the Meaning and Historical Background* (Lusaka, 1962), p. 9, that both the Lunda of Kazembe and the Bemba eulogize their ancestral rulers in Ciluba and not, as previously supposed, in Cilunda or Cibemba. Ciluba is now commonly used only by members of the royal families.

[78] Ann Tweedie, "Towards a History of the Bemba from Oral Tradition," in *Conference of the History of the Central African Peoples* (Lusaka, 1963), no pagination; F. M. Thomas, *Historical Notes on the Bisa Tribe, Northern Rhodesia* (Lusaka, 1958), pp. 7–9; C. M. N. White, "The Balovale Peoples and Their Historical Background," *The Rhodes-Livingstone Journal*, VIII (1949), pp. 36–37. Ian G. Cunnison, *The Luapula Peoples of Northern Rhodesia* (Manchester, 1959), p. 39, dates the migration of the Lunda of Kazembe into the Luapula region at about 1740. But he appears to base his evidence for this date solely upon the *very* approximate date given by Francisco João Pinto in Richard Burton (trans. and ed.), *The Lands of Cazembe* (London, 1873), p. 126.

non-existent. From about A.D. 900 to 1400, an agricultural people who made iron tools and weapons flourished on the plateau, near Kalomo in what is now southern Zambia. They lived in common rondavels, cultivated sorghum with iron hoes and wooden digging sticks, collected wild fruits, and kept short-horned cattle and small goats and/or sheep. Hunting added to their food resources. They fashioned figurines of clay that represented humans and cattle, and a few, conceivably only the leading families, decorated themselves with copper bangles and glass beads. There is some evidence, in the form of shells and beads, of trade contacts with the inhabitants of either or both coasts of southern Africa. It appears, too, that the way of life of these Kalomo people changed little over the five-hundred-year period revealed by pick and spade.

From about 1450 to 1650, a people—perhaps related to the modern Kunda of the Luangwa River valley—occupied a recently investigated site at Ingombe Ilede ("the place where the cow sleeps") down the Zambezi River from the Kariba dam in Zambia. Like the Kalomo people, the inhabitants of Ingombe Ilede used iron implements, grew sorghum, kept cattle and goats, hunted the largest of the wild animals, and rarely fished. Elephants provided ivory, the mines of what are now Katanga and Rhodesia, copper and gold, respectively, and the nearby Lusitu River (a tributary of the Zambezi), salt. Abundant supplies of these prime goods evidently permitted Ingombe Ilede to become an important entrepôt where Swahili- and Portuguese-speaking merchants from Sofala, and perhaps Mafia, bartered yards of cloth (although some cloth was manufactured locally) and quantities of glass beads for the products of the interior.

Commerce brought wealth to a few, undoubtedly the ruling class of what appears to have been a sharply segmented society. A minority of the residents of Ingombe Ilede were buried together with iron gongs—the ceremonial emblems of kingship—copper crosses, and quantities of undrawn copper wire. The limbs of a few skeletons were covered with cloth and copper bangles; their necks and waists were festooned with gold, colored glass beads, and expensive shells.[79] But most of the people of this riverain settlement were buried without decorations. They presumably benefited only indirectly from their community's profitable, possibly widespread, commercial contacts with the coast. Their relations to their rulers, and the relevance of Ingombe Ilede in the pre-colonial history of Central Africa, remain, however, speculative.

IV. The Peoples and Polities of the Northeast

If the chronicles of eastern Africa are obscure, records of many kinds of the same era fortunately permit us to reconstruct with confidence the history of Ethiopia and the Sudan in more than outline form. Indigenous as well as foreign reports abound; the traditions of northeastern Africa are susceptible to

---

[79] Brian M. Fagan, "The Iron Age Sequence in the Southern Province of Northern Rhodesia," *The Journal of African History*, IV (1963), pp. 160–173.

independent and, often, multiple corroboration, and a number of modern investigators have for some time directed their attentions to the relevant historiographical problems.

The reorientation of ethiopia

At the beginning of the sixteenth century, the empire of Ethiopia nominally extended from Massawa on the Red Sea to Lake Abaya; it encompassed the hostile tribesmen of Tigre, the various Sidama principalities, and the former Muslim kingdoms of Ifat, Fatajar, Dawaro, Bali, and Hadya. But the emperor of Ethiopia limited his government of the conquered provinces to the collection of tribute. Each of the Muslim sultanates retained its own ruling hierarchy and an autonomy that was almost total. Even within central Ethiopia, hostile tribesmen were rarely loath to take advantage of the emperor's inability to control his subjects. Beyond the limits of the empire, however, lay Ethiopia's greatest enemy, the Muslim sultanate of Adal. The sultan and the emperor had fought frequently during the fifteenth century, but those battles, and the decisive Ethiopian victory in 1516, proved but a prelude to the ruinous wars that followed.

In the second quarter of the sixteenth century, after the departure from Ethiopia of an abortive Portuguese embassy (it failed to conclude an alliance),[80] the emperor's army reopened the conflict with Adal. At this time, the Ottoman Turks—who were competing with Portugal for supremacy in the Red Sea, the Persian Gulf, and on the northern shores of the Indian Ocean—vigorously supported the generals of Adal against Christian Ethiopia. Together with merchants of Catalonia, the Turks supplied Adal with muskets, cannon, and detachments of experienced, disciplined soldiers and encouraged the Somali and Danakil leaders who had already rallied behind the militant banner of 'Ahmad ibn Ibrahim al-Ghazi (the famed 'Ahmad Grañ). A reformer who felt himself divinely appointed to conquer Christian Ethiopia, 'Ahmad refused to pay Adal's customary tribute to the emperor Lebna Dengel. In 1527 and 1529, he defeated the Ethiopian armies, but he was unable to launch an all-out attack until after he had consolidated his own power in Adal. Subsequently, 'Ahmad moved mercilessly against the Ethiopians. Between 1531 and 1536, his armies overran Dawaro, Shoa, Amhara, Lasta, Bali, Hadya, Sidama, and Tigre and, in time, occupied three-quarters of Ethiopia.[81] The emperor, harried from retreat to retreat, urged Portugal to come to his assistance. "All my chiefs have rebelled against me to help the Moors," he wrote, "and have wasted and violently taken possession of my countries." [82]

Portuguese reinforcements—four hundred gunners—did not arrive until 1541. In the next year, the combined regiments humbled 'Ahmad's soldiers, but with

[80] For the record of the embassy, see Francisco Álvares (trans. and eds. C. F. Beckingham and G. W. B. Huntingford), *The Prester John of the Indies* (Cambridge, Eng., 1961), 2v.

[81] See 'Ahmad ibn 'Abd al-Kadir (trans. René Basset), *Histoire de la conquête de l'Abyssinie* (Paris, 1897), I, pp. 130–141.

[82] Lebna Dengel to João Bermudez, *c.* 1540, in R. S. Whiteway (trans. and ed.), *The Portuguese Expedition to Abyssinia in 1541–3* (London, 1902), pp. 107–108.

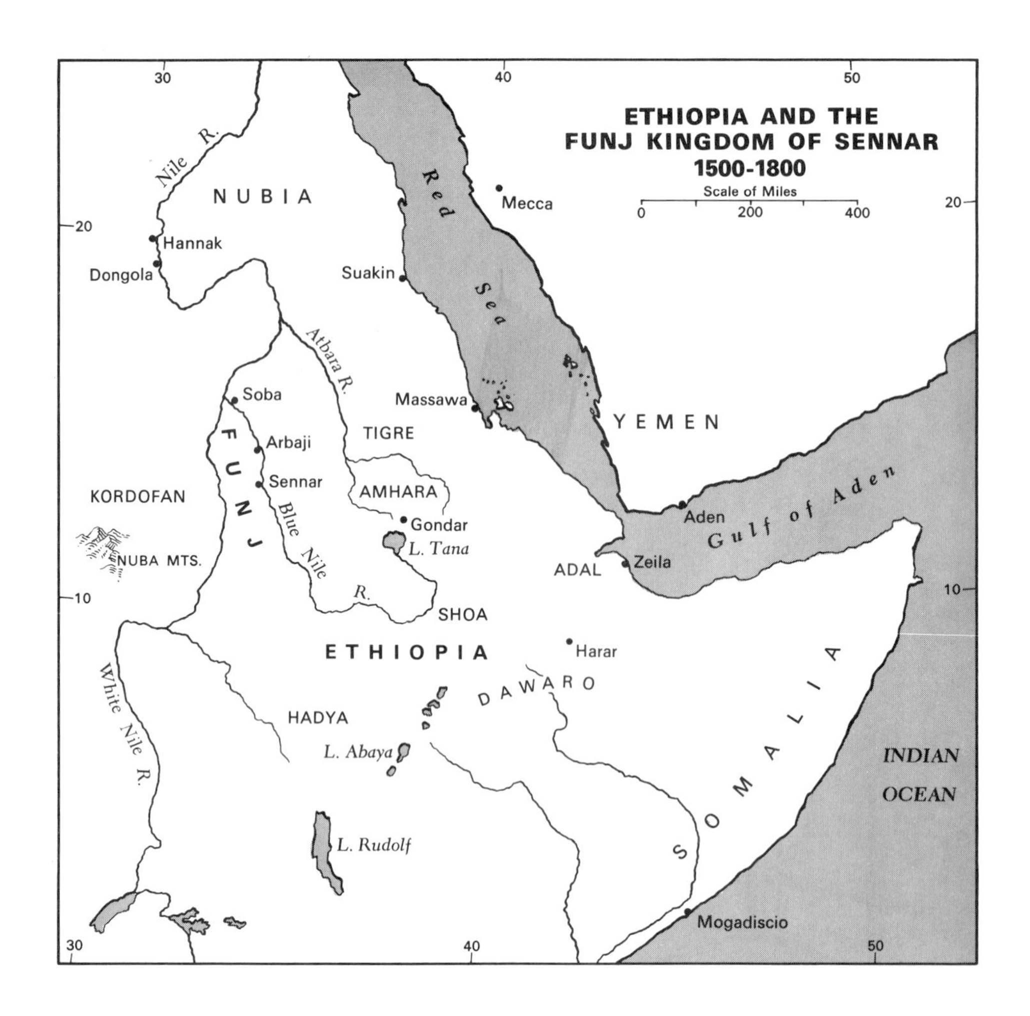

renewed Ottoman assistance—in particular, the services of nine hundred musketeers—'Ahmad quickly avenged his defeat. Finally, in early 1543, the remaining soldiers of Portugal and the warriors of the new emperor Galawdewos (1540–1559) killed the overconfident 'Ahmad and decisively defeated the Muslims at Wayna Daga, near Lake Tana.[83] Galawdewos soon ended the Muslim occupation of his empire, the monarchy and the Ethiopian church both emerging out of the long period of warfare stronger than before. In Wadj, the emperor built a magnificent church, a palace, a library, and an irrigation canal, and encouraged a spiritual and literary revival.[84]

But the long period of warfare brought an end to the old unity of Ethiopia. Throughout the remainder of his reign, the emperor Galawdewos fought the Turks, who occupied Massawa and Suakin and threatened Tigre, and he tried

[83] Jerome Lobo (trans. Samuel Johnson, ed. George Gleig), A *Voyage to Abyssinia* (London, 1789), pp. 88–95.

[84] William E. Conzelman (trans. and ed.), *Chronique de Galâwdêwos (Claudius), roi d'Éthiopie* (Paris, 1895), pp. 149–161.

Battles between Ethiopian Christian warriors and turbaned Muslims; in one case a Muslim, who is always seen only in profile, has evidently discarded a matchlock. From an early eighteenth-century manuscript. The British Museum, London.

desperately to forestall the Galla, who, pressed by the Somali, invaded the southern part of the empire as part of their migrations from the Ogaden. Later, the Galla conquered Harar, occupied the provinces of Gan and Angot, penetrated into Amhara and Shoa and, by the end of the century, controlled about one-third of the old Ethiopian empire and a part of what later became Somalia. Only during the latter part of the reign of the emperor Sartsa Dengel (1563–1597) were the fortunes of Ethiopia temporarily revived; he ousted the Turks from Tigre, temporarily stemmed the Galla tide, briefly contained the rebellious Falasha, Agau, and Sidama, and at least managed to forestall the complete disintegration of his Christian kingdom.

During the early seventeenth century, Sartsa Dengel's successors sought allies in their continuing struggle against the Muslim invaders. At the suggestion of the Jesuit priest Pêro Pais, the emperors Za Dengel (1603–1604) and Susneyos (1607–1632) both requested military assistance from Spain and religious instructors from Rome. Indeed, Susneyos even acknowledged the supremacy of the pope in order to obtain Spanish troops. He allowed the Jesuit Afonso Mendes, who succeeded Pais in 1626, to crusade against Monophysite Catholicism in order to cleanse it of foreign elements. A priest recorded:

> *The Christianity professed by the Abyssins is so corrupted with superstitions, errors, and heresies, and so mingled with ceremonies borrowed from the Jews, that little besides the name of Christianity is to be found here; and the thorns may be said to have choaked the grain.*[85]

[85] Lobo, *Abyssinia,* p. 66. See also pp. 76–79.

The Jesuits demanded the reordination of Ethiopian priests according to the Roman rite, the reconsecration of churches, the rebaptism of Christians, the introduction of graven images, the Roman calendar, and the Roman liturgy, the prohibition of circumcision, and the prohibition of the two-day sabbath. But these politically motivated acts naturally precipitated a war between the emperor and the conservative leaders of the indigenous church. Popular revolts followed which, in 1632, finally persuaded Susneyos to abandon the search for an alliance with Europe and to expel the Jesuits from Ethiopia. His more realistic son and heir, the emperor Fasiladas (1632–1667) explained:

> [*The people*] *detested nothing more, than the reiteration of Baptism, as if we had bin Heathens, before we had bin Baptiz'd by the Fathers. They* [*the Jesuits*] *re-ordain'd our Priests and Deacons, they burnt the wooden Chests of our Altars, and Consecrated some Altars of their own, as if ours had not bin consecrated before. . . . For now there is no returning to that, which all the whole Nation abhors and detests: for which reason, all farther Colloquies and Disputes will be in vain.*[86]

For the remainder of the seventeenth century, the emperors of Ethiopia sought to withdraw before dangerous foreign influences. Fasiladas retreated to Gondar—a town which eventually became renowned for its architectural elegance and literary accomplishments—where he established Ethiopia's first fixed, relatively secure capital in the heartland of Amhara. With the assistance of neighboring Islamic powers, he also tried to deny Portugal access to Ethiopia's Red Sea ports. Later, Johannes I expelled Roman Christians and, in order to counter the growth of Islam within the empire, compelled Muslims to live in segregated sections of villages and towns, where they joined the similarly penalized Armenians, Parsees, and Jews (some of whom were probably Falasha). But none of these measures could halt the spread of Islamic ideas and the growth of Galla power within the country. Indeed, once Fasiladas discarded the traditional practice of transferring capital sites periodically, concentrating the power and influence of the empire in remote Gondar, the rulers of Ethiopia grew more and more estranged from their subjects. Gondar, outwardly stable, was inwardly corrupt. Control of the far-flung empire from Gondar was impossible; apparent unity soon gave way, therefore, to anarchy.

Bereft of supporters and ringed by its enemies, the empire of Ethiopia expired during the eighteenth century. At first, its emperors attempted to forestall their demise by enlisting the support of Galla generals against their own independent-minded princes. But no combination of forces was sufficiently powerful to overcome the weaknesses inherent in Gondar's isolation. The armies of the Funj kingdom of the Sudan humbled the Ethiopian alliance; rebels organized their own provincial armies and successfully established their autonomy on a number of battlefields. Finally the Galla, who had steadily encroached upon the territories of the empire and had insinuated themselves

[86] Job Ludolphus (trans. John Phillips), *A New History of Ethiopia* (London, 1682), p. 364. See also pp. 339–351.

into the ruling circles of the capital, ousted the Christian Amhara chiefs from positions of prominence, and assumed control—although the Solomonid dynasty provided puppet kings—of what became the principality of Gondar. From 1769 to 1855, a number of princes governed the independent provinces of what had earlier been the Ethiopian empire.

The funj sultanate of sennar

Down the Blue Nile from Lake Tana—not far, as the crow flies, from Gondar—the Funj sultanate flourished during the times of difficulty in Ethiopia. Although their origins are excessively obscure, the black-skinned, seminomadic Funj rulers probably were descended from peoples who had long lived along the middle and upper Blue Nile and who had, at some earlier point in time, been associated with, or influenced by, the Lwo-speaking Shilluk of the White Nile.[87] Although the various recensions of the "Funj Chronicle," all of which date from the nineteenth century, say authoritatively that the sultanate and its capital at Sennar were founded in 1504, they refrain from offering an understandable account of the circumstances involved.[88] The available evidence indicates, however, that the Funj rulers established Sennar only after defeating the Arab nomads who had swept south from Nubia, overrunning the Christian kingdoms of Maqurra and 'Alwa. At Arbaji, about one hundred miles north of Sennar, the Funj armies apparently halted the thrust of the 'Abdullab Arabs early in the sixteenth century, thereby securing their own hegemony over the grazing lands of the Gezira plain.[89] Subsequently, the Funj armies consolidated their control over the area between the two Nile rivers and, during the long reign of *makk* Amara Dunqas, evidently conquered much of the Nilotic Sudan from Sennar to Hannak, near the Third Cataract. There the Ottoman armies supposedly prevented the Funj armies from continuing their march down the Nile. Shortly after this battle in about 1523, David Reubeni, a Jewish traveler from Arabia, visited Sennar. But he unfortunately says nothing about the conflicts of the time and little about the sultanate. He simply reported that Amara was black-skinned and that he ruled over people both black and white. Like a true nomadic chieftain, Amara traveled about his dominions "month by month from station to station," accompanied by his cavalry, camels, cattle, and sheep.[90]

---

[87] See the discussion in P. M. Holt, "Funj Origins: A Critique and New Evidence," *The Journal of African History*, IV (1963), pp. 46, 52. Holt sensibly handles the arguments in favor of Bornuese/Kanemi or Eritrean/Yemeni origin, as advanced primarily in A. J. Arkell, "Fung Origins," *Sudan Notes and Records*, XV (1932), pp. 201–250, and "More About Fung Origins," *ibid.*, XXVII (1946), pp. 87–97; Osbert G. S. Crawford, *The Fung Kingdom of Sennar* (Gloucester, Eng., 1951), pp. 143–162. See also H. C. Jackson, *Tooth of Fire: Being Some Account of the Ancient Kingdom of Sennâr* (Oxford, 1912), pp. 12–13, 99–101.

[88] Two of the more accessible versions are in Harold A. MacMichael (trans. and ed.), *A History of the Arabs in the Sudan* (Cambridge, Eng., 1922), II, p. 358; Holt, "Funj Origins," p. 51.

[89] James Bruce, *Travels to Discover the Source of the Nile* (Edinburgh, 1805), VI, pp. 369–370; MacMichael, *History*, p. 233; P. M. Holt, "A Sudanese Historical Legend: The Funj Conquest of Suba," *Bulletin of the School of Oriental and African Studies*, XXIII (1960), p. 11.

[90] See S. Hillelson, "David Reubeni: An Early Visitor to Sennar," *Sudan Notes and Records*, XVI (1933), p. 57. Reubeni indicates that Sennar was not then the capital (p. 60).

Of the sixteenth-century successors to Amara, we know little. *Makk* Dakin walad Nail, who reigned from about 1561 to 1576, was among the more powerful. He supposedly promulgated the first Funj code of laws and gave to the sultanate an administrative structure that may have corresponded with the shift of its ruling class from nomadic to more settled pursuits. Dakin appointed chiefs, many of whom appear to have possessed great power, to rule the various districts of the sultanate. The 'Abdullab sheikh Agib el Mangilak—among the more important of these district governors—may, during the sixteenth century, have helped to extend Funj rule to the Beja peoples of the Red Sea littoral. But his subsequent attempt to carve out an autonomous enclave was thwarted by the armies of the reigning *makk*, Adlan walad Aya.[91]

During the first half of the seventeenth century, the Funj sultanate reached the apparent zenith of its power. Although the Ethiopian army of Emperor Susneyos defeated the warriors of Funj in 1618/19 and conquered districts normally tributary to *makk* Rubat (*c.* 1616–1642), these reversals seem to have stimulated the growth of the sultanate's military machine. It raided along the White Nile, attacked the Shilluk, and moved west toward Kordofan. After a lengthy campaign in inhospitable territory, the Funj army conquered the inhabitants of the Nuba mountains and settled an old grievance with the Arab kingdom of Teqali. The Funj warriors took numerous prisoners, garrisoned the new provinces, and compelled the king of Teqali to pay annual tribute to Sennar. They also seem to have reclaimed territories along the upper Blue Nile from Ethiopia, and to have been widely feared in the area between the Nile and the Red Sea. But at some point during the last decades of the seventeenth century, the Funj lost control of the Dongola Reach—between the Third and the Fourth Cataracts—and with it, access to the supply of horses on which its army depended.[92]

Throughout the seventeenth century, the *makks* of Sennar welcomed a succession of seemingly notable Islamic visitors and, during the long reign of Badi Abu Duqn (*c.* 1642–1677), began to receive them in the style to which they were accustomed. His workmen constructed a great mosque, a royal palace of sun-dried brick, and two or three council chambers in which the *makk* and the "great men of the kingdom" considered their business. "Round the whole," the chronicler wrote, "he built a vast wall and made therein nine gates, and to each of the great men of his kingdom he appointed a special gate for entry or exit thereby . . . the ninth gate [being] reserved for the king himself. . . ."[93] But to Charles Poncet, the French physician who visited the Funj capital in 1699, Sennar presented itself in a rather mixed light. He wrote:

> *After holding on our journey for some time we came within sight of the city of Sennar, and were charm'd with its pleasant situation. This city, which contains near a league and a half of compass, is very populous, but has nothing of neatness*

[91] "Chronicle," in MacMichael, *History*, p. 360. A. E. D. Penn (ed.), "Traditional Stories of the 'Abdullab Tribe," *Sudan Notes and Records*, XVII (1934), pp. 61–64.
[92] See Crawford, *Fung Kingdom*, pp. 180–195.
[93] "Chronicle," in MacMichael, *History*, p. 363.

and besides is ill govern'd. They number in it near a hundred thousand souls. . . . The houses are only one storey high and are ill built; but the flat roof which covers them is very convenient. As to the suburbs, they are only wretched cottages, cover'd with reeds. The King's palace is surrounded with high walls of brick bak'd in the sun, but has nothing regular in it. You see nothing but a confus'd heap of buildings, without symmetry or beauty. The apartments of this palace are furnish'd richly enough with large carpets, after the manner of the Levant. . . . [The courtyard was] pav'd with little square tiles of different colours, after the manner of fayence.[94]

Poncet spent three months in Sennar. He observed the two important markets, where Funj merchants sold elephants' tusks, tamarind, civet, tobacco, gold dust, and slaves—the strongest of which were each worth ten écus or, in modern terms, about $135. From abroad, particularly from Arabia, the Funj imported spices, paper, brass, iron and iron ware, vermillion, arsenic, glass beads, and black with which to blacken their eyes and eyebrows. They also fished for pearls in the Red Sea. Ordinarily they drank coffee and a type of thick and, to Poncet, "ill-tasting" beer. While he called the people "naturally crafty and deceitful . . . and wedded to Mahometanism," he was pleased by the upper-class women:

The women of quality are cover'd with a silken vest, or of very fine calico, with large sleeves which hang down to the ground. Their hair is twisted, and set out with rings of silver, copper, brass, and ivory, or of glass of different colours. . . . Their arms, legs, ears, and even nostrils are cover'd with these rings.[95]

Badi el Ahmar ruled Sennar during Poncet's visit. Of him the French physician wrote: "He was black, but well shap'd and of a majestick presence; not having thick lips nor flat nose, like the rest of his subjects." He also possessed a piercing intelligence.

[Badi] was seated upon a rich bed under a canopy, with his legs across, after the oriental fashion; and round him twenty old men, seated after the same manner, but somewhat lower. He was cloath'd with a long vest of silk, embroider'd with gold, and girt with a kind of scarf made of fine calico. He had a white turban on his head. The old men were clad much after the same manner.[96]

According to Poncet, the *makk* regularly held councils in the mornings and evenings in order to see that justice was done to his subjects and that no crime went unpunished. For diversion he held shooting parties and contests with his nobles.

During the reign of Badi (*c.* 1680–1715), the Funj rulers began to lose control of the sultanate. As the chronicler wrote, "he was the first Funj king against

---

[94] "The Journey of Charles Jacques Poncet from Cairo into Abyssinia and Back," in William Foster (ed.), *The Red Sea and Adjacent Countries at the Close of the Seventeenth Century* (London, 1949), p. 102.

[95] *Ibid.*, p. 106.

[96] *Ibid.*, p. 103. Poncet does not mention the name of the reigning *makk*, but the description accords well with what we know of Badi. See Crawford, *Fung Kingdom*, p. 199.

whom a section of his people revolted." [97] Perhaps in 1705, after the young *makk* had angered some of the sheikhs of his court, a part of the army revolted, crowned a new *makk*, and inflicted a number of serious defeats upon the royalists. But Badi finally contrived to rout the rebels at a village on the right bank of the Blue Nile, north of Sennar.[98]

Despite the monarch's victory, this battle marked the beginning of the army's increasingly frequent interference in domestic politics. In about 1718, it ousted Badi's son and successor, the "frivolous and immoral" Ounsa, and thus ended the unbroken line of Funj kings. In his stead, the army installed Nul, a maternal relative of the royal family who received appointment because of his good sense and his religious orthodoxy. "And indeed," the chronicler said, "the common opinion of him was justified, for he showed himself just and steady in his conduct, and in his days the people had complete rest." [99] His son Badi abu Shelukh (*c.* 1723–1761/62) was, however, the last *makk* actually to rule the sultanate. During his day, the powerful Funj army, spearheaded by its regiments of Nuban Arabs, humbled the soldiers of Ethiopia (1743/44) and conquered Kordofan (*c.* 1747–1760) in a series of impressive campaigns. But at some point during these years, Badi forfeited the affection and the loyalty of his subjects. The chronicle said that he refused the advice of his vizier and thereafter changed many of the laws and the customs of the sultanate. He replaced the Funj nobles with Nubans, "consented to an evil policy of plunder and slaughter," and, in general, committed deeds of injustice and malice which "alienated the hearts of his people, and especially of the Funj nobility. . . ." [100] Thus, at the conclusion of the Kordofan wars, the warrior Muhammad Abu Likaylik, who commanded the crack Nuban regiments, besieged Sennar, ousted Badi, installed the first of a long line of puppet kings, and gave the reins of government to indigenous Hamaj sheikhs.

The Hamaj sheikhs ruled what remained of the Funj sultanate for sixty years. Until his death in 1776/77, Sheikh Muhammad controlled Sennar, where his brother acted as grand vizier, from Kordofan.[101] Together they and their successors made and unmade *makks*. But after the time of Sheikh Badi walad Regeb (*c.* 1777–1780), the sultanate fractured into a number of antagonistic parts. The Funj nobility fought the Hamaj regents; Kordofan, Shendi, 'Abdullab Gerri, and other principalities obtained their independence and, by so doing, hastened the breakup of the sultanate. Only Muhammad wad 'Adlan (1808–1821), the last of the Hamaj regents, was able to slow this decline. He brutally consolidated what little remained of the old sultanate, and then, shortly after his assassination in 1821, the Turco-Egyptian army of Muhammad 'Ali swept up the Nile to occupy Sennar and Kordofan.

---

[97] "Chronicle," in MacMichael, *History*, p. 363.

[98] *Ibid.*, pp. 363–364; *Tabakat wad Dayfulla*, in *ibid.*, pp. 249–250.

[99] "Chronicle," in *ibid.*, p. 364.

[100] *Ibid.*, pp. 365–366.

[101] But James Bruce, *Travels*, p. 391, who visited Sennar in 1772, said only that Sheikh Muhammad "maintained himself . . . independent of the king." Muhammad may therefore not have subordinated the *makks* completely until after Bruce's visit (see *ibid.*, p. 398).

The Negroes are so wilful and loth to leave their own country that they have often leap'd out of the canoes, boat and ship, into the sea, and kept under water till they were drowned, to avoid being taken up and saved by our boats, which pursued them; they having a more dreadful apprehension of Barbadoes than we can have of hell, tho' in reality they live much better there than in their own country; but home is home. . . .

—*Captain Thomas Phillips, 1693*

5 TROPICAL AFRICA AND THE WIDER WORLD: COMMERCIAL CONNECTIONS AND THE GROWTH OF THE SLAVE TRADE, 1600–1800

From the early years of the seventeenth century, the merchants and navies of other European nations successfully challenged the supremacy of Portugal along the coasts of the Atlantic and Indian oceans. The Dutch, the English, the Scots, the French, the Danes, the Swedes, and the Prussians all assumed a part of the lucrative commerce that Portugal had hitherto largely monopolized. The great national companies superseded the "interlopers" or buccaneers who had raided Portuguese and Spanish shipping for private gain during the sixteenth century and began, despite the antagonism of Spain, to trade directly with the New World. The newer naval powers were thus able to halt a long-term drain of specie and to reverse an unfavorable balance of payments position that, at the expense of France, England, and the cities of northern Europe, at first had benefited Portugal and Spain and, during the seventeenth century, the United Provinces of the Netherlands. Thereafter, England and France both tried to turn their American and African colonies into exclusive, protected markets and sources of raw materials. By so doing, they, like the earlier colonial powers, became committed economically to a system of tropical production that relied upon supplies of slave labor.

The Spaniards had been the first to take Africans to the New World. After learning that the indigenous inhabitants and their own settlers would not or could not successfully work the mines or the plantations of tropical America, they turned increasingly to Africa for assistance. The labor of African slaves thereafter enabled Spanish and, eventually, Portuguese, Dutch, English, and French settlers to exploit the virgin lands and mineral riches of the Americas and to grow sugar, tobacco, coffee, indigo, cotton, and a host of other crops profitably. Thus, Europe's exploitation of America presupposed an abundance of unskilled African laborers that naturally gave to the slave trade the status and the style of big business. During the seventeenth and eighteenth centuries, the nations of Europe competed among themselves for the black cargoes of Africa; they built forts or otherwise established themselves on the shores of Africa; they befriended indigenous middlemen or chiefs and encouraged them to enslave their fellows for shipment overseas. Until the nineteenth century, Europe was interested in tropical Africa primarily for the sake of America.

I. The Pursuit of Comparative Advantage

The export of slaves overseas began in 1441, when Nuno Tristão and Antão Gonçales captured a dozen Africans near Cape Blanc. Earlier, African chiefs and merchants had sold other Africans to Arabic- or Berber-speaking traders who in turn had offered them for sale in the markets of the Maghreb, the Levant, and Europe. Somehow African slaves even found themselves in China and India. The *Periplus of the Erythraean Sea* reported that the residents of the ports of northeastern Africa had traded slaves during the first century A.D.; before the end of the ninth century, slaves from East Africa had revolted in Basra, at the head of the Persian Gulf. But the export of slaves from Africa in pre-European times was generally incidental to the main currents of commerce. Indeed, there is little evidence of an extensive emigration of slaves from East Africa between the tenth and the seventeenth centuries; ivory was a more highly valued commodity. Similarly, the number of Africans forcibly transported from the Western Sudan to Fez and Cairo remained small. The trans-Saharan demand was never very great (Leo Africanus noted that one horse was worth fifteen or twenty Africans) because there were no plantations to be tilled and few mines to be exploited.[1]

Elsewhere in Africa, where there had been little contact with aliens, the buying and selling of humans was virtually unknown. In Angola, as late as the seventeenth century, the Portuguese learned to their astonishment that the Ndombe were unaccustomed "to sell each other." [2] Nonetheless, the institution of "slavery"—but not the export of slaves—probably existed throughout tropical Africa long before the arrival of the Portuguese in the fifteenth century. Africans captured in war or otherwise held hostage might have become the slaves of the chief or other members of the victorious tribe. Their masters expected captives to serve loyally—usually in combat—but slaves usually lost their mobility only.

---

[1] See G. S. P. Freeman-Grenville, "Swahili Literature and the History and Archaeology of the East African Coast," *Journal of the East African Swahili Committee*, 28/2 (1958), pp. 18–19; Leo Africanus (trans. John Pory), *The History and Description of Africa* (London, 1896), III, p. 833.

[2] Gladwyn Murray Childs, *Umbundu Kinship and Character* (London, 1949), p. 192.

They were free to marry, till their own fields, move freely within the tribal dominion, and live relatively normal lives among peoples possessing institutions similar to their own and holding analogous beliefs and customs. Indigenous society assimilated slaves and allowed them to rise to positions of power and influence. Occasionally, slaves even led revolutions and overthrew existing dynasties. Only infrequently were these slaves sold in the markets or transported to unfamiliar lands. The lot of the slave in Africa—compared with that of his descendant, the American field hand—was unfortunate and limiting, but rarely intolerable. An African freed slave later sought to impress the distinction upon his readers:

> *Those prisoners* [of war] *which were not sold or redeemed we kept as slaves: but, how different was their condition from that of the slaves in the West Indies! With us they do no more work than other members of the community, even their master. Their food, cloathing, and lodging, were nearly the same as ours, except that they were not permitted to eat with those who were free born; and there were scarce any other difference between them than a superior degree of importance which the head of a family possesses in our state, and that authority which, as such, he exercises over every part of his household. Some of these slaves have even slaves under them, as their property, and for their own use.*[3]

After 1441, however, the institution of African slavery was transformed with profound effect.

The quickening of europe's interest

In the years that followed the initial enslavement of Africans by Portuguese seamen, caravels carried them in ever greater numbers to the European ports of Lisbon and Lagos, where they were auctioned. There, and throughout Portugal, they received a warm welcome from employers short of willing agricultural and household labor. Both the church—in order to save "heathen" souls—and the monarchy encouraged this traffic, the ship captains of Portugal thereafter seeking vigorously by capture or purchase—depending upon the availability of slaves along the western shores of Africa—to meet the growing demand. They, and many of those Portuguese who subsequently bought Africans, treated their slaves humanely enough to mitigate somewhat the anxieties of transportation and the deprivation of individual freedom. In general, African slaves probably enjoyed greater privileges in Portugal than in America. Even so, Zurara's doleful description of the immediate human consequences of the slave trade deserves quotation:

> *But what heart could be so hard as not to be pierced with piteous feeling to see that company* [of slaves unloaded]*? For some kept their heads low and their faces bathed in tears, looking one upon another; others stood groaning very dolorously, looking up to the height of heaven, fixing their eyes upon it, crying out loudly, as if asking help of the Father of Nature; others struck their faces with the palms of*

[3] Olaudah Equiano, *The Interesting Narrative of the Life of Olaudah Equiano or Gustavus Vassa, the African* (Norwich, 1794), pp. 17–18.

their hands, throwing themselves at full length upon the ground; others made their lamentations in the manner of a dirge, after the custom of their country. And though we could not understand the words of their language, the sound of it right well accorded with the measure of their sadness. But to increase their sufferings still more, there now arrived those who had charge of the division of the captives, and who began to separate one from another, in order to make an equal partition of the fifths; and then was it needful to part fathers from sons, husbands from wives, brothers from brothers. No respect was shewn either to friends or relations, but each fell where his lot took him.

O powerful fortune, that with thy wheels doest and undoest, compassing the matters of this world as pleaseth thee, do thou at least put before the eyes of that miserable race some understanding of matters to come; they may receive some consolation in the midst of their great sorrow. And you who are so busy in making that division of the captives, look with pity upon so much misery; and see how they cling one to the other, so that you can hardly separate them.

And who could finish that partition without very great toil? For as often as they had placed them in one part the sons, seeing their fathers in another, rose with great energy and rushed over to them; the mothers clasped their other children in their arms, and threw themselves flat on the ground with them; receiving blows with little pity for their own flesh, if only they might not be torn from them.

And so troublously they finished the partition. . . .[4]

The Portuguese early discovered that slaves were most readily available along the so-called Gold and Slave Coasts of the Gulf of Guinea. The Grain Coast, partially on account of its dangerous shores and the sparse nature of indigenous settlement there, proved a secondary source, particularly after the end of the sixteenth century. To the south, the Cameroun region was increasingly involved in the trade, while Angola remained a rich field from the heyday of the *manikongo* Afonso until the late nineteenth century. East Africa and Madagascar became thoroughly enmeshed in the colonial trade only later, when Americans and Portuguese sought new sources of slaves. By the late seventeenth century, Europeans were also exporting slaves to the Mascarene Islands, and Arabs and Asians were engaged in transporting them to India, Persia, and Arabia.

The discovery of America added a new dimension to the demand for slaves. In 1502, partially at the behest of Bishop Bartolomé de las Casas, Africans began to replace Carib Indians in the plantation and pearl-fishing economy of Hispaniola.[5] At first many of these new laborers were trained and baptized in Iberia before being transported across the Atlantic Ocean. From 1513, however, the Spanish kings licensed the importation of Africans directly to America. The prevailing winds and currents made these voyages easy for sailing ships, and such voyages soon became sources of great profit for the entrepreneurs of

---

[4] Gomes Eanes de Zurara (trans. Charles Raymond Beazley and Edgar Prestage), *The Chronicle of the Discovery and Conquest of Guinea* (London, 1896), I, pp. 81–82 [xxv].

[5] Casas later changed his mind. See Georges Scelle, *La Traite négrière aux Indes de Castile: contrats et traités d'Asiento* (Paris, 1906), I, p. 122; Charles R. Boxer, *Salvador de Sá and the Struggle for Brazil and Angola, 1602–1686* (London, 1952), pp. 122, 236–237.

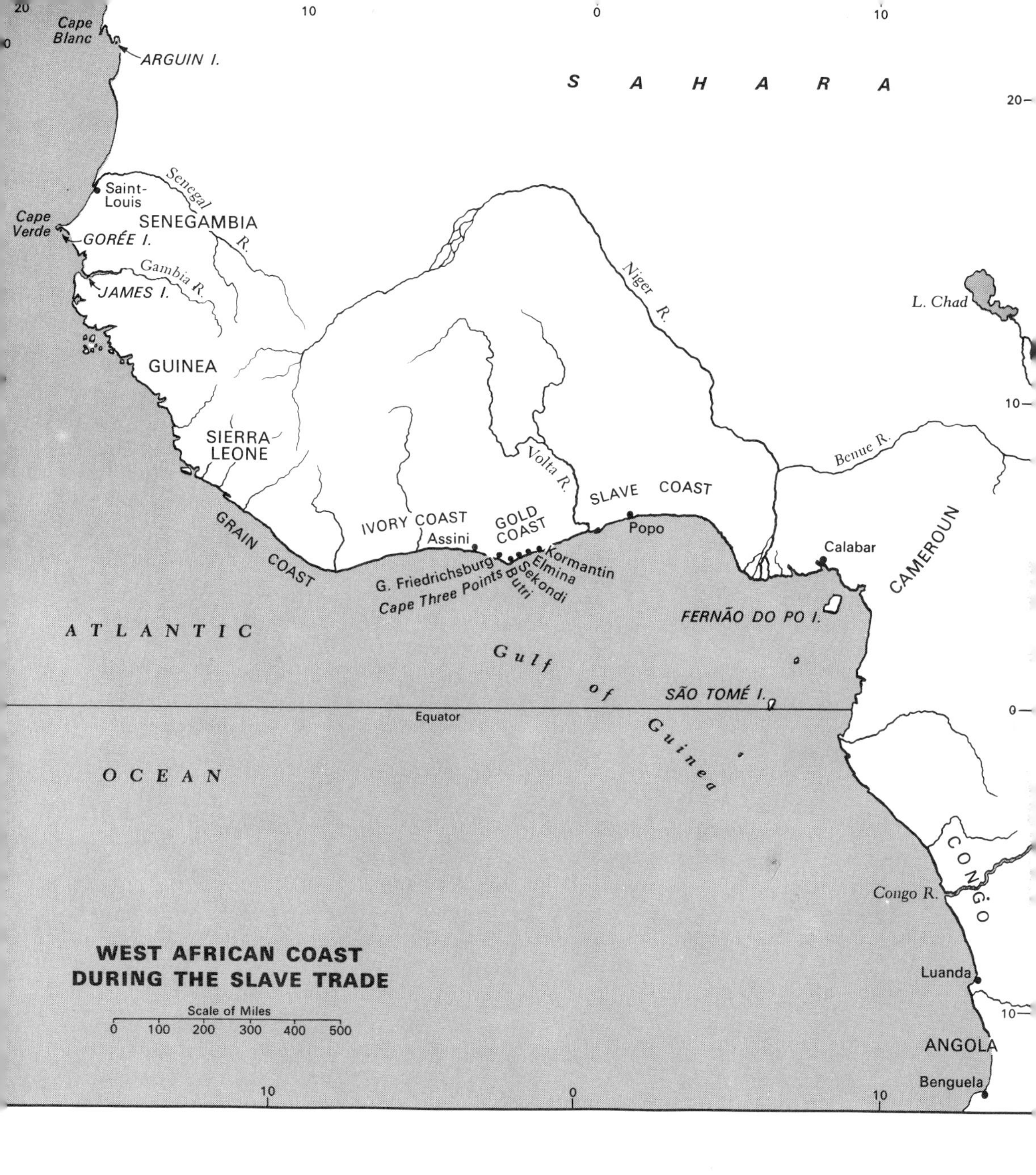

the day. Portuguese slavers meanwhile supplied the planters of Brazil and, unofficially, the mines of New Spain and the Andes with African laborers. The trade grew only gradually, however, until the last decades of the sixteenth century, when the American demand for slaves far outstripped the available supply. In 1593, Spain gave to the Portuguese merchant Pedro Gomes Reynal the exclusive privilege of importing slaves into its American colonies. He paid 900,000 ducats for the contract and promised to deliver 38,250 slaves in nine

Dutch ships trading along the Guinea coast. The engraving shows African merchants, apparently with satanic horns, the conveyance of goods from lighter to shore through the surf, and the local chief's customs shed. (De Bry, *Indiae Orientalis,* Part VI, Frankfurt, 1604)

years at an annual rate of 4,250, of which at least 3,500 were to be landed alive. He agreed that all the slaves would be "fresh from Africa"; mulattoes, Turks, and "Moors" were unacceptable.[6]

The captains and entrepreneurs of Portugal obtained slaves from numberless, scattered suppliers. But Gorée, Elmina, São Tomé, and Luanda were the main centers. The foundations of Angola in particular rested upon its trade in humans; in 1560, Roman Catholic priests "doubted that the people of the kingdom of Angola could be made Catholics unless the King [of Portugal] would allow the [slave] trade." [7] In those areas of sixteenth-century Angola that they dominated —Luanda and a wedge of territory about 150 miles long—Portuguese administrators enslaved and transported Africans as a matter of course. Local wars replenished the supply, and the needs of Brazil remained uppermost in the mind of the government. Early in the seventeenth century, however, the Dutch began to threaten Portugal's position throughout the Atlantic basin. Their mariners seized Portuguese vessels on the high seas, bombarded settlements along the African littoral, and established a fort on the Gold Coast. Furthermore,

[6] Elizabeth Donnan (ed.), *Documents Illustrative of the History of the Slave Trade to America* (Washington, 1930), I, pp. 17, 41–42. In the late sixteenth century, a ducat could buy about three chickens or six pounds of salt pork. Twenty-five pounds of dried codfish cost the equivalent of four ducats and a lamb, three. A ducat was a unit of account equivalent to 375 maravedis.

[7] Quoted in Childs, *Kinship,* p. 193.

their privateers captured a part of the slave traffic between Brazil and Angola and, in 1637, the Dutch navy conquered northeastern Brazil and Elmina on the Gold Coast. In order to ensure a steady supply from Angola—Brazil clearly depended economically upon the slaves of Angola—the Dutch added Luanda to their overseas dominions in 1641. Benguela fell in the same year. To the north, the United Provinces of the Netherlands also conquered all of the Portuguese bases from São Tomé to Arguin.[8]

Although Portugal lost its pre-eminent commercial position in West Africa, it soon regained control of Angola and Brazil. In 1648, troops commanded by the Brazilian landowner and admiral Salvador Correia de Sá e Benavides ousted the Dutch from Benguela and Luanda. His associates reclaimed northeastern Brazil in 1654. Sá renewed the flow of slaves to Brazil and rapidly sought to reimpose Portuguese standards throughout the colony.[9] He punished disloyal chiefs—even Afonso II of the Kongo was brought under direct administration—and extended the influence of Portugal to outlying districts. Moreover, in order to enlarge the effective limits of the colony and acquire greater numbers of slaves easily, he began a twenty-year war against the main independent African kingdoms. Portuguese troops defeated the Ndongo and the Kongolese in 1670/71 and humbled the people of Matamba during the subsequent decade. Sá's rule inaugurated an era of unparalleled prosperity in Portuguese Angola: the trade in slaves subsequently provided Lusitanian officials and merchants with great wealth and temporarily transformed Angola into little more than an appendage of Brazil.

Following the Dutch lead, a number of European nations competed during the seventeenth century for the produce of Africa. On the Gold Coast, after the Dutch West India Company had ousted the Portuguese from Elmina and had begun the construction of two new forts at Butri and Sekondi, a Swedish company, backed by Dutch capital, built three "lodges" and traded energetically between 1642 and 1657/58. In the latter years of this span, Danes captured the Swedish "lodges" and inaugurated their long period of influence on the Gold Coast. Later, in 1682/83, Friedrich, the elector of Brandenburg, sponsored a company that established settlements east of Axim. (Earlier, the German Duchy of Courland had traded with the peoples of Senegambia.) But the Prussian entrepôts proved expensive to maintain and commercially unproductive. In 1720, Brandenburg, which had now become Prussia, withdrew from its African venture and abandoned Gross-Friedrichsburg and Fort Sophie Louise to the Dutch.[10]

Norman merchants sailing individually or on behalf of commercial associa-

---

[8] Boxer, *de Sá*, pp. 46–51, 240–241; W. Walton Claridge, *A History of the Gold Coast and Ashanti* (London, 1915), I, pp. 80–89.

[9] Boxer, *de Sá*, pp. 273–276.

[10] Claridge, *History*, pp. 101–234; Arnold Walter Lawrence, *Trade Castles and Forts of West Africa* (London, 1963), pp. 223–224; Waldemar Westergaard, *The Danish West Indies Under Company Rule* (New York, 1917), p. 21; Mathew Nathan, "The Gold Coast at the End of the Seventeenth Century Under the Danes and the Dutch," *Journal of the African Society*, IV (1904), pp. 1–32; W. J. Varley, "The Castles and Forts of the Gold Coast," *Transactions of the Gold Coast and Togoland Historical Society*, I (1952), pp. 2–3.

Fort Elmina and Gross-Friedrichsburg. (J. Barbot, *Description of the Coasts of North and South Guinea,* in Churchill, *Collection,* London, 1732)

tions demonstrated a French interest in the African trade by sailing to Senegambia early in the seventeenth century. After 1626, three or four small ships traded annually up the Senegal and Gambia rivers and, in 1634/35, King Louis XIII licensed two commercial syndicates for the African trade, sanctioning voyages as far as Cape Lopez. From Senegambia and Guinea the two companies chiefly exported gum, millet, and slaves. In 1664, however, Jean-Baptiste Colbert, Louis XIV's finance minister, created the first of the great French trading organizations, the Compagnie des Indes Occidentales, thus initiating a profound reassessment of French aims and activities in West Africa.[11]

[11] Prosper Cultru, *Les Origines de l'Afrique occidentale: histoire du Sénégal du XVe siècle à 1870* (Paris, 1910), pp. 37–56; Stewart Lea Mims, *Colbert's West India Policy* (New Haven, 1912), pp. 68–69.

Colbert primarily wanted to supply the French sugar colonies in the West Indies with laborers transported from Africa in French bottoms. He therefore sought desperately and vainly to exclude the Dutch from the carrying trade, but at no time in the seventeenth century could the various French companies obtain slaves in sufficient quantity to satisfy the needs of their planters. Even after taking Arguin and Gorée from the Dutch in 1677/78 and turning their attention toward the Gold and Slave Coasts—where Africans generally could be obtained with ease—the French merchants remained unsuccessful. Dutch, English, and Portuguese competition proved too strong. Consequently, the French merchants concentrated their energies upon Senegambia, where they traded beads, brandy, and textiles for ivory, wax, pepper, dyewood, and gold. They established an important center at Saint-Louis, near the mouth of the Senegal River, and traded regularly with a network of factories upstream and down the coast toward the Gambia. But, despite royal backing and the efforts of several able administrators, the five French companies formed during the last half of the seventeenth century all failed to duplicate the Dutch mercantile successes.[12] It remained for the Compagnie Royale du Sénégal, Cap Nord, et Côte d'Afrique, to give meaning to the French presence in Africa after its incorporation in 1696.

During the seventeenth century, the English were the chief competitors of the Dutch.[13] As early as 1619, the sea captain George Thompson ventured up the Gambia River at the behest of the Governor and Company of Adventurers of London Trading to Gynney and Bynney. Richard Jobson sailed up the same river in 1620/21 and, upon his return, foretold a mutually profitable trade if the merchants of England were willing to respect and to deal fairly and openly with Africans.[14] The Adventurers exported a little gold and redwood from Sierra Leone, founded the first English post at Kormantin in the Gold Coast in 1631 and, thereafter, began to traffic in slaves. But not until the 1660's, after the Restoration had ushered in a period of political stability and had thereby encouraged English merchants again to look outward, and after the very profitable introduction of sugar cane cultivation into the West Indies had sharply increased the demand for slaves, did Englishmen enter the African trade vigorously and in comparatively large numbers. Backed by the Duke of York (later King James II), the Company of Royal Adventurers of England Trading to Africa sought gold and slaves and, by the terms of its Royal Charter (1663), obtained exclusive commercial rights to all of the western shores of Africa. In return, the Company promised each year to supply England's American colo-

---

[12] A detailed account of French activities in Senegambia during this period is contained in Abdoulaye Ly, *La Compagnie du Sénégal* (Paris, 1958), pp. 87–214.

[13] For England's earlier involvement, see Alice M. Kleist, "The English African Trade Under the Tudors," *Transactions of the Historical Society of Ghana*, III (1957), pp. 137–150.

[14] Richard Jobson, *The Golden Trade, or, a Discovery of the River Gambra, and the Golden Trade of the Aethiopians* (London, 1932 [first published, 1623]), pp. 210–212. For an account of the first English explorations of the hinterland of Senegambia, particularly Bambouk, see Thora G. Stone, "The Journey of Cornelius Hodges in Senegambia, 1689–90," *The English Historical Review*, XXXIX (1924), pp. 89–95.

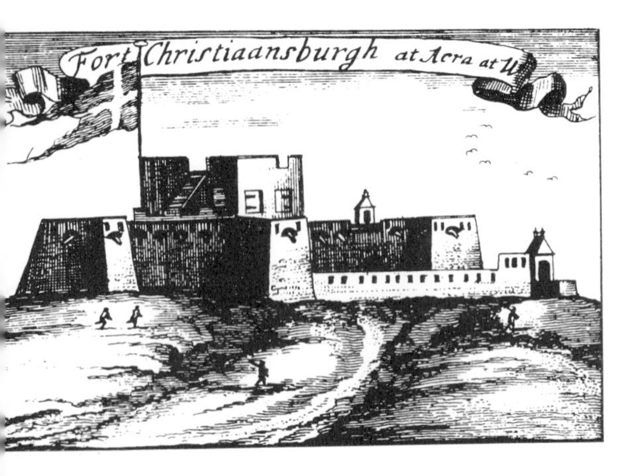

Christiansborg Castle and Fort James. (J. Barbot, *Description of the Coasts of North and South Guinea,* in Churchill, *Collection,* London, 1732)

nial possessions with three thousand slaves.[15] It occupied James Island, in the Gambia River, traded along the shores of Sierra Leone, and used the fort at Kormantin and a new one at Cape Coast. But the Dutch opposed the English visitors and, between 1663 and 1665, the two European nations fought an undeclared war from Cape Verde to Elmina. Hostilities increased between 1665 and 1667, the formal period of acknowledged enmity which bankrupted the Royal Adventurers and sharply reduced its influence in Senegambia and on the Gold Coast.

For the remainder of the seventeenth and the first part of the eighteenth centuries, the Royal African Company expressed England's commercial interests in western Africa. From its inception in 1672, the Company sought vainly to make its monopoly pay on the grand scale pioneered elsewhere in the world by similar trading organizations. It acquired the forts, factories, and retail outlets of the Royal Adventurers and exchanged woolens, textiles, beads, iron bars, guns, brass ware, cowrie shells, brandy, and hundreds of other European or Asian commodities for the gold, ivory, dyewood, hides, wax, and slaves of Africa. The Company transported the slaves directly to England's American and West Indian colonies—it delivered about ninety thousand between 1673 and 1711—and carried the other products of Africa to England.[16] In Africa, the Company also sponsored the cultivation of indigo and the manufacture of potash. It tried to develop a trade in locally made cotton cloth between Sierra Leone and the Gold Coast. It endeavored to stimulate new wants and satisfy the changing commercial tastes of its African customers. But the settled trade—from cantonments on the Gambia River or along the Guinea, Gold, and Slave

[15] See the declarations of the Company in Donnan, *Documents,* pp. 156–161. Cf. George Frederick Zook, *The Company of Royal Adventurers Trading into Africa* (Lancaster, Pa., 1919), pp. 82–83.

[16] K. G. Davies, *The Royal African Company* (London, 1957), pp. 213–232, 363.

Coasts—proved costly, and the so-called ship trade, which was carried on elsewhere by itinerant captains, was subject to continual uncertainties. Moreover, although slaves could be purchased, transported, and sold profitably, African merchants controlled the supply and successfully resisted every European attempt to engross or to rationalize it. Thus, because the trade was so marginal and their own positions so tenuous, the English, Dutch, French, and Danish companies (individual Portuguese, Spanish, Scottish, and Swedish sea captains also continued to interest themselves in the West African trade) all competed for the products and the custom of Africa. Throughout the seventeenth and eighteenth centuries, they each fought to keep merchants of other nationalities, and interlopers of their own, from taking any part of what each considered its own rightful trade. For all, however, the merchandising of slaves was, economically, the consuming passion.

II. The Export of Human Livestock

Despite the risks involved, the American demand for slaves was such that the transport of Africans thither appears to have enriched numberless white entrepreneurs during the sixteenth through nineteenth centuries. The available statistics are random and unsatisfactory. They suggest, however, the profits available to slave traders and illustrate both the importance and the scope of what was, after all, big business. John Hawkins, for example, admitted "prosperous successe and much gaine to himselfe" after selling African slaves to West Indian planters in 1562/63. His second voyage proved equally rewarding; according to Philip II's Spanish envoy to London, it "brought him 60 per cent profit." [17] During the same period, Portuguese slavers purchased Angolans or Dahomeans for a few yards of cloth and eventually sold them individually for four or five hundred pesos.[18] In the late seventeenth century, owners evidently paid the captains of English slave ships about £825 per voyage.[19] At that time, a cargo of "young" undernourished Africans from the Gold and Slave Coasts fetched £14 a head at Barbados. And in 1694, the Royal African Company valued each slave lost during the hazardous journey to America at about £10.[20] During the eighteenth century—when slaves from Senegambia were worth at least £20 each—traders from New England discovered that "niggers" could be sold at Paramaribo, in Surinam, for 150 to 200 "gilders" apiece, or about five times the price of a horse.[21] Between 1783 and 1793, ships registered in Liverpool transported more

[17] "The First Voyage of John Hawkins," in Richard Hakluyt (ed.), *The Principal Navigations, Voyages, Traffiques, and Discoveries of the English Nation* (Glasgow, 1903), X, pp. 7–8; Donnan, *Documents*, p. 59.

[18] Boxer, *de Sá*, p. 225.

[19] "Edwyn Stede and Stephen Gascoigne to the Royal African Company," in Donnan, *Documents*, p. 331.

[20] "William Hardringe and Nicholas Prideaux to the Royal African Company," in *ibid.*, p. 391; Thomas Phillips, *A Journal of a Voyage Made in the Hannibal . . . from England . . . to Barbadoes*, in Awnsham and John Churchill, *A Collection of Voyages and Travels* (London, 1732), VI, p. 236.

[21] George C. Mason, "The African Slave Trade in Colonial Times," *The American Historical*

than 300,000 slaves to America; the landed value of the slaves—which included a sizeable net profit—was £15,186,850.[22] In 1804, a single cargo of 342 slaves fetched £24,000 in the West Indies. Twenty-three years later, if Canot's account is true, 217 slaves landed at Cuba "yielded a clear profit on the voyage of forty-one thousand four hundred and thirty-eight dollars." [23]

The commerce of forts, creeks, and lagoons

The way in which the slave trade was organized in Africa is not yet known in detail. At first the African coastal peoples satisfied the European demand by selling either their own slaves or persons who had in some manner forfeited their individual freedom. When the demand outran the immediately available supply, however, African chiefs and merchants naturally sought to satisfy their customers by tapping new sources. Bartering cloth, cowrie shells, iron, or brass ware for individuals, indigenous entrepreneurs assembled small human caravans up-country and then marched them to the coast. On these occasions, the merchants often gathered slaves on behalf of a tribal chief who, in turn, protected the caravan and obtained a sizeable share of the resultant profits. Kidnapping was not an infrequent occurrence:

> Adam (A Congo) . . . boy . . . [relates that he] *came from a vast distance inland, was waylaid and stole, in the path about three miles from his own village, by one of his countrymen. It was early in the morning, and the man hid him all day in the woods, and marched him in the night. He was conducted in this manner for a month, and then sold to another Black man for a gun, some powder and shot, and a quantity of salt. He was sold a second time for a keg of brandy. His last-mentioned purchaser bought several other boys in the same manner, and when he had collected twenty, sent them down to the sea-coast, where they were sold to a captain of a ship.*[24]

The demand for slaves encouraged tribal wars. Indeed, Africans captured on the battlefield provided the main source of slaves shipped from the Gulf of Guinea during the eighteenth and nineteenth centuries. European factors resident along the coasts of Africa therefore generally bemoaned the absence of warfare in the interior. One of the more perceptive foreign residents stated the problem with simplicity:

> *It sometimes happens that when the In-land Countries are at Peace, here are no Slaves to be got: So that the Trade of this Place is utterly uncertain; and it only*

Record, I (1872), p. 316; Malachy Postlethwayt, *The Importance of the African Expedition Considered* (London, 1758), p. 73.

[22] Anonymous, *Liverpool and Slavery* (Liverpool, 1884), pp. 38–39, 100–117. See also George Francis Dow (ed.), *Slave Ships and Slaving* (Salem, 1927), p. 110; Robert Norris, *Memoirs of the Reign of Bossa Ahádee . . . and a Short Account of the African Slave Trade* (London, 1789), pp. 163–164. But see Davies, *Company*, pp. 335–336.

[23] Theodore Canot (ed. Malcolm Cowley), *Adventures of an African Slaver* (New York, 1935), p. 106; Dow, *Slave Ships*, p. 110. For a general discussion of this subject, see Eric Williams, *Capitalism and Slavery* (Chapel Hill, 1944), pp. 36–37.

[24] Bryan Edwards, *The History, Civil and Commercial, of the British Colonies in the West Indies* (London, 1794), II, p. 107. See also James Field Stanfield, *The Guinea Voyage* (Edinburgh, 1807), p. 61; Willem Bosman, *A New and Accurate Description of the Coast of Guinea* (London, 1705), p. 331; Equiano, *Narrative*, p. 32.

serves to touch at in our Passage this way, without depending on any thing from it.[25]

In order to eliminate these periods of peace and stabilize a trade subject to severe fluctuations, the European merchants often promised to give an annual allotment of guns to chiefs who would agree in turn to make war and provide white shippers with a yearly quota of captives. Never, however, were Africans willing to permit Europeans to interfere drastically with what amounted to a fixed commercial routine.[26]

In the Gold Coast, the presence of forts and castles permitted Europeans to pay fixed prices and accumulate a supply of slaves over a period of several months, or at least until an appropriate vessel appeared offshore. Most of the factors imprisoned female slaves within the castle courtyard and lodged male slaves beneath its outer walls. Thus they were able to diminish the expensive delays occasioned elsewhere by irregular supplies and suppliers.

Throughout most of the rest of western Africa, indigenous merchants maintained marshaling yards and *barracoons,* or warehouses, where slaves were fattened, oiled, and otherwise readied for white ship captains. Having anchored their ships and proceeded ashore, these slavers palavered with the local vendors. In 1699, for example, before James Barbot could collect slaves at Bandy, near Calabar, he conversed at length with the local merchants. Barbot wrote:

We fill'd them with drams of brandy and bowls of punch till night, at such a rate, that they all, being about fourteen with the king, had such loud clamorous tattling and discourses among themselves, as . . . were hardly to be endured.

Thus, with much patience, all our matters were adjusted indifferently, after their way . . . [and] the king order'd the publick cryer to proclaim the permission to trade with us; with the noise of his trumpets, being elephant's teeth . . . we paying 16 brass rings to the fellow for his fee. . . . We gave the usual presents to the king and his officers. . . . To the . . . king a hat, a firelock, and nine bunches of beads instead of a coat. . . . [To the others] two firelocks, eight hats, and nine narrow Guinea stuffs.

We also advanced to the king . . . the value of a hundred and fifty bars of iron, in sundry goods . . . in order to repair forthwith to the inland markets.[27]

The giving of "dash" always played a crucial part in the proceedings:

. . . to know how to make presents judiciously, is a very important part of the knowledge of [trading]. When the trader comes to see your goods he wants one; and when he receives payment another. The head slaves look for dashes. The pilots both in bringing you into and taking you out of the rivers, independent of

---

[25] Bosman, *Description,* p. 327. See also Anthony Benezet, *Some Historical Account of Guinea* (London, 1788), pp. 99–101.

[26] For a demonstration of John Conny's ability to force ship captains to submit to his rule at Cape Three Points in the Gold Coast, see John Atkins, *A Voyage to Guinea, Brasil, and the West-Indies* (London, 1737), pp. 75–78. See also Hugh Archibald Wyndham, *The Atlantic and Slavery* (London, 1935), pp. 59–66, 223–227; Phillips, *Journal,* p. 206.

[27] James Barbot, "A Voyage to New Calabar," in Churchill, *Collection,* pp. 459–460. Cf. Phillips, *Journal,* p. 217.

a fixed payment, receive dashes; indeed whatever the occasion of a black man's coming on board may be, a dash is always solicited. . . .[28]

Upon the conclusion of such preliminary ceremonies, the trading parties drew up a list of agreed prices for the various categories of slaves. In Senegambia and along the Windward Coast, these prices were usually expressed in terms of Swedish iron bars. In the Gold Coast, guns, perpetuanas (woolen fabrics), and beads were the usual media of exchange, and eastward, from Popo to Luanda, merchants expressed the prices of slaves in cowries, brass and copper manillas, and textiles.[29] Foreigners placed their highest value upon strong males in their middle twenties. They also wanted women capable of breeding and, occasionally, young children.

The European traders carefully examined the slaves offered for sale. In 1694, for example, Captain Thomas Phillips bargained with the "king" who, after "exact[ing] very high" customs fees, ordered his people to sell slaves:

. . . each brought out his slaves according to his degree and quality . . . and our surgeon examin'd them well in all kinds, to see that they were sound wind and limb, making them jump, stretch out their arms swiftly, looking in their mouths to judge of their age; for the [overseers] *are so cunning, that they shave them all close before we see them, so that let them be never so old we can see no grey hairs in their heads or beards; and then having liquor'd them well and sleek with palm oil, 'tis no easy matter to know an old one from a middle-age one . . . but our greatest care of all is to buy none that are pox'd, lest they should infect the rest aboard.*[30]

Ninety-five years later, an English surgeon, who had served aboard slave ships, reported that:

When the negroes . . . are shewn to the European purchasers, they first examine them relative to their age. They then minutely inspect their persons, and inquire into the state of their health . . . if they are lame, or weak in the joints, or distorted in the back, or are narrow in the chest; in short, if they have been or are afflicted in any manner, so as to render them incapable of much labour . . . they are rejected. . . .[31]

Each captain naturally tried to fill his ship with healthy slaves who would, he hoped, survive the voyage. Before departing with his quota, the crew branded the cargo:

The Invalides *and the Maimed being thrown out . . . the Remainder are numbred, and it is entred who delivered them. In the mean while a burning Iron,*

[28] J. Smith, *Trade and Travels in the Gulph of Guinea* (London, 1851), p. 186. "Dash" connotes bribery and apparently is either a corruption of the Portuguese word *doação* ("gift" or "present"), or the Fantse *ndase*, meaning "to thank."

[29] Davies, *Company*, pp. 234–238; Atkins, *Voyage*, pp. 159–166; A. F. C. Ryder, "An Early Portuguese Trading Voyage to the Forcados River," *Journal of the Historical Society of Nigeria*, I (1959), pp. 302–319; Nicholas Owen (ed. Eveline C. Martin), *Journal of a Slave-Dealer* (London, 1930), p. 46.

[30] Phillips, *Journal*, p. 218.

[31] Alexander Falconbridge, *An Account of the Slave Trade on the Coast of Africa* (London, 1788), p. 16.

with the Arms or Name of the Companies, lyes in the Fire; with which ours are marked on the Breast. This is done that we may distinguish them from the Slaves of the English, French *or others . . . and to prevent the* Negroes *exchanging them for worse; at which they have a good Hand.*

I doubt not but this Trade seems very barbarous to you, but since it is followed by meer necessity it must go on; but we yet take all possible care that they are not burned too hard, especially the Women, who are more tender than the Men.[32]

Farther south, in Angola, the Portuguese themselves usually raided the interior for slaves. They then marched their captives to Luanda, where Portuguese merchants fattened them in special warehouses and trained them for the plantation tasks that they would later be expected to perform in Brazil. Finally, before the slaves embarked upon their voyage across the Atlantic Ocean, "they were taken to a nearby church, or other convenient place, and there baptised by a parish priest in batches of hundreds at a time."

The ceremony did not take very long. The priest said to each slave in turn, your name is Peter, yours is John, yours Francis, and so on, giving each man a piece of paper with his name written on it, putting a little salt on his tongue, and then sprinkling holy water over the crowd with a hyssop. Then a Negro interpreter addressed them as follows: 'Look, you people are already children of God; you are going to the land of the [Spanish or Portuguese] where you will learn things of the Faith. Don't think any more about where you came from, and don't eat dogs, rats, or horses—now go with a good will.' [33]

The transport of slaves to america

The profound anguish undoubtedly experienced by slaves from the moment of their capture probably intensified after they were shaved, oiled, and sold in the coastal markets. They feared the passage to America for a number of obvious reasons. Many also believed that they were being transported across the Atlantic Ocean simply to be eaten by the supposedly cannibalistic whites.[34] They viewed their transfer from continent to continent with forebodings, and the rigors of the subsequent voyage only heightened their terror and increased their suffering. The slavers simply treated humans as livestock.

Small ships of between 40 and 400 tons burthen transported Africans to America. In the eighteenth century, the most common vessel was a "snow," a square-sterned ship weighing about 140 tons. It was fifty-seven feet long, with a twenty-one foot beam, nine feet deep holds, and a between-decks space of only five feet.[35] During the same period, slavers also used larger frigates of between 200 and 400 tons. In a ship of that size, the slaves occupied a below-decks space about seventy-seven feet long and ten feet wide that was divided into separate quarters for the men and the women and children. Although

---

[32] Bosman, *Description*, pp. 363–364.
[33] Boxer, *de Sá*, pp. 230–231.
[34] Equiano, *Narrative*, p. 47; Atkins, *Voyage*, p. 175.
[35] Edmund B. D'Auvergne, *Human Livestock* (London, 1933), p. 67. See also the measurements and diagram in *Liverpool and Slavery*, pp. 30–31.

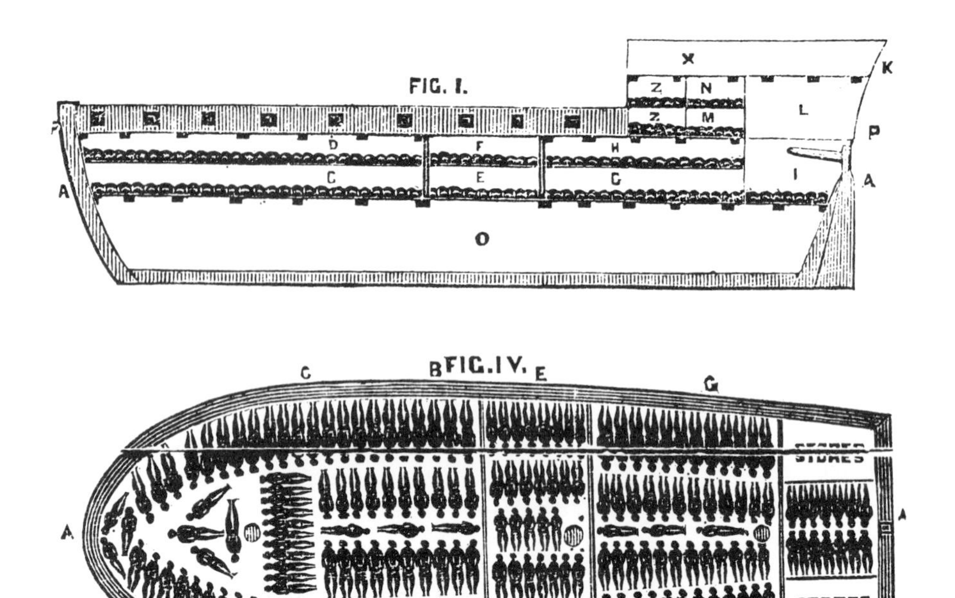

Diagram and loading plan of a slave ship. (Thomas Clarkson, "Abstract of the Evidence," delivered before the House of Commons in 1791)

they were legally allowed to carry only about 450 slaves, the captains of these larger ships often crammed their holds with as many as 1,000 captives. Smaller vessels wedged proportionally more into the limited space available.

Conditions aboard the slave ships almost defy imagination. In order to minimize the likelihood of an insurrection, slavers shackled the hands and feet of their male slaves. If the space between decks was particularly cramped, Africans often found themselves constrained to sit in each other's laps for the duration of the voyage. Sometimes—again whenever the shortage of space encouraged such expedients—captains forced their slaves to lie chained in a prone position, with one's head following another's feet. Little fresh air penetrated the slave quarters, which were consequently almost always intolerably hot. Sanitary provisions were primitive, even for the times, and surgeons responsible for the care of the cargo frequently found the dead chained to the living. One ship's surgeon wrote of slaves who fell ill:

> *The place allotted for the sick negroes is under the half deck, where they lie on the bare planks. By this means, those who are emaciated frequently have their skin, and even their flesh, entirely rubbed off, by the motion of the ship, from the prominent parts of the shoulders, elbows, and hips, so as to render the bones in those parts quite bare. And some of them, by constantly lying in the blood and mucus, that had flowed from those afflicted with the flux, and which, as before*

observed, is generally so violent as to prevent their being kept clean, have their flesh much sooner rubbed off, than those who have only to contend with the mere friction of the ship.[36]

From western Africa, slaves endured a passage to America that lasted from six to ten weeks; from eastern Africa and Madagascar, slave ships spent as long as four months at sea before reaching their destinations. During the journey, slaves often found that their opportunities for exercise were limited and that inclement weather and other contingencies frequently condemned them to long periods in cramped surroundings.[37] At the same time, their exercise often provided sport and amusement for the ship's captain.

Exercise being deemed necessary for the preservation of their health, they are sometimes obliged to dance, when the weather will permit their coming on deck. If they go about it reluctantly, or do not move with agility, they are flogged; a person standing by them all the time with a cat-o'-nine-tails in his hand for that purpose. . . . The poor wretches are frequently compelled to sing also; but when they do so, their songs are generally, as may naturally be expected, melancholy lamentations of their exile from their native country.[38]

Captains usually tried to keep their slaves alive during the voyage to America. Ships could rarely, however, carry both slaves and the requisite supplies of food and water. Moreover, good meal, or an adequate supply of yams, was expensive. Some captains therefore relied upon horse beans, which Africans appear to have detested.[39] Not surprisingly, Africans often refused to eat, in order to defy the slavers. Whenever they prolonged their obstinacy, however, captains used the *speculum oris*—an ingenious instrument sold in Liverpool and London—to pry open their mouths. During the late eighteenth century, a ship's surgeon witnessed other methods:

Upon the negroes refusing to take sustenance I have seen coals of fire, glowing hot, put on a shovel, and placed so near their lips, as to scorch and burn them. And this has been accompanied with threats, of forcing them to swallow the coals, if they any longer persisted in refusing to eat. These means have generally had the desired effect. I have also been credibly informed, that a certain captain in the slave trade, poured melted lead on such of the negroes as obstinately refused their food.[40]

Only between two-thirds and three-quarters of the slaves ever reached their destinations alive. And many of those who survived the passage to America

---

[36] Falconbridge, *Account*, pp. 27–28.

[37] During the somewhat shorter voyage from Angola to Brazil, captains rarely exercised their slaves for fear that they might mutiny or commit suicide. Boxer, *de Sá*, p. 232. See also James Duffy, *Portuguese Africa* (Cambridge, Mass., 1959), p. 141.

[38] Falconbridge, *Account*, p. 23.

[39] But see Edwards, *History*, p. 120; Atkins, *Voyage*, p. 171; James Barbot, "A Voyage to Congo," in Churchill, *Collection*, pp. 523, 545.

[40] Falconbridge, *Account*, p. 23. See also D'Auvergne, *Livestock*, p. 71; Thomas Clarkson, *The Substance of the Evidence of Sundry Persons on the Slave-Trade Collected in the Course of a Tour Made in the Autumn of the Year 1788* (London, 1789), p. 23.

arrived more dead than alive. Disease often ran uncontrolled through the ships. Smallpox took its toll and, in general, Africans who were undernourished and unaccustomed to the sea and the crowded, fetid quarters between the decks succumbed to all of the fevers and sicknesses that had been known to generations of sailors. In a long bill of lading dated 1676, a writer attributed the mortality aboard his slave ship to dropsy, "feavour," flux, "the cramp," "convultions," consumption, and "being consumed away untill life departed." [41]

Of the more frightening diseases, ophthalmia, which produced a temporary, although occasionally permanent, form of blindness, was common. According to the journal of a young cabin boy, an outbreak of ophthalmia disrupted the voyage of the slave ship *Le Rodeur.*

> *The negroes . . . were confined closely to the lower hold and this brought on a disease called ophthalmia, which produced blindness. The sailors, who sling down the provisions from the upper hold, report that the disease is spreading frightfully. . . .*
>
> *All the slaves and some of the crew are blind. . . . There is hardly enough men left . . . to work the ship. . . .*
>
> *All the crew are now blind but one man. The rest work under his orders like unconscious machines. . . . My own eyes begin to be affected; in a little while I shall see nothing but death. . . .*
>
> *We rolled along on our dreadful pain, with no other steersman than fate.*[42]

The obstacles to survival were many. Captains or seamen killed slaves in fits "of passion." They tortured their slaves and, despite a seeming self-interest in their remaining alive, drove some Africans to suicide. A one-time participant in the slave trade explained that "AVARICE, the author of the destructive business, when struggling with CRUELTY, loses its force and finds its powers of dominion foiled by the very monster it self produced." [43] If captains thought that their ships were overloaded, in danger of being captured, or otherwise in difficulty, they rarely hesitated to jettison all or a part of their human cargo. The more unscrupulous captains even tossed sick slaves overboard in order to claim insurance.[44]

Slaves often rebelled. From the moment that they found themselves forced to leave the shores of their native Africa, the helots sought—usually vainly—to escape from their fate. They dived overboard and fed themselves to the sharks. During the course of a voyage, despite the exercise of every precaution on the part of the crew, slaves somehow managed to challenge their captors. But these insurrections usually failed, and were repressed brutally. A late seventeenth-century account explains that:

> *About one in the afternoon . . . we according to custom caused them, one by one, to go down between decks, to have each his pint of water; most of them*

[41] "An Acc't of the Mortallity of Slaves Aboard the Shipp 'James,'" in Donnan, *Documents,* pp. 206–209. See also David Van Nyandael, in Bosman, *Description,* p. 429.

[42] J. B. Romaigne, quoted in Dow, *Slave Ships,* pp. xxxi–xxxii.

[43] Stanfield, *Voyage,* p. 72. See also Equiano, *Narrative,* p. 53.

[44] See Clarkson, *Evidence,* p. 14.

TO BE SOLD on board the Ship *Bance-Yland*, on tuefday the 6th of *May* next, at *Afhley-Ferry*; a choice cargo of about 250 fine healthy

NEGROES,

juft arrived from the Windward & Rice Coaft. —The utmoft care has already been taken, and fhall be continued, to keep them free from the leaft danger of being infected with the SMALL-POX, no boat having been on board, and all other communication with people from *Charles-Town* prevented.

Auftin, Laurens, & Appleby.

N. B. Full one Half of the above Negroes have had the SMALL-POX in their own Country.

An advertisement for a cargo of slaves aboard the *Bance Island*, anchored off Charleston, South Carolina, during an epidemic of smallpox. (From a Charleston newspaper, 1766)

> *were yet above deck, many of them . . . had pieces of iron they had torn off our forecastle door, as having premeditated a revolt, and seeing all the ship's company, at best but weak and many quite sick, they had also broken off the shackles from several of their companions feet. . . . Thus armed, they fell in crowds and parcels on our men, upon the deck unawares, and stabb'd one of the stoutest of us all . . . cut one of the [boatswain's] legs . . . round the bone. . . . Others cut our cook's throat to the pipe . . . we stood in arms, firing on the revolted slaves, of whom we kill'd some, and wounded many: which so terrify'd the rest, that they gave way . . . and many of the most mutinous, leapt overboard, and drown'd themselves in the ocean with much resolution.*[45]

When they reached America, the slaves who had survived the passage from Africa found that they remained objects of avarice. They were once again oiled and shaved and, after suitable announcement by "publick advertisement, specifying the number of Negroes imported, the country from whence, and day of sale," they were displayed to prospective purchasers. In the West Indies

> *It was the practice . . . to open the sale on ship-board, the males being arranged in one part of the ship, and the females in another: but, as visitors of all descriptions were admitted without hesitation or enquiry, it frequently happened . . . that such crowds of people went on board, and began so disgraceful a scramble, as to terrify the poor ignorant Africans with a notion that they were seized on by a herd of cannibals, and speedily to be devoured.*[46]

---

[45] James Barbot, "A Voyage to *Congo*," p. 513. See also Canot, *Adventures*, pp. 264–267; Claridge, *History*, pp. 175–176; William Snelgrave, *A New Account of Some Parts of Guinea and the Slave Trade* (London, 1734), pp. 161–167, 169–172, 190–191.

[46] Edwards, *History*, p. 127.

Everywhere there were similar scenes. Auctions or negotiated sales followed. The sale marked, however, only a final staging point down the road into slavery. Thereafter, Africans worked the sugar, tobacco, and cotton estates of colonial America, labored in its mills and mines and, in time, constituted a people estranged from both their past and present homelands.

The consequences of the slave trade

The available statistics permit no more than a rough, impressionistic assessment of the volume and consequences of the slave trade. In the last half of the fifteenth century, white merchants transported perhaps 5,000 slaves a year from the African mainland to its offshore islands and Europe. From Arguin alone, Portugal imported about 1,000 slaves a year.[47] During the early part of the sixteenth century, Spain's American colonies imported at least 4,000 slaves a year. Throughout the years between 1580 and 1680, Angola and the Congo supplied about 1,500,000 slaves to the planters of Brazil.[48] In the short period from 1680 to 1688, 249 ships of the Royal African Company successfully delivered about 41,000 slaves to America. Between 1722 and 1741, the Compagnie des Indes and private individuals introduced 136,000 Africans into the French American colonies.[49] During the early eighteenth century, Boston counted 1,514 slaves among its population; in 1794 it contained 4,449 slaves. In 1764, about 20,000 slaves lived in London.[50] In 1791, the slave population of the West Indies numbered about 900,000, and in 1801 about 400,000 slaves resided within the United States.[51] During the years from 1785 to 1788, a single slave entrepôt, Calabar, exported 5,511 slaves.[52] Into one Jamaican port, Montego Bay, thirty-eight shippers imported 9,993 Africans in a twenty-month period between 1789 and 1791.[53]

To generalize on the basis of such scattered evidence is dangerous. Nevertheless, it appears that white entrepreneurs probably transferred—conservatively speaking—at least twenty-five million slaves from western Africa to America before 1888, when Brazil officially abolished slavery.[54] But this figure does not include about ten million Africans who lost their lives during the voyages to America. It also excludes about ten million slaves who may have been exported from eastern Africa to Arabia and Asia. Tropical Africa was therefore deprived of about fifty million inhabitants because of the traffic in slaves.

---

[47] G. R. Crone (trans. and ed.), *The Voyages of Cadamosto* (London, 1937), p. 18 [ix]; Duarte Pacheco Pereira (trans. and ed. George H. T. Kimble), *Esmeraldo de Situ Orbis* (London, 1937), p. 101 [i, 33].

[48] Duffy, *Portuguese*, p. 138.

[49] Davies, *Company*, p. 362; Atkins, *Voyage*, p. 154; Pierre Dardel, *Navires et marchandises dans les ports de Rouen et du Havre au XVIIIe siècle* (Paris, 1963), p. 404, n. 2.

[50] Dow, *Slave Ships*, p. 269.

[51] Edwards, *History*, pp. 2–3.

[52] Daryll Forde (ed.), *Efik Traders of Old Calabar* (London, 1956), p. 7.

[53] Edwards, *History*, p. 123.

[54] About seven million slaves left Africa during the eighteenth century when the trade reached its peak. See Robert R. Kuczynski, *Population Movements* (Oxford, 1936), p. 12; J. D. Fage, *An Introduction to the History of West Africa* (Cambridge, Eng., 1959), pp. 82–84.

The consequences of the slave trade were many, but they did not arise solely or even mainly from the sheer numbers of the displacement. Although we can offer only crude estimates of the population of tropical Africa during the fifteenth through nineteenth centuries (even today it is known only imperfectly), the loss of fifty million Africans during the course of four centuries may have amounted to an annual defection of only 1 or 2 percent [55]—hardly sufficient to account for the great internal upheavals that are usually attributed to the slave trade. Moreover, in Africa the trade stimulated new investment and capital formation and accelerated the rise of new kingdoms. The areas hit hardest by the impact of the trade—the Gold and Slave Coasts and Angola—still, with the exception of Angola, possess large, densely settled populations.

Yet the slave trade tended to deprive tropical Africa of its most creative, adaptive, and reproductive human resources—the young and healthy. The slavers skimmed the cream, leaving behind those inhabitants who may well have been less able or willing to keep pace with the changing times. The slavers also encouraged Africans to substitute cheap European and Asian goods for local wares. Indigenous commercial activity declined. Knowledge of some of the old skills decayed. The traditional political processes, which had erected African states upon durable foundations, became less important than the new organization for war. The traffic in slaves therefore set in motion a train of ill-understood events, which together were more than the simple sum of Africa's numerical loss. In turn, by making possible the production of tropical crops in America, the slave trade played its part in stimulating the economic growth of both America and Europe; eventually it helped to spread Western ideas and material values throughout the world. Ultimately, too, the confrontation of Africa and the West in the setting of slavery contributed to the intensification of color prejudice and to those many and involved racial animosities which are so much a part of contemporary civilization.

III. A Further Commingling: The Intensification of the Commercial and Colonial Initiative

During the eighteenth century, the ties of tropical Africa to Arabia, India, Europe, and America grew stronger. The slave trade occupied the energies of many, brought wealth to Africa, and was particularly responsible for deepening traditional commercial commitments. Before the century ended, these commitments had ripened into European and Arabian colonial involvements on both coasts of Africa, which inaugurated, in their turn, a period during which foreigners set firm economic and political roots down into the fertile soil of the tropical parts of the "dark continent." If the nineteenth century was, in one sense, the period of Europe's scramble for Africa, then the activities of the eighteenth century set the stage for, and accustomed some of the main characters to their roles in, what was ultimately to become a complicated drama.

---

[55] *Ibid.*, p. 85.

Eastern africa in transition

The expulsion of Portugal from Fort Jesus in 1698 effectively ended the influence of Europe in eastern Africa north of Moçambique for more than a century. Already by 1640, European eyes had begun to look beyond Mombasa to the Orient. The needs and concerns of the East African littoral had, strategically at least, become peripheral to Europe's struggle for commercial dominance in southern Asia. White merchants had found the markets of eastern Africa less attractive than those of India and the East Indies, its inhabitants less hospitable, and its climate totally undesirable. Moreover, larger ships and experienced European sailors had begun to set a course for India that passed to the east of Madagascar. It was shorter and more convenient than the one that took advantage of the monsoon to follow the coast of eastern Africa from Moçambique to Mombasa and Goa. During the seventeenth and eighteenth centuries, the interests and the rivalries of the maritime powers of Europe therefore expressed themselves eastward from the Persian Gulf. The Dutch East India Company occupied Mauritius in 1644 and planted a colony near the Cape of Good Hope in 1652. French forces acquired Bourbon (the modern Réunion) in 1642 and later established a series of bases on Madagascar. The English, while settling in India between 1612 and 1665, attempted unsuccessfully to occupy their own permanent outposts on Madagascar. In 1715, France added the former Dutch settlements on Mauritius (calling it Île de France) to its holdings on Bourbon. Meanwhile, Portugal maintained its grip upon entrepôts in India and the Indies as well as Moçambique.

The ports of India—particularly Bombay, Calcutta, Madras, and Pondicherry—Ceylon, and the East Indies served as the terminal points of the magnet that drew European mariners into the Indian Ocean during the eighteenth century. In their individual ways, Basra, Muscat—a harbor of intrigue on the southeastern shores of Arabia—Mauritius, and Madagascar all played a strategic role in the struggle for supremacy in the East. Indeed, even Egypt was involved. During the American Revolutionary and Napoleonic Wars, Britain sought to safeguard her route to India by stationing a consul in Cairo, sending an agent to the shah of Persia, and appointing an "advisor" to the court of the imam of Oman and Muscat.

During this period, although their ships occasionally visited its ports, the United Provinces and England were little concerned with the affairs of eastern Africa.[56] North of Moçambique, Portugal tried halfheartedly to dominate her former subjects. Not until 1728/29, however, when an expedition from Goa succeeded in reoccupying Fort Jesus and in conquering Pate, could Portugal claim the loyalty of the coastal peoples.[57] But after the inhabitants of Mombasa had ousted the Portuguese garrison from Fort Jesus later in 1729, and other islanders had similarly driven the foreigners from their factories and strong-

[56] John Milner Gray, *History of Zanzibar from the Middle Ages to 1856* (London, 1962), pp. 89–98, notes the English and Dutch ships which visited Zanzibar during the eighteenth century.

[57] Justus Strandes (trans. Jean F. Wallwork), *The Portuguese Period in East Africa* (Nairobi, 1961), pp. 282–294.

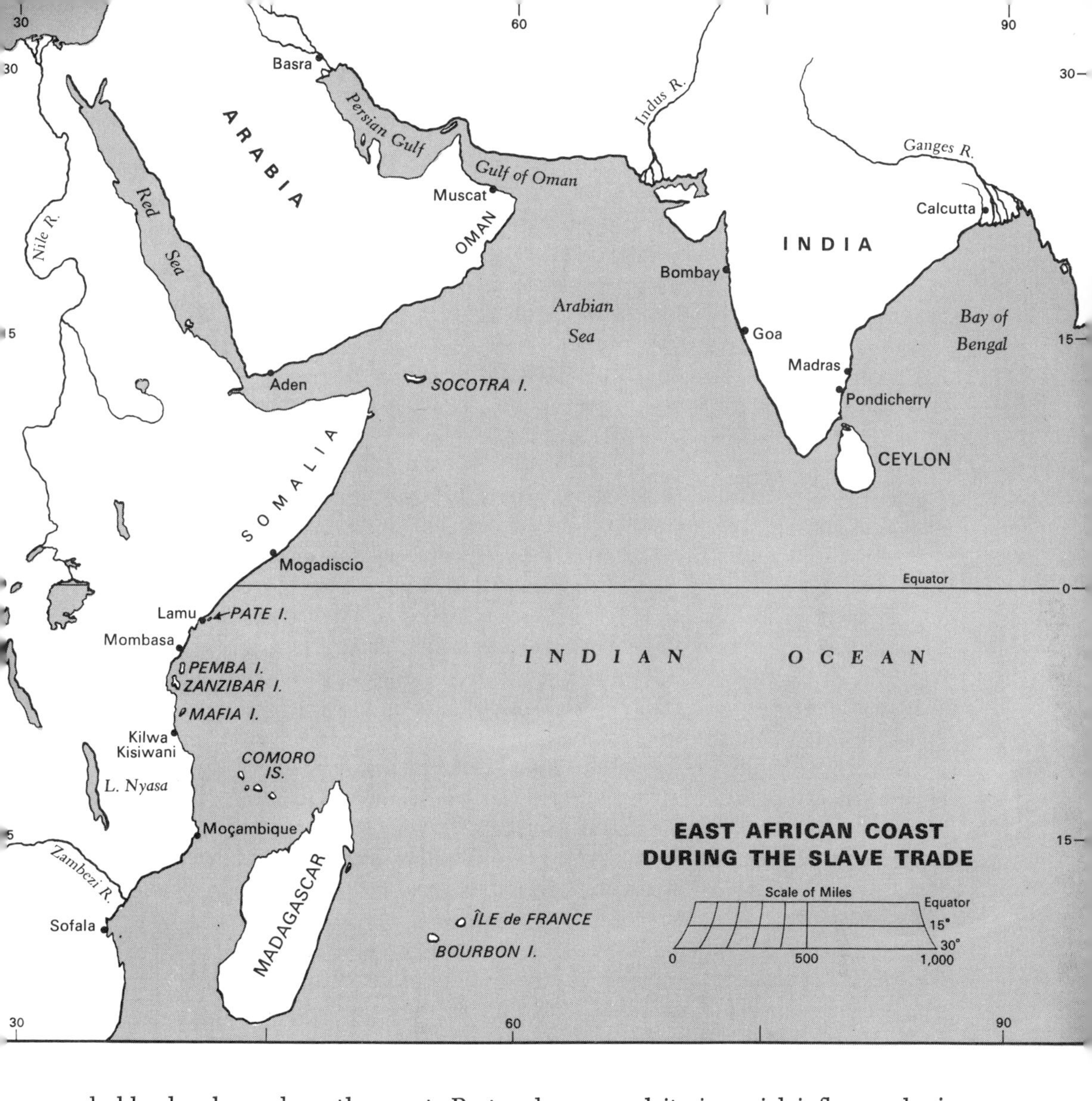

holds elsewhere along the coast, Portugal expressed its imperial influence hesitantly. From Moçambique its ambassadors and spies continued to visit the main East African ports. Its merchants traded with Kilwa, with whose sheikh the governor of Moçambique may have even negotiated a commercial treaty. From Moçambique Portuguese merchantmen occasionally sailed with economic intent to other East African entrepôts. And in 1769/70, the governor of Moçambique sought unsuccessfully to reconquer Mombasa.

The French Compagnie des Indes provided Portugal's main European competition. As early as 1739, the French wanted to assume the place of Portugal in East Africa in order to support the Compagnie's operations in Madagascar, Bourbon, and Île de France. Bertrand François de La Bourdonnais, the governor of Île de France and Bourbon, needed slaves to work their sugar, coffee, and cotton plantations. Like the Dutch before him, he first obtained such labor from Moçambique and Madagascar. But as these sources of labor became insufficient, French vessels began to compete with those of the Arabs for the slaves of East Africa. Indeed, in 1776 the sultan of Kilwa promised to supply the French trader known only as Morice with one thousand slaves a year.[58] Generally, however, most of East Africa's trade continued to be carried in Arabian and Indian dhows.

Throughout the eighteenth century, the imams of Muscat and Oman tried to rule the market towns of East Africa. After 1741, however, only Zanzibar remained loyal. By then the sheikhs of Kilwa, Lamu, Pate, Pemba, and a number of smaller islands had all successfully renounced the overlordship of the imams. And in that year Muhammad bin 'Uthman el-Mazrui, an Omani governor, declared Mombasa independent and proceeded to inaugurate the long, troubled reign of the Mazrui dynasty.[59] Thereafter, the armies of Pate and Mombasa competed for control of the food supplies of Pemba, eventually agreeing to share the island and its surplus of rice. In 1755, the sheikh of Mombasa attempted to conquer Zanzibar, but the supporters of the island's governor, who had been appointed by the ruling Busaidi family in Oman, repulsed the invaders.[60] This was only one of the many actions, however, that marked the bitter rivalry—a rivalry resolved only in the early years of the nineteenth century, when the Busaidi dynasty began to take an even greater interest in the affairs of Zanzibar and eastern Africa—between the Mazrui and Busaidi houses for power on the shores of the Indian Ocean.

Although detailed information about their activities is sparse, coastal merchants of eighteenth-century East Africa appear to have traded widely. The various towns all boasted markets where the ivory and slaves of the interior were exchanged for beads, blue and white Chinese porcelain, glazed ware from the Persian Gulf, rolls of Asian cloth, and coins from both foreign and indigenous mints. Lamu and Pate in the north, where the Tana River trade paths intersected the sea route to Arabia and India, and Mafia Island and Kilwa Kisiwani in the south were probably the centers of the coastal commercial complex. Lamu exported multicolored textiles, Kilwa and Mafia were probably in contact with the peoples of Lake Nyasa, and Bagamoyo may have traded with distant Karagwe.[61]

Colonial rivalries and senegambia

During the eighteenth century, Europe's commercial interest in western Africa found its fullest expression in Senegambia. There the merchants of France had begun to pose an effective challenge to those of England, Holland, and Portugal in 1697, after André Brüe assumed the directorship of the Com-

---

[58] See the documents in G. S. P. Freeman-Grenville (ed.), *The East African Coast* (Oxford, 1962), pp. 191, 193; John Milner Gray, "The French at Kilwa, 1776–1784," *Tanganyika Notes and Records*, 44 (1956), pp. 28–49.

[59] "A History of Mombasa," in Freeman-Grenville, *East African Coast*, p. 217.

[60] Gray, "The French," p. 88. The date is given as 1753 in a number of other sources.

[61] See *supra*, pp. 121–122.

pagnie Royale du Sénégal, Cap Nord, et Côte d'Afrique. He successfully inaugurated a long era of French hegemony on the Senegal River, extended French influence upstream, and generally asserted the economic claims of France vigorously throughout Senegambia. He reinstated the French presence on Gorée and in Saint-Louis and then sought to include the peoples living along the upper reaches of the Senegal River within his company's trading network. In order to further his program of development, Brüe himself undertook a series of hazardous journeys toward the gold fields of distant, little-known Bambouk and Kaarta. In 1697, he began the construction of a post at Goumel; in 1698, he reached Galam, located beyond the junction of the Falémé and Senegal rivers and nearly five hundred miles from Saint-Louis. There Brüe erected the fort that he vainly hoped would be the first of a number of French outposts on the way to the supposedly rich markets of the Western Sudan. At the same time, he increased the company's profitable export of slaves, ivory, gum, and ostrich feathers, encouraged the cultivation of cotton, indigo, and cacao, smoothed the ruffled relations of France with the indigenous inhabitants of Senegambia, and renewed his company's commercial ties with the traders of the Bijagós Islands.[62] But Brüe returned to France in 1702, and the directors who succeeded him failed to build upon the colonial foundations that he had successfully laid. Wars with England and the United Provinces also limited the growth of French trade.

Throughout the War of the Spanish Succession (1701–1714), English and French clashes in West Africa epitomized the economic struggle for Senegambia. Along the Gambia River, the two European powers fought to control Fort James, the entrepôt at Albreda on the right bank, and generally to monopolize the gum and slave trade of the upper river. While a French privateer captured and briefly held the fort, the Royal African Company managed in turn to oust the French from Galam for a time. But in 1713, the Treaty of Utrecht largely restored to Britain and France their previous spheres of influence.[63] The French and English factors both returned to the Gambia, where they continued to compete with each other, with privateers and interlopers, and with the Portuguese. Meanwhile, the French and the Dutch battled farther north on a number of occasions for control of Arguin; and, after 1724, the soldiers of France firmly claimed it and the gum trade of Mauritania as their own.[64] But except for a period between 1713 and 1725, when Africans living along the north bank of the Gambia River impartially attacked individual English and French traders and outposts, the inhabitants of Senegambia generally played no role in the European commercial wars. Some of their number supplied the human and material products of the region to white and mulatto

---

[62] The most complete treatment of Brüe's first directorship is contained in Étienne-Félix Berlioux, *André Brüe, ou l'origine de la colonie française du Sénégal* (Paris, 1874), pp. 43–190.

[63] John Milner Gray, *A History of the Gambia* (Cambridge, Eng., 1940), pp. 142, 150.

[64] André Delcourt, *La France et les établissements français au Sénégal entre 1713 et 1763* (Dakar, 1952), pp. 179–254.

traders and shippers and began to utilize European goods. Most, however, responded passively.

The British and French companies intensified their struggle for the supposed riches of Senegambia during the second quarter of the eighteenth century. Pierre-Félix David, the energetic director of the Compagnie des Indes in Senegambia from 1738 to 1746, attempted to reopen outposts and factories along the upper Senegal and the Falémé rivers as part of a larger plan to seek direct access and, conceivably, control of the gold mines of Bambouk. He increased and rationalized the Compagnie's exports of slaves, gum, and wax, closed the factories in the Bijagós Islands because of African hostility, and managed for a time to profit by trading slaves to the agents of the Royal African Company in return for the gum of the Gambia.[65] By an *ad hoc* treaty, he forestalled hostilities with the British during the War of the Austrian Succession (1740–1748). But after the Peace of Aix-la-Chappelle in 1748, the hallowed Anglo-French rivalry in Senegambia intensified to the point of all-out war. David's successors attempted to deprive Britain of its commercial pre-eminence along the Gambia River, and the British traders, in turn, tried to divert all of the trade of the interior away from the French factories and toward Fort James.[66] During the Seven Years' War, British warships endeavored on several occasions to take the more important of the French posts. In 1758, the navy finally conquered Saint-Louis, Gorée, and Albreda; it governed them for the balance of the war.

Elsewhere in West Africa, the Company of Merchants Trading to Africa—to which organization Parliament had, in 1750, transferred the liabilities and responsibilities of the Royal African Company—administered the British possessions. After the signing of the Treaty of Paris in 1763, the Committee of Merchants naturally sought, and in 1764 received, parliamentary permission to govern the conquered settlements. But the French tried forcibly to reclaim a part of the Senegambian trade and the Committee managed its new forts badly. As a result, the Board of Trade investigated the condition of the British settlements in West Africa and, in due course, recommended that Senegambia be revested in the Crown. In 1765, Parliament therefore transformed the Company's sphere of influence into Britain's first African colony.[67]

Lord Rockingham, Britain's principal minister, deliberately instituted a government modeled upon that of the Crown Colonies in America. A royally appointed governor and a nominated council of merchants exercised executive and legislative powers; a chief justice administered an elaborately conceived judicial system; and three specially raised military companies tried to maintain order, forestall a French invasion, and smooth the paths of commerce.[68] With their assistance, Colonel Charles O'Hara, the first governor, tried to tap new

[65] Cultru, *Les Origines*, pp. 195–196, 211–212. For a detailed contemporary English account, see Francis Moore, *Travels into the Inland Parts of Africa* (London, 1738), pp. 41–203.

[66] For the interesting views of England's commercial lobby, see Postlethwayt, *African Expedition*, pp. 4–5, 10–12, 35–38 ff.

[67] Eveline Christiana Martin, *The British West African Settlements, 1750–1821* (London, 1927), pp. 62–65.

[68] Gray, *Gambia*, pp. 234–235.

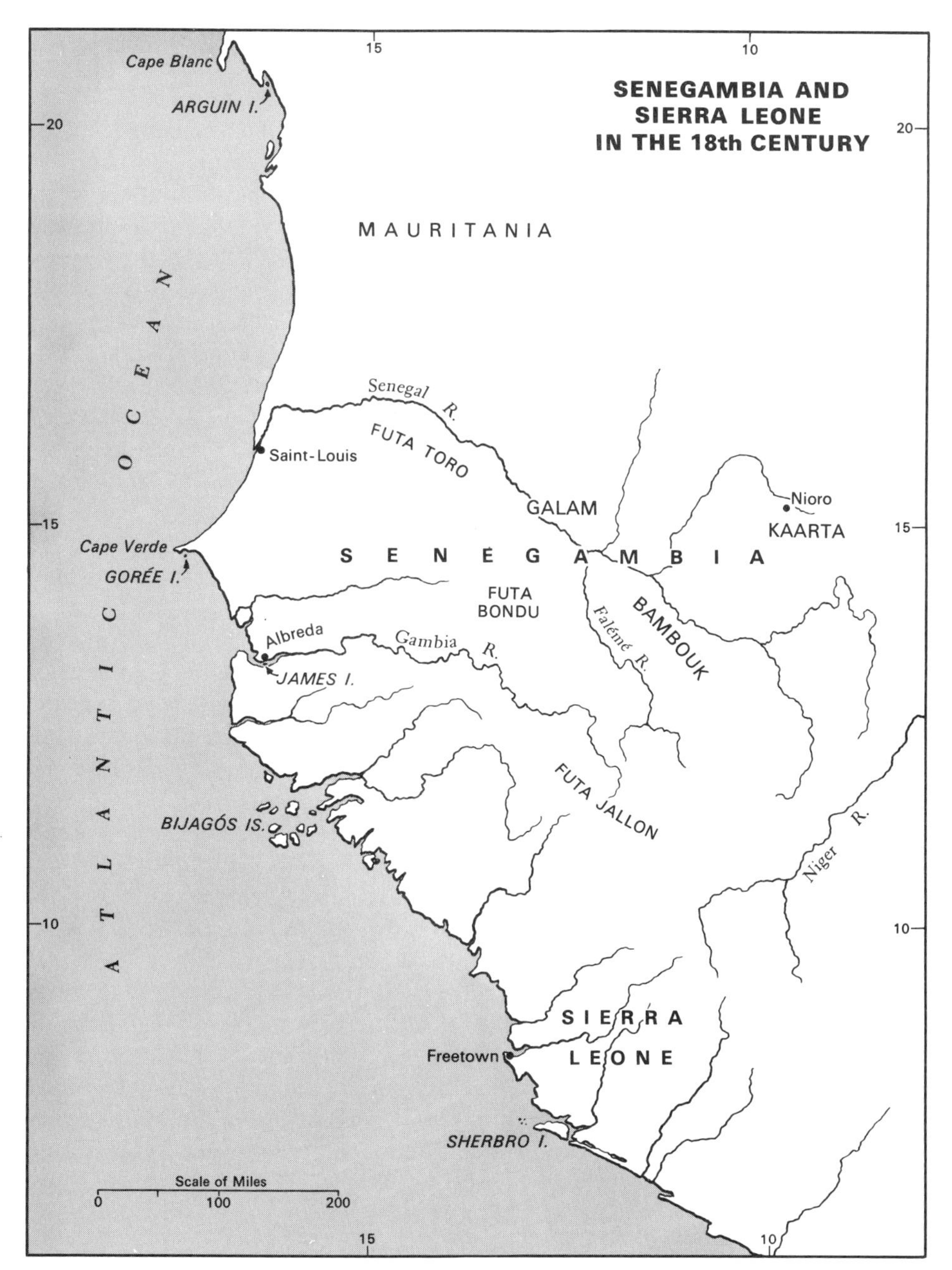

and to exploit old sources of export commodities; Rockingham expected—like many subsequent imperial ministers—that the governor would endeavor in every respect to pay the costs of the colonial administration from local import and export duties without drawing upon the British Treasury. For many of the same reasons, the governor of Senegambia also was instructed, and tried, to remain on friendly terms with the inhabitants of the colony.

These directives largely went for naught. The French merchants of Gorée (the fortified island had reverted to France by the terms of the Treaty of Paris) evaded British levies and managed, by sharp trading, to control most of the commerce of Senegambia. They were thus able to undermine the British colony, the administration of which would have been expensive even if its governors had not pursued personal gain more energetically than the promotion of the public interest. The officials were also evidently arbitrary to subordinates and cruel to individual Africans.[69] On the whole, the British colonial government of Senegambia, split as it was into two essentially riverain administrations with separate headquarters at Saint-Louis and Fort James, concerned itself almost exclusively with commercial routine, with securing its forts and factories against French depredations, and with the prevention of smuggling. Its officials cared little for Africans and African problems, except as commodities. Lacking the necessary means and more than a modest interest, they failed to incorporate the Senegambian hinterlands into the colony. Throughout the short period of its existence, British Senegambia consisted merely of a few forts, a number of small sloops, a handful of traders and factors, a somewhat unscrupulous administration, and a ragtag army of ex-convicts concerned only with serving their time in Africa quickly and, if possible, profitably.

The demise of the Province of Senegambia was a byproduct of the American Revolutionary War. In 1778, France agreed to join the thirteen colonies in their battle against Britain. Early in the next year, the French navy captured Saint-Louis, razed Fort James, and encouraged French merchantmen to challenge the British trading monopoly on the Gambia. Although a British contingent later conquered Gorée, the rule of Britain in Senegambia had come to an end. In 1783, by the terms of the Treaty of Versailles, Great Britain agreed to cede Arguin, Gorée, Saint-Louis, and all of its stations on the Senegal River to France. Its merchants retained their traditional prerogatives along the Gambia River and received recognition of their commercial rights to a share of the Senegalese gum trade. Thereafter, the British Crown removed itself temporarily from the exercise of colonial administration and once again devolved its expensive responsibilities in Senegambia to the Committee of the Company of Merchants Trading to Africa. The failure of Britain's earliest African colony demonstrated the inapplicability of the American colonial pattern to Africa and the inability of Britain to administer a tropical region devoid of white settlers. At that point in history, strategic considerations were clearly insufficient to justify colonial hegemony in Africa.

The province of freedom and the creation of sierra leone

Although they share only geographical and temporal affinity, Sierra Leone rightly follows Senegambia in the lexicon of colonial West Africa. Both colonies grew out of Britain's commercial relationships with Africa and America—the one an abortive attempt to secure the untrammeled exploitation of tropical

---

[69] See, for example, David Dean, "Joseph Wall of Gorée Island," *African Affairs*, LVII (1958), pp. 295–301; Gray, *Gambia*, pp. 238–265.

produce, the other a stratagem to relieve Britons of an acute source of social embarrassment.

Modern Sierra Leone is a product of the eighteenth-century currents of evangelical enthusiasm, a profound reassessment of the economic advantages of the slave trade, and a resulting intellectual climate distinctly favorable to an attack upon the institution of slavery and its commercial manifestations. Between 1765 and 1771, one man—Granville Sharp, a government clerk and self-taught man of letters—combined these various streams of conscience, compassion, and common sense. During those years, he personally marshaled the legal arguments against the status of slavery in England and procured in courts of law the liberation of at least six of the many slaves whom planters had brought to England from the West Indies. These judgments were nevertheless inconclusive. In 1772, however, Lord Chief Justice Sir James Mansfield finally agreed unequivocally with Sharp and his advocates that the slave James Somerset—and others held in like bondage—were free men in the light of English law. He ruled that slavery was illegal in England.

> *The exercise of the power of a master over his slave, must be supported by the laws of particular countries; but no foreigner can in England claim a right over a man: such a claim is not known to the laws of England.*
>
> *Immemorial usage preserves a positive law, after the occasion of accident which gave rise to it has been forgotten; and, tracing the subject to natural principles, the claim of slavery never can be supported. The power claimed never was in use here, or acknowledged by the law.*[70]

By this decision, more than fifteen thousand slaves obtained their freedom. In their new capacities, however, they remained unwanted and socially disadvantaged. After the conclusion of the American Revolutionary War, Negro loyalists—who had fought against the colonists in exchange for their freedom—joined the slaves freed by Mansfield's decision. In English eyes, this body of unemployed former slaves constituted a threat to law and order, particularly in London, and a general source of acute distress to those who had championed their cause and had endeavored to secure their liberation. In 1786, an *ad hoc* committee sought "to relieve the black poor" by raising funds, distributing food, and opening special hospitals for their benefit. These were stopgap measures, however, and the committee naturally wanted to effect a more permanent arrangement.[71]

In time the committee thought that the freed slaves should be transported overseas. As a likely destination, some men of influence suggested Nova Scotia, where many of the Negro loyalists had already settled. But the committee favored the proposal advanced by Henry Smeathman, a naturalist who had a passing acquaintance with West Africa. He offered—for a sizeable fee—to conduct free Negroes back to Africa and to establish a settlement along the Sierra

[70] Quoted in Prince Hoare (ed.), *Memoirs of Granville Sharp, Esq.* (London, 1820), p. 90. See also pp. 31–62, 69.

[71] Christopher Fyfe, *A History of Sierra Leone* (London, 1962), p. 14, Philip D. Curtin, *The Image of Africa: British Ideas and Action, 1780–1850* (Madison, Wisc., 1964), pp. 95–101.

Leone estuary.[72] This plan met with official support. In order to rid England of "black vagrants," the British Treasury promised to back the exodus financially. Many of the unemployed ex-slaves also looked upon the project with favor.[73] Indeed, by the time that the committee had begun to appreciate the dangers inherent in settling large numbers of Negroes in a distant, unprotected land, it was already too late to reconsider or modify a scheme that had seized the popular imagination.

More than four hundred persons sailed from England in 1787 to inaugurate the idealistic resettlement scheme known as the Province of Freedom.[74] After reaching the Sierra Leone estuary, also called St. George's Bay, the repatriates gave muskets, powder and shot, swords, lace hats, cotton goods, beads, iron bars, tobacco, and rum worth about £59 to three local Temne chiefs in exchange for ten miles of peninsula land along the estuary's southern shores. The settlers began, with high hopes and keen expectations, to build rude houses near the water and to create a new community for themselves. But many of the former slaves soon succumbed to fever and disease. They learned to their dismay that the soil of Africa was less fertile than they had expected. Their crops failed. Before long, in order to provide themselves with food and other resources, the newcomers sold their guns and other material possesions for rice grown by the Temne. Some among them even bought and sold slaves.

The Province of Freedom quickly reached a parlous state. In early 1788, only about 130 of the original settlers remained alive. Sharp, who had already done so much for the settlers, sent thirty-nine freed slaves to the settlement that had been named Granville Town in his honor. There its inhabitants treated again with the chiefs, giving the four Temne signatories new trade goods in exchange for another cession of the same land. This agreement marked the official beginning of the colony, but the settlers lacked the experience and the necessary capital both to develop their lands and to engage profitably in commerce. Moreover, the settlement was unable to protect itself from attack. Its existence was resented by slaving captains and the majority of the Temne who, in 1790, destroyed Granville Town, scattered the settlers, and abruptly terminated the experiment of the Province of Freedom.

Sharp and his supporters once again sought a sound solution to the problems of the liberated slaves. Together with the influential, evangelical-minded banker Henry Thornton and the abolitionists Thomas Clarkson and William Wilberforce, M.P., Sharp formed the St. George's Bay (later the Sierra Leone) Company to acquire and hold land and to rule ex-slaves in Africa.[75] At the same

---

[72] For a contemporary view of Sierra Leone see John Matthews, *A Voyage to the River Sierra-Leone, on the Coast of Africa* (London, 1791), pp. 10–24.

[73] Some of the "distressed blacks" may have been the first to suggest repatriation. Hoare, *Memoirs*, p. 260.

[74] The group that sailed included 290 black men, 41 black women, and 70 white prostitutes who willingly joined their friends and lovers. Fyfe, *Sierra Leone*, pp. 17, 19. But see Anna Mary Falconbridge, *Narrative of Two Voyages to the River Sierra Leone During the Years 1791–2–3* (London, 1802), pp. 65–66.

[75] Thornton became chairman of the board of the Company. See Standish Meacham, *Henry*

time, the freed slaves of Nova Scotia had become dissatisfied with their lot. They had been promised land there after fighting for Britain against the American colonists. But many of them were unable to obtain suitable farms; they disliked the climate, and willingly seized the opportunity to return to Africa.[76] With the support of the British Treasury, the Company collected those Nova Scotians favorably disposed to repatriation and, early in 1792, landed 1,123 former slaves and more than one hundred white Britons (including Superintendent John Clarkson) near the original site of Granville Town.[77]

Under Clarkson's energetic direction, the Nova Scotians created a new settlement named Freetown. He tried to allocate plots of land to the repatriates and encouraged them to build proper houses and combat the conditions that might encourage the spread of disease. By a display of force, he overawed the Temne. He also fought—although unsuccessfully—against corrupt practices that had bedeviled the original colony.

Although the upright, religious Nova Scotians welcomed Clarkson's initiative, they felt resentment against the Company. They had emigrated only after being assured that the Company would freely give each head of a household a large farm. Instead, they found that the presence of the Temne prevented the wholesale acquisition of land. Moreover, when Clarkson's successors eventually provided them with plots, the Company compelled the settlers to pay for the land during a period when funds were short and the possibilities for earning money were limited. The Nova Scotians thus accumulated a number of real grievances against the Company, each of which hung heavily in the confined, antagonistic air of the small, embryonic colony.[78]

The colonists engaged in an impassioned struggle against the Company. In 1796/97, Governor Zachary Macaulay tried to compel the settlers to pay quitrents for their lands. The enraged Nova Scotians refused, however, to submit to such levies. In 1799, when the Company, in desperation, imposed school fees, the settlers likewise refused to pay for the education of their children. Thereafter, in an attempt to obtain redress for their grievances, they vainly claimed a share in the government of the colony. They demanded their own judges. They urged the overthrow of Company rule. And in 1800, a small group of repatriates finally rebelled. But the governor quelled the rising with the assistance of 550 Maroons, whose coincidental arrival from Nova Scotia proved providential.[79]

Thornton of Clapham, 1760–1815 (Cambridge, Mass., 1964), pp. 102–114; Sharp to William Pitt, August 28, 1790, in Hoare, *Memoirs*, pp. 355–356.

[76] See Christopher Fyfe, "Thomas Peters: History and Legend," *Sierra Leone Studies*, 1 (1953), p. 6; G. Haliburton, "The Nova Scotia Settlers of 1792," *ibid.*, 9 (1957), pp. 16–17.

[77] For the re-establishment of Granville Town in 1791, see also Anna Falconbridge, *Narrative*, pp. 62–64.

[78] See *ibid.*, pp. 141, 152–153, 165–166, 188, 206, 214–216, 258–269.

[79] Hoare, *Memoirs*, p. 300. The Maroons were the descendants of slaves who had escaped to the mountains of Jamaica in the seventeenth century and who had, during the late eighteenth century, risen against the British. They were defeated and deported to Nova Scotia, which they detested. See the detailed reports contained in *The Proceedings of the Governor and Assembly of Jamaica, in Regard to the Maroon Negroes* (London, 1796).

During the early years of the nineteenth century, the colony of Sierra Leone failed to develop amicable relations with the indigenous peoples who surrounded Freetown. The settlers energetically defended themselves against the Temne in 1801/2 and later conquered a portion of Temneland. Beyond their coastal enclaves, however, the freed slaves exercised little influence. The few missionaries who ventured into the interior died there, returned disheartened, or traded in slaves. Freetown alone remained the center of British interest.

Between 1800 and 1808, the administration of Sierra Leone continued to prove a source of financial embarrassment to the Company. The British navy meanwhile sought a port from which its ships could patrol the African coast. At Thornton's insistence, the Company therefore transferred the government of the struggling settlement and its population to the British Crown. Subsequently, Freetown, a Crown Colony containing about two thousand settlers from America, came to play a major part in imperial considerations. It absorbed slaves freed at sea by the British navy's anti-slavery squadron and gradually developed significant commercial and social ties with the inhabitants of its hinterlands. At the same time, the colony remained the home of peoples who were both African and American, although distinctively neither.

We wish you to know our way of life. Our way of life is that of the Faith. It is our folk who have found the truth and we follow it.

—*Muhammadu Bello,* c. *1811*

POLITICAL CHANGE IN THE INTERIOR, 1800–1880

6

During the nineteenth century, change everywhere overtook the peoples of the interior. Before Europeans penetrated thither, Africans and Afro-Arabs themselves created new political and commercial empires. Intruders, they destroyed the power of pre-existing societies and imposed their own beliefs upon conquered peoples. They introduced new political and religious creeds and replaced traditional practices with new orthodoxies. In their day, because victory could change the character of society, warfare assumed a greater importance than before. Indeed, such forceful shattering of indigenous political and social foundations may well have contributed to the eventual success of the later European invasions.

I. Statecraft and Trade in Eastern Africa

During the nineteenth century, eastern Africa contained a welter of indigenous societies, many of which shared mainly geographic and historic affinities. In general, they possessed a common love for cattle and used similar techniques to till the soil. But they spoke radically different languages, favored different forms of social organization, and responded in surprisingly different ways to the stimulations of their environment. As a result, they each reacted idiosyncratically to the intrusion of outsiders. Some, like the Ganda and the Lozi, adapted themselves to change. Others, like the Masai, failed to adapt and were submerged or by-passed by the tide of events.

Developments in the lake regions

Throughout the nineteenth century, the interlacustrine powers vied for commercial and political ascendancy. In the north, Buganda built upon the firm foundations of its earlier successes and upon its unparalleled ecological advantages to become the most important. The Ganda army and navy first conquered the neighboring principalities of Kiziba and Koki, occupied the western marches of Busoga, and then brought Ihangiro and Karagwe, to the west of Victoria

Nyanza, within the *kabaka's* sphere of influence.[1] From 1832 to 1884, during the reigns of the powerful *kabakas* Suna and Mutesa, Ganda spearmen ranged far afield, gathering ivory, cattle, food supplies, and slaves from the distant inhabitants of the Ukerewe peninsula, the Kavirondo Gulf, the Buvuma Islands, Buzinza, Ankole, Toro, and Bunyoro. A proportion of the ivory and slaves later found its way to Zanzibar *via* Karagwe and Unyanyembe. In exchange, the *kabakas,* particularly Mutesa, obtained muskets with which to strengthen their positions internally and to protect the kingdom of Buganda from its enemies.

The organization of Buganda contributed significantly to its ability to dominate the western and northern borderlands of Victoria Nyanza. The *kabaka* ruled autocratically with the assistance of a centralized administrative hierarchy. Mutesa made the most of the ongoing system and, indeed, accelerated the processes that had already given such great power to his predecessors. He curbed the religious authority of the priests, deprived the clans of their lands, and replaced clan heads—the representatives of the "common Ganda"—with regional agents responsible only to himself. He created a modern army and gave new prominence to the court bureaucracy. Commoners could thereby obtain advancement and prestige more easily than they could in other areas of eastern Africa.[2] Ganda society was comparatively fluid and, consequently, proved receptive to the Muslim and Christian influences that later caused so much unrest. Thus, by helping to create conditions favorable to material and social change, Mutesa in many unwitting ways readied his people for the alterations and strains of the later period of partition.

Among Buganda's rivals, Bunyoro posed the most immediate threat. By the middle of the nineteenth century, it had largely recovered from a period of economic and political impoverishment and had begun, once again, to challenge the might of Buganda. Under the *omukamas* Kamurasi and Kabarega, Bunyoro dominated the commerce of the regions adjoining Lake Albert and Lake Kyoga—where Nyoro exchanged iron implements that they themselves had fashioned for produce and ivory—and, with Lango assistance, fought Buganda to a standstill. Kabarega, who began to rule in 1869, traded with the merchants of Khartoum who had followed the Nile route to Lake Albert, as well as with those of Zanzibar and Karagwe. From Khartoum, Kabarega obtained guns and, shortly after the period of the first European visits to Bunyoro, his armies actively began to enlarge the sphere of Bunyoro's effective influence.[3] For a time, in the face of Ganda opposition, Kabarega even re-imposed the rule of Bunyoro upon the breakaway principality of Toro, which lay astride Bunyoro's route to Karagwe. By 1880, however, Buganda had managed to install the ruler of its choice upon the throne of Toro, to check the expansion south-

---

[1] John Milner Gray, "Early History of Buganda," *The Uganda Journal,* II (1935), p. 269; J. Ford and R. de Z. Hall, "The History of Karagwe," *Tanganyika Notes and Records,* 24 (1947), p. 16.

[2] See Robert P. Ashe, *Two Kings of Uganda, or, Life by the Shores of Victoria Nyanza* (London, 1889), p. 53; Christopher Wrigley, "Buganda: An Outline Economic History," *The Economic History Review,* X (1957), pp. 71–74.

[3] Ruth H. Fisher, *Twilight Tales of the Black Baganda* (London, 1911), pp. 166–170.

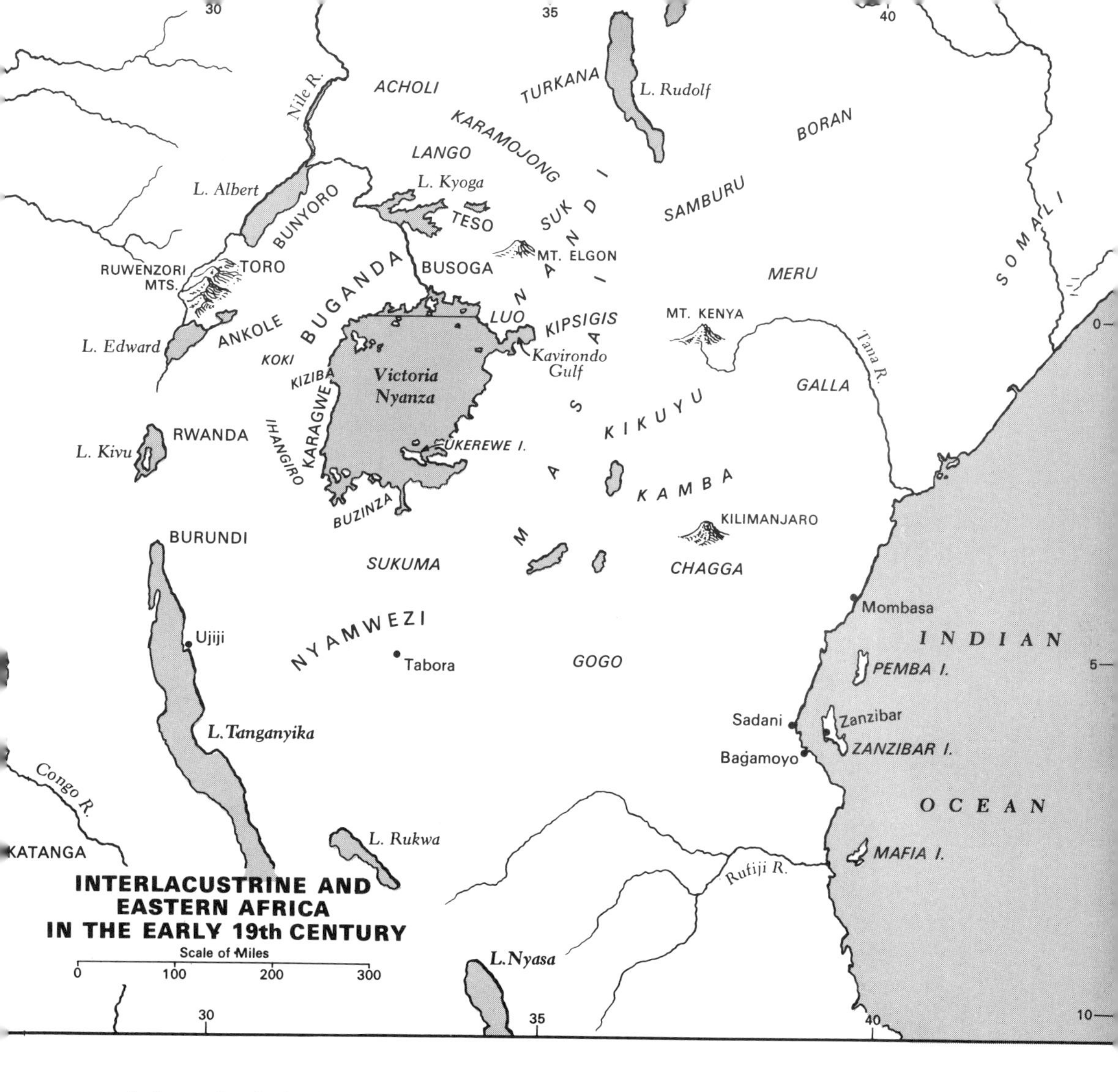

ward from the Lake Kyoga region of the numerous Teso and the Kumam and, thereby, to eclipse Bunyoro and effectively set the stage for further dramatic confrontations between the two northern lacustrine powers.

To the southwest, meanwhile, the *mugabes* of Ankole had managed to expand the borders of their state and to maintain their own independence in the face of repeated attacks by armies loyal to the *mwamis* of Rwanda. During the second half of the nineteenth century, *mwami* Kigeri IV ruthlessly transformed his small Tutsi-ruled kingdom into a major state with its center in the fertile hill region east of Lake Kivu. Using muskets purchased from Swahili-speaking traders, his soldiers continually tried to conquer Ankole, Kigezi, Bukiga, and Burundi. The Rwanda army was powerful and efficient; Kigeri, alone of the rulers of the region, had conscripted standing regiments and had devised a system whereby regiments could be rotated in order to permit the prosecution of remittent warfare. Nevertheless, Rwanda consistently acquired prestige and cattle more than territory.[4]

East of Victoria Nyanza, the Masai grazed their cattle within a large area that stretched from Mount Elgon to Kilimanjaro. The Great Rift Valley was theirs, and they both defended it against the designs of intruders and raided beyond its borders in search of the cattle with which to supplement their much valued herds. Furthermore, Masai boys, as they came of age, needed to demonstrate their manhood in war. Acting as age-groups, their prowess and vaunted military successes for long prevented the more numerous Kikuyu from leaving their own overcrowded lands near Mount Kenya for the fertile acres of the Rift Valley. For a time, the Masai also checked the swarming of the Nandi, on the western flank of the valley, and the invasions southward of the Suk and the Turkana, both of whom sought new pasture lands. For similar reasons, Swahili-speaking traders—often termed Zanzibaris—and the first European visitors generally avoided Masai country, following instead the safer and more easily accessible routes that skirted it to the south.[5]

At a time when the numbers and influence of the Masai began to decline as a result of civil wars between sections of the tribe and deaths due to disease, the Kikuyu and the Kamba grew progressively more powerful. An affluent people of the forest, who evidently held regular markets and traded, if reluctantly, with their neighbors and the Zanzibari travelers, the Kikuyu grew strikingly more numerous; in consequence, they cut down the forests of Kikuyuland and pushed southward to the edge of the Kenyan plains during the last half of the nineteenth century. During this latter phase, they purchased land—through a number of complicated transactions—from the Dorobo hunters. Despite what European settlers later believed, Kikuyu often bought their new lands outright. On one occasion, for example, a Kikuyu family exchanged about two hundred sheep and goats for land measuring one mile long by a half-mile wide.[6] The Kamba, of the hills and plains east of Kikuyuland, took to trading with less reluctance than their neighbors, partially because they lived in greater fear of famine. During the nineteenth century, their caravans conveyed hides and ivory to Mombasa, on the coast, where local merchants offered them cotton and calico piece goods, beads, wire, and salt in exchange. But Zanzibaris competed with the Kamba along the routes into the interior. If the Zanzibaris thought that they could avoid attacks by the Somali, who were then invading the area north of Mombasa, then they also followed the Tana River toward Mount Kenya, or beyond toward Mount Elgon. Others wended their way west through Chaggaland to Kilimanjaro and then, if the appropriate routes proved open,

[4] G. Pagès, *Un Royaume hamité au centre de l'Afrique* (Bruxelles, 1933), pp. 152–170; Jan Vansina, *L'Évolution du royaume Rwanda des origines à 1900* (Bruxelles, 1962), pp. 82, 89.

[5] For a summary of nineteenth-century developments among the Masai, the Kikuyu, the Kamba, and related peoples, see the account by D. Anthony Low, "The Northern Interior, 1840–1884," in Roland Oliver and Gervase Mathew (eds.), *History of East Africa* (Oxford, 1963),.I, pp. 300–308.

[6] Mervyn W. H. Beech, memorandum in the Dagoretti (Kenya) Record Book, December 12, 1912.

to Victoria Nyanza. Still others reached the shores of the Kavirondo Gulf, where Europeans later remarked upon their presence and their influence.[7]

Commercial ties similarly bound the African communities of the south to each other and to the coast. Swahili-speaking merchants penetrated the interior very early in search of markets and sources for exportable commodities. But the earliest large-scale entrepreneurs were Africans. From the late eighteenth century, if not before, Lunda and Bisa carriers transported the copper of Katanga and the ivory of the region between Lakes Mweru and Tanganyika to the Indian Ocean. Others went west to Luanda, where a number of trade paths converged.[8] Caravans also crossed Lake Nyasa at Kota Kota and continued down the Rovuma River toward Kilwa Kivinje. Parties of Yao trod the same paths from the environs of Lake Nyasa with loads of wax and ivory and files of slaves. Nonetheless, from Lake Tanganyika the main road to the coast began in Ujiji and passed—along the approximate route later taken by the railway—through Unyamwezi and Ugogo to the coastal entrepôts of Sadani and Bagamoyo.

The Nyamwezi, a people possessed of comparatively productive lands south of Victoria Nyanza, initially dominated the up-country sections of this route. Their merchants also ranged as far as Katanga, where Msiri, one of their number, later ruled.[9] The Nyamwezi also fought against Kazembe's Lunda for control of the commerce of the Luapula Valley.

From about the middle of the nineteenth century, Swahili-speaking entrepreneurs competed with the Nyamwezi. From Unyanyembe and Ujiji, their two most important settlements, they subsequently established outposts in Buganda, Bunyoro, Katanga, and the rich ivory-producing areas west of Lake Tanganyika. At first, the number of Zanzibaris in residence at the settlements may never have amounted to more than two hundred; nonetheless, their guns and their ability to extend large sums of credit for long periods gave these Zanzibaris wide contacts and a decided influence over the indigenous inhabitants of eastern Africa. Only Mirambo, chief of the Nyamwezi, successfully challenged and curtailed their ascendancy. During the years between 1870 and 1880, he dominated the central trade paths as well as the commercial routes that went north from Unyanyembe to Karagwe and Buganda.[10] Together with the fabled Tippu Tib, a Zanzibari who sold Congolese ivory and slaves and later governed a vast tract of land west of Lake Tanganyika, Mirambo was the last

[7] T. Wakefield, "Routes of Native Caravans from the Coast to the Interior of Eastern Africa, Chiefly from Information Given by Sádi Bin Ahédi, a Native of a District Near Gázi, in Udigo, a Little North of Zanzibar," *The Journal of the Royal Geographical Society*, XL (1870), pp. 303–328; Charles New, *Life, Wanderings and Labours in Eastern Africa* (London, 1873), pp. 358, 361.

[8] See Jan Vansina, "Long-Distance Trade-Routes in Central Africa," *The Journal of African History*, III (1962), pp. 382–388; John Hanning Speke, *What Led to the Discovery of the Source of the Nile* (Edinburgh, 1864), p. 199; Ian Cunnison, "Kazembe and the Arabs to 1870," in *Conference of the History of the Central African Peoples* (Lusaka, 1963), no pagination. See also António C. Pedroso Gamitto (trans. Ian Cunnison), *King Kazembe* (Lisboa, 1960 [orig. ed., Lisboa, 1854]), I, p. 66, II, p. 171.

[9] See *infra*, pp. 261–263.

[10] Norman R. Bennett, *Studies in East African History* (Boston, 1963), pp. 7–14.

A sketch of Tippu Tib, the fabled Zanzibari slave and ivory trader, *c.* 1885. (Heinrich Brode, *Tippoo Tib,* London, 1907)

of the great commercial warlords of the eastern interior to thrive before the coming of the Europeans.[11]

The zambezi hinterlands

Early in the nineteenth century, the irruption northward of the Nguni peoples of eastern South Africa decisively shattered the atmosphere of comparative calm that otherwise pervaded the highland areas drained by the Limpopo and Zambezi rivers. As a result of accumulated tensions, the most important Nguni chiefdoms began to compete vigorously among themselves. Out of their struggle for power, the Zulu, led by Shaka, emerged victorious. In 1819, armies loyal to Shaka overwhelmed Zwide's Ndandwe warriors and began a period of ruthless conquest that almost immediately dispersed the defeated branches of the Nguni nation to the far corners of southern Africa.

The subjugated Nguni groups split up into a number of sections, among which were the people later called Ngoni. In 1821, Zwangendaba, a subordinate of Zwide, led a section of the Ngoni out of Zululand into the Delagoa Bay region, where they met fellow refugees, including a Nguni group led by Soshangane. Together, Zwangendaba and Soshangane conquered and absorbed into

[11] For his activities, see Tippu Tib (trans. Wilfred H. Whiteley), *Maisha ya Hamed Bin Muhammed el Murjebi yaani Tippu Tib* (Nairobi, 1958–1959), pp. 125–137; Heinrich Brode (trans. H. Havelock), *Tippoo Tib: The Story of His Career in Central Africa* (London, 1907), pp. 59–155; *infra*, pp. 259, 263.

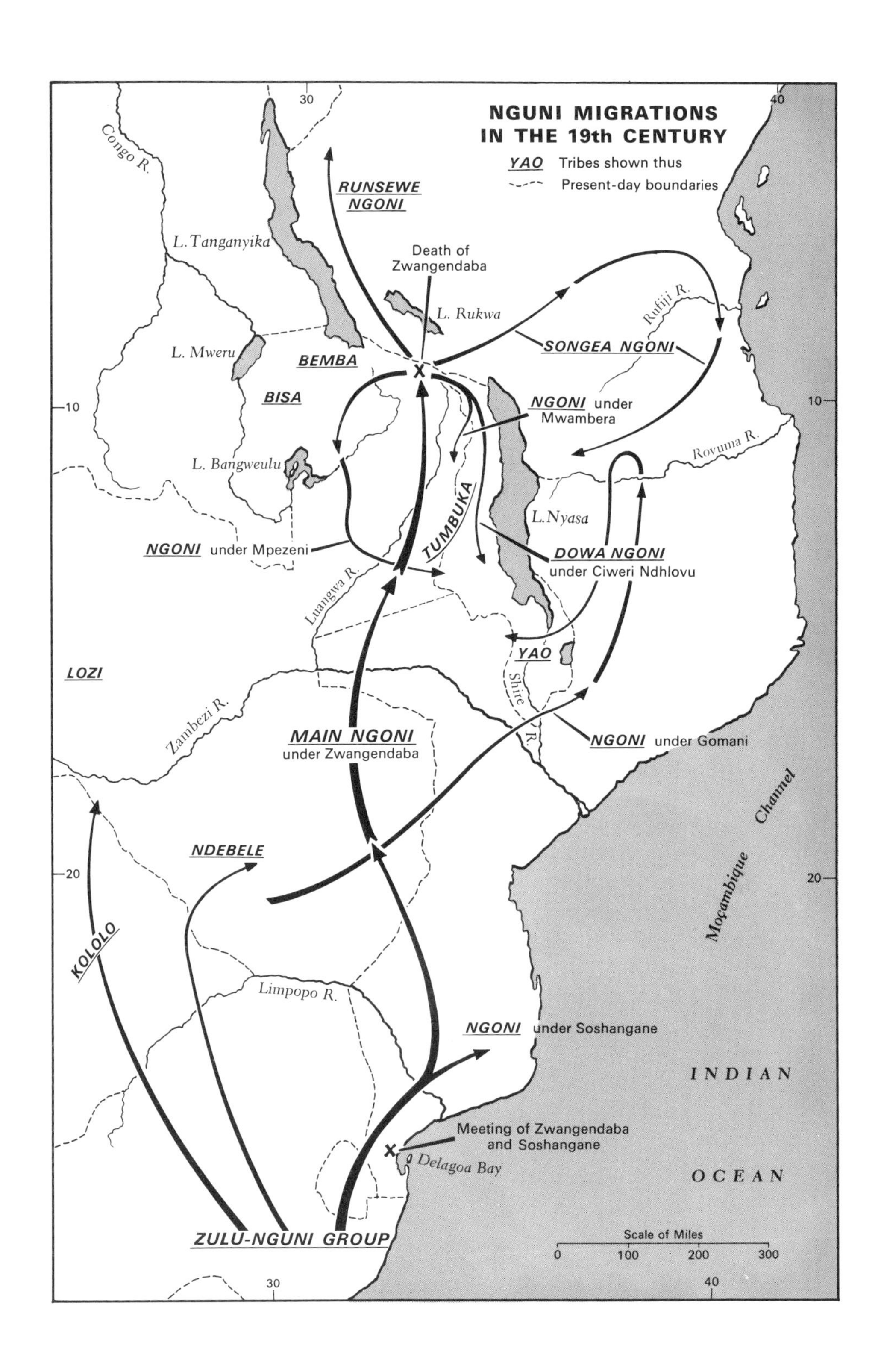
NGUNI MIGRATIONS
IN THE 19th CENTURY
YAO Tribes shown thus
Present-day boundaries
Congo R.
L. Tanganyika
RUNSEWE
NGONI
Death of
Zwangendaba
L. Rukwa
Rufiji R.
SONGEA NGONI
L. Mweru
BEMBA
BISA
NGONI under
Mwambera
L. Bangweulu
Rovuma R.
L. Nyasa
TUMBUKA
NGONI under Mpezeni
DOWA NGONI
under Ciweri Ndhlovu
Luangwa R.
YAO
LOZI
Shire R.
Zambezi R.
MAIN NGONI
under Zwangendaba
NGONI under Gomani
Moçambique Channel
NDEBELE
KOLOLO
Limpopo R.
NGONI under Soshangane
INDIAN
OCEAN
Meeting of Zwangendaba
and Soshangane
Delagoa Bay
ZULU-NGUNI GROUP
Scale of Miles
0
100
200
300
10
20
30
40

their own armies the indigenous Tsonga of the area. Then the two chiefs quarreled, and Zwangendaba and the Ngoni continued their journey northward across the Limpopo River into Shonaland.[12]

Throughout 1833 and 1834, the Ngoni raided and incorporated into their own ranks the inhabitants of Shonaland. In the process, they laid waste to the country through which they passed on their way toward the Zambezi River.[13] At about the same time, Soshangane conquered Gazaland in Moçambique, and Mzilikazi led the Ndebele—originally yet another section of the Nguni who had fled from the wrath of Shaka—to the banks of the Limpopo River. From a temporary center south of that river, Mzilikazi's warriors ranged far afield, overawing the surrounding Ngwato, Kgatla, Tswana, Kwena, and Shona. A few years later, after a group of Afrikaners had defeated the Ndebele in battle, Mzilikazi and his followers finally found a permanent home for themselves on the high veld beyond the Limpopo. From this general area, a division of Nguni previously loyal to Mzilikazi defected and, after traversing modern Rhodesia, Moçambique, and Malawi, penetrated into the Songea district of Tanganyika. Subsequently, this branch of the Nguni returned to Nyasaland, where they settled in the Ncheu district under the Gomani chiefs.[14]

Meanwhile, in 1835, the main branch of the Ngoni crossed the Zambezi River near its confluence with the Luangwa River and swept northward—everywhere incorporating adherents—through the lands of the Nsenga and the Cewa.[15] The latter two peoples had lived in the area for centuries.[16] The Cewa, in particular, were a section of the Malawi nation—in more recent times a cluster of tribal groups—whose rulers may have arrived from the Congo basin during an earlier period. Before the Ngoni invasions, the Malawi evidently dominated the region between the Luangwa River and Lake Nyasa (a lake previously known as Malawi), and shared control of the Shire River basin with the Yao, a people many of whom believed they had come originally from a hill named Yao in Moçambique.

Zwangendaba's Ngoni traversed the western marches of Malawi country during the years between 1839 and 1842. They settled for a time in Ufipa, near

[12] J. A. Barnes, *Politics in a Changing Society: A Political History of the Fort Jameson Ngoni* (Cape Town, 1954), p. 7; A. T. Bryant, *Olden Times in Zululand and Natal* (London, 1929), pp. 206–208, 459–461; Yesaya Mlonyeni Chibambo, *My Ngoni of Nyasaland* (London, 1942), pp. 8–10; D. Gordon Lancaster, "Tentative Chronology of the Ngoni: Genealogy of Their Chiefs, and Notes," *The Journal of the Royal Anthropological Institute,* LXVII (1937), p. 84.

[13] Frederick Courteney Selous, "Twenty Years in Zambezia," *The Geographical Journal,* I (1893), p. 318.

[14] Chibambo, *Ngoni,* p. 31; Margaret Read, "Tradition and Prestige Among the Ngoni," *Africa,* IX (1936), p. 464. But see Margaret Read, *The Ngoni of Nyasaland* (London, 1956), pp. 8, 207.

[15] Edward H. Lane Poole, "The Date of the Crossing of the Zambezi by the Ngoni," *Journal of the African Society,* XXIX (1930), p. 292.

[16] Raymond Apthorpe, "Problems of African History: The Nsenga of Northern Rhodesia," *The Rhodes-Livingstone Journal,* XXVIII (1960), pp. 59–63; M. G. Marwick, "History and Tradition in East Central Africa Through the Eyes of the Northern Rhodesia Cew̑a," *The Journal of African History,* IV (1963), pp. 378–379.

Lake Tanganyika. There Zwangendaba died, and one dissident segment continued north to Unyamwezi, where it later helped Mirambo to control the trade routes of the eastern interior.[17] Another segment went east, to attack the inhabitants of Bagamoyo and the lower Rufiji River districts before finally conquering and settling in Songea. The majority, however, followed Mpezeni, a chief who seems to have been the legitimate heir of Zwangendaba. He and most of the members of the main section of the Ngoni circled back through the country then dominated by the powerful Bemba—a tribe that had recently entered its third period of expansion—and the Bisa. The wanderings of the segments loyal to Mpezeni finally ended when the Ngoni crossed the Luangwa River into the eastern districts of what became Northern Rhodesia. Lastly, even before these segments had penetrated into Bembaland, Mwambera, a rival chief, had led a number of Mpezeni's erstwhile supporters onto the plateau lands west of Lake Nyasa. Another breakaway group ruled by Ciweri Ndhlovu, a Nsenga, followed a similar route down the west side of the lake into the Dowa district.

In this process of finding homes for themselves, these various groups had thrown the previous inhabitants of trans-Zambezia into turmoil. They had raided the lakeside Tonga, battled with the Tumbuka and the inhabitants of Nkamanga, and attacked the various Malawi peoples.[18] The Ngoni had pillaged, ravaged, and generally helped to disrupt the pre-existing social equilibrium. By so doing, they may well have smoothed the path for the eventual conquest by Europeans.

The various Ngoni chiefs each governed areas spatially separated but similarly composed of a heterogeneous collection of subject peoples. Indeed, the Ngoni created their states by adhering the conquered to the original, conquering nucleus. The conquered often outnumbered the conquerors; Ngoni warriors consequently took wives from the subject tribes. Eventually this process resulted in the partial absorption of the Ngoni by their subjects. In trans-Zambezia at least, the Ngoni children even adopted the languages of their non-Ngoni mothers, and the language of the Ngoni lost currency.

This process was foreign to the experience of the other Nguni intruders. By 1840, Mzilikazi's Ndebele had established themselves on the high veld north of the Matopo Hills; Inyati, and later Gbulawayo, became their capitals. Because the Ngoni loyal to Zwangendaba had previously destroyed the political and military power of the indigenous inhabitants of this region, the Ndebele conquered it easily. They reduced some of the remaining Shona to tribute-paying vassals. They assimilated others and raided some Shona, the Nyai, the Tonga, and the Ila in order to obtain cattle and produce. Their experience was,

---

[17] W. H. J. Rangeley, "Mtwalo," *The Nyasaland Journal,* V (1952), p. 60; G. W. Hatchell, "The Angoni of Tanganyika Territory," *Tanganyika Notes and Records,* 25 (1948), p. 70.

[18] Jaap van Velsen, "Notes on the History of the Lakeside Tonga of Nyasaland," *African Studies,* XVIII (1959), pp. 113–115; T. Cullen Young, "The 'Henga' People in Northern Nyasaland," *The Nyasaland Journal,* V (1952), p. 35. See also Hugh Stannus Stannus, "The Wayao of Nyasaland," *Harvard African Studies,* III (1922), pp. 231–232.

in general, largely unlike that of the Ngoni. The Ndebele retained their own language and customs; Mzilikazi's, much more than Mpezeni's and Mwambera's, was a simple conquest state. Mzilikazi ruled autocratically, and allegiance to his person provided the main unifying force. Mzilikazi commanded the army, made and interpreted the laws, and personally controlled the immense herds of cattle that symbolically testified to the might of the Ndebele nation.[19]

In 1870, when Lobengula succeeded Mzilikazi as chief of the Ndebele, he inherited a centralized tribal organization that had perfected the arts of war and plunder; his was probably the most powerful state between the Limpopo River and Unyamwezi. But the very manner in which Lobengula managed to obtain the throne, and the resultant participation of European concession hunters and missionaries in the affairs of the kingdom, served as a significant prelude to the eventual conquest of the Ndebele by white settlers from the south.[20]

To the northwest, an invading group similarly imposed its rule upon the inhabitants of Barotseland. Before about 1830, the Luyana, or Lozi ("Barotse"), whose own royal dynasty had probably arrived from the north during the early eighteenth century—perhaps as fugitives from the empire of *mwata yamvo*—occupied the flood plain of the upper Zambezi River and dominated the surrounding non-Luyana. Then, from about 1833 to 1835, the Kololo, a people who had fled Basutoland in the face of Shaka's hostility, plundered their way northward—under the leadership of Sebitwane—through Bechuanaland to the Zambezi, finally settling forcibly among the Tonga or Toka who grazed cattle on the river's northern shores. Soon the Kololo moved west to the flood plain, where Sebitwane's soldiers defeated those loyal to Mulambwa, the Lozi chief. Sebitwane thereafter ruled Barotseland. Several of the defeated *indunas*, or princes, resided with him in Naliele, but others governed independent chiefdoms beyond the northern limits of Kololo power.

Sebitwane, for whom David Livingstone expressed great affection, evidently ruled harshly and successfully. His son Sikeletu, however, and Mbololu, who soon succeeded Sikeletu, lost the confidence of their supporters as well as their subjects. In 1863/64, conditions therefore proved conducive to revolt. Njekwa, a leading Lozi commander, gathered a large following, obtained the support of Sipopa, a Lozi prince, and freed Barotseland from Kololo domination. Sipopa became *litunga*, or king, and, despite serious opposition from Mbunda and some Lozi, successfully enlarged the size and effective power of the Lozi state. During his reign, and the reigns of his successors Mwanawina and Lewanika, peoples living as far distant from Naliele as the Kafue and Chobe rivers acknowledged the might of the Lozi. It was only the Europeans who proved the undoing of Lewanika.[21]

---

[19] Thomas Morgan Thomas, *Eleven Years in Central South Africa* (London, 1872), pp. 226, 241–243; A. J. B. Hughes and Jaap van Velsen, *The Ndebele* (London, 1954), p. 63. But see Hugh Marshall Hole, *The Making of Rhodesia* (London, 1926), p. 45.

[20] Richard Brown, "The Ndebele Succession Crisis, 1868–1877," in *Historians in Tropical Africa* (Salisbury, S.R., 1962), pp. 163–172.

[21] Adolphe Jalla, *Litaba za Sicaba Sa Ma-Lozi* (Cape Town, 1951 [originally published in 1909]), pp. 32–53. (An anonymous translation, "The Story of the Barotse Nation," *c.* 1961, has

A sketch by Francis Moore of a Fulani village and its plantations, probably in the hinterland of Senegambia. (Francis Moore, *Travels into the Inland Part of Africa*, London, 1738)

II. Reconstruction in the West

Throughout the nineteenth century, a succession of militant Muslim reformers altered the course of history in the West African interior. They proclaimed *jihads* and led their followers against "unbelievers." They conquered these infidels, thereby introducing cultural orthodoxy into regions previously known for their forms of diversity. The conquering elites furthermore replaced older indigenous aristocracies and created empires that, for the most part, dominated the Western and Central Sudan until the coming of the European partitioners.

The creation of a fulani empire

During the last years of the eighteenth century, a spirit of religious revolution reached Hausaland from Futa Jallon and Futa Toro, where subject minorities had earlier ousted their overlords. In the first instance, Muslim Fulani pastoralists participated in a *jihad* against the pagan Mandingo; intermittently victorious in battles after 1726, they controlled sizeable enclaves by about 1745. About thirty years later, a learned member of the Tokolor clerical class returned from Futa Jallon to Futa Toro and led his people in another successful *jihad*,

been mimeographed by the Publications Bureau of Northern Rhodesia); David Livingstone, *Missionary Travels and Researches in South Africa* (London, 1857), pp. 84, 90; C. M. N. White, "The Ethno-history of the Upper Zambezi," *African Studies*, XXI (1962), pp. 11–14, 19; Gervas Clay, "Barotseland Between 1801 and 1864," in *Conference of the History of the Central African Peoples*, no pagination. On the early history of Barotseland, see Lishomwa S. Muuka, "The Colonization of Barotseland in the Seventeenth Century," in *ibid.*; Mutumba Mainga, "The Origin of the Lozi: Some Oral Traditions," in *ibid.*

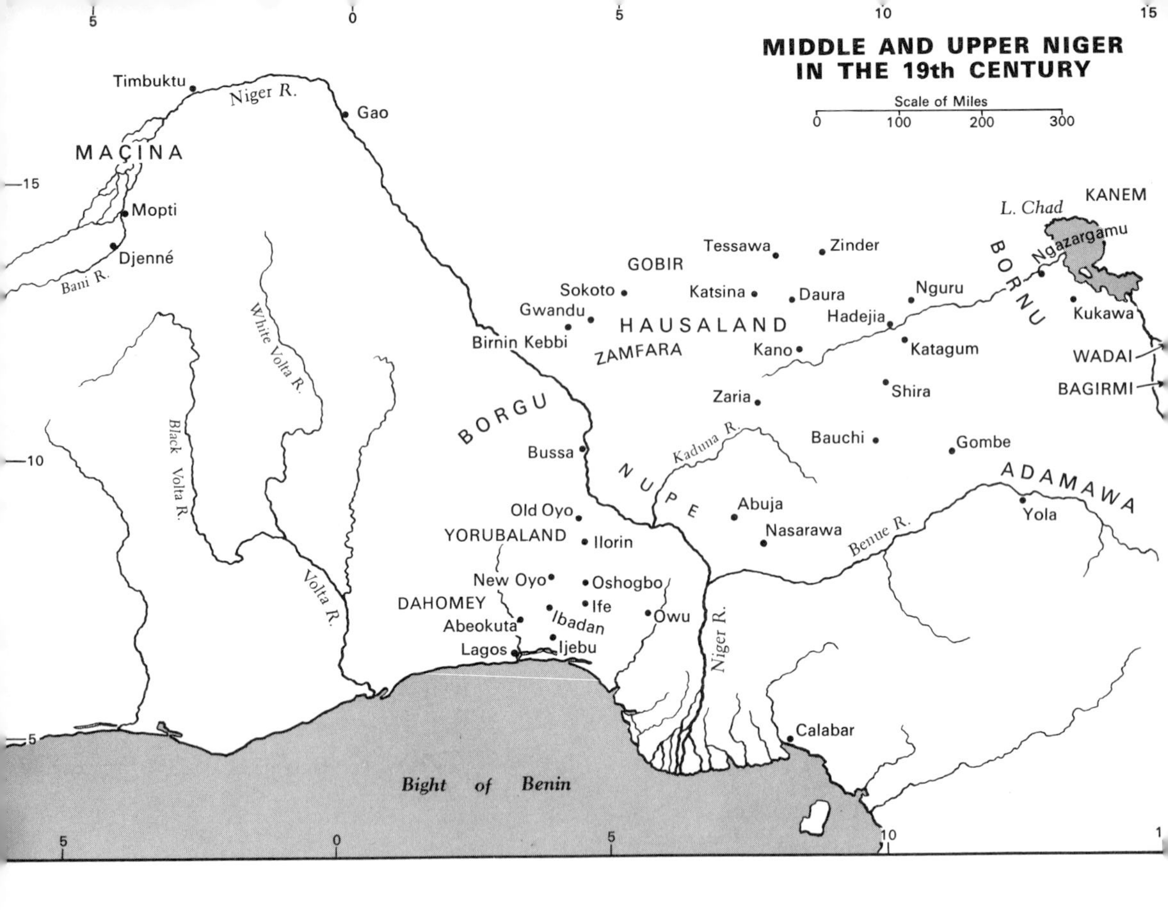

this time against the Fulani by whom Futa Toro was then ruled. In both cases, Muslim believers resented the social, political, and religious attributes of their subjection and, encouraged by positive spokesmen, acted to abolish it.

Similar tension existed in eighteenth-century Hausaland. Throughout the previous two centuries, the Fulani had immigrated into Hausaland from the west. Often converts to Islam, they had become subjects of Hausa *sarkuna* whose adherence to the same faith was evidently weak. The *sarkuna* generally refused to enforce the *Shari'a,* or Islamic code of laws, respect the teachings of a group of impressively learned Tokolor and Fulani clerics, or provide the Fulani with any opportunity to play significant roles in the processes of Hausa government.[22] Rightly or wrongly, the Fulani believed themselves to be seriously disadvantaged under Hausa rule.

In 1786, Usuman dan Fodio, one of the members of the clerical elite, began actively to preach reform in Gobir and Zamfara, two of the more important Hausa city-states. Then a tutor to the family of the *sarkin* Gobir, Usuman had

[22] A. D. H. Bivar and Mervyn Hiskett, "The Arabic Literature of Nigeria to 1804: A Provisional Account," *Bulletin of the School of Oriental and African Studies,* XXV (1962), pp. 142–143; Mervyn Hiskett, "An Islamic Tradition of Reform in the Western Sudan from the Sixteenth to the Eighteenth Century," *ibid.,* pp. 587–591.

studied in Agades and had already achieved a widespread reputation as an Islamic divine. Like the reformers in Futa Jallon and Futa Toro, and like the later Muslim evangelists in Libya, the Sudan, and Arabia, Usuman sought to recreate in the Central Sudan the reputedly ideal society of an earlier golden age of Islam.[23] He wanted to re-introduce into Hausaland a spirit of religious orthodoxy that was in keeping with the teachings of the Qur'an. He condemned the practice of paganism, emphasized the need for moral austerity, and accused the Hausa *sarkuna* of being unbelievers. In his "Admonition to the Brethren," Usuman wrote:

> *There is no dispute that the Hausa kings worshipped many places of idols, and trees, and rocks, and sacrificed to them. This constitutes Unbelief, according to the general opinion.*[24]

More specifically, Usuman accused the members of the Hausa ruling class of fulfilling only "their lusts, for they are like the beasts."

> . . . *whomsoever they wish to kill or exile or violate his honour or devour his wealth they do so in pursuit of their Lusts, without any right in the Shari'a.* . . .[25]

They imposed taxes on the people that were not laid down in the *Shari'a*. They ate forbidden food and drank forbidden beverages. Despite religious injunctions, these Hausa rulers rode whatever beasts they wished, dressed according to their whims, lived in decorated palaces wherein soft carpets were spread, and took numerous women into their homes without the sanction of a marriage contract. "[Some] of the ways of their government," Usuman declared, [are] "to change the laws of God" by taking the property of deceased persons—calling it inheritance—by compelling Muslims to serve in their armies or to pay a fine not imposed by the *Shari'a,* and by accepting bribes, particularly in cases of litigations. Usuman further accused the Hausa governments of shutting "the door in the face of the needy," forbidding worshipers of the Muslim God their sacrosanct beliefs, and refusing to end their traditional customs, among which he, like Ibn Battuta, singled out for particular mention the putting of dust upon their heads when giving a greeting[26] and, in tones that foreshadowed those of later Christian missionaries, the beating of drums for frivolous purposes. In sum, the evangelical Usuman warned the faithful that everyone who had followed the Hausa way had, in fact, "followed the way of Hell fire."[27]

---

[23] H. F. C. Smith, "A Neglected Theme of West African History: The Islamic Revolutions of the Nineteenth Century," *Journal of the Historical Society of Nigeria,* II (1961), pp. 176–177. See also Mervyn Hiskett, "Material Relating to the State of Learning Among the Fulani Before Their *Jihad,*" *Bulletin of the School of Oriental and African Studies,* XIX (1957), pp. 563–564, 566.

[24] Quoted in H. Richmond Palmer (trans. and ed.), "An Early Fulani Conception of Islam," *Journal of the African Society,* XIV (1914), p. 54.

[25] Mervyn Hiskett, "*Kitab al-Farq*: A Work on the Habe Kingdoms Attributed to 'Uthman dan Fodio," *Bulletin of the School of Oriental and African Studies,* XXIII (1960), p. 567. For the 'Abbasid provenance of Usuman's teachings, see Hiskett, "An Islamic Tradition of Reform," p. 592.

[26] H. A. R. Gibb (trans. and ed.), *The Travels of Ibn Battuta* (London, 1929), pp. 327, 330.

[27] Hiskett, "*Kitab al-Farq,*" pp. 567–569.

The *sarkin* Gobir tried vainly to counteract Usuman's appeal. He ordered converts to Islam to revert to traditional practices. He prohibited the wearing of the turban and the seclusion of women. But Usuman redoubled his efforts to "call all persons . . . to the Faith, and to expound to all whom he could reach, their duty to God, and . . . to deliver them from the doom to come and to save them, to keep alive the doctrines of Islam and to banish wickedness." [28] Significantly, he also protested against the "oppressive" taxes to which the Fulani and the Hausa were both subject. Usuman gathered a large number of followers and, by 1802 at least, openly espoused revolt against the autocratic rulers of Hausaland. Two years later, as a result of his subversion, a new *sarki* finally attacked Usuman and his followers, who fled from Degel to Gudu.

The flight from Degel transformed Usuman's program of reform into a revolutionary movement. He proclaimed a *jihad:*

> *. . . to make war upon the heathen king who does not say "There is no God but Allah" on account of the custom of his town . . . and who makes no profession of Islam, is . . . obligatory by assent; and that to take the government from him is obligatory by assent. . . .*
>
> *And that to make war against the king who is an apostate—who has not abandoned the religion of Islam as far as the profession of it is concerned, but who mingles the observances of Islam with the observances of heathendom, like the kings of Hausaland for the most part—is . . . obligatory by assent, and that to take the government from him is obligatory by assent. . . .*[29]

Shortly thereafter, at Tabkin Kwotto, near Gudu, Usuman and his followers defeated the pursuing cavalry of the *sarkin* Gobir; gathering adherents among Fulani and Hausa alike, the new soldiers of Islamic orthodoxy swiftly carried their revolution into the other states of Hausaland. In time, a number of young leaders even took Usuman's white banners (sometimes called flags) of authority, piety, and revolt into Bornu and Ilorin.[30]

Usuman's supporters soon overran Hausaland. They captured Birnin Kebbi and Zaria in 1805, entered Katsina city in 1807, and conquered Daura and the capital of Gobir in 1808. Kano finally fell in 1809. Farther east, in what became Adamawa, Modibbo Adama allied himself to Usuman, obtained the support of Fulani pastoralists who had installed themselves on the surrounding plateaux during the eighteenth century and, from about 1809, led a *jihad* that eventually gave his successors control of yet another Fulani state. The chief of Bauchi, who was not a Fulani, also rallied to Usuman's *jihad* and subdued the pagan tribes of the surrounding plateaux. Finally, Nupe and Ilorin capitulated to the Fulani cavalry after internal rivalries had vitiated the organization of their military defenses. The conquest of Bornu, however, eluded the Fulani.

---

[28] Quoted in Palmer, "Fulani Conception," XV (1915), p. 189.

[29] A. D. H. Bivar, "The *Wathiqat ahl al-Sudan*: A Manifesto of the Fulani *Jihad*," *The Journal of African History*, II (1961), p. 240. For the influence of the sixteenth-century reformer al-Maghili, see Hiskett, "An Islamic Tradition of Reform," pp. 585–586.

[30] S. J. Hogben, *The Muhammadan Emirates of Nigeria* (London, 1930), p. 111. For a general, revisionist critique of the revolution, see Marilyn Robinson Waldman, "A Re-Evaluation of the Nature and Bases of the Fulani *Jihad*" (unpub. honors thesis, Harvard, 1964).

By 1810, despite continued opposition from Katsina and Gobir, Usuman's victory had been won. From the newly created capital at Sokoto, he and his successors—as the Sarkin Musulmi, or "Commander of the Faithful"—ruled over a vast area that soon comprised about 180,000 square miles and fifteen emirates governed by Usuman's wartime lieutenants. They imposed a heavy-handed rule on the peasants and, after Usuman's return to a life of religious contemplation, the new Islamic veneer that covered the emirates merely helped to perpetuate many of the arbitrary governmental features that Usuman himself had earlier foresworn. A new aristocracy appropriated the traditional political institutions for their own purposes. Secular officials soon succeeded the early clerical governors. The revolution itself had simply replaced one ruling class with another; after Usuman's retirement, even irreligion flourished within the Fulani empire.

Throughout the nineteenth century, each of the individual emirs acknowledged and respected the overriding sovereignty of the Sarkin Musulmi. Their emirates paid tribute and, however autonomous they may have appeared to European observers, they regarded themselves as subordinates of an empire ruled from Sokoto.[31] For example, the Sarkin Musulmi regularly intervened in the politics and government of Zaria; he approved the accession of emirs, deposed them, and controlled appointments to certain principal offices. His representative installed the emir, initially in Zaria and later in Sokoto. The same representative visited Zaria regularly and maintained local agents who were responsible for supplying him with information. These agents twice annually forwarded tribute to Sokoto in the form of slaves, cloth, horses, mats, and cowrie currency, the sum of which tended to increase during the last half of the century. The emir of Zaria personally attended the court at Sokoto annually in order to report to the Sarkin Musulmi on the affairs of his emirate. At the request of the Sarkin Musulmi, he and the other emirs supplied the imperial power or their fellow emirs with military assistance when directed to do so by Sokoto. The court of the Sarkin Musulmi also derived considerable revenue from its share of the property of every deceased emir.

Within Zaria, the emir governed as he pleased. Without reference to Sokoto, he freely made war against non-Muslims, levied taxes and tribute, dispensed justice, and ruled seven subordinate vassals, each of whom possessed somewhat similar powers within their own areas. Economically, this intricate network of obligation and privilege depended upon the cultivation of cash crops by slaves and upon the sale of slaves; indeed, slave villages appear to have been one of the principal forms of capital investment. The overall impression is one of a high degree of internal security within nineteenth-century Zaria, and of a set of stabilized relations between Zaria and Sokoto that testify to the essential unity of Hausaland under the Sokoto Fulani.[32]

[31] See Heinrich Barth, *Travels and Discoveries in North and Central Africa* (London, 1857), III, pp. 10–11; Hugh Clapperton, *Journal of a Second Expedition into the Interior of Africa from the Bight of Benin to Soccatoo* (London, 1829), p. 215.

[32] Michael G. Smith, *Government in Zazzau, 1800–1950* (London, 1960), pp. 73–134.

The establishment of the Fulani empire, however its rulers ignored the precepts dear to Usuman, encouraged an intellectual renaissance throughout the Central and Western Sudan. Moreover, its creation ushered in a comparatively long era of peace that permitted the development of a free trade zone within Hausaland and encouraged the forging of new economic links beyond the confines of the empire.[33] In 1851, when Barth reached Kano, he found it a flourishing mercantile center where "commerce and manufactures [went] hand in hand . . . almost every family [having] its share in them." He noted that the inhabitants of Kano principally produced cotton cloth "in the form of . . . the oblong piece or dress of dark-blue colour worn by the women . . . or plaid, of various colours." They dyed their cloth in the deep pits of the town and exported it to Tripoli, Timbuktu, Nupe, and Calabar. They also exported tanned hides, red sheepskins, leather sandals, kola nuts, slaves, and natron and, in exchange, they imported salt, calico, and cotton prints from Manchester, glass beads from Trieste, sword blades from Solingen, and razors from Styria. In their markets, and in the markets of the other towns of Hausaland, horses, camels, ostriches, potash, lime, and slaves also found buyers. "There is something really grand," Barth concluded, "in this kind of industry, which spreads to the north as far as Murzuk, Ghat, and even Tripoli; to the west, not only to Timbuktu, but in some degree even as far as the shores of the Atlantic, the very inhabitants of Arguin dressing in the cloth woven and dyed in Kano; to the east all over Bornu . . . and to the south it maintains a rivalry with the native industry . . . while to the south-east it invades the whole of 'Adamawa, and is only limited by the nakedness of the pagan *sans-culottes*, who do not wear clothing." He continued:

> *In fact, if we consider that this industry is not carried on here as in Europe, in immense establishments, degrading man to the meanest condition of life, but that it gives employment and support to families without compelling them to sacrifice their domestic habits, we must presume that Kano ought to be one of the happiest countries in the world. . . .*[34]

Regeneration in bornu

The Fulani *jihad* brought war to a Bornu weakened by its earlier battles against Mandara. In 1805, after Usuman's emissaries had spread dissension, the Fulani resident in western Bornu revolted against the regime of *mai* Ahmad ibn 'Ali. Led by Ardo Lerlima, who carried one of Usuman's white banners, the Fulani irregulars first met defeat at the hands of the Bornuese army. Shortly thereafter, however, the Fulani defeated an army led by *mai* Ahmad in the battle of Nguru. From all classes the victors attracted adherents opposed to the autocratic rule of the *mais;* soon the fires of warfare had inflamed the western

---

[33] Thomas Hodgkin, *Nigerian Perspectives* (London, 1960), p. 41.

[34] Barth, *Travels*, II, pp. 125–128, 134. See also George Francis Lyon, *A Narrative of Travels in Northern Africa* (London, 1821), p. 139; Dixon Denham, Hugh Clapperton, and Walter Oudney, *Travels and Discoveries in Northern and Central Africa* (London, 1831 [first edition, 1826]) IV, pp. 47–51; Clapperton, *Journal*, pp. 221–223.

and southern marches of Bornu.[35] In the months that followed, the contagion spread, and the Fulani warriors, including many from Gombe and Katagum, defeated those military contingents that had remained loyal to the *mais*. They founded a number of small emirates within the borders of imperial Bornu and, in 1808, a force loyal to Gwoni Mukhtar, one of the leading flag-bearers of the *jihad*, finally occupied Ngazargamu, the capital of Bornu.

Their army and court put to flight, and their loyal subjects harassed unmercifully by the Fulani rebels, the *mai* and his councilors persuaded Muhammad al-Amin ibn Muhammad Ninga, known as Shehu al-Kanemi, to come to their assistance. Then about thirty years of age, al-Kanemi had been born in Fezzan of a Kanembu father and a local mother. He had subsequently lived and studied in Cairo and Medina and, after his return to Kanem, had married the daughter of a Bornuese provincial governor. In Kanem, he achieved an enviable reputation as a scholarly and pious cleric; he also appears to have gained a considerable secular following. From all accounts, al-Kanemi possessed abundant charisma; a European visitor later called his appearance "prepossessing . . . with an expressive countenance, and a benevolent smile." [36]

In the years immediately after the Fulani occupation of Ngazargamu, al-Kanemi organized a Kanembu army to defend Bornu. His cavalry forced the invaders to flee from central Bornu. In one important battle, Gwoni Mukhtar lost his life. After a period of peace, however, hostilities broke out anew. It was probably during the intervening period of comparative calm that al-Kanemi tried to understand why the Fulani chose to war against the rulers of Bornu and attempted to intervene diplomatically in order to arrest any further fighting. He therefore wrote the first of a series of revealing, persuasive letters to Usuman dan Fodio and Muhammadu Bello. "When the will of God brought me to the land of Bornu," he began, "I found the fire of discord had broken out between you and the people of this land."

> *I enquired the cause of this. Some persons informed me that oppression was the cause, others again that it was religion. We were, therefore, perplexed by this matter and I wrote a letter to your brethren who are my neighbours. I besought them to explain to me their reason and pretext for making war. . . . They sent me in reply a poor sort of answer, such as would not come from a wise man, much less from a learned one, and least of all from one who is reforming religion.*

"Will you," al-Kanemi continued, ". . . tell me the reason for your fighting with us?" The defenders of Bornu, he explained, were hardly heathen.

> *. . . heathenism is far from our thresholds. If indeed prayer and the giving of tithes and the knowledge of God and the fasting in Ramadan and the restoration of mosques, if these are heathenism, what then is Islam?*

Some Bornuese officials did, he admitted, take bribes. A few probably oppressed the peasants. Women, but not necessarily Muslim women, went unveiled. But

---

[35] Yves Urvoy, *Histoire de l'empire du Bornou* (Paris, 1949), pp. 97–99; Derrick J. Stenning, *Savannah Nomads* (London, 1959), pp. 30–35.

[36] Denham, Clapperton, and Oudney, *Travels*, I, p. 240.

in and of themselves, al-Kanemi protested, these practices did not constitute heathenism. "Better," he wrote to the rulers of Sokoto, "you should command him [who does these things] to do good, and forbid him to do evil, and if he refuses, leave him alone. That would be better than to make war on us as you are doing. The result of what you are doing . . . is that you are bringing distress and trouble on Muslims both in this world and in the next." Moreover, al-Kanemi accused the Fulani themselves of acting irreligiously:

> *You are destroying books; you are scattering them in the roads; you are throwing them in the dirt. But the name of God is on these books and you know that he who throws the name of God in the dirt is a heathen. Again, we have seen some of your folk make . . . oaths and then afterwards break these oaths. They slaughter men and capture women and children. We are astonished at this, since you started by being the reformers of knowledge and religion.*[37]

In reply, Muhammadu Bello warned his correspondent "that this holy war of ours [would be] fought with severity." He complained of the "inconsistency" and of the manifest "slander and hatred" of al-Kanemi's comments, and argued that the Fulani fought against the people and the rulers of Bornu because they had originally sided with the Hausa *sarkuna* against Usuman dan Fodio. Later, Usuman himself accused the people of Bornu of sacrificing to stones and trees and of worshiping idols. He also tried to persuade al-Kanemi to flee into a truly Muslim country.[38]

This interesting correspondence appears to have continued intermittently throughout different stages of the war. In 1811/12, Ibrahim Zaki, who had established the emirate of Katagum in 1810, led the Fulani *jihadi* once again into the heart of Bornu. He captured and sacked Ngazargamu, forcing *mai* Dunama Lefiami, Ahmad's son, both to flee and to summon al-Kanemi's martial assistance. The latter faithfully raised the green standard of the Prophet, rallied the Kanembu cavalry, and repulsed the Fulani. Partially in order to secure this reconquest, he and his followers settled in Bornu itself. Al-Kanemi founded the new capital of Kukawa, concluded a treaty of peace with Ibrahim, and established himself as the *de facto* ruler of Bornu. From *mai* Dunama, who retained only the trappings of traditional sovereignty, he obtained half of the revenues of Bornu's reconquered territories.

Shehu al-Kanemi governed Bornu until his death in 1835. He formally deposed Dunama in 1814 and, after Dunama had invaded Bornu at the head of a Bagirmi army, he ended Dunama's life in 1817.[39] The succeeding *mai*, Burra (Ibrahim) Aman Gana, remained a puppet ruler throughout his long reign. Denham epitomized the situation: "The sultanship of Bornou . . . is but a name: the court still keeps up considerable state, and adheres strictly to its

---

[37] Correspondence contained in Muhammadu Bello, "Infaq al-Maisuri," in H. Richmond Palmer (trans. and ed.), *The Bornu Sahara and Sudan* (London, 1936), pp. 260–261. A slightly different translation by H. F. C. Smith is contained in Hodgkin, *Perspectives*, pp. 199–201.

[38] Bello, in Palmer, *Bornu*, pp. 262–263, 267.

[39] But see Denham, Clapperton, and Oudney, *Travels*, III, p. 193.

The reigning *mai* of Bornu holding an audience, *c.* 1822. (Denham, Clapperton, and Oudney, *Narrative of Travels and Discoveries in Northern and Central Africa,* London, 1826)

ancient customs, and this is the only privilege left them."[40] Al-Kanemi meanwhile sought to recreate the empire of Bornu. He annexed Bagirmi and Wadai and tried, with intermittent success, to absorb the small emirates on Bornu's western and southern flanks. In 1824/25, Hadejia, the outer walls of which had been strengthened in anticipation of his assault, and Katagum both resisted his attack. Shira, however, fell in 1826. Damagaram and Tessawa soon succumbed. In 1829, the armies of Bornu even attacked Kano; there, however, they met the combined forces of Kano and Bauchi and, in 1830, al-Kanemi agreed to a peaceful delimitation of spheres of influence with the Sarkin Musulmi. He wrote to Muhammadu Bello:

> *We profess the same religion, and it is not fitting that our subjects should make war on each other. Between our two kingdoms are the pagan Bedde . . . on whom it is permissible to levy contribution: let us respect this limit: what lies to the east of their country shall be ours: what lies to the west shall be yours.*[41]

After al-Kanemi's death in 1835, his son 'Umar extinguished the Saifi line of *mais* and ruled Bornu autocratically. With the rulers of Kano and Katagum,

---

[40] *Ibid.,* pp. 193–194.
[41] Quoted in Palmer, *Bornu,* p. 269. But see Stenning, *Nomads,* p. 68; Clapperton, *Journal,* pp. 249, 252, 262.

A Bagirmi mounted lancer, *c.* 1823. Note the quilted protection reminiscent of the chain-mail armor of Hausaland. (Denham, Clapperton, and Oudney, *Narrative of Travels and Discoveries in Northern and Central Africa*, London, 1826)

he warred against Zinder, a new force in the Central Sudan and, in 1846, repelled an invasion mounted by the sultan of Wadai. After a number of other martial adventures, 'Umar retired to a life of religious contemplation. In his name, an increasingly influential palace claque of slaves, eunuchs, and other favorites of the nominal sovereign administered Bornu.[42] Under their rule, Bornu lost control of Kanem and its western tributary states and suffered periodic raids from Wadai. Within the reduced central kingdom, however, a standing army provided a modicum of security; agriculture and trade prospered, and the basically stratified organization of the state remained unchanged. After 'Umar's death in 1880, however, the fortunes of Bornu declined considerably. Weak rulers and a corrupt, luxury-loving bureaucracy proved no match for new conquerors. Rabih, a Sudanese slaver from Bahr el Ghazal, occupied Bagirmi in 1891 and then invaded Bornu, defeating the army of *shehu* Hashim and sacking Kukawa in 1893.[43] The history of Bornu was thereafter bound up with the course of the European partition.

The demise of oyo

Oyo lost its pre-eminent position in Yorubaland during the early years of the nineteenth century. Already, by 1800, the Dahomeans and Egba had successfully rid themselves of the overrule of the *alafin* of Oyo. At the same time, the

[42] Gustav Nachtigal, *Sahara und Sudan* (Berlin, 1881), I, pp. 708–724.
[43] See *infra*, pp. 257–259.

changed terms of overseas trade had begun to offer important new economic advantages to the *alafin's* subjects. These advantages, most of which resulted from America's demand for slaves, increased the importance of the southern states relative to that of Oyo, whose center was north of the forest near the Niger River, and contributed significantly to a weakening of their ties to, and their dependence upon, the *alafin*. The Yoruba sovereigns of the south consequently began to seek a fuller exercise of their own autonomy during a period when dynastic complications and internal controversies had weakened the *alafin's* ability to rule his subjects. Abiodun, who lived during the final years of the eighteenth century, thus proved to be the last *alafin* to enjoy a "long and prosperous reign" and to hold "the different parts of his kingdom together in one universal sway." With him, his chronicler recorded, "ended the tranquility and prosperity of the Yoruba country." [44]

Aole, the *alafin* who succeeded Abiodun, aroused the enmity of a number of powerful Yoruba, particularly the ambitious Afonja, *kakanfo* of Ilorin. With the support of Fulani clerics and Fulani and Hausa mercenaries, Afonja rebelled against Aole in 1817. He made real the independence of the state of Ilorin but, by so doing, he also ushered in a period of warfare that ultimately precipitated the dissolution of the unity of Yorubaland. But first Oyo and Ilorin continued to battle. Ojo Agunbambaru and his powerful army rallied to the cause of Oyo and, after ravaging the country between Oyo and Ilorin, laid siege to Afonja's capital. But Afonja managed to turn aside the besiegers and thereby to increase the extent of his own influence in the affairs of Yorubaland. Shortly thereafter, when Maku succeeded Aole as *alafin*, Afonja even possessed the arrogance to answer the traditional message announcing the installation of the *alafin*—"the New Moon has appeared"—with the command "Let that New Moon speedily set." [45] His army, with its shock regiments of Fulani and Hausa, subdued a number of Yoruba towns and city-states. In the process, the mercenaries looted and pillaged the regions through which they passed. They grew increasingly powerful until Afonja, recognizing in their independence a threat to his own régime, attempted to disband them. Resistant, naturally, the mercenaries deposed Afonja and installed first Alimi, Afonja's Fulani advisor, and then Abdussalami, Alimi's son, as the emir of Ilorin.

In a series of pitched battles between the cavalry of Fulani Ilorin and the foot soldiers of the briefly unified city-states of Yorubaland, the former won decisive victories. They laid siege to and conquered a number of walled Yoruba towns. The Fulani grip on Ilorin and northern Yorubaland simultaneously denied the southern states their customary supplies of Hausa slaves from across the Niger. Together, the collapse of the power of Oyo, the resultant Fulani attempt to conquer other Yoruba cities, and the new need to control sources of Yoruba slaves were factors that contributed decisively to the wars that did so much to accelerate the political disintegration of Yorubaland.

---

[44] Samuel Johnson (ed. O. Johnson), *The History of the Yorubas* (Lagos, 1921), pp. 186–187.
[45] *Ibid.*, p. 196.

From about 1820 to 1840, the newly independent city-states fought among themselves, and against the Fulani of Ilorin, for slaves, for control of the trade routes, and generally for political hegemony in Yorubaland. As a result, a variety of new city-states arose, often temporarily, to positions of prominence within the area once ruled so decisively by Oyo. The men of Owu, for example, were among the first to take advantage of Oyo's demise; wielding cutlasses, they conquered the armies of Ife and Ijebu. In time, however, they suffered defeat at the hands of a force composed of refugee gunners from Oyo and bowmen and spearmen from Ife and Ijebu. Ogbomosho humbled Ede. Later, in about 1830, the Egba fled their settlements near what is now Ibadan and established the modern city of Abeokuta. In the same year, many of the refugee soldiers from Oyo revolted against the rule of the *oni* of Ife and transformed a small village into the nucleus of the modern city of Ibadan. Thereafter, Ibadan exercised a preponderant influence within southern Yorubaland; in competition with Ijebu and Abeokuta, which also fought between themselves, its merchants sought to engross the supply and sale of slaves, and warfare naturally followed.

In the north, meanwhile, Ilorin attempted to build upon its initial victories over the Yoruba armies. In about 1833, its cavalry attacked Ijesa, but Fulani horses proved useless in a battle waged within the forest. The presence of the forest to some extent prevented the cavalry of Ilorin from conquering the divided cities of Yorubaland one by one. Usually, the Fulani could persuade at least one of the independent Yoruba cities to join them in making war upon another Yoruba city. In 1836/37, however, several Yoruba armies, led by the *alafin* of Oyo, marched together in a desperate attempt to crush the Fulani host. They possessed a numerical superiority as well as crack legions of fighting men. With victory in their grasp, however, they faltered, some among them defecting to the Fulani who had, in any event, summoned strong reinforcements from across the Niger. By this combination of circumstances, the Fulani repelled their attackers and, shortly thereafter, destroyed Oyo. The Fulani now poised themselves for the conquest of Yorubaland; indeed, it seems that they even hoped symbolically to touch the white flag of the *jihad* into the distant sea. In about 1840, the Fulani armies therefore laid siege to Oshogbo, whose defenders summoned assistance from Ibadan. Fearful of the Fulani cavalry, the soldiers of Ibadan and the new Oyo—established by refugees far to the south of the old—attacked the besiegers at night, freed Oshogbo, and ended, virtually for all time, the threat of a conquest of Yorubaland by Ilorin. Henceforth, Yoruba fought Yoruba in an interminable round of wars that lasted until the onset of British rule.

The creation of new states in the western sudan

The teachings and example of Usuman dan Fodio in Hausaland inspired two subsequent revolutions. In Maçina on the upper Niger, Muslims of Fulani and Soninke extraction lived uneasily as subjects of seemingly pagan Fulani, who were themselves vassals of the Bambara of Ségou. Onto this stage of tension stepped Ahmadu bin Hammadi Boubou, a Fulani cleric who had evidently studied under Usuman dan Fodio in Sokoto before returning home to the Maçina region, where he opened a Qur'an school and preached the gospel of Islamic reform. By so doing, he gained adherents sufficiently numerous to worry the rulers of Maçina and Ségou. In 1818, according to the "official" version of the story, they tried to imprison him, but Ahmadu proclaimed a *jihad* and quickly routed the Bambara and Fulani armies. He deposed the *ardo* of Maçina, ousted the authorities of Djenné and Mopti, established the capital town of Hamdullahi east of the Bani River, and proceeded to rule the old area of which Maçina had been the capital.[46] In 1826/27, Ahmadu extended his conquests to Timbuktu and the upper reaches of the Volta River.

Ahmadu governed strictly the five emirates into which he and his soldiers had carved up the new state of Maçina. He reorganized the existing systems of taxation and conscription, appointed new judges, and, in general, created an intolerant theocracy, as the rulers of which he and the members of his council of state largely ordered the daily lives of their subjects. They forcibly converted pagans and deprived their subjects of the pleasures of beer, tobacco, and dancing. According to Barth, Ahmadu even extended these strictures to Timbuktu:

> [The Fulani of Maçina became] *far more fanatical champions of the faith than the Arabs and Moors; and treating the inhabitants of the newly conquered city* [Timbuktu], *as well as the foreigners who used to visit it, with extreme rigour, according to the prejudices which they had imbibed, they could not fail to ruin almost the whole commercial activity of the place. Their oppression was not confined to the pagan traders . . . but extended even to the Mohammedan merchants from the north.*[47]

The very severity of the orthodox reformers invited further reaction. Although Ahmadu's son and grandson both attempted to consolidate their own positions within the theocratic state bequeathed to them, the inhabitants of Timbuktu and Maçina soon grew restless. With assistance from the Tuareg tribes of the nearby desert, Timbuktu rejected orthodox Muslim rule. Then Ahmadu III alienated anew a proportion of the learned community and the overwhelming majority of the ordinary people of his state. In 1862, therefore, they welcomed the activities of al-hajj 'Umar bin Sa'id, who invaded Maçina and ended the reign of Ahmadu.

A member of the Tokolor clerical class, 'Umar received his early education in Futa Toro. During the years from about 1820 to 1825, when he was approximately thirty years old, he undertook a pilgrimage to the Muslim Holy Cities.[48] There, no doubt, the militant struggle of the orthodox Wahhabi against their Turkish rulers influenced his own thoughts on Islamic reform. Even more

---

[46] Amadou Hampaté Ba and Jacques Daget, *L'Empire peul du Maçina, 1818–1853* (Paris, 1962), I, 29–42, 45–48; Charles Monteil, *Une Cité soudanaise: Djenné, métropole du delta central du Niger* (Paris, 1932), pp. 99–105. But see Maurice Delafosse, *Haut-Sénégal-Niger* (Paris, 1912), II, p. 236.

[47] Barth, *Travels*, IV, p. 434.

[48] J. Spencer Trimingham, *A History of Islam in West Africa* (Glasgow, 1962), p. 181, gives slightly different dates.

significantly, in Medina 'Umar became closely associated with the evangelical Tijaniyya brotherhood. Like Sheikh 'Ahmad al-Tijani, the founder of the brotherhood who died in 1815, 'Umar believed that divine grace had singled out the Tijanis—whatever sins they might commit—for salvation. He asserted the moral superiority of the Tijanis over all other Muslims.[49] Later, after 'Umar had returned to the Western Sudan, he propagated the doctrines of the new order and capitalized upon his own supposedly intimate relationship with the leaders of the brotherhood.

From 1826 until his return to the Western Sudan in 1838, 'Umar resided in Sokoto.[50] In Sokoto he influenced Muhammadu Bello, married his daughter, and conceivably may have converted the Sarkin Musulmi to the Tijaniyya. In their turn, the imperial successes of the Fulani and the military organization of their *jihad* impressed the erudite 'Umar. Meanwhile, his own religious ideas presumably developed into a political and social creed. He also attracted a number of Fulani and Hausa disciples and amassed a large fortune in cowries and slaves before moving westward.

After visiting Hamdullahi and being expelled from Ségou, 'Umar and a considerable entourage carefully tried to lay the groundwork for a revolution. He gathered a large number of new followers. He equipped these believers with modern firearms purchased from European traders and disciplined them in accord with the rather rigid precepts of the Tijaniyya brotherhood.

During the years between 1848 and 1852, 'Umar's movement gained momentum. At his staging camp in Dinguiraye, his army readied for combat and, it seems clear, 'Umar "deliberately created the conditions of tension which were the preliminary to *jihad*." [51] In 1852, his troops defeated an army loyal to the Bambara chiefs of Tamba. 'Umar thereupon proclaimed a *jihad* and his Tokolor, Fulani, and Hausa regiments, accompanied by Westernized artisans, quickly conquered Bambouk and invaded Kaarta. Nioro, the latter's capital, fell in 1854. To the west, 'Umar attacked Galam on the middle Senegal, but French forces forestalled this invasion during the years from 1857 to 1859.

The *jihadi* then moved east. In 1861, 'Umar took Ségou and, in the process, confronted troops loyal to Ahmadu III of Maçina. The armies of the two great modern Islamic reformers of the Western Sudan thereupon met in battle. But before they did so, Ahmadu III evidently wrote five letters to 'Umar protesting, in much the same vein as Shehu al-Kanemi had protested to Muhammadu Bello, that a *jihad* could not and should not be directed by one Islamic movement against another orthodox Muslim state like his own. In reply to these letters, 'Umar in turn echoed the style and content of Muhammadu Bello's

---

[49] Jamil Abun-Nasr, "Some Aspects of the Umari Branch of the Tijaniyya," *The Journal of African History*, III (1962), p. 329. Al-hajj 'Umar may have been influenced by the Tijaniyya before his visit to Medina.

[50] With regard to the first date, see Clapperton, *Journal*, p. 203. H. F. C. Smith, "Theme," p. 181, accepts it. But see Abun-Nasr, "Umari Branch," p. 329. See also the reference in Hajj Sa'id (trans. Octave Houdas), *Histoire du Sokoto* (Paris, 1901), p. 308.

[51] H. F. C. Smith, "Theme," p. 182. See also Frédéric Carrère and Paul Holle, *De la Sénégambie française* (Paris, 1855), pp. 195–208.

Infaq al-Maisur. 'Umar, like Muhammadu Bello, claimed that his own war against Ahmadu III derived its legitimacy from the assistance that Ahmadu had given to the "pagan" rulers of Ségou. In 1862/63, 'Umar therefore destroyed Hamdullahi, conquered Maçina, and sacked Timbuktu.[52]

For a period of months, 'Umar ruled supreme from Dinguiraye and Nioro to Timbuktu. Throughout this vast state, he attempted both to impose Tijani allegiance upon those who still adhered to the tenets of the older Islamic brotherhood, the Qaddiriyya, and to convert unbelievers by force. But his program of brazen reform met with serious opposition from the Fulani inhabitants of Maçina, who believed themselves to be Muslims superior to those who followed 'Umar. They refused to accept 'Umar's dogmatic dissemination of the Tijani creed with equanimity. In 1863/64, the Fulani and their allies rebelled, killed 'Umar, and ousted the Tokolor armies from much of Ahmadu's old state. Thereafter, 'Umar's son, also named Ahmadu, found it increasingly difficult to retain control over all of the empire that he had inherited. His brothers governed provinces of the empire largely without reference to him. Subject peoples frequently revolted; the French threatened his hegemony from the west. His followers also grew tired of war and evidently wished to till the soil so that they might reap the fruits of their hard-won victories. By 1874, although Ahmadu had managed to re-assert himself over portions of 'Umar's vast state, and had once again unified the petty kingdoms into which it had become fractured, he had come to depend more and more upon subject peoples and slaves for the administration of the central section of the old empire. The Tokolor lost their control and many of the attributes of their power. Soon French forces destroyed what remained of the old empire and, in time, apostasy even replaced conversion to Islam.

---

[52] Abun-Nasr, "Umari Branch," p. 331; Louis Tauxier, *Histoire des Bambara* (Paris, 1942), pp. 161–169. For the campaigns, see Delafosse, *Sénégal*, pp. 307–323.

If the English should meet with too great encouragement, they [will] come into [the] Soudan, one after another, until they [get] strong enough to seize on the country, and dispossess [its rulers], as they had . . . wrested [India] from the hands of the Mahometans.

—Attributed to Shehu al-Kanemi, c. *1824*

7 THE INTERACTION OF AFRICA AND EUROPE, 1788–1884

Until the end of the eighteenth century, the mutual interests of tropical Africa and Europe sought an almost exclusively commercial expression. The nations of the Northern Hemisphere traded guns, brandy, calicos, silks, beads, and metal bars for the gold, gum, and slaves of Africa. Liverpool, for example, thereby bound itself to Calabar; Abomey and Whydah likewise linked themselves to Montego Bay and Bordeaux. In large part, this interaction helped to encourage new kinds of African endeavor and to stimulate the emergence of new examples of indigenous and colonial statecraft. Subsequently, however, the invention of the steam engine, the European exploration of the interior of Africa, the abolition of the slave trade, the growth of industry in Europe, and the conquest of malaria through the use of quinine all acted to change the character of tropical trade and, with the emergence of new economic and political needs both in Europe and Africa, to inject Europe more completely than ever before into the fabric of African society. Thus the actions of explorers, abolitionists, missionaries, merchants, consulars of trade, and soldiers eventually played a significant part in creating a new understanding of, and effecting a rapprochement with, the tribes, kingdoms, and states of nineteenth-century Africa. By their responses to immediate events, they evoked an atmosphere conducive to the later era of scramble and partition; their first steps led ultimately to Europe's conquest of tropical Africa.

I. The Third Age of African Exploration

During the last years of the eighteenth century, Europeans actively started to seek accurate information about the interior of what had hitherto been regarded as the "dark continent." Of its configuration, they knew little more than Ptolemy, Idrisi, and Leo Africanus; indeed, their cartographers had habitually filled gaps in the maps of the day with "savage-pictures," placing "o'er uninhabitable downs . . . elephants for want of towns."[1] Their own economic disinterest, the relative lack of easy access to the interior, fears—dating at least from Strabo's day—about the harshness of the climate, and, in part, the hostility of the indigenous peoples had, except in Moçambique, Angola, and Ethiopia, effectively confined Europeans to the coastal regions of tropical Africa. Physically, deserts inhibited overland travel, and large rivers, often obscured at their mouths by sand bars or mazes of forest delta and blocked upstream by cataracts, failed to provide routes comparable to the Amazon, Mississippi, or Hudson. Furthermore, from the fifteenth through the eighteenth centuries, West African chiefs and middlemen had refused to permit a general advance by Europeans into the interior. They had controlled European settlements, prevented foreigners from tapping their own sources of slaves and gold directly, and had widely asserted their own numerical, economic, and, to a large extent, military superiority. The French, for example, paid tribute to Cayor and to a number of Wolof chiefs from the middle of the seventeenth century until 1854.[2] The indigenous inhabitants of tropical Africa thus retained the upper hand on the coast of West Africa and in the interior of tropical Africa until the efforts of individual explorers eventually dispelled Europe's ignorance and the actions of abolitionists and industrialists both ended the slave trade and encouraged the great expansion of "legitimate commerce" that transformed the positions of economic power in much of tropical Africa.

The intellectual and economic climate of late eighteenth- and early nineteenth-century Europe encouraged white men to seek answers to the riddles of Africa. Captain Cook's earlier voyage to *Terra Incognita Australis* had captured the public imagination and had encouraged others to imitate his exploits elsewhere. The manufacturers of Europe meanwhile sought new markets and, during an age of renewed evangelical fervor, missionaries looked for areas to which they could take the Gospel. For such a combination of reasons and, during the Victorian era in Britain, for social and political reasons as well, the exploration of Africa filled national needs and provided abundant opportunities for the achievement of great personal glory. Although exploration later became the servant of imperial expansion, at first the individual explorers and their sponsors sought more simply—but with commercial and scientific ends in mind—to answer the questions that had baffled both the ancient and the more modern writers: What was the source of the Nile River? Herodotus had failed to reach a satisfactory answer; Ptolemy had suggested great lakes fed by snow-capped mountains; others had traced its course from a marsh, had equated it with the Niger River, or had pictured it on their maps flowing across Africa from the Atlantic to the Indian oceans. Where did the Niger River go? Did it

[1] Jonathan Swift, *On Poetry: A Rhapsody* (London, 1733), l. 177. Cf. Ranulf Higden (trans. William Caxton), *Polychronicon* (London, 1480), cited in George H. T. Kimble, *Geography in the Middle Ages* (London, 1938), p. 212.

[2] On these points, see Robin Hallett, "The European Approach to the Interior of Africa in the Eighteenth Century," *The Journal of African History*, IV (1963), pp. 192–196; K. Onwuka Dike, *Trade and Politics in the Niger Delta, 1830–1885* (Oxford, 1956), pp. 4–10. See also Archibald Dalzel, *The History of Dahomey* (London, 1793), pp. 9–10, 44–45.

empty out into an ocean? Did it end in a great swamp or a desert? Or, as Leo Africanus suggested, did the Niger flow westward into the Atlantic from some interior source? Were the Congo and the Niger rivers one? Were there mountains near the equator, as Ptolemy had implied? Where were the so-called Mountains of the Moon? Were there great lakes in eastern Africa? Was inner

Africa desert or swamp? Who inhabited the African interior? Were there cannibals? [3]

The niger quest

In 1788, twelve British intellectuals, ten of whom were fellows of the Royal Society, formed the Association for Promoting the Discovery of the Interior Parts of Africa—the African Association—in order to seek answers to some of these questions. Encouraged by Sir Joseph Banks, who conceived the idea of such an association (he was a prominent botanist who had sailed to Australia with Cook and had subsequently become the president of the Royal Society and the director of the Kew Gardens), they sought to increase the extent of their own and of Europe's scientific knowledge of the unknown regions of Africa. They also wanted to turn to direct commercial use whatever discoveries might be made. Humanitarian and abolitionist sentiments apparently played no major part in their decision.[4] Specifically, at their second meeting, the members of the Association resolved that since the map of the interior of Africa was still "but a wide extended blank, on which the Geographer, on the authority of Leo Africanus . . . has traced, with a hesitating hand, a few names of unexplored rivers and of uncertain nations," and, especially, because its "places and termination, and even its existence as a separate stream" was still undetermined, the Association should initially attempt to unravel the riddle of the Niger.[5]

The Association sought direct evidence. To Cairo, Banks quickly despatched John Ledyard, an idiosyncratic American who had sailed with Cook to the Sandwich (Hawaiian) Islands and who had subsequently walked around the Gulf of Bothnia, from Stockholm to St. Petersburg, in midwinter. The Association directed Ledyard to traverse Africa from east to west "in the latitude attributed to the Niger." [6] To Simon Lucas, a sometime British vice consul in Morocco who spoke fluent Arabic, Banks entrusted the equally difficult task of following the caravan routes from Tripoli to Fezzan, and thence, *via* Timbuktu, to the Atlantic coast of Africa. In 1789, however, Ledyard died in Cairo before he could play a significant part in the quest for the Niger. In the same year, Lucas found the route to Fezzan blocked by rebellion.[7] He

[3] For a discussion of a number of these matters, see W. G. L. Randles, "South East Africa and the Empire of Monomotapa as Shown on Selected Printed Maps of the 16th Century," *Studia*, 1 (1958), pp. 126–129; Osbert Guy Stanhope Crawford, "Some Medieval Theories About the Nile," *The Geographical Journal*, CXIV (1949), pp. 18, 28–29. See also Isaac Vossius, *De Nili et Aliorum Fluminum Origine* (The Hague, 1666), pp. 69–70; Filippo Pigafetta (trans. Margarite Hutchinson), *A Report of the Kingdom of Congo and of the Surrounding Countries* (London, 1881 [original Italian edition, 1591]), pp. 129–132.

[4] A. Adu Boahen, "The African Association, 1788–1805," *Transactions of the Historical Society of Ghana*, V (1961), pp. 43–64. See also a statement of Joseph Banks, quoted in *Proceedings of the Association for Promoting the Discovery of the Interior Parts of Africa* (London, 1810), II, p. 5; *ibid.*, I, pp. 205, 258.

[5] *Proceedings of the Association for Promoting the Discovery of the Interior Parts of Africa* (London, 1790), p. 6.

[6] *Ibid.*, p. 20; Jared Sparks, *Life of John Ledyard: The American Traveller* (Boston, 1847), pp. 377, 388.

[7] Some of Lucas' findings are printed in *Proceedings of the Association* (1810), I, pp. 84–191.

thereupon returned to England. The Association next sent Major Daniel Francis Houghton, who had previously served the British government in Senegambia, up the Gambia River, which was thought by many learned Europeans to be the mouth of the Niger. In 1790/91, Houghton penetrated the interior of Senegambia at least as far as the gold fields of Bambouk. There, or subsequently *en route* to Timbuktu, he either died of fever or was killed by hostile Africans. Before Houghton met his death, however, he reported to the Association that the assumptions of Leo Africanus were probably false. Houghton suggested, and the Association accepted his finding, that the Niger flowed to the east, not to the west.[8] But if it did, he and his patrons wondered, where did the river go?

The pursuit of the Niger quest languished until 1795, by which time Houghton's death had been confirmed. In that year Mungo Park, a young Scottish doctor, returned from a long voyage to Sumatra. Banks suggested that Park should try to solve the baffling problem of the Niger. In the early summer of 1795, when he was twenty-four years old, Park therefore set sail for the Gambia River.

"My instructions," he wrote, "were very plain." The Association directed me " 'to pass on to the river Niger, either by the way of Bambouk, or by such other route as should be found most convenient.' " The Association hoped

> *That I should ascertain the course, and, if possible, the rise and termination of that river. That I should use my utmost exertions to visit the principal towns or cities in its neighbourhood. . . .*[9]

After spending five months in Senegambia learning local variations of Mande, Park proceeded eastward accompanied by two Africans. He followed well-established trade routes through Médine and the kingdom of Kaarta, where Africans robbed him of many of his possessions, to Benown, where the sultan kept Park captive for three long, unpleasant months. Escaping in the summer of 1796, Park stumbled toward Ségou, a Bambara market town on the Niger. Hungry and frightened, he eventually approached his objective. Then early one morning a passing African called to him:

> [*He said*] Geo Affili (*see the water*), *and looking forwards, I saw with infinite pleasure the great object of my mission—the long sought for majestic Niger, glittering to the morning sun, as broad as the Thames at Westminster, and flowing slowly to the eastward.*[10]

Park could learn little more of the Niger. After following it downstream for six days, he grew afraid of the "fanatical Moors" who inhabited the riverain regions beyond Djenné. He therefore retraced his steps to Ségou and hastily returned to the Gambia and England. Of the course of the Niger he knew

---

[8] *Ibid.*, I, pp. 256, 263.

[9] Ronald Miller (ed.), *Travels of Mungo Park* (London, 1954 [Park's original narrative was published in 1799]), pp. 1–2.

[10] *Ibid.*, p. 149. The comparison of the Niger with the Thames at Westminster is oddly foreshadowed in the *Proceedings of the Association* (1790), p. 123.

only that it continued beyond Timbuktu into Hausaland and then ran on to "the world's end." Park wrote:

> *Of the further progress of this great river, and its final exit, all the natives with whom I conversed seemed to be entirely ignorant. Their commercial pursuits seldom induce them to travel further than the cities of Timbuctoo and Houssa; and as the sole object of those journeys is the acquirement of wealth, they pay but little attention to the course of rivers, or the geography of countries. . . . All my informants agreed, that [the] many . . . Negro merchants who arrive at Timbuctoo and Houssa from the east . . . are ignorant of the termination of the river, for such of them as can speak Arabic, describe the amazing length of its course in very general terms, saying only that they believe it runs to the world's end.*[11]

Park, by virtue of his empirical evidence, had disproved Leo Africanus. If anything, however, his report made the question of the river's course and exit that much more tantalizing to the savants of Europe. On behalf of the Association, Friedrich Conrad Hornemann, a young German disguised as an Arab, followed the caravan trails from Cairo to Fezzan and then perhaps to Bornu and the Niger between 1798 and 1800. Like Herodotus, he believed the Niger and Nile rivers to be one.[12] But before he could prove or disprove his theory—or even send back an account of his journey—he succumbed to fever or dysentery somewhere south of Fezzan.

During the next few years, Britain's foremost armchair geographers took up the question of the Niger afresh. Some concluded that the Niger River flowed into a great swamp east of Timbuktu, where it slowly evaporated. They argued that if the well-known Oil Rivers were truly the delta of the Niger, they would widely be accepted as such. Others assumed that the Niger and the Congo rivers were one. Some continued to assert the unity of the Nile and the Niger. A lone German, whose views were widely discredited, held correctly that the Niger emptied into the Bight of Benin.[13] In order to resolve these perplexing theories once and for all, and to counter French designs upon the commerce of Senegambia and the Western Sudan, Mungo Park agreed to abandon his peacefully obscure medical practice in Scotland in order to lead a large party of explorers sponsored by the Colonial Office. In 1805, Park and forty-five other armed Britons thus proceeded up the Gambia and down the Niger.[14] One by one, the white members of his entourage lost their lives. And in the spring of 1806, after sailing downstream from Sansanding, Park and his few remaining

---

[11] Miller, *Mungo Park*, pp. 163–164.

[12] *Proceedings of the Association* (1810), I, pp. 202, 268. See also Francis Moore, *Travels into the Inland Parts of Africa* (London, 1738), p. 28.

[13] Christian Gottlieb Reichard, "Ueber die Vermuthung des Dr. *Seetzen* zu Jever, dass sich der *Niger* in Afrika vielleicht mit dem *Zaire* vereinigen könne," *Monatliche Correspondenz zur Beförderung der Erd-und Himmels-kunde,* V (1802), pp. 409–415. See the discussion of Reichard's contribution in Philip D. Curtin, *The Image of Africa: British Ideas and Action, 1780–1850* (Madison, Wisc., 1964), pp. 203–205.

[14] The expedition marked the first occasion on which the British government sponsored African exploration.

British companions perished near Bussa—probably after being received inhospitably by local Africans.[15] At the time, the officers of the Association and other Europeans failed to appreciate the magnitude of Park's achievement. No one knew precisely where Bussa was; many thought that it was no more than eighty, instead of eight hundred, miles downstream from Timbuktu.

After the conclusion of the Napoleonic Wars, Europeans continued to seek an understanding of the Niger's course. The British government urged Captain James Kingston Tuckey to ascend the Congo River in order to determine its relationship to the Niger and, in general, its place in the geography of the African interior.[16] Simultaneously, the government despatched two army officers to Senegambia, where they were expected to follow the course of the Niger downstream until they met Tuckey, hopefully proceeding upstream, or until they reached the Niger's outlet. But fever forced both expeditions back to the coast, with great loss of life, long before either had accomplished its major objectives.[17]

British travelers thereafter sought once again to follow the trans-Saharan trade routes that led, so they were told, to Timbuktu. In 1818, Joseph Ritchie and George Lyon traveled from Tripoli to Murzuk, in Fezzan, where Ritchie succumbed to an African illness. Lyon thereupon returned to Tripoli and to Britain, where, on the basis of information obtained in the markets of Murzuk, he espoused the hypothesis that the Niger and the Nile were different names for the same river.[18] Four years later, Major Dixon Denham, Lieutenant Hugh Clapperton, and Dr. Walter Oudney started across the desert from Tripoli at the behest of the British government. Successful, they became the first modern Europeans to espy Lake Chad and to traverse Bornu.[19] Denham later investigated the course of the Chari River and, after Oudney's death, Clapperton went on to Kano. In 1824, he continued westward to Sokoto, where Muhammadu Bello, Sarkin Musulmi, drew a map of the Niger in the sand and explained how easy it would be for the traders of Europe to reach Hausaland by sailing up the great river that emptied into the Gulf of Guinea.[20] At this point, Clapperton naturally wanted to proceed immediately to the river and, if Muhammadu Bello were right, to follow it downstream into the Gulf. But Muhammadu Bello categorically refused to permit Clapperton to continue beyond Sokoto to the Niger; Clapperton reluctantly returned to Kukawa and thence, in company with Denham, retraced his steps to Tripoli and London.

Clapperton's new information about the course of the Niger appeared to

---

[15] K. Lupton, "The Death of Mungo Park at Bussa," *Nigeria Magazine*, 72 (March, 1962), pp. 68–69. See also *Sixth Report of the Directors of the African Institution* (London, 1812), pp. 22–24.

[16] James Kingston Tuckey (ed. anonymously, but probably by Sir John Barrow), *Narrative of an Expedition to Explore the River Zaire, Usually Called the Congo, in South Africa* (London, 1818), pp. xxi–xxiii.

[17] Charles Hulbert (ed.), *African Fragments: Comprising Mr. William Lee's Narrative of Two Expeditions into the Interior of Africa, Etc.* (Shrewsbury, 1826), pp. 6–32.

[18] George Francis Lyon, A *Narrative of Travels in Northern Africa* (London, 1821), p. 148.

[19] Dixon Denham, Hugh Clapperton, and Walter Oudney, *Travels and Discoveries in Northern and Central Africa* (London, 1831 [first edition, 1826]), I, pp. 203–206.

[20] *Ibid.*, IV, pp. 100, 114–118.

The battle of Musfeia, a Fulani town in Mandara, as witnessed by Major Dixon Denham in 1823. Arab mercenaries in the employ of Bornu failed to overcome the stout resistance of the Fulani bowmen and, their superior firepower notwithstanding, fled after a combat of several hours. (Denham, Clapperton and Oudney, *Narrative of Travels and Discoveries in Northern and Central Africa,* London, 1826)

bear out the case put forward in 1821 by James MacQueen, a West Indian planter turned publicist. MacQueen had questioned his slaves, some of whom had supposedly heard of Mungo Park, and had—as early as 1816—surmised that the Oil Rivers were merely the lower reaches of the Niger.[21] In order to follow up this promising lead, the British government sent Clapperton and four other Britons, including Richard Lemon Lander, Clapperton's young Cornish servant, to the Oil Rivers. There, however, no one had heard of the ports that Muhammadu Bello had so confidently placed at the mouth of the Niger. Resolved, nonetheless, to test the veracity of Muhammadu Bello, Clapperton sailed to Badagri and, with Lander only, trekked northward through Yorubaland to Kano. Plagued by dysentery and fever, Clapperton then went on alone at the request of Muhammadu Bello to Sokoto, where he found that his former friends—preoccupied as they were by a war against Bornu—were no longer anxious to ally themselves to the nations of Europe.[22]

---

[21] James MacQueen, *A Geographical and Commercial View of Northern Central Africa: Containing a Particular Account of the Course and Termination of the Great River Niger in the Atlantic Ocean* (Edinburgh, 1821), pp. vii, 122–127. This obviously contained a new statement of Reichard's hypothesis.

[22] Hugh Clapperton, *Journal of A Second Expedition into the Interior of Africa from the Bight of Benin to Soccatoo* (London, 1829), pp. 199, 231, 234–235, 238.

After Clapperton's death there in 1827, Lander, then twenty-three years old, attempted to follow the Niger to its mouth. But the emir of Zaria prevented him from proceeding southward toward the Benue River; after a number of vicissitudes, Lander eventually made his way overland to Badagri and England.[23] In 1830, however, Lander and his brother John journeyed on foot from Badagri to Bussa, where they procured two leaky canoes. They paddled downstream and, after a number of adventures, reached Brass, on the Bight of Benin, having at long last proved that Park's Niger and the Oil Rivers were indeed identical.[24]

The Landers had demonstrated the existence of a seemingly easy route into the interior of West Africa. In addition, the Frenchman Gaspard Mollien had ascertained the sources of the Senegal and Gambia rivers in 1818, and both Alexander Gordon Laing, a Briton, and René Caillié, another Frenchman, had visited Timbuktu during the years between 1826 and 1828.[25] Together these different explorations encouraged European entrepreneurs to believe that they might, at last, tap the indigenous markets of which they had heard rumors for so long. In order to test their commercial feasibility, Macgregor Laird, a British shipbuilder, outfitted a new marine expedition and persuaded Richard Lander to guide it up the Niger. In 1832, Laird's two iron steamships struggled up the Niger to its confluence with the Benue at Lokoja. And during 1833, Lander and Richard Oldfield cruised up both rivers beyond Lokoja.[26] They obtained detailed information about African trade, but their reports dampened the enthusiasm of those who foresaw the Nigerian interior as a field into which European enterprise could profitably expand. Moreover, forty of the forty-nine Europeans who took part in the expedition, including Richard Lander, died.

For the next few years, British interests in this region owed their furtherance solely to the energy of John Beecroft, a Yorkshireman who had become the uncrowned king of Fernão do Pó. Privately financed by Robert Jamieson, a Liverpool palm oil trader, Beecroft ascended the Niger as far as Idah in 1835, explored the upper reaches of the Cross River in 1836 and, in 1840, proved that the Benin River was no more than an inlet of the sea.[27]

The British government, encouraged by Sir Thomas Fowell Buxton and the abolitionist movement, finally attempted to capitalize upon these many pio-

[23] "Journal of Richard Lander, Servant to the Late Captain Clapperton," in *ibid.*, pp. 298, 304.

[24] Richard and John Lander, *Journal of an Expedition to Explore the Course and Termination of the Niger* (London, 1832), III, pp. 231–234.

[25] Gaspard Théodore Mollien (trans. and ed. Thomas Edward Bowdich), *Travels in the Interior of Africa to the Sources of the Senegal and Gambia* (London, 1820), pp. 233–236, 262–263; Rĕné Caillié, *Travels Through Central Africa to Timbuctoo* (London, 1830), II, pp. 47–83. For the much earlier European travels to Tuat and Timbuktu, see Charles de la Roncière, *La Découverte de l'Afrique au Moyen Âge* (Cairo, 1924), I, pp. 143–166.

[26] Macgregor Laird and Richard A. K. Oldfield, *Narrative of an Expedition into the Interior of Africa by the River Niger in the Steam Vessels Quorra and Alburkah in 1832, 1833, and 1834* (London, 1837), II, pp. 353–404.

[27] K. Onwuka Dike, "John Beecroft, 1790–1854," *Journal of the Historical Society of Nigeria*, I (1956), p. 11.

Timbuktu as drawn by René Caillié after his visit there in 1828. Note the different types of housing and the three prominent mosques. (René Caillié, *Journal d'un voyage à Timboctou,* Paris, 1830)

neering ventures by establishing a colony of freed slaves near Lokoja. There Buxton envisaged the establishment of an agricultural settlement, the inhabitants of which would support themselves and thereby encourage the growth of legitimate Christian commerce as a civilizing substitute for slave trading.[28] To further their objectives, he and his supporters organized the Society for the Extinction of the Slave Trade and the Civilization of Africa, which in turn sponsored the large expedition that steamed up the Niger early in 1841. Despite the careful planning lavished upon it by British missionary societies and the Admiralty, however, 48 of the 145 whites who went upstream died of fever within two months of their arrival. (In all, 53 of the 303 original European and African members of the expedition lost their lives.) Before long, the Society evacuated the remaining members of the expedition, removed the farm equipment from Lokoja and, in 1842, finally ended Britain's most ambitious attempt

[28] For a discussion of "civilized trade" see Curtin, *Image,* pp. 255, 270, 301. See also John Gallagher, "Fowell Buxton and the New African Policy, 1838–1842," *The Cambridge Historical Journal,* X (1950), pp. 36–58. Robert Jamieson argued against it. See his *An Appeal to the Government and People of Great Britain Against the Proposed Niger Expedition* (London, 1840).

to exploit the discoveries of Richard and John Lander.[29] Only in 1854, when Dr. William Balfour Baikie guided the steamship *Pleïad* upstream to Lokoja and thence toward Yola on the Benue River, warding off the deadly fever by carefully administering quinine to his companions and crew, was the future of European navigation on the Niger assured.[30] Thereafter, steamships and traders plied the Niger, and European commercial enterprise, the forerunner of the partition of Africa, followed a course of perceptible expansion.

Simultaneously, a number of illustrious explorers filled in the missing details of the map of West Africa. Of these, Heinrich Barth, a German scholar of Arabic, proved the most perceptive. With the abolitionist James Richardson, a Briton, and Adolf Overweg, another German, he re-opened the trans-Saharan route for Great Britain, traversed the Western and Central Sudan during the years between 1850 and 1854, uncovered manuscripts of immeasurable historic value, and contributed impressively to Europe's subsequent understanding of the people and places of the African interior. He visited Agades, Kukawa, Katsina, Sokoto, and Timbuktu, investigated the upper reaches of the Benue River, and plotted the middle course of the Niger River.[31] Overweg, Barth's sometime companion, surveyed and navigated Lake Chad. In 1865, Gerhard Rohlfs, another German, reached Fezzan and Tibesti from Morocco and then went on to Kukawa and down the Benue to Lagos. Gustav Nachtigal traveled from Tripoli to Bornu in 1869, and contributed an important discourse on Bagirmi.[32] Later Paul Belloni du Chaillu, an American, explored Gabon; Captain Richard Francis Burton visited Cameroun and Dahomey; and, in 1873, Louis Eugène Dupont, the marquis de Compiègne, and Oskar Lenz explored the Ogooué River. Then in 1881, two Italians, Pellegrino Matteucci and Alfonso Maria Massari, crossed Africa from east to west—from Suakin to Brass. Theirs was, however, among the last of the major journeys undertaken simply in the service of West African exploration. Now that they and their predecessors had unmasked the main features of West Africa, treaty-makers gradually replaced simple explorers on the paths of the interior. As Africans had long

[29] But see C. C. Ifemesia, "The 'Civilizing' Mission of 1841: Aspects of an Episode in Anglo-Nigerian Relations," *Journal of the Historical Society of Nigeria*, II (1962), pp. 308–310. The detailed contemporary account is William Allen and T. R. H. Thomson, *A Narrative of the Expedition Sent by Her Majesty's Government to the River Niger in 1841* (London, 1848), 2v.

[30] See William Balfour Baikie, *Narrative of an Exploring Voyage up the Rivers Kwora and Binue* (*Commonly Known as the Niger and Tsadda*) *in 1854* (London, 1856); Philip D. Curtin, " 'The White Man's Grave': Image and Reality, 1780–1850," *The Journal of British Studies*, I (1961), pp. 108–109. Europeans generally refused to acknowledge the efficacy of quinine as a malarial prophylaxis until the early years of the twentieth century.

[31] Heinrich Barth, *Travels and Discoveries in North and Central Africa* (London, 1857/58), 5v. For an assessment, see A. Adu Boahen, *Britain, the Sahara, and the Western Sudan, 1788–1861* (Oxford, 1964), pp. 181–182. See also R. Mansell Prothero, "Heinrich Barth and the Western Sudan," *The Geographical Journal*, CXXIV (1958), pp. 326–337.

[32] Gerhard Rohlfs, *Quer durch Afrika: Reise vom Mittelmeer nach dem Tschad-See und zum Golf von Guinea* (Leipzig, 1875), II; Gustav Nachtigal, *Sahara und Sudan: Ergebnisse sechsjähriger Reisen in Afrika* (Berlin, 1881), II, pp. 477–728.

feared, these newcomers sought territorial concessions and, in time, soldiers and gunboats came in their train.

To the heart of africa

Beyond the Niger, the forest, savannah, and desert of eastern and Central Africa shrouded peoples and features as mysterious as those "discovered" in the west. Of the efforts of the early Portuguese adventurers, particularly those who traveled in the hinterland of Moçambique during the sixteenth and seventeenth centuries, little is known.[33] They failed, for the most part, to occasion any active official interest. The magnificent journey of James Bruce through the Sudan and Ethiopia in the years between 1769 and 1773 significantly furthered Europe's understanding of the political and natural history of both those areas. But many learned Britons greeted his exploits skeptically at first; his journals were not published, moreover, until after the formation of the African Association.[34] A far less successful expedition, that of the Lusitanian physician and governor of the Sena Rivers, Francisco José Maria de Lacerda e Almeida, likewise excited Europe little. In 1798, Lacerda reached the capital of the Lunda *mwata* Kazembe after an arduous trek from Tete, but he died there of fever before being able to proceed westward to Angola. Thereafter, two mixed-blood slave traders, Amaro José and Pedro João Baptista, traversed the continent from Luanda to Tete between 1802 and 1814 (Kazembe detained them twice for a total of four years), without arousing much comment. Then in 1831/32, two officers, Majors José Correia Monteiro and António Pedroso Gamitto, sought to discover an easy route from Moçambique to Angola that could help to bind together physically the two Portuguese possessions. But they failed to proceed beyond Lake Mweru.[35]

The explorations of David Livingstone kindled a renewed Western interest in the heart of Africa. At the age of ten, Livingstone went to work in a Scottish cotton mill. Later he studied medicine in Glasgow and, in time, joined the London Missionary Society (an English foundation) with the expectation of being sent to China. But the first Opium War intervened, and the secretary of the Society persuaded Livingstone to join Robert Moffat at its Kuruman mission station in Bechuanaland.[36] Soon he began looking for sites for new mission stations in the desiccated region north of Kuruman.

For Livingstone, "the end of the geographical feat [was] the beginning of

---

[33] For Ethiopia and the Sudan, see *supra*, pp. 74–75, 125–128.

[34] James Bruce, *Travels to Discover the Source of the Nile in the Years 1768, 1769, 1770, 1771, 1772 and 1773* (Edinburgh, 1790), 5v.

[35] See Richard Francis Burton (trans. and ed.), *The Lands of Cazembe* (London, 1873), pp. 55–105; Auguste Verbeken and M. Walraet (trans. and eds.), *La Première Traversée du Katanga en 1806* (Bruxelles, 1953), pp. 15–23, 37–117; António C. Pedroso Gamitto (trans. Ian Cunnison), *King Kazembe* (Lisboa, 1960 [orig. ed., Lisboa, 1854]), II, pp. 9–130; Ian Cunnison, "Kazembe and the Portuguese, 1798–1832," *The Journal of African History*, II (1961), pp. 65–76.

[36] See William Garden Blaikie, *The Personal Life of David Livingstone* (New York, 1881), p. 34; Cecil Northcott, *Robert Moffat: Pioneer in Africa* (London, 1961), pp. 173–180.

the missionary enterprise." [37] In 1849, after he had married Moffat's daughter and had established a station of his own, Livingstone guided the first successful European crossing of the Kalahari "thirstland" to Lake Ngami. But his hope that "the Ngami might be a highway, capable of being traversed by boats, to an unexplored and populous region" beyond proved illusory.[38] Later, in order to provide a new outlet for evangelical enterprise, he trekked northward across the "thirstland" toward the Chobe and Zambezi rivers. Upon reaching the banks of the latter in 1851, he realized for the first time that the Zambezi might prove to be an accessible avenue into the unevangelized heart of Africa. No longer, he hoped, would missionaries and explorers be forced to travel overland across the waterless wastes of the Kalahari. At the same time, Livingstone obtained his initial glimpse of the trade in slaves that he spent the remainder of his life seeking to eradicate. "Providence," he wrote, "seems to call me to the regions beyond." [39]

Livingstone became obsessed with a desire to open up the heart of Africa to new forms of commerce and religion in order to end the slave trade, foster the Christian endeavor, and destroy the several obstacles of ignorance, poverty, and isolation that blocked, he believed, the growth of "civilization" in Africa. Between 1853 and 1856, he therefore investigated the "unknown" regions of Central Africa. From Linyanti on the Chobe River, he traveled up the Zambezi River with a small company of local Lozi- and Kololo-speaking Africans. This, his first visit to Barotseland, prepared the way for the later settlement there by British and French Protestant missionaries. Wherever his party went, it was received hospitably. Of Barotseland, Livingstone, whose journals for this period record in minute detail the customs of the peoples and the features of the countries through which he passed, later wrote:

> *The people of every village treated us most liberally, presenting, besides oxen, butter, milk, and meal, more than we could stow away in our canoes. The cows in this valley are now yielding . . . more milk than the people could use, and both men and women present butter in such quantity, that I shall be able to refresh my men as we move along.*[40]

By the first weeks of 1854, Livingstone had entered the Lunda country beyond Barotseland. Plagued by illness, he followed African trade paths to Lake Dilolo and then crossed the Cuango River into Portuguese Angola. Finally he arrived at Luanda, on the Atlantic Ocean, in the late autumn of the same year. "Never," he wrote, "shall I forget the luxuriant pleasure I enjoyed in feeling myself again on a good English couch, after six months' sleeping on the ground." [41] Weak and in urgent need of rest, Livingstone remained in Luanda for four months. Many of his acquaintances, including the British consul,

---

[37] Quoted in George Seaver, *David Livingstone: His Life and Letters* (London, 1957), p. 267.
[38] David Livingstone, *Missionary Travels and Researches in South Africa* (London, 1857), p. 65.
[39] Quoted in Seaver, *David Livingstone*, p. 114.
[40] Livingstone, *Travels*, p. 246.
[41] *Ibid.*, p. 389.

sought to persuade him to return immediately to Britain in order to announce his discoveries to the world. But Livingstone chose instead to plunge back into the heart of Africa. He resolved to take his companions back to their chief, "with a view of trying to make a path from his country to the east coast by means of the great river Zambesi." [42]

Before long, Livingstone started down the Zambezi from Linyanti. On the way, he espied falls that he later named Victoria, after the reigning queen of England. Of his first glimpse of Mosioatunya ("smoke sounds there"), he wrote:

> *. . . we came in sight . . . of the columns of vapour, appropriately called "smoke," rising at a distance of five or six miles, exactly as when large tracts of grass are burned in Africa. Five columns now arose, and bending in the direction of the wind, they seemed placed against a low ridge covered with trees; the tops of the columns at this distance appeared to mingle with the clouds. . . . The whole scene was extremely beautiful. . . . It had never been seen before by European eyes. . . . But though we . . . were within a few yards of the [falls] . . . I believe that no one could perceive where the vast body of water went; it seemed to lose itself in the earth. . . . At least I did not comprehend it until, creeping with awe to the verge, I peered down into a large rent which had been made from bank to bank of the broad Zambesi, and saw that a stream of a thousand yards broad, leaped down a hundred feet, and then became suddenly compressed into a space of fifteen or twenty yards. . . . This . . . [was] the most wonderful sight I had witnessed in Africa.*[43]

Then, avoiding the country of the warlike Ila, he trekked across the Tonga plateau and eventually followed the course of the Zambezi River through Moçambique to Quelimane, on the Indian Ocean, where he arrived in May, 1856. In twenty months, he had negotiated the "dark continent" from west to east. Six months later, after the news of his travels had preceded him home, Livingstone arrived in London to receive Britain's highest honors and to set in motion a series of events that in time resulted in the introduction of commercial and missionary enterprises into the regions that he had explored.

Livingstone completely captured public sympathy. When he appealed for religious reinforcements and for a full-scale attack upon the slave trade, all of Britain listened. The famous speech at Cambridge epitomized his appeal:

> *I know that in a few years I shall be cut off in that country which is now open; do not let it be shut again. I go back to Africa to try to make an open path for Christianity. Do you carry out the work which I have begun. I leave it to you.*[44]

Livingstone's achievement encouraged others to seek answers to the many remaining mysteries of central and eastern Africa. Already in the years between 1848 and 1851, Ludwig Krapf and Johann Rebmann, German members of the Church Missionary Society stationed at Mombasa, had heard tales of the interior that appeared to confirm Ptolemy's description.[45] They reported

---

[42] *Ibid.*, p. 391.
[43] *Ibid.*, pp. 519–520.
[44] William Monk (ed.), *Dr. Livingstone's Cambridge Lectures* (London, 1860), p. 168.
[45] But see Crawford, "Medieval Theories," p. 19.

the existence of two snow-capped mountains near the equator; Rebmann personally sighted the slopes of Kilimanjaro. "One morning," he wrote,

> *I fancied I saw the summit of one of [the mountains of Chagga] covered with a dazzlingly white cloud. My guide called the white which I saw, merely* beredi, *cold; it was perfectly clear to me, however, that it could be nothing else but snow.*[46]

On the basis of their own experiences as well as African accounts, they reported the existence of a vast lake—the "Sea of Ujiji"—somewhere west of the coast. Startling though these revelations were, the learned "armchair geographers" of Europe largely discounted their credibility. Some of these theoreticians ridiculed the disclosures of Krapf and Rebmann and dilated at length upon their fraudulent character.[47] But even if untrue, the stories of snow-capped mountains echoed Ptolemy sufficiently to make others query the relationship between the mountains and the sources of the White Nile. Bruce had re-discovered the source of the Blue Nile, but as late as 1856, modern authors still wondered whether the White Nile sprung from the fountains of Herodotus or the lakes of Ptolemy.[48]

In 1855, Captain Richard Francis Burton of the Indian army—who had already visited the holy cities of Mecca and Medina in disguise and had made a dangerous foray to the "forbidden" city of Harar—proposed that he should lead an expedition into the heart of Africa primarily in order to ascertain the limits of Krapf and Rebmann's "Sea of Ujiji" and to "determine the exportable produce of the interior and the ethnography of its tribes." The Royal Geographical Society further instructed him to discover the location of the legendary "Mountains of the Moon" and, if possible, the source of the Nile.[49] In 1857, from Bagamoyo on the Indian Ocean, Burton, John Hanning Speke, also of the Indian army, and a Hindi-speaking African from the coast followed the traditional trade route to Unyanyembe (Speke's "Kazé"), where they arrived ten months later. They had already learned from Swahili-speaking merchants that the "Sea of Ujiji" was not one, but three lakes—the modern Nyasa, Tanganyika, and Victoria. Speke at least had also learned or surmised that from Ukerewe (Victoria) the Nile flowed north to Egypt.[50]

From Unyanyembe, where both Burton and Speke had begun to suffer remittent bouts of fever, they proceeded west to the trading town of Ujiji where, early in 1858, Burton (Speke had contracted ophthalmia) became the first European in modern times to view Lake Tanganyika. "Advancing a few yards,"

---

[46] In Ludwig Krapf, *Travels, Researches, and Missionary Labours, During an Eighteen Years' Residence in Eastern Africa* (Boston, 1860), p. 190. Krapf viewed Mt. Kenya himself in 1849.

[47] William Desborough Cooley, *Inner Africa Laid Open* (London, 1852), pp. 89–109. But see Krapf, *Travels,* p. 233.

[48] Herodotus, ii, 28; Ptolemy, i, 9.

[49] Reginald Coupland, *The Exploitation of East Africa, 1856–1890* (London, 1939), pp. 105–106; Byron Farwell, *Burton* (London, 1963), p. 137; John Hanning Speke, *What Led to the Discovery of the Source of the Nile* (Edinburgh, 1864), p. 191.

[50] *Ibid.,* pp. 198–200, 258–260.

Ganda warriors perform for their *kabaka*. The explorer John Hanning Speke, *en route* to discover the source of the White Nile, observes the display. (Bettmann Archive)

he wrote, "the whole scene suddenly burst upon my view, filling me with admiration, wonder, and delight. . . ." [51] Later, when Burton lay abed with malaria, Speke went on alone to Ukerewe. In the late African winter of 1858, he at last caught a murky glimpse of its southern waters through clouded eyes.[52]

Speke, although unable to continue his journey to the "fountains of the Nile," remained convinced that Ukerewe, which he now named Victoria, would prove the ultimate source of the mighty river. Burton, the careful, more literate geographer, was not altogether convinced. Nonetheless, the Royal Geographical Society commissioned Speke to demonstrate his belief that Victoria Nyanza fed the Nile. Accompanied by James Augustus Grant, Speke therefore returned to Unyanyembe in 1861. After some delay—warfare between the local Nyamwezi and the Swahili-speaking slavers depleted the supply of porters—Speke and Grant set out around the western side of Victoria Nyanza to Buganda, the capital of which they attained early in 1862. Of the Ganda, Speke spoke favorably:

> *I prepared for my first presentation at court, attired in my best, though in it I cut a poor figure in comparison with the display of the dressy Waganda. They wore neat bark cloaks resembling the best yellow corduroy cloth, crimp and well set, as if stiffened with starch, and over that, as upper-cloaks, a patchwork of small antelope skins, which I observed were sewn together as well as any English glovers*

[51] Richard Francis Burton, *The Lake Regions of Central Africa* (New York, 1961 [reprint of the 1860 edition]), II, p. 42.
[52] Speke, *What Led*, pp. 298, 305–308. But see Burton, *Lake Regions*, pp. 204–209.

could have pieced them; whilst their head-dresses, generally, were . . . turbans, set off with highly-polished boar-tusks, stick-charms, seeds, beads, or shells. . . .[53]

In July, Speke stood above a point where the waters of the Victoria Nyanza cascaded down the Job, or White Nile, on their way to Alexandria. "I saw," the exultant explorer wrote, "that old father Nile without any doubt [rose] in the Victoria N'yanza, and, as I had foretold, that [that] lake [was] the great source of the holy river which cradled the first expounder of our religious belief." [54] With Grant, who had rejoined him, Speke proceeded down the Nile, but they were inhibited from following its course, and from visiting other lakes of which they had heard rumor, by intertribal warfare. Leaving the valley of the Nile, they went north to Gondoroko, where they met Samuel White Baker, the son of a wealthy London merchant with West Indian and Mauritian sugar interests, and his Hungarian wife. Speke persuaded the persuadable Baker to follow up his own investigations by seeking definite evidence of the other lake that he thought would probably prove to constitute a part of the Nilotic system. And in 1864, after a particularly difficult journey southward along the trails used by slave traders, Baker corroborated Speke's supposition. Of his first sight of the waters of the lake that he named Albert, after Queen Victoria's consort, Baker wrote:

The glory of our prize burst suddenly upon me! There, like a sea of quick-silver, lay far beneath the grand expanse of water, a boundless sea . . . glittering in the noon-day sun. . . . It is impossible to describe the triumph of that moment; —here was the reward for all our labour. . . . England had won the sources of the Nile! [55]

Livingstone had meanwhile returned to his beloved Africa at the head of an expedition sponsored by the British government. On this occasion, he specifically sought ways whereby Christianity and commerce could most expeditiously be introduced into the heart of Africa. An attempt to ascend the Zambezi River by ship proved impossible, and Livingstone therefore concentrated his efforts upon what became Nyasaland. In 1859, he became the first Briton to describe Lakes Chilwa and Nyasa. During the course of the next four years, he and his white companions came to know intimately much of the Shire Highlands and the environs of Lake Nyasa. They assisted an abortive expedition to establish a Universities' Mission (Anglican) in the Highlands and contributed measurably to a growing British interest in the Nyasa region before the British government recalled them in 1863.[56]

---

[53] John Hanning Speke, *Journal of the Discovery of the Source of the Nile* (London, 1863), p. 285.

[54] *Ibid.*, p. 467. He named the falls Ripon, in honor of the president of the Royal Geographical Society.

[55] Samuel White Baker, *The Albert Nyanza, Great Basin of the Nile and Explorations of the Nile Sources* (New York, 1866), p. 331.

[56] For the expedition, see Reginald Coupland, *Kirk on the Zambesi* (Oxford, 1928), pp. 185–259; David and Charles Livingstone, *Narrative of an Expedition to the Zambesi and Its Tributaries* (London, 1865). Portuguese soldiers had already visited the lake.

David Livingstone and his Kololo-speaking men force their boat through a forest of papyrus along the upper Shire River before reaching and re-discovering Lake Nyasa. (Buell, *Heroes of the Dark Continent*, London, 1890)

Three years later, Livingstone again stopped in Zanzibar on his way into the heart of Africa. This time he was even more determined than before to seek information about the slave trade and about the configuration of the major watersheds of the continent. Although Speke and Baker had by this time seen what they affirmed to be the "main" sources of the White Nile, Livingstone and others refused to believe that the river's "true" sources had been found. He speculated that Lake Nyasa might drain north into Lake Tanganyika, which again might be linked to Lake Albert, and thence to the Nile. He also hoped to find the source of the Congo River, which in its turn, he thought, might eventually prove to be the "true source" of the Nile itself. He reasoned that if the Congo began in a series of "fountains"—as Africans supposedly said that it did—then these might also be the "fountains" from which Herodotus had suggested that the Nile rose.

Livingstone's last, desperate quest propelled him first from Zanzibar to Lakes Nyasa and Tanganyika. Growing steadily weaker in body and more obsessed in mind, he turned to the west, where, in 1867/68, he "discovered" Lake Mweru—which Lacerda had already visited—and Lake Bangweulu. Between 1868 and 1870, he investigated the river system that flowed north from Mweru and, in 1871, he reached the banks of the Lualaba or upper Congo River.[57] Later in the same year, he was "found" at Ujiji by Henry Morton Stanley, the young Anglo-American journalist whose publisher had sent him thither specifically to ascertain whether or not the great explorer, of whom no

[57] David Livingstone (ed. Horace Waller), *The Last Journals of David Livingstone in Central Africa* (London, 1874), I, pp. 337–344.

recent reports had reached Europe, still lived. Stanley later dramatized their actual meeting in front of Livingstone's house in Ujiji:

> *As I advanced slowly towards him I noticed he was pale, that he looked wearied and wan, that he had grey whiskers and moustache, that he wore a bluish cloth cap with a faded gold band on a red ground round it, and that he had on a red-sleeved waistcoat, and a pair of grey tweed trousers.*
>
> *I would have run to him, only I was a coward in the presence of* [the surrounding mob of traders]*—would have embraced him, but that I did not know how he would receive me; so I did what moral cowardice and false pride suggested was the best thing—walked deliberately to him, took off my hat, and said:*
>
> *"Dr. Livingstone, I presume?"*
>
> *"Yes," said he, with a kind, cordial smile, lifting his cap slightly.*
>
> *I replaced my hat on my head, and he replaced his cap, and we both grasped hands. I then said aloud: "I thank God, Doctor, I have been permitted to see you."* [58]

Together Livingstone and Stanley dispelled the former's pet theory of the interconnection of Lake Tanganyika and the Nile system. But this information in turn strengthened Livingstone's belief that Lake Mweru and some of the branches of the Congo River system fed the Nile. After Stanley had returned to Europe and America, Livingstone therefore plunged for the last time southwest toward Bangweulu and Katanga, where the "fountains" supposedly gushed forth to form the Congo. For another painful year he sought the fountains; sick physically and mentally discouraged, he nevertheless continued his quest throughout 1872 and the first months of the next year. But in May of 1873, his long search ended; he died near Lake Bangweulu.[59]

Livingstone had opened up the heart of Africa. Verney Lovett Cameron subsequently crossed Africa from Zanzibar to Luanda in 1873/74. During the next three years, Stanley, with characteristic efficiency, circumnavigated Lakes Tanganyika and Victoria, traced the Congo to its mouth, and in the process dramatically signaled the start of an era when explorers sought distinctly imperial goals.[60] A number of other white men later filled in the details while performing feats of physical endurance and mental agility. After 1876, their efforts were supplemented by the African International Association, a creation of King Léopold II of Belgium. In 1877, at its only plenary session, the Association proposed to seek the suppression of the slave trade and to establish a chain of posts from Zanzibar to the great lakes of the interior that would be manned by scientists trained to carry out astronomical, meteorological, ethnographical, biological, and linguistic research.[61] But in time, the explorations and activities

---

[58] Henry Morton Stanley, *How I Found Livingstone: Travels, Adventures, and Discoveries in Central Africa* (London, 1895), p. 331. See also Stanley, *The Autobiography* (Boston, 1909), pp. 255–267.

[59] A good narrative of this period is Reginald Coupland, *Livingstone's Last Journey* (London, 1945), pp. 216–246.

[60] For an account of their journeys, see Verney Lovett Cameron, *Across Africa* (London, 1877); Henry Morton Stanley, *Through the Dark Continent* (London, 1878), 2v.

[61] Auguste Roeykens, *Léopold II et l'Afrique, 1855–1880* (Bruxelles, 1958), pp. 189–224.

of the Association proved to be largely political. As such, they provided a collective prelude to the partition of tropical Africa.

II. The Establishment of Liberia

The Sierra Leone experiment stimulated, and the varied concerns of a number of prominent white Americans promoted, the schemes that ultimately resulted in the settlement of Liberia. As early as 1714, Americans interested in the "Negro question" suggested that all "men of color" should be removed beyond the borders of the then twelve colonies. Thomas Jefferson later favored a similar scheme and, in 1811, strongly urged its adoption. He wrote:

> *Nothing is more certainly written in the book of fate than that these peoples [the Negroes] are to be free; nor is it less certain that the two races, equally free, cannot live in the same government. Nature, habit, opinion have drawn indelible lines of distinction between them.*[62]

Meanwhile, Dr. Samuel Hopkins, an evangelical Congregational clergyman, had already expressed a second current of thought by training free Negroes as missionaries in order that they might go back to Africa in compensation for the "injury and injustice" of the slave trade.[63] Others assumed that the deportation of freed Negroes would alleviate racial conflict and thereby hasten the abolition of slavery in the southern United States. A Georgian newspaper editor, for example, felt that the choice was clear:

> *If the government will find means of conveying out of the country such slaves as may be emancipated and would likewise purchase annually a certain number, particularly females for transportation, it is believed our black population would soon become harmless if not extinct. To the importance of such an object the expense will bear no comparison. . . .*[64]

The american colonization society

To those who, for one reason or another, believed that the free Negro was anomalous in American society, the Sierra Leone example seemed eminently worthy of imitation. Robert Finley, a Presbyterian preacher who later became president of the University of Georgia, despaired of ameliorating the unhappy lot of free Negroes by any means short of transportation back to Africa. During the early years of the nineteenth century, Finley and others therefore explored the various alternatives then being considered by proponents of deportation.

---

[62] Quoted in Nnamdi Azikiwe, *Liberia in World Politics* (London, 1934), p. 40. See also Thomas Jefferson to Rufus King, July 13, 1802, in Albert Ellery Bergh (ed.), *The Writings of Thomas Jefferson* (Washington, 1907), IX, pp. 327–329; Jefferson to Joseph John Lynch, January 21, 1811, in *ibid.*, XIII, pp. 10–11; Henry Noble Sherwood, "Early Negro Deportation Projects," *The Mississippi Valley Historical Review*, II (1916), pp. 484–508; Sherwood, "The Formation of the American Colonization Society," *The Journal of Negro History*, II (1917), pp. 209–210.

[63] P. J. Staudenraus, *The African Colonization Movement, 1816–1865* (New York, 1961), p. 5.

[64] Quoted in Sherwood, "Formation," p. 217.

Finley encouraged Paul Cuffee, a Massachusetts Quaker of Amerindian and Negro extraction, to continue his search for a site in Africa where freed slaves might establish themselves. Cuffee, who had visited Sierra Leone in 1811, proposed to transport freed slaves thither and to profit personally from the resulting commercial concessions. Backed by a number of influential Americans, many of whom subsequently helped to found Liberia, Cuffee landed thirty-eight Negroes at Freetown in 1816.[65] But the British governor of Sierra Leone failed to welcome Cuffee's initiative. Nor did he like Cuffee's desire to compete economically with local traders. Instead, the governor suggested that the Americans would find a suitable site for a freed-slave settlement farther south along the coast of Africa near Cape Mesurado, where a group of English Swedenborgians had earlier hoped to establish a colony.

During the last weeks of 1816, advocates of these various sentiments jointly created the American Society for Colonizing the Free People of Color of the United States—later known simply as the American Colonization Society. In Washington, Finley and his brother-in-law Elias Caldwell, the clerk of the United States Supreme Court, persuaded Francis Scott Key, the wealthy lawyer and composer, Henry Clay, Speaker of the House of Representatives, Bushrod Washington, a Supreme Court justice and the heir of the first American president, Congressman John Randolph of Virginia, Senator Daniel Webster of New Hampshire, and a number of other influential legislators, clergymen, and bankers to sponsor the Society. Together they hoped that by "draining off" freed slaves to the lands of their fathers, the United States might be spared the "pernicious" consequences that could result from the continued residence within its borders of "free men of color." "Can there be," Clay asked, "a nobler cause than that which, whilst it proposed to rid our country of a useless and pernicious, if not dangerous portion of its population, contemplates the spreading of the arts of civilized life, and the possible redemption from ignorance and barbarism of a benighted quarter of the globe!" [66]

The new society raised funds and formed auxiliaries in the major cities of the eastern United States. It investigated conditions along the shores of western Africa and urgently sought official support from the government of the United States. Finally in 1819, President James Monroe reluctantly agreed to back the Society in its attempt to settle free Negroes in their ancestral homeland. But Monroe refused to commit the American government openly. In 1820, the first shipload of free Negroes therefore returned to Africa ostensibly as laborers employed to construct a base for ships of the American anti-slaving patrol.[67]

The efforts of the Society at first met with failure. At Sherbro Island, where the eighty 1820 settlers tried to establish a colony, they proved unable to with-

---

[65] Henry Noble Sherwood, "Paul Cuffe," *The Journal of Negro History,* VIII (1923), pp. 154–159; *Sixth Report of the Directors of the African Institution* (London, 1812), pp. 26–27. Cuffee spelled his name various ways.

[66] Quoted in Staudenraus, *Colonization,* p. 28.

[67] See the initial instructions in Charles Henry Huberich, *The Political and Legislative History of Liberia* (New York, 1947), I, pp. 73–76.

stand tropical diseases, assuage the hostility of local Africans, or obtain lands suitable for cultivation. Most of the colonists died, and those who remained soon sailed away to Fourah Bay on the Sierra Leone River. Early in 1821, representatives of the Society tried again, with the same result, to settle another shipload of thirty-three freed slaves in Africa. Finally, in the last month of 1821, Dr. Eli Ayres and Lieutenant Robert Stockton guided a third group of Negroes to Cape Mesurado (the site of modern Monrovia). There they both cajoled and threatened "Peter," a Bassa chief, to give or sell them the Cape. When he refused to do so and, in their eyes, added insult to injury by procrastinating, Ayres pointed a pistol at the chief's head and demanded "the country." A treaty signed by "Peter" thereupon transferred Cape Mesurado to the Society in exchange for muskets, beads, tobacco, gunpowder, clothing, food, and rum, together worth less than $300.[68]

In Washington, the managers of the Society agreed to the treaty. They called the settlement Liberia, a word that they derived from the Latin for "free," and issued a previously drafted constitution that gave sole authority in the colony to agents of the Society. The agents assumed the roles of governor, judge, legislator, and military commander in chief. The constitution also established the laws of the United States as the laws of the colony and prohibited the practice of slavery and the import of spirituous liquors. The Society even drafted the town plan for Monrovia in Washington.

Despite the Society's grandiose hopes, the history of Liberia began inauspiciously. Bassa warriors harassed and attacked the colony. Then in 1823, the settlers—whose numbers had increased to 150—complained vigorously about the way in which the agents of the Society treated them. Like the Nova Scotians in Sierra Leone, they were unwilling to exchange their American way of life for the indigenous customs of Africa. Their antagonism even took violent forms. In 1824, Lott Cary, a Baptist preacher from Virginia, led a revolt and forced the white agent in chief to flee. The colonists were momentarily free of outside control and, at this point in its history, Liberia might conceivably have sundered its direct connections with the United States. But President Monroe, after whom the Liberian capital had been named, despatched a warship to re-impose obedience to American law. At the same time, the Society sent a special agent to Liberia who managed to propitiate the rebellious settlers by granting them a share in the government of their new country.

During the next decade, Monrovia and Liberia both grew in size and influence. Swelled by the addition of new immigrants from the United States, slaves freed at sea, and tribesmen compelled to "consider themselves as Americans," the population of the colony grew from 150 to more than 2,000.[69] Using funds that the American government had appropriated for a campaign against the

---

[68] Staudenraus, *Colonization*, p. 65. But see Eli Ayres to the Society, December 11, 1821, in Huberich, *Liberia*, I, pp. 190–191. The treaty is in *ibid.*, pp. 195–196. For an early description of Cape Mesurado, see Nicolas Villault, *Relation des costes d'Afrique, appellées Guinée* (Paris, 1669), pp. 113–125.

[69] Staudenraus, *Colonization*, p. 289.

slave trade, the agents of the Society constructed permanent buildings and wharves in Monrovia and equipped and trained a small army. In command of the troops, various white agents in chief annexed strips of coastline south of Monrovia that had hitherto been controlled by indigenous Africans and French and Spanish merchants. Within the original colony, meanwhile, the settlers refused to regard themselves as Africans; they were, after all, not so much returned Africans as they were American colonials. They continued to obtain supplies of their staple foods from the United States. They shunned agricultural pursuits and soon found that it profited them greatly to trade with the peoples of the interior. Indeed, the sharpest colonials were soon exporting shiploads of ivory, camwood, and palm oil overseas.

During the 1830's, the state auxiliaries of the Society asserted their independence from Washington and sponsored their own separate colonization schemes. In 1834, abolitionists from Maryland settled a group of freed slaves near Cape Palmas. Once again local chiefs exchanged muskets, powder, cloth, beads, kettles, and pots for land. Like the earlier settlers of Monrovia, those of "Maryland in Liberia" sought to create a new America in Africa. They refused to till the soil and fought their own leaders, indigenous Africans, and whoever would give battle.[70] Later in the same year, the New York and Pennsylvania auxiliaries jointly established a small, religiously oriented colony on the St. John's River. Africans and slavers soon destroyed it, but the same state auxiliaries created another settlement in 1838. The Louisiana and Mississippi societies launched the Greenville colony in 1838, but its growth suffered from African raids and a lack of continuous American support. These various settlements and the original colony all competed commercially among themselves and warred separately against indigenous Africans.

Because of these conflicts of interest, the Society in Washington and the directors of the Pennsylvania, New York, Mississippi, and Louisiana auxiliaries agreed in 1839 to merge their colonies into the Commonwealth of Liberia. They also granted a new measure of responsibility to the colonial settlers and filled the office of the hitherto autocratic agent in chief with a somewhat more responsive governor.[71] Even so, rancor continued to pervade the colony; both the older and the newer settlers sought for themselves the spoils of control. At the same time, the equivocal status—neither colonial nor national—of the new Liberia encouraged British interlopers to poach upon the Commonwealth's economic preserve and to appeal for support to the British governors in Freetown. On several occasions, British officials even threatened to annex Liberia to Sierra Leone. In these circumstances, although the governors of Liberia looked to the United States for the protection and preservation of the colony, the administration in Washington continually refused either to annex

[70] John H. B. Latrobe, *Maryland in Liberia* (Baltimore, 1855), pp. 7–38; William D. Hoyt, Jr., "John McDonogh and Maryland Colonization in Liberia, 1834–35," *The Journal of Negro History*, XXIV (1939), pp. 440–453; Samuel W. Laughon, "Administrative Problems in Maryland in Liberia, 1836–51," *ibid.*, XXVI (1941), pp. 334–338, 342, 344–345.

[71] Huberich, *Liberia,* I, pp. 649–654, contains the text of the 1839 constitution.

Liberia directly or to demonstrate its concern in any overt manner. As a result, the Society finally decided to shed itself of all responsibility for the four thousand Afro-Americans of Liberia. In 1847, the parent therefore ordered its by now adolescent offspring to proclaim the independence of the Republic of Liberia.[72]

Joseph Jenkins Roberts, an octoroon émigré from Virginia, became the first president of the Republic under a constitution that denied indigenous Africans equal rights with Afro-American settlers.[73] Despite its independence, Liberia continued to occupy a precarious international position. Britain and France, with which Liberia had a number of outstanding border disagreements, finally recognized its assumption of sovereignty. But the government of the United States refused either to recognize Liberia or to enter into diplomatic relations with it until 1862, after opposition from American slave owners had finally been submerged in war.[74] In succeeding years, descendants of the earliest freed slaves consolidated their own control of the government of Liberia and enlarged the effective limits of the Republic by buying or conquering the lands of Gola, Kru, and Grebo tribesmen. During the balance of the nineteenth century, Liberians also engaged in a bitterly fought, parochial struggle for power in Monrovia.

III. The Imperialist Overture: New Colonies and Coastal Holdings

Despite the geographical exploits of their explorers in the interior of tropical Africa, the powers of nineteenth-century Europe initially directed their major economic and political energies toward the coastal areas with which whites had long traded. They banned and gradually halted the transportation of slaves overseas. Then they themselves came to have new economic needs and, often unwittingly, found satisfaction of those needs in the acquisition of hegemony in Africa. Yet this proved an *ad hoc* process; acquisition held different meaning for the leaders of different countries and, within the same country, for different groups at different periods. European statesmen constructed their colonial policies in the light of national or narrowly political considerations while—on another level entirely—their political and commercial representatives responded to the often distinctly parochial settings in which they found themselves. In those dissimilar arenas, the statecraft of African rulers and the actions of African merchants both evoked and provoked particular European responses. Africans first conducted the overture of imperialism; later, however, its final movements overwhelmed them.

---

[72] J. H. Mower, "The Republic of Liberia," *The Journal of Negro History*, XXXII (1947), pp. 268–269.

[73] Text in Huberich, *Liberia*, II, pp. 852–864. "Maryland in Liberia" maintained a separate existence until 1856.

[74] Charles H. Wesley, "The Struggle for the Recognition of Haiti and Liberia as Independent Republics," *The Journal of Negro History*, II (1917), pp. 377–381.

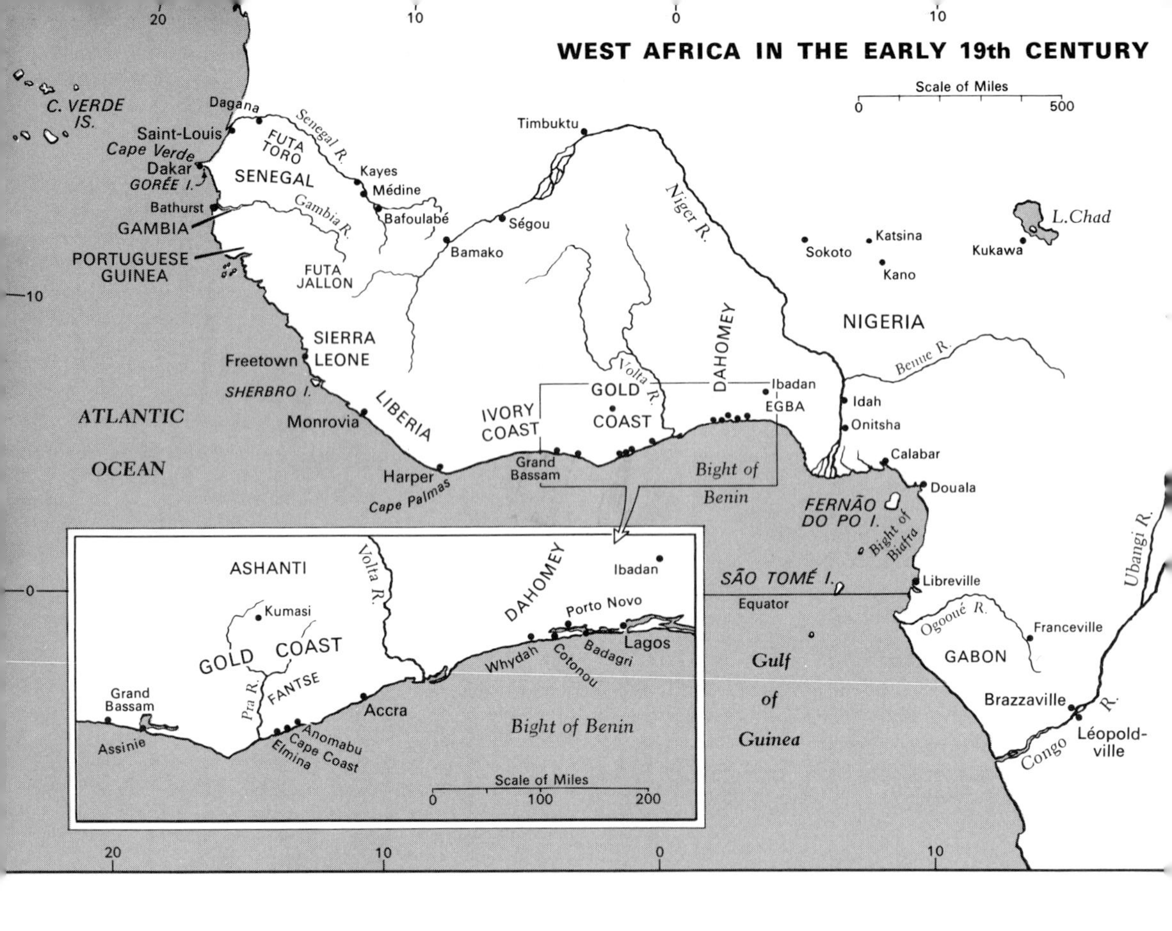

The french presence

At the end of the Napoleonic Wars, British troops and merchants withdrew from Gorée and Saint-Louis to the new settlement of Bathurst in the Gambia. French officials returned to Senegal and almost immediately attempted to transform a chain of trading posts into an agriculturally productive part of the empire. The first administrators therefore drew up ambitious plans for its settlement. They tried to attract colonists from France and to obtain the cooperation of the Africans who controlled suitable lands up-river from Saint-Louis. Their success, however, was limited. Although small groups of settlers opened up a few plantation areas and tried to grow indigo, sugar, coffee, and cotton, their products failed to thrive or compete with the varieties grown more economically in the West Indies. Furthermore, Africans regarded these schemes with hostility and acted accordingly. From this period, the French fought almost continually against the Muslim Oualo, Trarza, Brakna, Damga, and Fulani peoples who inhabited both banks of the Senegal River.

Undaunted, the energetic, autocratic Baron Jacques François Roger, who governed Senegal from 1822 to 1836, tried anew to make the colony pay. At the royal gardens in Dagana, he tried unsuccessfully to adapt a variety of exotic fruits to Senegalese conditions and encouraged the intensive cultivation of indigo, cotton, rice, and wattle for export. He attracted white settlers and recruited plantation labor by paying wages and ensuring conditions of employment better than those to which indigenous workers were accustomed.[75] Roger also tried to regulate and increase the commerce of the river. But from about 1830 to 1848, as a result of renewed African attacks and a lack of interest at home, the colony of Senegal abandoned its plantations and endured a period of economic stagnation. During this time, it once again comprised little more than a collection of riverain entrepôts and forts and the two small commercial settlements at Saint-Louis and Gorée, the merchants of which collected gum (used in the manufacture of calico prints), wax, hides, gold, and the first of the groundnuts that were later to revolutionize the economy of the territory. The French traders and officials quarreled incessantly with their African competitors and, along the Gambia, with Britons as well. Commercial success eluded the colony and its residents, most of whom came, by 1848, to believe that they would achieve commercial rewards only when France had mastered the riverain peoples of the hinterland.

Meanwhile, France had demonstrated an interest in the lands to the south of Senegal. From about 1831, ships based in Nantes, Le Havre, Bordeaux, and Marseille traded profitably along the shores of the Gulf of Guinea. But only after 1838, when a Marseille merchant house, the Chamber of Commerce of Bordeaux, and two serving naval officers, of whom Édouard Bouët (later Bouët-Willaumez) was one, persuaded the Ministry of the Marine to sponsor a voyage of commercial exploration to Gabon, did France demonstrate any official interest in new trading opportunities beyond Senegal. Bouët suggested that France establish centers of influence at Garroway west of Cape Palmas, at Grand Bassam and Assinie on the Ivory Coast, at Whydah, where Frenchmen had earlier possessed a post, and on the banks of the Gabon estuary, which would provide an excellent anchorage.[76] Indeed, Bouët appears to have persuaded the chiefs of Grand Bassam, Assinie, and Gabon to grant rights of occupation to France.

In the Ivory Coast, from 1841 to 1843, Bouët and other officials swiftly introduced the French presence. They erected forts, and at Gabon the French navy soon established a refueling depot for its anti-slave squadron. Almost simultaneously, the Marseille firm of Victor and Louis Régis re-opened France's historic commercial ties to Whydah. The brisk exchange of textiles, guns, and gunpowder for palm oil and ivory soon proved immensely profitable for the firm. But at Grand Bassam and Assinie, Africans offered strong resistance to the attempt by white merchants to concentrate the entire trade of the Ivory Coast in French hands. In Gabon, on the other hand, Africans apparently accepted the French initiative more readily. When Bouët created the freed-slave settlement of Libreville in 1849, they acquiesced. Subsequently, however,

---

[75] Georges Hardy, *La Mise en valeur du Sénégal de 1817 à 1854* (Paris, 1921), pp. 117–127, 143–151.

[76] See Édouard Bouët-Willaumez, *Commerce et traite des noirs aux côtes occidentales d'Afrique* (Paris, 1848), pp. 99–110, 151–156.

Africans regarded French efforts to penetrate the interior by Rio Muni, the Gabon River, and, finally, the Ogooué River, with undisguised animosity.[77]

From a French point of view, Senegal remained comparatively moribund until the arrival in Saint-Louis of Captain Louis Léon César Faidherbe. In 1854, Faidherbe, a young army engineer with experience in Algeria, assumed the governorship of the colony. Its economy, he found, depended largely upon gum —which faced stiff competition, in a declining market, from Egyptian suppliers and synthetic substitutes—and the continued friendliness of the Africans who provided the gum and permitted it to pass down the Senegal River to Saint-Louis. Powerless to protect their own traders, the French merchants feared the Muslim peoples who controlled the lower river and, indeed, encircled Saint-Louis. The growing revolutionary religious influence of al-hajj 'Umar also posed a threat to French interests in Senegal, although 'Umar himself seems to have regarded the French indifferently—primarily as his suppliers, not as his rivals.[78]

Faidherbe appreciated these various impediments to the vigorous assertion of a French presence. He championed the interests of the dominant local merchants, most of whom represented Bordeaux firms, and understood the commercial necessity of freeing the trade paths to the interior.[79] With a well-drilled army, he soon forced the Oualo to submit to French authority. Then he directed his regiments up-river, where they battled the Trarza and the Brakna for three years before finally winning a limited victory. French troops also attacked Futa Toro. Farther upstream, Faidherbe meanwhile established the garrison at Médine that successfully defended itself in 1857 against an assault by Tokolor troops loyal to 'Umar. Later, in 1860, Faidherbe and 'Umar negotiated mutually agreed spheres of influence in the Western Sudan. From Saint-Louis, Faidherbe then looked to the south, where he deposed the ruler of Cayor in order to secure the overland route to Gorée and Rufisque, established several new forts, and interfered with Portuguese privileges in Casamance.[80] By 1861, wherever the French had successfully conquered African territories, Faidherbe governed in a manner similar to that later styled indirect. Subject chiefs acknowledged French sovereignty and paid tribute to Saint-Louis or, at least, refrained from interfering with trade. But the colony remained economically dependent upon the export of gum.

From 1863 to 1865, during his second term as governor of Senegal, Faidherbe directed the attention of France toward the supposed riches of the Western Sudan. He hoped to conclude an alliance with 'Umar that would permit France to increase its commercial and political influence in the interior. To this end, Faidherbe sent Eugène Mage, a young naval officer, to outline his

[77] Bernard Schnapper, *La Politique et le commerce français dans le Golfe de Guinée de 1838 à 1871* (Paris, 1961), pp. 14–32, 59–72, 97–101, 144–148, 162–167; Paul Masson, *Marseille et la colonisation française* (Marseille, 1906), pp. 51–56.

[78] Prosper Cultru, *Les Origines de l'Afrique occidentale: histoire du Sénégal du XVe siècle à 1870* (Paris, 1910), p. 337.

[79] See Louis L. C. Faidherbe, *Le Sénégal: la France dans l'Afrique occidentale* (Paris, 1889), pp. 100–109.

[80] Cultru, *Les Origines*, p. 351; Paul Gaffarel, *Le Sénégal et le Soudan français* (Paris, 1890), pp. 116–118.

proposals for an alliance to the rulers of Ségou, 'Umar's capital. But this diplomatic venture into the interior accomplished little. The embassy met with poor response, and Mage returned empty-handed and disillusioned to Saint-Louis some months after Faidherbe had been replaced by a less visionary governor.[81] Only much later were other officers to make reality of Faidherbe's dreams of a Sudanic empire. Meanwhile, Faidherbe himself had also addressed his attentions to the Gambia, Portuguese Guinea, and the Ivory Coast. He coveted the trade of the first two, saw the Gambia River as an ideal route into the Western Sudan, and thought, logically, that the Gambia should be exchanged on practical grounds for the Ivory Coast, Porto Novo (where the French had recently imposed themselves), and Gabon. But the only immediate result of Faidherbe's interest in the Guinea coast was the French annexation, in 1867, of Mellacourie and the other Rivières du Sud.[82]

Faidherbe left to France the control of an area more than half the size of the mother country. His immediate successors brought new areas under the French flag—particularly in the Rivières du Sud—subdued a resistance movement in Cayor, and belatedly turned their attentions toward the Western Sudan in order to forestall British ventures in the same region. In 1876, Colonel Gaston Brière de l'Isle became governor of Senegal. A follower of Faidherbe, he proposed that France should build railways from Saint-Louis to Dakar, the new port on Cape Verde, from Saint-Louis to Médine or Kayes, on the upper Senegal, and from Kayes to the Niger near Bamako. In 1880, the French government authorized a limited version of this grand scheme; five years later, on the eve of the scramble for colonies, rails joined Dakar and Saint-Louis, and tracks stretched, in a tentative and incomplete fashion, southwestward from Kayes in the direction of Bafoulabé and Bamako. Only much later, however, did the French successfully link Saint-Louis to the Niger by rail.[83]

Meanwhile, under the governor's aegis, Captain Joseph Simon Galliéni, an impulsive marine who later governed Madagascar, sought by renewed martial exploits to introduce the French presence into the region of the upper Niger. In 1878, despite the stated antipathy of French traders, Galliéni defeated a Tokolor regiment and thereby acquired two small districts up-river from Médine.[84] At Bafoulabé, in territory nominally subject to the rule of Ahmadu, 'Umar's successor as ruler of the Tokolor empire, Galliéni soon built a fort. From it, he penetrated into the Tokolor regions and, with putative chiefs, concluded rather vague treaties that gave France the rights of a protector.[85] In exchange, Galliéni may have promised to support the chiefs against Ahmadu.

---

[81] Eugène Mage, *Voyage dans le Soudan occidental* (Paris, 1868), pp. 662–663; John D. Hargreaves, "Notes Towards a History of the Tokolor Empire of Ségou" (unpub. typescript, 1963), p. 6.

[82] John D. Hargreaves, "The French Occupation of the Mellacourie, 1865–67," *Sierra Leone Studies*, 9 (1957), p. 15; André Arcin, *Histoire de la Guinée française* (Paris, 1911), pp. 309–312, 317–326.

[83] See *infra*, p. 331.

[84] John D. Hargreaves, *Prelude to the Partition of West Africa* (London, 1963), p. 256.

[85] See Joseph Simon Galliéni, *Mission d'exploration du Haut-Niger: voyage au Soudan français* (Paris, 1885), pp. 150–154.

The Tokolor leader may have been aware of Galliéni's duplicity. The French had never respected the treaty that 'Umar had concluded with Faidherbe, and Ahmadu, not unnaturally, dealt warily with Galliéni's mission. He tried, once again, to negotiate with the French. But although the Tokolor supposedly liked the French, they did not trust them. And the French, while they trusted the Tokolor, did not like them.[86] Furthermore, Galliéni and his men were virtual prisoners of Ahmadu. As a result, the treaty of cooperation and friendship that Ahmadu eventually signed gave France much less than Galliéni had hoped. Later it even failed to receive official assent in Paris. But by then, indeed even before Galliéni had returned from the Niger, Colonel Gustave Borgnis-Desbordes had ignored instructions from Paris and had led a small army into upper Senegal. He feared that British initiative would wrest the commerce of the Niger away from France. In 1881/82, he and his soldiers therefore poised themselves upon the edge of the Western Sudan. Farther south, French competed energetically with British traders along the Gulf of Guinea, in the Oil Rivers, and in Gabon. As far as the French were concerned, the scramble had already begun.

The expansion of the british west african settlements

During the early years of the nineteenth century, the small colonial outpost in Sierra Leone, the fortified trading posts on the Gambia River and along the Gold Coast, and *barracoons* and other bases of commerce denoted the permanent interests of Britain in West Africa. From 1807, Parliament, by forbidding British subjects to transport slaves overseas, attempted to alter the character of Britain's earlier relationships with the peoples of these areas and to seek means by which its navy might curtail the sale of slaves to white entrepreneurs. Freetown became a depot of the Admiralty's African Squadron and a settlement for recaptives—as the new freed slaves were called. Groundnuts gradually replaced slaves in the list of commodities legally exported from the Gambia. Along the Slave and Niger Coasts, however, both African and European merchants had invested heavily in the transport of humans; therefore, as long as the American and Brazilian demand for agricultural field hands continued strong, the British government could hardly hope to persuade slave traders voluntarily to cease selling slaves. An African chief later summed up local opinion neatly:

> . . . *hitherto we thought it was so God's will that Black people should be slaves to White people. White people first told us we should sell slaves to them, and we sold them; and White people are now telling us not to sell slaves. . . . If White people give up buying, Black people will give up selling.*[87]

In the Gold Coast, Britain similarly pulled little upon the tides of profitable commerce. In this early period, the policies pursued by the Ashanti confederation exerted a greater influence.

[86] Quoted in Hargreaves, *Prelude*, p. 260.
[87] Quoted in the *Journal of the Rev. James Frederick Schön* (London, 1842), p. 70. K. Onwuka Dike, *Trade*, p. 48, includes a slightly different quotation and attributes it to *obi* Ossai of Abo.

By the beginning of the century, Ashanti had reached the height of its power and prosperity. At the same time, its differences with the Fantse (Fanti) states of the coast, the merchants of which had long acted as middlemen in the slave trade, approached a historic divide. In 1806, Ashanti soldiers administered a signal defeat to the Fantse armies at Abura, a few miles from Cape Coast, and then threatened the British and Dutch settlements, whose commanders had assisted the fleeing Fantse and the refugees from Asin. Kormantin, the Dutch fort, surrendered to Ashanti. The British at Anomabu chose, however, to support the Fantse defenders of their town. But the army of Ashanti overcame the Fantse and forced the governor, who administered the several British forts on behalf of the Company of Merchants Trading to Africa, to sue for peace. He also handed one of the Asin chiefs—who had fled for protection to Anomabu—over to the *asantehene* and agreed henceforth to pay rent for the forts to Ashanti. By so doing, the governor acknowledged Ashanti's paramountcy along the coast. "I took the English for my friends," the reigning *asantehene* supposedly said, "because I saw their object was trade only, and they did not care for the people." [88]

During the next ten years, the Ashanti consolidated their claims to the coast. In 1809, 1811, and again from 1814 to 1816, they fought against and defeated the armies of Fantse, Akim, Akwapim, and Wassaw. Thereafter, the victors regarded these vanquished peoples as subjects and their states as provinces of the Ashanti empire. From this period, Osei Tutu Kwamena, the *asantehene*, also held the African Company and its successors responsible for the good behavior of the Fantse, to whose chiefs the Company had reluctantly continued to extend its protection. At the same time, both Ashanti and the Company wanted the trade paths between the interior and the coast to remain open. But Ashanti wanted to continue to transport slaves down these paths to the coast and to sell slaves there to American, Brazilian, Portuguese, and Spanish merchants. The British, on the other hand, tried instead, as they had on the Niger coast, to encourage the export of "legitimate" tropical products like palm oil, ivory, and gold. These differences, and the invidious position of the Company *vis-à-vis* the Fantse, provided abundant sources of tension. At first, however, the Company chose to acknowledge the overweening power of the *asantehene*.

In 1817, the British governor in the Gold Coast sent an embassy to Kumasi, the members of which were the first Britons (a Dutch mission and at least one Dane preceded them) to observe the Ashanti court. The grandeur of the court impressed and overwhelmed their senses. One of the participants described the scene that they found:

> *Our observations en passant had taught us to conceive a spectacle far exceeding our original expectations; but they had not prepared us for the extent and display of the scene which here burst upon us; an area of nearly a mile in circumference was crowded with magnificence and novelty. The king, his tributaries, and cap-*

[88] Quoted in W. Walton Claridge, *A History of the Gold Coast and Ashanti* (London, 1915), I, p. 250.

tains, were resplendent in the distance, surrounded by attendants of every description, fronted by a mass of warriors which seemed to make our approach impervious. The sun was reflected, with a glare scarcely more supportable than the heat, from the massive gold ornaments, which glistened in every direction. More than a hundred bands burst at once on our arrival . . . the horns flourished their defiances, with the beating of innumerable drums and metal instruments, and then yielded for awhile to the soft breathings of their long flutes, which were truly harmonious. . . .

The caboceers, as did their superior captains and attendants, wore Ashantee cloths, of extravagant price . . . they were of an incredible size and weight, and thrown over the shoulder exactly like the Roman toga. . . . Some wore necklaces reaching to the navel entirely of aggrey beads; a band of gold and beads encircled the knee, from which several strings of the same depended; small circles of gold like guineas . . . were strung round their ankles; their sandals were of green, red, and delicate white leather . . . rude lumps of rock gold, hung from their left wrists. . . .[89]

In the eyes of the same writer, Osei Tutu Kwamena possessed all of the virtues that could be expected of an important potentate:

We cannot do justice to the King's sentiments either in detail or in expression; they were incredibly liberal, and would have ennobled the most civilized monarch; they seemed to break the spell which has shut the Interior.[90]

With Osei Tutu Kwamena, the members of the British embassy drank at least one toast to the "oneness" of Ashanti and Britain before eventually concluding a treaty of friendship and commerce between the two nations. In vague terms, the treaty provided that the British would protect Ashanti traders visiting the coasts and prevent the Fantse and other coastal peoples from attacking Ashanti. The *asantehene* agreed, in turn, to receive a permanent British official and to guarantee the safety of Cape Coast Castle against attack from Elmina.[91]

By the terms of the treaty of 1817, the Company had sought to accommodate itself to Ashanti power. But the changing trends of trade, abolitionist pressure from London, and disputes about British responsibility toward the Fantse all exacerbated their mutual antagonisms. The Company's governor, John Hope Smith, soon dishonored the provisions of the treaty by refusing to curb attacks by the coastal peoples against Ashanti. He publicly deprecated the *asantehene* and refused to receive messengers sent by him. Certainly from 1821, when the British government abolished the Company and vested the eight British forts in the Crown, the relationship of equals based upon commerce gradually "gave way to a situation in which one particular European nation . . . achieved *political* dominion over an area very much more extensive than that involved in the earlier sphere of *commercial* contact." [92]

[89] Thomas Edward Bowdich, *Mission from Cape Coast Castle to Ashantee* (London, 1819), pp. 34–35. With regard to the priority of this mission, see Curtin, *Image*, p. 20 n.

[90] Bowdich, *Mission*, p. 64.

[91] *Ibid.*, pp. 126–128, 149. For a discussion of the British mission to Kumasi, see Edmund Collins, "The Panic Element in Nineteenth-Century British Relations with Ashanti," *Transactions of the Historical Society of Ghana*, V (1962), pp. 106–138.

[92] John D. Fage, *Ghana: A Historical Interpretation* (Madison, Wisc., 1959), pp. 57–58.

In 1822, Sir Charles Macarthy became the joint governor of the Gambia, Sierra Leone, and the Gold Coast. Despite the contrary wishes of the Colonial Office, he had previously extended the authority of Britain beyond the then established borders of the colony of Sierra Leone. In the Gold Coast, his policies proved equally expansionist; upon his arrival, he immediately began to prepare for war. He refused to compromise, seek mediation, or conform in any normal way to the proprieties of coastal diplomacy. Instead, he enlisted the support of the Ga people and aroused the Fantse spirit sufficiently to threaten peace with Ashanti. The campaigns of 1823/24 followed, the Ashanti overwhelmed the British regiments along with their Fantse supporters, and Macarthy lost his own life on the banks of the Bonsa River. In 1826, however, British troops and those of their coastal allies avenged themselves at Katamansu, north of Accra.[93] The British no longer paid rent for their forts to the Ashanti; their forces had at last humbled the northern warriors and, by so doing, they obtained consideration for the wishes of imperial Britain in the subsequent affairs of the Gold Coast. Peace, however, eluded the victors.

Only George Maclean, who in 1830 became the first permanent president of the Council of Merchants, proved diplomat enough to smooth the paths of peace in the Gold Coast. Three years before, the British government had tired of the wars against the Ashanti and the expenses connected with its administration of the Gold Coast forts. It had therefore transferred its responsibilities to a committee of resident traders—the Council of Merchants—and had provided a proportion of the funds required for their execution. Maclean, the choice of the Council, had previously visited the Gold Coast with the acting governor of Sierra Leone. A soldier, he seems to have possessed an especial pragmatic sensitivity to the problems of Anglo-African relations. The pursuit of trade, he understood, required conditions of stability. Toward this end, he finally persuaded Britain's coastal allies, particularly the Fantse, that they should offer the weakened Ashanti a just rather than a punitive, and therefore unsignable, treaty. In 1831, the *asantehene* renounced his sovereignty over the Fantse, surrendered six hundred ounces of gold and two hostages as security for the future behavior of the Ashanti, and signed agreements that committed the various African parties to refer acts of aggression to Maclean for arbitration. The agreements also provided that the flow of trade was to be unrestricted and unhindered by any artificial obstacles. Maclean explained that the importance of the agreements lay in the confidence that they gave to the traders of Kumasi. By the terms of the treaty, Maclean had eliminated middlemen:

> *. . . the Ashantees . . . have a free communication secured to them with the sea, without interruption by the intermediate tribes who have hitherto required that the trade from the interior should pass through their hands.*[94]

Maclean's efforts ensured a comparatively long period of peace in the Gold Coast. Africans called him Badayi, "the White man in whose time all men slept

---

[93] For details, see Claridge, *History*, pp. 339–352, 383–391.

[94] Quoted in George E. Metcalfe, *Maclean of the Gold Coast* (London, 1962), p. 89.

sound." [95] The better to induce "sleep," Maclean extended his judicial authority—restricted in theory to the "forts and roadsteads or harbours thereunto adjoining"—beyond Cape Coast Castle to the local tribes with whom he had alliances.[96] Their chiefs became his dependents, their subjects equally his. Upon them, Maclean successfully imposed British ideas of morality. By dint of a forceful, indeed authoritarian personality, a reputation for impartiality, the prestige of his peacemaking with the Ashanti, and careful displays of British might, he soon created an informal "protectorate" out of the effective sphere of his own personal influence. Indeed, a number of Fantse chiefs and the *denkyerahene* acknowledged this extension of British jurisdiction beyond the coastal settlements. In 1844, they even signed a casually worded bond (one of many between Africans and Britons) that for some years remained the only legal justification for the exercise of British sovereignty in the Gold Coast. Its terms were later seen to have constituted a recognition by Britain of the authority and independence of the signatories and of the limited nature of British rights.[97] But for the moment, the bond simply signified an offhand acceptance of the existing arrangements for law and order.

From Maclean's day, Britain in effect governed the Gold Coast between the Pra and Densa rivers—except for the Dutch and Danish enclaves—and from the borders of Ashantiland to the coast. By 1840, the influence of Maclean had helped to treble the trade of the Gold Coast; its value was even greater than that of Sierra Leone. Maclean encouraged the production of palm oil, timber, and indigo, introduced a cowrie currency to replace pinches of gold dust, and contrived to provide the measure of internal security that was so essential to the free flow of commerce.[98] He encouraged Africans to keep open the paths of trade between Kumasi and Cape Coast and, when necessary, interceded forcefully in the cause of commercial justice. But the concentration of so extensive an authority in private hands dismayed Maclean's detractors in Britain and in the Gold Coast. British officials also wondered if Maclean's government had sought with sufficient vigilance to eradicate the slave trade. Although a Select Committee of the House of Commons finally praised Maclean's efforts, the Crown, in 1843, resumed direct administration over the settlements in the Gold Coast. Beyond the settlements, it agreed to continue the extra-territorial jurisdiction exercised so profitably by Maclean. Indeed, although Maclean lost the presidency of the Council of Merchants, he remained on the coast for a short time as the judicial assessor and interpreter of customary law in the "protectorate" that he himself had created. And for the next thirty years, Britain attempted, with but little success, to translate Maclean's personal influence into formal and enduring institutional arrangements.

---

[95] *Ibid.*, p. vi.

[96] Quoted in *ibid.*, p. 66.

[97] Joseph B. Danquah, "The Historical Significance of the Bond of 1844," *Transactions of the Historical Society of Ghana*, III (1957), pp. 6–9.

[98] Metcalfe, *Maclean*, p. 115; John D. Fage, "The Administration of George Maclean on the Gold Coast, 1830–44," *Transactions of the Gold Coast and Togoland Historical Society*, I (1955), pp. 104–118.

In the Niger and Slave Coasts, British merchants had meanwhile turned to "legitimate" trade. They had sought to replace the sale and conveyance of humans with the export of palm oil, ivory, timber, pepper, rice, and gum. Of these products, the first was by far the most important. But even as the British demand for palm oil increased because of new standards of European cleanliness and industrial efficiency, so its production remained unimportant wherever slavers continued their activities. Although the British navy blockaded the coast and its officers attempted to interfere with the organization of coastal distribution centers frequented by the slavers, its inability to deal a death blow to the trade was widely known. In 1827, the Admiralty even established a base on Fernão do Pó in order to provide protection for "legitimate" traders. This action, and the energy with which the African Squadron pursued slavers, temporarily increased the export of palm products to Britain. But the base on Fernão do Pó reverted to Spain in 1834; thereafter, the sale of slaves threatened once again to halt the export of palm oil and palm kernels from the Bight of Benin.

From 1836 to 1849, Britain interfered forcefully along the Niger coast in order to encourage the growth of "legitimate" commerce. With naval assistance, its several agents attempted, by the expedients of treaty and subsidy, to persuade city-states and trading houses to cease dealing in slaves. They also obtained agreements that were designed to ensure commercial freedom for Britons. On a number of occasions, British officials also interfered more actively in the affairs of these coastal entrepôts. They removed those indigenous leaders who chose to oppose the growth along the coast of Britain's hesitant, informal, but growing paramountcy. In 1847, for example, Lord Palmerston sanctioned the removal of Awanta, the high priest of Bonny, after Awanta had aroused Africans against British merchants and property there.[99]

Pressed by abolitionist interests in Britain, free traders, and the commercial communities of both England and the Niger coast, Lord Palmerston finally settled upon a policy of intervention. In 1849, he therefore appointed a consul to the states bordering upon the Bights of Benin and Biafra. John Beecroft, the consul, had long been privately active in these regions.[100] He was particularly well versed in the canons of coastal politics and commerce; middlemen and chiefs knew him well. For five years he utilized the art of palaver and the bluster of gunboats to acquaint African merchant oligarchies with British pre-eminence and power. He forcibly removed obstinate rulers of creeks and ports or otherwise compelled them to recognize Palmerstonian principles of "free trade." He would tolerate no chief "who took an independent line or showed signs of an anti-British attitude in trade or politics." [101]

In the Slave Coast, similar policies gradually gave Britain the semblance of paramountcy. In 1842, Maclean and the Methodist missionary Thomas Birch Freeman proposed the establishment of a number of anti-slavery stations between Accra and Lagos. Maclean even stationed a detachment of marines

---

99 Dike, *Trade*, pp. 88–92.
100 See *supra*, p. 198.
101 Dike, *Trade*, pp. 129–130.

An altarpiece, probably nineteenth century, for the yam spirit Ifijioku, from the Kwale Ibo, Nigeria. The family head, flanked by his wives, is seated in front of the altar and is about to sacrifice a fowl to the yam spirit. The British Museum, London.

in Badagri until the Foreign Office instructed him to withdraw them. In order to protect a "legitimate" British emporium, it at first tended to prefer persuasion to force. After 1849, both Beecroft and John Duncan, the British vice consul at Whydah, therefore tried without success to interest the king of Dahomey in the virtues of "legitimate" trade. At the same time, British merchants and missionaries attempted to entrench their own economic positions in Abeokuta by strengthening the Egba against the Dahomeans. And Abeokuta's natural port was Lagos, where slavers exercised control. Thomas Hutton, an influential British merchant with interests in the Slave Coast, articulated the case for Abeokuta:

> *One thing alone is wanting to compel [the king of Dahomey] to stop the [slave] trade, that is, to get possession of Lagos, and either by treaty or force utterly extinguish the Slave Trade there.*[102]

Together, these different currents of interest led to the annexation of Lagos. Beecroft and Hutton persuaded the Foreign Office and the Admiralty that such an action was both necessary and expedient. To Beecroft, Lagos held the solution to Britain's commercial problems along the coast. All of the rulers of the

[102] Quoted in Colin W. Newbury, *The Western Slave Coast and Its Rulers* (Oxford, 1961), p. 53. Cf. Alan Burns, *History of Nigeria* (London, 1955), p. 112.

coast "want coercion," he wrote, "but Lagos ought not to be allowed to escape; place the right person there, all is well." [103] He therefore decided to oust Kosoko, then the ruler of Lagos, and to install in his place Akitoye, whom Kosoko had deposed in 1845. Akitoye resided in Badagri, where he had remained in contact with the local British merchants and missionaries. In exchange for British assistance in regaining his position in Lagos, he willingly promised to suppress the slave trade. In late 1851, with the ex-ruler's agreement secured, Beecroft and British marines invaded Lagos, put Kosoko to flight, and restored Akitoye to the throne.[104]

During the next decade, Britain "protected" Lagos, and the British consulate became the center of power in the port. While British, French, German, Italian, Brazilian, Sierra Leonean, and indigenous traders competed among themselves, the consulate prevented invasion from without or "subversion" from within.[105] But under combined rule by consul and chief, the administration of Lagos continued to be chaotic; in the realm of commerce, confusion reigned in the absence of law and order. Furthermore, in 1859 the Egba and the Egbado closed the trade routes from Abeokuta to the coast in the face of British protests. Uncertainty hurt trade. In 1861, in order to support "lawful commerce" and assist the ending of the slave trade, chief Docemo ceded Lagos to Britain. This action, and a treaty made with the ruler of Badagri, supported British merchants and missionaries in Abeokuta and, in theory, assured an uninterrupted flow of palm oil from the interior to the Niger and Slave Coasts. Yet Lagos remained dependent upon its relations with peoples who lived beyond British control. And to the British Colonial Office, Lagos, quite justifiably, was a "deadly gift" that would soon "join the queue of West African pauper possessions lining up for a Parliamentary grant-in-aid." [106] That very dependence would, moreover, soon mean a further extension of British influence to the Yoruba settlements on the Lagos lagoon, and then northward and westward to Ibadan and Badagri.

Elsewhere the British government accepted the fact of its paramountcy with ambivalence. On the Gambia, officials in Bathurst gradually extended their influence to the peoples living along the middle and upper reaches of the river. Yet on a number of occasions, the government in London seriously considered transferring its rights on the Gambia to France in exchange for a territorial settlement of the kind first proposed by Faidherbe and later re-introduced by others. In Sierra Leone, governors interfered in the Rivières du Sud on behalf of Creole traders, and annexed Sherbro Island, the mainland opposite that island, and several chiefdoms of the interior, despite the evident disinterest of the Colonial Office. Indeed, the latter refused for a time to administer these new territories. In the Gold Coast, however, Britain purchased the Danish forts,

---

[103] Quoted in Newbury, *Slave Coast*, p. 54.

[104] Burns, *Nigeria*, pp. 117–122, text of treaty with Akitoye at pp. 313–315.

[105] Fearing her "subversion," Consul Benjamin Campbell even expelled Madam Tinubu, a leading trader, from Lagos in 1856.

[106] Quoted in Ronald Robinson and John Gallagher, *Africa and the Victorians: The Climax of Imperialism in the Dark Continent* (New York, 1961), p. 36.

including Christiansborg, in order to eliminate jurisdictional conflicts between Britons and Danes and prevent the French from obtaining a foothold on the coast. In 1853, in an attempt to appease the resident merchants and minimize the expenses connected with administration of the Gold Coast settlements, Britain even began to collect a poll tax, to the imposition of which the chiefs and headmen of the protectorate had previously agreed when meeting as the first Gold Coast Legislative Assembly. According to their resolutions, the funds raised by the tax were to be used for the "public good, in the education of the people, in the general improvement and extension of the judicial system, in affording greater facilities of internal communication, in increased medical aid, and in such other measures of improvement and utility as the state of social progress may render necessary." [107] At the same time, Britain was reluctant to increase its overseas commitments; in the Gold Coast, it refused either to restrain the local inhabitants from interfering with Ashanti trade or to defend the protectorate against Ashanti attack. Britain also declined to withdraw from its position of paramountcy; instead, the queen's officials temporized. By so doing, they violated the spirit, if not the letter, of Maclean's treaty. The last of a number of trivial incidents resulted in another war with Ashanti and an overwhelming defeat for Britain and its allies in 1863/64. The *asantehene*, in remarking upon the British fiasco, supposedly commented pithily that "the white men bring many cannon to the bush, but the bush is stronger than the cannon." [108]

Britain thereafter tried to eliminate commitments that could lead to further wars against African armies. In 1865, a parliamentary Select Committee recommended that the government of Britain should ultimately divest itself of its West African responsibilities. It advanced the opinion that "all further extension of territory or assumption of Government, or new treaties offering any protection to native tribes, would be inexpedient." Furthermore, the committee decided that the paternal object of British policy with regard to the Gambia, Sierra Leone, the Gold Coast, and Lagos "should be to encourage in the natives the exercise of those qualities which may render it possible for us more and more to transfer to them the administration of all the Governments, with a view to our ultimate withdrawal. . . ." [109] This was, however, more an expression of pious imperial compromise than an analysis of local realities.

In practice, the denial of 1865 meant little. Although Africans and officials in London had welcomed it, the "men on the spot" advanced instead of withdrawing. They wanted to strengthen, not weaken, their influence by introducing European trade goods and Christianity into the interior of West Africa. Baikie had already demonstrated the ease with which whites could navigate the Niger River. After 1865, British consuls took steps both to ensure the accessibility

---

[107] Quoted in David Kimble, *A Political History of Ghana: The Rise of Gold Coast Nationalism, 1850–1928* (Oxford, 1963), p. 173. See also Curtin, *Image*, pp. 455–456. The tax was collected, in declining amounts, until 1861.

[108] Attributed to Kwaku Dua, in Claridge, *History*, p. 529.

[109] Quoted in Kimble, *Political History of Ghana*, p. 208; Hargreaves, *Prelude*, pp. 76–77. For the antecedents of this policy, see Curtin, *Image*, p. 278.

of coastal markets and to restrain, however imperfectly, the virulent opposition of African middlemen to the further penetration of the interior by European traders. Of these middlemen, Ja Ja exerted the most influence. Through sheer ability and a modicum of intrigue, he had risen from slavery to lead the Bonny house, or trading association, of Anna Pepple. He had reorganized the economic and political affairs of that house and had amalgamated it with others in order to form an African cartel. But because of his success, a middlemen's war ensued. Seemingly defeated, Ja Ja nonetheless emerged from it as the ruler of Opobo, a creek that lay to the east of Bonny. After 1870, he swiftly directed the flow of palm oil toward Opobo; by dint of skillful trading, he bankrupted British firms and created an entirely new locus of power on the Niger coast.[110]

During the same years, various forms of British "protection" accompanied the commercial frontier as it moved up the Niger. Merchants moored their hulks near Onitsha and Idah, on the lower Niger River, and along the Benue; consular officials and Admiralty gunboats soon followed. Between 1867 and 1869—when African hostility caused it to be abandoned—Britons even manned a consulate at Lokoja. And in 1870, Britain symbolically transferred its consular headquarters for the Bights of Benin and Biafra from Fernão do Pó to Calabar. British consuls and captains thereafter guarded the Delta and the rivers, periodically destroying many of the towns whose rulers hindered the pursuit of "free trade" or threatened the lives and property of British traders. In 1879, for instance, a British warship bombarded Onitsha for three days. On this occasion, the British consul observed: "Our proceedings . . . will have a most salutary effect up and down the Niger, and the Missionaries and Traders unanimously gave us their thanks for our promptness and decision." [111]

In the Gold Coast, meanwhile, the British "men on the spot" refused immediately to advance. Partially for this reason, Fantse chiefs and influential commoners acted together after 1867 in order to protect what they believed to be their own interests. In Fantse eyes, the local Britons appeared both unable and unwilling—particularly in light of the report of the parliamentary Select Committee—to exercise their imperial power in the ways foreshadowed in the bond of 1844. The Fantse thus banded together, first informally, in a war against the Dutch (which led, in 1872, to the withdrawal of the Dutch from the Gold Coast [112]), and then formally, in the interests of long-range peace and stability on the coast. In 1871, at Mankessim, thirty-one signatories therefore united "for offensive and defensive purposes against their common enemy [Ashanti]" and agreed to govern the so-called Fantse Confederation according to the decisions of a common assembly and a constitutional monarch to be elected from among their own number.[113] They envisaged a confederal government that would make roads, establish schools, provide a judicial system, promote agricultural and

---

[110] Dike, *Trade*, pp. 192–196. See also *infra*, p. 248.

[111] Quoted in *ibid.*, p. 207.

[112] Douglas Coombs, *The Gold Coast, Britain and the Netherlands, 1850–1874* (London, 1963), pp. 107–119.

[113] Joseph Ephraim Casely Hayford, *Gold Coast Native Institutions* (London, 1903), pp. 328–329; Kimble, *Political History of Ghana*, pp. 247–249.

industrial pursuits, and develop the mineral resources of the country. Theirs was, in sum, an honest attempt to avoid chaos on the coast by welding a collection of principalities into one superstate bound, nevertheless, to Britain and beholden to Britain for "protection." The Crown might indeed have welcomed their initiative, but C. S. Salmon, then the acting administrator, instead regarded the Mankessim agreements as both a personal affront to his dignity and a conspiracy against British rule in the Gold Coast. He arrested the principal architects of the proposed confederation and charged them with treason. As a result, the idea of an autonomous African confederation—the first major expression of political modernity in the Gold Coast—came to naught. New forces were, in any event, transforming the relationships between the peoples of the Gold Coast and Great Britain.

Another Ashanti war, which had been simmering since 1867, boiled over into the protectorate in 1873/74. Unwilling to suffer any longer the indignity and economic dislocation caused by such frequent "invasions" of the protectorate, the then administrator obtained imperial reinforcements and London's agreement to a "war to end wars." Led by Major General Sir Garnet Wolseley, who planned his campaign in great detail beforehand, British-officered African levies and British troops and marines quickly crossed the Pra River and fought their way to Kumasi, which they looted and burned. Wolseley failed, however, to depose the *asantehene*. Shortly thereafter, the British government, in order to defend the people of the coast against a resurgence of Ashanti power, reluctantly agreed to annex the protectorate and to create in its place the new Gold Coast Colony (which at first included Lagos). Sir Robert Herbert, the Under-Secretary of State for the Colonies, voiced the British rationale for annexation:

> *It is difficult to see how any half measures with regard to the Government of the Protectorate can be made to suffice. Unless we directly govern, up to the Prah, we can have no guarantee against wars and disturbances. I am not at all sure that the annexation of the whole Protectorate (which I look upon with horror) is not the only cheap and safe alternative to retirement from all the coast. . . .*[114]

In another's terms, total abandonment simply was "too charming to be capable of execution." [115] Thus the Fantse, who had envisaged the queen of England as a guardian rather than as a sovereign, henceforth found that her government had deprived them of their status and privileges as protected allies. A half-century of imperial vacillation had resulted in the assumption by Britain of a new form of colonial hegemony. Indeed, before long the colonial logic led to the annexation of Ashanti.

Zanzibar and the eastern coast

At the close of the Napoleonic Wars, Seyyid Said bin Sultan, the sultan of Muscat and Oman, claimed sovereignty over Zanzibar, Pemba, and a number

[114] Quoted in William E. F. Ward, *A History of Ghana* (London, 1958), p. 262.
[115] Quoted in Robinson and Gallagher, *Africa and the Victorians*, p. 31. See also Hargreaves, *Prelude*, p. 71.

of the other island-states of the East African coast as a result of the conquests of his dynastic predecessors in the seventeenth and eighteenth centuries. In the greater Indian Ocean basin, however, Seyyid Said's power suffered no comparison with that of the British government, whose fleet dominated the eastern seas in order to protect the route to India. The importance of India conditioned British imperial thinking: Britain occupied Mauritius and warily watched the French, who controlled Réunion and played an increasingly important role in Madagascar and the Comoro Islands. In East Africa, Britain at first chose to exercise only limited, informal influence of a kind sufficient to protect India; at the same time, it attempted to curtail the export of slaves from East Africa. But the pursuit of these two policies contained the seeds of inherent contradiction.

In general, the British government was unwilling to concern itself deeply with the problems of East Africa. Yet in 1822, Captain Fairfax Moresby, who was acting on behalf of the governor of Mauritius, obtained Seyyid Said's signature to an anti-slavery treaty. It purported to end the export of slaves from all of Said's dependencies and dominions. It gave to the British government the privilege of posting an agent in Zanzibar "for the purpose of having intelligence and watching the traffic in slaves with Christian nations." [116] By implication, the treaty also recognized Said's sovereignty over the entire coast of eastern Africa from Cape Guardafui to Cape Delgado. In 1823, the Mazrui family, who ruled Mombasa in the face of Said's displeasure, nevertheless appealed to the British government for protection against the navy of Muscat and Oman. "Beneath [your flag's] protecting shade," they wrote to Bombay, one of the seats of the government of British India, "we may defy our enemies. As the lamb trembles at the lion's roar, so will the Imam [sultan] shrink from that which is the terror of the world." [117] In reply, the British government refused to ignore its treaty obligations to Said. At this time, it also wished to avoid intimate connections with any East African polity.

Considerations of state reckoned, however, without the actions of a "man on the spot." Captain William Fitzwilliam Owen had already acted in the Gulf of Guinea against slave traders. As an earnest of British abolitionist and commercial concern for Africa, he had then begun to chart the coasts, rivers, and ports of Africa. In 1823, *en route* from Cape Town to Muscat, he surveyed Delagoa Bay and there obtained a rather suspect cession of the surrounding land from the chiefs then in control. Later, on his own initiative, he imperiously demanded that Seyyid Said should strictly observe the provisions of the Moresby treaty (which had not yet been enforced). Owen next sailed to Mombasa, where he found Said's navy locked in combat with forces loyal to the Mazrui family. He naturally showed partiality for the Mazrui and, in defiance of settled British policy, Owen signed an agreement with the rulers of Mombasa that exchanged

---

[116] Quoted in Reginald Coupland, *East Africa and Its Invaders from the Earliest Times to the Death of Seyyid Said in 1856* (Oxford, 1938), p. 215.

[117] Quoted in *ibid.*, p. 225. Cf. John Milner Gray, *The British in Mombasa, 1824–1826* (London, 1957), p. 21.

imperial protection for a promise to end the slave trade. Both parties agreed to share customs revenues. "It is as clear as the sun," Owen wrote, "that God has prepared the dominion of East Africa for [Great Britain] the only nation on the earth which has public virtue enough to govern it for its own benefit."[118]

Owen agreed to support the Mazrui against the ruler of Muscat and Oman. Between 1824 and 1826, a small detachment of British naval officers therefore "protected" Mombasa from Muscat. In Bombay, however, the government of British India expressed its disapproval, and Lord Bathurst, at the Colonial Office in London, declared that the British government preferred to support the claims of the sultan. Further British involvement in Mombasa was, he said, unwarranted. Britain had no real interests there and wanted none. The naval officers reluctantly withdrew, and this first direct British colonial essay in East Africa, like a similar suggestion in 1838, came to naught in the face of London's lack of interest.

With British support, Said simultaneously increased the extent of his influence in East Africa. After Owen's departure, he carried the war against Mombasa to fruition, occupying that island-state briefly in 1827/28 and permanently in 1837. Said also sought alliances with Ranavolana I, the powerful queen of the Merina people of Madagascar. He signed a treaty with the United States, whose traders were already active in East Africa, and permitted it to establish a consulate on Zanzibar in 1837. Finally in 1841, Said transferred his permanent residence from Muscat to Zanzibar, where the climate suited him and the possibilities of trade intrigued him. "I am nothing but a merchant," he later averred.[119] He transformed Zanzibar into a money and produce market for the traders of the mainland and consequently made it the economic center of East Africa. He also encouraged the Arabs of Zanzibar assiduously to cultivate the clove tree that French visitors had previously introduced from Mauritius and the Far East. The small unopened buds of the common-looking clove tree brought great wealth to Said personally and to the other plantation owners of the island. Indeed, the economy of Zanzibar soon depended primarily upon their export.

From 1841 to 1854, a British resident "advised" and guided Sultan Said. He maintained him in power, exercising in effect an informal, but nonetheless effective paramountcy in Zanzibar and wherever the sultan's writ ran along the coast of East Africa. Yet even as the British government supported the sultan as the strongest power on the western shores of the Indian Ocean, so it undercut the slave trade on which that strength was based. Slaves from the mainland cultivated and picked the clove trees. The entrepreneurs of the island had invested heavily in slaves, and many of the sultan's subjects were to some extent involved in the transportation and sale of slaves. The British government nevertheless demanded that Said should curtail the slave trade within his dominions. In 1845, it even persuaded him to sign a treaty which purported to prohibit the transport of slaves between Zanzibar and Muscat. Afterwards, however, many

---

[118] Quoted in Coupland, *Invaders*, pp. 237–238.
[119] Quoted in *ibid.*, p. 299.

The town of Zanzibar in the time of Sultan Seyyid Said. His residence lies to the center right. At the left, an American vessel lies at anchor. (Painting by C. P. Brown, 1878, Peabody Museum, Salem, Mass.)

questioned whether or not the sultan—even if he wanted to—would be able to enforce the provisions of the treaty in the face of the overwhelming opposition of his subjects. But Lord Palmerston refused to brook delay. He thus imperiously instructed the British consul to Zanzibar:

> *You will take every opportunity of impressing upon these Arabs that the nations of Europe are destined to put an end to the African Slave Trade, and that Great Britain is the main instrument in the hand of Providence for the accomplishment of this purpose; that it is in vain for these Arabs to endeavour to resist the consummation of that which is written in the book of fate; that they ought to bow to superior power, to leave off a pursuit which is doomed to annihilation, and a perseverance which will only involve them in pecuniary losses and in various other evils; and that they should hasten to betake themselves to the cultivation of the soil and to lawful and innocent commerce.*[120]

After 1856, when the weak Sultan Majid acceded to the throne of Zanzibar, now separated from Muscat and Oman, Britain's consular presence increased in importance. The British agents prevented Thuwain, the brother of Majid who ruled in Muscat, from conquering Zanzibar and thereby reuniting the two Albusaid kingdoms. Moreover, by the terms of the subsequent arbitration agreement, the British government agreed to maintain the position of the sultan of Zanzibar. Thus, in late 1859, they also safeguarded the pliant Majid when yet another brother, the petulant Barghash, intrigued with the local French consul and raised the banner of revolt.

> *My brother Majid's wish is to give the country to the English. . . . We, however, will not give our country either to the English or to the French or to the*

[120] Quoted in John Milner Gray, *History of Zanzibar from the Middle Ages to 1856* (London, 1962), p. 250.

Americans or to anyone else; but, if we sell it, we shall do so only at the cost of our blood and of war to the death.[121]

Captain Christopher Palmer Rigby and a detachment of British marines arrested Barghash and exiled him to Bombay. And by the bilateral declaration of 1862, both the French and British governments promised thereafter to respect the separate independence of the sultan of Zanzibar and the imam of Muscat and Oman.[122]

In 1870, at the death of Majid, Britain almost literally governed Zanzibar. The British consul installed Barghash as sultan and then tried to persuade him to abolish the still flourishing slave trade. As British pressure increased, so Barghash grew increasingly obstinate. He and his advisors understandably feared that, dependent as they were on slaves, the agricultural and commercial economies of Zanzibar could hardly continue without such labor. The sultan even tried to deny the validity of the agreements made with the British government by his predecessors. The Foreign Office held, however, to the principles of Lord Palmerston; pressed by Parliament, it urgently sought a new agreement that would really end the trade in slaves. Sir Bartle Frere, a special British envoy, cajoled and threatened Barghash. But the sultan and his counselors believed that they would court disaster less by incurring the enmity of Britain than by tampering with the profitable machinery of slavery. Barghash's reply to Frere had also received expression earlier in West Africa:

We have considered what has been said, and we are convinced it involves destruction to us. It is quite in your power to destroy us, but you ask us to destroy ourselves, and that we cannot do.[123]

For a few months, Barghash managed to sustain his refusal. But in early 1873, Frere ordered the British navy forcibly to halt the transportation of slaves from Kilwa Kivinje and elsewhere along the coast to Zanzibar. Dr. John Kirk, the British consul at Zanzibar, also threatened to blockade Zanzibar totally, whereupon Barghash soon signed the necessary treaty. He agreed to prevent the "export of slaves from the coast . . . of Africa, whether destined for transport from one part of the Sultan's dominions to another or for conveyance to foreign parts." [124] He closed the public slave markets and, in time, the Universities' Mission to Central Africa built an Anglican cathedral upon the site of the main emporium.

Barghash had learned to play the British game. Kirk saw the sultan's correspondence, and even transmitted exact copies to the Foreign Office. Zanzibaris came to regard Kirk as the sultan's prime minister. Together they outlawed the overland conveyance of slaves and, with Kirk's support, Barghash further directed his governors to imprison any who continued to trade in slaves. When revolts followed these proclamations against the trade, ships of the British navy attacked

[121] Quoted in Coupland, *Exploitation*, p. 32. See also Lillian M. Russell (ed.), *General Rigby, Zanzibar and the Slave Trade* (London, 1935), pp. 118–123.

[122] The declaration of 1862 followed the pattern set by the Anglo-French declaration of 1843, which had guaranteed the independence of the Sandwich (later Hawaiian) Islands.

[123] Quoted in Coupland, *Exploitation*, p. 189.

[124] Quoted in *ibid.*, p. 212.

the coastal centers of disaffection. The Foreign Office also supplied Zanzibar with a small British-officered army to deal with further outbreaks against the new régime.

The army successfully upheld Barghash's sovereignty in the face of a variety of challenges from independent-minded sheikhs of the mainland and others who threatened to destroy the balance of power on the East African coast. The British government itself refused to assume territorial commitments. Yet from about 1876, Britain clearly dominated Zanzibar and the nearby littoral by virtue of its hold over Barghash. The Foreign Office even refused to encourage the working of a private concession of mainland territory that Barghash agreed, in 1877, to give to Sir William Mackinnon. No other powers threatened Britain's position in East Africa and, on the eve of the partition, only the importance of the Suez Canal and German intrigue could compel Britons to scramble for slices of the interior.

Intruders in the northeast

In the chronicle of the nineteenth-century invaders of tropical Africa, a place belongs to the Turkish-speaking soldiers loyal to Muhammad 'Ali, viceroy of Egypt under the Ottomans. Muhammad 'Ali dreamed of the supposed gold of the Sudan, coveted its supply of black slaves so that he might replenish the ranks of his military establishment, and feared the Mamluks who had fled from Lower Egypt into the Dongola region of the upper Nile River. For all these complex reasons, the viceroy sent a well-equipped army under the command of his son Isma'il south from Aswan into Nubia, Dongola, and the Funj-controlled regions beyond. In 1820/21, without meeting appreciable resistance, this force imposed the rule of Muhammad 'Ali's Egypt upon the peoples living between Sennar and Wadi Halfa. They also conquered Kordofan, but failed—at this time—to annex Darfur. The Sudan thus became a distant dependency of Egypt, itself a dependency of the Ottoman Empire.

The Sudanese knew the resultant administration of these Turco-Egyptians—most of whom were neither Turkish nor Egyptian—as the *Turkiyya.* In the years immediately after the conquest, they resented the exorbitant taxes and the tribute demanded from them in the form of slaves and recruits for the Egyptian army. The peoples of the old Funj sultanate revolted in 1822, killing Isma'il. But they were able to forestall a permanent re-establishment of Muhammad 'Ali's sovereignty in the region only until 1824, by which time the troops of *Turkiyya* had desolated the rich grain-producing areas between the White and Blue Niles, forced the Funj to retire southward into the mountains, and destroyed Sennar. Thereafter, the next Turco-Egyptian governors-general of the Sudan exacted a high price from their new subjects. Muhammad 'Ali, like the later British Chancellors of the Exchequer, presumed that the Sudan would pay its own way. Agents of the *Turkiyya* collected—usually with difficulty—taxes in kind, in cattle, and in slaves. Tax-gathering evidently was a grim affair in the prosecution of which force of arms and military raids played a substantial part.[125]

[125] Richard Hill, *Egypt in the Sudan, 1820–1881* (London, 1959), p. 40. Hill's book contains the fullest treatment of the history of the *Turkiyya.*

Yet as much as the viceroy welcomed the fruits of such administrative ardor, he tended to temper its harsher excesses. He forbade his governors-general to imprison or harass their subjects without cause. He even allowed local Sudanese to assume civil and military positions in their own country.

Under the early *Turkiyya*, the Sudanese, along with new immigrants from Egypt, began to increase the level of their internal trade and to improve the quality of their agricultural production. The Turco-Egyptians particularly encouraged the growth of cotton—in time the Sudan's most important export—sugar cane, and indigo. They developed the export of ostrich feathers and gum, and profited greatly by the sale of Sudanese ivory. At the same time, they failed to exploit the salt deposits of the Red Sea littoral and discovered, to Muhammad 'Ali's disappointment, that the iron deposits of Kordofan were too expensive to be worked on a large scale and that the dreams of large gold deposits were illusory.

In contemporaneous Ethiopia, only the Monophysite Catholic Church held together the disparate sections of what had once been a powerful empire. In Tigre, Shoa, Amhara, and the other regions, autonomous princes ruled Christian peoples speaking different languages and practicing divergent customs. This atmosphere bred warfare and warlords. During the 1840's, Kassa, one of the more remarkable of these warlords, rose to prominence in western Ethiopia by defeating the prince of Gojjam and ending the Galla influence in Amhara. He naturally turned his attentions next to Tigre, where in 1855 he imposed his influence. Later in that year—even before turning his attentions to Shoa—Kassa persuaded the *abuna*, or head, of the church to install him as the king of kings—the emperor of all of Ethiopia. Assuming the name of Theodorus II, which to Ethiopians conjured up visions of a messianic, all conquering ruler, he soon annexed Shoa and thereafter governed a reunited empire. At this time, the resident British consul wrote:

> *Theodorus . . . is persuaded that he is destined to restore the glories of the Ethiopian Empire, and to achieve great conquests; [he is young in years], of untiring energy . . . his personal and moral daring are boundless. . . . When aroused, his wrath is terrible, and all tremble. . . .*[126]

Since James Bruce's day, Britons had expressed an interest in Ethiopia. During the first decade of the nineteenth century, private men of influence and the East India Company had interested themselves in its muddled affairs. On two occasions, Henry Salt, an English draughtsman, spent time in Tigre; his account of the trade of Adowa is particularly valuable. He also recommended that the British government should take possession of the Ethiopian coast in order to increase the extent of its trade with the peoples of the interior.[127] After him, Nathaniel Pearce, another Briton, lived for fourteen years in Massawa and in Gondar, the old imperial capital and then the capital of Amhara. Missionaries

---

[126] Trevor Chichele Plowden (ed.), *Travels in Abyssinia and the Galla Country, with an Account of a Mission to Ras Ali in 1848* (London, 1868), pp. 455–456.

[127] Henry Salt, *A Voyage to Abyssinia and Travels into the Interior of That Country* (London, 1814), pp. 496–498.

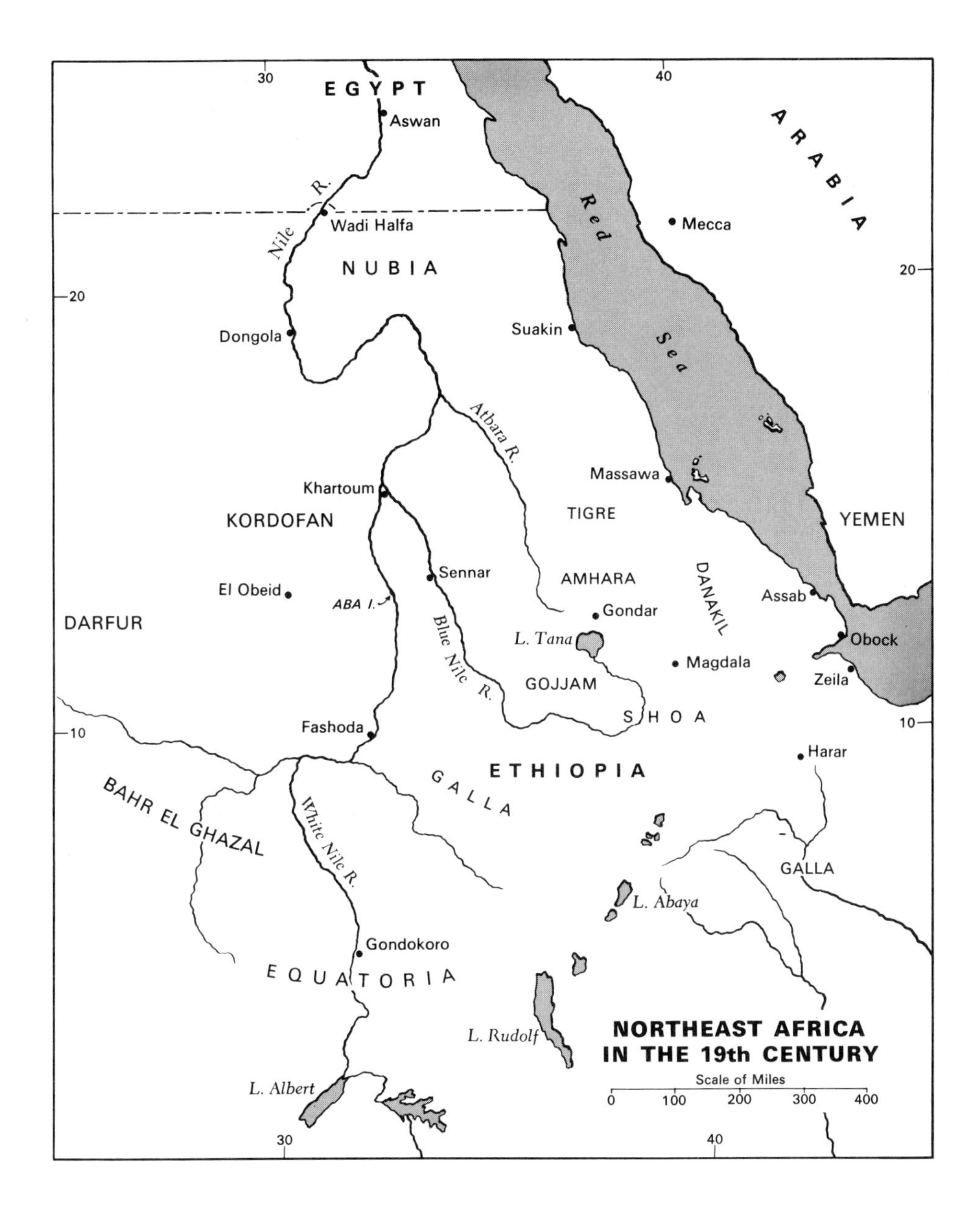

followed, French and German travelers and foreign artisans entered the highlands of Ethiopia and, in 1841, a British military expedition concluded a treaty of friendship and commerce with Sahela Selassie, the ruler of Shoa. Seven years later, Lord Palmerston sent Walter Chichele Plowden and John Bell, two young Englishmen, to represent the interests of Britain in Gondar. They witnessed Kassa's rise to power and, to him, they evinced the interest of Queen Victoria in the affairs of the empire of Ethiopia.

After his accession to the throne of all Ethiopia, Theodorus appears to have

The imperial quarter of Gondar in the late eighteenth century, showing the castles of the emperors Fasiladas (1632–1667),[1] Iyasu I (1682–1706),[3] and Bakaffa (1721–1730),[10] and of Empress Mentuab (1721–1755).[11] (A. A. Monte della Corte, *I Castelli di Gondar,* Rome, 1939)

initiated a series of administrative reforms designed to reduce the arbitrary powers of the feudal nobility. He cruelly crushed revolts in various sections of the empire and, by 1862, had moved his capital from Gondar to Magdala in Lasta, which proved to be more centrally situated and easily fortified. At this time Theodorus, who had become increasingly unreasonable and neurotic in his actions and beliefs, sought to further his connections with Europe and to obtain European military and commercial manufactures. Piqued by Queen Victoria's failure to answer his letters, and perhaps suspicious of British, Egyptian, and Turkish intentions in the Red Sea basin, Theodorus imprisoned Charles Duncan Cameron, the British consul, and his associates at Magdala.

From Aden, two other British officials tried, in 1866, to negotiate the release of the original captives. One of these officials later left a description of the emperor:

> *The expression of his dark eyes, slightly depressed, was strange; if he was in good humour they were soft, with a kind of gazelle-like timidity about them that made one love him; but when angry the fierce and bloodshot eyes seemed to shed fire. In moments of violent passion his whole aspect was frightful: his black visage acquired an ashy hue, his thin compressed lips left but a whitish margin around the mouth, his very hair stood erect, and his whole deportment was a terrible illustration of savage and ungovernable fury.*[128]

[128] Henry Blanc, *A Narrative of Captivity in Abyssinia* (London, 1868), p. 10. On this period, see also Richard Pankhurst, "The Role of Foreigners in Nineteenth-Century Ethiopia Prior to the Rise of Menelik" (unpub. paper, 1963), pp. 11–20.

Theodorus II, emperor of Ethiopia, as he appeared in a drawing in 1868. (Bettmann Archive)

Despite the fact that they at first proved compatible personalities, Theodorus imprisoned these emissaries and thereafter held a number of European missionaries in captivity as well.

Theodorus had affronted the queen of England and had compromised the imperial image of Britain, particularly in India. Early in 1868, Sir Robert Napier therefore landed at Zeila and marched his sixty-two thousand men over the Danakil plain and into the highlands of Lasta. Theodorus recognized his nadir:

> *Believing myself to be a great lord, I gave [the English] battle; but, by reason of the worthlessness of my artillery, all my pains were as nought. . . . I had intended, if God had so decreed, to conquer the whole world. . . . You people, who have passed the night in joy, may God do unto you as He has done unto me.*[129]

---

[129] Quoted in Clements R. Markham, *A History of the Abyssinian Expedition* (London, 1869), p. 331. See also James R. Hooker, "The Foreign Office and the 'Abyssinian Captives,'" *The Journal of African History*, II (1961), pp. 245–258; Alaqâ Walda Maryam (trans. H. Weld Blundell), "History of King Theodore," *Journal of the African Society*, VI (1906), pp. 36–40.

Magdala fell easily and Theodorus committed suicide. Thereafter, although the British forces quickly withdrew, the powers of Europe continued to interest themselves in the fortunes of Ethiopia.

After the death of Theodorus, Johannes IV, the former prince of Tigre, struggled for power; after 1872 he governed Ethiopia for seventeen years. At the same time, Menelik, prince of Shoa and a claimant to the imperial throne, acquired a large measure of autonomy in the south. In Johannes' day, the Ethiopians repulsed two Turco-Egyptian invasions and began to treat continuously with Europeans of many nationalities. France had acquired the port of Obock in 1862, an Italian firm had purchased Assab in 1869, and another Turco-Egyptian force occupied Harar from 1874 to 1884. Napier had demonstrated the weakness of the Ethiopian position. Others soon took advantage of his discovery.

Meanwhile, slaves had increasingly provided the economic lifeblood of the Sudan. After about 1853, even the European and Levantine merchants of Khartoum had participated. Like the Turco-Egyptians and the Sudanese, they enslaved Lwo- and Bantu-speaking Africans, sending their captives north to Cairo and, more commonly after about 1860, across the Red Sea to Arabia. In 1854, Muhammad Sa'id, who had become viceroy of Egypt, tried to halt the traffic in slaves. But even his influence, and the establishment of a control post at Fashoda on the White Nile, could not alter established custom. Slave traders penetrated into the Bahr el Ghazal and as far as, if not beyond, Gondokoro on the White Nile. In this vast region, these brigands came to exert an idiosyncratic power. Each trader had his fortified headquarters and outlying camps; he led private armies whose firearms and modern forms of organization gave them a superiority over the indigenous inhabitants.

At the instigation of Khedive Isma'il, the administrators of the *Turkiyya* redoubled their efforts after 1863 to curtail this trade. The governor-general of the Sudan created and took control of a new province in the lands of the Shilluk. Its capital was Fashoda. Officials of the *Turkiyya* also tried to police the river from armed launches. But the slavers managed to elude the patrols, to bribe officials, and in many other ways to continue their profitable trade with little interruption. Indeed, at times the government of the Sudan itself connived at the continuation of the traffic in slaves. Musa Hamdi, the governor-general between 1863 and 1865, even sent his own troops to participate in raids for Dinka captives. Finally, however, the *Turkiyya* extended its administrative boundaries to Gondokoro and the headwaters of the Nile. And in 1871, on behalf of Isma'il, Sir Samuel Baker organized the government of what was to become the Equatoria province of the Sudan. Nevertheless, despite the expenditure of much energy, if not intelligence, he failed to curb the trade in slaves. Indeed, in Bahr el Ghazal, the private army of Zubair Rahma Mansur, a slave trader, defeated a detachment of Turco-Egyptian troops that had been sent to introduce the fiat of the governor-general there. As a result, in 1873 the governor-general appointed Zubair governor of Bahr el Ghazal. Early in the next year, Zubair conquered a Fur army; representatives of the governor-general thereafter administered the province of Darfur from El Fasher.

But the slave trade still flourished. Even Colonel Charles George Gordon, of China and the Crimea, while governing Equatoria from 1874 to 1876, failed lamentably to subordinate the dictates of commerce to his own rule of law. On the other hand, he extended the influence of the *Turkiyya* into Buganda and Bunyoro, sponsored new explorations of the upper Nile region, suggested an unhappy expedition by which the khedive attempted to annex a portion of the East African littoral, and established new forts and the Turco-Egyptian presence in the heart of Equatoria. Later he demanded and obtained the governor-generalship of the entire Sudan. In that capacity, between 1877 and 1879, he sought by the expenditure of immense personal energy to crush the slave traders and to re-unite a dependency patently slipping from the grip of the Turco-Egyptian administration. Gordon quelled a revolt in Darfur, humbled Sulaiman, the son of Zubair and the latter's successor as the uncrowned king of Bahr el Ghazal, and prevented the emperors of Ethiopia from encroaching upon the eastern marches of the Sudan. Gordon was everywhere at once and tried, sometimes succeeding, to be all things to all men. Yet the Sudan still seethed with revolt when Gordon finally returned to England in late 1879.[130] Thereafter, despite all of his efforts, the administrators continued to be corrupt, the brigands remained supreme unto themselves, and the slavers still herded their captives across the desert wastes.

Already the Mahdi, as well as the forces that gave the Mahdi his strength, had introduced himself. The Baqqara nomads hated the taxes of the *Turkiyya* and reacted hostilely to the other manifestations of settled government to which they had been subjected. Others, particularly those who held an economic stake in the success of the slave trade, resented the efforts of Isma'il and Gordon to diminish their prosperity. A third element decried sins against Islam, sought to introduce reform, and hoped to impose a divine fundamentalism upon the peoples of the Sudan. For their various reasons, these groups welcomed Muhammad 'Ahmad ibn 'Abdallah when he proclaimed himself the Mahdi, or the saviour of the Sudan, in 1881. At Aba on the White Nile, warriors loyal to him defeated Turco-Egyptian troops and then established themselves in a remote section of Kordofan. There the Mahdi assembled, trained, and preached to his followers, repulsed another punitive expedition in 1882, and finally mounted an offensive against the centers of alien authority. Throughout Kordofan the fires of revolt flared. Early in 1883, El Obeid, the capital of the province, capitulated. In the Gezira and near Sennar, the rebels harried the agents of the *Turkiyya*. In 1883, again in Kordofan, they overwhelmed a large Turco-Egyptian army. The governors of Darfur and Bahr el Ghazal thereafter acknowledged the rule of the Mahdi, and the followers of the new prophet extended their swath of conquest to the borders of Suakin on the Red Sea.[131]

At this point, the British government, which had previously made itself responsible for the administration of Egypt and the dependencies of Egypt,

[130] Bernard M. Allen, *Gordon and the Sudan* (London, 1931), pp. 114–153, contains the best account of Gordon's activities during this period.

[131] Peter M. Holt, *The Mahdist State in the Sudan, 1881–1898* (Oxford, 1958), pp. 42–78, is complete.

sent Gordon back to Khartoum ostensibly to evacuate the remaining Turco-Egyptian garrisons. William Gladstone, at least, sympathized with the revolutionary aims of the Mahdi.[132] But Gordon, and possibly the khedive, seems also to have wanted to re-establish the authority of the *Turkiyya.* Gordon evidently hoped for reinforcements and, when they failed to come, he insisted fatalistically upon remaining in Khartoum until the time when either a relief column or regiments loyal to the Mahdi would enter the city. The latter arrived first. Early in 1885, Khartoum fell, Gordon perished, and the Mahdi reigned supreme from Dongola and the outskirts of Suakin to the farthest limits of the Bahr el Ghazal. Only Equatoria and northern Nubia remained in other hands.

The eve of the scramble

During the early 1880's, the powers of Europe began to gather together their various strands of African interest. France and Britain asserted their especial claims vigorously and, particularly after the British government entered Egypt militarily in 1882, clashed commercially and diplomatically throughout western Africa. Both—perhaps France more than Britain—wanted to control the course of the Niger River; each also feared that the other, or a third hostile power, would somehow gain control of the trade of the Congo River. Both nations, and their merchants, competed elsewhere along the coasts; they sought commercial hegemony more than territorial concessions, justifying—more willingly than previously—their acquisitions of sovereignty on economic grounds.

By 1880, it was clear that conditions along the Niger River posed a colonial dilemma for Britain: trade there, however insignificant in terms of Britain's overall balance of payments, produced profits for a few firms and appeared capable of even greater exploitation. At the same time, competition between Europeans and Africans, and of both parties among themselves, had created conditions of commercial instability that had tended to vitiate the economic potential of the region. During a visit to the Niger in 1877/78, George Dashwood Goldie Taubman came to understand these problems. After a childhood spent on the Isle of Man and romantic adventures in the Sudan and Paris, Goldie, as he preferred to be known, had gone out to Africa to inspect the affairs of a palm oil trading firm with which his family had long-standing connections.[133] Within two years he managed to stifle competition among the European firms active on the middle river by associating the four largest British companies, which together formed the United African Company (subsequently the National African Company and finally the Royal Niger Company). During the next few years, Goldie established more than one hundred trading posts along the Niger and Benue rivers. His agents also concluded thirty-seven treaties with African chiefs; they gave to the United African Company a monopoly of the riverine trade and control of certain tracts of land. In 1881, Goldie even offered, on

[132] John Morley, *The Life of William Ewart Gladstone* (London, 1908), II, p. 288.
[133] After being knighted in 1887, George Dashwood Goldie Taubman styled himself Sir George Goldie. He was a member of a family that had long been prominent on the Isle of Man. The standard biography is John Flint, *Sir George Goldie and the Making of Nigeria* (London, 1960).

behalf of the British government, to create and administer a protectorate over territories on either side of the lower river. But London at first refused to meddle in the commercial affairs of Nigeria. The threat of France had not yet manifested itself.

By this time, the designs of France had become widely extended. French officials strengthened their influence in the Rivières du Sud and advanced into the Futa Jallon region of Guinée. On the Ivory Coast, French merchants continued to play a prominent role at Assinie and Grand Bassam. Marcel Treich-Laplène, one of the traders involved, even added to the French sphere by obtaining treaties of friendship—some of which granted exclusive commercial rights to France—from a number of the tribal peoples situated northward from the coast on the road to the upper Niger. In 1883, in the western Slave Coast, the French navy forcefully occupied Porto Novo and Cotonou in order to forestall British interests in Lagos. And in the equatorial regions where Pierre Savorgnan de Brazza had already followed the Ogooué River from the shores of Gabon to the Congo River, emissaries of the French government competed for priority of "discovery" with agents of King Léopold of the Belgians. In 1880, Brazza therefore traversed Gabon a second time, established a post (later called Franceville) on the banks of the upper Ogooué River, and finally persuaded the paramount chief of the Tyo (Téké) people to accept the "protection" of France and to permit another European outpost (now named Brazzaville) to be established on the northern bank of the Congo River.[134] Shortly thereafter, Stanley gained the Congo for the second time and, on behalf of Léopold, claimed a site opposite Brazzaville for the future Léopoldville.

Brazza's acquisitions on the northern bank of the Congo River worried both Léopold and the government of Portugal, which, on the grounds of prior "discovery," claimed the river as its own. In 1882, Portugal sought recognition of its "rights." It negotiated with the governments of Great Britain and France, both of which wanted to use the Portuguese as pawns in their still silent struggle against one another. Lisbon vacillated between London and Paris in 1883 and finally, in 1884, persuaded the British government to accede to a treaty of recognition in exchange for a number of concessions that, in the eyes of Portugal, served virtually to emasculate the purpose supposedly served by the treaty.[135] Moreover, it appeared to further the interests of Britain on the Congo River. This possibility naturally worried the other powers of Europe, and the publication of the Anglo-Portuguese treaty ultimately encouraged the various interested parties to resolve their differences at a meeting in Berlin.

Brazza, who envisaged a colony on the Congo River as the first step in a concerted exercise by which France might obtain control over the potential

[134] Napoléon Ney (ed.), *Conférence et lettres de Pierre Savorgnan de Brazza* (Paris, 1887), pp. 156–162; R. de Lannoy de Bissy, "Recent French Explorations in the Ogowe-Congo Region," *Proceedings of the Royal Geographical Society*, VIII (1886), pp. 770–778; Henri Brunschwig, *L'Avènement de l'Afrique noire du XIXe siècle à nos jours* (Paris, 1963), pp. 146–148.

[135] Roger T. Anstey, *Britain and the Congo in the Nineteenth Century* (Oxford, 1962), pp. 139–167; Edward S. Hertslet, *The Map of Africa by Treaty* (London, 1896), II, pp. 713–714.

wealth of the interior, had meanwhile returned to Africa in 1883 as a commissioner for the Third Republic. Assisted by sixty French soldiers and civilians, he opened a number of new stations along the Ogooué River and proclaimed a protectorate over the Loango people of the Niari valley. He reasserted the French presence in Tyo country and sent Albert Dolisie north to explore the valleys of the Sangha and Ubangi rivers. By these actions, Brazza provided France with a definite claim to portions of Equatoria. On the eve of the conference in Berlin, he had established twenty-one posts in a rough triangular salient that stretched from the Atlantic Ocean to the confluence of the Ubangi and Congo rivers.

On the Niger, Goldie simultaneously waged a vicious economic war with the French merchants who had lately threatened to destroy the commercial monopoly of the United African Company. Their success in turn gradually stimulated the British government to regard the French interests there as dangerous. In 1884, Consul Edward Hewett thus began to gather cessions of land from Africans living in the Niger Delta, along the shores of the Bight of Biafra, and in Cameroun. At the same time, the National African Company (as it had become known) ousted its French competitors on the lower Niger. Up-country, Joseph Thomson, Goldie's agent, also managed to obtain the signatures of the Sarkin Musulmi to treaties that, on the eve of the partition of tropical Africa, gave Britain reasonably good paper rights to a large portion of what became Northern Nigeria. Of his successful venture to Sokoto, Thomson wrote:

> *'Twere needless to tell how I traversed 500 miles on horseback, and exactly three months from my leaving England reached the famous city of Sokoto, and there bloomed forth in all the glories of a diplomatist. . . . In consideration of a yearly subsidy, Umuru [of Sokoto] agreed to hand over irrevocably to the National African Company all his rights to the banks of the river Binue and its tributaries . . . to give them absolute monopoly of all trading and mineral rights throughout his entire dominions, and to make the company the sole medium in his intercourse with foreigners. . . .*[136]

On their different errands, Hewett and Thomson both strove to strike agreements with indigenous leaders before rival Germans proved in a position to make similar claims. Already, in order to discomfort Britain and appease the commercial and evangelical groups within his own country who favored colonies, Otto von Bismarck, the German chancellor, had backed German-speaking merchants in Southwest Africa. Early in 1884, although few wanted it for its own sake and the indigenous population evinced a noticeable antipathy toward foreign intervention, Germany simply annexed Southwest Africa.[137] At the same time—perhaps because he believed that involvements in Africa would redound to his diplomatic favor in Europe—Bismarck allowed his agents to play the

[136] Letters from Joseph Thomson, quoted in James Baird Thomson, *Joseph Thomson: African Explorer* (London, 1896), pp. 160, 162.

[137] Amelia Lawrence Hodge, *Angra Pequena* (München, 1936), pp. 17–38; William Osgood Aydelotte, "The First German Colony and Its Diplomatic Consequences," *The Cambridge Historical Journal,* V (1937), pp. 293–295.

imperial game in West Africa. Germans had involved themselves in the affairs of the Volta River region since 1847, when the Nordeutsche Missionsgesellschaft opened its first stations. Merchants had followed and had opened trading posts along the Togo coast. By 1883, they had captured the major portion of the palm oil trade of that area and had profited from the sale of arms and spirits.[138] In Cameroun, a number of German firms—of which the most influential was directed by Adolf Woermann of Hamburg—had similarly prospered in the face of increasing British competition.[139] In 1883, both groups of merchants apparently urged the government of Germany to annex their respective areas. They thus added a further dimension to Bismarck's own intrigue with Paris and London. In July, 1884, Germany proclaimed a protectorate over the Togo coast and, days before the arrival of Hewett, Gustav Nachtigal, the German consul, agreed to protect the chiefs of Douala in Cameroun who, at the behest of Woermann and the other traders, had previously requested such oversight.[140]

German businessmen and explorers had long interested themselves in the affairs of East Africa. But only the actions of Carl Peters gave Germany a territorial stake in the interior. In 1883, Peters returned home to Germany after a long visit to Britain, where he had been infected by the fever of imperialism. He dreamed of colonial adventure, helped a number of older men of influence to form a new German colonization society, and finally turned his attentions toward East Africa.[141] In the autumn of 1884, after Bismarck had tried to dissuade them, Peters, Count Joachim Pfeil, Dr. Karl Jühlke, and August Otto secretly traveled from Hamburg to Aden, where they took deck-class accommodations for the voyage to Zanzibar. Still incognito, they arrived there only to find a cable from Bismarck warning them that Germany could not back their plans for colonial adventure. Undaunted, Peters and his companions quickly crossed to the African mainland and followed the valley of the Wami River toward modern Kilosa. In return for trinkets and alcohol, African chiefs and headmen unwittingly signed away their lands; by December, 1884, Peters had obtained 124 "treaties" giving him exclusive sovereignty over about 2,500 square miles of eastern Tanganyika. Whether Bismarck realized it or not, these actions had already given Germany new colonial responsibilities.[142] The partition of Africa had begun.

---

[138] Newbury, *Slave Coast,* pp. 101 ff.

[139] Adolf Woermann, the proprietor of the firm in question, reputedly was a close friend of Bismarck. See Alfred Zimmermann, *Die Geschichte der deutschen Kolonialpolitik* (Berlin, 1914), pp. 46–49.

[140] By the terms of the treaty of July 12, 1884, the chiefs of Douala made their request for protection conditional upon a German promise to refrain from interfering with the customs, lands, or trade of the indigenous peoples. For the treaty, see Harry R. Rudin, *Germans in the Cameroons, 1884–1914* (London, 1938), pp. 31–36. The Togo treaty is in Newbury, *Slave Coast,* pp. 209–210.

[141] Before thinking of East Africa, Peters and his compatriots had planned to establish a colony at St. Lucia Bay in Natal. See Herman Krätschell, *Carl Peters, 1856–1918* (Berlin, 1959), pp. 12–31; Fritz Ferdinand Müller, *Deutschland—Zanzibar—Ostafrika* (Berlin, 1959), pp. 97–112.

[142] For the treaties, see Max von Koschitzky, *Deutsche Kolonialgeschichte* (Leipzig, 1888), II, pp. 117, 123, 131–174; André Chéradame, *La Colonisation et les colonies allemandes* (Paris, 1905), pp. 85–89.

The European governments have recently decided to take Africa from the Africans, so that this continent, in the latest maps, can be seen coloured red, white and blue according to the nation claiming the territory. The African kings themselves, of course, were not consulted in these deliberations and they have had to submit.

—Frederick Stanley Arnot, 1894

THE PERIOD OF THE EUROPEAN PARTITION, 1885–1902

8 By 1884, the nations of Europe openly contemplated the wholesale conquest of the interior of tropical Africa. For reasons essentially diplomatic and mercantile, they individually sought places in what they assumed to be the lucrative African sweepstakes. Their peoples and their statesmen dreamed of the wealth and glory that African victories might bring; some of the statesmen also hoped to use Africa as a foil with which to wage and win the battles of Europe itself. Indeed, from that time the fates of Africa and Europe remained mutually intertwined in ways that occasioned the partition itself, the colonial interlude, and the eventual recrudescence of indigenous nationalism.

In Europe, Otto von Bismarck, the chancellor of imperial Germany, had already achieved the mastery of Europe that had eluded the grasp of Napoleon. In part by the continued manipulation of colonial issues, he expected to embarrass Britain and France and thus to maintain that mastery. He also wanted to fan the flames of Anglo-French conflict. At the same time, it seemed to serve his purpose to neutralize the pretensions of Portugal in the Congo and, indeed, consequently to bolster the ambitions of King Léopold II of the Belgians who —although few then appreciated the extent of his ambition—coveted the reputed wealth of the Congo basin for himself. In turn, by using the seemingly virtuous African International Association as a convenient façade, Léopold persuaded France in 1884 to support his claims to the Congo. The good offices of a number of friendly Americans also allowed him successfully to woo the United States.[1]

With French support, Bismarck convened the West African Conference at Berlin ostensibly in order to prevent an intra-European war for Africa. In a

[1] The Americans, led by Henry Shelton Sanford, a sometime ambassador to Brussels, negotiated United States recognition of Léopold's Association. Many of the Americans appear to have been directly in Léopold's pay.

sense, he wanted the conferees to partition tropical Africa in Berlin rather than to scramble for its choice segments overseas. For thirteen weeks in 1884/85, the representatives of fourteen European nations and the United States therefore considered the establishment of freedom of commerce in the basin and mouth of the Congo River, freedom of navigation on both the Congo and Niger rivers, and a definition of what constituted effective occupation of African territory. On maps in Berlin, they delimited the geographical basin of the Congo. For purposes of trade, they also included in the "conventional basin" of the Congo lands lying as far from the mouth of the Congo as southern Somalia and northern Moçambique. Within the "conventional basin" of the Congo, the conferees forbade the exercise of monopolies of trade and the imposition of a number of specific duties. At the behest of Bismarck, they opened the waterways and future roads and railways of the Congo freely to the traffic of all. Britain and France similarly promised to permit free navigation of the portions of the Niger that each controlled.

During the second half of the conference, Germany and France, in an attempt to curtail what they regarded as Britain's ambitions in Africa, proposed that future European territorial extensions along the coasts of the "dark continent" be regarded as rightfully alienated only when the power concerned had effectively occupied the tracts in question. (The French government persuaded Bismarck to confine the doctrine of effective occupation only to the coasts in order to safeguard its own claims to the interior.) The British government refused at first to agree; later, after it had obtained a general recognition of the supposed difference between possessions (wherein Britain assumed territorial sovereignty) and protectorates (wherein Britain theoretically assumed no more rights than those necessary to maintain the paramount authority) and had persuaded the delegates assembled in Berlin to exclude protectorates from the provisions of the eventual agreement, it signed a protocol that contained little of substance. The first article of the declaration simply provided for the notification of other powers whenever one of their number annexed land along the African coasts. The second recognized an "obligation to ensure the establishment of authority in regions occupied by [the powers of Europe] on the coasts of the African continent . . . sufficient to protect existing rights. . . ."[2] "Effective occupation" later became a useful shibboleth, but it possessed little juridical meaning and, in essence, simply rationalized the inability of the powers to act decisively. Indeed, outside of the deliberations proper, but nonetheless within their purview,

[2] "Declaration Relative to the Essential Conditions to Be Observed in Order That New Occupations on the Coasts of the African Continent May Be Held to Be Effective," chap. VI of the General Act of the Conference of Berlin. Text in Arthur Berriedale Keith, *The Belgian Congo and the Berlin Act* (Oxford, 1919), p. 315. The declaration had been foreshadowed by Britain's note to Portugal of 1877, wherein Her Majesty's Government chose not to admit "that the idea of sovereignty [could] be disassociated from that of *bona fide* occupation and *de facto* jurisdiction of a continuous and non-intermittent kind" in the "vast interior of the African continent, respecting which no Treaties exist. . . ." The most complete study in English of the West African Conference at Berlin is contained in Sybil Eyre Crowe, *The Berlin West African Conference, 1884–1885* (London, 1942), esp. pp. 95–118, 178–179, 186.

Léopold managed to obtain general cognizance of his claims to the left bank of the Congo River from Stanley Pool to Banana. With German assistance (the British representatives acquiesced), he thus acquired "the rights" to a sizeable African demesne by negotiation in Europe. Instead of curtailing it, the West African Conference in Berlin distinctly recognized and provided the formal rules for a scramble for territory in tropical Africa that in time divided tribes indiscriminately, disrupted traditional patterns of migratory drift, and resulted in the partition of tropical Africa into arbitrary, untidy colonial aggregates of heterogenous territory.

I. The Conquest of West Africa

Before the Berlin conference, the governments of Britain, France, and Germany had all acquired control over sections of coastal West Africa by force of arms or the agreements made between indigenous leaders and European emissaries. In addition, Britain and France already possessed historic associations with parts of West Africa of a kind that gave a peculiar added significance to their own successful efforts to partition Africa. For them, and to a lesser extent for Germany, the actual actions of partition simply continued a process that their military leaders and "men on the spot" had previously begun in an essentially *ad hoc* manner.

The Germans had established a secure foothold in Togo and Cameroun. While the West African Conference remained in session, their local representatives quelled a rebellion led by Lock Priso of Hickory Town on the Cameroons estuary, ousted a number of British Baptist missionaries from lower Cameroun, and simultaneously extended their influence into the interior of Togo. Thereafter, the Germans persuaded both the British and French to withdraw their own claims to coastal Cameroun and to sign a series of protocols that, collectively, had the effect of giving a distinct outline to the territory that now calls itself Cameroun. None of the powers had as yet, however, appropriated the Camerounian interior. The German traders, who had been largely responsible for encouraging Bismarck to "protect" Cameroun in early 1885, urged their new governor to extend this privilege to the peoples living between Douala and the Sangha and Ubangi rivers and in Adamawa, farther to the northeast. These traders knew that ivory and palm products abounded there. They appreciated the extent to which the merchants of Britain and France had also interested themselves in these regions. Furthermore, the first German settlers sought to obtain sufficient labor to man their plantations on and near Mount Cameroons. Together, these various factors combined neatly to set into motion a small, secondary scramble for the Camerounian interior and the basin of Lake Chad.

In competition with their British and French rivals, German traders—initially without direct support from the German government itself—overcame the serious resistance of the Koko people and, in 1888, established the modern Yaoundé as a center from which they could tap the ivory trade of the interior. They later persuaded the emir of Yola to open up Adamawa to their caravans;

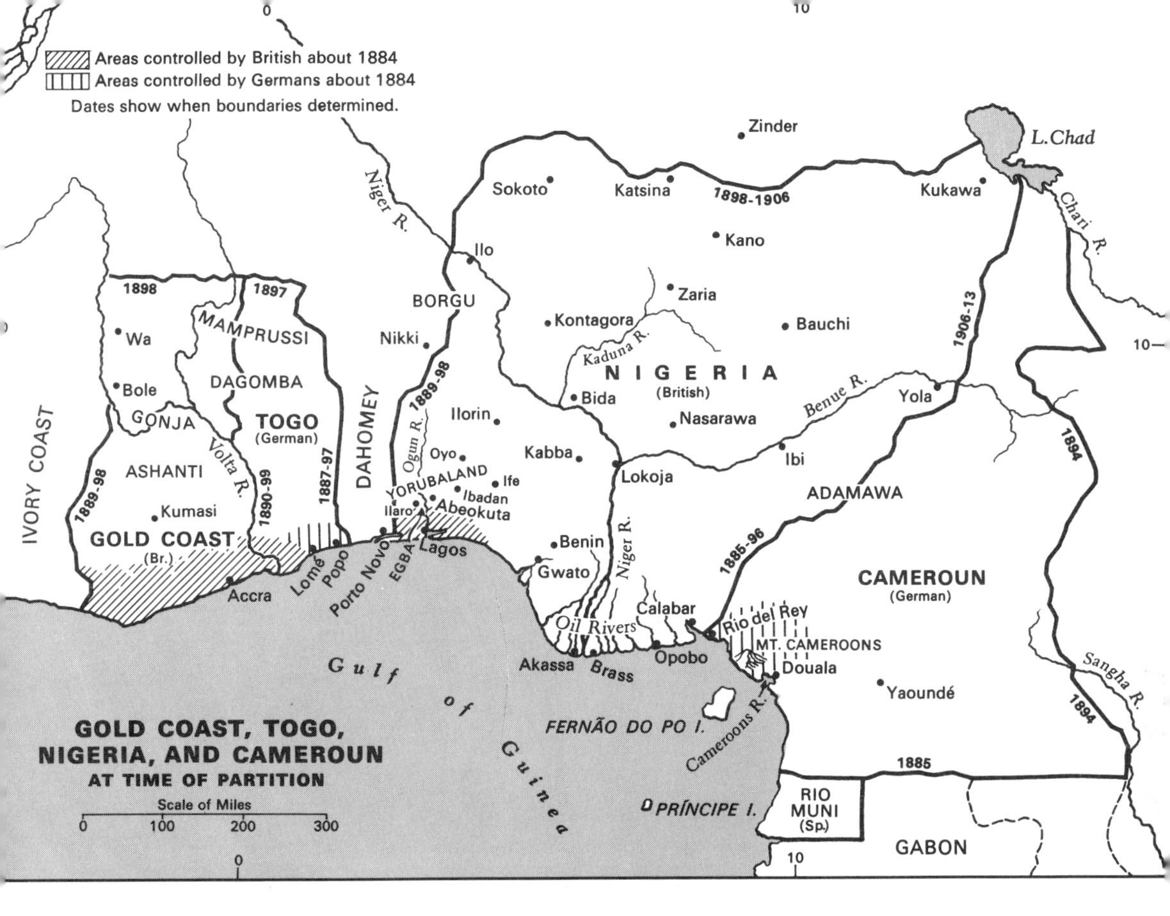

in the late 1890's, under the energetic direction of Governor Jesko von Puttkamer, the Germans finally conquered—with attendant loss of black men's blood—the lands between Yaoundé and Lake Chad that treaties with France and Britain had assigned to them.[3] Puttkamer directed the trade of Adamawa toward the German entrepôts on the coast, sent his soldiers to acquire control over the rubber-producing lands of southeastern Cameroun before either the Belgians or the French could forestall them and, in general, heralded an era during which Germans tried systematically to exploit the riches of Cameroun in a thoroughgoing colonial fashion.

Painting the map of west africa british red

Britons meanwhile sought to make good their claims to the Niger and Volta river basins in the face of African hostility and French and German military and diplomatic competition. In 1885, a few months after the conclusion of the Berlin conference, the government of Britain unilaterally decided to declare a

[3] For the treaties, see Edward S. Hertslet, *The Map of Africa by Treaty* (London, 1896), II, pp. 658–662, III, pp. 999–1003. See also Harry R. Rudin, *Germans in the Cameroons, 1884–1914* (London, 1938), pp. 182–212; A. H. M. Kirk-Greene, *Adamawa: Past and Present* (London, 1958), pp. 32–37.

protectorate over the Niger districts; within it British cartographers later included the shoreline from the Lagos colony to Rio del Rey, and all of the riverain territories from the mouth of the Niger to Lokoja, and thence up the Benue to Ibi.[4] This action seemingly permitted Britain early in the next year to sub-contract its obligations in the Niger districts to Sir George Goldie's Royal Niger Company. Despite German and some British commercial opposition, Her Majesty's Government chartered the Niger Company and gave it a tacit monopoly of the up-country trade of Nigeria. In exchange, the Company agreed to rule most of the territory included in the Niger districts on behalf of Britain and therein to abolish slavery, maintain order, oversee the performance of treaty obligations, and raise revenues only in order to defray administrative expenses.[5]

In the delta of the Niger and along the shores of the Gulf of Guinea, British pretensions naturally posed an immediate economic and political threat to a number of African merchant princes. In particular, Ja Ja, who reigned at Opobo, refused to relinquish his own economic prerogatives without a struggle. When European traders disregarded his very lucrative control of the up-country supplies of palm oil, he blocked the trade paths and interfered vigorously with their attempts to by-pass the "regular" channels of trade. By way of retaliation, the main British firms formed the so-called African Association and then agreed to pay less than before for Opobo's oil. But Ja Ja induced one of these concerns to break with the cartel and to pay the regular price in exchange for exclusive rights to the oil.

These successful machinations antagonized the African Association. In 1887, their pleas for assistance evoked an official response in London. The Foreign Office asked Henry Hamilton (later Sir Harry) Johnston, its vice consul in the Cameroons, to remove all obstructions to "free trade" at Opobo. And before long, Ja Ja fell into Johnston's hands. A court in Accra tried Ja Ja and then deported him to the West Indies in order to satisfy both the avarice of British commerce and Johnston's personal ideas of right and wrong. Lord Salisbury, then the British Foreign Secretary, observed: "We need not discuss the principles . . . . They amount to this, that when a merchant differs from a native chief as to their respective rights, the native chief is to be deported."[6] The British government had simply "protected" eastern Nigeria even more thoroughly than before.

The needs of commerce similarly encouraged the expansion of British power

---

[4] See Hertslet, *Map*, II, p. 445.

[5] For the text, see John Flint, *Sir George Goldie and the Making of Nigeria* (London, 1960), pp. 330–336.

[6] Lord Salisbury's minute on a despatch from Johnston, quoted in Roland Oliver, *Sir Harry Johnston and the Scramble for Africa* (London, 1957), p. 118. See also Arthur Norton Cook, *British Enterprise in Nigeria* (Philadelphia, 1943), pp. 63–65; William Neville M. Geary, *Nigeria Under British Rule* (London, 1927), pp. 275–294; A. A. Nwafor Orizu, *Without Bitterness* (New York, 1944), p. 247; C. J. Gertzel, "Commercial Organization on the Niger Coast, 1852–1891," in *Historians in Tropical Africa* (Salisbury, S.R., 1962), pp. 301–302. For Ja Ja, see *supra*, p. 227.

into Yorubaland. The port of Lagos served as a clear-cut commercial excuse. Its trade centered upon the exchange of palm products from Yorubaland for cheap articles from industrial Lancashire. Wars between some of the more important Yoruba city-states, when they disrupted the smooth flow of trade, thus affected Lagos. The British authorities at Lagos also concerned themselves with the growth of French influence in Porto Novo to the west. In 1888, after Édouard Viard, a French explorer and entrepreneur, had obtained a treaty of friendship with the Egba of Abeokuta, the British establishment in Lagos realized more fully than before how easily the French could sever its commercial lifeline. Alfred Moloney, then the British governor of Lagos, quickly obtained similar treaties from the rulers of Ilaro, Igbessa, Oyo, and Ife. Igbessa even included itself within the colony proper and, in order to avoid ruinous strife, the French and the British soon agreed on the borders of respective spheres of influence.[7]

The British businessmen based in Lagos nonetheless continued to complain. Their competitors imported goods into Yorubaland more cheaply through Porto Novo, where the tariff remained low and, at the same time, the internal wars of Yorubaland had begun to prevent trade caravans from reaching Lagos. Britons also feared that the impending French conquest of Dahomey would threaten anew their control of the "natural" commercial hinterland of Lagos. In 1891, George C. Denton, the acting governor of the colony, therefore annexed several nearby city-states. His successor, Governor Sir Gilbert Carter, forcibly pacified the Ijebu people who had blocked the trade routes to the north, deposed the ruler of Addo and, by so doing, persuaded the Egba, who had previously closed the vital Ogun River to commerce, to forswear their opposition to the British in exchange for British recognition of the independence of Egbaland. Ibadan subsequently acknowledged British might and, in 1895, British troops conquered Oyo, thereby completing the subjection of the Yoruba city-states.[8]

Britain meanwhile reorganized its administration of the Oil Rivers. Under a commissioner and consul-general, six British vice consuls patrolled the various commercially important rivers and creeks with armed launches. Together, they raised a constabulary and with it deposed recalcitrant chiefs, like Nana of the Jekri, along the Benin River, who had refused to accept British economic control. Similarly, in 1895, after raiders from Brass attacked the Niger Company's depot at Akassa in the Delta (the Company having previously excluded the men of Brass from their traditional markets), the consul-general demanded that the people of Brass surrender the raiders and pay a large fine in addition.

---

[7] See Samuel Johnson (ed. O. Johnson), *The History of the Yorubas* (Lagos, 1921), pp. 571–572; Colin W. Newbury, *The Western Slave Coast and Its Rulers* (Oxford, 1961), pp. 94–95, 133. For the treaties, see Hertslet, *Map*, I, pp. 425–430, 567.

[8] Newbury, *Slave Coast*, pp. 136–138; A. B. Aderibigbe, "The Ijebu Expedition, 1892: An Episode in the British Penetration of Nigeria Reconsidered," in *Historians in Tropical Africa*, pp. 267–282; Johnson, *Yorubas*, pp. 570, 573, 582, 595–597, 611, 625, 638–642. Texts in Hertslet, *Map*, I, p. 432; Alan Burns, *History of Nigeria* (London, 1955), pp. 332–333.

King Koko's men of Brass on their way down the Niger River to attack depots of the Royal Niger Company in 1895. (Culver Pictures)

When the people of Brass failed to comply, British guns razed their main towns, finally forcing them to submit to Britain's suzerainty.[9]

In Southern Nigeria, only Benin, by this time a comparatively insignificant state, remained effectively independent. Although its ruler, *oba* Ovonramwen, had in 1892 promised to permit free trade within his dominions, he had instead tried to withdraw since then from active participation in the new, British-dominated Nigerian world. The entreaties of British consuls failed to persuade him to do otherwise. As a result, in 1897 they sent a large, but apparently unarmed, expedition to Benin. Its leader, J. B. Phillips, evidently hoped by such a show of numbers to persuade the *oba* to re-open his commercial routes into the interior. Instead, Phillips and most of his party fell in an ambush on the road between Gwato and Benin. In 1898, British troops naturally retaliated, easily overrunning Benin and its satellite villages and towns.[10] British officials thereafter regarded their conquest of Southern Nigeria as complete.

In the Gold Coast as well as in Nigeria, concern with the growth and extension of trade remained uppermost in the minds of British merchants and

[9] Henry Galway, "The Rising of the Brassmen," *Journal of the African Society*, XXXIV (1935), pp. 149–160; Harold Bindloss, *In the Niger Country* (Edinburgh, 1898), pp. 205–216.

[10] Felix N. Roth, "A Diary of a Surgeon with the Benin Punitive Expedition," in H. Ling Roth, *Great Benin* (Halifax, Eng., 1903), pp. ii–xii.

One of several sixteenth- or seventeenth-century ivory masks found in the bedchamber of *oba* Ovonramwen when the British punitive expedition conquered Benin in 1898. The stylized Portuguese heads in the tiara and the forehead markings are characteristic of the earliest periods in Benin ivory carving. The British Museum, London.

their colonial compatriots. The prosperity of the Gold Coast largely depended upon the steady flow of goods from Ashantiland; thus, when civil wars erupted there in 1886/87, Britons resident on the coast urged their governors to intervene directly in the affairs of the Ashanti nation. At first the governors spurned such entreaties. Instead, they attempted to weaken the power of the Ashanti nation by weaning its dissident factions away from allegiance to the *asantehene*, despite his warning that such a policy of "divide and rule" would encourage a further deterioration of trade. The destruction of Ashanti power, the *asantehene* argued impressively, would probably cause a severe diminution in the flow of goods from the interior to the coast. "When all my subjects have come to the Protectorate," he complained to the governor, "where is then trade; for once they have crossed to you, they shall fear to cross over and pass on my land to the interior to trade." [11] But the governor took little heed. His merchant advisors regarded such arguments as mere casuistry. Moreover, they feared that the French and the Germans would soon encircle the Gold Coast, thereby cutting its economic arteries to the north. In 1890, Governor Sir Brandford Griffith consequently attempted to persuade the *asantehene* to submit voluntarily to British "protection." Instead, the *asantehene* attacked the various vassal kingdoms that had renounced their allegiance to the Ashanti golden stool in

[11] Kwaku Dua III to Frederic M. Hodgson, December 27, 1889, quoted in W. Walton Claridge, *A History of the Gold Coast and Ashanti* (London, 1915), II, p. 341.

favor of the British might. He also reminded Griffith that his people hoped always to remain independent:

> *The suggestion that Ashanti in its present state should come and enjoy the protection of Her Majesty the Queen and Empress of India, I may say this is a matter of serious consideration, and which I am happy to say we have arrived at this conclusion, that my kingdom of Ashanti will never commit itself to any such policy; Ashanti must remain independent as of old, at the same time to remain friendly with all white men. I do not write this with a boastful spirit, but in the clear sense of its meaning. Ashanti is an independent kingdom. . . .*[12]

Most merchants hoped that Britain would act decisively to resolve the impasse. But the Secretary of State for the Colonies would not at first commit his government to aggressive action. He instead suggested that the *asantehene* should promise not to make war on peoples friendly to Britain and that he should further take advice from a Briton who would reside in Kumasi. But the Ashanti recognized that their acceptance of such proposals would lead before long to the very "protection" that they so dreaded. At the same time, they feared Britain's wrath. Instead of replying negatively or affirmatively, they engaged in an endless round of seemingly fruitless consultations that exhausted the patience of British businessmen and officials. In 1895, Governor William Maxwell despatched an ultimatum to the *asantehene*. Because of the *asantehene's* failure to keep open the trade routes to the interior, pay the indemnity of 1874, and prevent "human sacrifice," it ordered him to receive a British "resident" and to agree forthwith to "protection" by the government of Queen Victoria.[13]

Maxwell wanted a pretext to intervene. The *asantehene* obliged by signifying his unwillingness to accept the British demands. Three thousand British-officered troops thereupon marched to Kumasi, met little opposition, and occupied it early in 1896. There, in the central square of the Ashanti capital, Maxwell held an audience designed thoroughly to humble and humiliate the rulers of the Ashanti nation. The governor encouraged the *asantehene* to demonstrate total fealty to the British regime. When, in a remarkable gesture, the *asantehene* did so, Maxwell still demanded that the Ashanti should pay an exorbitant indemnity in gold. Their inability to comply meant the deportation of their leaders, and Maxwell soon exiled the *asantehene*, the queen mother, and a number of chiefs to the Seychelles.[14] British troops seized the royal palace and mausoleum, destroyed temples and sacred trees and, at least in their own minds, ended the power of Ashanti. In its proud center, only grievances remained.

The Ashanti no longer blocked the paths to the Western Sudan. British troops soon occupied a number of the smaller city-states in the savannah region

---

[12] Quoted in *ibid.*, p. 359.

[13] For a discussion of "human sacrifice," see Robert S. Rattray, *Religion and Art in Ashanti* (Oxford, 1927), pp. 139–143.

[14] William Tordoff, "The Exile and Repatriation of Nana Prempeh I of Ashanti," *Transactions of the Historical Society of Ghana*, IV (1960), pp. 33–55; George Clark Musgrave, *To Kumassi with Scott* (London, 1896), pp. 177–183.

beyond Kumasi, conquered Bole and Wa and, in 1898, manned posts in the Dagomba, Gonja, and Mamprussi countries of the far north. By so doing, they excluded the French and Germans and kept the wealth of this distant region for British merchants. The British Crown concluded border agreements with both European powers and, thereafter, created of its new territories the Northern Territories district of the Gold Coast.[15]

In Ashantiland, British administrators had meanwhile exacerbated local enmities by vigorously suppressing the selling and keeping of slaves. They had also conscripted labor for public purposes. Then, in 1900, Governor Sir Frederic Hodgson decided to tax the people of Ashanti. He also told their chiefs that the British government would never reinstate the *asantehene*, that the British resident would continue to exercise his powers, and that the Ashanti would remain liable for forced labor. With an audacity that horrified them, he further asked for the golden stool—in their eyes the symbol that embodied the nationhood of Ashanti. A few weeks later, the Ashanti rebelled. Within the fort of Kumasi they imprisoned the governor and his retinue, several missionaries, and more than seven hundred troops. They demanded that the governor release the *asantehene*, renew the traffic in slaves, forbid compulsory labor, and expel all strangers, both European and Fantse, from Ashantiland. But the governor and other whites finally escaped from the besieged fort and, two months after the beginning of the rebellion, fourteen hundred British-officered soldiers relieved Kumasi.[16] Fierce fighting continued, and a number of Ashanti continued to harass the British regiments until early in the next year. Finally, in 1901, the governor again arrived in Kumasi, this time in order to accept a final submission from the Ashanti and to nominate new chiefs to replace those who had led the revolt. And in 1902, Britain formally annexed Ashanti as a Crown Colony, thus carrying its support of economic interest and love of order to their logical conclusions.

Throughout the 1890's, British troops fought to secure the claims of the Crown and the Royal Niger Company to Northern Nigeria before the French could make good their own pretensions to parts of the same area. Although Britain and France had each agreed by the treaty of 1890 to respect the exclusive rights of the other to territories that lay to either side of a latitudinal line that they drew through Hausaland and Bornu, control over the middle Niger remained in dispute.[17] In 1894, Captain Frederick (later Lord) Lugard reached Nikki, in Borgu, before his French opposite number and thus won the first part of the race for Britain. Thereafter, he and other British officers led their armies against the Fulani-governed city-states. In 1897, forces of the Royal Niger Company took Bida and Ilorin after weeks of heavy combat. War with France might have followed, but in 1898 France and Britain instead signed a

[15] For the treaties, see Hertslet, *Map* (1909), III, p. 920.
[16] B. Wasserman, "The Ashanti War of 1900: A Study in Cultural Conflict," *Africa*, XXXI (1961), pp. 169–175; Claridge, *History*, pp. 446–566; C. H. Armitage and Arthur Forbes Montanaro, *The Ashanti Campaign of 1900* (London, 1901), pp. 122–132.
[17] For the text, see Hertslet, *Map* (1896), II, p. 572.

convention that divided the controversial area of Borgu and gave what became northern Dahomey to France. Britain retained the western reaches of what became Northern Nigeria.[18]

After the conclusion of the British war against the Ashanti, Lugard turned in earnest to his conquest of the remainder of Northern Nigeria. Kontagora and Nupe successfully resisted him for a time, but his troops finally occupied the capitals of these two emirates in late 1901. Several other emirs thereafter accepted their new overlord and voluntarily opened trade paths, received British residents, and garrisoned British levies within the walls of their towns. In this way, Lugard soon "protected" Borgu, Kabba, Zaria, Nasarawa, and Muri. He retained their indigenous rulers, imposed a system of laws based upon British practice, and installed individual Britons as administrators. These administrators governed in the style that later came to be called indirect. But in practice they intervened directly whenever they deemed such action necessary. At the head of British-officered columns, they pacified their respective emirates and sought to end slave-raiding. In general, while the administrators took into account local pressures and political variations in the various emirates, they each established Britain's protectorate in accord with Lugard's all encompassing design.

Some areas of Northern Nigeria nonetheless refused to recognize the tide of political power. At first, warriors loyal to the emirs of Yola and Bauchi harassed the stations of the Royal Niger Company, closed their markets to Britons, and refused to regard themselves as vassals of Queen Victoria. Then, after some hard fighting, Lugard deposed the two emirs and proceeded to rule their territories directly.[19] Sokoto and Kano, however, still remained proudly independent. The Sarkin Musulmi, ruler of all Hausaland, had already made known his unwillingness to deal with the British. In the course of a letter to Lugard, he supposedly wrote:

> *I do not consent that any one from you should ever dwell with us. I will never agree with you. I will have nothing ever to do with you. Between us and you there are no dealings except as between [Muslims] and Unbelievers, War, as God Almighty has enjoined on us. There is no power or strength save in God on high. This with salutations.*[20]

Thus two forces, one indigenous and declining, the other *arriviste* and ascendant, clashed when total control of all of what is now Northern Nigeria seemed at stake. Toward the end of 1902, the emir of Kano attacked the British garrison in Zaria. In the next year, Lugard retaliated; his expeditionary force

---

[18] *Ibid.* (1909), II, pp. 785–793; Margery Perham, *Lugard: The Years of Adventure* (London, 1956), pp. 505–518.

[19] Charles W. J. Orr, *The Making of Northern Nigeria* (London, 1911), pp. 100–101.

[20] The Sarkin Musulmi to Lugard, May, 1902, quoted in *Journal of the African Society,* XXVII (1929), p. 218. Margery Perham, *Lugard: The Years of Authority* (London, 1960), p. 90; Burns, *Nigeria,* p. 183, contain slightly different versions of the same letter. David J. Muffett, *Concerning Brave Captains: Being a History of the British Occupation of Kano and Sokoto and of the Last Stand of the Fulani Forces* (London, 1964), pp. 44–49, argues that the letter was a forgery.

A section of the city of Kano. The buildings are all constructed of mud baked dry by the sun. In 1903, when Frederick Lugard conquered Kano, the city may have looked little different from the modern view at right. (Nigerian Consulate)

reached Kano without encountering significant opposition, breached the walls of the town, and soon occupied its central market place. Katsina, which had refrained from war, submitted to Britain. A few weeks later, Sokoto itself fell, and Lugard rejoiced in the conquest of all of Hausaland. He brought the beginnings of British rule to many who had long held Europeans in contempt.

The french thrust into the interior

Since the early eighteenth century, French officials had schemed to acquire the fabled riches of the Western Sudan. Throughout the nineteenth century, they made steady progress toward their goal. But the great expansion of France into the heart of Africa awaited the conditions that materialized during the two decades after the Berlin conference. Thenceforth, French civil and military officials energetically attempted to realize a grand vision of outright conquest. They sought to link the hinterland of western Africa to coastal territories that they already controlled, thereby linking Algiers and Tunis across the Sahara to Dakar and Brazzaville. Three main concerns dominated French thought: its leaders wanted to join their West and Equatorial African possessions at Lake Chad, to join French West and French East Africa across the upper Nile River, and to control as much as possible of the upper and middle reaches of the Niger River.

By the end of the Berlin conference in 1885, the generals of France had placed a gunboat on the Niger. It signified the extent of their position in the Western Sudan. During the next five years, they rapidly consolidated that position in a series of campaigns against Africans, who bitterly resented their intrusion. In 1886, for example, Mahmadou Lamine, a prominent Galami *marabout*, attacked French outposts in the upper Gambia region. The French retaliated with alacrity, and fought repeated battles with the followers of

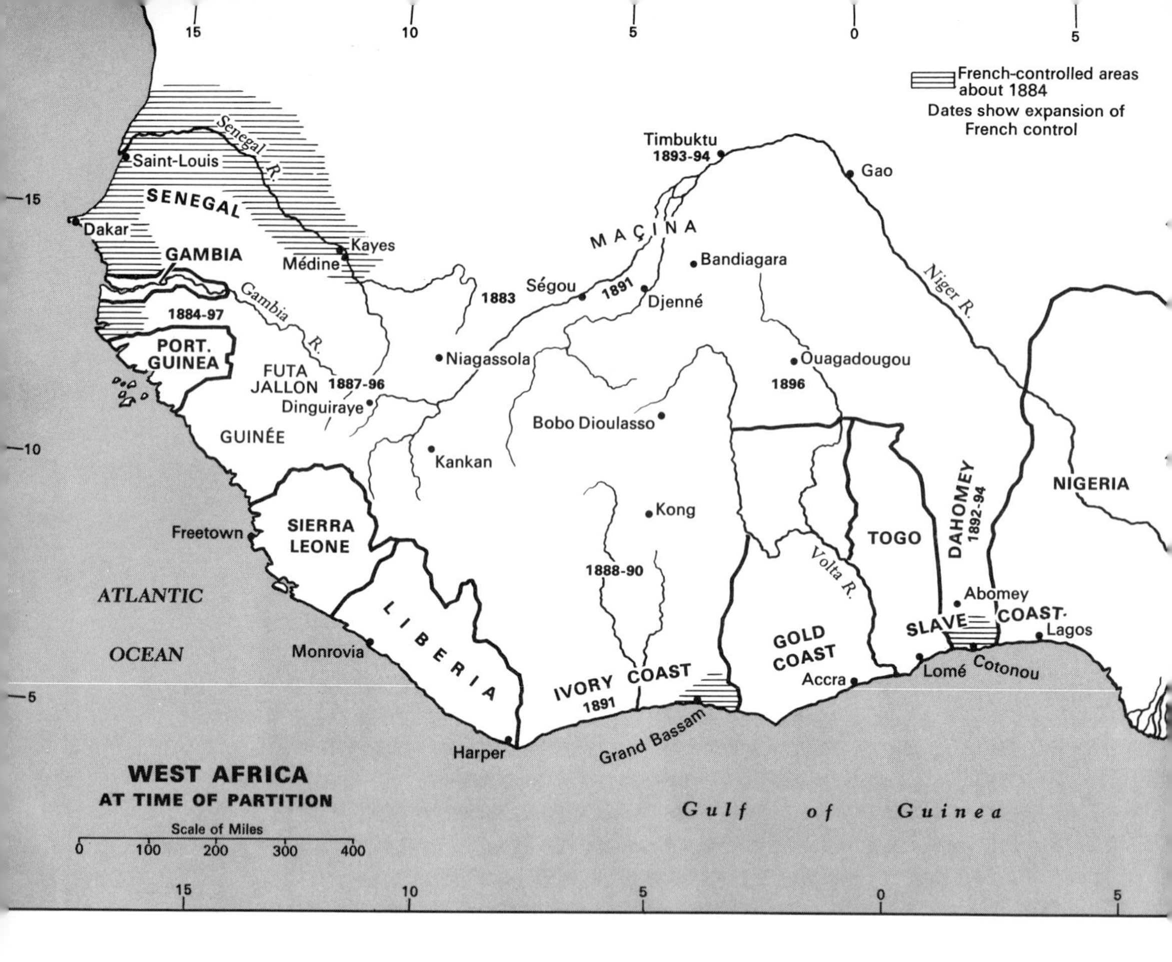

Mahmadou before finally quelling their resistance in late 1887. At about the same time, the French also conquered the Futa Jallon and the lands that surrounded the headwaters of both the Niger and Senegal rivers.

Only with difficulty, however, could the French generals cope with Samori ibn Lafiya Ture, a Mande-speaking warlord who harassed their armies and refused ever to acknowledge their rule in the Western Sudan. Earlier he had imposed his own rule on upper Guinée and a part of the Sudan. Starting with the control of a small Mande chieftaincy in the Kankan district, he began, in about 1866, to construct an empire by joining to his own a number of the neighboring principalities. In 1873, he overran Kankan itself and thus opened an era marked by almost continuous warfare, first against his African enemies and then against the French.[21] In 1886, Samori sued for peace after a French victory at Niagassola. In the next year, after the French victories against Mahmadou Lamine, Samori signed a treaty whereby he supposedly accepted French "protection." In fact, he only intended to buy time. Soon Samori and his followers

[21] Étienne Péroz, *Au Soudan français: souvenirs de guerre et de mission* (Paris, 1889), pp. 388–400; Amadou Kouroubari, "Histoire de l'imam Samori," *Bulletin de l'Institut Français d'Afrique Noire*, XXI (1959), pp. 545–554; André Mévil, *Samory* (Paris, n.d., but 1899), pp. 4–29.

began afresh to attack the French and their allies. At Kenedougou, however, Samori lost again and, in 1889, he promised to refrain from troubling the French further.

In the equatorial regions of Africa, Savorgnan de Brazza had meanwhile attempted to consolidate the position of France in Gabon and on the right bank of the Congo River. In order to protect his northern hinterland from Belgian and German encroachments and, if possible, to link forces with the French in West Africa, he had pushed rapidly forward into the little-known regions beyond the confluence of the Ubangi and Congo rivers. Under Brazza's direction, Paul Crampel explored the basin of the Sangha River, obtaining treaties of "friendship and cession" from fourteen chiefs *en route*. In 1889, Albert Dolisie, another of Brazza's lieutenants, founded Bangui, the future capital of the Central African Republic, on the banks of the Ubangi. And as the French began to administer this region, the explorers proceeded northward along the Chari River toward Lake Chad and Adamawa. But Rabih, a slave-raiding general from the eastern Sudan who commanded Bornu and Kanem, blocked their way to the lake and, in 1891, killed Crampel.[22]

The respite afforded by the agreement with Samori had, in the west, permitted the leader of the French forces to focus his attention upon another opponent of the French—Ahmadu, the son of al-hajj 'Umar and leader of the Tokolor. In 1890, French troops marched on Dinguiraye, easily occupied Ségou, and forced Ahmadu to flee.[23] Beyond, fabled Timbuktu beckoned. The French army moved slowly downstream, in the manner of Ghanaian and Songhaian armies centuries before. In 1893, France conquered Djenné, Bandiagara, and Maçina. In the next year, they gained Timbuktu, but the Tuareg disputed their suzerainty there for the next eleven years. In 1896/97, French troops also occupied Ouagadougou and Bobo Dioulasso—the Mossi peoples continued to resist foreign domination, however, until 1902—and, in 1899, they pacified Gao and Zinder, thus bringing the flag of France almost to the shores of Lake Chad.

As France had conquered the Western Sudan and much of Guinée, so it subdued the peoples of the forest and endeavored to make the two thrusts one. In 1885, by an agreement with Britain, France began to control the Slave Coast town of Katanou in addition to Cotonou and Porto Novo. During the succeeding five years, the French gradually usurped the powers that the kingdom of Dahomey had itself long exercised on the coast. At this time, Dahomey no longer appeared to be a great state. After the cessation of the slave trade, it had been unable to compete successfully with others better placed to supply Western buyers with tropical products. Wars against Yoruba and Egbado armies had ended disastrously. The French supported peoples of the coast who had long

---

[22] For Rabih, see Julius Lippert, "Rabah," *Mitteilungen des Seminars für orientalische Sprachen*, II (1899), pp. 242–256; Yves Urvoy, *Histoire de l'empire du Bornou* (Paris, 1949), pp. 126–130; Rudolf C. Slatin (trans. F. R. Wingate), *Fire and Sword in the Sudan: A Personal Narrative of Fighting and Serving the Dervishes, 1879–1895* (London, 1896), pp. 23–26.

[23] Jacques Ménioud, *Les Pioneers du Soudan avant, avec, et après Archinard* (Paris, 1931), I, pp. 179–194; Louis Tauxier, *Histoire des Bambara* (Paris, 1942), pp. 180–193.

been vassals of the Fon kings. Finally, French officials replaced Fon customs agents with their own appointees and, in general, posed problems of commercial and political prominence that could be resolved only by resort to arms. King Behanzin, who acceded to the throne in 1889, spoiled for war. He engaged in slave-raiding and, in 1892, fired on a French lieutenant-governor. France welcomed the convenient pretext for revenge and, later in the same year, occupied Abomey, the capital of the kingdom of Dahomey. The two parties continued to fight until 1894, and indeed in some parts of Dahomey until 1911, but the French began to govern the kingdom itself, and its southern vassals, from 1893.[24]

Thereafter, except for skirmishes in the Ivory Coast and confrontations with the Mossi and the Tuareg, French troops in West Africa met their only serious opposition from Samori. Refusing to confine his followers in fortresses, he retained his mobility and carefully avoided the direct battles with the French or British armies that would have probably resulted in his defeat. Withal, he led the French a merry chase in the years after 1891, when Colonel Archinard occupied Kankan. Samori and his followers thereafter terrorized the area eastward from Sierra Leone to Ouagadougou and the northwestern border of the Gold Coast. In 1896, he even besieged a French administrator for more than two months. Two years later, however, after he had engaged British troops in the Gold Coast, Samori was finally cornered and captured by a French force at Goulemou, in the environs of the Kong region of the Ivory Coast.[25]

The armies of France, having conquered the peoples of the Western Sudan, the forests of the south, and the river basins of Equatoria, next turned toward the Nile River. Their strategists hoped to inject the French presence into the area of the upper White Nile and, by controlling a blue route between Lake Chad and Djibouti, the main French port on the Somali coast, to truncate the line of British red, and thus to threaten Britain's paramountcy in Egypt.[26] But Captain Jean-Gabriel Marchand's expedition proved a glorious failure at Fashoda; the British diplomatic victory there turned France away from the Nile forever. Instead, French generals returned to the conquest of Chad. By this time, Rabih controlled large areas in what later became Cameroun, Chad, and Nigeria, and the French respected the prowess of his army. Indeed, after troops led by Émile Gentil skirmished indecisively with Rabih's forces in 1899, the French mounted an all-out offensive to remove this last obstacle to their control of the Chad basin. In 1900, Major L. J. M. Lamy crossed the Sahara from the oases of Algeria with reinforcements, another detachment converged upon Chad

---

[24] Colin W. Newbury, "A Note on the Abomey Protectorate," *Africa*, XXIX (1959), pp. 146–150; Édouard Dunglas, "Contribution à l'histoire du Moyen-Dahomey," *Études Dahoméennes*, XXI (1958), pp. 20–21.

[25] Mévil, *Samory*, pp. 241–261.

[26] Because red is a dominant basic color, British publishers apparently used it to make their own islands stand out on early colored and printed maps; Britain's colonial possessions naturally received the same treatment. Similarly, French acquisitions took the blue-purple (a strong color combination useful in the representation of a small area) of their own mother country.

from the middle Niger, and Gentil continued to lead his assaults from Ubangi-Chari. These three columns finally overwhelmed Rabih and, at long last, France managed to make its West and Equatorial African empires one.[27]

II. The Conquest of the Congo

At the conclusion of the conference in Berlin, King Léopold II swiftly sought to exploit the favorable position that he had attained with respect to the Congo. He first persuaded a reluctant Belgian parliament to permit him to declare himself sovereign of the territories claimed by the African International Association in the geographical basin of the Congo. This deed accomplished, Léopold next created, and in a ceremony near Banana proclaimed the existence of, the Independent State of the Congo without bothering to consult the members of the Association.[28] His subjects—although they at first refused to acknowledge such a relationship—numbered about ten million, including Swahili- and Arabic-speaking slavers from Tanganyika and Zanzibar who had previously established themselves as the *de facto* overlords of the area between the Stanley Falls on the upper Congo River and the great lakes of the continental rift. During the late 1880's, while Léopold concerned himself primarily with the lower Congo, these interlopers enslaved the peoples of the eastern Congo and marched them to the Indian Ocean markets. Fearful of their raids, Africans slept in canoes and were reduced to eating berries, roots, and water lilies for want of ordinary field crops.[29] In 1886, on behalf of Léopold, Henry Morton Stanley, who was then leading the Emin Pasha Relief Expedition, tried to end the slave raids by putting Tippu Tib, the leading Arab slaver, on Léopold's payroll.[30] In exchange, Tippu Tib supposedly promised to cease slaving himself and to prevent others from slaving as well.

Léopold meanwhile attracted Belgian capital to the lower Congo and, in 1889, promises of continuing aid during the succeeding ten-year period. In return, Léopold agreed to cede the entire Congo to Belgium upon his death.[31] He thus forged strong colonial links between the private colony and the mother country, of which he also remained sovereign. In time, these ties made nonsense out of the international economic and political ideals on which the growth of the Congo had at first appeared to be based. But in the short run, Belgium provided both the manpower by which Léopold administered the Independent State and the funds with which he financed the construction of the important railway between the Stanley Pool and Matadi. Stanley had earlier declared that "the Congo basin was not worth a two-shilling piece" without a railway connecting the lower and upper Congos and, in 1890, the actual construction

[27] Émile Gentil, *La Chute de l'empire de Rabah* (Paris, 1902), pp. 211–224; Max G. von Oppenheim, *Rabeh und das Tschadseegebiet* (Berlin, 1902), pp. 103–112.
[28] Britons and Americans for long erroneously called it the Congo Free State.
[29] W. Holman Bentley, *Pioneering on the Congo* (New York, 1900), II, pp. 96–110.
[30] For Tippu Tib, see *supra*, pp. 169–170.
[31] Louis de Lichtervelde, *Léopold II* (Bruxelles, 1935), pp. 257–267.

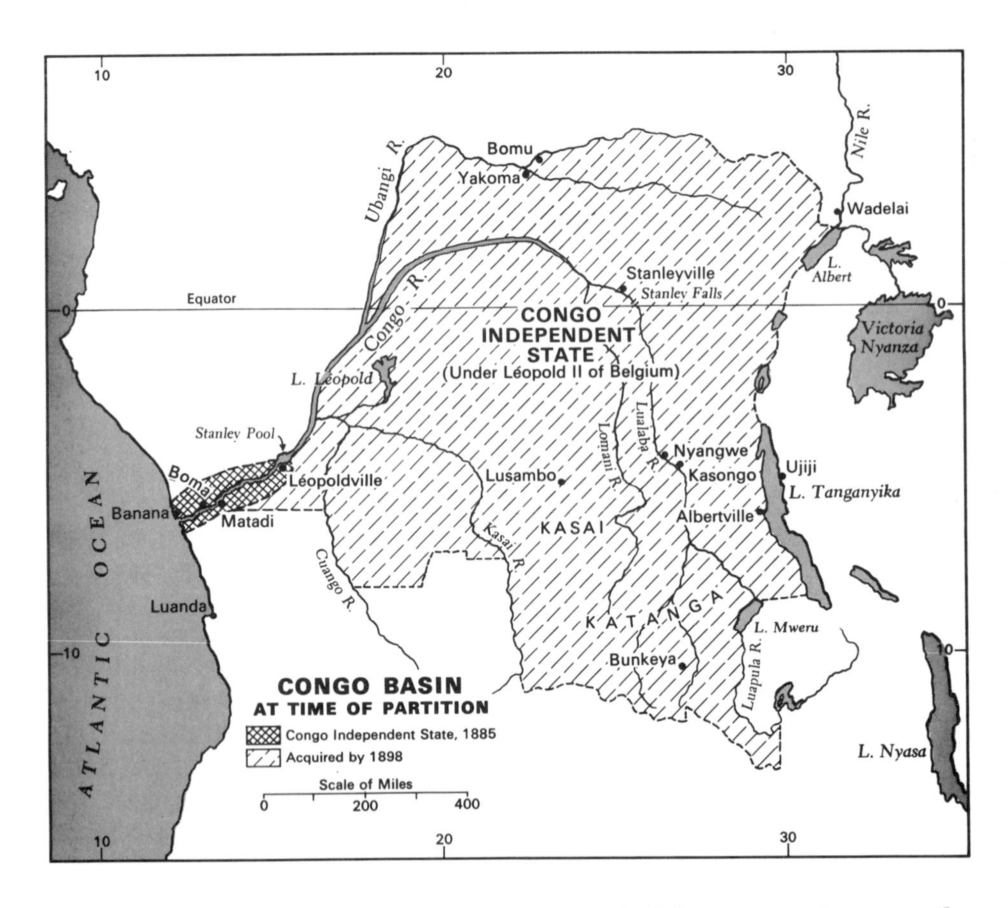

of the line began.[32] A shortage of local labor limited its progress, however, the work proceeding only after the arrival in the lower Congo of Africans from Senegal, the Gambia, Sierra Leone, Liberia, and Nigeria, Barbadans from the West Indies, Piedmontese from Italy, and Cantonese from China. Between 1890 and 1892, the Belgians employed seven thousand men on the railway. Of this number about half died or deserted, and another fifteen hundred returned home before the expiration of their contracts. Indeed, mortality rates remained at this high level until 1898, when the rails finally reached Léopoldville, on the Stanley Pool.[33] During the same period, the new state established a steamship service on the upper Congo River and inaugurated a system of postal and telegraphic communications.

The race for katanga

Léopold naturally wanted to engross all of the wealth of the Congo. The British explorers David Livingstone and Verney Lovett Cameron, the Germans

[32] Henry Morton Stanley, *The Congo and the Founding of Its Free State* (New York, 1885), I, p. 463, II, pp. 370–372.
[33] Fritz Masoin, *Histoire de l'état indépendant du Congo* (Namur, 1912), I, pp. 360–369.

African laborers extend the main quais at Léopoldville on Stanley Pool. This photograph, taken in 1903, is one of the earliest taken in the area. (Brown Brothers)

Paul Reichard and Richard Böhm, and the Portuguese Hermenigildo Capelo and Roberto Ivens, had all written of the minerals of Katanga, but to this potentially rich section of the Congo, Léopold was least sure of his claims and control.[34] There Msiri ruled. Msiri also presided over a lucrative commercial network that linked both Zanzibar and Luanda to Bunkeya, his capital. In exchange for ivory and slaves, Msiri received cloth, and the guns and powder with which he overawed his neighbors. In 1886, at a time when Msiri sought the means whereby he might reduce the power of the Arabs in Bunkeya, a British missionary, Frederick Stanley Arnot, arrived to preach the Gospel and establish new stations on behalf of the Plymouth Brethren, a Protestant fundamentalist movement of which he had become a leading member. Arnot lived in Katanga for two years, but failed to create a religious beachhead. Charles Swan and Henry Faulkner, the two British Plymouth Brethren who succeeded to his witness, remained in Katanga from 1888 to 1891. They made few Christian conquests, but Swan, in particular, became a confidant and aide of Msiri.[35]

The activities of the missionaries caused Léopold serious concern. He feared that they might persuade Msiri to invite another European power into Katanga. In particular, Léopold rightly suspected that the British, who had already displayed an interest in trans-Zambezia, might try to capture Katanga. George Cawston, a director of the British South Africa Company, meanwhile convinced Cecil John Rhodes, its founder, that Katanga contained supplies of valuable

[34] David Livingstone (ed. Horace Waller), *The Last Journals of David Livingstone in Central Africa* (London, 1874), II, p. 120; Verney Lovett Cameron, *Across Africa* (New York, 1877), pp. 298, 353, 358, 475; Hermenegildo Capello and Roberto Ivens (trans. Alfred Elwes), *From Benguella to the Territory of Yacca* (London, 1882), I, p. 223.

[35] For a fuller discussion, see Robert I. Rotberg, "Plymouth Brethren and the Occupation of Katanga, 1886–1907," *The Journal of African History*, V (1964), pp. 285–290.

Msiri, ruler of Katanga, during the last half of the nineteenth century. In this portrait, based on a photograph taken by Roberto Ivens, Msiri wears a Portuguese hat; his clothes may also have come from Portugal. (Auguste Verbeken, *Msiri, roi de Garenganze*, Brussels, 1956)

copper. In turn, Rhodes asked the Scottish explorer Joseph Thomson to "get M'siri's. . . . I mean Katanga. The King of the Belgians has already floated a company for it, presumably, because he does not possess it. . . . You must go and get Katanga." [36] But Thomson, hindered by an epidemic of smallpox *en route*, failed to reach his goal. Instead, later in the same year, Alfred Sharpe, the British vice consul in Nyasaland, arrived in Bunkeya to claim Katanga on behalf of both Rhodes and Queen Victoria. But Msiri reacted hostilely to Sharpe's suggestion that he should sign away his sovereignty to the Company. Swan, who acted as the chief's translator, proved unsympathetic to Sharpe and, in a diplomatic sense, totally unhelpful.

In 1891, the Belgians finally mounted a counteroffensive. Paul le Marinel led the first of three groups thither in April, but Msiri refused to accept his offer of Belgian protection. By the time that Alexandre Delcommune and his expedition attained Bunkeya in October, civil war had overtaken Katanga. The Sanga had revolted against Msiri's rule and, after again demonstrating his unwillingness to sign a treaty with the Congo Independent State, Msiri decided

[36] Cecil Rhodes to Joseph Thomson, July, 1890, quoted in James Baird Thomson, *Joseph Thomson: African Explorer* (London, 1896), p. 269. See also the Cawston Papers: George Cawston to Cecil Rhodes, February 6, and March 14, 1890, Rhodes House, Oxford; FO 2/55: H. H. Johnston to Rhodes, October 8, 1893.

to invite Sharpe to return to Bunkeya.[37] At this juncture, the chief evidently feared an unholy Belgian alliance with the Sanga. Unfortunately for his own plans, a letter destined for Sharpe instead reached William Grant Stairs, a Nova Scotian in Léopold's employ. Stairs intercepted the letter while *en route* to Bunkeya from the east. In December, after arriving in Bunkeya, Stairs unavailingly attempted to persuade Msiri to agree to join the Congo Independent State. But the chief persisted in his refusal to acknowledge the sovereignty of King Léopold. In order to end the impasse, Stairs, who wanted with equal determination to accomplish his mission, finally effected Msiri's murder a few days before Christmas.[38] Léopold ruled Katanga.

By this time, Tippu Tib had relinquished his role in the eastern Congo, and Belgian soldiers and entrepreneurs had begun to campaign against its remaining warlords. In 1892, these skirmishes turned into an all-out war. After the Arabs had been harried by troops under the command of Barons Adolphe Descamps and Jules Marie Alphonse Jacques de Dixmude, they retaliated by ambushing two Belgian expeditions on the Congo and Lomani rivers. By mid 1892, the Belgians had abandoned every post above Stanley Falls. Soon, however, Baron Francis Dhanis counterattacked at the head of a detachment of Zanzibari soldiers. In rapid succession, he recaptured the area later known as the Kasai and occupied the important slaving camps of Nyangwe and Kasongo. By early 1894, the Belgians controlled the eastern Congo. Although fighting between Arabs and Belgians continued for another six years, and their own African troops rebelled several times between 1895 and 1900, Léopold could justifiably claim to have broken the hold of the slavers for good. The cost, however, had been high. Both sides had perpetrated atrocities and had laid waste to extensive acreage from the Stanley Falls to Lake Tanganyika.[39]

During the next seven years, the troops of the Congo Independent State made good their claims to the far corners of the Congo basin. Lucien Bia and Clement Brasseur, for example, forcefully established Léopold's rule of law in the environs of Lake Mweru and along the Luapula River. Others, like Edgar Antoine Auguste Verdick and Charles Lemaire, implanted the flag of the Congo on the high plateaux of northern Katanga. For a time, Léopold's army also occupied the Bahr el Ghazal and Equatoria provinces of the Sudan. In the south, his followers advanced up the Cuango and Kasai rivers until the diplomats of the Congo and Portugal arbitrarily demarcated a border in order to

---

[37] Daniel Crawford, *Thinking Black: Twenty-Two Years Without a Break in the Long Grass of Central Africa* (London, 1913), pp. 301–302; René Cornet, *Katanga* (Bruxelles, 1946), pp. 145–151; Alexandre Delcommune, *Vingt années de vie africaine* (Bruxelles, 1922), II, pp. 257–286.

[38] The precise circumstances of Msiri's death remain uncertain. See William Stairs to Frederick Arnot, December 20, 1891, in *Echoes of Service* (July, 1892), p. 161; Daniel Crawford, letters and diary, in *Echoes of Service* (December, 1891), pp. 299–300 (November, 1892), pp. 258–259; Auguste Verbeken, *Msiri: roi du Garenganze* (Bruxelles, 1956), pp. 229–242; Joseph Augustus Moloney, *With Captain Stairs to Katanga* (London, 1893), pp. 183–190.

[39] Sidney Langford Hinde, *The Fall of the Congo Arabs* (New York, 1897), pp. 153–177; R. P. P. Ceulemans, *La Question arabe et le Congo, 1883–1892* (Bruxelles, 1959), pp. 269–357.

prevent conflicts between Europeans. Indeed, the outline of the modern Congo gradually took shape as much as a result of activity in remote European chanceries as of the process of "effective occupation" in Africa itself. Whatever their provenance, by the end of the nineteenth century, these various factors had combined to make Léopold personally the master of an area of the heart of Africa about one-quarter the size of the continental United States.

III. The Conquest of Central Africa

David Livingstone, the Scottish explorer, interested Europeans in the future of Central Africa. The example of his life and the loss occasioned by his death subsequently evoked an evangelical outpouring that encouraged the forces of "Christianity and commerce" to establish themselves in Central Africa in order to labor there in his memory. In 1875/76, the Free Church and the Established Church of Scotland both despatched missionaries into the area that later became Nyasaland. A Scottish commercial concern, the Livingstonia Central Africa Company (later the African Lakes Company), soon joined the missionaries in an attempt to suppress the slave trade and persuade Africans to exchange their "heathen" customs for Western virtues. During the 1880's, in emulation of this Presbyterian endeavor, other Protestant and Roman Catholic church groups also entered Central Africa. Some settled near Lake Nyasa, others built stations on the southern shores of Lake Tanganyika or along the Zambezi River in distant Barotseland. Individually and collectively, they represented the West in a part of tropical Africa where the presence of whites remained novel. The missions had, perforce, to act independently. They maintained their own supply routes to the coast, attempted forcibly to impose their own concepts of law and order and, in certain circumstances, even assumed a measure of temporal power and suzerainty over Africans. Rudimentary hospitals and networks of schools demonstrated their industry and benevolent intentions. Each station's stock of trade goods testified to the importance of the missionaries in the economic life of the area. They preceded and encouraged the later partitioners.

The protection of trans-zambezia

The presence of Scottish missionaries in the environs of Lake Nyasa worried the Portuguese. On the basis of prior interest and exploration, they had traditionally regarded that area and, indeed, all of Central Africa as their own. After 1880, despite the British government's refusal to recognize Portuguese sovereignty in the interior wherever *bona fide* occupation and *de facto* jurisdiction "of a continuous and non-intermittent kind" did not exist, the government of Portugal asserted its claims with renewed vigor. In turn, the Scottish missions asked for "a kind of British Protectorate," and, in 1883, the British government sent its first consul to "the territories of the African Kings and Chiefs in the districts adjacent to Lake Nyasa." [40] But this appointment only served to in-

[40] Alexander John Hanna, *The Beginnings of Nyasaland and North-Eastern Rhodesia* (Oxford, 1956), pp. 62–64, 111.

crease Portugal's concern. After 1884, Portuguese officials in Moçambique tried to impose their authority over the Nyasa regions to the detriment of what Britons regarded as their commercial and evangelical freedom in the interior. Indeed, in 1887 Portugal obtained the assent of a number of African chiefs to treaties that purportedly supported its territorial claims to the entire Zambezi basin.[41] During the next two years, the Portuguese government of Moçambique interfered with the passage of vessels and equipment to Nyasaland, hindered the African Lakes Company in its efforts to win a war against Arab slavers, and attempted to gain control of the areas in question.[42]

The Scottish missions and traders tried vainly to persuade their government to "protect" Nyasaland. They wrote of its economic and strategic potential and of the evangelical advantages that might be lost if the Portuguese succeeded in realizing their territorial pretensions. But successive British foreign secretaries at first shrugged their official shoulders. Protectorates cost too much. And Lord Salisbury answered the Christian argument:

> *It is not our duty to [establish a protectorate]. We should be risking tremendous sacrifices for a very doubtful gain. . . . We must leave the dispersal of this terrible army of wickedness to the gradual advancement of civilisation and Christianity.*[43]

Soon, however, when the circumstances of power altered, Nyasaland came to strike its own minor humanitarian note in Britain's imperial symphony of conquest.

The governments of the Afrikaner Republic of the Transvaal and the British-backed Cape Colony meanwhile coveted the potential riches of the trans-Limpopo River regions known as Matabeleland and Mashonaland. In 1887, Lobengula, chief of the Ndebele, signed a treaty of friendship with the Transvaal. In 1888, he concluded a similar agreement with a representative of the Cape Colony. To an emissary of Cecil Rhodes, the chief also gave "complete and exclusive" mineral rights to Matabeleland.[44] But Rhodes required imperial protection to secure the concession against Portuguese and Afrikaner designs. In turn, Lord Salisbury welcomed his assistance in keeping the interior of Central Africa—the red route from the Cape to Cairo—free of foreign domination.[45]

Early in 1889, Rhodes, then thirty-six years old and worth millions, came to London from Cape Town. In exchange for the support of the British govern-

---

[41] Texts in Hertslet, *Map* (1896), I, pp. 325 ff.

[42] For the war against the Arabs, see FO 84/1883 and FO 84/1942; Hanna, *Beginnings*, pp. 79–105; Perham, *Lugard: The Years of Adventure*, pp. 106–126.

[43] Lord Salisbury, speaking in Parliament, quoted in Ronald Robinson and John Gallagher, *Africa and the Victorians: The Climax of Imperialism in the Dark Continent* (New York, 1961), p. 224.

[44] Richard Brown, "The Scramble and African Politics in Matabeleland," in *Conference of the History of the Central African Peoples* (Lusaka, 1963), no pagination.

[45] The "Cape to Cairo" expression, usually credited to Cecil Rhodes, appears to have originated with Henry Hamilton (later Sir Harry) Johnston. See "African Explorer" (a pseudonym used by Johnston), "Great Britain's Policy in Africa," *Times* (London), August 22, 1888; Harry Johnston, *The Story of My Life* (Indianapolis, 1923), p. 205; FO 2/55: Johnston to Rhodes, October 8, 1893.

ment in Matabeleland, he offered to pay for the colonization and administration of both the Bechuanaland Protectorate and Matabeleland, to extend the existing rail and telegraph lines to the Zambezi River, and to obtain for the Crown, without cost to the Crown, trans-Zambezia and Nyasaland. With that abundant resolution of which Livingstone would have approved, Rhodes simply proposed to paint the heart of Africa British red with his own financial brush. It seemed in Lord Salisbury's interest to let him do so. Later in the year, a few, swift strokes of Salisbury's pen chartered Rhodes's British South Africa Company and authorized it to govern and administer trans-Zambezia, where Rhodes suspected the existence of copper, as well as Matabeleland and Mashonaland, where he hoped to find gold.[46] Partially in exchange, Rhodes promised to support financially the imperial activities of Harry Johnston, the first British commissioner and consul-general in Nyasaland, and to defray his future administrative costs.

During a dramatic early morning encounter in London, Johnston and Rhodes each reinforced the other's conception of Britain's imperial role in Central Africa: "We settled as we thought the immediate line of action. . . ."[47] A few months later, Johnston arrived in the Shire Highlands region of southern Nyasaland determined to implement "the line of action" that he had discussed with Rhodes and, in part, with Lord Salisbury. Almost immediately, he authorized the declaration of a protectorate over the Shire Highlands in order to prevent a similar assertion of hegemony there by Portugal. With the assistance of Alfred Sharpe, who was soon to treat with Msiri, and Joseph Thomson, he also negotiated an array of agreements with many of the indigenous chiefs who ruled in the vast territory that stretched westward from the Shire River to Lake Mweru. These treaties, like many similar instruments of Western diplomacy in Africa, bound the chiefs to seek the approval of Queen Victoria before ceding territory or sovereignty to another foreign power. They also affirmed the existence of peace between a particular tribe and the Queen, promised not to hinder the passage through their domains of British subjects, and accorded to the Queen's government jurisdiction in all disputes that arose between the indigenous inhabitants and Britons. The treaties neither promised nor conferred protection.[48] On the other hand, they could be used to support the claims of Britain in its conflict with Portugal. And early in 1890, Lord Salisbury resolved that conflict by threatening to despatch gunboats to Moçambique. He ordered Portugal to remove its troops from the Shire Highlands and Mashonaland forthwith, or face war. Portugal submitted and, in the eyes of Europe, Britain thereafter became the unquestioned mistress of what was soon known as Central Africa.

As Johnston's activities in the east had brought such success, so Rhodes's similar efforts in the west were crowned equally with success. There, in Barotse-

---

[46] Texts in Hertslet, *Map* (1896), I, pp. 174–182.
[47] Johnston, *Story of My Life*, p. 219.
[48] Hertslet, *Map* (1896), I, pp. 187–190.

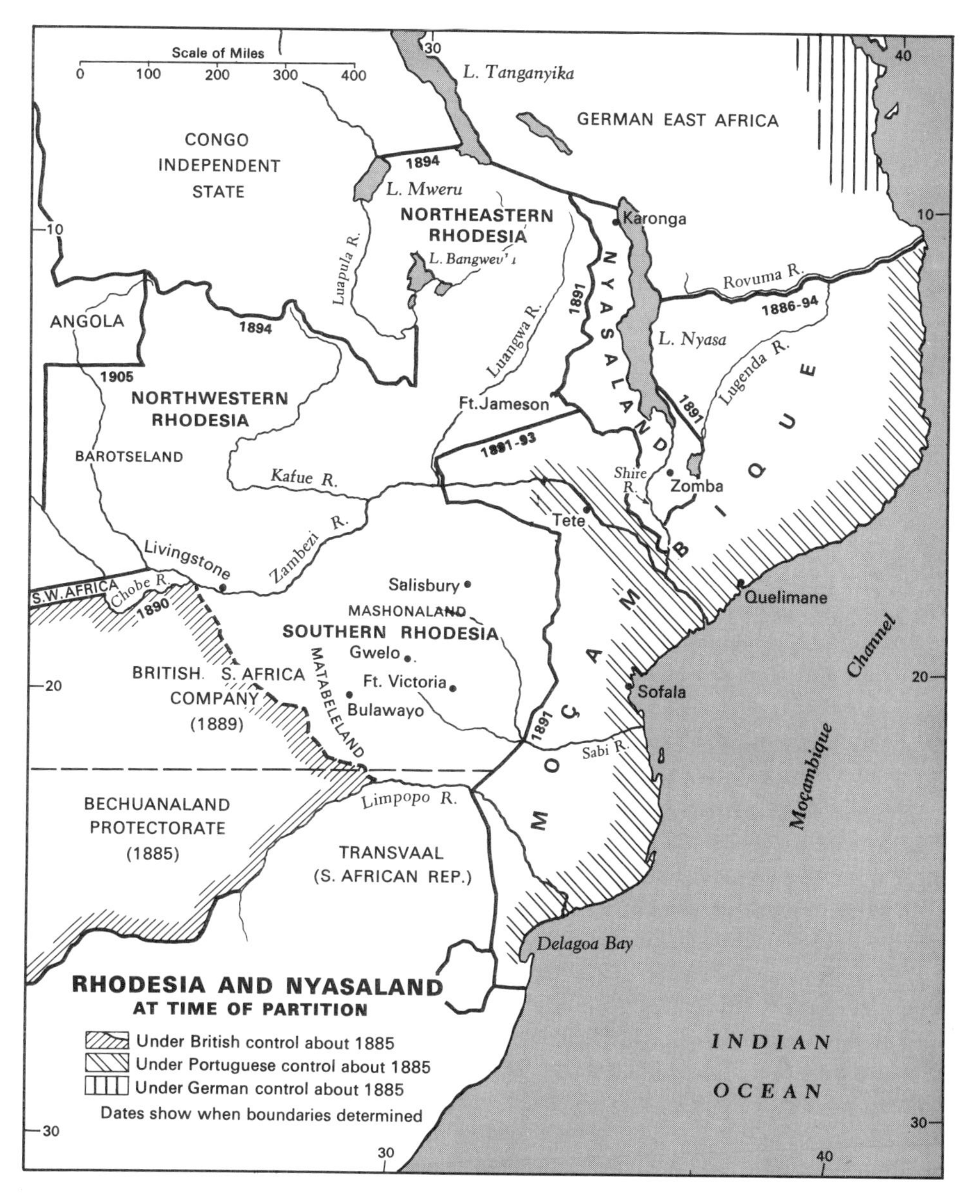

land, Mwanawina Lewanika, *litunga* of the Lozi, ruled much of what became Northwestern Rhodesia, eastern Angola, northern Bechuanaland, and the Caprivi Strip of Southwest Africa.[49] Of the missionaries who had preached in his kingdom, none had achieved a greater measure of influence than François Coillard of the Paris Missionary Society. Coillard had married a Scot. He feared that the Germans or Portuguese might acquire Barotseland and limit missionary

[49] On the controversial extent of Lewanika's influence, see A/2/1/1: memorandum by Frank V. Worthington, June 5, 1908, Lusaka archives.

freedom. Thus, when Rhodes wanted Barotseland for its supposed store of minerals, he persuaded Coillard to intercede with Lewanika, who in turn desired to interpose the British presence between his own people and Lobengula's fearsome Ndebele.[50]

In mid 1890, Coillard helped Frank Lochner, a representative of Rhodes, to obtain Lewanika's signature to a treaty that, in Lozi eyes, gave them a direct relationship with Queen Victoria. Later, when they learned that they had instead forfeited control of their land and their sub-soil rights to a commercial company, their anger knew no bounds. Nonetheless, the so-called Lochner treaty provided the original basis for the British South Africa Company's subsequent assumption of direct rule in western trans-Zambezia and, wrongly, for its rights to the lucrative ores that have since permitted Zambia to become the world's second largest producer of copper.[51]

In 1891, Rhodes, Johnston, and Salisbury divided trans-Zambezia into the three protectorates of Nyasaland (then the so-called British Central Africa Protectorate), Northeastern, and Northwestern Rhodesia. At first, Johnston governed both Nyasaland and Northeastern Rhodesia from Zomba while the Company exercised its responsibilities in Northwestern Rhodesia by the despatch of representatives to Lewanika. Johnston believed that tropical Africa "must be ruled by whites, developed by Indians, and worked by blacks." [52] To further this plan, he advocated cooperation with missionaries, encouraged the settlement of whites within his dominions, and imported Sikhs and other Asians to police and organize the commercial life of the protectorates. With the help of the Sikhs, he subdued the many chiefs and peoples who refused to accept the British declaration of "protection." When the Company began to govern Northeastern Rhodesia directly, its administrators similarly vanquished the Ngoni under Mpezeni and the Lunda under Kazembe. By 1901, all of the peoples of trans-Zambezia thus became "protected" persons under the aegis of the Crown.

The creation of a colony

Rhodes, despite the staunch opposition of Lobengula and the Ndebele, had meanwhile set in motion the train of events that led, in time, to the colonial occupation of Matabeleland and Mashonaland. In 1890, despite the treaties that he had signed with white diplomats and prospectors, Lobengula still reigned supreme over the lands that lay between the Limpopo and Zambezi rivers. The Ndebele *impi*, or raiding parties, ranged far afield, everywhere enhancing their reputations as the pre-eminent warriors of Central Africa. The Shona, among others, fearfully paid them tribute and allegiance. In these circumstances, Rhodes and his advisors proposed to settle white farmers and prospectors on the high, well-watered central plateaux of Mashonaland. There

---

[50] Coillard Papers: Coillard to Sir Sidney Shippard, January 8, 1889; Kgama to Lewanika, July 17, 1889, Salisbury archives.

[51] *Africa South*, 414, no. 245 (encl.), contains a copy of the treaty.

[52] FO 2/55: Harry Johnston to Sir Percy Anderson, October 10, 1893.

they might find gold. By occupying a part of the territory, they would also safeguard the interests of the Cape Colony and serve as an effective counterpoise to the Portuguese and Afrikaners.

The "pioneer column" that occupied Mashonaland looms large in the mythology of the white man in Africa. It consisted of a carefully chosen cadre of South Africans and Britons, led by Colonel Leander Starr Jameson, guided by the experienced hunter, Frederick Courteney Selous, and accompanied by five hundred white policemen. In 1890, this column crossed from Bechuanaland into Matabeleland, ignoring the protests of Lobengula. It kept well wide of his capital and, a few months later, established Fort Salisbury in the far interior. It simply "took possession of Mashonaland in the name of the Queen." [53] The members of the "pioneer column," who were soon joined by other whites from South Africa, thereafter forcefully acquired lands that belonged to the Shona, built new forts, and gradually consolidated their grip upon Mashonaland. The forerunners of the white-dominated cities of the twentieth century began at this time as collections of mud and thatch huts.

The spectre of war soon rose on the horizon. In the eyes of the settlers, Mashonaland had failed to fulfill its promise. Its soil seemed unsuited to intensive farming or grazing, costs remained high since consumer goods reached them only after traveling more than a thousand miles over difficult terrain from Vryburg, in South Africa, and prospectors had failed to locate workable gold in the quantities expected. On the other hand, the pioneers believed that Matabeleland contained good pastures and abundant gold. For their part, the Ndebele feared that the whites might take their land. They felt that the whites had treacherously defied Lobengula and had sheltered the Shona, the tribesmen whom the Ndebele had traditionally regarded as their natural prey. In such an atmosphere of tension, the settlers and the Ndebele tacitly demarcated a border that they hoped would separate the contending parties. But when white prospectors and African raiding parties persistently violated the boundaries, even a delimitation of territory could hardly postpone the outbreak of war for long.

In 1893, a large Ndebele *impi*, presumably intent upon punishing "disrespectful" Shona who lived near Fort Victoria, attacked white-owned farms, stole white-owned cattle, and killed a number of African laborers. It also entered the town of Fort Victoria. Although no whites lost their lives, the Ndebele evidently continued to terrorize the inhabitants of Fort Victoria for about a week.[54] In these circumstances, Jameson, the administrator of the colony, ordered the *impi* to return to Matabeleland forthwith. When it tarried instead, whites attacked the regiment and hurried it toward Gbulawayo, Lobengula's capital. Alarmed, the chief warned the whites that their actions might escalate the conflict beyond control. "I thought you came to dig gold," he wrote to Jameson, "but it seems that you have come to rob me of my people and country

[53] Hugh Marshall Hole, *The Making of Rhodesia* (London, 1926), p. 146; Frederick Courteney Selous, *Travel and Adventure in South-East Africa* (London, 1893), pp. 356–382. See also Hugh Marshall Hole, *Old Rhodesian Days* (London, 1928), pp. 10–28.

[54] Details in Hole, *Making,* pp. 286–298.

as well . . . you are like a child playing with edged tools."[55] The British Secretary of State for the Colonies refused to support any aggressive action in Rhodesia. But Rhodes purchased horses for the British South Africa Company's mounted police; the settlers, in the manner of colonials everywhere, demanded that the "natives" be "taught a lesson"; and Lobengula, distraught, recalled regiments that had embarked upon a campaign against the Lozi. "To whom," Lobengula's emissary asked, "do the Mashona belong?"[56] Finally, in late 1893, white soldiers dragged their cannon and machine guns toward Gbulawayo. In a few desultory battles, many Africans and a few whites lost their lives. Lobengula escaped to the north—where he apparently died early in 1894—and his followers sued for peace. Subjugation soon followed.

For the conquered, the conditions of the peace that succeeded the war belied the calm assurances that Jameson had given to the Ndebele leaders at the time of their surrender. The settlers herded the Ndebele into reserves where the soil was poor and supplies of water short. As reparations, they took cattle belonging to the Ndebele and compelled many Ndebele to work on their newly established farms. The settlers also imposed a tax upon the conquered people. In time, too, Ndebele leaders accused white farmers and white-employed Shona policemen of treating them harshly and molesting their women.[57] In innumerable ways, the Ndebele and the Shona both suffered humiliation at the hands of their new white overlords. To them, such treatment seemed unjust, the more so because both the Ndebele and the Shona had originally trusted the white man's fine words and lofty promises. And then, to make matters worse, the gods—or so it seemed to the Africans—brought famine and pestilence where there had previously been plenty. A contemporary observer in Company employ summarized the depths of the Ndebele discontent:

> *Faced with a grain famine, robbed of their newly-acquired cattle, importuned in season and out . . . to provide unaccustomed labour, bullied by their former tribesmen and slaves who had enlisted in the Police Force . . . what wonder if the [Ndebele] . . . began to seek a short cut out of their troubles. . . .*[58]

In early 1896, at a time when many of the Company police had gone south to participate in Jameson's ill-starred raid on Johannesburg, the Ndebele rose against white rule. Within a week, whites residing on isolated homesteads had lost their lives. Many of the remaining settlers *laagered* in Bulawayo (newly established near the old Gbulawayo) and in Gwelo, only occasionally sending out patrols into the rural areas of Matabeleland. But by the middle of the year, two thousand armed whites had taken the field against the marauding Ndebele. Then, at a time when the settlers thought that they could end the rebellion, the Shona, who had harbored their own grievances, rose in the north. Salisbury, like Bulawayo earlier, fortified itself. On two fronts, black fought white for

---

[55] Quoted in Philip Mason, *The Birth of a Dilemma* (London, 1958), p. 170.
[56] *Ibid.*, pp. 172–173.
[57] See Charles Freer Andrews, *John White of Mashonaland* (London, 1935), pp. 50–56.
[58] Hole, *Making*, p. 349.

control of Rhodesia: the Ndebele, even after suffering an overwhelming defeat in July, battled on from the fastnesses of the Matopo Hills until Rhodes, in this his finest hour, personally persuaded their chiefs to disarm and to accept the pay and the rule of the Company. Throughout the end of 1896, the Shona, however, continued to harry the whites in the north. Finally, during the first months of 1897, white patrols managed to capture most of the rebellious chiefs and to flush defiant tribesmen from caves and the farthest crags of inaccessible kopjes. In the process, whites and Africans both perpetrated atrocities; even the best white officers killed prisoners without fair trial and submitted Africans to indignities.[59] But the whites had at last demonstrated their superiority. In the next year, with the blessing of Rhodes, the settlers began to govern themselves as a colony theoretically subject to, but practically divorced from, the fiat of Queen Victoria.

IV. The Conquest of East Africa

At the conclusion of the Berlin conference, Bismarck unilaterally recognized the activities and territorial acquisitions of Carl Peters in East Africa. To Peters' Society for German Colonization, he gave an imperial German *Schutzbrief*, or charter, that caused consternation both in London and in Zanzibar. By the terms of the *Schutzbrief*, and on behalf of the Society, Germany claimed and "protected" all of the lands that lay roughly between Lake Tanganyika and the dominions of the sultan of Zanzibar. Without qualification, it furthermore gave "jurisdiction over both the natives and the subjects of Germany and of other nations established . . . or sojourning there for commercial or other purposes." [60] By the wording of the charter, no caveats hindered the exercise of sovereignty by Peters and his colleagues. No fulsome phrases urged due care for the "welfare of the natives." Peters thus proceeded to include new territories within his colonial empire and to administer the parts of Tanganyika that he already controlled.

An anglo-german rivalry

The precise magnitude of the German claims remained obscure. Sultan Seyyid Barghash of Zanzibar presumed that he still ruled all of Tanganyika and that the Germans were therefore little more than trespassers. He protested vigorously to the Kaiser and then despatched Lloyd William Mathews, the

---

[59] For contemporary accounts of the risings, see Frederick Courteney Selous, *Sunshine and Storm in Rhodesia* (London, 1896); Robert S. S. Baden-Powell, *The Matabeleland Campaign* (London, 1897); Edwin Alfred Alderson, *With the Mounted Infantry and the Mashonaland Field Force, 1896* (London, 1898). See also Basil Williams, *Cecil Rhodes* (London, 1919), pp. 287–291; Terence O. Ranger, "The Organization of the Rebellions of 1896 and 1897," in *Conference of the History of the Central African Peoples*, no pagination.

[60] For the text in the original, see Alfred Zimmerman *et al.*, *Die deutsche Kolonialgesetzgebung* (Berlin, 1893), I, p. 323. Reginald Coupland, *The Exploitation of East Africa, 1856–1890* (London, 1939), p. 405, contains a translation.

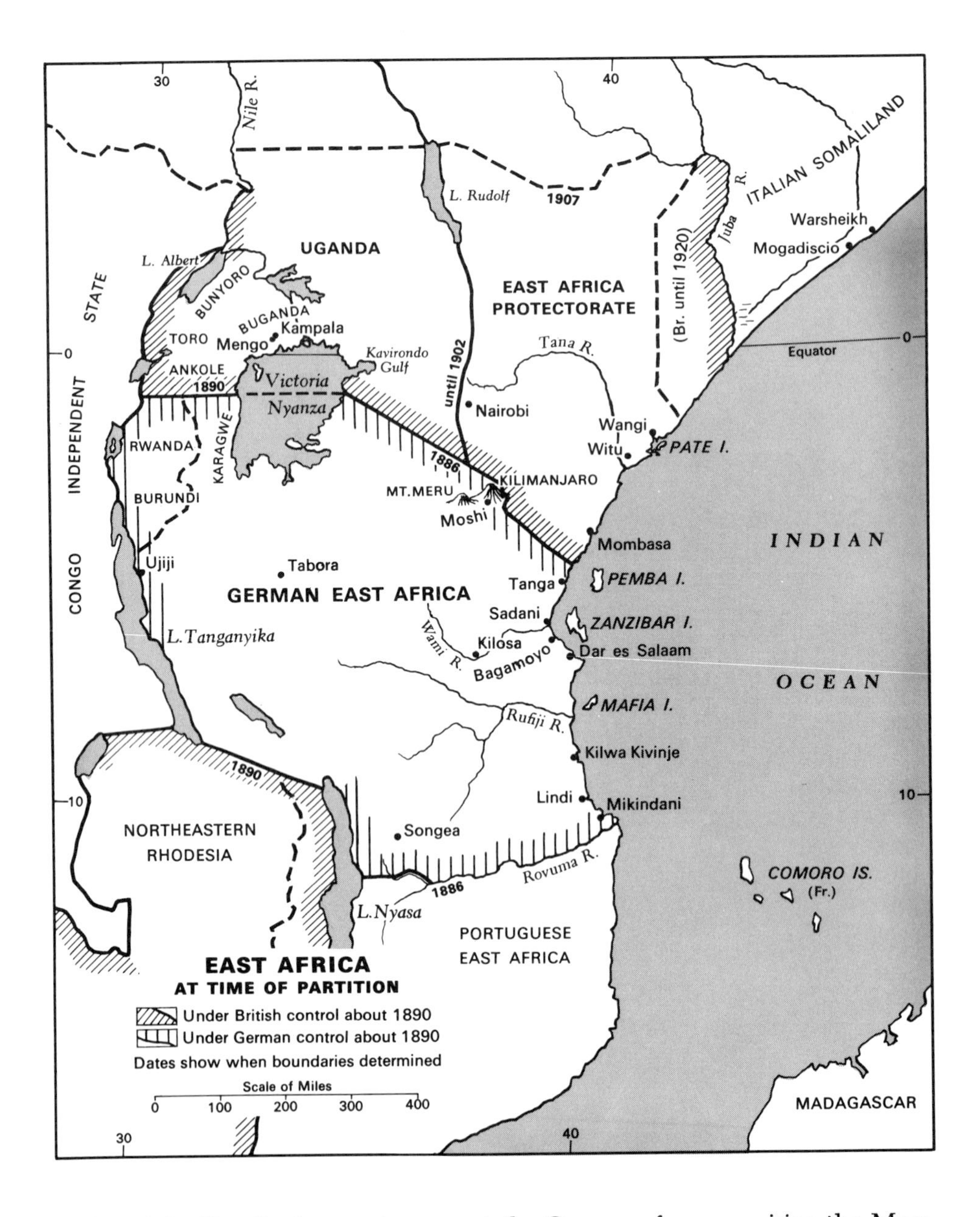

leader of the Zanzibari army, to prevent the Germans from acquiring the Mombasa and Kilimanjaro areas.[61] In turn, Frederick Holmwood, a British consular official home on leave from East Africa, tried to persuade Sir William Mackinnon, the shipping magnate, and James H. Hutton, a former president of the Manchester Chamber of Commerce and a director of Goldie's National

---

[61] Robert Nunez Lyne, *An Apostle of Empire: Being the Life of Sir Lloyd William Mathews, K.C.M.G.* (London, 1936), pp. 68–74.

African Company, to establish a chartered company that could wrest control of the peoples of the Kilimanjaro area from the Germans. Earlier, Joseph Thomson and Harry Johnston had both visited and reported favorably upon Kilimanjaro's economic prospects.[62] Holmwood and other officials of the British Foreign Office encouraged the financiers to organize and operate a European colony in East Africa along the lines of the old, profitable East India Company. Hutton, Mackinnon, Lord Aberdare, the chairman of the National African Company, and five other influential Britons agreed that they should try to obtain concessions in East Africa in order to "maintain and extend British influence . . . to develop British trade, and to deal in a practical manner with the Slave Trade. . . ." [63] But the highest circles in Whitehall, embarrassed by recent affairs in Afghanistan and the Sudan, feared Bismarck's reaction and, for the sake of his continued diplomatic support for the British role in Egypt, they refused officially to back the Holmwood scheme.

In East Africa, meanwhile, the Germans forged ahead. The brothers Clemens and Gustav Denhardt obtained signatures from its "sultan" and "protected" Witu and the adjacent islands. A few months later, Karl Jühlke, a compatriot of Peters, persuaded Africans to sign away the Kilimanjaro and Usambara districts to Germany. Throughout the last half of 1885, a number of Germans obtained treaties of cession from peoples living near the Tana River, between the Wami and Rovuma rivers, and westward toward Lake Nyasa. Not necessarily by the use of the peaceful methods that had served Peters well, still others collected signatures to similar treaties from chiefs or sheikhs who ruled sections of the Tanganyika coast and the Somali littoral from Warsheikh to Berbera.

The sultan of Zanzibar complained, and Sir John Kirk, his British advisor, urged the British government to intervene on behalf of the sultan and Britain's own position in East Africa. But the publication of the German *Schutzbrief* had already marked the end of Britain's unquestioned paramountcy in East Africa. For long content with limited hegemony, the British still believed that their interest in East Africa remained marginal. "I do not quite see our interest in this Zanzibar quarrel," Salisbury wrote. "Keeping every other nation out on the bare chance that some day . . . our traders will pluck up heart to go in is a poor policy." [64] A few weeks before, the presence of German warships in the harbor of Zanzibar had encouraged Sultan Barghash to recognize Germany's pre-eminent position in Tanganyika and in East Africa generally, thereby also effecting a change in British attitudes.

The powers of Europe quickly dismembered the empire of Zanzibar. After a commission composed of representatives from Britain, France, and Germany had, with little reference to the actual state of affairs, decided to its own satis-

---

[62] Oliver, *Sir Harry Johnston*, pp. 59–77; Harry Johnston, "The Kilimanjaro Expedition," *Proceedings of the Royal Geographical Society*, VII (1885), pp. 139–141; Thomson, *Joseph Thomson*, pp. 100–123.

[63] Quoted in Coupland, *Exploitation*, p. 427.

[64] A minute by Lord Salisbury on a despatch from Sir John Kirk, September 17/18, 1885, quoted in *ibid.*, p. 433.

faction the extent to which the sultan of Zanzibar ruled parts of the mainland of East Africa, the governments of Britain and Germany arbitrarily agreed to recognize his sovereignty along the coast only between the Tana and Rovuma rivers. They decreed that his authority was limited to an inland depth of no more than ten miles. In 1886, the same Anglo-German agreement gave Germany control over the Witu protectorate north of the Tana River. South of that river, it divided the British and German spheres of influence in East Africa by a line that ran northwesterly from Vanga on the Umba River to a point approximately midway between the northern and southern ends of the eastern shore of Victoria Nyanza. Beyond that point, the respective spheres remained unapportioned.[65] France received a protectorate over the Comoro Islands. And Barghash, powerless without British support, bowed reluctantly to this foreign partition of his lands.

Yet the sultan and a number of Britons hoped that they might still preserve a British initiative in East Africa. In 1887, Barghash gave Mackinnon's newly formed British East Africa Association full political and jural authority over his mainland possessions from Kipini to Vanga in exchange for a yearly cash payment equal to the amount that the sultan habitually collected from the region in customs fees.[66] During the remainder of the year, the agents of the Association collected treaties from leading chiefs of the interior; they thereby claimed two hundred miles of territory inland from the coast.

By about this same time, Lord Salisbury had come to appreciate that Britain would be unable in the near future to withdraw from Egypt. His government at last regarded the occupation of Egypt as a long-term affair. Consequently, the interests of Egypt in the source and flow of the Nile River equally became the interests of Britain. Its government therefore wanted to protect the upper reaches of the river, to keep other European powers out of Uganda and the Sudan, and carefully to safeguard all of the possible approaches to the White Nile. In 1888, Lord Salisbury thus gave a charter to the Imperial British East Africa Company—as the East Africa Association had become—that empowered it to seize and govern as much territory as possible within the British sphere; the financial risk was to belong strictly to its promoters.[67] In the same year, the Germans forced the sultan of Zanzibar to grant them a lease to his mainland possessions in Tanganyika.

The interior enticed the two powers of Europe. Because of its reputed wealth and strategic position near the headwaters of the Nile, the German and British companies particularly coveted Buganda, then rent by a bitter internecine struggle between the supporters of different religious factions. In 1888, *kabaka* Mwanga attempted to deprive the Anglican, Roman Catholic, and

[65] Hertslet, *Map* (1896), II, p. 615; Philip Magnus, *Kitchener: Portrait of an Imperialist* (London, 1961), pp. 76–77; Coupland, *Exploitation*, pp. 448–468. The Anglo-French treaty of 1862 respecting East Africa had envisaged the constitution of a commission similar to that called in 1885.

[66] See P. L. McDermott, *British East Africa, or Ibea* (London, 1893), pp. 263–275.

[67] Texts in *ibid.*, pp. 282–291; Hertslet, *Map* (1896), I, pp. 345–359.

Muslim parties of their growing influence at his court. But the monotheistic parties, uniting temporarily, deposed Mwanga in favor of his elder brother Kiwewa. In turn, the Arab-led Muslims, anxious here as elsewhere to preserve their commercial dominance in the face of increasing European competition, ousted the Christian chiefs from Mengo, the capital of Buganda, and replaced Kiwewa by his more pliant brother, *kabaka* Kalema. But in 1889, Mwanga, supported by the Christian Ganda who had taken refuge from the Arabs in Ankole and Karagwe, and assisted by Charles Stokes, a former lay Anglican missionary turned trader and gunrunner, ousted the Muslims from Mengo.[68] A few weeks later, the Muslims and the forces of *omukama* Kabarega of Bunyoro reversed the position and again turned the Christians out of the capital. Finally, in early 1890, Mwanga and his Christian supporters won a lasting victory over the Muslims and occupied Mengo for good. His kingdom, however, remained divided.

European interest in the affairs of Buganda had already intensified. In early 1889, when Stanley was still engaged in his "rescue" of Emin Pasha from the Equatoria province of the Sudan, a private German committee for the relief of Emin Pasha sent Carl Peters on the same errand. Many Britons suspected that Peters' activities would be used by Germany to acquire new territories along the Nile. The British Imperial East Africa Company consequently despatched Frederick Jackson toward the upper Nile so that he could watch Peters and, if necessary, render support to Stanley. In fact, Stanley had already accomplished his mission and, unbeknown to Europeans on the coast, had started to return to Zanzibar. Thus, when Peters and Jackson later learned of Stanley's success, they turned their attentions to Buganda. In late 1889, during the second period of Arab ascendancy, Mwanga and the Anglican missionaries also appealed for assistance to Jackson, who was then based at Chief Mumia's village in upper Kavirondo. Before he managed to reach Buganda, however, Peters stopped at Mumia's, read the correspondence between Mwanga and Jackson, and seized the opportunity to make Buganda German.[69] He trekked posthaste to Mengo, where Mwanga had recently recovered his throne. There Peters quickly persuaded Mwanga to sign a treaty of friendship with the Kaiser. Jackson soon followed and, after Peters had gone south, he offered Mwanga a treaty that the *kabaka* felt unable to accept.[70]

The German threat to British control over the Nile increasingly appeared serious. The Germans had begun to govern Tanganyika directly, replacing the officers of the Company by an imperial commissioner. In the spring of 1890, his administration openly displayed its continued interest in Buganda. In turn,

---

[68] The government of the Congo Independent State later executed Stokes for supplying arms and ammunition to Arab slavers. For the religious wars, see John Milner Gray, "The Year of the Three Kings of Buganda," *The Uganda Journal*, XIV (1950), pp. 29–49; D. Anthony Low, *Religion and Society in Buganda, 1875–1900* (Kampala, 1956), pp. 8–10.

[69] But see Carl Peters (trans. H. W. Dulcken), *New Light on Dark Africa* (London, 1891), pp. 313–329.

[70] It contained provisions that the missionaries regarded as unduly harsh. Roland Oliver, *The Missionary Factor in East Africa* (London, 1952), p. 139.

the British government grew alarmed. The Imperial British East Africa Company sent Captain Frederick Lugard and a column of African troops to establish its authority there, and before long Lord Salisbury used diplomatic means to keep the Germans away from the Nile. By the omnibus Anglo-German treaty of 1890, Lord Salisbury acquired the future Uganda, the hitherto German protectorate over Witu, and recognition of Britain's especial interests in Zanzibar and Pemba (which it "protected" in the same year) in exchange for Heligoland, the small but strategically important North Sea island that commanded the Elbe estuary. Germany also obtained "rights" to the Karagwe and Haya countries of Tanganyika, Rwanda, and Burundi, and a thin wedge of territory—the Caprivi Strip—that thereafter connected Southwest Africa to the Zambezi River at Katima Mulilo.[71] Salisbury further urged the sultan of Zanzibar to sell his Tanganyikan coastal strip to the Germans. The British government gave away much; it even ended dreams of an all red route from the Cape to Cairo. But Salisbury successfully safeguarded the Nile and took the first of several steps that eventually eliminated foreign rivalry in the area between Victoria Nyanza and the Mediterranean Sea.

The mastery of tanganyika and uganda

From the first, Germany maintained its position in Tanganyika by force of arms. In late 1888, after the Germans had begun to occupy the port towns of Tanganyika for the first time, Abushiri ibn Salim al-Harthi, a member of a prominent Pangani family, inspired and led a resistance movement that swept the coast and the interior. His followers attacked mission stations and the German fort at Dar es Salaam, repulsed a landing party at Kilwa Kivinje, and compelled the Germans to evacuate Mikindani and Lindi. But during the next year, after Britain, Italy, Portugal, and Germany had blockaded the coast and had thereby denied Abushiri supplies of arms and ammunition, German-officered troops routed the indigenous defenders in a series of battles near Bagamoyo and inland. At the end of 1889, the Germans finally captured and hanged Abushiri. Bwana Kheri, a Zigua chief, continued the battle against the Germans, occupying Sadani. But the Germans managed to retake Kilwa, Lindi, and Mikindani and, before too long, to establish their rule over the sullen peoples of the coast.[72]

Up-country, the Hehe actively resisted the Germans between 1891 and 1894, when Kalenga, their main fort, fell before a determined German onslaught. Emin Pasha and Peters cruelly subdued the Gogo people of central Tanganyika. Peters similarly terrified the Chagga, during which time he and his successor, Ulbrecht von Bülow, established the position of Germany in the Kilimanjaro district. Hermann von Wissmann conquered the remote areas between

[71] Hertslet, *Map* (1896), II, pp. 642–657; William Roger Louis, *Ruanda-Urundi, 1884–1919* (Oxford, 1963), pp. 18–28. But see D. R. Gillard, "Salisbury's African Policy and the Heligoland Offer of 1890," *The English Historical Review*, LXXV (1960), pp. 649–653.

[72] See Hemedi bin Abdallah bin Said el Buhriy (trans. and ed. J. W. T. Allen), *Utenzi wa Vita vya Wadachi kutamalaki Mrima* (Dar es Salaam, 1960), pp. 66–77.

Lakes Nyasa and Tanganyika. In 1894/95, the Germans also overcame two separate Yao resistance movements along the southern coast. Wissmann continued the pacification of the Chagga and constructed a strong fort at Moshi. Others subjugated the Arusha and built a stockade on the slopes of Mount Meru. In the deep south, the Germans erected another fort at Songea and proceeded to end the resistance of the Ngoni led by chiefs Chabruma and Mharuli. Mkwawa, the fugitive Hehe chief, continued actively to oppose their rule until 1898. Thereafter, although the conquest of Burundi and Rwanda had yet to occur, the Germans justifiably considered themselves to be the masters of practically all of their East African sphere of influence.

The Imperial British East Africa Company, with its headquarters in Mombasa, had meanwhile stationed customs collectors in the small ports along the coast and agents in the depots or forts along the caravan route to Victoria Nyanza. At first, the Company and its employees up-country exerted very little influence upon the peoples in whose territories they had established their way stations. Later the Company backed the Masai and the Kamba and began to use force to protect its critical position on the southern borders of Kikuyuland. It thereby came into open conflict with the Kikuyu. Even so, throughout the 1890's, Britons concerned themselves primarily with Buganda and the establishment of their authority around the northern rim of Victoria Nyanza.

In late 1890, Lugard entered Buganda determined to preserve and widen Britain's influence there. He soon persuaded Mwanga and the leading Ganda chiefs to accord "suzerainty" over Buganda to the Company for a period limited to two years. In 1891, after failing to reconcile the conflicting positions of the Catholic and Anglican parties, he led a Christian army to a decisive victory against the Muslims, thus removing the fears that had hitherto served to limit conflict between the two Christian camps. Thereafter, during the course of a long tour through the western kingdoms, Lugard attempted to isolate Bunyoro by curtailing the arms traffic from the south. To this end, he negotiated a treaty that bound the *omugabe* of Ankole to act against the gunrunners and that gave British "protection" to the peoples of his country. Because Bunyoro regarded Toro as a subjugated province, Lugard also restored the royal line there and established a line of forts along the border between Toro and Bunyoro.

The Company had meanwhile admitted its parlous financial state. Basically, it seemed unable to obtain or entertain prospects of revenue sufficient to attract new investment. In the summer of 1891, its directors therefore decided to withdraw from Buganda and to abandon their concessions on the coast. An attempt to acquire a parliamentary subsidy failed. The Anglican Church Missionary Society's solicitation of private funds with which to support the Company proved equally unsuccessful. Early in 1892, after Lugard had returned to Buganda, he learned that the Company expected to end its occupation of Buganda later in the year. Already, however, he had apparently decided to impose the authority of the Company on the *kabaka* and the leaders of the Catholic and Anglican factions. An unimportant incident provided the necessary pretext; Lugard then distributed arms to his Anglican supporters, precipitated

THE WHITE ELEPHANT
Present Proprietor: "See Here, Governor! He's a likely-looking Animal,—but I can't manage him! If you won't take him, I must let him go!"

During the British debate on the future of Uganda, *Punch* published this African cartoon, which shows a conversation between the "Present Proprietor," i.e., the British East Africa Company and John Bull, i.e., the British government. (*Punch,* 1892)

a war, and overwhelmed Mwanga and the Catholics. As a result, the *kabaka* and the leading chiefs of both parties confirmed the authority of the Company in Buganda and accepted a geographical partition of the kingdom that favored the Anglicans. In addition, Mwanga himself espoused the Anglican faith.[73]

The Company still intended to withdraw from Buganda. Neither Lugard nor Lord Rosebery, the new British Foreign Minister, wanted Britain to lose its pre-eminent position there, however, and together they campaigned publicly and privately in favor of retention. During the summer and autumn of 1892, Rosebery tried to persuade his fellow cabinet ministers to back the Company in Buganda in the Salisbury manner. Lugard and others meanwhile encouraged influential newspapers to express themselves strongly in favor of the continued protection of Buganda and the wisdom of constructing a railway from the East African coast to Victoria Nyanza. Church and missionary groups and the important Anti-Slavery Society—indeed most humanitarian organizations—agitated on behalf of benighted Buganda, carefully converting the already converted and strengthening Rosebery's hand within a hostile cabinet that continued to be more concerned about Ireland than Africa.[74] By the end of the year, the cabinet finally agreed merely to send a commissioner to investigate "with an open mind"

---

[73] See Mwanga to Henry Colvile, July 24, 1894, quoted in Oliver, *Missionary Factor*, p. 149n; Perham, *Lugard: The Years of Adventure*, pp. 288–302; Alfred Tucker, *Eighteen Years in Uganda and East Africa* (London, 1911), I, pp. 60–72. The text of the agreement may be found in McDermott, *Ibea*, pp. 329–332.

[74] D. Anthony Low, "British Public Opinion and the Uganda Question, October–December, 1892," *The Uganda Journal*, XVIII (1954), pp. 81–100; Perham, *Lugard: The Years of Adventure*, pp. 447–469; Robert Rhodes James, *Rosebery* (London, 1963), pp. 274–275, 351.

and to report on the situation in Buganda. Rosebery in turn asked Sir Gerald Portal, then his consul-general in Zanzibar and a public supporter of retention, to undertake the mission. With Portal, Rosebery had a private understanding; both men expected the eventual report to favor the continued "protection" of Buganda.

In the spring of 1893, Portal reached Buganda, learned that the leading Anglican and Roman Catholic missionaries favored the further extension of British rule there and, on the flagstaff of the fort at Kampala, replaced the banner of the Company with the Union Jack. Mwanga and his leading chiefs signed another treaty giving the British government the status of "protector." The *kabaka* surrendered his power to make agreements with other foreign nations and transferred to the British government his right to collect taxes.[75] As part of a revised settlement, Portal also saw that the Catholic party regained a measure of equal status within the Buganda government and control over additional lands. In his report, which Rosebery influenced if not wrote, Portal argued mildly for retention in the interests of Britain's strategic needs in Egypt. In 1894, after British diplomacy had failed to keep other foreign powers from advancing toward the upper Nile, Parliament officially approved the inauguration of a protectorate over what was erroneously termed Uganda.[76] In 1895, Parliament likewise established the East Africa Protectorate (later known as Kenya).

While the diplomats and statesmen pondered the future of Uganda, the soldiers on the spot had acted. The Christian Ganda, with British support, suppressed a rebellion by the Muslim Ganda that had spread from Buganda to Toro. In 1893, when the Nyoro army attacked Toro, forcing its ruler to flee into the nearby mountains, and another Nyoro army poised itself for an attack upon Busoga, British officers led a Ganda army into Bunyoro. After a prolonged war that laid waste to much of its heartland, the *omukama* Kabarega fled across the Nile, and Buganda emerged victorious. As a result, the Ganda thereafter occupied some of the richest agricultural lands of a shrunken Bunyoro—including the area in which its royal tombs lay; the British gave other parts of Bunyoro to Toro and again bolstered the fortunes of its ruler.[77]

In Buganda, the British administration backed the Christian oligarchy and eroded further the basis of Mwanga's traditional authority. The *kabaka* gradually became little more than a constitutional monarch.[78] He in turn fought a silent struggle against the British commissioners throughout 1896 and then, in mid 1897, fled from Mengo into Buddu. There he and his numerous sup-

[75] Text in Hertslet, *Map* (1896), III, pp. 995–997.

[76] James, *Rosebery*, pp. 284–285; Perham, *Lugard: The Years of Adventure*, pp. 451–457; A. J. P. Taylor, "Prelude to Fashoda: The Question of the Upper Nile, 1894–1895," *The English Historical Review*, LXV (1950), pp. 53–68.

[77] Henry Colvile, *The Land of the Nile Springs* (London, 1895), pp. 116–120 ff.; Mai Bovill and G. R. Askwith, *Roddy Owen* (London, 1897), pp. 85–148; J. W. Gregory, *The Foundation of British East Africa* (London, 1901), pp. 212–218; A. R. Dunbar, "The British and Bunyoro-Kitara, 1891 to 1899," *The Uganda Journal*, XXIV (1960), pp. 232–236.

[78] Marie de Kiewiet Hemphill, "The British Sphere, 1884–1894," in Roland Oliver and Gervase Mathew (eds.), *History of East Africa* (Oxford, 1963), I, p. 427.

porters battled fiercely against the troops of the Protectorate. But without the support of the Christian chiefs, who remained loyal to Britain, Mwanga soon found his mutinous position militarily untenable. After exiling him, the British administrator appointed Daudi Chwa, the *kabaka's* infant son, ruler of Buganda. During the minority of the new *kabaka,* a British commissioner governed Buganda with the assistance of three regents among whom Apolo Kagwa, the *katikiro,* or prime minister, exercised a predominant influence.

During the next few years, Britons subjugated most of the remainder of modern Uganda beyond Buganda. They concluded a number of treaties with the leaders of the Acholi and other peoples that carried the flag and guns of Britain as far as Fashoda. In Bunyoro, a British officer ruled absolutely and gave a number of new privileges to Ganda settlers. Semei Kakunguru, an outstanding Ganda general, had on his own behalf, and subsequently on behalf of Britain, begun to control large parts of the Teso and Lango countries. Only the Kiga in the far southwest, the Alur and the Bari across the Nile, and the Karamojong in the far northeast remained outside of the British sphere. By 1900, Britain had thus successfully "protected" most of Uganda.[79]

V. The Struggle for Northeastern Africa

In 1885, the Italian government, which already possessed a colony at Assab, gained control of Massawa on the Red Sea coast of Ethiopia. With British encouragement, its soldiers thereafter pushed inland across the hot desert toward the highland borders of Tigre, where Emperor Johannes IV reigned. Italian and French emissaries also contacted Menelik II, who ruled Shoa and expected to become emperor of Ethiopia after Johannes. Along the Adeni coast of Somalia, Britons simultaneously negotiated treaties with local sheikhs and, in 1887, officially "protected" the peoples of the region between the French sphere of influence, at Djibouti, and Bender Ziada to the east.

The foreign powers threatened to encircle Ethiopia. Emperor Johannes, whose position in Tigre seemed vulnerable, appreciated the extent to which these new pressures mortgaged the future of his country. The Italians had occupied Massawa without his leave. They had also advanced toward his capital of Adowa, near historic Axum, in a manner that belied their peaceful overtures. In 1887, an Italian military detachment marched up-country to relieve a small party of "scientists" who had been imprisoned in Tigre. It failed, however, to repeat General Sir Robert Napier's success at Magdala; this time, in an engagement at Dogali, the Ethiopian army overwhelmed the foreign host, killed most of the invaders, and drove the remainder back to Massawa. Johannes knew that the Italians would return; he had, however, won a considerable reprieve.[80] In the

[79] H. B. Thomas, "Capax Imperii: The Story of Semei Kakunguru," *The Uganda Journal,* VI (1939), pp. 125–136; J. C. D. Lawrance, "A History of Teso to 1937," *ibid.,* XIX (1955), pp. 20–25.

[80] Gerald H. Portal, *My Mission to Abyssinia* (London, 1892), pp. 157–162; Sven Rubenson, "Some Aspects of the Survival of Ethiopian Independence in the Period of the Scramble for Africa," in *Historians in Tropical Africa,* pp. 258–259.

interim, the discomforted Italians attempted to intrigue with Menelik. He, in turn, took their bribes and kept their guns, but refused to join the Italians in combat against his emperor.

Johannes and Ethiopia next faced the threat of an invasion by the Sudanese, their traditional enemies. In 1885, after the death of the Mahdi, his various followers had reluctantly recognized the supreme leadership of Khalifa 'Abdallahi, who commanded the armies of Baqqari nomads and had served as the Mahdi's administrative vizier. With consummate skill, he outwitted his rivals, many of whom represented the Mahdi's own kin, and consolidated his position among the Ansar, as the mass of the Mahdist revolutionaries were known. At the same time, 'Abdallahi attempted to complete the work of the Mahdi by extending the rule of purified Islam—the Mahdiya—throughout the remainder of northeastern Africa. In 1887, his armies overcame a revolt by the Fur and pacified the province of Darfur. A year later, Abu Jummayza, another messianic figure, claimed to be a khalifa worthy of succession to the Mahdi's authority. Only after he succumbed to smallpox could the army of the recognized khalifa re-impose its mandate in the troubled province.[81]

During this period of warfare in the western areas of the Sudan, hostilities of a traditional kind continued along the marches of Ethiopia. In 1887, Ethiopian troops based in Amhara defeated the Ansar, who were stationed in Gallabat, an outpost across the border in the Sudan. To avenge this defeat, 'Abdallahi sent reinforcements who succeeded in pillaging western Amhara and in penetrating as far into Ethiopia as Gondar. Two years later, after 'Abdallahi had refused to treat for peace with Emperor Johannes, the Christian and Muslim armies prepared for war. Johannes personally led his troops to Gallabat, where the Ethiopians initially appeared to possess the advantage. A Mahdist gunman fatally wounded the emperor, however, and the Ethiopians, dismayed, gave the victory to the Sudanese. Emboldened, the Ansar attempted in the following months, on the distant northern front, to conquer Egypt. But near Tushki on the Nile, an Anglo-Egyptian force ended such Sudanese pretensions forever. And in the east, the Mahdist forces under 'Uthman Diqna repeatedly failed to take Suakin from its British defenders; indeed, to add to the humiliation of their defeat at Tushki, the Sudanese soldiery, in 1891, lost a decisive battle near the Red Sea to an Anglo-Egyptian detachment under the command of Colonel Herbert Horatio Kitchener. He successfully opened up a second front and permanently put the followers of 'Abdallahi on the defensive.[82]

The unexpected death of Johannes had meanwhile caused consternation in Ethiopia. With Italian diplomatic support, and by demonstrating the prowess of his Shoan army, Menelik had succeeded to the throne of Ethiopia despite the pretensions of Ras Mangasha of Tigre, Johannes' deathbed nominee. Afterwards, since Shoa was far from Massawa and was within Mangasha's natural hinterland, Menelik accepted Italy's colonial ambitions in the Asmara highlands.

---

[81] Peter M. Holt, *The Mahdist State in the Sudan, 1881–1898* (Oxford, 1958), pp. 136–140.
[82] *Ibid.*, p. 173.

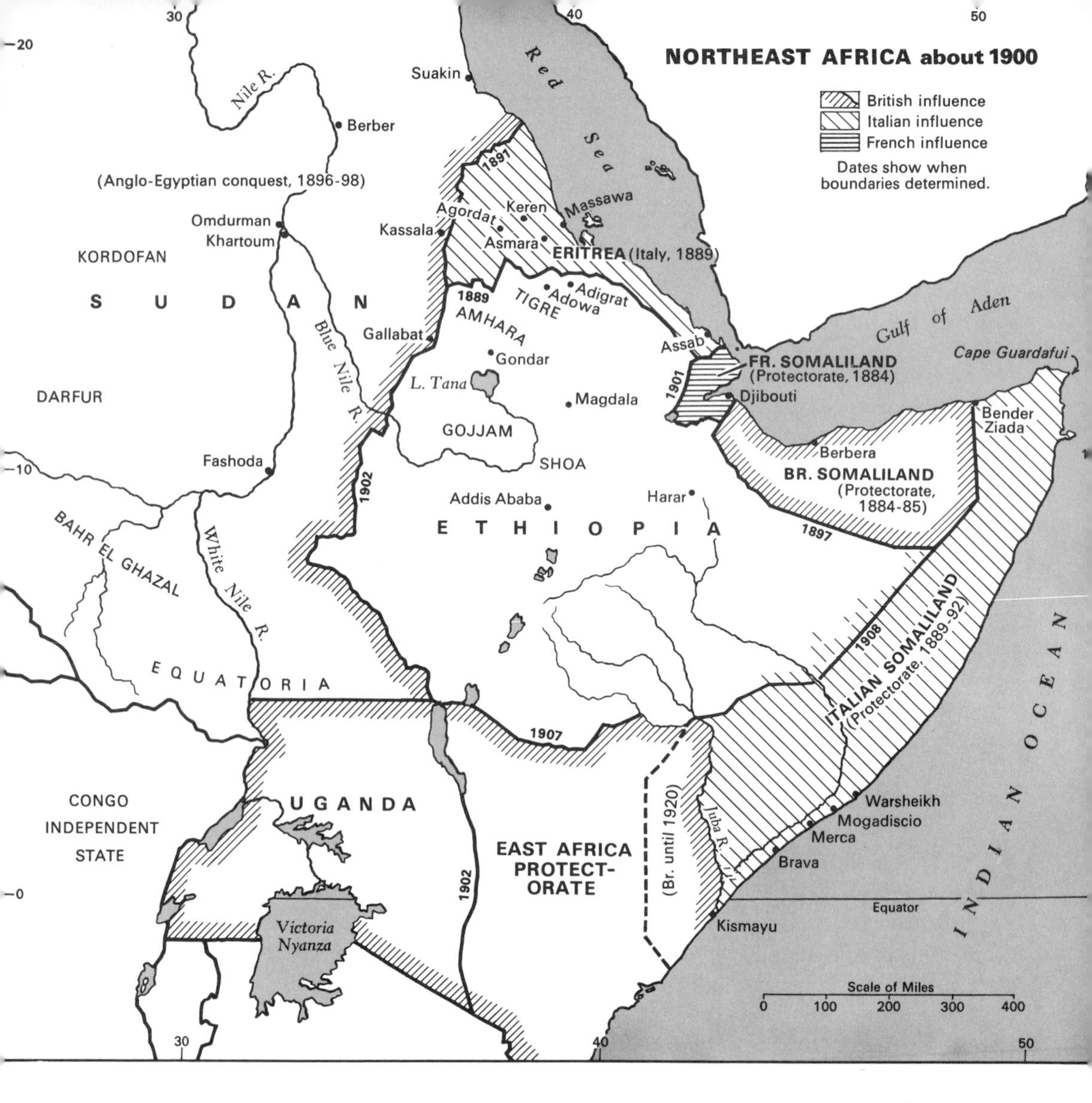

To his later annoyance, he also signed the Treaty of Wichale (Ucciali), which, in an article of its Amharic version, stated no more than that the emperor *might* conduct his foreign relations through the offices of the Italian government. The Italian text, however, allowed the government of Italy to assert that it *had* acquired a protectorate over all of Ethiopia.[83]

The Italians proceeded to occupy the area along the Red Sea that they named Eritrea. With little opposition, they tied Assab to Massawa, took Keren and Agordat, and approached Axum. Although irrelevant to Menelik and to their specific strategy in Ethiopia as well, the Italians, by agreement with the

[83] Sven Rubenson, "The Protectorate Paragraph of the Wichale Treaty," *The Journal of African History*, V (1964), pp. 243–282.

Menelik, emperor of Ethiopia, photographed about 1900.
(Bettmann Archive)

sultan of Zanzibar and the Imperial British East Africa Company, had also acquired control over the Benadir Somali towns of Warsheikh, Mogadiscio, Merca, and Brava, and had obtained a foothold in Kismayu. In 1889, agreements made with several important sultans gave the Italians additional influence in northern Somalia.[84]

By 1891, the Italian flag fluttered over most of the port towns between Cape Guardafui and the Juba River. Within another three years, the Italians had also implanted it in the Sudan. There, since 1891, 'Abdallahi had ruled autocratically and without serious challengers over the Mahdist Sudan. But in 1893, his commander in the east miscalculated and attacked Eritrea. At Agordat, his troops fell easily before the Italians, who soon pressed their advantage and, in 1894, occupied Kassala, a garrison town across the Sudanese border.[85] Europeans, some of whom were also active in the distant, disaffected provinces of Bahr el Ghazal and Equatoria, once again poised themselves for the reconquest.

The Italians had meanwhile exhausted the patience of Menelik. In 1893, perhaps at the instigation of his French advisors, Menelik denounced the Treaty of Wichale. During the next year, Eritrean allies of Mangasha revolted against the Italians; after quelling several similar manifestations of discontent, the

[84] Hertslet, *Map* (1896), III, pp. 1123–1124.
[85] For the khalifa's reaction to the loss of Kassala, see Slatin, *Fire and Sword*, pp. 504–506.

Italians carried their campaign into Tigre. Mangasha pleaded for peace, but the Italians instead occupied Adigrat, on the road to Adowa. At this juncture, Menelik and Mangasha resolved their differences. Throughout most of 1895, they prepared for the continuation of the Italian campaign. Under one banner, Menelik gathered the soldiers of Shoa, Harar, Tigre, and Gojjam, and the Galla cavalry.

Oreste Baratieri, the Italian general, underestimated Ethiopian strength. His own men numbered only 20,000 compared to the 100,000 or more that Menelik had at his disposal. Baratieri also failed to remember the cannon and guns that successive Italian governments had given to Menelik, and he and his generals lacked an adequate knowledge of the terrain over which they fought. Their intelligence lacked precision generally, and their scouts reported hearsay and obscured fact. When the Italian army finally attacked Adowa in 1896, it suffered a calamitous defeat. About eight thousand Italians and four thousand African *askari*, or soldiers, lost their lives.[86] Italy annulled the pact of Wichale, recognized the independence of Ethiopia and, surprisingly, was allowed to retain Eritrea. Together with emissaries from other countries of Europe, the Italians thereafter paid court to Menelik in his new capital of Addis Ababa.

Menelik's victory at Adowa precipitated the Anglo-Egyptian campaign that resulted in time in the fall of Omdurman.[87] In the spring of 1896, Kitchener, who had anxiously awaited the moment when he might lead a reconquest, started up the Nile from Wadi Halfa at the head of a large, well-disciplined army and a corps of engineers that constructed a railway as the troops rapidly pushed the badly organized Sudanese defenders back toward the great bend of the Nile River. Dongola province soon fell to the invaders; by autumn Kitchener's column had penetrated almost to the Fourth Cataract. During 1897, the invaders constructed another supporting rail line across the desert from Wadi Halfa to Abu Hamed. In that year, after disaffected Ansar had revolted in a number of different centers north of Omdurman, the Anglo-Egyptian army occupied Berber and thereafter easily controlled the Nile from Berber more than half of the distance to Omdurman. At al-Rajjaf, a Belgian force almost simultaneously routed the last of the Ansar in the far south. At this time, a shortage of grain limited the effectiveness of 'Abdallahi's troops. Furthermore, for several years, and particularly since the defeat at Kassala, his authoritarian régime had lost much of its popular appeal. No longer did the Ansar exhibit the fanatic fortitude that had carried them to victory under the Mahdi.

In 1898, the Mahdiya finally succumbed to the forces of internal division and external determination. In the autumn of the year, after 'Abdallahi had failed to utilize his remaining strategic advantages, the large Anglo-Egyptian army, supported by three new gunboats, advanced unhindered up the Nile. Its cannon bombarded the town of Omdurman, and its machine guns slaughtered

---

[86] Cf. George F-H. Berkeley, *The Campaign of Adowa and the Rise of Menelik* (London, 1902), pp. 261–347.

[87] See J. A. S. Grenville, *Lord Salisbury and Foreign Policy: The Close of the Nineteenth Century* (London, 1964), pp. 115–120.

the Ansar in a decisive battle at Karai, north of 'Abdallahi's capital. Eleven thousand Sudanese lost their lives, sixteen thousand lay wounded, while fewer than one hundred of the attackers suffered death or injury. The British soon occupied Omdurman, and Kitchener, after he had successfully disputed with Marchand at Fashoda, began to rule the Sudan in accord with the Anglo-Egyptian condominium agreements. In 1899, the Khalifa 'Abdallahi, who had fled after the fall of Omdurman to rally a small army of followers, finally lost his life in a battle against a British force near Aba Island, where the Mahdi had originally preached his *jihad*.[88]

---

[88] A. B. Theobald, *The Mahdiya: A History of the Anglo-Egyptian Sudan, 1881–1899* (London, 1951), pp. 189–236; Ronald Wingate, *Wingate of the Sudan: The Life and Times of General Sir Reginald Wingate* (London, 1955), pp. 105–126; G. N. Sanderson, "Contributions from African Sources to the Military and Diplomatic History of European Competition in the Upper Valley of the Nile," in *Historians in Tropical Africa*, pp. 235–243.

From Negrophobism, colour prejudice, oppression and deceit, Good Lord Deliver Us.

—The Times of Nigeria, *March 24, 1914*

THE CONSOLIDATION OF THE COLONIAL INITIATIVE, 1891–1918

9

At the beginning of the twentieth century, the body of tropical Africa lay divided into colonies, protectorates, enclaves, and the two independent states of Ethiopia and Liberia. By then, white foreigners had either demarcated or accepted the borders between these entities; within each of the dependencies, they had subdued African defenders and had forcefully asserted their own claims to rule. On or near the coasts, they had already introduced Africans to the concepts and demands of their sovereignty. But in the interior, European control remained essentially *ad hoc* and, for the most part, superficial. Both the new and the old colonial powers thus concerned themselves essentially with the extension of their individual African frontiers and with the consolidation, and further elaboration, of their existing, if ambiguous, positions of power. Throughout, these concerns remained uppermost in the official minds of imperialism. Africans, who themselves cared deeply about their own fates, meanwhile continued for the most part to resist European-sponsored change and, in whatever ways they could, attempted to maintain the integrity of their own societies. This confrontation of European and African imperatives occupied the remainder of the colonial period.

In governing their new African dependencies, the main colonial powers followed no set pattern. The nature of the particular conquest, the length of association between mother country and colony, the national goals involved, the initial response of the indigenous inhabitants, the presence or absence of easily exploited tropical products, the suitability of the climate and terrain for settlers, and the predilections of the first administrative "men on the spot" all conditioned the ways in which Europeans began or continued to rule tropical Africa. In response to these variables, their approach expressed a variety of social philosophies. National notions of law, representation, property, and justice further differentiated colonies; only some of the powers viewed their role in a basically custodial and tutorial light. Some, particularly the ones that governed territories where an indigenous elite—whether Westernized or traditional—had long existed, recognized the ultimate legitimacy of African aspirations and allowed their own internal policies to follow lines that contributed, if inadvertently, to the rise of nationalism.

I. The French Colonial System

France made of its vast West and Equatorial African empire two centrally run federations. From their respective capitals of Dakar and Brazzaville, two governors-general and subordinate colonial governors ruled the indigenous inhabitants of these federations in accord with integrated policies enunciated in Paris and interpreted in Africa.[1] As this system of government developed, it provided for the direct administration of the peoples of the interior by officials who expected to transform their African wards into loyal black Frenchmen. In the selection of chiefs, for example, tribal legitimacy mattered less than an ability to speak and write French and to understand French administrative procedures. Indeed, in most areas the chiefs occupied administrative positions clearly subordinate to those of the French officers serving there. A decree promulgated in 1912 promised to grant French citizenship to those West Africans who approached the French in education, adopted their civilization and customs, or distinguished themselves by service to the state.[2] But few Africans either "assimilated" or "associated" themselves in this way immediately, and during the ten years after 1912, fewer than one hundred Africans took advantage of the naturalization provisions of the law.

By contrast, the indigenous inhabitants of urban Senegal had long possessed substantive rights. Under the Second Republic, they elected a deputy to the French National Assembly. After the fall of the Second Empire, the government of the Third Republic restored this privilege and conferred political and civil rights identical to those possessed by the residents of municipalities in metropolitan France upon the people who lived within the four communes of Saint-Louis, Gorée, Rufisque, and Dakar. Indeed, in 1914 the voters of Senegal elected Blaise Diagne, an African customs official, to the National Assembly and re-elected him for many years thereafter. With their support, Diagne also became the mayor of Dakar and the leader of the first modern political organization in French West Africa.[3] For the most part, however, he eschewed nationalism and accepted the full logic of assimilation.

---

[1] See Colin W. Newbury, "The Formation of the Government General of French West Africa," *The Journal of African History*, I (1960), pp. 115–117; Raymond Leslie Buell, *The Native Problem in Africa* (New York, 1928), II, pp. 115–130.

[2] For general discussions of the French policies of assimilation and association, see Raymond Betts, *Assimilation and Association in French Colonial Theory, 1890–1914* (New York, 1961), pp. 10–32, 106–132; Martin Deming Lewis, "One Hundred Million Frenchmen: The 'Assimilation' Theory in French Colonial Policy," *Comparative Studies in Society and History*, IV (1962), pp. 149–152; Arthur Girault, *Principes de colonisation et de législation coloniale* (Paris, 1927), II, pp. 571–576. See also Michael Crowder, "Indirect Rule, French and British Style," *Africa*, XXXIV (1964), pp. 200–203.

[3] Kenneth Robinson, "Senegal: The Elections to the Territorial Assembly, March 1957," in W. J. M. Mackenzie and Kenneth Robinson (eds.), *Five Elections in Africa* (Oxford, 1960),

Side by side with their attempt to introduce unified administrative methods into the interior of their empire, the French continued the conquest that they had begun during the period of the European partition. Between 1904 and 1910, they added Mauritania and the northern portions of modern Mali and Niger to their West African Federation. In campaigns that lasted until 1916, the French army finally humbled the peoples of the Ivory Coast and Guinée. Similarly, in Equatoria French soldiers forcibly asserted their authority over tribesmen who lived along the Sangha River in the Moyen Congo and Ubangi-Chari. Between 1909 and 1912, they overcame the resistance of the inhabitants of the eastern area of what has since become the Central African Republic. In southern Chad, the French gradually usurped the powers of the sultans of Bagirmi and Wadai. Between 1909 and 1919, they also fought the powerful Sanusi of Cyrenaica for control of the Bourkou, Ennedi, and Tibesti regions of northern Chad. Only after World War I, when the Italians conquered Cyrenaica, could the French finally pacify Tibesti, the most remote of these three territories, and thus complete their occupation of Equatorial Africa.[4]

The French had coveted the wealth of Africa, but their colonies contained few mineral resources. Administrators therefore attempted instead to exploit the potential agricultural riches of their domains. Unhappily, while parts of Equatoria appeared comparatively lush, French West Africa contained lands in the interior of low carrying capacity and a potentially productive coastal forest belt capable of being exploited only if cultivated skillfully. Moreover, the population of French West Africa was comparatively small, and there seemed little likelihood that whites could be encouraged to settle in any numbers. For these reasons, the French colonial machine subordinated the economic program of its different parts to an overall plan; each colony grew for commercial sale only what the government-general thought that it could sell most profitably.

Governors delegated to Africans the production of the raw materials that could be both consumed in France and sold for foreign exchange. Their administrations forcibly conscripted labor for use on private plantations in West Africa. In Equatoria, even before the end of the nineteenth century, the French government had alienated much of Gabon, the Moyen Congo, and Ubangi-Chari to private concessionaires. In return for the payment of a rental fee and a percentage of their gross profits, the government of France gave to these private concerns the freedom to exploit the entire agricultural, animal, forest, and industrial wealth of their respective regions. By the terms of the grants, African produce belonged to the companies in whose concessions it was grown. Moreover, Africans could "legally" sell tropical products only at the artificial prices set by whites. The government of French Equatorial Africa also taxed

---

pp. 306–307; André Villard, *Histoire du Sénégal* (Dakar, 1943), p. 179; Pierre Mille, "The 'Black Vote' in Senegal," *Journal of the African Society*, I (1901), p. 75.

[4] For a detailed account of the pacification, see Auguste Terrier, "Afrique équatoriale française," in Gabriel Hanotaux and Alfred Martineau (eds.), *Histoire des colonies françaises et de l'expansion de la France dans le monde* (Paris, 1931), IV, pp. 540–541.

its subjects in order to encourage them to work for the concessionaires. (The concessionaires provided a source of cash with which to pay the tax collector.)

Whenever Africans refused to carry ivory or gather rubber for foreign entrepreneurs, government officials and company agents used force to persuade them to cooperate. Frenchmen incarcerated Africans without water or food, held their wives and children hostage, and frequently used whips and guns to damaging effect. In the process, numerous Africans lost their lives. These methods helped most of the companies to operate their concessions profitably. But they also incurred the wrath of the indigenous people.

Revolts followed. From the banks of the Ogooué to the shores of the Ubangi, Africans killed whites indiscriminately. Along the upper Chari River, Africans displayed their dissatisfaction with white enterprise by stuffing the skulls of dead traders with rubber.[5] Following an investigation by Savorgnan de Brazza, the government of France finally agreed to supervise the activities of the concession companies more closely. It also reorganized the administration of its equatorial possessions. But as far as the mass of the Africans could see, their own conditions of life improved little.

II. The British in West Africa

Compared to the French, the British approached colonial problems pragmatically. Although the Colonial Office in London provided its overseas representatives with general policy guidelines, the "men on the spot" often modified or interpreted these directives to suit their peculiar local situations. Indeed, the actions of British governors usually developed primarily as responses to the pressure of events. As a result, each of the British dependencies assumed a largely idiosyncratic character.

In West Africa, the Gambia, Sierra Leone, the Gold Coast, Southern Nigeria, and Northern Nigeria usually went their separate ways. Yet during the earliest years of the colonial period, British officials in each of these places attempted to make of their disjointed possessions an integrated, viable colony of the Crown. They occupied their respective hinterlands, subdued resentful Africans, introduced patterns of administration later labeled direct and indirect, built railways and, in order to satisfy the British Treasury, tried to defray the cost of their activities by raising revenues locally. In Sierra Leone, after it had signed border agreements with France and Liberia, the British government unilaterally annexed a rich inland area to its old, impoverished coastal colony. In 1896, Britain thus created a new protectorate. Within it, comparatively few Britons and a number of indigenous chiefs governed. Later, in order to support its activities, the British régime taxed the inhabitants of the Sierra Leone Protectorate and, in 1898, provoked a war that broke out in the Mende, Bulom, and Krim countries. More than one thousand Creole traders and white missionaries

[5] Jules Lefébure, *Le Régime des concessions au Congo* (Paris, 1904), pp. 101–114; Félicien Challaye, *Le Congo français: la question internationale du Congo* (Paris, 1909), pp. 101–236; A. H. Savage Landor, *Across Widest Africa* (London, 1907), II, pp. 103–109.

lost their lives before British troops could restore order, capture the leading chiefs (including Bai Bureh), and restore British authority up-country.[6]

The government of Sierra Leone thereafter rigorously introduced the peoples of the new Protectorate to the elements and form of British administration and justice. It created a number of new districts, over which white officers presided. More than their predecessors, they controlled the chiefs and gradually eliminated overt centers of disaffection while ensuring the regular collection of the disliked tax on an individual's huts. At the same time, the government of Sierra Leone constructed a railway from Freetown to Bo and Pendembu in order to "open up" the interior to commerce and provide an outlet for the export of its palm products. At Bo, it also opened an important school. In a sense, the railway linked the Protectorate economically to the Colony; but commercial and political integration followed only after World War I, when Africans first began to influence the affairs of the Colony significantly.

In the Gold Coast, Britons had begun to administer the conquered areas of Ashanti and the Northern Territories in ways that would have seemed familiar to the peoples of Sierra Leone and the Gambia. In the coastal areas of the Colony, however, the relations between African subjects and their foreign rulers had become increasingly complicated. During the last years of the nineteenth century, the indigenous intelligentsia, many of whose members had long played a prominent part in the government and development of the Gold Coast, sensed a change in their relations with the leading British officials of the Colony. Whereas Africans had once filled many of the senior positions in the government, Britons had begun to ease these same Africans out of their jobs. The administration failed to advance educated Africans to positions of authority; there seemed a new, to them "unnatural," bar between the "native" and the "European" branches of the civil service.[7] The local Legislative Council, while it contained African members throughout this period, remained—like nearly all similar deliberative bodies in Britain's African empire—essentially impotent.[8] At the same time, its mere existence and the possibility of its further transformation into a true representative assembly inspired and focused the aspirations of those many African lawyers and businessmen who wanted desperately to participate in the modernization of their country. They tried, despite some opposition from local Britons, to organize themselves at the municipal level.

Throughout the early colonial period, the Gold Coast Aborigines' Rights Protection Society expressed the grievances of Africans. It had been formed in 1897 by Joseph W. de Graft-Johnson, James Mensah Sarbah, Chief J. D.

---

[6] David Chalmers, *Report by Her Majesty's Commissioner and Correspondence on the Subject of the Insurrection in the Sierra Leone Protectorate, Minutes and Evidence*, Cmd. 9388, 9391 (1899), pp. 50–51; John D. Hargreaves, "The Establishment of the Sierra Leone Protectorate and the Insurrection of 1898," *The Cambridge Historical Journal*, XII (1956), pp. 56–80.

[7] David Kimble, *A Political History of Ghana: The Rise of Gold Coast Nationalism, 1850–1928* (Oxford, 1963), pp. 94–100.

[8] Martin Wight, *The Gold Coast Legislative Council* (London, 1947), pp. 21–26.

Abraham, and a number of other prominent residents of Cape Coast and Axim in order that they might oppose more effectively the promulgation of legislation that threatened to deprive the inhabitants of the Gold Coast of their land. Chiefs also supported the Society. Its agitation, and the protests of British firms, won the day. Thereafter, the Society continued to keep a sharp watch for legislation that might prove inimical to Africans. It fought the application of municipal rates to Sekondi and Cape Coast, defeated an ordinance that apparently affected indigenous land rights, and generally mobilized public opinion whenever the white-run government threatened to deny to Africans the privileges that they had long enjoyed. Generally, the Society attempted to promote "right understanding" and to be the means of communication between the government and the people. It also wanted to educate its members, chiefs, and Britons about the way in which mutually advantageous ties between the two countries had developed.[9] In a real sense, the Society represented merely one of the earliest of a number of voluntary associations formed for limited political purposes in nearly all of the British African colonies. Other, more militant groups soon succeeded it.

Despite politics, neither Africans nor Britons had neglected to develop the Gold Coast economically. During the late nineteenth century, missionaries and Africans first began to plant cacao trees there. It seemed an ideal smallholder's crop, requiring modest capital and a good supply of patience rather than intensive cultivation. In 1885, the Colony exported five long tons; by 1900, more than two hundred long tons of cocoa left the country. During the next fifteen years, production soared and firms based in the Gold Coast sold about fifty thousand tons on the world market. Africans also gathered rubber and continued to mine gold profitably. In order to further the exploitation of gold as well as manganese and diamonds, the government constructed the Gold Coast's first railway from Sekondi to Tarkwa, which was located in the center of the mining area. Later the railway also helped to transport harvested cocoa from Kumasi, the Ashanti capital, to the coast.[10]

After the conquest of Northern Nigeria, Sir Frederick (later Lord) Lugard brought to the organization of its government an administrative philosophy that later guided the efforts of Britons almost everywhere in tropical Africa. Essentially, in the interests of efficiency he superimposed an alien superstructure onto the existing foundations of indigenous authority. Lugard assumed the powers of the Sarkin Musulmi but chose to support the traditional authority of the various subordinate Fulani emirs within their own provinces. But in order to supervise and guide each of these emirs, Lugard installed British residents, most of whom were first recruited from the ranks of the British army and later from the universities. They preserved law and order—their "first duty consisted

[9] Kimble, *Political History of Ghana*, p. 362.

[10] Polly Hill, *The Gold Coast Cocoa Farmer* (London, 1956), pp. 40–47, 103–113; *The Gold Coast Handbook* (London, 1937), p. 38; G. Keith Allen, "Gold Mining in Ghana," *African Affairs*, LVII (1958), pp. 224–240.

in seeing that the Emirs and Chiefs and native officials carried out their administrative duties with justice and without oppression." [11]

Residents personally tried offenders, commanded the civil police and the jailors, and dealt with a number of other, seemingly extraneous matters, such as the regulation of prices in local markets. They organized and ran the provincial post offices, took the census, and surveyed the land. Lugard also hoped that the residents would promote trade, encourage modern methods of agriculture, and prevent the misuse of the forests. In addition, he expected from his residents a mass of routine, detailed reports. Thus the residents carried what eventually seemed an intolerable burden. Reluctantly, Lugard therefore decided to permit them to share a greater proportion of their many responsibilities with the emirs. At this time, he also drafted the detailed memoranda that explained and later served as the scriptures of "indirect rule." To Lugard, indirect rule seemed a necessary expedient; by using the authority inherent in traditional institutions, his administration could conserve scarce colonial funds and make the best use of a very few, overworked British officials.[12]

In the south, Britain at first generally refused to experiment with such *ad hoc* administrative measures. In 1906, after joining the old colony of Lagos to the Protectorate of Southern Nigeria, it divided the territory of Southern Nigeria into three provinces, and subsequently ruled the new central and eastern regions in the usual direct way. In the east, British-led soldiers also subdued the last pockets of African resistance to white rule. But in the western region, where the Yoruba-speaking people lived, the government ruled through the chiefs. Indeed, the Egba continued to regard themselves as independent. Their government in Abeokuta exercised a large measure of local autonomy, dispensed justice in accord with its own system of values, and levied and spent its own taxes. In this way, it appeared to threaten the paramountcy of British interests in Nigeria.[13]

The existence of the two separate administrative entities of Northern and Southern Nigeria reflected British experiences during the period of the European partition. In the twentieth century, however, the red line that encompassed the king of England's largest chunk of West Africa encouraged cooperation and unity. Both Nigerias shared customs revenues and common rail and river transport, and drew upon the same pool of troops. Unification made administrative and financial sense, and the British Treasury naturally welcomed an opportunity to saddle the comparatively wealthy south with the deficit-ridden north. It also assumed that a single Nigerian government would be less costly to run.

In 1912, the British government called Lugard back from Hong Kong, where he had governed since 1906, to merge Northern and Southern Nigeria.[14] With

---

[11] Charles W. J. Orr, *The Making of Northern Nigeria* (London, 1911), p. 137.
[12] Margery Perham, *Native Administration in Nigeria* (London, 1937), pp. 43–60.
[13] Ajayi Kolawole Ajisafe, *History of Abeokuta* (Bungay, Eng., 1924), pp. 187–195.
[14] See Lord Louis Harcourt, in *Parliamentary Debates*, June 27, 1913, quoted in Margery Perham, *Lugard: The Years of Authority* (London, 1960), p. 418.

characteristic industry, he devised a scheme of amalgamation and, in 1914, unified the country. Thereafter, he visited the outlying districts, planned wholesale reforms in the south, cleverly stretched his limited funds, and wrote endless memoranda on a variety of subjects. The customs, rail, telegraph, and postal systems received a common direction. But to the detriment of thoroughgoing unity, Lugard preserved the separate administrative services and practices of the north and the south. In the south, he also ignored the treaty of 1893 and brought the Egba unreservedly under the government of Nigeria.[15] He likewise terminated agreements made by his predecessors with the neighboring kingdoms of Yorubaland. In the east, he instructed his subordinates to find and make new chiefs where none had ever existed.

Lugard changed Nigeria's hitherto sacrosanct judicial system. He reduced the jurisdiction of the Lagos Supreme Court and, despite the vehement opposition of African and British barristers, substituted "political" for "professional" justice in the rural areas of Southern Nigeria. He replaced judges with administrative officers who, at the provincial level, henceforth combined, as they long had in the north, the roles of prosecutor, attorney for the defense (defendants were not allowed to employ counsel), and magistrate. These same officials also supervised the "native courts" over which traditional chiefs presided. By giving the chiefs such responsibility, Lugard hoped "to create the rudiments of law and order, to inculcate a sense of responsibility, and [to] evolve among a primitive community some sense of discipline and respect for authority." [16] Whether or not he succeeded, his philosophy of justice exerted a strong influence upon all of the other British African colonies.

Lugard believed that the "primary function of education should . . . be to fit the ordinary individual to fill a useful part in his environment . . . and to ensure that the exceptional individual shall use his abilities for the advancement of the community and not . . . to the subversion of constituted authority." [17] The paucity of educational opportunities for Nigerians consequently appalled him. In the south, less than 1 percent of the school-age population attended class.[18] He therefore encouraged Christian missionary groups to increase the number of their teaching institutions. He urged them to improve the quality of the generally lamentable "bush" schools. He also supported a government secondary school in Lagos. But his attempt to educate the people of the north foundered upon the shoals of indirect rule. His subordinates, entrenched as they were in isolated emirates, wanted to resist the changes that widespread schooling might bring. Perhaps even more fervidly than the emirs themselves, they feared that the creation of an indigenous intelligentsia might eventually subvert what seemed to them a perfectly stable, ideally arranged society. A few schools there were, but they for long remained isolated oases in the desert of

---

[15] Ajisafe, *Abeokuta*, pp. 238–240; Perham, *Lugard: The Years of Authority*, pp. 436, 450.

[16] Quoted in Perham, *Lugard: The Years of Authority*, p. 462. See also William Nevill Montgomerie Geary, *Nigeria Under British Rule* (London, 1927), p. 270.

[17] Quoted in Perham, *Lugard: The Years of Authority*, p. 491.

[18] James Coleman, *Nigeria: Background to Nationalism* (Berkeley, 1960), p. 94.

traditionalism. Despite Lugard, Nigeria thus stayed unified more in name than in common experience.

Lugard contributed the philosophy and machinery of indirect rule to the development of Nigeria and, in large part, to all of British Africa. He introduced it in Northern Nigeria and, during the period of his governor-generalship, tried to make it work equally well in the south. But among the Yoruba- and Ibo-speaking peoples, these concepts never found favor. In particular, they resisted the regular collection of taxes—an essential element in the apparatus of indirect rule. In 1916, and again in 1918, the people of Iseyin, Lagos, and Abeokuta rioted. The educated elite protested verbally. The Nigerian "yellow press" continually excoriated Lugard. Not all of his reforms and innovations stood the test of time and the predilections of his successors during the "administrative interlude." But the content of his experiences in Nigeria influenced an entire generation of British colonial administrators and, by default, generations of Africans as well.

III. The German Régime

In the years after 1900, the Germans devoted themselves energetically to the development of their tropical African possessions. Except in northern Cameroun, where Fulani emirs retained much of their power, German officers and their appointed African assistants briskly administered Togo, Cameroun, and

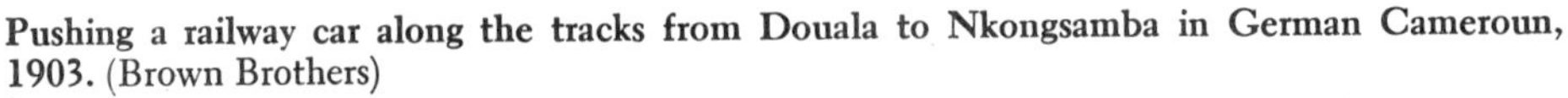

Pushing a railway car along the tracks from Douala to Nkongsamba in German Cameroun, 1903. (Brown Brothers)

Tanganyika as conquered provinces of the empire. Like many of their British and French counterparts, these agents of government tried cases between Africans, maintained order, recruited and transported labor to the main centers of employment and, in general, directly supervised the various affairs of their individual districts. In Togo, the German government also appointed senior chiefs to oversee groups of headmen who had previously recognized no superior indigenous authority. As employes of the administration, these chiefs also heard civil disputes and conscripted labor for road-building and other rural improvement projects. In the process, customary law became subordinate at every level to German civil and criminal codes. The government also instituted "improvement camps" to punish those Togolese who resisted the increasingly heavy hand of the German occupation. In Tanganyika and Cameroun, Africans similarly resented the obligation of compulsory labor and the imposition of alien laws and new tax obligations. In Cameroun, while the German government outlawed "barbarous" customs, it allowed African levies to keep the women that they captured in combat. At least during the period of the governorship of Jesko von Puttkamer, the administration also sanctioned regular extramarital relations between European men and African women. According to Puttkamer, this practice "kept a girl out of a cruel harem, made her envied by other native women, gave her a good living, and made for friendly relations between whites and natives." [19]

In general, the Germans abused Africans. In Cameroun, they shanghaied laborers, shackled them together, and marched them long distances to work for whites. Then the laborers succumbed to disease, overwork, lack of food, or excessive discipline in such numbers that the government eventually suggested that plantation managers provide their own cemeteries for Africans. Porters also complained that whites compelled them to carry too much too often, and to work without remuneration or any provision of food and water along the route of their march. Tanganyikans told similar tales.

In West Africa, a great expansion of trade followed the extension of German administration to the peoples of the interior. The Germans cut footpaths and, after 1905, motor roads between the Camerounian coast and the important centers of inland commerce. At a high cost in African lives, they built railways between Douala and Nkongsamba and Douala and the Njong River,[20] and from Lomé, the capital of Togo, to Atakpamé and Palimé up-country. Both areas provided palm oil and palm kernels. In Cameroun, the administration also extorted Africans to gather wild rubber and carry ivory. But cultivated crops gradually occupied a more important place on the list of agricultural exports. In Togo, where the government urged Africans to diversify, smallholders began to grow coffee, cocoa, coconuts, maize, and cotton.[21] In Cameroun, by the eve of World War I, nearly two hundred whites employed almost eighteen thou-

[19] Jesko von Puttkamer to Hohenlohe, December 7, 1896, quoted in Harry R. Rudin, *Germans in the Cameroons, 1884–1914* (London, 1938), pp. 304–305.
[20] For figures, see *ibid.*, pp. 91, 237, 241.
[21] See Colin Newbury, *The Western Slave Coast and Its Rulers* (Oxford, 1961), pp. 176–177.

sand Africans on plantations along the fertile, well-watered lower slopes of Mount Cameroons. There they grew cacao, kola, and rubber, the colony's most important export, and unsuccessfully experimented with cotton, tobacco, ramie (a fibrous plant), and coffee. Even so, only Togo produced profits for Germany; by comparison Cameroun, with its comparatively extensive school system and communications network, always remained a drain on the imperial treasury.

The African inhabitants of Togo, Cameroun, and Tanganyika reacted coldly to the oppressive features of German colonial rule. In the late 1890's, Togolese fought unsuccessfully on two important occasions to oust their conquerors. In Cameroun, sporadic warfare between 1888 and 1914 testified to the continuity of African discontent. Only Tanganyika, however, experienced a full-scale uprising. By the end of 1904, dissatisfaction there seemed general. Africans resented the imposition of taxes and the regular use of harsh methods to recruit labor. Encouraged by medicine men, who agitated against European domination and persuaded their compatriots to drink potions that reputedly turned the bullets fired by white men into water (*maji*), the various peoples of southern Tanganyika made a bold attempt to reclaim their freedom. In 1905, the spark of the "Maji-Maji" war ignited the villages in the Matumbi Hills of the Rufiji district. Soon the contagion spread to Morogoro and Mahenge in the north and west, and southward to Liwale, where a group of German missionaries lost their lives. The rebels cut telegraph lines and occupied Lindi and Kilwa Kivinje. Terming themselves *askari ya mungu*, the soldiers of God, they demonstrated in Bagamoyo and threatened Dar es Salaam on the coast, besieged Mahenge and Songea in the far interior, destroyed mission stations in the south, and burned Kilosa, the former German capital.

For a time, the *askari ya mungu*, who included in their number members of different tribal groups, effectively eliminated the hated German overrule in a large part of strife-torn southern Tanganyika. But in the end, the Germans proved too powerful. Although the efforts of their army at first proved no match for the guerilla tactics of the Maji-Maji, they eventually undertook to contain the revolt by firing crops and villages throughout southern Tanganyika. This scorched-earth policy brought results. By the end of 1907, the Germans had devastated a large part of the rebel-held territory and had starved its inhabitants into submission. At least 75,000 Africans lost their lives before the Germans finally restored order, if not the settled conditions of peace, to the beleaguered region.[22]

In the wake of the Maji-Maji, the German government attempted to redress the grievances of its African subjects. Dr. Bernhard Dernburg, the new German Minister for Colonies, instituted sweeping reforms and strove to transform the actions of his overseas subordinates in accord with the benevolent conception

---

[22] For the detailed, German official account, see Gustav Adolf von Götzen, *Deutsch-Ostafrika im Aufstand, 1905/06* (Berlin, 1909). See also in Abdul Karim bin Jamaliddini (trans. Wilfred H. Whiteley), *Utenzi wa Vita vya Maji-Maji* (Arusha, 1957), pp. 8–16; R. M. Bell, "The Maji-Maji Rebellion in the Liwale District," *Tanganyika Notes and Records*, 28 (1950), pp. 40–50.

Lessons in Swahili at a government school in Dar es Salaam, the capital of German East Africa, photographed in 1903. Note the pictures of Kaiser William II and Kaiserin Augusta Victoria on the wall. (Brown Brothers)

of "scientific colonization" upon which he himself so frequently dilated. He encouraged the development of indigenous agriculture, promoted the cultivation of cotton in particular, eschewed the employment of compulsory labor, and regarded Africans as assets whose assistance should be won, not coerced. But German settlers, particularly in Tanganyika, successfully resisted the Dernburg program of reform and continued to exploit the natural and physical resources of the colony. There the overt expression of discontent no longer hindered economic development. The administration completed the construction of railways from Dar es Salaam to Kigoma and from Tanga to Moshi. It assisted the sisal growers of the coast and experimented with the production of coffee in the highlands.

Just as the events in Europe influenced the birth of the German colonies in Africa, so they also brought about their liquidation. In 1914, a few weeks after war broke out in Europe, French and British troops occupied Togo and attacked the Germans in Cameroun. In the larger colony, the Germans fought a losing battle for two years and then, after exhausting their supply of ammunition, retreated into Spanish-held Rio Muni. In East Africa, the Germans held the upper hand until the end of 1915, when the British navy finally managed to overpower them along the coast. The main Allied campaign on land began early in the next year when General Jan Christian Smuts, fresh from victories over the Germans in Southwest Africa, led South African, Rhodesian, East African,

West Indian, West African, and Indian troops against the German bases in the Kilimanjaro region. His successes there equaled those of the Belgians in western Tanganyika, and most of the defenders retreated rapidly toward the Rovuma River. By late 1916, the Allies occupied all of Tanganyika, Rwanda, and Burundi. But a small German detachment under the able leadership of General Paul von Lettow-Vorbeck thereafter managed to engage the attentions of a very much larger Allied army throughout 1917 and 1918. With great tactical skill, Lettow-Vorbeck led his motley force into Moçambique, where he caused turmoil in the poorly defended hinterland of Quelimane, and threatened to invade Nyasaland. During the last weeks of the European war, he even managed to capture Fife and Kasama, two of the more important administrative centers in Northeastern Rhodesia, before surrendering to British officers at a ford over the Chambeshi River.[23]

As a result of the war, France and Britain divided Togo and Cameroun into unequal parts and established new colonial régimes that later became mandates of the League of Nations. Although it later attempted to persuade first Italy and then the United States to take control of German East Africa, Britain retained its control over Tanganyika—which it had governed since late 1916—at the insistence of Ugandan and Kenyan settlers as well as General Smuts.[24] By the same division, Belgium claimed Rwanda and Burundi, both of which, along with Tanganyika, later became mandates under the League.

IV. The Liquidation of the Congo Independent State

After about 1891, the indigenous inhabitants of the Congo found themselves at the mercy of the Europeans who administered the various *postes, secteurs,* and zones into which the government of King Léopold II had divided the Independent State. Samples of the white man's brand of justice disillusioned them, and their occasional attempts to redress grievances in the Belgian-run courts produced little satisfaction. In every way, the state harassed them. At the pleasure of the local district commissioners, it conscripted African men between the ages of fifteen and thirty. After freeing slaves from the Arabs, the state retained them in compulsory employment for seven years.[25] It also acquired a commercial monopoly over ivory, copal, and wild rubber, tropical products heretofore gathered freely by Africans, Arabs, and Europeans. In flagrant viola-

---

[23] Charles Prestwood Lucas, *The Empire at War* (London, 1924), IV, pp. 34–53, 67–120, 151–199, 249–314; C. J. Charlewood, "Naval Actions on the Tanganyika Coast," *Tanganyika Notes and Records,* 55 (1960), pp. 153–168; Paul von Lettow-Vorbeck, *My Reminiscences of East Africa* (London, 1920), pp. 307–322. At different stages in the campaign, the Allies put nearly 100,000 men in the field. Lettow-Vorbeck rarely commanded more than 3,000.

[24] George Louis Beer (ed. Louis Herbert Gray), *African Questions at the Paris Peace Conference* (New York, 1923), pp. 61–67, 424, 433–438; David Lloyd George, *Memoirs of the Peace Conference* (New Haven, 1939), I, pp. 66–77; James T. Shotwell, *At the Paris Peace Conference* (New York, 1937), p. 159.

[25] *The Congo: A Report of the Commission of Inquiry* (New York, 1906), p. 32; *Report on the Congo Independent State,* Cmd. 8649 (1898), pp. 8–11.

tion of provisions contained in the Berlin Act, the government of the Congo decreed that all of the exploitable crops of the northern districts of Ubangi, Uele, and Aruwimi were its property. The state furthermore forbade Africans to sell or traders to buy the products of those districts. Instead, it granted concessions to a number of Belgian companies. In addition, King Léopold appropriated a large private domain for his own use. From it he derived the wherewithal to build palaces and monuments in Belgium, to live luxuriously, and to keep his mistresses content.[26]

The various European-run enterprises in the Congo depended for their success upon the physical effort of Africans. But since many Africans refused to offer themselves as laborers, the government of the Independent State permitted its local administrators and commercial agents to exact taxes in the form of forced labor and the compulsory collection of rubber. These local officials also flogged, mutilated, and killed the Congolese who attempted to resist the demands of the white-run régime.[27] The government, in sum, totally subordinated the interests of Africans to its own exploitation of the resources of the Congo.

Léopold's oppressive régime could hardly escape the public criticism of Europeans indefinitely. As early as 1890, British and American Protestant missionaries exposed conditions in the Congo. Businessmen complained about restrictive commercial practices. Suspicion of the activities in the Congo in humanitarian circles grew after 1895, when an investigation into the death of a British trader occasioned questions in the Belgian Chamber of Deputies and the British House of Commons. An authoritative report by William Clayton Pickersgill, the British consul at Luanda, added considerable fuel to the fires of disclosure. In 1900, William Henry Sheppard, an American missionary, wrote an eye-witness account of the atrocities and Belgian-sponsored slave raids. Henry Richard Fox-Bourne, the secretary of the British Aborigines' Protection Society, gathered further evidence of Belgian wrongdoing.[28]

After 1900, humanitarians waged a war of words against King Léopold's administration of the Congo. Edmund Dene Morel, an Anglo-French shipping clerk, actively led the attack. In England, he organized the Congo Reform Association and, in the best muckraking style, wrote numerous books and pamphlets to support his crusade. The exposés of Guy Burrows and Fox-Bourne measurably assisted his cause, but official Britain became aroused only after Roger Casement, then the British consul at Boma, on the Congo, rendered a

---

[26] Émile Vandervelde, *La Belgique et le Congo* (Paris, 1911), p. 140; Neal Ascherson, *The King Incorporated: Leopold II in the Age of Trusts* (London, 1963), pp. 186, 212, 292–296.

[27] Alain Stenmans, *La Reprise du Congo par la Belgique: essai d'histoire parlementaire et diplomatique* (Bruxelles, 1949), pp. 208–213; Ruth Slade, *King Leopold's Congo* (London, 1962), pp. 240–246; *The Congo: A Report of the Commission of Inquiry*, pp. 66–70, 112–114; Arthur Berriedale Keith, *The Belgian Congo and the Berlin Act* (Oxford, 1919), p. 124.

[28] Ruth Slade, "English Missionaries and the Beginning of the Anti-Congolese Campaign in England," *Revue Belge de Philologie et d'Histoire*, XXXIII (1955), pp. 35–73; D. C. Rankin, "Atrocities in the Kongo Free State," *The Independent* (New York), February 1, 1900.

A Protestant missionary baptizes converts in the Belgian Congo, 1904. (United Press International)

detailed report of atrocities and malpractices up-river.[29] Casement's report contained evidence sufficiently damaging to persuade King Léopold to appoint a Commission of Inquiry; in 1905, the Commission endorsed the complaints of the humanitarians, and the king thereupon ordered an impressive number of reforms that, had they been implemented, would have successfully disarmed his critics.[30] But missionaries and Morel continued to demonstrate the paper nature of the reforms. Forced labor, excessive taxation, and abuses, such as the chaining of women hostages, occurred as often as before. Through diplomatic channels, the governments of Britain and the United States therefore argued that annexation to Belgium would prove the only readily available solution to the problems of the Congo. Many Belgians objected on financial and practical grounds to this proposed retrocession. In 1908, however, the Belgian parliament

---

[29] *Correspondence and Report from Her Majesty's Consul at Boma Respecting the Administration of the Independent State of the Congo*, Cmd. 1933 (1904); Henry Richard Fox-Bourne, *Civilisation in Congoland: A Story of International Wrongdoing* (London, 1903); Guy Burrows, *The Curse of Central Africa* (London, 1903); Edmund Morel, *King Leopold's Rule in Africa* (London, 1904); Morel, *Red Rubber* (London, 1906). See also Mark Twain, *King Leopold's Soliloquy* (Boston, 1905); William Roger Louis, "Roger Casement and the Congo," *The Journal of African History*, V (1964), pp. 99–107.

[30] Jean Stengers, "La Rôle de la Commission d'Enquête de 1904–05 au Congo," *Annuaire de l'Institut de Philologie et d'Histoire Orientales et Slaves*, X (1950), pp. 701–726.

reluctantly agreed, and the Congo Independent State became the Belgian Congo.

The government of Belgium slowly brought a measure of reform to the Congo. Under the Colonial Charter of 1908—the Congo's constitution—a governor-general resident in Boma (later in Léopoldville) administered the colony on behalf of Belgium. In turn, the four (later six) provinces of the Congo were each ruled somewhat autonomously by subordinate figures who possessed vast authority over their subjects. They took advice occasionally from a local Council of Government and individual provincial councils whose membership consisted primarily of Belgian officials and businessmen. For a time, a commercial concern even governed Katanga. Overall, the absence of real consultative machinery was marked. It contributed to a monolithic control of the destiny of the Congo and acted eventually to discourage indigenous participation in the affairs of the state.

The Colonial Charter prohibited the exercise of administrative functions by agents of the concession companies and envisaged a "new deal" for Africans. By 1910, the new government of the Congo had officially curtailed the use of forced labor and had repealed the onerous labor tax. During the next few years, it abolished producer monopolies, permitted individuals to gather and trade tropical crops freely, and reduced the extent of the areas controlled directly by the large concessionary companies. But many administrators continued to exercise their powers arbitrarily, and to exhibit the kind of behavior toward Africans that had been popular during the era of the Independent State.[31] A few years after the end of Léopold's rule, an American missionary reported that "veiled slavery" still existed.

> *During the month of June a raid was made near Luebo by a State officer. Men and women, boys and girls were taken by force; villages were pillaged; two were burnt; women were raped; chiefs tied up and taken away. . . . Now, the question is, how long will all this keep up? How long can the native races stand this drain? I am sorry to say that so far I can see no material change in the situation under the so-called Belgian regime.*[32]

Under Belgium, the Congo remained a fertile field for the promotion of economic projects beneficial to foreign investors and the state itself. Like Léopold, the Belgian government of the Congo preferred an entrepreneurial to a strictly custodial role. But whereas the Independent State had tapped the natural agricultural wealth of the Congo, the Belgian administration carefully constructed an impressive economic edifice based upon the exploitation of mineral resources, the development of plantation crops, and the provision of an efficient system of transport. By the end of 1910, locomotives of the Rhodesia Railway had reached Elisabethville, in the heart of Katanga; thereafter, the production of copper kept pace with the rapid expansion of the rail network and ultimately made Katanga one of Africa's richest regions. At the same time,

[31] But see George Van Der Kerken, *La Politique coloniale Belge* (Anvers, 1943), p. 139.
[32] Quoted in Colin Legum, *Congo Disaster* (Harmondsworth, 1961), p. 34.

Lever Brothers of England (now Unilever) began to grow oil palms on a plantation larger than the state of Delaware.[33] Other firms envied, and before long emulated, this first of the new generation of successful concessionaires.

V. The Portuguese Possessions of Angola and Moçambique

Africans had not been party to the European agreements that confirmed Portugal's traditional claims to the hinterlands of Angola and Moçambique. And during the last years of the nineteenth century, they resisted the occupation of the interior by Portuguese armies. In 1890/91, the Bihe chief Ndunduma blocked the main route from Luanda to Barotseland before Portuguese soldiers and Afrikaner marksmen (who had been employed as mercenaries) won a bloody war for the possession of his country.[34] They also occupied the nearby territory of Bailundu. There, in 1902, Africans rose in a forlorn attempt to redress the wrongful excesses that had accompanied the recruitment of labor. Mutu ya Kevela led the vengeful Bailundu against the Portuguese; his followers killed a number of white traders and destroyed their stores. Soon the spirit of rebellion spread beyond Bailundu toward Bié. But Portuguese troops from Benguela and Moçamedes marched against them, burnt their villages and, by the end of 1903, had quenched the fires of revolt.[35]

Elsewhere in Angola, Africans similarly tried to resist the coming of white rule. In the south, the Cuanhama remained unsubdued between 1890 and 1915, during which time they inflicted a series of defeats upon successive Portuguese punitive expeditions. In 1897, after they had refused to have their cattle vaccinated, Cuanhama warriors routed a Portuguese garrison. Then in 1904, after an interlude of peace, the Cuanhama again attacked the Portuguese, persisting in their opposition until the Portuguese won a decisive battle near Roçadas. Between 1907 and 1910, Portuguese troops from Luanda had meanwhile captured the powerful chiefs of the Dembos region—where a modern revolution erupted in 1961—and gradually subdued their numerous recalcitrant followers.

The Portuguese mounted similar offensives in Moçambique. In 1895, after pacifying the area near Lourenço Marques, they defeated Gungunhana, a descendant of Soshangane, in the battle of Manjacaze and subsequently occupied Gazaland. Yet until 1897, his successors continued to dispute Portugal on the battlefield, winning occasional victories but finally succumbing before an army led by the renowned officer Joaquim Augusto Mousinho de Albuquerque.[36]

[33] Charles Wilson, *The History of Unilever: A Study in Economic Growth and Social Change* (London, 1954), I, pp. 165–176.

[34] Frederick Arnot, a letter of Feb. 14, 1889, in *Echoes of Service* (May, 1890), pp. 178–180; James Johnston, *Reality Versus Romance in South Central Africa* (London, 1893), pp. 59–62. For the role of António Francisco da Silva Porto, see Frederick Arnot, a letter of March 31, 1889, in *Echoes of Service* (July, 1890), pp. 219–220.

[35] James Duffy, *Portuguese Africa* (Cambridge, Mass., 1959), p. 228; John T. Tucker, *Drums in the Darkness* (New York, 1927), pp. 120–136.

[36] For Gungunhana's earlier relations with Cecil Rhodes and the British government, see Philip R. Warhurst, *Anglo-Portuguese Relations in South-Central Africa, 1890–1900* (London, 1962), pp. 81–107.

Between 1897 and 1900, the Portuguese also conquered the Nyanja-speaking peoples of the north and destroyed pockets of African resistance along the Zambezi River between Chinde and Sena. In 1902, they occupied the Gorongosa district and gained control of the peoples who lived between Tete and the border with Nyasaland. Angoche, an Arab-run island entrepôt, fell to the Portuguese in 1910. But only in 1912, after they had overcome the resistance of the Yao and Gua peoples of the Lujenda River basin and captured Mataka, a leading Yao chief, could Portugal justifiably claim to administer all of Moçambique.

In both colonies, a reform of administrative practices succeeded the conquest. In theory, the Portuguese intended to rule Africans paternally and to extend to them the benefits of a "civilizing tutelage." [37] But foreign observers reported that the governments of Angola and Moçambique had continued instead to follow the traditional paths of colonial oppression. The Portuguese believed that the state as "a depository of social authority" should oblige the "rude Negroes" of Africa to work, "that is . . . to civilize themselves through work. . . ." Compulsory labor even received official sanction:

> *. . . all natives of Portuguese overseas provinces are subject to the obligation, moral and legal, of attempting to obtain through work the means that they lack to subsist and to better their social condition. They have full liberty to choose the method of fulfilling this obligation, but if they do not fulfill it public authority may force a fulfillment.*[38]

During the early years of this century, Portuguese administrators sent Africans "on contract" to the cacao and sugar plantations of distant São Tomé and Réunion. They supplied laborers to mine gold in South Africa. At home, like their fellow Europeans in the Congo and in French Equatoria, they compelled Africans to gather rubber. They also allowed plantation managers in the two Portuguese colonies to "buy" laborers from the state. According to one account:

> *It was the custom in those days to give [the contracted laborers] the rudest and most difficult work, in domestic service as well as in the fields and factories, above all in the matter of porterage, in which they took the role of humble animals.*
>
> *For the slightest fault they were often cruelly punished by being beaten with the hippopotamus-hide whip which cut their skin horribly. Very frequently one heard in the late hour of a warm mysterious African night piercing shrieks of pain from the poor wretches who were being beaten by the company officers or head men, generally hard-hearted mulattoes.*[39]

This type of oppression, and conditions that amounted to "a modern slavery," received further confirmation *ad nauseam*. The accusations of the journalist Henry Nevinson inspired William Cadbury, a British Quaker chocolate manufacturer, to sponsor an investigation of the governance of Angola and São Tomé.

---

[37] Duffy, *Portuguese*, p. 243.

[38] Quoted in *ibid.*, p. 155. See also Lucy P. Mair, *Native Policies in Africa* (London, 1936), pp. 251–252.

[39] Quoted in Duffy, *Portuguese*, p. 154.

What he learned persuaded his firm and other chocolate companies to refuse to buy supplies of cocoa that were grown in Portugal's overseas empire.[40]

Laws enacted in 1911 and 1915 reflected these criticisms. Yet they still imposed "correctional labor penalties" upon those Africans who seemed to require a betterment of their "social condition." This legislation embodied safeguards theoretically sufficient to protect the natural rights of indigenous labor. But characteristic excesses, and a neglect of the "civilizing" aspects of labor recruitment, continued to make mockery of carefully drafted provisions.[41]

VI. The British Presence in the East

During the years immediately following the fall of Omdurman, the defeat of *mwata* Kazembe, and the final conquest of Matabeleland, Britain began to rule the different peoples of the Sudan, East Africa, and Central Africa. Within each of these areas, its officials attempted to satisfy the competing demands of the indigenous inhabitants, the white settlers, the white-run businesses, and the policies of the Empire. Out of the resultant crucible of compromise emerged the distinctive features that for long characterized their respective governmental experiences and provided fuel for the subsequent fires of nationalism.

Kenya and the Rhodesias became settler countries. In 1901, after Anglo-Indian troops had pacified the Mazrui, Giriama, and Somali people of the East African coast and had similarly subdued those Kikuyu, Kamba, and Nandi tribesmen who had attempted to resist the tide of the white advance inland, Britons finally completed the construction of a railway between Mombasa on the Indian Ocean and Kisumu on the Kavirondo Gulf of Victoria Nyanza.[42] Thereafter, to the detriment of subsequent unity in East Africa, the British Foreign Office transferred to the future administration of Kenya (then still the East Africa Protectorate) the fertile highland areas northwest of Lake Naivasha through which the railway passed.[43]

Sir Charles Eliot, then the commissioner of the East Africa Protectorate, became responsible for making the new railroad pay. By the promotion of indigenous agriculture in the productive Kikuyu uplands, Eliot might have satisfied his financial objectives. But in the eyes of most Europeans, the peoples who lived in this area were too disorganized and uncooperative to boost the new state economically. Ignoring the possibility that any other scheme might cause fewer problems for the future, Eliot instead decided to settle whites in

---

[40] Henry Nevinson, *A Modern Slavery* (London, 1906), pp. 180–208; William Cadbury, *Labour in Portuguese West Africa* (London, 1910), pp. 71–74, 81–96.

[41] See John Harris, *Portuguese Slavery: Britain's Dilemma* (London, 1913), pp. 10–81.

[42] Although Britons termed it the Uganda Railway, locomotives only later ran thither. The laying of the rails between Mombasa and Nairobi and Nairobi and Kisumu cost the lives of many Asians. See Mervyn F. Hill, *Permanent Way: The Story of the Kenya and Uganda Railway* (Nairobi, 1950), pp. 242–243.

[43] Sir Harry Johnston, then in charge in Uganda, opposed the transfer. He instead suggested that the Uganda and East Africa Protectorates should be governed by a high commissioner common to both. See Roland Oliver, *Sir Harry Johnston and the Scramble for Africa* (London, 1957), pp. 334–336.

the highlands that seemed climatically and ecologically suitable for farming by Europeans. "We had," wrote Eliot, "the rare experience of dealing with a *tabula rasa*, an almost untouched and sparsely inhabited country, where we [could] do [what seemed] best." [44]

By the end of 1904, the government of the East Africa Protectorate had alienated nearly a million acres of choice land to fewer than four hundred British farmers and South African stockmen.[45] In so doing, it acted as if African land rights had never existed. It apparently chose to ignore the traditional Kikuyu system of individual tenure and the fact that many Kikuyu had purchased their lands outright from the Dorobo. Eliot's administration further refused to acknowledge Masai claims to land in the valley of the continental rift. It failed to realize that Africans had reserved a proportion of the so-called empty lands for their future use or for the periodic, rather than the continual, grazing or watering of cattle. "Emptiness" was a relative concept, and Eliot and the earliest settlers allowed their own economic needs to override the views of a number of white district commissioners who had lived for some time among Africans and who had come to appreciate their attachment to the land.[46]

Europeans deprived Africans of their land. They then confined them to crowded reserves that generally represented inadequate compensation. In successive stages, the government of the Protectorate thus moved the Masai out of the Rift Valley to make room for whites. It also created reserves for the Kikuyu, Embu, and Meru peoples. But even the existence of "reserved" land failed to prevent the Protectorate from later alienating further portions of the patrimony of the Kikuyu to white settlers. Moreover, according to its own officers, "the principle line of policy laid down by the government for the native reserves . . . may be said to consist of the collection of revenue and the provision of labour for private employers." [47]

In the Rhodesias, where the British South Africa Company governed, white settlers and Africans similarly coveted the most suitable agricultural and pastoral lands. The Company created reserves and, in Southern Rhodesia, alienated well-watered lands near the railway for European settlement exclusively. An official explained that, by creating reserves, the Company minimized conflict between Africans and Europeans:

> *It is within these reserves that it is, on general administrative grounds, desirable that native communities . . . should be established. Their establishment out-*

[44] Charles Eliot, *The East Africa Protectorate* (London, 1905), pp. 208–209.

[45] *Report of the Kenya Land Commission: Evidence and Memoranda*, Cmd. 4556 (1934), I, p. 54. See also *ibid.*, pp. 204–214, 258 ff.

[46] By virtue of its own Regulation No. 12 of 1897, the government of the East Africa Protectorate had admitted the principle of individual African ownership of land. It had even issued regulations respecting the sale of land by Africans to immigrants. For contemporary evidence, see *supra*, p. 168; C. W. Hobley, "Confidential Memorandum Regarding Settlement of Native Rights and Future Settlement of Labour Colonies on Farms," December 28, 1911, in Kiambu (Kenya) Records; W. McGregor Ross, *Kenya from Within* (London, 1927), pp. 44–45; Mervyn W. H. Beech, "Kikuyu System of Land Tenure," *Journal of the African Society*, XVII (1917), pp. 47–55.

[47] Memorandum to the governor of Kenya, signed by the five district commissioners responsible for sections of Kikuyuland, December 10, 1924, in Kiambu Records.

side the reserves on land available for European settlers would tend to produce that conflict of interests between European and native communities which it is the object of good administration to avoid.[48]

Where Africans "squatted" in an area scheduled for whites, they paid rent. Generally, however, spatial segregation was the goal of the Company, and it assumed that Africans who lived or worked on European-owned farms, or who resided in the towns in order to accept employment by whites, were temporary residents. It thus compelled Africans to carry "passes" or identification certificates, forbade most forms of racial mixing and, in Salisbury, the capital of Southern Rhodesia, passed laws that prohibited Africans from standing on the sidewalks.

In Nyasaland, where the zone of white interpenetration remained narrow, Africans living on alienated land were encouraged to remain in a rent-paying capacity. Otherwise, the government evicted them. A missionary commented:

On the face of it, it is an anomaly that the native should in this way have to buy back land which was once his own. Where once he had fixity of tenure he now has to pay for it at the rate of four shillings per annum. It is an anomaly, but one of those anomalies which must be allowed for.[49]

Whites in eastern Africa generally refused to indulge in manual labor. They argued that the employment of Africans presented a "civilizing opportunity" and urged their respective governments somehow to persuade members of the otherwise indifferent indigenous population to offer their physical services. Two of the early white settlers in the highlands of the East Africa Protectorate averred that "a good sound system of compulsory labour would do more to raise the nigger in five years than all the millions that have been sunk in missionary efforts for the last fifty. . . ."

Then let the native be compelled to work so many months in the year at a fixed and reasonable rate, and call it compulsory education, as we call our weekly bonnet parades church. Under such a title, surely the most delicate British conscience may be at rest.[50]

In 1908, Sir James Hayes Sadler, Eliot's successor, bowed to white opinion and began to tax Africans heavily in order to make them offer their labor to white employers. Already, in the Rhodesias and in Nyasaland, the other governments had anticipated such needs and had acted accordingly. In Nyasaland, officers of the government burned down the huts of tax defaulters or held their wives hostage. In Northern Rhodesia, a settler of experience wrote:

Poor villagers . . . their tax [has been] put up from 5/- to 10/- a year as a reward for being loyal. It's the good old policy of exploiting the black man; in this case

[48] White Papers: C. P. Millar to Marshall Hartley, December 30, 1918, Methodist Missionary Society archives.

[49] Quoted in George Shepperson and Thomas Price, *Independent African* (Edinburgh, 1958), p. 144.

[50] Ewart S. Grogan and Arthur H. Sharp, *From the Cape to Cairo* (London, 1900), p. 360.

it's intended to drive him down to the mines in Southern Rhodesia, 1500 miles away, where they're short of labour. . . .[51]

In all the settled areas, white farmers, often with government connivance, obtained African assistance by a variety of means that approximated compulsory labor. In Southern Rhodesia, the Company asked its so-called Native Commissioners to see that chiefs supplied "boys" for work on the white-owned farms. Otherwise, an official of the Company assumed that the commissioners "knew what to do." [52] Thus, because whites forced Africans to work, because Africans sought money with which to pay their taxes, and because they or their wives acquired new wants, Africans gradually decided to offer their labor in the white-run market. But they never worked in sufficient number, nor diligently enough, to please their employers.

The introduction of the white man's code of justice failed to redress the grievances accumulated by Africans. No matter how flagrant the crime, few courts convicted whites in cases involving African plaintiffs. In Southern Rhodesia, although the law did not reserve the penalty of death for rape and attempted rape to Africans alone, no white man ever lost his life for assaults on African women. On the other hand, innumerable Africans forfeited theirs for offenses against white women. And in all of the settler-dominated areas of eastern Africa, whites freely used the whip and other *ad hoc* methods to control the activities of their African neighbors and employes.[53]

White settlers played a potent political role in all of Britain's mainland colonies south of the Sudan. In the East Africa Protectorate, they successfully organized themselves into an influential pressure group—the Convention of Associations—that British governors ignored at their peril.[54] Under the leadership of Lord Delamere, the Convention became the main forum for the expression of the views of the local white population. The tiny white farming and trading groups of Nyasaland, Northern Rhodesia, and Uganda similarly formed themselves into chambers of commerce and planters' associations. They, too, demanded and, except for the Northern Rhodesians, received a measure of representation in the legislative councils of their respective territories. But for the most part, the official communities of civil servants effectively retained ultimate authority and, in Nyasaland and Uganda, used their power to resist the more outrageous white attempts to deprive Africans of their natural rights.

---

[51] Gore-Browne Papers: Stewart Gore-Browne to Dame Ethel Locke-King, June 15, 1921, privately held.

[52] Philip Mason, *The Birth of a Dilemma* (London, 1958), pp. 221–222. See also Buell, *Native Problem*, I, pp. 233–237. For a discussion of taxation, see FO 2/699: "Native Labour and Hut Tax, 1900–1902"; FO 2/605: Alfred Sharpe to Sir Clement Hill, April 3, 1902.

[53] Mason, *Birth*, pp. 295–311; Robert I. Rotberg, "Missionaries as Chiefs and Entrepreneurs: Northern Rhodesia, 1882–1924," in Jeffrey Butler (ed.), *Boston University Papers in African History* (Boston, 1964), I, pp. 204–208; *Correspondence Relating to the Flogging of Natives by Certain Europeans at Nairobi*, Cmd. 3562 (1907), pp. 19 ff.

[54] George Bennett, "The Development of Political Organizations in Kenya," *Political Studies*, V (1957), pp. 113–114; Marjorie Ruth Dilley, *British Policy in Kenya Colony* (New York, 1937), p. 41; Elspeth Huxley, *White Man's Country* (London, 1935), I, pp. 261–262.

In Southern Rhodesia, meanwhile, the white settlers in effect governed the colony themselves. In 1907, they obtained a majority of the seats in the Legislative Council and regularly encouraged the Company to administer the country solely on behalf of whites.

Of the British East and Central African colonies and protectorates, only Uganda preserved the pre-eminent position of Africans. Its earliest commissioners fondly expected that Uganda would become a center of European settlement; they intended the railway, and a set of favorable land ordinances, to serve such ends. But despite the enthusiasm of Sir Harry Johnston for the development of white plantations, and the abortive attempt to create a Zionist homeland in Uganda, the climate and potential of the Protectorate attracted few white farmers to the fertile lands north of Victoria Nyanza.[55] Transport from Uganda to the coast remained expensive and, under Eliot and his successors, the highlands of the East Africa Protectorate proved far more enticing than the plateau sites available in Uganda. Moreover, in 1905, Commissioner (later Governor) Sir Hesketh Bell explicitly stated that large-scale white settlement would be unwelcome in Uganda.[56]

The presence of a powerful, sophisticated African state influenced Bell's decision to maintain the indigenous character of Uganda. In 1900, Johnston had transformed Buganda into a constitutional monarchy, entrenched its landed gentry and, with unforeseen future consequences, denied the traditional Ganda usufruct. In sum, by the terms of the Uganda Agreement of that year, he created a state within a state. Thereafter, power within Buganda remained unnaturally centralized; Ganda bureaucrats gained control in a manner that later accelerated centrifugal tendencies within the kingdom. Until 1914, the government of Uganda exercised a benign oversight of affairs within a Buganda that continued to be ruled by the oligarchy of its secular leaders.[57]

Beyond Buganda, the British administration ruled either directly or through the agency of Ganda chiefs. Even after Britons nominally governed Teso country, Ganda helped to administer the area with the assistance of Teso district councils. Ganda officials likewise ran the Lango district on Britain's behalf. Later, British forces moved into Acholi, established an outpost at Gulu, and overcame local resistance at Lamogi and Kitgum. By 1914, all of the peoples of Uganda, except the Karamojong and the Turkana in the east, had succumbed to British might.[58]

---

[55] Kenneth Ingham, *The Making of Modern Uganda* (London, 1958), p. 105. But see Oliver, *Sir Harry Johnston*, p. 333. On Zionism, see Eliot, *East Africa Protectorate*, p. 177. See also Jacob de Haas, *Theodor Herzl* (New York, 1927), II, pp. 157–213; Raphael Patai (ed.), *The Complete Diaries of Theodor Herzl* (New York, 1960), IV, pp. 1294, 1473, 1487, 1498, 1501, 1558, 1599.

[56] Hesketh Bell, *Glimpses of a Governor's Life* (London, 1946), pp. 121–122.

[57] D. Anthony Low and R. Cranford Pratt, *Buganda and British Overrule* (London, 1960), pp. 128–136, 350–366.

[58] A. L. Kitching, *On the Backwaters of the Nile* (London, 1912), pp. 260–262; Kenneth Ingham, "British Administration in Lango District, 1907–1935," *The Uganda Journal*, XIX (1955), pp. 156–160; R. M. Bere, "An Outline of Acholi History," *ibid.*, XI (1947), pp. 5–8; A. B. Adimola, "The Lamogi Rebellion, 1911–12," *ibid.*, XVIII (1954), pp. 169–176;

In Somaliland and the Sudan, the British government likewise attempted to consolidate its position during the crucial years before the end of World War I. After the death of the Khalifa, messianic pretenders led a series of minor revolts in Kordofan and along the Blue Nile. In the Gezira, a disappointed former Mahdist official inspired a locally important uprising. But Anglo-Egyptian troops always seemed equal to the task of suppression. Likewise, the government of the Sudan gradually regained respect and authority in the Nuba Hills and the equatorial south. In Darfur, however, Sultan 'Ali Dinar had reigned supreme since the end of the Mahdiya. The British government waited until 1916; nearly three thousand troops, accompanied by airplanes, then overcame the Fur army, occupied El Fasher, and at last ended the independence of the sultanate.[59] Thereafter, Britons, subordinate Egyptians and Lebanese, and a few Sudanese governed the vast country of the Condominium; they regarded it, however, as virtually two nations—the Arab north and the African south—and tended to isolate the one from the other to the detriment of the development of the latter.

Despite its victory in the Sudan, the government of Britain spent the first two decades of the twentieth century attempting to quell a Mahdist uprising in Somaliland. Between 1895 and 1899, Sayid Muhammad ibn 'Abdullah Hassan, the so-called Mad Mullah, urged the Muslim Somali of Berbera to purge their faith of its impurities. In 1899, after he and his followers had retreated inland, they occupied Burao and conquered groups unwilling to accept the tenets of revivalism. Sayid Muhammad announced himself to be the Mahdi and declared a *jihad* against the infidels. Within months, the predominantly Darod Somali warriors, who supported Sayid Muhammad, gained control over the grazing grounds and trade routes of greater Somalia. Between 1901 and 1904, a number of British- and Ethiopian-sponsored military expeditions failed to curtail their operations. For a time, Muhammad moved into Italian Somaliland. In 1909, however, he resumed his operations in British territory, and the British thereafter governed only the coastal towns of Somaliland. Indeed, not until the conclusion of World War I could British-officered troops from Somaliland, India, and Central Africa finally overthrow this second Mahdiya and gradually regain control of their section of Somalia.[60]

The subsequent prosperity of both the Sudan and Uganda depended upon the cultivation of cotton by Africans. In 1904, with the support of the British Cotton Growing Association, an Anglican missionary introduced its commercial cultivation to the inhabitants of Buganda. Soon the people of Busoga, Bukedi, Teso, and Lango also planted cotton. In this process, the backing of the important chiefs, official financial and legislative support, and the willingness of the

J. P. Barber, "The Karamoja District of Uganda: A Pastoral People Under Colonial Rule," *The Journal of African History*, III (1962), pp. 111–114; John R. P. Postlethwaite, *I Look Back* (London, 1947), pp. 54–56.

[59] Ronald Wingate, *Wingate of the Sudan: The Life and Times of General Sir Reginald Wingate* (London, 1955), pp. 183–186; Peter M. Holt, *A Modern History of the Sudan* (London, 1961), p. 124; A. B. Theobald, "Darfur and Its Neighbours Under Sultan 'Ali Dinar, 1898–1916," *Sudan Notes and Records*, XL (1959), p. 120.

[60] Douglas Jardine, *The Mad Mullah of Somaliland* (London, 1923), pp. 264–280.

government of the Protectorate to construct good roads and a railway from Busoga to Jinja all contributed in a crucial manner to the rapid rise in the value of Uganda's cotton exports. After 1911, when more than thirteen thousand bales reached the world market, it preceded ivory, hides and skins, and chillies on the list of Uganda's most lucrative cash crops. By this time, the American and Egyptian cotton crops had both failed in the same year. The Cotton Growing Association therefore urged the government of the Sudan to irrigate the Gezira with the waters of the Nile and, therein, to grow cotton. An American entrepreneur had already demonstrated the potential for cotton at a small plantation on the Atbara River. Benefiting by his experience, in 1911, the government, which had expanded the railway network of the country and had even joined El Obeid in Kordofan to Port Sudan on the Red Sea, started its own irrigation scheme along the Blue Nile. It proved immediately successful and provided the foundations for the development of the Gezira plain during the years after World War I.[61]

The government of the East Africa Protectorate neglected to develop African agriculture. Nevertheless, Africans continued to grow cotton along the shores of Victoria Nyanza and coconuts along the Indian Ocean littoral. They exported hides and skins and, despite its general exclusion from the market economy, the indigenous sector apparently accounted for about half of the country's total export production.[62] Delamere meanwhile pioneered an agricultural revolution. His experiments with wheat and cattle and his persistence and energy brought a new prosperity to the farmers of the East African highlands. Other whites also began to grow potatoes, maize, sisal, and coffee, which soon became their most valuable crop. In Nyasaland, tea replaced coffee as the most important plantation-grown commodity. Whites cultivated tobacco and maize in Southern Rhodesia and mined a little gold. The great economic growth of Northern Rhodesia awaited the completion in 1906 of a railway to Broken Hill, where lead and zinc were mined, and its extension to Bwana Mkuba in the heart of the copper country. Only later, however, after the development of new techniques for the separation of copper from its ore, could Rhodesia's copper production come into its own.

Despite the economic development of their homelands, Africans throughout the areas dominated by English-speaking settlers refused ultimately to accept the extent to which they had become second-class citizens. Their protest took many verbal forms. Separatists founded African-run churches in the Rhodesias and Nyasaland. Millennial preachers pursued the kingdom beyond colonialism and, like Elliot Kenan Kamwana of Nyasaland, promised the coming of a new, tax-free, independent Africa. After Armageddon, he said, the white govern-

---

[61] Arthur Gaitskell, *Gezira: A Story of the Development in the Sudan* (London, 1959), pp. 51–73; Christopher C. Wrigley, *Crops and Wealth in Uganda: A Short Agrarian History* (Kampala, 1959), pp. 14–21; D. Anthony Low, "The Advent of Populism in Buganda," *Comparative Studies in Society and History,* VI (1964), p. 429n.

[62] The collection of taxes from Africans also helped to support the government of the East Africa Protectorate. See Kenneth Ingham, *A History of East Africa* (London, 1962), pp. 221–222.

ment would go. "We shall build our own ships, make our own powder, import our own guns." [63] Charles Domingo, another Nyasa evangelist, decried the practice of crude discrimination. He and others wearied of the onerous daily confrontation of race realities that can never be conveyed fully on paper. "There is too much failure among all Europeans," he said. "The three combined bodies, Missionaries, Government and Companies, or gainers of money, do form the same rule to look upon the native with mockery eyes. . . . [T]he life of the three combined bodies is altogether too cheaty, too thefty, too mockery. Instead of "Give" they say "Take away from." [64]

John Chilembwe, a Nyasa separatist church leader who had studied in America, experienced a similar disenchantment with white rule. Either because he was more intelligent and courageous than other educated Africans, or perhaps because he had become persuaded of his own charisma and understanding of the destiny of Africa, Chilembwe actively opposed governmental measures that he deemed of affront to Nyasas. He protested the employment of African troops in "imperialist" wars. He championed Nyasaland's landless proletariat. He opposed tax increases. Foreshadowing similar activity years later among the Kikuyu, he established a chain of independent churches and schools. During the first weeks of World War I, Britons conscripted Africans to help fight the Germans on Lake Nyasa. At about this same time, and evidently because of the war, Chilembwe began to understand the importance of making a dramatic protest against white rule. He apparently welcomed martyrdom. He may possibly have envisaged himself as the future leader of an independent African Nyasaland. In any event, the government ignored his warning:

> *We understand that we have been invited to shed our innocent blood in this world's war which is now in progress. . . . A number of our people have already shed their blood, while some are crippled for life. . . . Police are marching in various villages persuading well-built natives to join in the war. . . .* [*But*] *will there be any good prospects for the natives after the end of the war? Shall we be recognized as anybody in the interests of civilization and Christianity after the great struggle is ended?*
>
> . . . we are imposed upon more than any other nationality under the sun. [*We*] . . . *have been loyal since the commencement of this government. . . . And no time have we ever been known to betray any trust, national or otherwise, confided to us. . . . For our part we . . . have unreservedly stepped to the firing line in every conflict and played a patriot's part with the Spirit of true gallantry. But in time of peace the Government failed to help the underdog. In time of peace everything* [*is*] *for Europeans only. . . .*[65]

Early in 1915, Chilembwe directed his Christian followers in a brief, completely unsuccessful rising against British rule in Nyasaland. A few whites lost

---

[63] Quoted in George Shepperson, "The Politics of African Church Separatist Movements in British Central Africa, 1892–1916," *Africa*, XXIV (1954), p. 239.

[64] *Ibid.*, pp. 240–241.

[65] GOA 2/4/14: John Chilembwe to the *Nyasaland Times*, Zomba archives. See also Shepperson and Price, *Independent African*, pp. 234–235 ff.

their lives, and the actual skirmishes lasted less than a week. In the immediate context, Chilembwe accomplished nothing. He nevertheless shattered the widespread aura of white complacency. He destroyed the notion that "the natives were happy" under British domination. Unfortunately, however, his government and other governments learned this lesson imperfectly. The rising of 1915 failed to change the course of colonial rule in Africa. Only later, in a revolutionary age, did Chilembwe's forlorn example provide the text for a genuine movement of independence.

VII. Ethiopia Under Menelik

Ethiopia remained free. After the Italian debacle at Adowa in 1896, Emperor Menelik II had, without compromising the integrity of his kingdom, skillfully extended his contacts with the powers of Europe. For a time, he seemed to favor the French. They won a concession to build the railway that, in 1918, eventually reached Addis Ababa, the capital, from Djibouti, and also introduced the telegraph, telephone, and electric light to some of the main centers of the country. To representatives of other European nations, Menelik sold a vast array of additional privileges; various firms received the right to export coffee, cotton, wax, skins and hides, imaginary minerals, and non-existent rubber. Throughout his reign, Addis Ababa naturally attracted concession-hunters, freebooters, "advisors" of one kind or another, bankers, soldiers, and diplomats.

The French again played the most important military role. With the help of French soldiers, Menelik consolidated his position in the old empire and made new conquests that eventually extended the borders of the new. Before the turn of the century, he annexed the domain of the Wallamo Galla. In the manner of the European partitioners, he next conquered the Beni Shangul who lived along the western marches of the Sudan. The Ethiopian army forced the king of Kaffa to submit to the authority of the emperor; another contingent gave him control over the Ogaden, where Ethiopians later fought Somali who were loyal to the Mahdi of Somalia. In the south, Ethiopia also forcibly subdued Sidamo and the Boran Galla, and carried the authority of the emperor for the first time to the shores of Lake Rudolf. But throughout this area, Ethiopian rule initially affected the local people little. Few roads, and even fewer economic reasons, connected them to the Shoan and Amharan centers of the state.

While the soldiers fought, the diplomats compromised. In order to safeguard his conquests, Menelik made a number of treaties with the nations of Europe. With Britain he delimited the borders of the East Africa Protectorate, the Sudan, and Somaliland. He also agreed to recognize the peculiar British interest in the headwaters of the Blue Nile at Lake Tana, and promised not to impede the flow of the river downstream to Egypt.[66] With the French

[66] Edward S. Hertslet, *The Map of Africa by Treaty* (London, 1909), II, pp. 432–435, 445–446.

Lij Jasu, briefly emperor of Ethiopia, from a photograph by Colonel R. J. Stordy taken about 1911/12, when Lij Jasu was the heir apparent to Menelik. (Lord Cranworth, *Kenya Chronicles,* Macmillan & Co., Ltd. London, 1939)

and the Italians, he determined the remainder of the outline of modern Ethiopia. Of these many delimitations, only the Italian border eventually caused difficulty.

While Menelik remained unaware, because he had weakened physically, the ambassadors to his country from Britain, France, and Italy anxiously watched the Germans gain a surprising influence within the imperial court. In 1906, the three Allied powers thus decided among themselves to counter the German threat by acknowledging the independence of Ethiopia. But at the same time, they divided the empire into three spheres of European influence and promised to protect their own nationals if the political situation in Ethiopia ever deteriorated. Each promised further to intervene in the internal affairs of the country only with the consent of the other signatories to the so-called Tripartite Treaty.[67] Later in the year, Menelik, who had already begun to suffer acutely from an illness that had left him partly paralysed, reluctantly acknowledged these arrangements.

During the next year, Menelik's health gave increasing cause for alarm. In 1907, he provided for the succession by nominating Lij Jasu, his twelve-year-old grandson, and the son of a Muslim nobleman, as heir. Intrigue thereafter occu-

[67] *Ibid.,* pp. 436–444.

pied persons of prominence throughout the empire. Menelik's fourth wife, Empress Taitu, shrewdly attempted to gain control; as the heir presumptive she nominated Zauditu, a daughter of one of Menelik's earlier wives. She also supported the Germans, and thereby worried the representatives of the other European powers. But she overreached herself and, with Menelik lying alive but essentially unable to exercise his power, conditions in central Ethiopia approximated chaos. Gunrunning and slave-trading occupied Ethiopians and Europeans alike; even the closure of the French port of Djibouti improved matters little.

In 1911, Lij Jasu began to exercise the power that became fully his two years later, after the death of Menelik. He first flirted with and then openly espoused the religion of Islam. He denounced his Solomonid ancestry and claimed descent from the Prophet Muhammad, rejected his Christian wife and collected a harem, and entered into relations with the Ottoman caliphate in Turkey. At this point, the signatories to the Tripartite Treaty naturally worried about the stability of Ethiopia. Since the Ottoman Empire and the Allies were at war, they also feared that Lij Jasu might assist the Germans in Tanganyika and the Turks in the Middle East. Before they could act, however, the Shoan princes and the leaders of the Ethiopian church independently altered the course of Ethiopia's future. In 1916, during a period when Lij Jasu was away in the east, they marched on Addis Ababa and, with the blessing of the *abuna* or head of the church, elevated Zauditu to the throne. Ras Tafari, the future Haile Selassie and then the governor of Harar, became the regent and active ruler of the empire. Meanwhile, after the former emperor had been excommunicated by the *abuna*, he was pursued by the Shoan princes into Danakil country. He died some years later in captivity.

There certainly are some progressive ideas among the Europeans. They include the ideas of material prosperity, of medicine, and hygiene, and literacy which enables people to take part in world culture. But so far the Europeans . . . have not been conspicuously zealous in imparting these parts of their inheritance to the Africans, and seem to think that the only way to do it is by police discipline and armed force. They speak as if it was somehow beneficial to an African to work for them instead of for himself, and to make sure . . . they . . . take away his land . . . they rob him of his government, condemn his religious ideas, and ignore his fundamental conceptions of justice and morals. . . . Europeans have robbed [the African] of the material foundations of his culture, and reduced him to a state of serfdom incompatible with human happiness. The African . . . realises that he must fight unceasingly for his own complete emancipation; for without this he is doomed to remain the prey of rival imperialisms, which in every successive year will drive their fangs more deeply into his vitality and strength.

—*Jomo Kenyatta, 1938*

10 *THE ADMINISTRATIVE INTERLUDE, 1919–1939*

For the peoples of tropical Africa, the years between the two world wars constituted a period of adjustment. Their white rulers had clearly come, for all intents and purposes, to stay. A new generation grew up that had never known any life other than that ultimately directed by whites. They, along with some of their elders, accepted the new, imposed societal framework and, for the most part, faithfully attempted to remain within its perimeter. Many adapted easily: the African in the administrative age learned the language, customs, and organizational methods of his rulers. He studied in schools staffed by European secular and clerical teachers, worked for white district officers, road foremen, traders, and missionaries, and attended to the household needs of their families. All these experiences naturally provided grist for the mills of personal change. Africans generally tried to become "good" citizens and, if they followed the paths of the

West, relied upon the patronage of colonists to advance their own careers. Whites encouraged this type of response, but they generally discouraged assimilation and, in an unpremeditated way, concentrated upon administration. They developed their colonies economically, they experimented with a variety of political rearrangements, and they cared for and tutored those whom they considered to be their charges or wards. The colonial approach remained, however, essentially static and divorced from the social and economic changes taking place in the respective mother countries. This divorce from reality nonetheless continued to define the context within which Africans lived. It also molded their aspirations.

I. The Governance of Colonies

No dramatic shifts in colonial policy distinguish the "administrative interlude" from its predecessor. The major foreign powers elaborated the rule that they had already consolidated, extended their efforts to profit from the resources of tropical Africa, and improved the quality of their cultural and social services. In some areas, settlers gained increasing power. In all, Africans realized that they had become objects rather than subjects; their ability to withstand the tide of events consequently suffered an apparent decline. There seemed, during this period, few temporal or other limitations to the exercise of sovereignty by foreigners in tropical Africa.

The pattern of rule

Throughout the interwar period, Europeans generally administered their colonial subjects directly. Under the French system of rigid administrative centralization, traditional rule rarely found a place. The French consciously attempted in many areas to eradicate it, to rearrange pre-colonial political units, and to focus indigenous loyalties afresh. The functions of legitimate chiefs generally "were reduced to that of a mouthpiece for orders emanating from outside." [1] Except in parts of Chad, Ubangi-Chari, and Cameroun, the French themselves appointed and deposed chiefs. They also recruited replacements without reference to their tribal backgrounds or affiliations, and transformed the institution of chieftaincy into a branch of the overall administrative bureaucracy. Chiefs acted as agents of the government: they kept order, collected taxes, and recruited labor on behalf of superior white officials. In many areas, the chiefs were strangers to their districts and no more effective than the French in winning the allegiance of peoples who preferred their own traditions to those of a foreign design. Even in the cases where pre-colonial legitimacy and French choice coincided, the new role of the "made" chiefs compromised their positions in indigenous society.

Like the French, the Belgians initially sought to destroy the power of the more important Congolese chiefs. But by fragmenting the larger tribes and

[1] Lucy P. Mair, *Native Policies in Africa* (London, 1936), p. 210.

appointing chiefs whose positions—and nickel-alloy badges of office—depended upon Belgian largesse rather than tribal sanction, the government of the Congo apparently created conditions of disorder that approximated anarchy. After World War I, the Belgians therefore attempted to restore the importance of legitimate tribal authority and to transfer to it some of the powers that had been usurped by the white chain of command. They returned the primary jurisdiction in jural matters involving Africans to tribal courts, but nevertheless retained for themselves the prerogative of trying Africans summarily. In a few provinces, they allowed tribal treasuries to retain and use—in accord with the theories of Lord Lugard—a percentage of the taxes collected locally. Some African units of government maintained their own public works. Yet until about 1955, the Belgian administration, like the French, regarded indigenous officials as no more than its mouthpieces. Few thought of allowing them to speak responsibly on behalf of the African population of the Congo. In the cities, the Belgians gave even less encouragement to the exercise of African authority or to the development of any non-judicial forms of modern government. Throughout the Congo, the Belgian form of direct rule thus facilitated the rapid growth of the economy. Sterile but effective, it permitted a seemingly stable, carefully regulated administrative grid to mask widespread discontent.

In its African colonies, the government of Portugal carefully distinguished between its subjects. If assimilated, "civilized" Africans officially became legally equal to Europeans. In 1933, the administration decided that it would grant the cachet of assimilation to those educated Africans of "good character" and reasonable means who spoke and wrote Portuguese fluently and had become thoroughgoing Christians. But the Portuguese intended that this evolutionary process should take place slowly and carefully, and that it should be selective. In the short run, it meant little to the mass of the indigenous inhabitants of Angola, Moçambique, and Portuguese Guinea. Even as recently as 1950, *assimilados* numbered only about fifty thousand among the seven million inhabitants of Angola and Moçambique.[2] To observers, the vaunted lack of a color bar appeared to constitute fiction more than fact. Assimilation and unrestricted miscegenation thus served the Portuguese régime more as conceptual façades than as practical demonstrations of equality.

Between the two wars, Portugal administered the non-assimilated majority of its African subjects in the usual direct fashion. In the various provinces and regions, Portuguese officials and their African assistants exercised a supreme authority. In order to leave tribes leaderless, they attempted ruthlessly to destroy the bases of indigenous authority. Unlike the British, they refused to recognize the validity of custom; instead, they subjected disputes among Africans to the common law of Portugal. They regulated African mobility strictly. The state also constructed an apparatus of repression in order to contain indigenous insubordination and protest. The régime summarily punished those who dared to agitate; it despatched the recalcitrants to labor "correction" camps on São

[2] Eduardo Moreira, "Portuguese Colonial Policy," *Africa*, XVII (1947), pp. 185–186; James Duffy, *Portuguese Africa* (Cambridge, Mass., 1959), p. 295.

Tomé or imprisoned them at home. In the cities and districts, administrators introduced painful modes of corporal punishment. They employed the *cikoti*, a hippopotamus-hide whip, and the *palmatória*, a wooden paddle with holes that raised welts, in order to encourage African obedience. The indigenous inhabitants of Angola, Moçambique, and Guinea thereby endured a rule as strict as any in Africa; indeed, under Prime Minister António Oliveira da Salazar, the government of Portugal brought a police-state efficiency to an "informal apparatus of terror." [3]

In British Africa, a variety of administrators attempted to adapt Lugard's philosophy of indirect rule to the needs of their own colonial situations. They praised its flexibility and the promise of evolutionary development that served as its theoretical foundation. Experience in "native authorities," or indigenous local governments, promised to prepare Africans for the eventual problems of home rule and, in the process, to preserve the "best elements" of traditional life. The aura of indirect rule, however, increasingly seemed more important than the realities inherent in Lugard's original administrative experiment. Indeed, although nearly all of the British colonies at one time or another during the years between the wars attempted to change from direct to indirect forms of government, the preconditions for the necessary devolution of authority existed in their ideal form only in Northern Nigeria. There, Britons had entrenched the practice of indirect rule; in company with the emirs, whom they "advised," they valued the traditional organization of society and actively resisted change. For these reasons, they tolerated corrupt and inefficient rule and joined the emirs in perpetuating personal expressions of power.[4]

Lugard himself extended indirect rule to Southern Nigeria. Under his successors, however, individual administrators often blurred the distinctions between "advice" and "supervision." Whatever the logic of the theory of indirection might imply, these men ruled in fact if not always in name. In eastern Nigeria, however, they originally grouped the indigenous inhabitants under the jurisdiction of alien "warrant" chiefs who owed their appointments and power to the central government. When the administration also began to tax these Ibo- and Ibibio-speaking peoples, they protested. In 1929/30, the women of Aba and Opobo rioted against white rule, the new "native authorities," and direct taxes.[5] Much of eastern Nigeria was affected. Thereafter, the government largely dropped the pretense of indirect rule, and white district commissioners themselves administered the peoples of the east without the intervention of an artificial class of chiefs. Indirect rule had failed. Only modern institutions of local government later suited the proclivities of these Nigerians.

---

[3] *Ibid.*, p. 304; Basil Davidson, *The African Awakening* (London, 1955), pp. 204, 217–218; Marvin Harris, "Portugal's African 'Wards,' " *Africa Today*, V (November–December, 1958), pp. 11–12.

[4] W. R. Crocker, *Nigeria: A Critique of British Colonial Administration* (London, 1936), p. 215; Arthur Norton Cook, *British Enterprise in Nigeria* (Philadelphia, 1943), p. 251; L. Gray Cowan, *Local Government in West Africa* (New York, 1958), p. 25.

[5] Margery Perham, *Native Administration in Nigeria* (London, 1937), pp. 206–220; Lord Hailey, *Native Administration in the British African Territories* (London, 1951), III, p. 159.

Outside of Nigeria, Tanganyika provided the setting for the most ambitious attempt to transform the mystique of indirect rule into actual administrative machinery. When Administrator (later Governor) Horace Byatt realized that he could not govern Tanganyika cheaply and efficiently by overworking his few district officers and their Asian and Arab assistants, he empowered African courts to hear minor cases and recognized the local authority of traditional headmen. In this *ad hoc* fashion, he laid the foundations of indirect rule. In 1925, Governor Sir Donald Cameron, who had served under Lugard in Nigeria, succeeded him and immediately built upon them. His first memorandum set the tone:

> *We must not, in fact, destroy the African atmosphere, the African mind, the whole foundations of his race. . . . [Instead] we [endeavour] to purge the native system of its abuses, to graft our higher civilisation upon the soundly rooted native stock . . . that [has] its foundations in the hearts and minds and thoughts of the people.*[6]

The Native Authorities Ordinance of 1926 gave indirect rule to Tanganyika. Cameron thereafter instructed his district officers to locate the repositories of indigenous power and to constitute them "native authorities." Unfortunately, however, the indigenous societies of Tanganyika failed to duplicate the hierarchical model of Northern Nigeria. Many appeared fragmented; others possessed chiefs who acted only on behalf of their traditional councils. Some tribes could boast no chiefs whatsoever. The Masai, for example, recognized the influence of religious figures, but no chiefs. Even peoples who demonstrably had chiefs often refused to call anyone paramount chief. Along the coast, too, the indigenous inhabitants accepted the judgments of *liwali,* or headmen, but the concept of a "native authority" seemed foreign. Nevertheless, by the end of 1927, district officers had gazetted nearly two hundred "superior" and five hundred "subordinate" authorities in thirty-three districts.[7] During the next few years, British administrators attempted to reduce this proliferation of "government" by amalgamating many of the smaller units. Such a policy, however, inevitably implied the merging of unrelated ethnic groups or the equally disruptive linking of peoples who shared common customs and language but no tradition of common chieftaincy.

Cameron's team went about its task with energy and enthusiasm. Africans began to exercise a measure of home rule and the edifice of indirection grew correspondingly. Even so, the "native authorities," however sincerely constituted, remained creatures of the British administration. By the terms of the legislation of 1926, British district officers in Tanganyika, like their Ugandan counterparts, could direct "native authorities" to issue, enforce, or cancel legislation "whenever

---

[6] Quoted in Raymond Leslie Buell, *The Native Problem in Africa* (New York, 1928), I, pp. 451–452. See also Margaret L. Bates, "Tanganyika Under British Administration, 1920–1955" (unpub. D. Phil. thesis, Oxford, 1957), pp. 49–53, 84–85; Donald Cameron, *My Tanganyika Service and Some Nigeria* (London, 1939), pp. 31–35; Horace Byatt, "Tanganyika," *Journal of the African Society,* XXIV (1924), pp. 4, 8.

[7] Bates, "Tanganyika," p. 94. See also Margery Perham, "The System of Native Administration in Tanganyika," *Africa,* II (1931), pp. 303–312.

it [was] expedient for good order and government." [8] They thus encouraged the new councils to jettison traditional procedures in favor of British practices. Furthermore, although financial independence and the development of "native treasuries" had occupied a crucial position in the Lugardian catechism, the British officials retained control of the local purse-strings and the responsibility for collecting taxes. Cameron, who later dismantled Lugard's legal system in Nigeria, also placed African courts under the supervision of district officers as representatives of the hand of the executive. After 1936, the government even gazetted a few white administrators as "native authorities." [9]

In Nyasaland and Northern Rhodesia, in the years after World War I, colonial officials realized that by governing Africans directly they had weakened what a perceptive judge called "tribal feeling." [10] To many, these methods of administration seemed to deny the principles of imperial trust by which Britons had originally justified the protection of trans-Zambezia. In 1930 and 1933, the governments of Northern Rhodesia and Nyasaland thus turned to indirect rule. But like the experiments elsewhere in British Africa, these new forms of colonialism made little difference to the actual administration of rural areas. Indirect rule was rarely real. District commissioners remained reluctant to transfer any of their important governmental functions to Africans for fear that the "native authorities" would perform the required tasks inefficiently and incompetently. They did not want to "hurry" the development of the "native authorities." They further refused to "jeopardize the success" of indirect rule by entrusting "native authorities" with responsibilities that they were "not fit to exercise." Despite Colonial Office insistence that the governments of Northern Rhodesia and Nyasaland should transfer the task of collecting taxes to Africans—"this not only enhances [the] . . . importance [of the "native authority"] in the eyes of the native population, but provides the most valuable part of their education in administrative responsibility"—the district commissioners and their superiors regularly resisted such a devolution of power. In practice, indirect rule therefore meant just as little to the peoples of Central as of East or most of West Africa. "Every service which has been 'taken over' by the chiefs," an official commented, "is in actual fact largely carried out by the District Commissioner." [11]

During the years immediately following World War I, the Ganda, alone among the British-dominated non-Nigerian peoples, could legitimately claim to rule themselves. But before long, and despite lip service paid to indirect rule, the government of Uganda successfully compromised the independence of the kingdom of Buganda. Within the Protectorate of Uganda, Britons wanted to integrate the kingdom as fully as possible. They influenced the actions of the

---

[8] Bates, "Tanganyika," pp. 92–93; Buell, *Native Problem*, I, p. 454.

[9] Lord Hailey, *An African Survey* (London, 1938), p. 569; Bates, "Tanganyika," p. 151; J. P. Moffett, "A History of the Development of Native Courts from German Times," *The Journal of African Administration*, IV (1952), p. 21.

[10] ZA 1/9/39: Philip Macdonnell to James Moffat Thomson, February 13, 1927, Lusaka archives.

[11] NC 1/20/1–3, Zomba archives; Sec/Nat/274, Lusaka archives. But see Michael Crowder, "Indirect Rule, French and British Style," *Africa*, XXXIV (1964), pp. 199, 205.

Lukiiko, Buganda's parliament, usurped the powers of appointment hitherto reserved to the government of Buganda and, particularly during the 1930's, tended more and more to ignore and to circumvent the authority of the *kabaka*. The most dramatic clash between the two systems occurred in 1926, when John R. P. Postlethwaite, the provincial commissioner responsible for Buganda, decided to end the influence of Sir Apolo Kagwa, the experienced prime minister and dominant figure in the kingdom. Postlethwaite, with the eventual support of his governor, asserted the right of the government of the Protectorate to give "advice" and to expect that Ganda officials would heed such advice. Kagwa wearily resigned, despite his own feeling that he, and others similarly experienced, could best govern Buganda alone. "I cannot believe," he wrote naively, "that His Majesty's Government will follow the unjust advice of its junior official who has served for only sixteen years [in Uganda] against one of his chief officials a native of the country, more experienced and trusted." [12] Thereafter, while the indigenous government of Buganda retained the raiments of independence, the Protectorate of Uganda possessed its substance and ruled the kingdom in a fashion that was not discernibly different from its rule of the other provinces of Uganda. A memorandum drafted by members of the Ganda hierarchy underscored this shift away from the *laissez faire* attitude that had previously characterized Anglo-Gandan relations. "At present," the memorandum declared,

> *The Kabaka occupies a position which is tantamount to that of an ordinary Paramount Chief of one of the second-rate native tribes of Africa. He no longer has any power or control over his own chiefs and all and sundry officers of the Protectorate Government appear to possess the right to "have direct access" to the Kabaka, which right was exclusively reserved to the Governor alone. This practice is clearly contrary to the old native principles . . . and is certainly in direct conflict with the terms of the Uganda Agreement of 1900. . . . The Provincial Commissioner is now the direct ruler of the native chiefs of Buganda. . . .* [13]

Central or metropolitan governments made policy in their dependencies. African leaders accordingly altered the focus of their loyalties and, in some of the French and British colonies, they participated to a degree in the governmental process. As members of British legislative councils and French *conseils colonial* and *conseils d'administration*, they collectively advised governors and "were consulted" upon matters "of importance." They deliberated, criticized, proposed, resolved, and occasionally blocked financial measures but, despite the English name, they never really legislated. Only British and French governors, their executive councils, and the French Minister of the Colonies possessed that authority. Notwithstanding this absence of real power, Africans welcomed the opportunity to represent their people on the councils.

---

[12] Quoted in D. Anthony Low and R. Cranford Pratt, *Buganda and British Overrule* (London, 1960), p. 217. See also David Apter, *The Political Kingdom in Uganda* (Princeton, 1961), pp. 151–157; John R. P. Postlethwaite, *I Look Back* (London, 1947), pp. 106–112.

[13] Quoted in Buell, *Native Problem*, I, pp. 576–577.

Inhabitants of the Gold Coast had served on its Legislative Council since 1850. After 1916, three chiefs joined three African appointees from the urban areas and three white businessmen on its unofficial benches. Nine years later, the number of African councilors increased and, for the first time, townsmen elected their own representatives. But the officials continued to hold a majority of the seats until after World War II.[14] Similarly, from 1922, the residents of Lagos and Calabar together elected four Africans to the Legislative Council of Nigeria. The governor appointed the rest of the members: the other six African councilors—all of whom represented Southern Nigeria—eight white businessmen, and thirty white officials.[15] In Sierra Leone, after 1924, three of the ten unofficial members of the Legislative Council owed their seats to the electors in Freetown. Of the others, three were paramount chiefs from the Protectorate and four, including two businessmen, nominees from the Colony. In French West Africa, a small group of whites and Africans also elected Africans to the various *conseils d'administration*. The Senegalese, because of their different status, possessed a slightly more important *conseil colonial* composed of forty members, half of whom (later twenty-six) were elected by the citizens of the four communes. Provincial and cantonal chiefs filled the other seats. At the federal level, a Conseil du Gouvernement contained delegates from these various subordinate *conseils*.[16] In Britain's East and Central African colonies, Africans had to wait until World War II to play any direct part in the activity of their respective councils. Instead, settlers and a few Asians mixed with the official community; occasionally a nominated missionary or a sympathetic settler attempted to represent "African interests."

The settler factor

White settlers played a potent political role within the six territories that comprised British East and Central Africa. They governed Southern Rhodesia, received sympathetic consideration for their views from successive governors of Kenya, Northern Rhodesia, and Nyasaland, and gradually occupied a less important position in Tanganyika and Uganda. Their representatives sat on the six legislative councils, ran the towns and municipalities, formed political parties and special interest pressure groups, and everywhere spoke vociferously in order to increase the ascendance of the white man's sun over tropical Africa. Generally, the British determinedly asserted their superiority and urged their governments at all costs to deny the aspirations of the indigenous majority. They feared for their positions of privilege, and sought continually to extend the defenses of discrimination by legislation or by ending the authority of Whitehall in the colonies.

Conditions in Southern Rhodesia elicited envy among settlers elsewhere in

---

[14] Martin Wight, *The Gold Coast Legislative Council* (London, 1947), pp. 208–238.

[15] Joan Wheare, *The Nigerian Legislative Council* (London, 1950), pp. 203–204.

[16] Kenneth Robinson, "Political Developments in French West Africa," in Calvin Stillman (ed.), *Africa in the Modern World* (Chicago, 1955), p. 146; F. J. Amon d'Aby, *La Côte d'Ivoire dans la cité africaine* (Paris, 1951), p. 51.

tropical Africa. In 1922, white Rhodesians had voted against joining South Africa and in favor of home rule. Toward the end of the next year, on the thirty-third anniversary of the establishment of Fort Salisbury, His Majesty's Government formally annexed Southern Rhodesia, and ended the power there of the British South Africa Company. Subject to ineffective limitations with regard to African rights, the Crown immediately allowed the settlers to rule their own internal affairs. They, and the governments that they elected, naturally attempted both to design their racial policies to cater to the economic interests of white Rhodesians and to keep the majority and minority cultures as distant from each other as possible.

Land rights remained a source of friction. As a result of recommendations made by a commission headed by Sir Morris Carter, whites deprived Africans of further arable land. By the terms of the Land Apportionment Act of 1930, they also prohibited Africans from living in so-called settled areas.[17] In the towns, Africans could reside, usually singly, only on the premises of their white employers or in the urban "locations." Africans shuttled between urban areas, where their labor met with favor, and the reserves, where their families remained. And in the crowded, badly watered, overstocked reserves, pressure on the land grew until it reached alarming proportions. In 1931, half of the ninety-six million acres in Southern Rhodesia were controlled by fifty thousand whites. About one million Africans possessed rights to twenty-eight million acres. Towns and land unsuitable for agricultural purposes comprised the remainder.[18]

Despite the strictures of the Land Apportionment Act, the economy of the Rhodesias obviously depended upon African labor. Nyasas and Africans from the two Rhodesias dug the minerals and picked the tobacco that provided Southern Rhodesia's export earnings. They similarly supported the railway, the professions, and the government. Indeed, European endeavor in its widest context became possible only because of the broad base of economically inexperienced Africans who, at every stage, bolstered the European economy. In a complementary way, skilled workers remained few and the wages paid to whites correspondingly inflated. The government also reserved a number of occupations to whites; although Africans drove the locomotives of Nyasaland and the Congo, for example, whites monopolized these positions on the Rhodesia Railway despite the considerable savings that might have resulted from the employment of Africans.[19]

---

[17] *Report of the Land Commission, 1925* (Salisbury, C.S.R. 3-1926); Richard Gray, *The Two Nations: Aspects of the Development of Race Relations in the Rhodesias and Nyasaland* (London, 1960), pp. 48–49; Colin Leys, *European Politics in Southern Rhodesia* (Oxford, 1959), p. 28. But also see A. C. Jennings, "Land Apportionment in Southern Rhodesia," *Journal of the African Society*, XXXIV (1935), pp. 298–308; Lewis H. Gann, "The Southern Rhodesia Land Apportionment Act, 1930: An Essay in Trusteeship," *Occasional Papers of the National Archives of Rhodesia and Nyasaland*, I (1963), pp. 75–87.

[18] Leys, *European Politics*, p. 14; Montague Yudelman, *Africans on the Land* (Cambridge, Mass., 1964), pp. 68–84.

[19] C. H. Thompson and H. W. Woodruff, *Economic Development in Rhodesia and Nyasaland* (London, 1954), pp. 69–72; William J. Barber, *The Economy of British Central Africa* (London, 1961), pp. 30–31, 41–42.

Dr. Godfrey Huggins (later Lord Malvern) became the architect of a white Rhodesia. From 1933 to 1953, he remained prime minister of Southern Rhodesia. He espoused a "two-pyramid" scheme of parallel racial development and appealed to the white electorate on segregationist platforms. In 1936, his government tightened the "pass" laws that had already restricted African movement within the colony. Like the similar legislation that aroused African resentment in Kenya, Northern Rhodesia, and South Africa, it required male Africans to carry a registration certificate at all times. To it, officials affixed tax receipts and contracts of service with white employers. In addition, the law asked Africans to display any number of other certificates if they wanted to seek employment or remain at work in an urban area. And in order to make the expression of displeasure punishable, the Sedition Act of the same year declared that it would henceforth be illegal "to engender feelings of hostility between Europeans and others." [20]

To the north, the annexation in 1920 of the East Africa Protectorate to the Crown as the Kenya Colony symbolized a white settler triumph and marked the beginning of an era of unequaled dominance for twelve thousand white settlers.[21] At their insistence, the government excluded Asians and Africans from fertile highlands, introduced the *kipande*, or pass, in order to give settlers added control over indigenous labor and, for a period, even encouraged its district officers to requisition laborers on behalf of white farmers.[22] Land also continued to constitute a source of conflict between white and black. Africans wanted assurances that the whites would alienate no more of their land. But the government, while promising not to take any more, continued to give portions of the crowded reserves to whites. By the beginning of World War II, Africans had lost nearly seventeen thousand square miles of the Colony of Kenya. The government had restricted indigenous holdings to less than half of the arable land, and the best 35 or 40 percent had become the property of about two thousand white settlers.[23] Yet despite their prominent role in the affairs of the Colony, the settlers failed to obtain absolute control. Like their fellow whites in Northern Rhodesia, they never managed to persuade the British government to grant home rule. Indeed, in 1923, when the Duke of Devonshire adroitly resolved a serious dispute between Asians and whites by declaring Kenya to be "primarily . . . an African territory [where] the interests of the African natives must be paramount," he denied, perhaps unintentionally, the pretensions of whites for all time. "In the administration of Kenya," he wrote, "His Majesty's Govern-

---

[20] Gray, *Two Nations*, pp. 155–156.

[21] Lord Lugard, among others, regarded the establishment of the Colony as premature. Frederick D. Lugard, *The Dual Mandate in British Tropical Africa* (London, 1923), p. 321.

[22] For the Elgin pledge, see *Tenure of Land in the East Africa Protectorate*, Cmd. 4117 (1908), p. 33. On labor, see W. McGregor Ross, *Kenya from Within* (London, 1927), p. 450; Buell, *Native Problem*, I, pp. 332–342; Marjorie Ruth Dilley, *British Policy in Kenya Colony* (New York, 1937), p. 224.

[23] MAA/2/5/8/1–6, Kenya archives, contains an accumulation of petitions that testify to African discontent over land. See also Martin Kilson, "Land and Politics in Kenya: An Analysis of African Politics in a Plural Society," *The Western Political Quarterly*, X (1957), pp. 565–568; Norman Leys, *Kenya* (London, 1925), pp. 79, 101.

ment regard themselves as exercising a trust on behalf of the African population, and they are unable to delegate or share this trust, the object of which may be defined as the protection and advancement of the native races."[24]

Particularly in Kenya and Northern Rhodesia, and to a lesser extent in Nyasaland, these views obscured white hopes for the future. A prominent Northern Rhodesian reiterated oft-heard sentiments:

> *We white people have not come to this country solely and even mainly to raise the native in the scale of civilization. Our main objective is to survive ourselves, to improve our conditions if we can, and . . . to raise a family and perpetuate our race.*[25]

During the years before World War II, whites therefore attempted to effect the amalgamation of the Rhodesias and Nyasaland and to associate the three British East African dependencies, or the protectorates of East and Central Africa, into a wider union that they could dominate. For a time, leading British officials also favored a closer union of East Africa, but the opposition of Africans in Uganda and Kenya, and the apprehensions voiced by liberals in Britain, prevented their plans from reaching fruition. In Central Africa, however, the government of Southern Rhodesia and the settler community of Northern Rhodesia conspired together. In 1936, their representatives met at the Victoria Falls and agreed that "amalgamation" would be in the "best interests of all the [white] inhabitants of both colonies." Thereafter, Huggins and others promoted "amalgamation" in Rhodesia and in Britain. But on the eve of World War II, a visiting royal commission chaired by Lord Bledisloe heard ambiguous evidence. While settlers universally praised the proposed closer association of the Rhodesias and Nyasaland; liberal Europeans and Africans seriously questioned whether the British government should, in fairness, allow settlers to rule the protected peoples of Nyasaland and Northern Rhodesia. Southern Rhodesians, said an African who gave evidence before the commission, "do not look upon the black man as a person, they just treat them as dogs. The only time they look after them, is when they want money from them. I am a person, not a dog."[26] The commission agreed that racial policies of the colony were restrictive; in a labored, ambiguous way, its members therefore urged the British government to defer the implementation of real unity indefinitely.[27] For a time, its recommendations, and the outbreak of the war, thus frustrated settler designs on Central Africa.

---

[24] *Indians in Kenya,* Cmd. 1922 (1923), p. 10. Joseph H. Oldham, then the secretary of the International Missionary Council, evidently fathered the paramountcy declaration; Roland Oliver, *The Missionary Factor in East Africa* (London, 1952), pp. 261–262; George Bennett, "Paramountcy to Partnership: J. H. Oldham and Africa," *Africa,* XXX (1960), p. 357.

[25] Leopold Moore, speaking in the Legislative Council of Northern Rhodesia, May 29, 1933, quoted in J. W. Davidson, *The Northern Rhodesian Legislative Council* (London, 1948), p. 94.

[26] Evidence to the Bledisloe Commission, quoted in Gray, *Two Nations,* p. 192.

[27] *Report of the Rhodesia-Nyasaland Royal Commission,* Cmd. 5949 (1939), pp. 214–218, 252; Robert I. Rotberg, "The Federation Movement in British East and Central Africa, 1889–1953," *The Journal of Commonwealth Political Studies,* II (1964), pp. 152–154.

Development and exploitation in the colonies

The powers of Europe took the progressive ideas of their civilization to Africa. They opened schools and hospitals, introduced entrepreneurial concepts, built roads and railways, erected impressive buildings, extracted minerals, and planted profitable crops. Everywhere they advanced the cause of materialism. During the "administrative interlude," more and more Africans became enmeshed in this web of the West. They alone made development and exploitation possible.

As an integral part of their evangelical endeavor, missionaries started the first schools and hospitals in much of tropical Africa. In the villages, these centers of instruction consisted of little more than "a fence of grass, six feet high, surrounding some big trees, [with] a few poles laid across short forked sticks for seats, and a mass of wriggling, chocolate brown, youthful humanity. . . ." [28] There, Africans learned how to count and to read and write their own or the metropolitan language. They drew, sang, mapped the physical terrain of the mother country, and memorized selected portions of the Bible. The lucky few later continued their education in a higher primary or secondary school, where they received an introduction to the history of their colonial rulers, advanced lessons in the geography of the mother country, and further drill in mathematics, the relevant foreign language, and the Scriptures. Many also learned an industrial or agricultural skill.

By Western standards, the educational systems of tropical Africa remained rudimentary, and Africans often complained that although white men spoke glibly of their "civilizing mission," they limited its benefits to a few and neglected the secondary and higher levels of instruction. Before 1939, colonial Africa could claim fewer than ten real secondary schools in addition to a small number of post-primary teacher- and professional-training institutions. In West and Equatorial Africa, the French designed a pyramidal system of education that, through an orderly succession of village, district, and regional primary schools, emphasized the superiority of the French culture and language. The École William Ponty, near Dakar, constituted the apex of the pyramid and, until World War II, it offered French Africa's only university-entrance courses. In Equatorial Africa, the sole higher primary school stayed shut between 1927 and 1935. The government of the Congo similarly allowed its subjects to remain largely uneducated; Roman Catholic missionary orders largely controlled its school system—the state spent little. Indeed, the Belgians expected Africans to develop only gradually, at their "own pace." [29] In order to strengthen their grip in Angola, Moçambique, and Guinea, the Portuguese consciously restricted the educational opportunities available to Africans and hampered the Protestant

---

[28] William Lammond, letter of April 22, 1920, in *Echoes of Service* (August, 1920), pp. 185–186.

[29] Lord Hailey, *An African Survey* (London, 1957), p. 1209; Pierre Ryckmans, "Belgian 'Colonialism,'" *Foreign Affairs*, XXXIV (1955), p. 100; George Van Der Kerken, *La Politique coloniale Belge* (Anvers, 1943), pp. 187–194.

A classroom in western Nigeria, 1958. Similar classroom scenes were common during the administrative interlude. (Nigerian Consulate)

missions that attempted to fill the consequent vacuum.[30] In British Central Africa, neither the missions nor the governments opened a full secondary school until World War II.

The British fostered educational advancement only in their West African colonies, Uganda, and the Sudan. Governor Frederick Gordon Guggisberg of the Gold Coast believed that education was "the keystone of progress." In the early 1920's, he encouraged a widespread expansion and improvement in the already comparatively excellent school system of that colony. He also founded the Prince of Wales College at Achimota, where, after 1926, Africans lived and studied in model surroundings under the direction of a well-qualified staff. The college patterned itself upon an English public school; yet it included primary, commercial, agricultural, and teacher-training sections, and it welcomed applicants of both sexes. In 1938, the college enrolled nearly seven hundred pupils, more than two hundred of whom were girls.[31] It later proved the germ of the University of Ghana. And in Uganda, where Roman Catholic and Anglican missionary orders each founded secondary schools, the government consciously

[30] Eduardo Moreira, *Portuguese East Africa* (London, 1936), p. 51; Duffy, *Portuguese*, p. 374; Harris, "African 'Wards,'" p. 16.

[31] F. M. Bourret, *Ghana: The Road to Independence, 1919–1957* (London, 1960), p. 137. See also Thomas Jesse Jones (ed.), *Education in Africa: A Study of West, South and Equatorial Africa* (New York, 1922), pp. 66–68, 142–144.

transformed its own Makerere College into the first university college in eastern Africa.[32]

The quality of these various educational systems often depended upon the extent to which each of the colonies paid its way. Both Uganda and the Gold Coast, for example, prospered during the inter-war period. In Uganda, Africans planted coffee in addition to cotton, and successfully managed to weather periodic slumps in world commodity prices. In order to facilitate the marketing of these peasant-grown crops, the government of the Protectorate at last extended the so-called Uganda Railway from the Kenya highlands to Kampala and gradually constructed one of the finest road systems in tropical Africa. Guggisberg meanwhile based his plans for the rapid development of the Gold Coast upon its cocoa, which in 1925 supplied nearly one-half of the requirements of the world. He linked Accra to Kumasi by rail, improved or constructed nearly five thousand miles of earth or macadam arteries, and made the old roadstead of Takoradi into the dependency's first proper harbor. Nevertheless, he and his successors failed in their attempts to diversify the economy of the country; cocoa remained cyclically vulnerable. They also permitted white-owned gold, diamond, and manganese mining companies to escape significant royalty payments or taxation of a kind that benefited the Gold Coast directly.[33]

The birth of a mining industry significantly altered the character of life in the Rhodesias. Although the copper deposits of Northern Rhodesia and Katanga had long interested both Africans and Europeans, a full-scale exploitation of the Northern Rhodesian lode took place only after 1924, when a rising world demand encouraged British and American financiers to re-investigate its potential. An American engineer discovered that a rich zone of sulphide ore lay below the surface supplies of oxidized, poor-quality copper. In 1929/30, the Rhodesian Copperbelt, as it had come to be called, experienced a period of boom. White and African labor migrated thither from all over southern Africa; whole towns grew where few persons had ever lived before. During the first years of the world depression, the boom abated, but the Rhodesian companies weathered the crisis more easily than their competitors and emerged as low-cost producers dependent upon abundant supplies of comparatively cheap African labor and ores that submitted easily to technical treatment. The onset of World War II, and subsequent demands for copper, brought great wealth to Northern Rhodesia. At the same time, the mines proved a magnet for migratory labor, and helped to denude rural Nyasaland and Northern Rhodesia of the male members of their population. Copper thus transformed an essentially agricultural people into an underpaid urban proletariat that often lived on the tenuous margin between employment and unemployment. In the towns, too, Africans experienced their inferiority in oppressive new ways. Segregation appeared more onerous than before. Indeed, the African Copperbelt strikes and riots of 1935

[32] See *Report of the Commission on Higher Education in East Africa,* Col. No. 142 (1937).

[33] Bourret, *Ghana,* pp. 30, 124–128; W. Keith Hancock, *Survey of British Commonwealth Affairs,* II (London, 1942), pp. 186, 209–212, 248–258.

One of Africa's first international personalities, Dr. James Emman Kwegyir Aggrey (1875–1927) was a member of the Phelps-Stokes educational commissions and, until his death, deputy vice-principal of The Prince of Wales College at Achimota, the Gold Coast. (Photo taken in 1925. Courtesy of O. Rudolph Aggrey)

and 1940 signified a discontent generated as much by the pricks of discrimination as by sharp economic grievances.[34]

In addition to copper, Africans in the Congo also mined a large percentage of the world's cobalt, uranium, and industrial diamonds, and smaller quantities of gold, zinc, cadmium, manganese, columbium, and tantalum. The construction of a railway from Elisabethville in Katanga to Benguela in Angola, and the extension of the line from Rhodesia into the diamond country of the Kasai basin, assisted the exploitation of these minerals. The great Belgian companies that controlled this wealth were joined by others that established palm oil, rubber, cacao, and coffee plantations throughout the breadth of the Congo. As a result, whites lived well. By the end of World War II, the Congo could boast a corps of efficient white technocrats, an impressive collection of public works and urban locations, one of the best transportation systems in Africa and, in Léopoldville, one of the most modern of tropical African cities.

The managers of the Congo drew Africans into the lower levels of this transplanted economy. Whereas the Independent State had exploited its subjects crudely, the Belgian administration used African labor in a sophisticated way. An official directive early encouraged district administrators to become "penetrated with the idea that [their] reason for existence is to favor and develop [the Belgian] occupation. . . ." The governor-general instructed:

---

[34] For the opening up of the Copperbelt, see E. A. G. Robinson, "The Economic Problem," in J. Merle Davis (ed.), *Modern Industry and the African* (London, 1933), pp. 141–145.

You will be apostles of labor . . . not of accidental labor which is content with paying taxes, but a persevering labor, which is the basis of all prosperity, development and civilization.

It is a mistake to believe . . . that once taxes are paid and other legal obligations met, the native may remain inactive. . . . In every case I should consider this to be a lack of discipline violating the recommendations of the government and our most positive duties toward our black subjects. . . .

"The moral authority of the magistrate and administrator, persuasion, encouragement, favors; and if these do not succeed, marks of displeasure" would turn idle Africans into workers.[35]

The Belgians thus obliged Africans to perform "communal" tasks or "civil requisitions" that, the Colonial Charter to the contrary, amounted to compulsory labor. Although legislation limited the amount of time that Africans could be forced to spend on public projects, impressed Africans often maintained the roads and railways of the state. The administration forcibly conscripted Africans into the *force publique,* or militia, and sent them to the mines or to distant plantation centers.[36] The state also compelled Africans to cultivate rice, cotton, and other cash crops. At the same time, the government of the Congo, like that of Kenya, discouraged Africans from planting coffee, which it reserved exclusively for the exploitation of Europeans.

The economy of the Portuguese colonies similarly depended upon the labor of Africans. District officials used force to recruit laborers for local projects. They shipped Africans "under contract" to white-run plantations or diamond mines, where the workers, contrary to their inclinations, often remained for long periods of time. A former Portuguese colonial official contributed his own indictment:

In some ways the situation is worse than simple slavery. Under slavery, after all, the Native is bought as an animal: his owner prefers him to remain as fit as a horse or an ox. Yet here the Native is not bought—he is hired from the State, although he is called a free man. And his employer cares little if he sickens or dies, once he is working, because when he sickens or dies his employer will simply ask for another.[37]

In Moçambique, the state, like the administration in the Congo, also compelled Africans to grow cotton to the detriment of their own way of life. It captured "idlers" and transformed them into "laborers," and regularly recruited Africans for work in the mines of South Africa.[38]

Like the other colonial powers of Europe, France depended upon its African empire for a supply of raw materials that could be consumed at home and sold abroad. French administrators consequently used a variety of means to ensure

---

[35] Quoted in Buell, *Native Problem,* II, pp. 539, 540–541.

[36] See Octave Louwers, "La Question sociale au Congo," *Congo: Revue Générale de la Colonie Belge,* II (1924), p. 480; Guy Malengreau, *Ver paysannat indigène: les lotissements agricoles au Congo belge* (Bruxelles, 1949), p. 343.

[37] From an unpublished report of Henrique Galvão, dated January 22, 1947, quoted in Basil Davidson, *Awakening,* p. 205. See also F. Clement C. Egerton, *Angola in Perspective* (London, 1957), p. 220.

[38] Harris, "African 'Wards,' " pp. 5, 24.

Examples of mud and thatch village housing on the great inland plateau of Nigeria. (British Information Services)

that the indigenous inhabitants of the empire would play their expected role. In West Africa, they conscripted laborers for work on privately owned cotton plantations in the Soudan, for the timber-extraction industry of the Ivory Coast, and for the fisheries of Mauritania. Before a mutiny brought reforms, Frenchmen also freely used the whip to hasten the efforts of African railway construction gangs. In Equatoria, the criticisms of the novelist André Gide publicized the existence of conditions that seemed inhumane. In 1927, he made it clear that French concessionaires had merely refined their techniques of exploitation since the scandals and reforms of the period between 1904 and 1910. They still compelled villagers to sell home-grown tropical products at an artificially low rate. They continued to expect Africans to gather rubber. Gide wrote of private stockades, of starvation prisons, and of one village where Africans who had not filled their quotas had to march around and around all day carrying heavy wooden beams on their shoulders. When they fell, guards flogged them with a *cikoti* until they rose, or died.[39] He, and others who investigated conditions in Equatoria during the 1930's, saw women and children working in road gangs. These visitors wrote of whole neighborhoods that had been deprived of able-bodied men, of the flight of frightened Africans to Rio Muni, of the violent protest that gripped Ubangi-Chari between 1927 and 1930, and of the rapacity of the French overseas administration. A later observer also criticized the high death toll that accompanied the construction of the rail line between Pointe Noire and Brazzaville: seventeen thousand Africans lost their lives in order to lay about one hundred miles of track through the equatorial forest.[40] At the

[39] André Gide, *Voyage au Congo* (Paris, 1927), pp. 23, 92.
[40] Marcel Homet, *Congo: terre de souffrances* (Paris, 1934), pp. 35–41. See also Negley Farson, *Behind God's Back* (New York, 1941), pp. 491–496, 508. Other important exposés in-

same time, Equatorial Africa remained France's "cinderella" colony. Its government neglected the minerals of Gabon, discouraged Africans from cultivating cash crops like cocoa, and constructed few proper roads.

The italian conquest of ethiopia

Between 1916 and 1928, Ras Tafari, the regent of Ethiopia, yearly grew more influential. Nonetheless, his modernist views, his evident abilities, and his ambition for power aroused the animosity of the empress and many of the more important members of the imperial oligarchy. They objected to his flirtations with the West, his willingness to reform the administrative and social services of the province of Harar, and his decision in 1923 to join Ethiopia to the League of Nations. Even then, Tafari understood the extent to which his militarily weak nation remained prey to the designs of Europeans; at the time, he hoped that the League could, if the need arose, successfully protect smaller countries from aggression. Three years later, he in fact used the platform provided by the League to denounce renewed Anglo-Italian recognition of mutual spheres of influence in Ethiopia. But divided within, the vulnerability of the empire seemed apparent.

Toward the end of 1928, Ras Tafari became the uncrowned ruler of Ethiopia. After the death of the powerful war minister, the regent gained control of a number of the important provinces of the empire and won the loyalty of their soldiery. He overawed the governors of Tigre and Sidamo, outmaneuvered the empress, and foiled the so-called palace revolt of nobles. Later, when the governor of Begemder led an insurrection in the north, his troops quelled it with ease. Shortly thereafter, the empress died and, in the spring of 1930, Tafari became Haile Selassie I, king of kings and the unquestioned monarch of Ethiopia. With deliberation, he began to knit the disparate sections of the empire together more tightly than ever before. He gave advisors of many nationalities positions of prominence in the government and relied upon them to train the army and the police. He sponsored an extension of the limited Ethiopian educational system and personally sent a number of supporters to universities overseas. He abolished slavery and even attempted to modernize the Church. In 1931, he granted a constitution to the people of the empire; for long, however, it remained a paper reform.

Despite the Italo-Ethiopian Treaty of Friendship in 1928, relations between the two countries deteriorated alarmingly. The Italians nursed a number of grievances with regard to the still unsettled border between Italian Somaliland and Ethiopia. They also claimed that the Ethiopians had defaulted on an agreement to construct a road between Addis Ababa and Assab in Eritrea. Nevertheless, in 1934, Mussolini and Haile Selassie supposedly resolved their differences by reaffirming the earlier treaty of friendship. But toward the end of 1934, a group of Ethiopians attacked the Italian consulate at Gondar. A few

---

cluded: Albert Londres, *Terre d'ebène* (Paris, 1929); Pierre Fontaine, *Le Mort mysterieuse du Gouverneur-Général Renard* (Paris, 1943); Marcel Sauvage, *Sous le feu de l'équateur: les secrets de l'Afrique noire* (Paris, 1947).

Haile Selassie I, emperor of Ethiopia, on his way to the League of Nations in 1936 in a forlorn attempt to save his country from being conquered by the Italian Fascists. (Wide World)

weeks later, an Anglo-Ethiopian boundary demarcation commission, then surveying the border between Ethiopia and Somaliland, visited the oasis of Walwal in the Ogaden. Walwal occupied a position well inside of Ethiopia, but the Italians had nonetheless long considered it theirs and, since 1930, had occupied it. In any event, the Italians in charge at Walwal hampered the activities of the commission and clashed with its escort of Ethiopian troops. Italy demanded apologies and compensation. It also refused to submit the dispute to arbitration, and Mussolini became more and more belligerent.

Haile Selassie hopefully turned to the League of Nations. But the nations of Europe hesitated. Throughout the first half of 1935, they temporized. The Council of the League met in January without taking up the matter. In April, after the governments of France and Italy had drawn closer together politically, the foreign ministers of Britain, France, and Italy—the three signatories of the Tripartite Treaty of 1906—met at Stresa and publicly said nothing about the dispute over the Ogaden. In May, the Council of the League set in motion the arbitration machinery that had been mentioned in the treaty of 1928. But the Italians obstructed the resultant conciliation commission and tried to confine any public discussion to the events at Walwal; Ethiopia naturally demanded a settlement of questions regarding the entire frontier and sought to achieve a public declaration from the League that Ethiopian independence would be protected. In July, the League agreed to examine any questions still outstanding between the two countries. By then, however, the Fascist army had mobilized and the foreign minister of France had secretly agreed, and had persuaded the British foreign minister, to acquiesce in the Italian invasion.[41]

[41] See Arnold Toynbee, *Survey of International Affairs, 1935* (London, 1936), II, pp. 188–189.

An Ethiopian chieftain with his armed band of warriors, typical of the tribesmen who fought shoulder to shoulder with Haile Selassie's troops. (United Press International)

Mussolini, determined to aggrandize, meanwhile rode high upon a crest of public opinion at home. Revenge for a long list of seeming insults and for the defeat long ago at Adowa, the desire to add the highlands of Ethiopia to their arid strips of colonial coastline, and a lust for the fruits of victory all moved the Italians.

In October, 1935, they entered Ethiopia. Like earlier invaders, the Italians followed the road from Asmara toward Adowa and Axum, persuaded Haile Selassie's enemies to defect, and easily occupied Tigre. From the south, other Italians advanced into the Ogaden and headed for Harar. At the same time, the European nations that comprised the League, and the United States, talked much but acted little. They failed to impose the type of sanction—particularly an embargo on oil—that would have damaged Italy's ability to wage war. As a result, the Italians quickly capitalized upon their initial military successes. At a battle on the road to, ironically enough, Magdala, the Italians administered a decisive defeat to forces personally led by Haile Selassie. In the weeks that followed, their airplanes dropped bombs and poison gas, while Ethiopians loyal to the emperor fought on. In April, 1936, Mussolini's generals captured Gondar and Dessye. In May, the southern and northern armies joined forces at Dire Dawa and, within days, entered Addis Ababa and Harar. The emperor fled to Palestine and then to Britain.[42] Mussolini meanwhile annexed the oldest

[42] For a detailed account of the war, see George L. Steer, *Caesar in Abyssinia* (London, 1936), *passim;* E. W. Polson Newman, *Italy's Conquest of Abyssinia* (London, 1937), pp. 82–283.

independent African state and, despite periodic revolts, ruled it until British forces fought their way to Asmara and Addis Ababa in 1941.

The maintenance of liberia's independence

From the beginning of the twentieth century, Liberia again looked to the United States for assistance. In 1912, after the Liberians had quarreled with British concessionaires and the agencies with which their government had previously negotiated a disastrous loan, the American administration persuaded private banks to fund the back debts and provide a new supply of capital. The banks installed a financial advisor to guide the economy of the country and customs supervisors to safeguard their lien.[43] During World War I, when the Kru people of the coast rose against their Americo-Liberian rulers, the United States supplied arms and ammunition that were used to suppress the rebellion. In exchange, the American Secretary of State demanded that the government of Liberia should reform. As a result, conditions in the interior, where the rule of Americo-Liberians had long been despotic, improved, and the central administration tried to eliminate corruption in the towns.

The course of national politics nonetheless continued to follow its accustomed path. The oligarchy of Americo-Liberian planters that controlled the True Whig party remained in power. The president of the country and most of the members of Liberia's small bicameral congress came from its ranks. At each election, more Liberians often marked ballots than actually possessed the right to vote. According to the report of one observer:

> *. . . Natives were forced . . . to appear at the polls on election day and there with soldiers at their backs, place ballots in the boxes, ballots which they were unable to read, and practically all of which were marked with [the president's] name.*
>
> *There has been no legal registration in the interior. Pseudo names were entered in the registration books and the practice was to vote as many as could be secured over and over again until the lists were exhausted. . . . Another method was to place hundreds of ballots in the boxes before voting began, or to create an excitement and in the confusion put in several hands-full of tickets.*[44]

During the period between the two world wars, Liberia's bonds to the United States became tighter. With official encouragement, the Firestone Rubber Company and its subsidiaries established plantations, constructed roads, provided local revenue and, after 1926, dominated the economy of the country.[45] Before long, the Company occupied more than 200,000 acres of land, ran the banks, developed the port of Monrovia and, in general, provided the stabilizing factor

---

[43] George W. Brown, *The Economic History of Liberia* (Washington, 1941), pp. 164–170.

[44] Quoted in Buell, *Native Problem*, II, p. 715. See also Arthur Hayman and Harold Preece, *Lighting up Liberia* (New York, 1943), pp. 16–67.

[45] See *ibid.*, p. 845; William E. Burghardt Du Bois, "Liberia, The League and the United States," in *Africa Seen by American Negroes* (Paris, 1958), pp. 331–334; Charles Morrow Wilson, *Liberia* (New York, 1947), pp. 80–146. See also B. Nnamdi Azikiwe, *Liberia in World Politics* (London, 1934), pp. 144–167.

so necessary for the financial rehabilitation of the country. In consort with the National City Bank of New York, it also backed a new loan that bolstered the economy of Liberia at the onset of the world depression.

American influence thus helped to modernize Liberia. But the injection of new capital served merely to reinforce the traditional system of politics and government. The True Whigs maintained their power and successfully resisted the formation of opposition parties. They also enriched themselves at the expense of their constituents. According to the report of an investigation conducted at American and British insistence for the League of Nations, officials of the government of Liberia had often forced chiefs or used troops to collect laborers for shipment to Fernão do Pó or Gabon. There these Liberian "recruits" worked "under contract" on the plantations while in Monrovia members of the government pocketed the profits. The League investigators even accused the president and vice president of Liberia of participating directly in this new form of the slave trade. Their report further noted that the government had forced laborers to work on its own roads. It also cited instances of extortion, illegal taxation, and maladministration of the tribal areas of the interior. "Not only have the native village classes been intimidated and terrorized by a display of force, cruelty and suppression," the report read, "but the chiefs themselves, men whom the people not so many years ago looked up to . . . have been so systematically humiliated, degraded and robbed of their power that now they are mere go-betweens, paid by the Government to coerce and rob the people." [46]

The leaders of Liberia reluctantly resigned. Under pressure from the United States and the League, the new government enacted a number of reforms that promised much but produced little. The League even planned a program of direct international administration, in some ways foreshadowing the subsequent actions of the United Nations in the Congo, but Liberia persisted in its refusal to accept such outside supervision, particularly on the terms proposed by the Firestone Company, and thus avoided a period of "international colonialism" that could conceivably have cost Liberia its independence.[47] Thereafter, the state employed a number of American advisors, but the True Whigs retained real power in their own hands until World War II when the triumph of nationalism elsewhere transformed Liberia, under the leadership of President William V. Shadrach Tubman, into an influential member of the Afro-Asian bloc.

II. The Stirrings of Discontent

Colonial rule, with its many coercive demands and regulations, encouraged a hostile response. Throughout tropical Africa, the indigenous inhabitants contrasted Biblical teachings of equality with the actual performance of the Europeans who had chosen to settle in their midst. Not unnaturally, they also queried

---

[46] League of Nations, *Report of the International Commission of Enquiry into the Existence of Slavery and Forced Labour in the Republic of Liberia*, c. 658, m. 272, VI (1930), p. 86.
[47] William Koren, Jr., "Liberia, the League and the United States," *Foreign Policy Reports*, X (1934), pp. 239–248.

their own initially rather mute acceptance of the superiority of the white man's approach to modern life. These winds of thought, often influenced by the social or economic circumstances of particular Euro-African confrontations or by the force of external ideological stimuli, at first stirred gently. In time, however, Africans grafted a wide range of political and religious expression onto the frail stock of tentative protest.

The prophets of the new jerusalem

Wherever Africans felt unable to express their reaction to Western rule openly, or wherever healthy protest failed to produce any visible amelioration of their lot, they clothed their rejection of colonialism in religious dress. Throughout the "administrative interlude," separatist and chiliastic sects thus increased in number and influence. For many of the aggrieved, the formation of these organizations provided the only satisfactory means by which Africans might reject foreign domination, voice aspirations displeasing to their rulers, and achieve prominence independent of the colonial context. They constituted forms of sublimation and, like the related cargo cults of Oceania and the ghost groups of Indian America, demonstrated the need among subject peoples for religious experiences that corresponded to widely held aspirations.[48]

Millenarian preachers gained a widespread following throughout southern and Central Africa in the years after World War I. In Northern Rhodesia, for example, converts to the African Watch Tower, or Kitawala, movement returned in 1917 from Southern Rhodesia to their homes in Northern Rhodesia. There they found that their contemporaries resented the treatment that they had received during the war, and that they willingly received the new doctrines of disobedience; the Kitawalans spoke persuasively of the imminent end of the world, when "the last [i.e., the oppressed Africans] would be first," and of the destruction of the then prevalent system of colonial overrule. Since the apocalypse appeared to be near at hand, they argued, Africans should prepare themselves for the coming of the new age by accepting baptism, by severing their polygynous bonds, by forsaking their huts for the forests, and by praying vigilantly there until judgment day. It followed that the cultivation of crops and care of livestock were superfluous pursuits. These preachers also urged their adherents to refuse either to labor for or obey chiefs and European officials. They accused white missionaries of preaching deceitfully and of expounding only half-truths. Hanoc Sindano, a leading Kitawalan, voiced the thoughts of many:

> *God made [Europeans] know Africans and sent them with goods and many things we see to come and give us free, and teach us about God, and when they get into this country, they hide everything, and teach us very little about God; they teach us how to write but they did not tell us what God sent them here for, and they*

[48] Lucy P. Mair, "Independent Religious Movements in Three Continents," *Comparative Studies in Society and History*, I (1959), p. 135. See also Michael Banton, "African Prophets," *Race*, V (1963), p. 54; Bengt G. M. Sundkler, *Bantu Prophets in South Africa* (London, 1948), p. 297.

could not give us the things free what God gave them to give us. They make us work very very hard and give us little for the work we have done to them, and therefore if we pray very hard with all our hearts, God will hear our prayer and will clear all the Europeans back home to England and everything will be ours, and we will be [as] rich as they are.[49]

Early in 1919, the government of Northern Rhodesia arrested more than one hundred of the more influential Kitawalans; it found Sindano in his prophetically named village of Jordan, near the shores of Lake Tanganyika. In the High Court of the territory, the chief justice later sentenced most of these chiliastic enthusiasts to short terms of imprisonment. He and other members of the government confidently anticipated that such a demonstration of authority would rapidly halt the spread of Watch Tower doctrines.

But neither the sentences nor subsequent acts of suppression halted a widespread African search for religious means of expressing their despair. Throughout the Congo, the Rhodesias, and Nyasaland, the gospel of the Watch Tower remained popular. In its name, itinerant Africans baptized and held revivals, taunted chiefs, flaunted white authority, and preached what governments considered sedition. They offered a millenarian solution—despite the frequent postponement of the judgment day—to the economic and political ills of which Africans continued to be only too conscious. And, at least during the years between the two world wars, this solution owed only its inspiration to the Jehovah's Witnesses and America.[50] The African Watch Tower movement had its own prophets, its own distinctive means of expression, its own forms of ritual, and its own peculiar interpretations of Scriptural revelation.

Africans of almost every tribal and socioeconomic background gratefully accepted Watch Tower teaching. Many of their number became active preachers, achieved a certain notoriety and, between about 1930 and 1939, often gave to the standard message and the usual texts a decidedly political twist. In 1932, Joseph Sibakwe told an audience in the mining town of Broken Hill, Northern Rhodesia, that "the present government was no good and that during the [next] year a new one was coming from America and [that it] would be made up of natives only. . . . Next year all the trains will be stopped and all the Europeans will leave the country to the natives who will then be able to live their own life." In Barotseland, Mulemwa—who wore his hair long and carried a gold-topped cane—said that he had come "to abolish everything." He promised that there would be no more taxation, "nor carrying work, no more arrests, no more dying. Everybody will be baptised at the Jordan River . . . [and] . . . the missionaries are thieves. . . ." [51] On the border between Nyasaland and Northern Rhodesia, Africans began to expect that, "when Jesus comes," Europeans would "eat from the same plate as the natives. . . ." [52]

---

[49] ZA 9/2/2/2: quoted in a memorandum prepared by Hugh Charles Marshall, August 15, 1919, Lusaka archives. See also testimony in ZA 1/10.

[50] See George Shepperson, "Nyasaland and the Millennium," in Sylvia L. Thrupp (ed.), *Millennial Dreams in Action* (The Hague, 1962), p. 156.

[51] Sec/Nat/393: report of the trials of Joseph Sibakwe and Mulemwa, Lusaka archives. Both Sibakwe and Mulemwa languished for a time in prison.

[52] Sec/Nat/314: statement attributed to John Kayo, August 4, 1934, Lusaka archives.

Associated with the growth of chiliastic separatism were the messianic movements that concentrated upon the exorcism of witchcraft. They represented a recurring theme: prophets frequently proclaimed a magic method whereby witches might be found and human suffering eliminated. They offered their adherents an easy eschatological escape from fearful everyday problems. Theirs was, in sum, the welcome message of speedy salvation.

In the years after World War I, the Belgian authorities became alarmed at the evangelical activities of Simon Kimbangu in the lower Congo. During World War I, he attended classes conducted near Thysville by the Baptist Missionary Society; later he worked in the house of one of the missionaries without calling particular attention to himself. About this time, however, he began to hear voices and have visions. The voices commanded him to help his people by studying and preaching the word of the Bible. In 1921, they ordered him to heal a sick child. He did so, and the local populace soon accepted him as a prophet and redeemer. "They rejoiced to think that . . . not only white people could be great and powerful, for a mighty one, a man worthy of note, could arise from the ranks of the Africans whom they had scorned." [53] Kimbangu rapidly gathered numerous adherents on both sides of the Congo River. He denounced witchcraft, cured the sick and the lame, and energetically spread the Gospel. But he refused to establish his own church or to break with the missionaries, and he failed to denounce the Europeans. For a time, indeed, he supported received Christianity openly, and his followers packed the Protestant churches in an enthusiastic spirit of revival.

The administration of the Congo, Roman Catholic missionaries, and a number of white businessmen grew anxious. Africans left their jobs and flocked to Kimbangu. Their ecstasy seemed dangerous and, if Kimbangu failed to take advantage of his undoubted influence, other Africans apparently fanned the nationalist flames. In some areas of the lower Congo, Kimbangists refused to pay taxes; others threatened to withdraw their labor from European-backed construction projects. In a manner reminiscent of the Mahdist period in the Sudan, new prophets announced themselves and attempted to establish an exclusively African church with Kimbangu as its saviour. In the spring of 1921, the Belgians therefore arrested Kimbangu. But he escaped from custody and intensified his evangelical activities. In the autumn, the government of the Congo declared martial law in the Thysville region and mounted a full pursuit of the prophet, who eventually submitted voluntarily. A hostile court pronounced Kimbangu guilty of sedition and treason, and condemned him to death. King Albert of the Belgians commuted this sentence to life imprisonment, but the prophet, who languished in an Elisabethville jail until his death in 1951, nonetheless was thought by his followers to have been martyred. The governments of the Belgian and French Congo subsequently drove the movement underground. There it grew increasingly revolutionary and xenophobic, and its many leaders

[53] Efraim Andersson, *Messianic Popular Movements in the Lower Congo* (Uppsala, 1958), p. 57. See also Georges Balandier, *Sociologie actuelle de l'Afrique noire* (Paris, 1955), pp. 427–433; É. de Jonghe, "Formations récentes de sociétés secrètes au Congo belge," *Africa*, IX (1936), pp. 56–63.

continued to proclaim the imminence of the Second Coming and the consequent end of white rule in Africa.

In 1936, Simon-Pierre Mpadi, a junior member of the Salvation Army, experienced a revelation, broke with his white mission superiors, and organized an important neo-Kimbangist revival in the lower Congo. Three years later he founded the *mission des noirs* in order to herald the imminent resurrection of Kimbangu and, in the interim, the revival of his church. Harassed by the Belgians, Mpadi crossed the river into the Moyen Congo, and organized his followers, called Khakists because of the color of their uniforms, into a xenophobic movement that introduced nationalistic sentiments into many of the areas of the Moyen Congo and Ubangi-Chari.[54]

More prosaic in the expression of discontent than the millenarians, numerous Africans demonstrated their equally vehement rejection of colonial society by the establishment of a number of separatist sects.[55] These took different forms, but each emphasized the control by Africans of the religious present and offered to their adherents an avenue of advancement that rivaled that of the European mission churches. For the most part, they resembled religious versions of the secular protest movements common to much of tropical Africa during the inter-war years. Indeed, in many cases the leadership of voluntary associations and separatist churches was identical; for educated men, most of whom had received their instruction from European missionaries and had worked, in one capacity or another, for the missionaries, it seemed as appropriate and necessary to establish "breakaway" churches in opposition to the missions as it did to organize themselves in opposition to colonial rule. In both cases, they responded bitterly to the way in which Europeans discriminated against and prevented Africans from sharing the cultural and material riches of white society.

In the late 1920's, Reuben Spartas Mukasa, a well-educated Anglican convert from Buganda who had seen service in the King's African Rifles, learned of Marcus Garvey's Universal Negro Improvement Association and of the American African Orthodox Church, a group that had broken away from the American Protestant Episcopal Church. In Buganda, he founded an African Progressive Association and, in a letter to George Alexander McGuire, the Antiguan archbishop of the African Orthodox Church, promised "to go to hell, jail or die for the redemption of Africa." [56] He also established a short-lived Christian Army for the Salvation of Africa. Then, in 1929, after receiving encouragement from McGuire, he denounced Anglicanism and started a branch of the African Orthodox Church in Uganda. In his eyes, it was a church "for all right-thinking Africans, men who wish to be free in their own house, not always being thought

---

[54] See Balandier, *Sociologie*, pp. 447–455; Jean Comhaire, "Sociétés secrètes et mouvements prophétiques au Congo belge," *Africa*, XXV (1955), p. 56.

[55] While the use of the terms "Ethiopian" and "Zionist" in order to categorize African religious movements may originally have served a useful, if limited, function, it no longer seems appropriate either to label them in such a misleading fashion or to draw sharp distinctions between the two supposed divisions.

[56] Quoted in F. B. Welbourn, *East African Rebels: A Study of Some Independent Churches* (London, 1961), p. 81.

of as boys." [57] He later told the archbishop of Canterbury that he had left the Anglican Church in order to enter the "true church"; indeed, the African Greek Orthodox Church in Uganda, as it had become, subsequently sought and obtained recognition by the Alexandrine patriarch. After 1933, African Roman Catholics, Anglicans, and pagans all joined Mukasa's schism. It spread from Buganda into Busoga and Lango, and then into the Nyanza area of Kenya. Among the Kikuyu, a religious movement of separate provenance meanwhile attracted a wide following and, like Mukasa's church, opened schools and, in numerous ways, remained critical of colonial rule.

In other parts of tropical Africa, similar breakaway churches prospered during the years between the wars. Many, however, boasted an independent invention, a unique name, and an idiosyncratic organization. In northern Nyasaland, for example, Jordan Msuma broke away from the Livingstonia Mission of the United Free Church of Scotland in order to found the Last Church of God and His Christ. He and his followers acknowledged the authority of the New Testament only; during their services they sang hymns of their own inspiration and read particular, selected extracts from the Gospels. In direct opposition to the Presbyterian missionaries, they baptized immediately upon a sinner's confession of faith and sanctioned, even commended, the practice of polygynous marriage. The constitution of the Last Church justified this departure from accepted Christian custom in terms that reflected indigenous reactions to the rule of Europeans:

> *Africa is in need of a church that would correspond with her God-given customs and manners. We believe the commission of the Christian church to Africa was to impart Christ and education in such a way as to fit in with the manners and the customs of the people and not that it should impose on the Africans the unnecessary and impractical methods of European countries, such as having one wife. . . .*

The Last Church also believed—"unlike the missionaries"—"in the fatherhood of God and the brotherhood of man regardless of colour and creed. . . ." [58] Content in their sublimation, the followers of the many separatist and millennial movements chose to escape from the realities of colonial rule by taking alternative paths that led, they thought, to the political, as well as the spiritual, salvation of a subjected Africa.

The expression of incipient nationalism

During the years between the two world wars, Africans sought, in every conceivable constitutional way, to better the colonial political, social, and economic order. In an implicit recognition of the fact that the governments of Europe had come to stay and that the imposed codes of law could not be removed easily, Africans tried to work within the colonial context. Using the political concepts and languages of their respective rulers, they unsuccessfully

[57] *Ibid.*

[58] NN/1/20/3: constitution of the Last Church of God and His Christ, Zomba archives.

claimed a democratic right to participate in the governing process. At first they wanted to achieve no more than the right to have their collective voice heard in matters directly affecting the lives and actions of the indigenous population. To this end, those Africans (primarily educated lawyers, doctors, businessmen, clerks, evangelists, teachers, and journalists) to whom the white man's ways had become most familiar, formed organizations in order to help themselves to express their mutual pleas for reform and consideration.

In most of tropical Africa, particularly in the settler-dominated sections of eastern Africa, the Congo, the Portuguese possessions, and French Equatorial Africa, the establishment of voluntary associations played an important role in the development and eventual emergence of the avowedly nationalist movements of the 1940's. For more than twenty years, the associations sought redress for grievances allegedly endured by Africans. They urged reform upon hostile or amused governments. In East and Central Africa, they countered every public move made by the settler associations to entrench white privilege at the expense of Africans. They reacted strongly against settler agitation in favor of amalgamation or closer union. They also concerned themselves continually with matters of immediate, even parochial, consequence to the otherwise unrepresented indigenous populations of these dependencies. In Gabon, for example, Gallicized Africans formed a branch of the French Ligue des Droits de l'Homme et du Citoyen. It expressed protest in a "constructive" manner permitted by the administration. Similarly, when the youthful leaders of Port Gentil and Libreville established the short-lived Jeune Gabonais, they too understood that the French administration would accept only carefully articulated forms of criticism. In Luanda and Lourenço Marques, the Liga Africana, originally a Portuguese creation, decried official actions in a muted voice. Perhaps unintentionally, these gentle skirmishes with authority represented an intermediate phase in the history of the rise of nationalism during which the indigenous leadership came gradually to appreciate the essential futility of a strictly constitutional, *ad hoc*, and basically elitist approach to the problems posed for subject peoples by colonial rule.[59]

In the Rhodesias, Nyasaland, Tanganyika, Uganda, the Sudan, the Congo, Angola, Moçambique, and much of French Africa, the various African voluntary associations refrained from speaking publicly of self-government, and by 1939 they had alluded only in the most tangential manner to the possibility that Africans might one day be represented on legislative or executive bodies by persons of their own choice. Their leaders spoke rarely of "freedom" or of the stratagems that might ultimately return the various colonies to indigenous control. At the onset of World War II, they still craved equality of opportunity more than power, and status within the existing society more than its wholesale transformation. Yet their actions kept alive the fires of protest. Associational activity also provided training for future politicians. In many ways, the

[59] Some of these matters are discussed more fully in Robert I. Rotberg, "The Rise of African Nationalism: The Case of East and Central Africa," *World Politics*, XV (1962), pp. 78–83.

associations may thus be considered the logical progenitors of the nationalist-minded political parties of the 1940's and 1950's.

Before World War II, in only comparatively few areas of tropical Africa had Africans agitated militantly, used the available weapons of mass protest, or demanded their "freedom." In Senegal, where politics constituted a well-established part of the life of the communes, and the Ivory Coast, Africans formed branches of the Section Française de l'International Ouvrière, the French Socialist party, during the last years of the Third Republic. In Paris, meanwhile, André Matswa, a sometime customs official from the Moyen Congo, lived amidst the ferment of his time. In 1925/26, he formed the Société Amicale des Originaires de l'Afrique Equatoriale Française in order to redress the grievances of his fellow Congolese. While Matswa protested in Paris against discrimination in Equatoria, his followers in Libreville, Bangui, and Brazzaville began passively to resist a number of governmental regulations. In 1930, the French therefore tried Matswa in Brazzaville and later exiled him to Chad. But the persecution of Matswa only increased the popularity of his movement. Violent demonstrations by the Kongo people soon became common. Indeed, Matswanism cut across tribal lines and, in Equatorial Africa, provided the only sustained opposition to French rule before World War II.[60]

In Kenya, where the alienation of land constituted a major grievance, Kikuyu chiefs and commoners protested unavailingly on a number of occasions before and during World War I. When they failed to obtain any satisfaction from the government, a number of Kikuyu chiefs established the Kikuyu Association, which generally spoke bluntly about the land problem but otherwise conformed to the essentially hesitant pattern of proto-political activity throughout tropical Africa. Meanwhile, Harry Thuku, a Kikuyu telephone switchboard operator, had resented being called a native. He disliked the decision of the government of Kenya to make Africans carry a pass, and he, like many of his compatriots, complained when the administration arbitrarily increased hut and poll taxes and reduced the scale of African wages in order to accommodate white settlers during a period of economic recession. Moreover, he believed that the imperial power would "listen to reason" when it learned of the extent of African discontent.[61] In 1921, Thuku formed the Young Kikuyu Association and, with some Asian and European financial assistance, gathered a large following in Nairobi, Kisumu, and some of the other urban centers of Kenya. At open-air meetings, he emphasized the dissatisfaction of Africans and, to some extent, used platform techniques similar to those employed much later by other Kenyans. Soon, however, the government of Kenya thought that Thuku constituted a danger to the peace and good order of the Colony. Without the formality of a trial, Thuku was sent into exile, where he spent the next eight years of his life.[62] Meanwhile, his arrest provoked disturbances in Nairobi.

[60] Balandier, *Sociologie*, pp. 397–412.

[61] Harry Thuku, interview with the author (Kambui, September 14, 1961); Ross, *Kenya*, pp. 217–228, 233.

[62] After being released from detention, Thuku took an increasingly moderate political line. After World War II, he also became a prosperous coffee farmer.

After a brief hiatus, the movement begun by Thuku re-emerged as the Kikuyu Central Association. It demanded Thuku's release, complained about the continued alienation of African land, and vainly asked the government to allow Africans to plant coffee in competition with Europeans. Throughout the inter-war period, it grew increasingly more representative of the Kikuyu: from 1929, it championed female circumcision, a traditional *rite de passage*, in the face of missionary and administrative attempts to prohibit its practice. During the 1930's, members of the Association played a prominent part in the establishment of the independent schools and religious sects that proved so important to the subsequent rise of modern Kenyan nationalism.[63] Jomo Kenyatta, the secretary of the Association, gained prominence during the campaign over circumcision, and he drafted and personally took petitions of protest to the British Secretary of State for the Colonies and to the British Parliament. Of the astounded Secretary of State, he demanded the direct election of Africans to the Legislative Council of Kenya. Throughout the 1930's, during a period of voluntary exile and study in Britain, Kenyatta continued to promote the case for reform. His letters appeared in the correspondence columns of numerous British newspapers and periodicals; with other nationalists, he discussed the various ways by which the peoples of Africa might someday free themselves from the rule of Europeans. Meanwhile, at home the Kikuyu Central Association carried on unspectacularly without Kenyatta until the government of the Colony decided in 1940 to ban the Association for the duration of World War II.

The peoples of the old colonial areas of British West Africa had long possessed a tradition of indigenous political expression. At the close of World War I, the intelligentsia of this region gained inspiration from the activities of the All-India Congress and the liberal sentiments so loftily expressed by President Woodrow Wilson and Prime Minister David Lloyd George. For some, Wilson's "self-determination" struck a very responsive chord. In 1920, largely at the instigation of Joseph Ephraim Casely Hayford, a Gold Coast lawyer, a comparatively small group of educated Africans from the Gambia, Sierra Leone, the Gold Coast, and Nigeria met in Accra and formed the National Congress of British West Africa. Casely Hayford and a few others intended to work for the eventual union of the four colonies. At their inaugural meeting, the members of the Congress demanded substantial reforms in legislative representation, urged the foundation of a university for British West Africa, asked for the appointment of African lawyers and doctors to the judiciary and the colonial medical service, decried segregation, condemned the partition of Togo and Cameroun, and implied a definite interest in self-determination.[64]

---

[63] See Jomo Kenyatta, *Facting Mount Kenya* (London, 1938), pp. 130–138, 273–279; Welbourn, *Rebels*, pp. 135–161; Ralph J. Bunche, "The Irua Ceremony Among the Kikuyu of Kiambu District, Kenya," *The Journal of Negro History*, XXVI (1941), pp. 46–65.

[64] David Kimble, A *Political History of Ghana: The Rise of Gold Coast Nationalism, 1850–1928* (Oxford, 1963), pp. 383–385.

The formation of the Congress made an immediate impact in British official circles. The members of the Congress envisaged the eventual grant of local self-government. But although they claimed to speak for all, their authority was challenged in the Gold Coast by a number of influential chiefs. Moreover, the members of the Congress sought most of all to advance the claims of the intelligentsia and to obtain a restoration of their own economic and human rights more than the rights of the masses. Its cross-territorial ambitions also appeared unwarranted; the Congress never found much support in Nigeria, Sierra Leone, and the Gambia, where Africans largely concerned themselves with local problems. For a few years, it played an active part in the affairs of the Gold Coast, but Casely Hayford antagonized a number of his erstwhile supporters and, although it met periodically, the Congress gradually became an empty vehicle of protest. With Casely Hayford's death in 1930, it lost its one significant voice.

Before his death, Casely Hayford had employed Joseph Kwame Kyeretwie Boakye Danquah, a lawyer of the royal family of Akim Abuakwa who had taken a Ph.D. at the University of London, to write for his newspaper, the *Gold Coast Leader*. In 1929, they together founded the Gold Coast Youth Conference. Under Danquah, it became the most important of a number of associations that agitated, albeit mildly, for improved employment opportunities and a general amelioration in relations between the government and the indigenous inhabitants of the Gold Coast. Danquah later insisted that the Conference had pressed for self-government as such,[65] but even after he revitalized it in the late 1930's, the Conference continued to give priority to social and economic advance. In 1943, the Youth Conference still sought a definite policy. Critics accused it of "yapping" much and doing nothing, of drifting comfortably without proposing significant change. At the time, Danquah and Komla Agbeli Gbedemah, later Ghana's Minister of Finance, advocated "raising the status of this country . . . industrially and economically" by setting up a national council of chiefs and educated Africans. Refusing to talk of self-government, Danquah still hoped to emulate the achievements of the whites. "Let them try as hard as they can," Danquah wrote, "but none can succeed to take away the sight of the White Man from the mind of the Gold Coast People. Churchill said the future of the world belongs to the educated race. In Africa the future belongs to him who fastens his sight on the White Man, the Economic individual." [66]

In Nigeria, meanwhile, Herbert Samuel Heracles Macaulay, a civil engineer, journalist, and grandson of the country's first African bishop, had in 1923 founded the Nigerian National Democratic party in order to contest the first elections to the Legislative Council. The Democratic party wanted "to secure the . . . welfare of the people of Nigeria as an integral part of the British Imperial Commonwealth and to carry the banner of 'Right, Truth, Liberty, and Justice' to the empyrean heights of Democracy until the realisation of its ambi-

[65] The late Dr. Joseph Danquah, personal interview with the author (Accra, June 29, 1961).
[66] Joseph Danquah, *Self-Help and Expansion* (Accra, 1943), p. 25.

tious goal of 'A Government of the People, by the People, for the People. . . .' "[67] In spite of these lofty ideals, Macaulay's party never managed to obtain a national following. Until the beginning of World War II, it continued to be led by educated, middle-class Nigerians who naturally concerned themselves more with the affairs of Lagos, the country's capital, than with the rural areas where Britons habitually bolstered traditional authorities. The Democratic party tried and failed to establish branches in Abeokuta, Ibadan, and Kano. Calabar and several of the smaller southern towns boasted their own, largely parochial parties. Until 1938, nothing could induce the smaller urban areas to subordinate local interests to a movement directed from Lagos. Few national issues excited rural leaders to the extent that they stirred the more politically conscious Lagosians. There were, furthermore, few forums where they might meet.

Except for periodic electoral fever in Lagos, and the consequent activities of the Democratic party, the "administrative interlude" was pre-eminently a period of nationalist gestation. Many of the important developments during these years took place overseas. For Nigerians, the Nigerian Progress Union (later the West African Students' Union) of London provided a hostel where West African students met and shared their hopes and frustrations. It published a magazine that reflected the rising pride and racial consciousness of African intellectuals. In general, it stimulated thought about the future of English-speaking Africa and disseminated a new radical racialism among Britain's large Nigerian student population.[68]

In 1934, a number of educated Nigerians campaigned vigorously against the allegedly poor quality of the new Yaba Higher College and, in the process, formed the Lagos Youth Movement. They also tried to alter legislation that discriminated against African truck drivers, agitated for equal advancement opportunities in the civil service, and, in 1936, called their growing organization the Nigerian Youth Movement. But until 1938, the Movement remained essentially a club of middle-class Lagosians. In that year, the Movement, infused with new radical blood, "threw its doors open to workers . . . for the first time" and ended Macaulay's grip on the Lagos Town Council.[69]

Benjamin Nnamdi Azikiwe (later the president of Nigeria) and H. Oladipo Davies had come home to supply the new blood. Davies, of a prominent Lagos family, returned from the London School of Economics, where he had studied under Professor Harold Laski and shared a room with Jomo Kenyatta. After completing his education at Storer College and Lincoln (where he also taught), Howard, Columbia, and Pennsylvania universities in the United States, Azikiwe had written bitter editorials for the *African Morning Post* of Accra and, in 1937, had founded the *West African Pilot*, Nigeria's first national newspaper. It soon made "Zikism" a household word.

---

[67] Quoted in Buell, *Native Problem*, I, p. 743.

[68] Philip Garigue, "The West African Students' Union," *Africa*, XXIII (1953), p. 56.

[69] Chief H. O. Davies, *in litt.*, May 7, 1962. See also Obafemi Awolowo, *Awo* (Cambridge, Eng., 1960), p. 116.

Inspired by Azikiwe and Davies, the Youth Movement advocated "complete independence in the local management of our affairs" and "complete antonomy within the British Empire." [70] It established more than fifty branches in the major cities of the country. Within the Movement, however, there developed personal and ethnic antagonisms that, by 1941, had vitiated its effectiveness nationally. Azikiwe became more and more estranged from the conservative faction within the Movement; Yoruba-speaking Africans dominated it to the annoyance of those Nigerians from other regions. During World War II, it played a diminishing role in the affairs of the country at a time when Azikiwe and others in Brazzaville, Blantyre, Khartoum, and Nairobi had begun to seek means of expressing their needs nationalistically.

---

[70] *Ibid.*, pp. 121–123; James Coleman, *Nigeria: Background to Nationalism* (Berkeley, 1960), p. 225.

When is Africa going to be freed? Where is that freedom promised to the world, when is it going to come to be enjoyed by everyone living on this earth?

—Charles Wesley Mlanga, 1946

11 *THE TRIUMPH OF NATIONALISM, 1940–1965*

The turmoil and the propaganda of World War II provided a climate of opinion and a range of new experience conducive to the rise of nationalism in tropical Africa. The stirring pronouncements of President Franklin D. Roosevelt and Prime Minister Winston S. Churchill, the appeal of General Charles de Gaulle, and the agitation in India and Palestine encouraged Africans of every station. The "Four Freedoms" became a household phrase. Moreover, African soldiers served with the Allied armies in Asia, North and northeastern Africa, and Europe. They fought the Japanese, the Italians, and the Germans and returned home with a new sense of self-respect. Within the colonies themselves, they helped the Gaullists to eliminate the influence of Vichy France in Equatorial Africa; thereafter it, like so much else of colonial Africa, provided the bases for Allied airplanes and ships that incidentally afforded opportunities for the mixing of white troops and Africans on relatively equal terms. The impact of the war also persuaded colonial governments and several far-seeing administrators, such as Felix Éboué in Equatorial Africa and Sir Alan Maxwell Burns in the Gold Coast, to promise and indeed to introduce a number of reforms; they thereby tried to give urban and rural Africans a greater sense of participation in the affairs of state. In general, this combination of circumstances encouraged educated Africans to take heart and to seek new ways to demonstrate their dissatisfaction with colonial rule.

I. The Tempest of Change

In 1943/44, after Roosevelt and Churchill had enunciated the principles of the Atlantic Charter and the Allies had effectively eliminated the threat of an Axis conquest of Africa, Sudanese, Nigerians, and Nyasas separately found new organizational ways in which to express the political thoughts of the day. In the Sudan, the Graduates' General Congress, originally an association of civil servants, had unsuccessfully demanded the right to self-determination after the war. As a result, Isma'il al-Azhari transformed a section of the Congress into the pro-Egyptian Ashiqqa' (Brothers) party; his opponents formed the more moderate Umma (Nation) party under the patronage of a descendant of the Mahdi. In Nigeria, youth organizations and the Nigerian Union of Students meanwhile encouraged Nnamdi Azikiwe, Herbert Macaulay, the leaders of the Nigerian Youth Movement, and several other prominent personalities to consider ways by which they might further the political evolution of their country. In 1944, after lengthy consultations, they thus organized the Nigeria National Council (later the National Council of Nigeria and the Cameroons). Macaulay became its president and Azikiwe its secretary. Two months later, in response to a call from James Frederick Sangala, who had earlier held office in different voluntary associations, a number of civil servants and chiefs established the Nyasaland African Congress. Levi Mumba, its first president, denounced the continued "exploitation" of Africans by Europeans. Africans desired, he said, all the attributes of full citizenship and, in a perhaps conscious echo of Roosevelt, "opportunities for all regardless of race, colour, or creed." He also demanded the representation of Africans by Africans in the Protectorate's Legislative Council. The delegates to the inaugural meeting of the Congress condemned the color bar, deplored the restrictions that reduced Africans to a state of social inferiority, and humbly requested the government to permit Africans to enter movie theatres, to purchase goods from European-owned stores without being forced to ask for them through a hatchway, and to wear shoes and hats in the presence of whites.[1] Like the Nigerian Council, however, the Nyasaland Congress was designed organizationally as an umbrella under which constituent bodies could find shelter. Neither enrolled individuals. Instead the Nigerian Council counted trade unions, literary societies, professional groups of herbalists and "native therapeutists," social clubs, and ethnic unions among its numerous affiliates.

Before the Nigerians and the Nyasas had actually established their respective political bodies, Éboué and a number of other French officials became aware of the political awakening of tropical Africa. In 1944, at a conference in Brazzaville, they attempted to contain indigenous aspirations by recasting the heretofore common forms of the colonial mold. They recommended that the post-war government of France should provide its African subjects with improved educational and medical facilities, prohibit the *corvée* and other types of compulsory labor, and give flexibility to marketing arrangements so that the agricultural economies of the colonies might cope more easily with cyclical fluctuations in demand. At the same time, the conferees unequivocally rejected the idea of either immediate or eventual self-government for France's overseas dependencies. They instead foresaw the need to loosen administrative ties between Paris and the colonial capitals and suggested that a special assembly sitting in Paris should legislate on behalf of the territories, each of which would

[1] Minutes printed in a pamphlet entitled *African Congress: First Annual Meeting* (Blantyre, 1944), p. 16.

possess its own local legislative council composed of Africans and Europeans. Indeed, they sketched out a plan of "association" that in many ways foreshadowed the framework of the later French Union.[2]

However paternal in approach, the conclusions of the Brazzaville conference marked the first public avowal of the need for change in French-speaking Africa. After the war, and largely because of the spirit engendered at Brazzaville, the support of the French Communist party, and the persuasive arguments of Félix Houphouët-Boigny of the Ivory Coast, Léopold-Sédar Senghor and Lamine Guèye of Senegal, Yacine Diallo of Guinée, and Léon Mba of Gabon, the constitution of the Fourth Republic instituted a number of radical reforms. It abolished forced labor in the colonies and gave to all of the inhabitants of overseas France the status of full citizens. It furthermore established the former colonies of the two African federations as territories with rights similar to those possessed by the old communes of Senegal. Deputies and senators from each of these dependencies sat in the French National Assembly and the Council of the Republic respectively. The colonies boasted their own local assemblies; subject to the deliberations of a Grand Council that met either in Dakar or Brazzaville, and the Assembly of the French Union that sat in Paris, each colony even controlled its own national budget. But within the individual territories, the constitution failed to provide for the establishment of local governments. Moreover, the existence of a qualified franchise and communal representation made its implementation in the colonies less progressive than it otherwise might have been.[3]

Although these rearrangements and reforms gave the inhabitants of the colonies considerable hope for the future, the apparent hostility of the voters of metropolitan France to the dismemberment of the empire encouraged the new leaders of French Africa to organize themselves politically. Lamine Guèye, the mayor of Dakar; Houphouët-Boigny, a *chef de canton*; Diallo; Fily Dabo Sissoko, from the Soudan; Jean-Félix Tchikaya, from the Moyen Congo; and Gabriel d'Arboussier, a part-Soudanaise former member of the French colonial civil service, jointly called a meeting of all of the groups that sought political and social democracy in French Africa.[4] In 1946, eight hundred delegates from all of French West and Equatorial Africa, except Gabon and Ubangi-Chari

---

[2] Jean-Hilaire Aubame, "La Conférence de Brazzaville," in Eugène Guernier (ed.), *Afrique équatoriale française* (Paris, 1950), pp. 183–186.

[3] Kenneth Robinson, "Political Developments in French West Africa," in Calvin Stillman (ed.), *Africa in the Modern World* (Chicago, 1955), pp. 159–168; Virginia Thompson and Richard Adloff, *French West Africa* (Stanford, 1958), pp. 54–63; Michel Devèze, *La France d'outre-mer de l'empire colonial à l'union française, 1938–1947* (Paris, 1948), pp. 280–281, 285–290; Robert Bourcart, *Le Grand Conseil de l'Afrique occidentale française* (Paris, 1956), *passim*.

[4] "Manifeste du Rassemblement Démocratique Africain, Septembre 1946," in *Le Rassemblement Démocratique Africain dans la lutte anti-impérialiste* (Paris, 1948), quoted in Robinson, "Political Developments," p. 173. For a discussion of the role played by the Groupe d'Études Communistes, see Kenneth Robinson, "Senegal: The Elections to the Territorial Assembly, March 1957," in W. J. M. Mackenzie and Kenneth Robinson (eds.), *Five Elections in Africa* (Oxford, 1960), p. 311.

(Senghor, Guèye, and the Socialists of Senegal withdrew) responded to the call and met in Bamako. There they listened to impassioned condemnations of the colonial system; then, in order to fight the elections of 1946 and to achieve the abolition of all forms of discrimination and the employment of greater numbers of Africans in government positions, they organized a political party, the Rassemblement Démocratique Africain, across territorial lines. At first, the party refrained from making "nationalist" demands; its leaders essentially desired to be treated as Frenchmen. They wanted improved conditions of life and liberty, not self-government. "In seeking to achieve its dual aim," read their manifesto, "—the union of Africans, and their alliance with French democrats—the RDA is also seeking to achieve a real French Union—of different peoples who are free, and equal in their rights and duties—and likewise ensuring the participation of Africa in the anti-imperialist struggle. . . ."[5]

Elsewhere in tropical Africa, the end of World War II likewise quickened the pace of change. In 1946, a number of Northern Rhodesians formed a territorial Federation of African Welfare Societies, the forerunner of their later Congress and, like the Nyasaland African Congress, the Federation attempted to combat the pretensions of local white settler politicians. In Buganda, riots that expressed rural discontent and displeasure with the government of the *kabaka* led to the formation of the Butaka Union. The Union preached a kind of rural fundamentalism and expressed opposition to the enhanced position of Buganda's oligarchy of chiefs. Although the aims of the Union transcended the narrow interests of Buganda's peasant leadership and, for the first time, represented welfare associations and recreation societies without regard to religious affiliation, under the leadership of Jemusi Miti and Cesario Ssemakula Mulumba it remained an interest group within Buganda rather than a national party. In the neighboring colony, however, Jomo Kenyatta returned from London in 1946 to assume the presidency of the Kenya African Union, a national organization that younger Kikuyu, Kamba, and Luo had formed from the shell of the Kenya African Study Union which Eliud Mathu had founded in 1944. After his long exile, Kenyatta evinced a determination to seek the immediate political kingdom. He brought together the Kikuyu independent schools, age-groups, ex-soldiers' clubs, and trade unions. At the same time, he alienated some of his more influential non-Kikuyu supporters and, during the next few years, the Kenya African Union found the largest number of its followers in Kikuyuland.

Untroubled by the settler factor, Sudanese politicians had meanwhile made rapid strides in the direction of self-government. In 1946, the British government promised to let the Sudanese someday rule themselves. At the same time, since the government of Egypt still theoretically shared sovereign rights in the Sudan and worried about the integrity of the Nile Valley, the emergence of the Sudanese nation contained its Anglo-Egyptian as well as its Anglo-Sudanese

---

[5] Quoted in Thomas Hodgkin, "From Brazzaville to Bamako," *West Africa* (January 23, 1954), p. 54.

Jomo Kenyatta and Tom Mboya, then the president and the secretary general, respectively, of the Kenya African National Union, acknowledge cheers of victory after the Union's overwhelming victory in the Kenya parliamentary elections of 1963. (Wide World)

aspects. Thereafter, while the British government bargained fruitlessly with its Egyptian counterpart, it simultaneously accepted the conclusions of an Anglo-Sudanese consultative conference and, in 1948, gave to the Sudan a forward-looking constitution that provided, in effect, for the assumption of considerable powers of decision by Sudanese. It also established a new Legislative Assembly; the Ashiqqa' boycotted and the Umma won the subsequent elections that filled its seats. The Umma consequently provided the leader of the Assembly and most of the members of the governor-general's new Executive Council. Thereafter, as the Egyptians strenuously attempted to assert their own authority over the Sudan, so the British government localized the civil service, tried to integrate the south and the north, provided new cultural and social facilities, and demonstrated a willingness to take the Sudanese farther along the road to independence. In 1952, when politicians elsewhere in tropical Africa envisaged the achievement of home rule more in terms of decades than of years, Britain agreed to let the Sudan govern itself.[6] Because of the peculiar local circum-

[6] J. S. R. Duncan, *The Sudan's Path to Independence* (Edinburgh, 1957), pp. 149–152.

stances and the traditional administrative separation of the Sudan, however, this achievement of the Sudanese seemed more isolated and made less of an impact upon the rest of the continent than events to the west.

In Nigeria, the National Council of Nigeria and the Cameroons became the spearhead of African opposition to British rule during the period immediately after World War II. Azikiwe, who had captured the imagination of the people of Nigeria by his outspoken championship of their cause, led his Council in protests against continued foreign domination. In 1946, he and other prominent nationalists denounced a new quasi-federal constitution that Governor Sir Arthur Richards (later Lord Milverton) had introduced the previous year. They resented the way in which it had been conceived: "We appreciate," they wrote, "the energy dissipated in order to prepare this historic document . . . but we regret to observe the unilateral way the whole proposals were prepared without consulting the people and natural rulers of this country. . . ."[7] Furthermore, the constitution said nothing about self-government. Azikiwe led a very successful eight-month tour of the entire country in order to arouse antigovernment sentiment and to raise funds with which to send a delegation of protest to London. After he easily won one of the Lagos seats in the Legislative Council elections of 1947—his party also took the other two—a delegation from the National Council of Nigeria and the Cameroons presented the Secretary of State for the Colonies with demands for a new, more forward-looking constitution. It thereby further dramatized the cause of nationalism.

The British government had meanwhile given the Gold Coast a constitution that similarly left the reins of power firmly in official hands. Moreover, the local Legislative Council continued to reflect the views of conservatives during a time of severe economic dislocation. Cocoa farmers suffered a sharp drop in income due to the rapid spread of a virus disease, and a shortage of consumer goods and food produced inflation. In addition, demobilized servicemen unwilling to revert to their positions of minimal status, middle-school and secondary-school graduates who failed to find acceptable white collar positions, and wealthy merchants and professional men who felt themselves increasingly denied any substantial economic or political role all experienced pangs of discontent. As a result, Joseph Danquah, the lawyer and politician, A. George Grant, a wealthy timber trader from Sekondi, and Francis A. Awooner-Williams and R. S. Blay, both lawyers, decided to organize a new movement that could express this prevalent dissatisfaction and also bring together the members of the moribund Gold Coast Youth Conference and the country's numerous voluntary associations. In 1947, they and others founded the United Gold Coast Convention and, at its inaugural meeting at Saltpond, advocated that the "government should pass into the hands of the people and their chiefs in the shortest possible time." And to achieve such self-government, they called for the use of legitimate and constitutional means only.[8]

---

[7] Quoted in Joan Wheare, *The Nigerian Legislative Council* (London, 1950), p. 178.
[8] Dennis Austin, "The Working Committee of the United Gold Coast Convention," *The Journal of African History*, II (1961), p. 280.

The rise of nkrumah

Danquah and his colleagues had responded to the mood of the Gold Coast. They proceeded to organize the Convention as an effective political movement, and soon took a step of crucial importance to the subsequent emergence of modern Ghana. Only with the undivided attention of a full-time, paid secretary and organizer, they thought, could the Convention succeed in its attempt to achieve self-government rapidly. Danquah, for long the administrator of unions, associations, and groups of every description, seemed the logical choice. He preferred, however, to guide the destinies of the Convention in a part-time capacity and to allow a younger man to direct activities that would no doubt be strenuous. "I felt," he later said, "that I had been secretary too long and that there should be a change of personnel in order to bring new blood into the organization." [9] Danquah offered the job to Ako Adjei, a young lawyer who had recently returned from Britain, but Adjei, who subsequently became the foreign minister of Ghana, instead urged the Convention to offer the position to Kwame Nkrumah, with whom he had studied at Lincoln University in the United States before World War II.

After some hesitation, the Working Committee of the Convention agreed to ask the comparatively unknown Nkrumah, then deeply involved in African expatriate politics in London, to take the secretaryship. He, in turn, only reluctantly decided to return home. The Committee and Nkrumah disagreed about the rate of his emoluments. It also remained unsure whether the new secretary should be an executive officer or a mere organizing agent. To this end, the members of the Committee queried his political affiliations and finally managed to satisfy themselves that Nkrumah believed in "territorial before inter-territorial solidarity" and that he had not been tinted with ideas too radical for the Convention.[10]

Throughout the first months of 1948, Danquah, Nkrumah, and the other leaders of the Convention addressed public meetings and spoke generally of self-government. Nkrumah, at least, also praised boycotts, strikes, and demonstrations as the only weapons capable of supporting pressure for self-government in the Gold Coast. He and several others probably fished "in troubled waters"; [11] they supported a consumer campaign against high prices in Accra and urged the Ex-Servicemen's Union to present the grievances of its members to the government. On a fateful Saturday afternoon late in February, 1948, the failure of the merchants of Accra to lower their prices appreciably, and discontent of a general kind, gave rise to riots that passed the immediate political initiative to the masses. Crowds looted European-owned stores, broke into the Central

---

[9] Joseph Danquah, interview with the author (Accra, June 30, 1961). The Nyasaland African Congress had earlier refused to employ a full-time organizing secretary, despite the willingness of Dr. H. Kamuzu Banda to pay the salary of such a person.

[10] Austin, "Working Committee," p. 281. But see Kwame Nkrumah, *Ghana: The Autobiography of Kwame Nkrumah* (Edinburgh, 1957), p. 70.

[11] George Padmore, *The Gold Coast Revolution: The Struggle of an African People from Slavery to Freedom* (London, 1953), p. 62.

Statue of Kwame Nkrumah in front of the Parliament House in Accra. (United Nations Photo)

Prison and freed prisoners, and apparently accompanied the ex-servicemen when they marched upon Christiansborg Castle, the residence of the governor, and elicited gunfire from its police guard. Accra remained in turmoil over the weekend, and nearby towns and distant Kumasi caught the fever of revolt during the succeeding week. Danquah and Nkrumah meanwhile stated the Convention's willingness to restore order and to govern the Gold Coast in place of Britons.[12] As a result, Danquah and five other members of the Working Committee spent a short period in jail.

From the February disturbances to their final break fourteen months later, Nkrumah and the older, more conservative leaders of the Convention formed what remained, at best, an uneasy alliance. Nkrumah's style and evident ability appealed to the younger, more virulently anti-colonial elements of the population. He organized a number of new branches of the Convention in the months after the riots and, by so doing, diffused his own personal influence throughout the dependency. He sponsored a Ghana National College for students who had been expelled at Cape Coast after a political strike. In the autumn of 1948, he founded the *Evening News* of Accra; it became an effective vehicle of per-

[12] The text of the Nkrumah/Danquah cablegram to the Secretary of State for the Colonies is contained in *Report of the Commission of Enquiry into Disturbances in the Gold Coast,* Col. No. 231 (1948), p. 94.

sonal expression. Meanwhile, the Working Committee had become increasingly suspicious of Nkrumah, of his alleged Communist views, and of his penchant for seeking support for himself rather than for the policies of the Convention.

When a British Commission of Enquiry subsequently accused the Convention of fomenting the riots, Nkrumah welcomed the opprobrium while the members of the Working Committee recoiled from such notoriety.[13] The members also agreed to serve on a new committee that the governor of the Gold Coast had established to examine the constitutional proposals contained in the report of the Commission of Enquiry. By doing so, Danquah, Grant, Ebeneezer Odartei Obetsibi Lamptey, and Edward Akufo Addo associated themselves with the constitutional, and hence the moderate, roads to reform. As Danquah later realized, this action tied the older members of the Convention to a constant round of committee meetings and "diminished the enormous prestige won by their detention earlier in the year." [14] Nkrumah, whom the governor purposely excluded from the committee, therefore remained free to take a more radical tangent.

With Komla Agbeli Gbedemah and Kojo Botsio, he organized the Committee on Youth Organization within the framework of the Convention. Theoretically allies, they quickly alienated themselves from the leaders of the Convention. The Youth Committee preached a message of self-government "now, now, now," while the Working Committee of the Convention disavowed such sentiments. Nkrumah's newspaper endlessly criticized the members of the Working Committee; he and Gbedemah spoke throughout the Gold Coast and everywhere found the masses ideologically prepared for rapid political change.

In the spring of 1949, the leaders of the Convention finally decided to purge themselves of the man who had troubled them for so long. They thought that a simple dismissal of Nkrumah, coupled with a disavowal of the Youth Committee, would suffice. But their opponents had already anticipated the break and had made their own plans to leave the ranks of the by now uninspired and essentially discredited Convention. Before an audience of about sixty thousand people in Accra, Nkrumah, ". . . on behalf of the Committee on Youth Organization, in the name of the chiefs, the people, the rank and file of the Convention, the Labour Movement, our valiant ex-servicemen, the youth movement throughout the country, the man in the street, our children and those yet unborn, the new Ghana that is to be, . . . [the] comrades who died at the cross roads of Christiansborg during the 1948 riot, and in the name of God Almighty and humanity," transformed the Youth Committee into a political party "with the object of promoting the fight for full self-government now." [15]

---

[13] The Commission called Nkrumah a Communist and suggested that he might personally have instigated the riots, *ibid.*, pp. 17–19. See also Kwame Nkrumah, *I Speak of Freedom* (New York, 1961), p. 8.

[14] Quoted in Austin, "Working Committee," p. 287.

[15] Nkrumah, *Autobiography*, p. 105. The use of the name "Ghana" linked the Gold Coast romantically with the African state that had flourished farther north about one thousand years before. W. T. Balmer, *A History of the Akan Peoples of the Gold Coast* (London, 1925), pp. 26–28, originally suggested that the peoples of the Gold Coast might be related

Although the final rupture with the older politicians actually took place several months later, Nkrumah had already cast the die of political change.

The Convention People's party of the Gold Coast emerged at an appropriate time. The rural and urban masses, a proportion of the middle-class professionals, a number of the intelligentsia, and some of the educated chiefs favored self-government. It was Nkrumah's genius that he understood the nature of the ground swell, and that he allowed himself to be borne upon its crest toward power. Taking an important leaf from Mahatma Gandhi's book, he began to threaten "positive action"—strikes, boycotts, and demonstrative non-cooperation based upon the principle of "absolute non-violence"—if the administration of the Gold Coast refused to grant home rule to its subjects before the end of 1949. But the governor deferred elections until 1951, and Nkrumah led a not altogether non-violent strike that began early in 1950. The governor arrested Nkrumah and several of his colleagues and banned the *Evening News*. But while Nkrumah languished in jail, Gbedemah and others ably canvassed the country on behalf of the party. They easily succeeded in obtaining support for a "modernist" platform that demanded improved educational facilities, equal political and economic opportunity, and the immediate grant of self-government. In early 1951, the party won thirty-four of the thirty-eight seats in the colony's Legislative Council. Nkrumah, who had campaigned from prison, captured a pivotal seat in Accra. The Convention pleased the voters in only three constituencies, and an independent candidate was returned in another area.

In these circumstances, Sir Charles Noble Arden-Clarke, then the governor of the Gold Coast, realized that it would be folly to oppose the wishes of the electorate. "I released Dr. Nkrumah," he later wrote, "as an 'act of grace.' "

> *My choice was fairly simple: if I did not release him we would not even make a start with working the Constitution; and if I did release him, he would find it very difficult to refuse to work the Constitution or give it a trial, even though it might be called 'bogus and fraudulent.' So he was released. He came up to see me, and I asked him to form a Government.*[16]

Arden-Clarke named Nkrumah the "leader of Government business" in the Legislative Council and, under the provisions of the new constitution, appointed five other members of the party to ministerial portfolios. The Gold Coast thus entered the tutelary interlude known as "responsible government." A number of other British colonial territories subsequently followed the same pattern of transition.

---

to those of ancient Ghana. In 1944, Danquah revived the idea of calling an independent Gold Coast "Ghana." He also informed the Commission of Enquiry in 1948 that the use of "Ghana" would "make a clean break away from the memories of the old days of exploitation and imperialism, and the colonial adjective Gold Coast will give way to the substantive name of the people and country, Ghana and Ghanaland." See also David Apter, *The Gold Coast in Transition* (Princeton, 1955), p. 22n.

[16] Charles Arden-Clarke, "Gold Coast into Ghana," *International Affairs*, XXXIV (1958), p. 51. Cf. Charles Arden-Clarke, "Eight Years of Transition in Ghana," *African Affairs*, LVII (1958), pp. 31–33. See also Nkrumah, *Autobiography*, pp. 117–122; Bankole Timothy, *Kwame Nkrumah: His Rise to Power* (London, 1963), pp. 103–106.

The resurgence of parties

The Bamako conference of 1946 had already launched the Rassemblement Démocratique Africain, with its impressive chain of village committees and urban "sections," throughout French West Africa (except Mauritania) and into Cameroun, Chad, and Ubangi-Chari. Under the leadership of Houphouët-Boigny and d'Arboussier, five members of the Rassemblement sat in the French National Assembly, and the party as a whole played an important part in the political life of nearly all of the French African colonies. In 1948, it claimed more than 700,000 members. Yet in succeeding years, the appeal of the Rassemblement tended to be more territorial than federal, and it became a collection of affiliates more than an integrated party. Moreover, as d'Arboussier forged stronger and stronger links to the French Communist party, so the Rassemblement began to lose some of its following except in the Ivory Coast. Indeed, by 1950, ties to the French Communists had become a liability. A rightward swing in French metropolitan politics and the open hostility of administrators in Africa also persuaded the leadership of the Rassemblement carefully to weigh the advantages and disadvantages of its continued connection with the Communists. In 1950, Houphouët-Boigny thus severed the formal ties between the two parties. After the Rassemblement fared poorly in the 1951 elections, Houphouët-Boigny also broke openly with d'Arboussier; the terms of their estrangement heightened Houphouët-Boigny's decision to eschew an ideological approach to politics. Instead, he adopted a more practical frame of reference. "You want," he wrote to d'Arboussier, "an Africa totally free of colonial rule."

> *We have a less noble but more practical and immediate goal, also a more modest one. Certainly we want social emancipation, but within the framework of the French Union. In the present national and international situation, continuation of the French experiment is the only proper position . . . it is the immediate future that now concerns us, and that is to bring into being honestly the French Union through mutual understanding. . . .*[17]

In Nigeria, politics had assumed an increasingly regional character that was reflected in the "wretched compromise" constitution of 1951. Azikiwe's National Council of Nigeria and the Cameroons catered—or at least seemed to cater—more and more to the Ibo- and Ibibio-speaking peoples of the Eastern Region and, as a result, had begun to lose the support of a number of educated Yoruba- and Hausa-speaking Nigerians. Inhabitants of most of the Western Region, where Yoruba predominated, followed Obafemi Awolowo, an Ijebu trader who had long distrusted Azikiwe. "In 1948," he later wrote, "it was clear . . . from the general political and journalistic manoeuvres of Dr. Azikiwe over the years that his great objective was to set himself up as a dictator . . . and to make the Ibo nation the master race." [18] In that year, Awolowo helped to form the politically important Egbe Omo Oduduwa, the Society of the Descendants of Oduduwa; [19] three years later he emerged as the leader of a new

[17] Quoted in Thompson and Adloff, *West Africa*, p. 91.
[18] Obafemi Awolowo, *Awo* (Cambridge, Eng., 1960), p. 172.
[19] Oduduwa supposedly begat the Yoruba-speaking people. See *supra*, p. 105.

President William V. S. Tubman of Liberia (left) and President Felix Houphouët-Boigny of the Ivory Coast (right) with Emperor Haile Selassie I of Ethiopia during the African "summit" conference in Addis Ababa, May, 1963. (Wide World)

party, the Action Group, that sought power solely within the Western Region. In elections there in 1951, Action Group candidates easily defeated their National Council opponents and gained control of the regional assembly, thereby signaling the rise of local, rather than territorial nationalism. In the Northern Region, meanwhile, Abubakar Tafawa Balewa and Amino Kano, two teachers, had, with encouragement from Azikiwe, founded the Northern Peoples' Congress. Supported by the emirs, in 1951 it easily gained a firm control over the Northern House of Assembly and the Northern delegation to the national House of Representatives. Thereafter, it championed regional autonomy; the Northerners clearly feared Ibo and Yoruba pretensions far more than British overrule.[20] Divisive regionalism had come home to roost.

By 1950, on the other side of the continent, Kenyatta's Kenya African Union had, preceding political parties elsewhere in the eastern colonies, begun to urge its government to provide for the direct election of Africans to the Legislative Council on a universal franchise. Although critics later decided that appearances had deceived, most of its members still spoke and acted constitutionally.[21]

---

[20] See the quotations in James Coleman, *Nigeria: Background to Nationalism* (Berkeley, 1960), pp. 361–362.

[21] See F. D. Corfield, *Historical Survey of the Origins and Growth of Mau Mau*, Cmd. 1030 (1960), pp. 57–63. Cf. F. B. Welbourn, "Comment on Corfield," *Race*, II (1961), pp. 7–27. See also George Bennett and Carl Rosberg, *The Kenyatta Election* (London, 1961), pp. 37–45.

Meanwhile, some Kikuyu had begun taking and administering the secret oaths that, by 1952, had ripened into violent manifestations of semi-religious xenophobia. In that year, after disorders had begun to shatter the quiet of Kikuyuland, the government formally recognized the existence of Mau Mau—as the organization of oath-takers was called—and proclaimed an emergency. The government accused Kenyatta of managing Mau Mau; after a much-criticized trial that was held under extremely difficult conditions, a presiding magistrate sentenced Kenyatta and five others to imprisonment and, until 1961, virtual exile.[22]

By this time, the British government had decided to allow white settlers to control the destinies of the African population of the Rhodesias and Nyasaland. Despite the vehement opposition of the indigenous leadership of the three colonies, and a modicum of liberal disenchantment in the United Kingdom, it made plans to provide Central Africa with a federated government in theory predicated upon a partnership between white and black. Britons wanted to create a multiracial island in a sea beset by the strong contrary tides of African and Afrikaner nationalism. They saw great economic advantages in the federation of the three territories. They also trusted the good intentions of settlers whose motives had, at least to Africans, always seemed suspect. Harry Mwaanga Nkumbula, who had studied at the London School of Economics before returning home to Northern Rhodesia to command its African National Congress, based his opposition to the proposed federal scheme on the fact that the settlers and the British government were patently aiming "at a complete domination and exploitation of the Black people of Central Africa." He condemned Sir Godfrey Huggins and Roy Welensky, the leading Rhodesian white politicians, and spoke for many who felt that the federal scheme sold Africans into slavery and deferred home rule indefinitely. In 1952, before a large public meeting of the Congress near Lusaka, Nkumbula argued for them all:

> *Ladies and gentlemen, we are being betrayed by the British government and it is high time that we tell the white people . . . that their support of this plan is not only dangerous to us but to their well being and happiness in this country. This is our country. There is no mistake about that. I have time and time again stated that the imposition of this scheme against the wishes . . . of Africans will make life intolerable for the whites in Central Africa. . . . I cannot help thinking . . . that . . . the best government for the black people is a government fully manned and run by the black people of Africa. . . .*[23]

The British government paid almost no attention to such expressions of discontent at a time when the settlers themselves repeatedly confirmed Africans in the worst of their fears. Welensky, for example, publicly admitted that "if there is going to be domination, it is going to be my own [white] race that will

---

[22] See Jomo Kenyatta, quoted in Montagu Slater, *The Trial of Jomo Kenyatta* (London, 1959), pp. 240–242. Cf. Corfield, *Mau Mau*, pp. 158–162. The name "Mau Mau" is of uncertain provenance.

[23] N/0001/2/5: report of a meeting of June 26, 1952, Lusaka archives.

Dr. Kenneth Kaunda, then president of Northern Rhodesia's United National Independence party, pleads his country's case for independence before the United Nations Special Committee on Colonialism in April, 1962. He is flanked and supported by Sir Stewart Gore-Browne, and Arthur Wina. (United Nations Photo)

dominate. The African is unfit . . . to be a full partner." [24] Henry Hopkinson (later Lord Colyton), the British Minister of State for Colonial Affairs, toured Central Africa but refused to believe that African opinion on the subject of federation even existed.[25] In early 1953, the British government and delegates from the Rhodesias and Nyasaland approved a constitution for the Federation that contained few effective safeguards for African rights.

Africans warned the British government of the consequences that would follow the forceful imposition of the federal plan. Sooner or later, they said, blood would flow. Joshua Nkomo of Southern Rhodesia promised that Africans would struggle. "Let us not be blamed that the Africans resort to savagery again. . . . We refuse," he said, "to be bound by unjust laws." [26] Further verbal protest availed Africans little and, in the autumn of 1953, the government of the Federation of Rhodesia and Nyasaland officially began to rule Central Africa. Its creation marked the end of one fruitless campaign of protest and the beginning of an unremitting local struggle against any kind of alien rule whatsoever. Instead of ensuring white domination forever, the federal gambit materially hastened the day when Nyasas and Rhodesians would govern themselves.

The threat of another federation gave added impetus to the rise of the nationalist spirit in Uganda. In the summer of 1953, the Secretary of State for the Colonies spoke generally of the possibility that the British government

---

[24] *Northern News,* July 22, 1952.
[25] *East Africa and Rhodesia,* September 4, 1952.
[26] 2/14: verbatim report of a public meeting held at Church House, Westminster, London, January 23, 1953, Lusaka archives.

might someday unify or federate its East African possessions. He thereby aroused all of the old fears of threats to the privileged position of Uganda. Africans there wanted to remain separated from Kenya, where whites still ruled, and the government of Buganda, in particular, feared for its special relationship with the Crown. Sir Andrew Cohen, then the governor of Uganda, had earlier attempted, despite the hostility of the Buganda oligarchy, to develop Uganda as a unitary state, to subordinate the role of the *kabaka*, and to introduce progressive reforms without popular support.[27] The crisis over the "federation" thus gave Mutesa II, the *kabaka* of Buganda, an opportunity to oppose Cohen over unification. He accordingly called for the independence of Buganda and attempted, by the employment of a number of stratagems, to reassert a claim to the loyalties of his subjects and to the prerogatives of an autonomous ruler. But Cohen felt that he could not permit this reaffirmation of separatism and, after the *kabaka* refused to remain silent, the governor decreed a state of emergency and deported Mutesa to Britain.[28] This action combined with a number of other local irritations to give a decided fillip to the pretensions of the Uganda National Congress, the first of the Protectorate's many political organizations to claim a true national following. Ignatius Musazi and Abu Mayanja, two Ganda, had formed the Congress during the previous year. It participated fully in the protests that followed Mutesa's deportation and, along with the Progressive party of Eridadi Mulira, helped to make of it a national, rather than a regional issue. To the leaders of the Congress, and to Ugandans generally, the deportation symbolized a basic British contempt for traditional institutions and indigenous ways of life.

II. The Achievement of Independence

At the beginning of 1954, few appreciated that, with the exception of the Portuguese and Spanish possessions and Southern Rhodesia, the succeeding ten years would constitute tropical Africa's last decade of dependence. Although the Sudan had already begun to govern itself and the Gold Coast soon followed suit, the Mau Mau emergency still engulfed Kenya, and Tanganyikans and Congolese, among others, had not yet demonstrated their political aspirations nationally.[29] Well-meaning Africans, Europeans, and Americans envisaged a gradual, almost imperceptible, devolution of authority throughout much of this area. They prophesied independence in terms of half-centuries, not years, and failed to understand the extent to which the first transfers of power would have a decided demonstration effect upon the transformation of all of the other colonies.

[27] D. Anthony Low and R. Cranford Pratt, *Buganda and British Overrule* (London, 1960), pp. 319–326.

[28] See *ibid.*, pp. 331–332; D. Anthony Low, "The Advent of Populism in Buganda," *Comparative Studies in Society and History*, VI (1964), pp. 437–438.

[29] Within Tanganyika, however, the leaders of the Lake Province branch of the Tanganyika African Association had, from 1952, agitated for self-government. Later in the year, when Julius Nyerere returned home from the University of Edinburgh, he formulated his own political ideas with an awareness of this local ferment.

Independence came easily to the Sudan. In 1953, Azhari's Egyptian-backed National Unionist party, which had replaced the Ashiqqa', won a clear majority of the seats in the two houses of the local Parliament. The Umma party went reluctantly into opposition and, during the first week of 1954, Azhari became prime minister. Azhari and his party ostensibly remained committed to a program of Nile Valley unity. However, strong opposition within the country, the rise of Colonel Gamal Abdel Nasser to power in Egypt, and Azhari's party's natural unwillingness to cast aside the prerogatives of office all caused them to concern themselves primarily with the integrity of the Sudan. In 1955, Parliament demanded the evacuation of British and Egyptian troops; after this deed had been accomplished, and after the general acquiescence of the governments of Britain and Egypt had been secured, Parliament next declared the Sudan independent and, on the first day of 1956, transformed it into a republic. But the ascendancy of Parliament and the politicians lasted only three years; in late 1958, after a coalition led by 'Abdallah Khalil of the Umma party had succeeded Azhari's government, after relations with Egypt had once again become tense, and after the country had entered a period of economic crisis, General Ibrahim 'Abbud and a small group of military officers arrested the politicians, occupied the administrative and legislative offices in Khartoum and the radio station in Omdurman and, until late 1964, governed the Republic in the name of the army.[30]

Once Nkrumah had begun to participate in the affairs of state, the Gold Coast became Ghana with a minimum of friction. From 1951, when he agreed to work within a framework that he had earlier characterized as "bogus," Nkrumah and his ministerial colleagues gradually assumed more and more of the responsibilities heretofore exercised by the governor and British civil servants. In the Legislative Council, his majority initiated local government reforms that gave a democratic basis to the "native authorities" and, except in the northern districts, replaced chiefs by elected executive officers. At the same time, the government of the Gold Coast progressively advanced Africans to senior administrative and technical positions and established training schools to accelerate the transition from tutelage to independence. Overall, the leaders of the Convention People's party exhibited an ability to rule themselves; in 1954, Britain therefore permitted the Gold Coast to proceed from "responsible-" to "self-government." In the elections of that year the Convention won more than two-thirds of the seats in the Legislative Council. Its main opposition came from conservative regionalists in the north and in Ashanti.

During the next three years of self-government, the gulf between the supporters of the ruling Convention and its opponents grew steadily wider. In Ashanti, the National Liberation Movement, which the *asantehene* supported, focused this dissatisfaction with Nkrumah's policies and vigorously campaigned for regional autonomy. But Nkrumah flatly rejected all such separatist proposals. Despite the poor showing of the Convention in Ashanti and the Northern

---

[30] For the *coup d'état*, see Peter Kilner, "A Year of Army Rule in the Sudan," *The World Today*, XV (1959), pp. 432–434.

Territories, its otherwise overwhelming success in the elections of 1956 strengthened his hand considerably and led, in 1957, to the birth of an independent Ghana. Nkrumah, after a brief wait in the political wings, thereby became the leading African nationalist. In succeeding years, politicians elsewhere in British Africa sought to emulate his success and to make of his *ad hoc* responses to colonialism a theory of political struggle.

In West and Equatorial Africa, the government of France had increasingly shared its control of local territorial affairs with a new generation of indigenous leaders. In 1956, the passage by the French National Assembly of a *loi-cadre* permitted the subsequent granting of increased powers to overseas territorial assemblies, virtually eliminated the authority of the two governments-general, and gave to African-dominated embryo cabinets a substantial measure of authority within the individual colonies. It also introduced universal suffrage. France still ruled, however, and before 1958 only Sékou Touré, a descendant of Samori and the leader of the Parti Démocratique de Guinée, and Sylvanus Olympio, the leader of the Comité de l'Unité Togolaise, openly demanded independence. The others—particularly Houphouët-Boigny, who had helped to draft the *loi-cadre*—continued to value the French connection and to concern themselves with territorial rather than anti-colonial rivalries. In 1958, when General de Gaulle allowed each of the overseas territories to vote for or against the constitution of the Fifth Republic, and *oui* or *non* on the question of membership in the new French Community, only Guinée (Togo and Cameroun remained outside of the Community because they were United Nations trust territories) rejected France and became independent. The others all cast *oui* ballots, became self-governing (Senegal and the Soudan formed the short-lived Mali Federation) and, along with Togo and Cameroun, attained independence at various times during 1960.

In 1958, the vehicle of independence began to hurl itself forward with increasing speed. Dr. H. Kamuzu Banda returned home after an absence of more than forty years, assumed the leadership of the Nyasaland African Congress and, with the active assistance of Dunduzu Chisiza, Masauko Chipembere, and W. Kanyama Chiume, campaigned energetically against his people's continued subservience to the governments of the Federation of Rhodesia and Nyasaland and of Great Britain. In neighboring Northern Rhodesia, Kenneth Kaunda, who formed the Zambia National Congress after breaking with Nkumbula, took a similar position. To the south, Joshua Nkomo had become president of the Southern Rhodesian African National Congress. The Tanganyika African National Union, which Julius Nyerere and Oscar Kambona had established in 1954, won a critical "multi-racial" election for seats on that trust territory's Legislative Council, and thereafter pushed rapidly toward the goal of independence. In Uganda, seven of the non-Ganda victors in similar elections formed the Uganda People's Union and soon merged it with the more militant wing of the Uganda National Congress, then led by Milton Obote, a Lango who had worked in Kenya. Together, these two groups formed the Uganda People's Congress. Within Uganda, its main opposition came from the Demo-

After forty years Dr. H. Kamuzu Banda returns to Nyasaland, July 6, 1958, to lead the African Congress in its struggle against British rule. (Colin Legum)

cratic party, which received substantial support from the Roman Catholic Church, and the Uganda National Movement, which served the interests of the political leaders of Buganda. Although isolated Mau Mau terrorists still continued to threaten the peace of Kikuyuland, the Kenya emergency had ended in all but name after thirteen thousand Africans and ninety-five whites had lost their lives. Thereafter, Clement Argwings-Kodhek, Tom Mboya, and a number of other Africans revived nationalist political activity in Nairobi and, in time, elsewhere in Kenya.

The Congolese, quiet politically for so long, had meanwhile begun to stir. In late 1955, Antoine van Bilsen, a Belgian professor, published "A Thirty-Year Plan for the Political Emancipation of the Congo and Ruanda-Urundi." It recognized African aspirations, criticized the policies of the government of the Congo, suggested that the "colonial imperialism" of the twentieth century was no longer valid, and urged the rapid creation of representative, indigenous-controlled political institutions.[31] The Congolese themselves greeted the plan enthusiastically, and Belgians at home accepted a number of its suggestions.

[31] A. A. J. van Bilsen, "Een Dertigjarenplan voor de politieke Outvoogding van Belgisch Afrika," *De Gids op Maatschappelijk Gebied*, XLVI (1955), pp. 999–1028. A translation later appeared in French as "Un Plan de trente ans pour l'émancipation de l'Afrique belge," *Les Dossiers de l'Action Sociale Catholique*, XXXIII (1956), pp. 83–111.

A colonial legislature is transformed into the parliament of an independent state. Here, during the Tanganyikan independence ceremonies of December, 1961, behind Speaker Abdulkarim Y. A. Karimjee, who opens the proceedings, is H. R. H. Prince Philip, Duke of Edinburgh. Prime Minister Dr. Julius Nyerere is third from the rear on the front bench to the Speaker's right. (United Nations Photo)

It apparently also stimulated a group of African Roman Catholic intellectuals to make modest demands within the thirty-year framework. They called upon Europeans to abandon racial segregation and to avoid humiliation of the Congolese. "We do not enjoy always being treated as children," they wrote.[32] In reply, Joseph Kasavubu, who in 1952 had founded the Association pour le Maintien, l'Unité et l'Expansion de la Langue Kikongo—the Abako party—declared that thirty years was too long to wait. He demanded the immediate grant of full political rights, freedom of assembly, freedom of thought, and freedom of the press. He also envisaged an African-run federation of the Belgian Congo.

Despite the hostility of the government of the Belgian Congo, the next few years saw rapid political change. The Belgians created a spidery superstructure of indigenous aspiration and alien inspiration: on the one hand, they encouraged the tentative expression of indigenous discontent; on the other, they

[32] Jean Labrique, *Congo politique* (Léopoldville, 1957), pp. 251–275, contains the text of this manifesto. It is also quoted in part in Stewart C. Easton, *The Twilight of European Colonialism* (New York, 1960), p. 462.

believed that simply by modernizing their paternal approach they would be able to continue to rule the Congo for at least another thirty years. In 1957, when the Belgian Congo experienced its local elections, Kasavubu's party won most of the city council seats in Léopoldville. He and other nationalist spokesmen also looked on enviously when the peoples of the Moyen Congo voted in the French referendum of 1958. By then, a number of the African politicians of the Belgian Congo had committed themselves to a full-scale campaign against colonial domination.

At the end of 1958, nationalists from all over Africa went to Accra and participated in the sessions of the first All-African People's Conference. Patrice Lumumba represented the Congo (its government prevented Kasavubu, whom the administrators believed to be "most dangerous," from going), Banda attended from Nyasaland, and both Kaunda and Nkumbula led separate Northern Rhodesian delegations. Except for Nkumbula, they returned to their respective countries more determined than before to carry the battle against white rule forward to its ultimate conclusion—whatever that might be. In Accra, they had received ample moral support from other African nationalists; Nkrumah, Nasser, and other leaders may have promised to supply some of the necessary funds. At home, Banda said that he meant henceforth to fight the Federation with violence only if all other avenues to freedom appeared blocked. He invited arrest, and repeatedly reiterated his willingness to die if it would further African opposition to white rule. "Whatever the consequences," Kaunda told his followers, "we are prepared to pay the price of freedom." [33] Lumumba, in turn, returned to the Congo convinced that only a national campaign could succeed against the Belgians. He also began to advocate "immediate independence" for the whole of the colony.

On the eve of 1959, the Congo erupted into violence. Although only a few Europeans and Africans lost their lives, the ferocity with which the rioters expressed their hatred of whites overwhelmed the Belgians and contributed subsequently to the swift pace of political devolution there. At the end of 1959, Lumumba's Mouvement National Congolais and the administration-backed Parti National du Progrès emerged victorious after territorial elections. (Kasavubu's party had boycotted the elections on the grounds that they would permit only a gradual transfer of power.) [34] Early in 1960, King Baudouin sponsored a representative conference in Brussels to decide how next to proceed. There the Belgians agreed to give the Congo its independence. They presumed that Baudouin would remain king of the Congo and that a series of careful pre-independence agreements would assure future Belgo-Congolese amity.[35] The administration also sought to isolate Kasavubu and to transfer sovereignty gradually. But in the end, independence came all in a rush, leaving future re-

---

[33] *Northern News*, February 16, 1959.

[34] For the elections of 1959 and 1960, see Daniel Biebuyck and Mary Douglas, *Congo: Tribes and Parties* (London, 1961), pp. 9, 26–41.

[35] See A. A. J. van Bilsen, "Some Aspects of the Congo Problem," *International Affairs*, XXXVIII (1962), p. 42.

Prime Minister Moise Tshombe of the Congo (Léopoldville) greeting the public with Antoine Gizenga after the latter's release from prison in July, 1964. (Wide World)

lationships unclear, leaders untrained, and the Congo in a state of confusion. In rapid succession, the Congolese thereafter moved from crisis to crisis. The central government quickly lost control of provincial affairs; Lumumba, the first premier, was killed; Katanga seceded under Moise Tshombe; and the United Nations entered the country in order to restore essential services. Eventually, the United Nations also acted to end Katanga's separation and to unify the Congo. But in 1964, rebels threatened to divide the young nation afresh.

In 1959, unrest and militant agitation gripped Nyasaland and Northern Rhodesia as well. Nyasas began deliberately to defy the government, to hold meetings without permission, to ignore conservation laws, and to welcome official retaliation. "We mean to embarrass the . . . Nyasaland Government and the British Government about our demands," Yatuta Chisiza, later the Minister of Home Affairs, said. "This is the only way. Negotiations won't do. But we mean to create disturbances . . . even if it means every person in the country dies." [36] Africans burned mission buildings, stoned the police, destroyed government property, and blocked the roads. By the beginning of March, they had demonstrated their ability to tie up the security resources of the country. They had also committed Southern Rhodesian troops. As a result, the Prime Minister of that neighboring colony proclaimed an emergency, banned Nkomo's Congress, and arrested about five hundred of its members. Finally, in March, 1959, the government of Nyasaland, with encouragement from Welensky, then the prime minister of the Rhodesian Federation, followed suit. It too declared an emergency, banned the Nyasa movement, and arrested Banda and more than one thousand of his followers. More violence ensued, and fifty Africans

[36] *Report of the Nyasaland Commission of Inquiry,* Cmd. 814 (1959), p. 71.

died before troops could restore peace. Northern Rhodesians also demonstrated discontent, if comparatively mildly, and Kaunda urged Africans to boycott the forthcoming elections to the territorial Legislative Council. Before polling day, however, the governor of the Protectorate compared the Zambia Congress to America's "Murder, Inc." and detained Kaunda and his fellow Zambians.

Whites hoped that life would continue as before. They saw in the actions of the three Central African governments what they had long hoped to see—the death of nationalism and the vindication of the decisions that had resulted in the formation of the Federation. In fact, unbeknown to them, the violence and retaliation of 1959 marked the beginning rather than the end of the final phase of the nationalist struggle. The British cabinet thereafter realized that it could only hope to govern its African dependencies with the consent of the governed. It also at last understood the depth of African resistance to the Federation and, generally, to settler rule. As Banda, Kaunda, Kenyatta, and others knew, British governments traditionally respected only those of their subjects who had actually shown the stuff of contention and the potential for leadership. Banda and Kaunda confidently expected that months spent in prisons would qualify them—like so many others—to accede, in decent time, to prime ministerships.

After Nigeria—which had enjoyed full regional self-government since 1957/58 and a "national government" under Prime Minister Balewa since 1957—had celebrated its independence in 1960, the British government next advanced Sierra Leone and Tanganyika. Sierra Leone had enjoyed a full measure of responsible government since 1958. It became self-governing in 1960. In the same year, after Nyerere's party had demonstrated overwhelming electoral support, he became the chief minister of Tanganyika. Sierra Leone achieved its independence in the spring of 1961; after a short period of "self-government," Tanganyika reached the same status.

Nyasaland, Uganda, and Kenya meanwhile held elections. In Nyasaland, Banda led his new Malawi Congress party to an almost total victory. He thereafter steadily gathered more and more of the reins of rule in his own hands and occupied the position of prime minister long before he received it in name. In 1961, the Democratic party formed the government of Uganda. In Kenya, although the African National Union had won a plurality of the Legislative Council places, it refused to enter the government until Britain released Kenyatta from detention. Instead, the minority Kenya African Democratic Union governed and campaigned for "regionalization" in order to obviate the likelihood of an independent Kenya in which the National Union, backed by the large Kikuyu and Luo tribes, could dominate. Later in the year, the governor of Kenya released Kenyatta and, in 1962, persuaded both the Democratic and the National Unions to form a coalition government. A few months later, fresh balloting in Uganda gave an alliance between Obote's Congress and the supporters of the *kabaka* of Buganda a clear majority in the national legislature. Obote became prime minister and, in the autumn, Uganda joined the ranks of the other independent African states.

In 1962/63, the voters of Kenya and Northern Rhodesia demonstrated their

Turkana women, carrying their voting registration cards in cleft sticks, are entering a polling booth in Lokitaung, Kenya, during the 1961 elections. (Wide World)

faith in militant nationalism. Kenyatta's African Union won a clear electoral victory in early 1963 and thereafter rode the tide of victory that carried Kenya to independence later in the same year. Kaunda's United National Independence party, however, formed a coalition government with Nkumbula's Congress in order to prevent the white settlers, who still held a sizeable proportion of the seats in the Protectorate's Legislative Council, from taking its place. Throughout the rest of 1963, both Banda and Kaunda pressed their respective claims for independence and, in the process, toppled the structure of the Federation, which ceased to exist at the end of the year.

Zanzibar, where severe rioting in 1961 had demonstrated the existence of widespread racial and political animosity, also gained its independence in late 1963 after a small plurality of the voters had reaffirmed the political ascendancy of Sheikh Ali Muhsin's Arab-dominated Zanzibar Nationalist party. Before it had begun to rule, however, John Okello, a self-appointed revolutionary general, led a movement that overthrew the administration of Sheikh Ali Muhsin and, early in 1964, gave the powers of government to Abeid Karume, the leader of the heretofore opposition Afro-Shirazi party, which claimed to represent the predominantly African masses. Karume subsequently merged Zanzibar with Tanganyika to form the United Republic of Tanganyika and Zanzibar (later Tanzania) under the presidency of Nyerere.

While Zanzibaris revolted, Northern Rhodesians voted. Early in 1964, in an election in which an African ballot at last counted as much as one cast by a white, Kaunda's party demonstrated its widespread support, and he himself became the first prime minister of Northern Rhodesia. A few months later, Nyasaland shed its colonial name and emerged as the independent nation of Malawi. In the autumn, Northern Rhodesia achieved the same status. It simultaneously became a republic, discarded colonial memories, and henceforth called itself Zambia. Only the Gambia, which expected to become independent in 1965, Southern Rhodesia (now plain Rhodesia), the Portuguese possessions (a revolt still simmered in Angola and Guinea), and Spanish Africa remained under the control of whites.

BIBLIOGRAPHY

Although extensive, the bibliography that follows contains only a fraction of the published literature relevant to the history of tropical Africa. I have attempted to list only those books and articles known to me personally. Because they are generally available, I have omitted many standard works and those that appeal essentially to a popular audience. I have also omitted reference material, texts, many compendia and anthologies and, overall, articles and books that, in the judgment of the author, seemed of only passing interest. Of the many criteria used to justify selection, intrinsic quality and lasting value were uppermost. Publications of very particular significance or interest are noted with a †. The symbol * indicates a publication to which persons new to the field of study should turn first. Space limitations preclude a more complete annotation.

The entries below have been verified and put into the forms that agree with the manner of their listing in the union catalogue of the Harvard University Library system or the printed catalogues of the British Museum, the Library of Congress, and the Biblioteque Nationale. Under individual authors, entries have been listed chronologically.

For ease of reference, the books and articles below have been assigned to the categories listed in the following table of contents. Although various items might legitimately fall under more than one heading, entries have been included in the most appropriate section only.

The bibliography includes a number of recently published books and articles that were unavailable to the author during the period when he was completing his own manuscript.

The edition used in the preparation of the manuscript is not necessarily the same as that listed in the bibliography. The bibliography cites first editions, except where the book has been subject to important revision.

CONTENTS

I. Ancient Africa

Arkell, Anthony John, *Early Khartoum* (Oxford, 1949).

* ———, *A History of the Sudan from the Earliest Times to 1821* (London, 1961).

Carcopino, Jérôme, *Le Maroc antique* (Paris, 1943).

Carpenter, Rhys, "A Trans-Saharan Caravan Route in Herodotus," *American Journal of Archaeology*, LX (1956), pp. 231–242.

* Cary, Max Otto, and Eric H. Warmington, *The Ancient Explorers* (London, 1929).

Clark, J. Desmond, *Prehistoric Cultures of Northeast Angola and Their Significance in Tropical Africa* (Lisboa, 1963), 2v.

———, "The Prehistoric Origins of African Culture," *The Journal of African History*, V (1964), pp. 161–183.

Clarke, Somers, "Ancient Egyptian Frontier Fortresses," *The Journal of Egyptian Archaeology*, III (1916), pp. 155–179.

Crowfoot, J. W., *The Island of Meroë . . . and Meroitic Inscriptions* (London, 1911), 4v.

Dale, Ivan R., "The Indian Origins of Some African Cultivated Plants and African Cattle," *The Uganda Journal*, XIX (1955), pp. 67–72.

Davies, Oliver, "The Neolithic Revolution in Tropical Africa," *Transactions of the Historical Society of Ghana*, IV (1960), pp. 14–20.

Dunham, Dows, "Notes on the History of Kush 850 B.C.–A.D. 350," *American Journal of Archaeology*, L (1946), pp. 378–388.

———, *Royal Cemeteries of Kush*: I. El Kurru, II. Nuri, III. Decorated Chapels of the Meroitic Pyramids at Meroë and Barkal, by Suzanne E. Chapman, IV. Royal Tombs at Meroë and Barkal, V. The West and South Cemeteries at Meroë Excavated by the late George Reisner (Cambridge, Mass., 1950–1963), 5v.

Emery, Walter B., "A Preliminary Report on the Excavations at Buhen," *Kush*, VII (1959), pp. 7–14; X (1962), pp. 106–108; XI (1963), pp. 116–120.

Fagg, Bernard E. B., "The Nok Culture in Prehistory," *Journal of the Historical Society of Nigeria*, I (1959), pp. 288–293.

* Fairservis, Walter A., *The Ancient Kingdoms of the Nile and the Doomed Monuments of Nubia* (New York, 1962).

Gadallah, Fawzi F., "Meroitic Problems and a Comprehensive Meroitic Bibliography," *Kush*, XI (1963), pp. 196–216.

Gaffarel, R., *Eudoxe de Cyzique et le périple de l'Afrique dans l'antiquité* (London, 1873).

Garstang, John, Alexander Henry Sayce, and F. Lloyd Griffith, *Meroë, the City of the Ethiopians: Being an Account of a First Season's Excavations on the Site, 1909–1910* (Oxford, 1911).

Garstang, John, Alexander Henry Sayce, and W. J. Phythian Adams, "Fifth Interim Report on the Excavations at Meroë," *University of Liverpool: Annals of Archaeology and Anthropology*, VII (1914–1916), pp. 1–24.

Gautier, Émile Félix, *L'Afrique noire occidentale: esquisse des cadres géographiques* (Paris, 1935).

† Germain, Gabriel, "Qu'est-ce que le *Périple* d'Hannon? Document, amplification littéraire ou faux intégral?" *Hespéris*, XLIV (1957), pp. 205–248.

Greenberg, Joseph Harold, *Studies in African Linguistic Classification* (New Haven, 1955).

———, "Languages and History in Africa," *Présence Africaine*, XVII (1963), pp. 114–122.

———, *The Languages of Africa* (Bloomington, Ill., 1963).

Griffith, F. Lloyd, "Meroitic Studies IV," *The Journal of Egyptian Archaeology*, IV (1917), pp. 159–173.

Gsell, Stéphane, *Histoire ancienne de l'Afrique du Nord* (Paris, 1920–1921), 4v.

Guthrie, Malcolm, "Bantu Origins: A Tentative New Hypothesis," *The Journal of African Languages*, I (1962), pp. 9–21.

———, "A Two-Stage Method of Comparative Bantu Study," *African Language Studies*, III (1962), pp. 1–24.

Habachi, Labib, "The First Two Viceroys of Kush and Their Family," *Kush*, VII (1959), pp. 45–62.

Hanno (trans. Wilfred H. Schoff), *The Periplus of Hanno* (Philadelphia, 1913).

Hansberry, William Leo, "Ancient Kush, Old Aetheopia, and the Balad es Sudan," *Journal of Human Relations*, VIII (1960), pp. 357–387.

Hennig, Richard, "Hannos 'Götterwagen,'" *Geographische Zeitschrift*, XXXIII (1927), pp. 378–392.

Hornell, James, "Sea-Trade in Early Times," *Antiquity*, XV (1941), pp. 233–256.

Jeffreys, M. D. W., "How Ancient Is West African Maize?" *Africa*, XXXIII (1963), pp. 115–131.

Junker, Hermann, "The First Appearance of the Negroes in History," *The Journal*

of Egyptian Archaeology, VII (1921), pp. 121–132.
Kirwan, L. P., "Comments on the Origins and History of the Nobatae of Procopius," *Kush,* VI (1958), pp. 69–73.
———, "The International Position of Sudan in Roman and Medieval Times," *Sudan Notes and Records,* XI (1959), pp. 23–37.
———, "The Decline and Fall of Meroë," *Kush,* VIII (1960), pp. 163–173.
Kwapong, A. A., "Africa Antiqua," *Transactions of the Gold Coast and Togoland Historical Society,* II (1956), pp. 1–11.
Low, Charles Rathbone, *Maritime Discovery: A History of Nautical Exploration from the Earliest Times* (London, 1881), 2v.
McMaster, D. N., "Speculations on the Coming of the Banana to Uganda," *The Journal of Tropical Geography,* XVI (1962), pp. 57–69.
Mauny, Raymond, "Que faut-il appeler 'pierres' d'aigris?" *Notes Africaines,* 42 (April, 1949), pp. 33–36.
———, "Note sur le périple d'Hannon," *Comptes rendues: Première Conférence Internationale des Africanistes de l'Ouest* (Paris, 1951), II, pp. 509–530.
Miracle, Marvin P., "Interpretation of Evidence on the Introduction of Maize into West Africa," *Africa,* XXXIII (1963), pp. 132–135.
Monneret de Villard, Ugo, *La Nubia romana* (Roma, 1941).
Posener, Georges, "Pour une localisation du pays Koush au Moyen Empire," *Kush,* VI (1958), pp. 39–65.
Posnansky, Merrick, "Bantu Genesis," *The Uganda Journal,* XXV (1961), pp. 86–93.
Reisner, George A., "Preliminary Report on the Harvard-Boston Excavations at Nûri: The Kings of Ethiopia After Tirhaga," *Harvard African Studies,* II (1918), pp. 1–64.
———, "The Viceroys of Ethiopia," *The Journal of Egyptian Archaeology,* VI (1920), pp. 28–55, 73–88.
———, *Excavations at Kerma* (Cambridge, Mass., 1923), 2v.
———, "The Meroitic Kingdom of Ethiopia: A Chronological Outline," *The Journal of Egyptian Archaeology,* IX (1923), pp. 34–77, 157–160.
———, "The Egyptian Forts from Halfa to Semna," *Kush,* VIII (1960), pp. 11–24.
Sauneron, Serge, and Jean Yoyotte, "La Campagne nubienne de Psammétique II et sa signification historique," *Bulletin de l'Institut Français d'Archéologie Orientale,* L (1952), pp. 157–207.
Sayce, Alexander Henry, "Second Interim Report on the Excavations at Meroë in Ethiopia: Part II. The Historical Results," *University of Liverpool: Annals of Archaeology and Anthropology,* IV (1911), pp. 53–65.
Shinnie, Peter L., "The Fall of Meroë," *Kush,* III (1955), pp. 82–85.
Smith, H. F. C., "The Transfer of the Capital of Kush from Napata to Meroë," *Kush,* III (1955), pp. 20–25.
Snowden, Frank M., Jr., "Some Greek and Roman Observations on the Ethiopian," *Tradito,* XVI (1960), pp. 19–38.
Thabit, T. H., "International Relations of the Sudan in Napatan Times," *Sudan Notes and Records,* XL (1959), pp. 19–22.
Ullendorff, Edward, "The Gold of Kush," *Kush,* VII (1959), pp. 120–153.
Vercoutter, Jean, "Ancient Egyptian Influence in the Sudan," *Sudan Notes and Records,* XL (1959), pp. 8–18.
Vivien de Saint-Martin, Louis, *Le Nord de l'Afrique dans l'Antiquité, grecque et romaine: étude historique et géographique* (Paris, 1863).
Vycichl, Werner, "Hindu Influence in Meroitic Art," *Kush,* VI (1958), pp. 74–81.
Wainwright, Gerard A., "Iron in the Napatan and Meroitic Ages," *Sudan Notes and Records,* XXVI (1945), pp. 5–36.
Webb, E. J., "The Alleged Phoenician Circumnavigation of Africa," *The English Historical Review,* XXII (1907), pp. 1–14.
Wheeler, Mortimer, *Rome Beyond the Imperial Frontiers* (London, 1954).
Willett, Frank, "The Introduction of Maize into West Africa: An Assessment of Recent Evidence," *Africa,* XXXII (1962), pp. 1–13.
† Wrigley, Christopher C., "Speculations on the Economic Prehistory of Africa," *The Journal of African History,* I (1960), pp. 189–203.

II. Early Modern Africa

A. Contemporary Writings

Africanus, Leo (trans. John Pory), *The History and Description of Africa* (London, 1896), 3v.
al-Bakri, 'Abu 'Ubayd Abdallah Ibn 'Abdal 'Aziz (trans. MacGuckin de Slane), *De-*

scription de l'Afrique septentrionale (Alger, 1913).
Conzelman, William E. (trans. and ed.), *Chronique de Galâwdêwos (Claudius), roi d'Éthiopie* (Paris, 1895).
al-Fida, 'Abu (trans. and ed. Joseph Toussaint Reinaud), *Géographie* (Paris, 1848–1883), 2v.
al-Hakam, Ibn 'Abd al-Rahman (trans. Charles Cutler Torrey), "The Mohammedan Conquest of Egypt and North Africa," *Biblical and Semitic Studies . . . of Yale University* (New York, 1902).
——— (trans. Albert Gateau), *Conquête de l'Afrique du Nord et de l'Espagne* (Alger, 1947).
Ibn Battuta, Muhammed ibn 'Abd Allah (trans. and ed. Hamilton A. R. Gibb), *Ibn Battuta: Travels in Asia and Africa* (London, 1929).
——— (trans. Hamilton A. R. Gibb), *The Travels of Ibn Battuta* (Cambridge, Eng., 1962), II.
Ibn Fartua, 'Ahmed (trans. and ed. H. Richmond Palmer), *History of the First Twelve Years of the Reign of Mai Idris Alooma of Bornu (1571–1583)* (Lagos, 1926).
Ibn Hawqal, Muhammad (trans. MacGuckin de Slane), "Description de l'Afrique," *Journal Asiatique*, XIII (1842), pp. 153–196, 209–258.
Ibn Khaldun, 'Abd al-Rahman (trans. MacGuckin de Slane), *Histoire des Berbères et des dynasties musulmanes de l'Afrique septentrionale* (Alger, 1852–1856), 4v.
Ibn Raziq, Salil (trans. and ed. George Percy Badger), *History of the Imâms and Seyyids of 'Oman* (London, 1871).
al-Idrisi, 'Abu 'Abdullah Muhammad (trans. Pierre Amédéé Jaubert), *Géographie* (Paris, 1836–1840), 2v.
——— (trans. R. Dozy and M. J. de Goeje), *Description de l'Afrique* (Leiden, 1866).
Joannus, Bishop of Ephesus (trans. and ed. Robert Payne Smith), *The Third Part of the Ecclesiastical History* (Oxford, 1860).
al-Kati, Mahmud (trans. Octave Houdas and Maurice Delafosse), *Tarikh el-Fettach* (Paris, 1913).
McCrindle, J. W. (trans. and ed.), *The Christian Topography of Cosmas, an Egyptian Monk* (London, 1897).
al-Maqrizi, Taki-ed-Din-Ahmed (trans. M. Quatremère), *Histoire des sultans Mamlouks, de l'Égypte* (Paris, 1837–1845), 2v.
——— (trans. Urbain Bouriant), *Description topographique et historique de l'Égypte* (Paris, 1900), 3v.
al-Mas'udi, 'Ali ibn al-Husain (trans. G. Barbier de Meynard and Pavet de Courteille), *Les Prairies d'or* (Paris, 1861–1877), 9v.
al-Muqadassi, Abu 'Abd Allah Muhammad ibn 'Ahmad (trans. Charles Pellat), *Description de l'occident musulman* (Alger, 1950).
Periplus of the Erythraean Sea. The translated and edited versions by Hjalmar Frisk (Göteborg, 1927), J. W. McCrindle (London, 1879), Wilfred H. Schoff (New York, 1912), and William Vincent (London, 1800–1805), 2v.
Perruchon, Jules (trans. and ed.), "Histoire des guerres d'Amda Syon, roi d'Éthiopie," *Journal Asiatique*, XIV (1889), pp. 237–363, 441–483.
———, *Vie de Lalibela, roi d'Éthiopie*, (Alger, 1892).
———, *Les Chroniques de Zar'a Yâ'eqôb et de Ba'eda Mâryâm, roi d'Éthiopie de 1434 à 1478* (Paris, 1893).
Renaudot, Eusèbe (ed.), *Historia Patriarcharum Alexandrinorum Jacobitarum* (Paris, 1713).
as-Sa'di, 'Abd al-Rahman bin 'Amir (trans. Octave Houdas), *Tarikh es-Soudan* (Paris, 1900).
Sa'id, Hajj (trans. Octave Houdas), *Histoire du Sokoto* (Paris, 1901).
Salih, Abu al-Armani (trans. and ed. Basil Thomas Alfred Evetts), *The Churches and Monasteries of Egypt and Some Neighbouring Countries* (Oxford, 1895).
al-Tonbukti, 'Abd al-Rahman ibn 'Abdallah (trans. Octave Houdas), *Tedzkiret en-Nisian fi Akhbar Molouk es-Soudan* [*Reminders of the Forgetful and The History of the Princes of the Sudan*] (Paris, 1901).
al-'Umari, Ibn Fadl 'Allah (trans. Maurice Gaudefroy-Demombynes), *L'Afrique, moins l'Égypte* (Paris, 1927).
Winstedt, Eric Otto (ed.), *The Christian Topography of Cosmas Indicopleustes* (Cambridge, Eng., 1909).
al-Ya'qubi, 'Ahmad ibn Wadih al-Katib al-'Abbasi (ed. Th. Houtsma), *Historiae* (Leiden, 1883), 2v.
——— (trans. Gaston Wiet), *Les Pays* (Cairo, 1937).

B. The East, the Island States, and the Interior

'Abd al-Magid, 'Abdin, "Some General Aspects of the Arabisation of the Sudan," *Sudan Notes and Records*, XL (1959), pp. 48–74.

Abdallah, Yohanna B. (trans. and ed. G. Meredith Sanderson), *Chikala cha Wayao* (Zomba, 1919).

Abdallah bin Hemedi, 'lAjjemy (trans. and ed. J. W. T. Allen and William Kimweri bin Mabogo), *The Kilindi* (Nairobi, 1963).

Abraham, D. P., "The Principality of Maungwe: Its History and Traditions," *Nada*, XXVIII (1951), pp. 56–83.

———, "The Monomotapa Dynasty," *ibid.*, XXXVI (1959), pp. 59–84.

———, "Maramuca: An Exercise in the Combined Use of Portuguese Records and Oral Tradition," *The Journal of African History*, II (1961), pp. 211–225.

† ———, "The Early Political History of the Kingdoms of Mwene Mutapa, 850–1589," *Historians in Tropical Africa* (Salisbury, S.R., 1962), pp. 61–92.

Aešcoly, A. Z., "Notices sur les Falacha ou Juifs d'Abyssinie, d'après le journal de voyage d'Antoine d'Abadie," *Cahiers d'Études Africaines*, 5 (1961), pp. 84–140.

Alaqâ, Walda Maryam (trans. H. Weld Blundell), "History of King Theodore," *Journal of the African Society*, VI (1906), pp. 12–42.

Allen, J. W. T., "Rhapta," *Tanganyika Notes and Records*, 27 (1949), pp. 52–59.

Apthorpe, Raymond, "Problems of African History: The Nsenga of Northern Rhodesia," *The Rhodes-Livingstone Journal*, XXVIII (1960), pp. 47–67.

Arkell, Anthony John, "Fung Origins," *Sudan Notes and Records*, XV (1932), pp. 201–250.

———, "More About Fung Origins," *ibid.*, XXVII (1946), pp. 87–97.

———, "The History of Darfur 1200–1700 A.D.," *ibid.*, XXXII (1951), pp. 37–70, 207–238; XXXIII (1952), pp. 129–155, 244–275.

———, "A Christian Church and Monastery at Ain Farah, Darfur," *Kush*, VII (1959), pp. 115–119.

———, "The Medieval History of Darfur in Its Relation to Other Cultures and to the Nilotic Sudan," *Sudan Notes and Records*, XL (1959), pp. 44–47.

Avelot, René, "Les Grands Mouvements de peuples en Afrique: Jaga et Zimba," *Bulletin de Géographie Historique et Descriptive*, I (1912), pp. 75–216.

Baker, E. C., "Notes on the History of the Wasegeju," *Tanganyika Notes and Records*, 27 (1949), pp. 16–41.

Barnes, John A., *Politics in a Changing Society: A Political History of the Fort Jameson Ngoni* (Cape Town, 1954).

Beattie, J. H. M., "Bunyoro: An African Feudality," *The Journal of African History*, V (1964), pp. 25–35.

Beidelman, Thomas O., "A History of Ukagura: 1857–1916," *Tanganyika Notes and Records*, 58/59 (1962), pp. 11–39.

Bent, James Theodore, *The Ruined Cities of Mashonaland: Being a Record of Excavation and Exploration in 1891* (London, 1892).

Bere, R. M., "Awich: A Biographical Note and a Chapter of Acholi History," *The Uganda Journal*, X (1946), pp. 76–78.

———, "An Outline of Acholi History," *ibid.*, XI (1947), pp. 1–8.

Bidder, Irmgard (trans. R. Grabham-Hortmann), *Lalibela: The Monolithic Churches of Ethiopia* (New York, 1959).

Biebuyck, Daniel, "Fondements de l'organisation politique des Lunda du Mwaantayaav en territoire de Kapanga," *Zaïre*, XI (1957), pp. 787–817.

Bikunya, P., *Kyabakame bya Bunyoro* (Kampala, 1927).

Birch, J. P., "Migration Movements of the Madi, with Some Tentative Conclusions," *The Uganda Journal*, VI (1938), pp. 119–122.

Brothwell, D. R., "Evidence of Early Population Change in Central and Southern Africa: Doubts and Problems," *Man*, LXIII, 132 (1963), pp. 101–104.

Bruwer, J., "Notes on Maravi Origin and Migration," *African Studies*, IX (1950), pp. 32–34.

Bryant, Alfred T., *Olden Times in Zululand and Natal: Containing Earlier Political History of the Eastern-Nguni Clans* (London, 1929).

Budge, Ernest Alfred Wallis (trans. and ed.), *Kebra Nagast: The Queen of Sheba and Her Only Son Menyelek; Being the History of the Departure of God and His Ark of the Covenant from Jerusalem to Ethiopia, and the Establishment of the Religion of the Hebrews and the Solomonic Line of Kings in That Country* (London, 1922).

———, *A History of Ethiopia, Nubia and Abyssinia According to the Hieroglyphic Inscriptions of Egypt and Nubia, and the Ethiopian Chronicles* (London, 1928).

——— (trans.), *Mashafa Sĕnekĕsâr: The Book of the Saints of the Ethiopian Church; a Translation of the Ethiopic Synaxarium . . . Made from the Manuscripts Oriental 660 and 661 in the*

British Museum (Cambridge, Eng., 1928), 4v.
Caquot, André, and Jean Leclant, "La Reine de Saba et le bois de la croix: selun une tradition éthiopienne," *Annales d'Éthiopie*, I (1955), pp. 137–147.
———, "Histoire amharique de Gran et des Gallas," *ibid.*, II (1957), pp. 123–143.
———, "La Royauté sacrale en Éthiopie," *ibid.*, pp. 205–218.
———, "Éthiopie et Cyrénaïque? À propos d'un texte de Synésius," *ibid.*, III (1959), pp. 173–177.
Caton-Thompson, Gertrude, *The Zimbabwe Culture: Ruins and Reactions* (Oxford, 1931).
Cerulli, Enrico, *Somalia: Scitti Vari Editi ed Inediti* (Roma, 1957–1959), 2v.
Césard, Edmond, "Le Muhaya," *Anthropos*, XXXII (1937), pp. 15–60.
Chibanza, S. J., "Kaonde History," *Central Bantu Historical Texts* (Lusaka, 1961), I.
Chittick, H. Neville, "Notes on Kilwa," *Tanganyika Notes and Records*, 53 (1959), pp. 179–203.
———, *Kisimani Mafia: Excavations at an Islamic Settlement on the East African Coast* (Dar es Salaam, 1961).
† ———, "Kilwa and the Arab Settlement of the East African Coast," *The Journal of African History*, IV (1963), pp. 179–190.
———, "The Last Christian Stronghold in the Sudan," *Kush*, XI (1963), pp. 264–272.
Chiwale, Jacques Chileya (trans. and ed.), *Central Bantu Historical Texts, III: Royal Praises and Praise Names of the Lunda Kazembe of Northern Rhodesia, the Meaning and Historical Background* (Lusaka, 1962).
Clark, J. Desmond, "A Note on the Pre-Bantu Inhabitants of Northern Rhodesia and Nyasaland," *South African Journal of Science*, XLVII (1950–1951), pp. 80–85.
———, "The Spread of Food Production in Sub-Saharan Africa," *The Journal of African History*, III (1962), pp. 211–228.
Clarke, Somers, *Christian Antiquities in the Nile Valley: A Contribution Towards the Study of the Ancient Churches* (Oxford, 1912).
Clay, Gervas, "Barotseland Between 1801 and 1864," *Conference of the History of the Central African Peoples* (Lusaka, 1963), no pagination.
Contenson, Henri de, "Aperçus sur les fouilles à Axoum et dans la région d'Axoum en 1958 et 1959," *Annales d'Éthiopie*, III (1959), pp. 101–106.
———, "Les Premiers Rois d'Axoum d'après les découvertes récentes," *Journal Asiatique*, CCXLIX (1961), pp. 441–459.
Conti Rossini, Carlo, *Storia d'Etiopia* (Milano, 1928).
Cox, A. H., "The Growth and Expansion of Buganda," *The Uganda Journal*, XIV (1950), pp. 153–159.
Crawford, Osbert Guy Stanhope, "Some Medieval Theories About the Nile," *The Geographical Journal*, CXIV (1949), pp. 6–29.
———, "The Strange Adventures of Zaga Christ," *Sudan Notes and Records*, XXXI (1950), pp. 287–296.
———, *The Fung Kingdom of Sennar, with a Geographical Account of the Middle Nile Region* (Gloucester, Eng., 1951).
———, *Castles and Churches in the Middle Nile Region* (Khartoum, 1961).
Crazzolara, J. Pasquale, "The Lwoo People," *The Uganda Journal*, V (1937), pp. 1–21.
———, *The Lwoo* (Verona, 1950–1954), 3v.
———, "Lwoo Migrations," *The Uganda Journal*, XXV (1961), pp. 136–148.
Culwick, A. T. and G. M., "Indonesian Echoes in Central Tanganyika," *Tanganyika Notes and Records*, 2 (1936), pp. 60–66.
Cunnison, Ian G., *The Luapula Peoples of Northern Rhodesia* (Manchester, 1959).
———, "Kazembe and the Portuguese, 1798–1832," *The Journal of African History*, II (1961), pp. 61–76.
——— (trans. and ed.), *Central Bantu Historical Texts, II: Historical Traditions of the Eastern Lunda* (Lusaka, 1962).
———, "Kazembe and the Arabs to 1870," *Conference of the History of the Central African Peoples* (Lusaka, 1963), no pagination.
Devic, L. Marcel, *Le Pays des Zendjs, ou la côte orientale d'Afrique au Moyen Âge* (Paris, 1883).
Doresse, Jean, *Au pays de la Reine de Saba: l'Éthiopie, antique et moderne* (Paris, 1956).
———, *L'Empire du Prêtre-Jean* (Paris, 1957), 2v.
———, "L'Éthiopie et l'Arabie méridionale, aux IIIe et IVe siècles A.D., d'après les découvertes récentes," *Kush*, V (1957), pp. 49–60.
Dorman, M. H., "The Kilwa Civilization and the Kilwa Ruins," *Tanganyika Notes and Records*, 6 (1938), pp. 61–71.

Drake, St. Clair, "The Responsibility of Men of Culture for Destroying the 'Hamitic Myth,'" *Présence Africaine,* I (1959), pp. 228–243.

Drewes, A. J., "Les Inscriptions de Melazo," *Annales d'Éthiopie,* III (1959), pp. 83–99.

Dundas, Charles Cecil Farquharson, *Kilimanjaro and Its People: A History of the Wachagga, Their Laws, Customs and Legends, Together with Some Account of the Highest Mountain in Africa* (London, 1924).

Duyvendak, Jan Julius L., "The True Dates of the Chinese Maritime Expeditions in the Early Fifteenth Century," *T'oung Pao,* XXXIV (1939), pp. 341–412.

———, *China's Discovery of Africa* (London, 1959).

Evans-Pritchard, E. E., "The Zande State," *The Journal of the Royal Anthropological Institute,* XCIII (1963), pp. 134–154.

Fagan, Brian M., "Pre-European Iron Working in Central Africa with Special Reference to Northern Rhodesia," *The Journal of African History,* II (1961), pp. 199–210.

† ———, "The Iron Age Sequence in the Southern Province of Northern Rhodesia," *ibid.,* IV (1963), pp. 157–177.

———, "The Greeswald Sequence: Bambandyanalo and Mapungubwe," *ibid.,* V (1964), pp. 337–361.

Fallers, Lloyd (ed.), *The King's Men: Leadership and Status in Buganda on the Eve of Independence* (London, 1964).

Ferrand, Gabriel (trans. and ed.), *Relations de voyages et textes géographiques: Arabes, Persans et Turks relatifs à l'Extrême-Orient* (Paris, 1913–1914), 2v.

Ferry, Robert, "Quelques hypothèses sur les origines des conquêtes musulmanes en Abyssinie au XVIe siècle," *Cahiers d'Études Africaines,* 5 (1961), pp. 24–36.

Filesi, Teobaldi, *Le Relazioni della cina con l'Africa nel Medio-Evo* (Milano, 1962).

Fisher, Ruth Hurditch, *Twilight Tales of the Black Baganda* (London, 1911).

Ford, J., and R. de Z. Hall, "The History of Karagwe (Bukoba District)," *Tanganyika Notes and Records,* 24 (1947), pp. 3–27.

Fortune, George, "The Contributions of Linguistics to Ethnohistory," *Historians in Tropical Africa* (Salisbury, S.R., 1962), pp. 17–30.

Fosbrooke, Henry A., "An Administrative Survey of the Masai Social System," *Tanganyika Notes and Records,* 26 (1948), pp. 1–50.

——— (ed.), "Tanganyika Rock Paintings," *ibid.,* 29 (1950), pp. 1–61.

Freeman-Grenville, G. S. P., "Coinage in East Africa Before Portuguese Times," *The Numismatic Chronicle,* XVII (1957), pp. 151–179.

———, "Swahili Literature and the History and Archaeology of the East African Coast," *Journal of the East African Swahili Committee,* 28/2 (1958), pp. 7–25.

———, "Medieval Evidence for Swahili," *Swahili,* 29/1 (1959), pp. 10–23.

———, "East African Coin Finds and Their Historical Significance," *The Journal of African History,* I (1960), pp. 31–43.

———, "Historiography of the East African Coast," *Tanganyika Notes and Records,* 55 (1960), pp. 279–289.

———, *The Medieval History of the Coast of Tanganyika* (London, 1962).

Furley, O. W., "Kasagama of Toro," *The Uganda Journal,* XXV (1961), pp. 184–198.

Gadallah, F. F., "The Egyptian Contribution to Nubian Christianity," *Sudan Notes and Records,* XL (1959), pp. 38–43.

Gorju, Julien L., *Entre le Victoria l'Albert et l'Édouard* (Rennes, 1920).

Gray, John Milner, "Early History of Buganda," *The Uganda Journal,* II (1935), pp. 259–271.

———, "The Basoga," *ibid.,* III (1936), pp. 308–312.

———, "Ahmed bin Ibrahim: The First Arab to Reach Buganda," *ibid.,* XI (1947), pp. 80–97.

———, "Portuguese Records Relating to the Wasegeju," *Tanganyika Notes and Records,* 29 (1950), pp. 85–97.

———, "Arabs on Lake Victoria, Some Revisions," *The Uganda Journal,* XXII (1958), pp. 76–81.

———, "A History of Ibanda, Saza of Mitoma, Ankole," *ibid.,* XXIV (1960), pp. 166–182.

———, *History of Zanzibar from the Middle Ages to 1856* (London, 1962).

Gray, Richard, *A History of the Southern Sudan, 1839–1889* (London, 1961).

Gray, Robert F., "The Mbugwe Tribe: Origin and Development," *Tanganyika Notes and Records,* 38 (1955), pp. 39–50.

Guillain, Charles (ed.), *Documents sur l'histoire, la géographie et le commerce de l'Afrique orientale* (Paris, 1856), 3v.

Gulliver, Philip H., "A History of the Songea Ngoni," *Tanganyika Notes and Records,* 41 (1955), pp. 16–30.

Hall, Richard Nicklin, and W. G. Neal, *The Ancient Ruins of Rhodesia* (London, 1902).
Harries, Lyndon, *Swahili Poetry* (Oxford, 1962).
——— (ed.), "The Founding of Rabai: A Swahili Chronicle by Midani bin Mwidad," *Swahili*, 31 (1960), pp. 140–149.
Harvey, Ronald J., "Mirambo," *Tanganyika Notes and Records*, 28 (1950), pp. 10–28.
Hatchell, G. W., "The Angoni of Tanganyika Territory," *Tanganyika Notes and Records*, 25 (1948), pp. 69–71.
Hiernaux, J., and E. Maquet, "Cultures préhistoriques de l'âge des métaux au Ruanda-Urundi et au Kivu," *Bulletin des Séances de l'Académie des Sciences Coloniales* (Bruxelles, 1956), pp. 1126–1149.
Hirth, Friedrich, "Early Chinese Notices of East African Territories," *Journal of the American Oriental Society*, XXX (1909–1910), pp. 46–57.
———, "The Mystery of Fu-lin," *ibid.*, pp. 1–31.
———, and William Woodville Rockhill (trans. and ed.), *Chao Ju-Kua: His Work on the Chinese and Arab Trade in the Twelfth and Thirteenth Centuries, Entitled Chu-fan-chi* (St. Petersburg, 1911).
Hollis, Alfred Claud, *The Masai: Their Language and Folklore* (Oxford, 1905).
———, *The Nandi: Their Language and Folklore* (Oxford, 1909).
Holt, Peter Malcolm, "A Sudanese Historical Legend: The Funj Conquest of Suba," *Bulletin of the School of Oriental and African Studies*, XXIII (1960), pp. 1–12.
† ———, "Funj Origins: A Critique and New Evidence," *The Journal of African History*, IV (1963), pp. 39–55.
Hornell, James, "Indonesian Influence on East African Culture," *The Journal of the Royal Anthropological Institute*, LXIV (1934), pp. 305–332.
Huntingford, G. W. B., "The Azanian Civilization of Kenya," *Antiquity*, VII (1933), pp. 153–165.
Jackson, Henry Cecil, *Tooth of Fire: Being Some Account of the Ancient Kingdom of Sennâr* (Oxford, 1912).
——— (trans. and ed.), *Black Ivory and White, or the Story of El Zubeir [Zubair ibn Rahmat] Pasha, Slaver and Sultan, as Told by Himself* (London, 1913).
Jeffreys, M. D. W., "Negro Influences on Indonesia," *African Music*, 11 (1961), pp. 10–16.
* Jones, A. H. M., and Elizabeth Monroe, *A History of Ethiopia* (Oxford, 1955).
Jones, A. M., "Indonesia and Africa: The Xylophone as Culture-Indicator," *The Journal of the Royal Anthropological Institute*, LXXXIX (1959), pp. 155–168.
Junod, Henri Philippe, "A Contribution to the Study of Ndau Demography, Totemism and History," *Bantu Studies*, VIII (1934), pp. 17–37.
Kabuga, Charles E. S., "The Genealogy of Kabaka Kintu and the Early Bakabaka of Buganda," *The Uganda Journal*, XXVII (1963), pp. 205–216.
Kagame, Alexis, *Le Code des institutions politiques du Rwanda précolonial* (Bruxelles, 1952).
———, *L'Histoire des armées bovines dans l'ancien Rwanda* (Bruxelles, 1961).
———, *Les Milices du Rwanda précolonial* (Bruxelles, 1963).
Kagwa, Apolo, *Ebika bya Buganda* (Mengo, 1912).
———, *Ekitabo kya Basekabaka Bebuganda, Nâbebunyoro, Nabekoki, Nabetoro, Nabenkole [History of the Kings of Buganda, etc.]* (London, 1912).
——— (ed. Ernest Millar), *Ekitabo kya Bakabaka Bebuganda [The Book of the Kings of Buganda]* (London, 1901).
Kammerer, A., *Essai sur l'histoire antique d'Abyssinie: le Royaume d'Askum et ses voisins d'Arabie et de Meroë* (Paris, 1926).
Kanyamunyu, Perezi K., "The Tradition of the Coming of the Abalisa Clan to Buhwezu, Ankole," *The Uganda Journal*, XV (1951), pp. 191–192.
Katate, A. G., and L. Kamugungunu, *Abagabe b'Ankole* (Kampala, 1955), 2v.
———, and Kesi K. Nganwa, *Abakozire eby'Okutangaza Omuri Ankole* (Nairobi, 1948).
Kirkman, James S., *The Arab City of Gedi: Excavations at the Great Mosque, Architecture and Finds* (London, 1954).
———, "Historical Archaeology in Kenya, 1948–1956," *Antiquaries' Journal*, XXXVII (1957), pp. 16–18.
———, "The Excavations at Ras Mkumbuu on the Island of Pemba," *Tanganyika Notes and Records*, 53 (1959), pp. 161–178.
———, *The Tomb of the Dated Inscription at Gedi* (London, 1960).
———, *Gedi: The Palace* (The Hague, 1963).
———, *Men and Monuments on the East African Coast* (London, 1964).
Kirwan, L. P., "A Contemporary Account

of the Conversion of the Sudan to Christianity," *Sudan Notes and Records*, XX (1937), pp. 289–295.
———, "A Survey of Nubian Origins," *ibid.*, pp. 47–62.
al-Lamuy, Shaibu Faraji bin Hamed al-Bakariy (trans. William Hichens), "Khabar al-Lamu: A Chronicle of Lamu," *Bantu Studies*, XII (1938), pp. 1–33.
Lancaster, D. Gordon, "Tentative Chronology of the Ngoni: Genealogy of Their Chiefs, and Notes," *The Journal of the Royal Anthropological Institute*, LXVII (1937), pp. 77–90.
Lanning, E. C., "Ancient Earthworks in Western Uganda," *The Uganda Journal*, XVII (1953), pp. 51–62.
———, "Masaka Hill: An Ancient Centre of Worship," *ibid.*, XVIII (1954), pp. 24–30.
———, "Notes on the History of Koki," *ibid.*, XXIII (1959), pp. 162–172.
———, "The Earthworks of Kibengo, Mubende District," *ibid.*, XXIV (1960), pp. 183–196.
Lawrance, J. C. D., "A History of Teso to 1937," *The Uganda Journal*, XIX (1955), pp. 7–40.
———, *The Iteso: Fifty Years of Change in a Nilo-Hamitic Tribe of Uganda* (London, 1957).
LeBaron, Richard, Jr., and Frank P. Albright, *Archaeological Discoveries in South Arabia* (Philadelphia, 1958).
Lewis, I. M., "The Somali Conquest of the Horn of Africa," *The Journal of African History*, I (1960), pp. 213–230.
MacGaffey, Wyatt, "The History of Negro Migrations in the Northern Sudan," *Southwestern Journal of Anthropology*, XVII (1961), pp. 178–197.
MacMichael, Harold A. (trans. and ed.), *A History of the Arabs in the Sudan and of the Tribes Inhabiting Darfur* (Cambridge, Eng., 1922), 2v.
Mainga, Mutumba, "The Origin of the Lozi: Some Oral Traditions," *Conference of the History of the Central African Peoples* (Lusaka, 1963), no pagination.
Maquet, Jacques Jerome, *Le Système des relations sociales dans le Ruanda ancien* (Tervuren, 1954).
Marealle, Chief Petro I. (trans. R. D. Swai), "Notes on Chagga Customs," *Tanganyika Notes and Records*, 60 (1963), pp. 67–90.
Marwick, M. G., "History and Tradition in East Central Africa Through the Eyes of the Northern Rhodesia Ceŵa," *The Journal of African History*, IV (1963), pp. 375–390.
Mathew, Gervase, "Recent Discoveries in East African Archaeology," *Antiquity*, XXVII (1953), pp. 212–218.
———, "Chinese Porcelain in East Africa and on the Coast of South Arabia," *Oriental Art*, II (Summer, 1956), pp. 50–55.
———, "The Culture of the East African Coast in the Seventeenth and Eighteenth Centuries in the Light of Recent Archaeological Discoveries," *Man*, LVI, 61 (1956), pp. 65–68.
———, "Songo Mnara," *Tanganyika Notes and Records*, 53 (1959), pp. 155–160.
Mathews, Derek, and Antonio Mordini, *The Monastery of Debra Damo, Ethiopia* (Oxford, 1959).
Mayers, W. F., "Chinese Explorations of the Indian Ocean During the Fifteenth Century," *The China Review*, III (1874–1875), pp. 219–225, 321–331; IV (1875–1876), pp. 61–67, 173–190.
Miracle, Marvin P., "Aboriginal Trade Among the Senga and Nsenga of Northern Rhodesia," *Ethnology*, I (1962), pp. 212–222.
Mondon-Vidailhet, Casimir (trans.), *Chronique de Théodoros II, roi des rois d'Éthiopie (1853–1868), d'après un manuscrit original* (Paris, 1905).
† Monneret de Villard, Ugo, *Storia della Nubia cristiana* (Roma, 1938).
Morris, H. F., "The Kingdom of Mpororo," *The Uganda Journal*, XIX (1955), pp. 204–207.
———, *A History of Ankole* (Kampala, 1962).
———, *The Heroic Recitations of the Bahima of Ankole* (Oxford, 1964).
Mungonya, Z. C. K., "The Bacwezi in Ankole," *The Uganda Journal*, XXII (1958), pp. 18–21.
Musad, Mustafa M., "The Downfall of the Christian Nubian Kingdoms," *Sudan Notes and Records*, XL (1959), pp. 124–128.
Nenquin, Jacques, *Excavations at Sanga, 1957: The Protohistoric Necropolis* (Tervuren, 1963).
Nyakatura, J. W., *Abakama ba Bunyoro-Kitara* (Kampala, 1947).
Nyirenda, Saulos (trans. and ed. T. Cullen Young), "History of the Tumbuka-Henga People," *Bantu Studies*, V (1931), pp. 1–75.
Ogot, Bethwell A., "Kingship and Statelessness Among the Nilotes," *The Histo-

rian in Tropical Africa (London, 1964), pp. 284–300.
Oliver, Roland, "A Question About the Bachwezi," *The Uganda Journal,* XVII (1953), pp. 135–137.
———, "The Baganda and the Bakonjo," *ibid.,* XVIII (1954), pp. 31–33.
———, "The Traditional Histories of Buganda, Bunyoro, and Nkole," *The Journal of the Royal Anthropological Institute,* LXXXV (1955), pp. 111–117.
———, "Ancient Capital Sites of Ankole," *The Uganda Journal,* XXIII (1959), pp. 51–63.
———, "The Royal Tombs of Buganda," *ibid.,* pp. 124–133.
———, "Reflections on the Sources of Evidence for the Precolonial History of East Africa," *Historians in Tropical Africa* (Salisbury, S.R., 1962), pp. 322–336.
———, and Gervase Mathew (eds.), *History of East Africa* (Oxford, 1963).
Orchardson, Ian Q. (ed. A. T. Matson), *The Kipsigis* (Nairobi, 1961).
Pages, A., *Un Royaume hamité au centre de l'Afrique* (Bruxelles, 1933).
Pankhurst, Estelle Sylvia, *Ethiopia: A Cultural History* (Woodford Green, 1955).
Pankhurst, Richard, *An Introduction to the Economic History of Ethiopia from Early Times to 1800* (London, 1961).
———, "Menelik and the Foundation of Addis Ababa," *The Journal of African History,* II (1961), pp. 103–117.
Paul, Andrew, *A History of the Beja Tribes of the Sudan* (Cambridge, Eng., 1954).
Pearce, Francis Barrow, *Zanzibar: The Island Metropolis of Eastern Africa* (London, 1920).
Pelliot, Paul, "Les Grands Voyages maritimes chinois au début du XVe siècle," *ibid.,* XXX (1933), pp. 237–455.
———, "Notes additionnelles sur Tcheng Houo et sur ses voyages," *T'oung Pao,* XXXI (1934–1935), pp. 274–314.
Penn, A. E. D. (ed.), "Traditional Stories of the 'Abdullab Tribe," *Sudan Notes and Records,* XVII (1934), pp. 59–82.
Phillips, Wendell, *Qataban and Sheba* (New York, 1955).
Piggott, D. W. I., "History of Mafia," *Tanganyika Notes and Records,* 11 (1941), pp. 35–40.
Pirenne, Jacqueline, *La Grèce et Saba* (Paris, 1955).
† ———, *Le Royaume sud-arabe de Qatabân et sa datation d'après l'archéologie et les sources classiques jusqu'au Périple de la mer Erythrée* (Louvain, 1961).
———, "Un Problème-clef pour la chronologie de l'Orient: la date du 'Périple de la mer Erythrée,'" *Journal Asiatique,* CCXLIX (1961), pp. 441–459.
Posnansky, Merrick, "Pottery Types from Archaeological Sites in East Africa," *The Journal of African History,* II (1961), pp. 177–198.
———, "The Traditional History of the Hereditary Kingdoms of the Western Lacustrine Bantu and Rwanda," *Conference of the History of the Central African Peoples* (Lusaka, 1963), no pagination.
Price, Thomas, "The Meaning of Mang'anja," *The Nyasaland Journal,* XVI (1963), pp. 74–79.
Prins, Adriaan Hendrik Johan, "On Swahili Historiography," *Journal of the East African Swahili Committee,* 28/2 (1958), pp. 26–40.
———, "Uncertainties in Coastal Cultural History: The 'Ngalawa' and the 'Mtepe,'" *Tanganyika Notes and Records,* 53 (1959), pp. 204–213.
———, *The Swahili-speaking Peoples of Zanzibar and the East African Coast: Arabs, Shirazi and Swahili* (London, 1961).
Pumphrey, M. E. C., "The Shilluk Tribe," *Sudan Notes and Records,* XXIV (1941), pp. 1–45.
Randles, W. G. L., "South East Africa and the Empire of Monomotapa as Shown on Selected Printed Maps of the Sixteenth Century," *Studia,* 1 (1958), pp. 103–163.
———, "Matériaux pour une histoire du Sud-Est africain jusqu'au XVIIIe siècle," *Annales: Économies, Sociétés, Civilisations,* XVIII (1963), pp. 956–980.
Rangeley, W. H. J., "Mtawalo," *The Nyasaland Journal,* V (1952), pp. 55–70.
Read, Margaret, "Tradition and Prestige Among the Ngoni," *Africa,* IX (1936), pp. 453–484.
———, *The Ngoni of Nyasaland* (London, 1956).
Revington, T. H., "Some Notes on the Mafia Island Group," *Tanganyika Notes and Records,* 1 (1936), pp. 33–37.
Roberts, D. R., "Serology and the History of the Northern Nilotes," *The Journal of African History,* III (1962), pp. 301–305.
Robinson, Arthur E., "The Arab Dynasty of Dar For (Darfur), A.D. 1448–1874 or A.H. 852–1201," *Journal of the African Society,* XXVII (1927–1928), pp. 353–363; XXVIII (1928–1929), pp. 55–67, 274–280, 379–384; XXIX (1929–1930), pp. 53–70, 164–180.

———, "The Shirazi Colonization of East Africa: Vumba," *Tanganyika Notes and Records*, 7 (1939), pp. 92–112.

Robinson, Keith R., *Khami Ruins: Report on Excavations Undertaken for the Commission for the Preservation of Natural and Historical Monuments and Relics, Southern Rhodesia, 1947–1955* (Cambridge, Eng., 1959).

———, "The Archaeology of the Rozwi," *Conference of the History of the Central African Peoples* (Lusaka, 1963), no pagination.

Rockhill, William Woodville, "Notes on the Relations and Trade of China with the Eastern Archipelago and the Coasts of the Indian Ocean During the Fourteenth Century," *T'oung Pao*, XV (1914), pp. 419–447; XVI (1915), pp. 61–84, 236–271, 374–392, 435–467, 604–626.

Roland, Hadelin, "Résumé de l'histoire ancienne du Katanga," *Problèmes Sociaux Congolais*, 61 (1963), pp. 3–41.

Roscoe, John, *The Baganda: An Account of Their Native Customs and Beliefs* (London, 1911).

———, *The Bakitara or Banyoro: The First Part of the Report of the Mackie Ethnological Expedition to Central Africa* (Cambridge, Eng., 1923).

Routledge, William Scoresby and Katherine, *With a Prehistoric People: The Akikúyu of British East Africa, Being Some Account of the Method of Life and Mode of Thought Found Existent Amongst a Nation on Its First Contact with European Civilisation* (London, 1910).

Sauter, R., "Où en est notre connaissance des églises rupestres d'Éthiopie," *Annales d'Éthiopie*, V (1963), pp. 235–292.

Shinnie, Peter L., *Excavations at Soba* (Khartoum, 1955).

———, "Excavations at Bigo, 1957," *The Uganda Journal*, XXIV (1960), pp. 16–28.

Sicard, Harald von, "The Ancient Sabi-Zimbabwe Trade Route," *Nada*, XL (1963), pp. 6–16.

Sigola, Simon, "How Lobengula Came to Rule the Matabele," *Nada*, XXXVI (1959), pp. 87–91.

Southall, Aidan W., "Alur Tradition and Its Historical Significance," *The Uganda Journal*, XVIII (1954), pp. 137–165.

Stahl, Kathleen M., *History of the Chagga People of Kilimanjaro* (The Hague, 1964).

Stiffe, Arthur W., "Ancient Trading Centres of the Persian Gulf," *The Geographical Journal:* I. Siráf, VI (1895), pp. 166–173; II. Kais, or al-Kais, VII (1896), pp. 644–649; III. Pre-Mohammedan Settlements, IX (1897), pp. 309–314; IV. Maskat, X (1897), pp. 608–618; Persian Gulf Notes, Khanag Island, XII (1898), pp. 179–182; V. Kung, XIII (1899), pp. 294–297; VI. Bandar 'Abbas, XVI (1900), pp. 211–215; VII. Bahrein, XVIII (1901), pp. 291–294.

Stigand, C. H., *The Land of Zinj: Being an Account of British East Africa, Its Ancient History and Present Inhabitants* (London, 1913).

Strandes, Justus, *Die Portugiesenzeit von Deutsch- und Englisch-Ostafrika* (Berlin, 1899).

——— (trans. Jean F. Wallwork), *The Portuguese Period in East Africa* (Nairobi, 1961).

Strong, S. Arthur (ed.), "The History of Kilwa," *The Journal of the Royal Asiatic Society*, XX (1895), pp. 385–430.

Summers, Roger, "Carl Mauch on Zimbabwe Ruins," *Nada*, XXIX (1952), pp. 9–17.

———, *Inyanga: Prehistoric Settlements in Southern Rhodesia* (Cambridge, Eng., 1958).

———, "The Southern Rhodesian Iron Age," *The Journal of African History*, II (1961), pp. 1–13.

* ———, *Zimbabwe: A Rhodesian Mystery* (Johannesburg, 1963).

† ———, K. R. Robinson, and Anthony Whitty, *Zimbabwe Excavations, 1958* (Salisbury, S.R., 1961).

Tarantino, A., "The Origin of the Lango," *The Uganda Journal*, X (1946), pp. 12–16.

Thomas, F. M., *Historical Notes on the Bisa Tribe, Northern Rhodesia* (Lusaka, 1958).

Torrend, Julius (trans. and ed.), *Specimens of Bantu Folk-Lore from Northern Rhodesia* (London, 1921).

Trimingham, J. Spencer, *Islam in the Sudan* (London, 1949).

———, *Islam in Ethiopia* (London, 1952).

———, *Islam in East Africa* (London, 1964).

Turner, V. W. (trans. and ed.), "A Lunda Love Story and Its Consequences: Selected Texts from Traditions Collected by Henrique dias de Carvalho at the Court of Mwatianvwa in 1887," *The Rhodes-Livingstone Journal*, XIX (1955), pp. 1–26.

Tweedie, Ann, "Towards a History of the Bemba from Oral Tradition," *Confer-*

ence of the History of the Central African Peoples (Lusaka, 1963), no pagination.
Ullendorff, Edward, *The Semitic Languages of Ethiopia* (London, 1955).
———, "Hebraic-Jewish Elements in Abyssinian (Monophysite) Christianity," *Journal of Semitic Studies,* I (1956), pp. 216–256.
Vansina, Jan, "Notes sur l'histoire du Burundi," *Aequatoria,* XXIV (1961), pp. 1–10.
* ———, *L'Évolution du royaume Rwanda des origines à 1900* (Bruxelles, 1962).
† ———, "La Fondation du royaume de Kasanje," *Aequatoria,* XXV (1962), pp. 45–62.
———, "Long-Distance Trade-Routes in Central Africa," *The Journal of African History,* III (1962), pp. 375–390.
———, *Geschiedenis van de Kuba van ongeveer 1500 tot 1904* (Tervuren, 1963).
Van Velsen, Jaap, "Notes on the History of the Lakeside Tonga of Nyasaland," *African Studies,* XVIII (1959), pp. 105–117.
Velten, Carl (trans. and ed.), *Prosa und Poesie der Suaheli* (Berlin, 1907).
Verhulpen, Edmond, *Baluba et Balubaïsés du Katanga* (Anvers, 1936).
Vycichl, Werner, "Le Titre de roi des rois: étude historique et comparative sur la monarchie en Éthiopie," *Annales d'Éthiopie,* I (1955), pp. 192–218.
Wainwright, Gerald A., "Early Foreign Trade in East Africa," *Man,* XLVII, 161 (1947), pp. 143–148.
Wakefield, T., "Routes of Native Caravans from the Coast to the Interior of Eastern Africa, Chiefly from Information Given by Sádi Bin Ahédi, a Native of a District Near Gázi, in Udigo, a Little North of Zanzibar," *The Journal of the Royal Geographical Society,* XL (1870), pp. 303–339.
Walker, John, "The History and Coinage of the Sultans of Kilwa," *The Numismatic Chronicle,* XVI (1936), pp. 43–81.
Wayland, E. J., "Notes on the Biggo bya Mugenyi: Some Ancient Earthworks in Northern Buddu," *The Uganda Journal,* II (1934), pp. 21–32.
Weatherby, J. M., "Inter-tribal Warfare on Mount Elgon in the Nineteenth and Twentieth Centuries (with Particular Reference to the Part Played by the Sebei-speaking Groups)," *The Uganda Journal,* XXVI (1962), pp. 200–212.
———, B. E. Kipkorir, and J. E. Sutton, "The Sirikwa," *ibid.,* XXVIII (1964), pp. 61–74.
Werner, Alice (ed.), "A Swahili History of Pate," *Journal of the African Society,* XIV (1914–1915), pp. 148–161, 278–297, 392–413.
Wheatley, Paul, "The Land of Zanj: Exegetical Notes on Chinese Knowledge of East Africa Prior to A.D. 1500," Robert W. Steel and R. Mansell Prothero (eds.), *Geographers and the Tropics: Liverpool Essays* (London, 1964), pp. 139–188.
White, C. M. N., "The Balovale Peoples and Their Historical Background," *The Rhodes-Livingstone Journal,* VIII (1949), pp. 26–41.
———, "The Ethno-History of the Upper Zambezi," *African Studies,* XXI (1962), pp. 10–27.
Whiteley, Wilfred H., "Swahili and the Classical Tradition," *Tanganyika Notes and Records,* 53 (1959), pp. 214–223.
——— (ed.), *A Selection of African Prose: Traditional Oral Texts* (Oxford, 1964).
Wieschhoff, Heinrich Albert, *The Zimbabwe-Monomotapa Culture in Southeast Africa* (Menasha, Wisc., 1941).
Wilson, G. E. H., "The Ancient Civilization of the Rift Valley," *Man* XXXII, 298 (1932), pp. 250–257.
K. W. [Tito Winyi, *omukama* of Bunyoro], "The Kings of Bunyoro-Kitara," *The Uganda Journal,* III (1935), pp. 155–160; IV (1936), pp. 75–83; V (1937), pp. 53–84.
Worsley, P. M., and J. P. Rumberger, "Remains of an Earlier People in Uhehe," *Tanganyika Notes and Records,* 27 (1949), pp. 42–46.
Wrigley, Christopher C., "Buganda: An Outline Economic History," *The Economic History Review,* X (1957), pp. 69–80.
———, "Some Thoughts on the Bacwezi," *The Uganda Journal,* XXII (1958), pp. 11–17.
———, "Kimera," *ibid.,* XXIII (1959), pp. 38–43.
Young, T. Cullen, *Notes on the Speech and History of the Tumbuka-Henga Peoples* (Livingstonia, 1923).
———, *Notes on the Customs and Folk-Lore of the Tumbuka-Kamanga Peoples* (Livingstonia, 1931).
———, "The 'Henga' People in Northern Nyasaland," *The Nyasaland Journal,* V (1952), pp. 33–37.

C. The Western Sudan and Forest

Abdullah ibn Muhammad (trans. and ed. Mervyn Hiskett), *Tazyin al Waraqat* (Ibadan, 1964).

Abun-Nasr, Jamil, "Some Aspects of the Umari Branch of the Tijaniyya," *The Journal of African History,* III (1962), pp. 329–331.

Adegbamigbe, A. A., *History, Laws and Customs of the Ile-Oluji* (Ibadan, 1962).

Agyeman-Duah, J., "Mampong, Ashanti: A Traditional History to the Reign of Nana Safo Kantanka," *Transactions of the Historical Society of Ghana,* IV (1960), pp. 21–25.

Ajayi, J. F. Ade, and Robert S. Smith, *Yoruba Warfare in the Nineteenth Century* (Cambridge, Eng., 1964).

Ajisafe, Ajayi Kolawole, *History of Abeokuta* (Bungay, Eng., 1924).

Akindélé, Adolphe, and C. Aguessy, *Contribution à l'étude de l'histoire de l'ancien royaume de Porto Novo* (Dakar, 1953).

Amangala, G. L., *A Short History of Ijaw* (Port Harcourt, 1954).

Aubert, A., "Légendes historiques et traditions orales recueillies dans la Haute-Gambie," *Bulletin du Comité d'Études Historiques et Scientifiques de l'Afrique Occidentale Française,* VI (1923), pp. 384–428.

† Ba, Amadou Hampaté, and Jacques Daget, *L'Empire peul du Maçina, 1818–1853* (Paris, 1962), I.

Bâ, Tamsir Ousmane, "Essai historique sur le Rip (Sénégal)," *Bulletin de l'Institut Français d'Afrique Noire,* XIX (1957), pp. 564–591.

Balmer, William Turnbull, *A History of the Akan Peoples of the Gold Coast* (London, 1925).

Beckingham, Charles F., "The Pilgrimage and Death of Sakura, King of Mali," *Bulletin of the School of Oriental and African Studies,* XV (1953), pp. 391–393.

Beier, H. Ulli, "Before Oduduwa," *Odù,* 3 (1956), pp. 25–32.

Biobaku, Saburi O., "The Problem of Traditional History, with Special Reference to Yoruba Traditions," *Journal of the Historical Society of Nigeria,* I (1956), pp. 43–47.

———, "An Historical Sketch of the Peoples of Western Nigeria," *Odù,* 6 (1958), pp. 24–28.

Bivar, A. D. H., "Arabic Documents of Northern Nigeria," *Bulletin of the School of Oriental and African Studies,* XXII (1959), pp. 324–349.

† ———, "The *Wathiqat ahl al-Sudan:* A Manifesto of the Fulani *Jihad,*" *The Journal of African History,* II (1961), pp. 235–243.

† ———, and Mervyn Hiskett, "The Arabic Literature of Nigeria to 1804: A Provisional Account," *Bulletin of the School of Oriental and African Studies,* XXV (1962), pp. 104–148.

———, and P. L. Shinnie, "Old Kanuri Capitals," *The Journal of African History,* III (1962), pp. 1–10.

Blanc, E., "Notes sur les Diawara," *Bulletin du Comité d'Études Historiques et Scientifiques de l'Afrique Occidentale Française,* VII (1924), pp. 84–99.

Bonnel de Mézières, Albert, *Recherches de l'emplacement de Ghana (fouilles à Koumbi et à Settah), et sur l'emplacement de Tekrour* (Paris, 1923).

Boulnois, Jean, and Hamma Boubou, *L'empire de Gao: histoire, coutumes et magie des Sonrai* (Paris, 1931).

Bovill, Edward William, "The Moorish Invasion of the Sudan," *Journal of the African Society,* XXVI (1926–1927), pp. 245–262; XXVII (1927–1928), pp. 47–56.

———, *Caravans of the Old Sahara: An Introduction to the History of the Western Sudan* (London, 1933).

———, "The Camel and the Garamantes," *Antiquity,* XXX (1956), pp. 19–21.

* ———, *The Golden Trade of the Moors* (London, 1958).

Bowdich, Thomas Edward, *An Essay on the Superstitions, Customs, and Arts Common to the Ancient Egyptians, Abyssinians, and Ashantees* (Paris, 1821).

Boyer, Gaston, *Un Peuple de l'Ouest soudanais, les Diawara* (Dakar, 1953).

Bradbury, R. E., *The Benin Kingdom and the Edo-speaking Peoples of Southwestern Nigeria* (London, 1957).

———, "Chronological Problems in the Study of Benin History," *Journal of the Historical Society of Nigeria,* I (1959), pp. 263–287.

Bruce-Myers, J. M., "The Origin of the Gãs," *Journal of the African Society,* XXVII (1927–1928), pp. 69–76, 167–173.

Cardinall, Allan Wolsey (ed.), *Tales Told in Togoland . . . to Which Is Added the Mythical and Traditional History of Dagomba by E. F. Tamakloe* (London, 1931).

Castries, Henri de, "La Conquête du Soudan par el-Mansour (1591)," *Hespéris,* III (1923), pp. 433–488.

Chenguiti [al-Shinqiti], Ahmed Lamine Ech (trans. and ed. Mourad Teffahi), *El Wasît: littérature, histoire, géographie, moeurs et coutumes des habitants de la Mauritanie* (Saint-Louis, Senegal, 1953).

Chéron, Georges, "Contribution à l'histoire du Mossi: traditions relatives au cercle de Kaya," *Bulletin du Comité d'Études Historiques et Scientifiques de l'Afrique Occidentale Française*, VII (1924), pp. 635–691.

Childs, Gladwyn Murray, *Umbundu Kinship and Character* (London, 1949).

———, "The Kingdom of Wambu (Huambo): A Tentative Chronology," *The Journal of African History*, V (1964), pp. 367–379.

Chilver, Elizabeth M., "Nineteenth-Century Trade in the Bamenda Grassfields, Southern Cameroons," *Afrika und Übersee*, XLV (1961–1962), pp. 233–258.

———, and Phyllis Kaberry, "Traditional Government in Bafut, West Cameroon," *Nigerian Field*, XXVIII (1963), pp. 4–30.

Clinton, J. V., "King Eyo Honesty II of Creek Town," *Nigeria Magazine*, 19 (1961), pp. 182–188.

Cohen, Ronald, "The Just-so So? A Spurious Tribal Group in Western Sudanic History," *Man*, LXII, 239 (1962), pp. 153–154.

Collieaux, M., "Contribution à l'étude de l'histoire de l'ancien royaume de Kénédougou," *Bulletin du Comité d'Études Historiques et Scientifiques de l'Afrique Occidentale Française*, VII (1924), pp. 128–181.

Cooley, William Desborough, *The Negroland of the Arabs Examined and Explained, or an Inquiry into the Early History and Geography of Central Africa* (London, 1841).

Cornevin, Robert, *Histoire du Dahomey* (Paris, 1962).

———, "Notes sur le cercle de Dapango (Républic du Togo) et l'histoire de ses habitants," *Le Monde non Chrétien*, 67 (1963), pp. 168–186.

Daaku, K. Yeboa, "Pre-European Currencies of West Africa and Western Sudan," *Ghana Notes and Queries*, 2 (1961), pp. 12–14.

Daget, Jacques, and Z. Ligers, "Une Ancienne Industrie malienne: les pipes en terre," *Bulletin de l'Institut Français d'Afrique Noire*, XXIV (1962), pp. 12–53.

Dalzel, Archibald, *The History of Dahomey, an Inland Kingdom of Africa: Compiled from Authentic Memoirs, with an Introduction and Notes* (London, 1793).

Danquah, Joseph Boakye, *Gold Coast: Akan Laws and Customs and the Akim Abuakwa Constitution* (London, 1928).

———, "The Culture of Akan," *Africa*, XXII (1952), pp. 360–366.

Decraene, Philippe, "Le Mali médiéval," *Civilisations*, XII (1962), pp. 250–258.

De Graft-Johnson, John Coleman, *African Glory: The Story of Vanished Negro Civilizations* (London, 1954).

Delafosse, Maurice, *Les Frontières de la Côte d'Ivoire, de la Côte d'Or et du Soudan* (Paris, 1908).

———, *Haut-Sénégal-Niger* (Paris, 1912), 3v.

———, "Les Relations du Maroc avec le Soudan à travers les âges," *Hespéris*, IV (1924), pp. 153–174.

——— (trans. F. Fligelman), *The Negroes of Africa: History and Culture* (Washington, 1931).

Denis, Paul, *Histoire des Mangbetu et des Matshaga jusqu'à l'arrivée des Belges* (Tervuren, 1961).

Deschamps, Hubert Jules, *Traditions orales et archives au Gabon: contribution à l'ethno-histoire* (Paris, 1962).

Desplagnes, Louis, *Le Plateau central nigerien* (Paris, 1907).

Dike, K. Onwuka, "Benin: A Great Forest Kingdom of Medieval Nigeria," *Practical Anthropology*, VIII (1961), pp. 31–35.

Dim Delobsom, A. A., *L'Empire du Mogho-Naba: coutumes des Mossi de la Haute-Volta* (Paris, 1932).

Dorjahn, V. R., "A Brief History of the Temne of Yoni," *Sierra Leone Studies*, 14 (1960), pp. 80–89.

† Dunglas, Édouard, "Contribution à l'histoire du Moyen-Dahmoey," *Études Dahoméennes*, XIX–XXI (1957–1958), *passim*.

Dupuis-Yakouba, Auguste (trans. and ed.), *Les Gow: ou chasseurs du Niger; légendes Songhaï de la région de Tombouctou* (Paris, 1911).

Egharevba, Jacob V., *A Short History of Benin* (Ibadan, 1960).

Engeström, Tor, "Origin of Pre-Islamic Architecture in West Africa," *Ethnos*, XXIV (1959), pp. 64–69.

† Fage, John D., "Ancient Ghana: A Review of the Evidence," *Transactions of the Historical Society of Ghana*, III (1957), pp. 77–98.

———, "The Use of Oral Evidence in West African History," *Bulletin of the Institute of Historical Research*, XXXI (1958), pp. 33–35.

Fagg, Bernard E. B. and William Buller, "The Ritual Stools of Ancient Ife," *Man*, LX, 155 (1960), pp. 113–115.

Fagg, William Buller, and Frank Willett, "Ancient Ife: An Ethnographical Summary," *Odù*, 8 (1960), pp. 21–35.

Frobenius, Leo (trans. Rudolf Blind), *The Voice of Africa: Being an Account of the Travels of the German Inner African Expedition in the Years 1910–1912* (London, 1913), 2v.

Fuller, Francis, *A Vanished Dynasty: Ashanti* (London, 1921).

Gaillard, M., "Niani, ancienne capitale de l'empire Mandingue," *Bulletin du Comité d'Études Historiques et Scientifiques de l'Afrique Occidentale Française*, VI (1923), pp. 620–636.

Gautier, E. F., "L'Or du Soudan dans l'histoire," *Annales d'Histoire Économique et Sociale*, VII (1935), pp. 113–123.

Geay, J., "Origine, formation et histoire du royaume de Porto-Novo," *Bulletin du Comité d'Études Historiques et Scientifiques de l'Afrique Occidentale Française*, VII (1924), pp. 619–634.

Gerbeau, H., "Ancienne Route d'invasions, zone marginale des grands empires soudanais, trait d'union entre le Maçina et Tombouctou: la région de l'Issa-Ber," *Études d'Outre-Mer*, 42 (1959), pp. 51–58.

Goodwin, A. J. H., "Archaeology and Benin Architecture," *Journal of the Historical Society of Nigeria*, I (1957), pp. 65–85.

Goody, Jack [John Rankine], "Ethnohistory and the Akan of Ghana," *Africa*, XXIX (1959), pp. 67–81.

Gouilly, Alphonse, *L'Islam dans l'Afrique occidentale française* (Paris, 1952).

Greenberg, Joseph, "The Negro Kingdoms of the Sudan," *Transactions of the New York Academy of Sciences*, XI (1949), pp. 126–135.

———, "Linguistic Evidence for the Influence of the Kanuri on the Hausa," *The Journal of African History*, I (1960), pp. 205–212.

Hair, P. E. H., "Notes on the Discovery of the Vai Script with a Bibliography," *Sierra Leone Language Review*, 2 (1963), pp. 36–49.

Hau, Kathleen, "Evidence of the Use of Pre-Portuguese Written Characters by the Bini?" *Bulletin de l'Institut Français d'Afrique Noire*, XXI (1959), pp. 109–154.

Herissé, A. le, *L'Ancien Royaume de Dahomey* (Paris, 1911).

* Herskovits, Melville J., *Dahomey: An Ancient West African Kingdom* (New York, 1938), 2v.

Hervé, H., "Niani: ex-capitale de l'empire Manding," *Notes Africaines*, 82 (1959), pp. 51–55.

Hiernaux, C. R., "Notes sur l'évolution des Gagou," *Bulletin de l'Institut Français d'Afrique Noire*, XII (1950), pp. 488–512.

Hilton, T. E., "Notes on the History of Kusasi," *Transactions of the Historical Society of Ghana*, VI (1962), pp. 79–86.

Hiskett, Mervyn, "Material Relating to the State of Learning Among the Fulani Before Their *Jihād*," *Bulletin of the School of Oriental and African Studies*, XIX (1957), pp. 550–578.

† ———, "*Kitab al-farq*: A Work on the Habe Kingdoms Attributed to Uthman dan Fodio," *ibid.*, XXIII (1960), pp. 558–579.

† ———, "An Islamic Tradition of Reform in the Western Sudan from the Sixteenth to the Eighteenth Century," *ibid.*, XXV (1962), pp. 577–596.

* Hodgkin, Thomas (ed.), *Nigerian Perspectives: An Historical Anthology* (London, 1960).

Hogben, Sidney John, *The Muhammadan Emirates of Nigeria* (London, 1930).

Holas, Bohumil, *Cultures matérielles de la Côte d'Ivoire* (Paris, 1960).

Houis, Maurice, "Notes sur le Songay," *Bulletin de l'Institut Français d'Afrique Noire*, XX (1958), pp. 225–240.

Hunwick, J. O., "Ahmad Baba and the Moroccan Invasion of the Sudan," *Journal of the Historical Society of Nigeria*, II (1962), pp. 311–328.

———, "A New Source for the Biography of Ahmad Baba al-Tinbuktu (1556–1627)," *Bulletin of the School of Oriental and African Studies*, XXVII (1964), pp. 568–593.

Igwebe, R. O., *The Original History of Arondizuogu from 1635 to 1960* (Aba, 1962).

Jeffreys, M. D. W., "Speculative Origins of the Fulani Language," *Africa*, XVII (1947), pp. 47–54.

———, "Two Arabic Documents," *African Studies*, IX (1950), pp. 77–85.

———, "The Origins of the Benin Bronzes," *ibid.*, X (1951), pp. 87–92.

———, "Some Historical Notes on the Ntem," *Journal of the Historical Society of Nigeria*, II (1961), pp. 260–276.

———, "Traditional Sources Prior to 1890 for the Grassfield Bali of Northwestern Cameroons," *Afrika und Übersee*, XLVI (1962–1963), pp. 168–199, 296–313.

Johnson, Samuel (ed. O. Johnson), *The*

History of the Yorubas from the Earliest Times to the Beginning of the British Protectorate (Lagos, 1921).
Jones, D. H., "Jakpa and the Foundation of Gonja," *Transactions of the Historical Society of Ghana,* VI (1962), pp. 1–29.
† Jones, Gwilyn Iwan, *The Trading States of the Oil Rivers: A Study of Political Development in Eastern Nigeria* (London, 1963).
Kabore, Gomkoudougou V., "Caractère 'féodal' du système politique Mossi," *Cahiers d'Études Africaines,* 2 (1962), pp. 609–623.
Ketchuua, T., *Contribution à l'histoire du Cameroun de 450 avant Jesus-Christ à nos jours* (Yaoundé, 1962).
Koelle, Sigismund Wilhelm, *Narrative of an Expedition into the Vy Country of West Africa, and the Discovery of a System of Syllabic Writing Recently Invented by the Natives of the Vy Tribe* (London, 1849).
Kouroubari, Amadou, "Histoire de l'imam Samori," *Bulletin de l'Institut Français d'Afrique Noire,* XXI (1959), pp. 544–571.
Krieger, Kurt, *Geschichte von Zamfara, Sokoto-Provinz, Nordnigeria* (Berlin, 1959).
Kup, A. Peter, *A History of Sierra Leone, 1400–1787* (Cambridge, Eng., 1961).
Lebeuf, Jean-Paul, "Fouilles archéologiques dans la région du Tchad," *Zaïre,* I (1947), pp. 543–553.
———, "The Site of Wara (Republic of Chad)," *Journal of the Historical Society of Nigeria,* II (1962), pp. 396–399.
———, and Annie Masson-Detourbet, *La Civilisation du Tchad* (Paris, 1950).
Lewicki, Tadeusz, "L'État nord-africain de Tāhert et ses relations avec le Soudan occidental à la fin du VIIIe aux IXe siècle," *Cahiers d'Études Africaines,* 2 (1962), pp. 513–535.
Lloyd, Peter C., "Yoruba Myths: A Sociologist's Interpretation," *Odù,* 2 (1956), pp. 20–28.
———, "Sacred Kingship and Government Among the Yoruba," *Africa,* XXX (1960), pp. 221–237.
———, "The Itsekiri in the Nineteenth Century: An Outline Social History," *The Journal of African History,* IV (1963), pp. 207–232.
Lombard, Jacques, "La Vie politique dans une ancienne société de type féodal: les Bariba du Dahomey," *Cahiers d'Études Africaines,* 1 (1960), pp. 5–45.
McCall, Daniel F., "The Traditions of the Founding of Sijilmassa and Ghana," *Transactions of the Historical Society of Ghana,* V (1961), pp. 3–32.
———, *Africa in Time-Perspective: A Discussion of Historical Reconstruction from Unwritten Sources* (Boston, 1964).
Marc, Lucien, *Le Pays Mossi* (Paris, 1909).
Marty, Paul, *Études sur l'Islam au Sénégal* (Paris, 1917).
———, *Études sur l'Islam et les tribus du Soudan* (Paris, 1920–1921), 4v.
———, *L'Islam en Guinée* (Paris, 1921).
———, *Études sur l'Islam en Côte d'Ivoire* (Paris, 1922).
Mathews, A. B., "The Kisra Legend," *African Studies,* IX (1950), pp. 144–147.
Mauny, Raymond A., "Une Route préhistorique à travers le Sahara occidental," *Bulletin de l'Institut Français d'Afrique Noire,* IX (1947), pp. 341–357.
———, "L'Expédition marocaine d'Ouadane (Mauritanie) vers 1543–44," *ibid.,* XI (1949), pp. 129–140.
———, "Le Judaïsme, les Juifs et l'Afrique occidentale," *ibid.,* pp. 354–378.
———, "Un Âge du cuivre au Sahara occidental?" *ibid.,* XIII (1951), pp. 168–180.
———, "The Question of Ghana," *Africa,* XXIV (1954), pp. 200–213.
† ———, *Tableau géographique de l'Ouest africain au Moyen Âge d'après les sources écrites, la tradition, et l'archéologie* (Dakar, 1961).
Meek, Charles Kingsley, *The Northern Tribes of Nigeria: An Ethnographical Account of the Northern Provinces of Nigeria* (London, 1925).
Meyerowitz, Eva L. R., "The Akan and Ghana," *Man,* LVII, 99 (1957), pp. 83–88.
———, *The Akan of Ghana: Their Ancient Beliefs* (London, 1958).
———, *The Divine Kingship in Ghana and Ancient Egypt* (London, 1960).
———, "The Tradition of Tafo (Ashanti)," *Transactions of the Historical Society of Ghana,* LV (1960), pp. 30–32.
Migeod, F. W. H., "The Ancient So People of Bornu," *Journal of the African Society,* XXIII (1923), pp. 19–29.
Monteil, Charles, *Les Bambara du Ségou et du Kaarta: étude historique, ethnographique et littéraire d'une peuplade du Soudan français* (Paris, 1924).
———, "Les Empires du Mali," *Bulletin du Comité d'Études Historiques et Scientifiques de l'Afrique Occidentale Française,* XII (1929), pp. 291–447.
———, *Une Cité soudanaise: Djenné,*

métropole du delta central du Niger (Paris, 1932).
———, "La Légende du Ouagadou et l'origine des Sarakolé," *Memoires de l'Institut Français d'Afrique Noire,* XXIII (1954), pp. 359–408.
Mouezy, Henri, *Histoire des coutumes du pays d'Assinie et du royaume de Krinjabo (fondation de la Côte d'Ivoire)* (Paris, 1942).
Murray, K. C., "Nigerian Bronzes: Work from Ife," *Antiquity,* XV (1941), pp. 71–80.
Mveng, Engelbert, *Histoire du Cameroun* (Paris, 1963).
Nadel, Siegfried Frederick, *A Black Byzantium: The Kingdom of Nupe in Nigeria* (Oxford, 1942).
Newbury, Colin W., *The Western Slave Coast and Its Rulers* (Oxford, 1961).
† Niane, Djbril Tamsir, *Soundjata, ou l'épopée mandingue* (Paris, 1960).
———, "Recherches sur l'empire du Mali au Moyen Âge," *Recherches Africaines,* 2 (1961), pp. 31–51.
Obio-Effiong, U. E. E., *A First Step to the Study of Ibibio History* (Aba, 1958).
Ogunkoya, T. O., "The Early History of Ijebu," *Journal of the Historical Society of Nigeria,* I (1956), pp. 48–58.
Olunlade, E. A. [Otun Seriki of Ede], *Ede: A Short History* (Ibadan, 1961).
Ozanne, Paul, "Notes on the Early Historic Archaeology of Accra," *Transactions of the Historical Society of Ghana,* VI (1962), pp. 51–70.
Pageard, Robert, "La Marche orientale du Mali (Ségou-Djenné) en 1644 d'après le Tarikh es-Soudan," *Journal de la Société des Africanistes,* XXXI (1961), pp. 73–81.
———, "Soundiata Keita and the Oral Tradition," *Présence Africaine,* VIII (1961), pp. 53–72.
———, "Contribution critique à la chronologie historique de l'Ouest africain, suivie d'une traduction des tables chronologiques de Barth," *Journal de la Société des Africanistes,* XXXII (1962), pp. 91–177.
Palau Marti, Montserrat, *Le Roi-Dieu au Benin* (Paris, 1964).
Palmer, Herbert Richmond, "An Early Fulani Conception of Islam," *Journal of the African Society,* XXIII (1913–1914), pp. 407–414; XIV (1914–1915), pp. 53–59, 185–192.
———, "The 'Fulas' and Their Language," *ibid.,* XXII (1922–1923), pp. 121–130.
——— (trans. and ed.), *Sudanese Memoirs: Being Mainly Translations of a Number of Arabic Manuscripts Relating to the Central and Western Sudan* (Lagos, 1928), 3v.
———, *The Bornu Sahara and Sudan* (London, 1936).
Paques, Viviana, *Les Bambara* (Paris, 1954).
Pauvert, Jean-Claude, "L'Évolution politique des Ewé," *Cahiers d'Études Africaines,* 1 (1960), pp. 161–192.
† Person, Yves, "Les Ancêtres de Samori," *Cahiers d'Études Africaines,* 4 (1963), pp. 125–156.
Pottier, René, *Histoire du Sahara* (Paris, 1947).
† Priestley, Margaret, and Ivor Wilks, "The Ashanti Kings in the Eighteenth Century: A Revised Chronology," *The Journal of African History,* I (1960), pp. 83–92.
Prost, A., "Légendes Songay," *Bulletin de l'Institut Français d'Afrique Noire,* XVIII (1956), pp. 188–201.
Proyart, Liévain Bonaventure, *Histoire de Loango, Kakongo, et autres royaumes d'Afrique: rédigée d'après les mémoires des préfets apostoliques de la mission française* (Paris, 1776).
Raponda-Walker, André, *Notes d'histoire du Gabon* (Montpellier, 1960).
Rattray, Robert Sutherland, *Ashanti* (Oxford, 1923).
———, *Religion and Art in Ashanti* (Oxford, 1927).
———, *The Tribes of the Ashanti Hinterland* (Oxford, 1932).
Redhouse, James William, *Translations from the Original Arabic of a History and Journal of the Events Which Occurred During Seven Expeditions in the Land of Kanim, Against the Tribes of Bulala, etc., by the Sultan of Burnu, Idris the Pilgrim, Son of ʿAli, Preceded by Some Details of the Sultan's Ancestors* (London, 1861).
Reindorf, Carl-Christian, *History of the Gold Coast and Asante* (Basel, 1895).
Rennell Rodd, Francis James Baron, *People of the Veil: Being an Account of the Habits, Organisation, and History of the Wandering Tuareg Tribes Which Inhabit the Mountains of Air or Asben in the Central Sahara* (Cairo, 1924), 3v.
Riad, Mohamed, "The Jukun: An Example of African Migrations in the Sixteenth Century," *Wiener Völkerkundliche Mitteilungen,* VII (1959), pp. 37–44.
Robinson, Charles Henry, *Specimens of*

Hausa Literature (Cambridge, Eng., 1896).

Rodinson, M., and Jean-Paul Lebeuf, "L'Origine et les souverains du Mandara," *Bulletin de l'Institut Français d'Afrique Noire*, XVIII (1956), pp. 227–255.

Roncière, Charles de la, *La Découverte de l'Afrique au Moyen Âge* (Cairo, 1924), 3v.

Roth, Henry Ling, *Great Benin: Its Customs, Art and Horrors* (Halifax, Eng., 1903).

† Rouch, Jean, *Contribution à l'histoire des Songhay* (Dakar, 1953).

Saint-Père, "Création du royaume du Fouta Djallon," *Bulletin du Comité d'Études Historiques et Scientifiques de l'Afrique Occidentale Française*, XII (1929), pp. 484–555.

Sarbah, John Mensah, *Fanti Customary Laws: A Brief Introduction to the Principles of the Native Laws and Customs of the Fanti and Akan Districts of the Gold Coast, with a Report of Some Cases Thereon Decided in the Law Courts* (London, 1929).

Sauvaget, J., "Les Épitaphes royales de Gao," *Bulletin de l'Institut Français d'Afrique Noire*, XII (1950), pp. 418–440.

Shabeeny [Shabini], el-Hage Abd Salam (trans. James G. Jackson), *An Account of Timbuctoo and Housa, Territories in the Interior of Africa, with Notes, Critical and Explanatory* (London, 1820).

Shaw, Thurstan, *Excavation at Dawu: Report on an Excavation in a Mound at Dawu, Akuapim, Ghana* (Edinburgh, 1961).

Shinnie, Peter L., and Paul Ozanne, "Excavation at Yendi Dabari," *Transactions of the Historical Society of Ghana*, VI (1962), pp. 87–118.

Sidibé, Mamby, "Soundiata Keita: héros historique et légendaire, empereur du Manding," *Notes Africaines*, 82 (April, 1959), pp. 41–51.

Siré, Abbas Soh (trans. and ed. Maurice Delafosse and Gebri Gaden), *Chroniques du Fouta sénégalaises* (Paris, 1913).

Skinner, Elliott Percival, "The Mossi and Traditional Sudanese History," *The Journal of Negro History*, XLIII (1958), pp. 121–131.

Smith, H. F. C., "Source Material for the History of the Western Sudan," *Journal of the Historical Society of Nigeria*, I (1957), pp. 238–248.

† ———, "A Neglected Theme of West African History: The Islamic Revolutions of the Nineteenth Century," *ibid.*, II (1961), pp. 169–185.

Smith, Michael G., *Government in Zazzau, 1800–1950* (London, 1960).

Sossouhounto, M. F., "Les Anciens Rois de la dynastie d'Abomey," *Études Dahoméennes*, XIII (1955), pp. 23–30.

Stafford, A. O., "The Tarik É Soudan," *The Journal of Negro History*, II (1917), pp. 139–146.

Staude, Wilhelm, "La Légende royale des Kouroumba," *Journal de la Société des Africanistes*, XXXI (1961), pp. 209–259.

Talbot, Percy Amaury, *The Peoples of Southern Nigeria: A Sketch of Their History, Ethnology and Languages* (London, 1926), 4v.

Tardieu, Amédée, *Sénégambie et Guinée* (Paris, 1847).

Tardits, Claude, "Religion, épopée, histoire: notes sur les fonctions latentes des cultes dans les civilisations du Bénin," *Diogène*, XXXVII (1962), pp. 17–28.

Tauxier, Louis, *Le Noir du Soudan: pays Mossi et Gourounsi* (Paris, 1912).

———, *Le Noir du Yatenga* (Paris, 1917).

———, *Nouvelles notes sur le Mossi et le Gourounsi* (Paris, 1924).

———, *Moeurs et histoire des Peuls* (Paris, 1937).

———, *Histoire des Bambara* (Paris, 1942).

Temple, Charles Lindsay, *Native Races and Their Rulers: Sketches and Studies of Official Life and Administrative Problems in Nigeria* (Cape Town, 1918).

Tepowa, Adebiyi, "A Short History of Brass and Its People," *Journal of the African Society*, VII (1907), pp. 32–88.

Thomas, Benjamin Earl, *Trade Routes of Algeria and the Sahara* (Berkeley, 1957).

Thomassey, Paul, and Raymond Mauny, "Campagne de fouilles à Koumbi Saleh," *Bulletin de l'Institut Français d'Afrique Noire*, XIII (1951), pp. 438–462.

———, "Campagne de fouilles de 1950 à Koumbi Saleh (Ghana?)," *ibid.*, XVIII (1956), pp. 117–140.

Tordoff, William, "The Ashanti Confederacy," *The Journal of African History*, III (1962), pp. 399–417.

Trautmann, René, *La Littérature populaire à la Côte des Esclaves: contes, proverbes, devinettes* (Paris, 1927).

* Trimingham, J. Spencer, *A History of Islam in West Africa* (Glasgow, 1962).

Tubiana, Marie-José and Joseph (eds.), "Un Document inédit sur les sultans du Wadday," *Cahiers d'Études Africaines*, 2 (1960), pp. 49–112.

———, *Contes Zaghawa: trente-sept contes et deux légendes recueillis au Tchad* (Paris, 1961).

Urvoy, Yves, *Histoire des populations du Soudan central (colonie du Niger)* (Paris, 1936).

———, *Histoire de l'empire du Bornou* (Paris, 1949).

Vansina, Jan, "A Comparison of African Kingdoms," *Africa,* XXXII (1962), pp. 324–335.

———, "The Functions of Oral Traditions and Their Influence on the Historical Content of These Sources," *Historians in Tropical Africa* (Salisbury, S.R., 1962), pp. 119–126.

———, "Notes sur l'origine du royaume de Kongo," *The Journal of African History,* IV (1963), pp. 33–38.

———, Raymond Mauny, and L. V. Thomas (eds.), *The Historian in Tropical Africa* (London, 1964).

Vidal, J., "Au sujet de l'emplacement de Mali (ou Melli)," *Bulletin du Comité d'Études Historiques et Scientifiques de l'Afrique Occidentale Française,* VI (1923), pp. 251–268.

———, "La Légende officielle de Soudiata, fondateur de l'empire Manding," *ibid.,* VII (1924), pp. 317–328.

Westcott, Roger W., "Did the Yoruba Come from Egypt?" *Odù,* 4 (1956), pp. 10–15.

† Wilks, Ivor, "The Rise of the Akwamu Empire, 1650–1710," *Transactions of the Historical Society of Ghana,* III (1957), pp. 99–136.

———, "Akwamu and Otublohum: An Eighteenth-Century Akan Marriage Arrangement," *Africa,* XXIX (1959), pp. 391–404.

———, "A Note on the Traditional History of Mampong," *Transactions of the Historical Society of Ghana,* IV (1960), pp. 26–29.

† ———, *The Northern Factor in Ashanti History* (Legon, 1961).

——— (ed.) (trans. Mahmoud El-Wakkad), "Qissatu Salaga Tarikhu Gonja: The Story of Salaga and the History of Gonja," *Ghana Notes and Queries,* 3 (1961), pp. 8–31; 4 (1962), pp. 6–25.

Willett, Frank, "The Discovery of New Brass Figures at Ife," *Odù,* 6 (1958), pp. 29–54.

———, "Ife and Its Archaeology," *The Journal of African History,* I (1960), pp. 231–248.

———, "Investigations at Old Oyo, 1956–1957: An Interim Report," *Journal of the Historical Society of Nigeria,* II (1960), pp. 59–77.

Zahan, Dominique, "Pour une histoire des Mossi de Yatenga," *L'Homme: Revue Française d'Anthropologie,* I, 2 (1961), pp. 5–22.

Zohoncon, Célestin Adjolohoun, "À propos de l'histoire de Cotonou," *Études Dahoméennes,* XIII (1955), pp. 7–9.

III. The Euro-African Interaction

A. Contemporary Accounts Before 1800

Adanson, Michel, *A Voyage to Senegal, the Isle of Goree and the River Gambia* (London, 1759).

Ahmad ibn Majid (trans. T. A. Shumouskii), *Tri Neizvestnye Lozii* (Moskva, 1957).

Álvares, Francisco (trans. and eds. Charles F. Beckingham and G. W. B. Huntingford), *The Prester John of the Indies* (Cambridge, Eng., 1961), 2v.

Atkins, John, *A Voyage to Guinea, Brasil, and the West-Indies* (London, 1737).

Barbot, James, "An Abstract of a Voyage to Congo River," Awnsham and John Churchill, *A Collection of Voyages and Travels* (London, 1732), V.

Barbot, John, *A Description of the Coasts of North and South Guinea, and of Ethiopia Inferior, Vulgarly Angola,* Awnsham and John Churchill, *A Collection of Voyages and Travels* (London, 1732), V.

Barros, João de, *Deçadas da Asia* (Lisboa and Madrid, 1552–1615), 4v.

Beckingham, Charles F., and G. W. B. Huntingford (trans. and eds.), *Some Records of Ethiopia, 1593–1646* (London, 1954).

Birch, Walter de Gray (trans. and ed.), *The Commentaries of the Great Afonso d'Alboquerque* (London, 1875).

Bosman, Willem, *A New and Accurate Description of the Coast of Guinea Divided into the Gold, the Slave, and the Ivory Coasts* (London, 1705).

Bruce, James, *Travels to Discover the Source of the Nile in the Years 1768, 1769, 1770, 1771, 1772, and 1773* (Edinburgh, 1790), 5v.

Burnell, Arthur Coke, and P. A. Teile (eds.), *The Voyage of John Huyghen van Linschoten to the East Indies* (London, 1884–1885), 2v.

Castro, João de, *Le Routier de Dom Joam de Castro: l'exploration de la mer Rouge par les Portugais en 1541* (Paris, 1936).

Collis, M., *The Grand Perigrenation: Being the Life and Adventures of Fernão Mendes Pinto* (London, 1949).

Correa, Gaspar (trans. and ed. H. E. J. Stanley), *The Three Voyages of Vasco da Gama* (London, 1869).

Crawford, Osbert Guy Stanhope (ed.), *Ethiopian Itineraries, Circa 1400–1524* (Cambridge, Eng., 1958).

Crone, G. R. (trans. and ed.), *The Voyages of Cadamosto* (London, 1937).

Dames, Mansel Longworth (trans. and ed.), *The Book of Duarte Barbosa: An Account of the Countries Bordering on the Indian Ocean and Their Inhabitants* (London, 1918–1921), 2v.

Dapper, Olfert, *Naukeurige Beschrijvinge der Afrikaensche Gewesten van Egypten, Barbaryen, Lybien, Biledulgerid, Negroslant, Guinea, Ethiopien, Abyssinie*: Together with *Naukeurige Beschrijvinge der Afrikaensche Eylanden als Madagaskar, Sant Laurens, Sant Thomee, d'Eilanden van Kanarien, Kaep de Verd, Malta, en Andere* (Amsterdam, 1676).

——— (trans. and abridged from Flemish), *Description de l'Afrique* (Amsterdam, 1686).

Equiano, Olaudah, *The Interesting Narrative of the Life of Olaudah Equiano, or Gustavus Vassa, the African* (London, 1789), 2v.

Fernandes, Valentim (trans. and ed. P. de Cenival and Théodore Monod), *Description de la côte d'Afrique de Ceuta au Sénégal, 1506–1507* (Paris, 1938).

——— (eds. Théodore Monod and Raymond Mauny), *Description de la côte occidentale d'Afrique (Sénégal au Cap de Monte Archipels, etc.)* (Bissau, 1951).

Foster, William (ed.), *The Voyages of Sir James Lancaster to Brazil and the East Indies, 1591–1603* (London, 1940).

———, *The Red Sea and Adjacent Countries at the Close of the Seventeenth Century, as Described by Joseph Pitts, William Daniel, and Charles Jacques Poncet* (London, 1949).

Galvão, Antonio (trans. and ed. C. R. Drinkwater Bethune), *The Discoveries of the World, from Their First Original unto the Year of Our Lord 1555* (London, 1862).

Gama, Vasco da (trans. and ed. Ernst Georg Ravenstein), *A Journal of the First Voyage of Vasco da Gama, 1497–1499* (London, 1898).

Gomes, Diogo (trans. and eds. Théodore Monod, Raymond Mauny, and G. Duval), *De la première découverte de la Guinée* (Bissau, 1959).

Greenlee, William Brooks (trans.), *The Voyage of Pedro Álvares Cabral to Brazil and India* (London, 1938).

Hallett, Robin (ed.), *Records of the African Association, 1788–1831* (London, 1964).

Hamilton, Alexander (ed. William Foster), *A New Account of the East Indies* (London, 1930 [orig. ed., Edinburgh, 1727]), 2v.

Hawkins, Joseph, *A History of a Voyage to the Coast of Africa* (Troy, N.Y., 1797).

Jobson, Richard, *The Golden Trade, or a Discovery of the River Gambra, and the Golden Trade of the Aethiopians* (London, 1932 [first published, 1623]).

al-Kadir, Shihab al-Din 'Ahmad ibn 'Abd (trans. René Basset), *Histoire de la conquête de l'Abyssinie* (Paris, 1897–1909), 2v.

Labat, Jean-Baptiste, *Nouvelle relation de l'Afrique occidentale: contenant une description exacte du Sénégal et des peus situés entre Cap-Blanc et la rivière de Serrelionne* (compiled from the notes of André Brüe, Paris, 1728).

Le Maire, Jacques Joseph, *Voyages aux Îles Canaries, Cap Verd, Sénégal et Gambie* (Paris, 1695).

Lobo, Jerome (trans. Samuel Johnson, ed. George Gleig), *A Voyage to Abyssinia: Containing the History, Natural, Civil and Ecclesiastical, of that Remote and Unfrequented Country, Continued down to the Beginning of the Eighteenth Century* (London, 1789).

Marees, Pieter de, *Description et récit historical du riche royaume d'or de Gunea* (Amsterdam, 1605).

——— (ed. S. P. L'Honoré Naber), *Beschryvinghe ende historische Verhael van het gout Koninckrijck van Gunea anders de Gont-Custe de Mina genaemt liggende in bet deel van Africa* (s'Gravenhage, 1912).

Matthews, John, *A Voyage to the River Sierra-Leone, on the Coast of Africa: Containing an Account of the Trade and Productions of the Country, etc., in the Years 1785–1787, with an Additional Letter on the Subject of the African Slave Trade* (London, 1791).

Moore, Francis, *Travels into the Inland Parts of Africa: Containing a Description of the Several Nations for the Space of Six Hundred Miles up the River Gambia*

. . . *to Which Is Added, Captain Shibbo's Voyage up the Gambia in the Year 1723* (London, 1738).

Park, Mungo, *Travels in the Interior Districts of Africa in the Years 1795, 1796, and 1797* (London, 1799).

Paulinus, a Sancto Bartolmaeo (trans. William Johnston), *A Voyage to the East Indies . . . Observations . . . Between 1776 and 1789 . . .* (London, 1800).

Phillips, Thomas, "Journal of a Voyage from England to Africa . . . and So Forward to Barbadoes in the Years 1693 and 1694," Awnsham and John Churchill, *A Collection of Voyages and Travels* (London, 1732), IV, pp. 173–239.

Pigafetta, Filippo (trans. Margarite Hutchinson), *A Report [by Duarte Lopez] of the Kingdom of Congo and of the Surrounding Countries* (London, 1881 [orig. Italian ed., 1591]).

——— (trans. and ed. Willy Bal), *Description du royaume de Congo et des contrées environnantes, par Filippo Pigafetta et Duarte Lopez* (Louvain, 1963).

Pires, Tomé (trans. and ed. Armando Cortesão), *The Suma Oriental of Tomé Pires* (London, 1944), 2v.

Ravenstein, Ernst Georg, "The Voyages of Diogo Cao and Bartholomeu Dias, 1482–1488," *The Geographical Journal*, XVI (1900), pp. 625–655.

——— (ed.), *The Strange Adventures of Andrew Battell of Leigh* (London, 1901).

Ruyters, Dierick (ed. S. P. L'Honoré Naber), *Toortse der Zee Varet* (s'Gravenhage, 1913).

Santos, João dos, *Ethiopia oriental, e varia historia de cousas notaveis do Oriente* (Evora, 1609), 2v.

Smith, William, *A New Voyage to Guinea: Describing the Customs, Manners, Soil, Climate, Habits, Buildings, Education . . . Habitations, Diversions, Marriages, and Whatever Else Is Memorable Among the Inhabitants* (London, 1744).

Snelgrave, William, *A New Account of Some Parts of Guinea and the Slave Trade* (London, 1734).

Varthema, Ludovico de (trans. John Winter Jones, ed. George Percy Badger), *The Travels of Ludovico di Varthema in Egypt, Syria, Arabia Deserta and Arabia Felix, Persia, India, and Ethiopia, A.D. 1503 to 1508* (London, 1863).

Villault, Nicolas Sieur, *Relation des costes d'Afrique, appellées Guinée, avec la description du pays, moeurs et façons de vivre des habitans, des productions de la terre, et des merchandises qu'on en apporte, avec les remarques historiques sur ces costes* (Paris, 1669).

Zurara, Gomes Eanes de (trans. Charles Raymond Beazley and Edgar Prestage), *The Chronicle of the Discovery and Conquest of Guinea* (London, 1896–1899), 2v.

——— (trans. Léon Bourdon and Robert Ricard), *Chronique de Guinée* (Dakar, 1960).

B. Later Personal Narratives

Adams, John, *Remarks on the Country Extending from Cape Palmas to the River Congo* (London, 1823).

Adams, Robert (ed. S. Cock), *The Narrative of Robert Adams* (London, 1816).

Ahuma, S. Attoh R. B., *Memoirs of West African Celebrities, 1700–1850* (Liverpool, 1905).

Alexander, James Edward, *Narrative of a Voyage of Observation Among the Colonies of Western Africa in the Flag-Ship "Thalia"* (London, 1837), 2v.

Allen, William, and Thomas Richard Heywood Thomson, *A Narrative of the Expedition Sent by Her Majesty's Government to the River Niger in 1841* (London, 1848), 2v.

Arnot, Frederick Stanley, *Garenganze, or Seven Years' Pioneer Mission Work in Central Africa* (London, 1889).

Baikie, William Balfour, *Narrative of an Exploring Voyage up the Rivers Kwora and Binue (Commonly Known as the Niger and Tsadda) in 1854* (London, 1856).

Baker, Samuel White, *The Albert Nyanza, Great Basin of the Nile and Explorations of the Nile Sources* (New York, 1866).

———, *The Nile Tributaries of Abyssinia, and the Sword Hunters of the Hamran Arabs* (London, 1868).

———, *Ismaïlia: A Narrative of the Expedition to Central Africa for the Suppression of the Slave Trade* (London, 1874), 2v.

† Barth, Heinrich, *Travels and Discoveries in North and Central Africa . . . 1849–1855* (London, 1857–1858), 5v.

Bellefonds, Louis Maurice Adolphe Linant de (ed. Margaret Shinnie), *Journal d'un voyage à Méroë dans les années 1821 et 1822* (Khartoum, 1958).

Bindloss, Harold, *In the Niger Country* (Edinburgh, 1898).

Blanc, Henry, *A Narrative of Captivity in Abyssinia* (London, 1868).

Bouët-Willaumez, Édouard, *Commerce et traite des noirs aux côtes occidentales d'Afrique* (Paris, 1848).
Bovill, E. W. (ed.), *Missions to the Niger: The Journal of Friedrich Hornemann's Travels . . . [and] the Letters of Major Alexander Gordon Laing* (Cambridge, Eng., 1964).
Bowdich, Thomas Edward, *Mission from Cape Coast Castle to Ashantee, with a Statistical Account of the Kingdom, and Geographical Notices of Other Parts of the Interior of Africa* (London, 1819).
Burckhardt, John Lewis, *Travels in Nubia* (London, 1819).
Burdo, Adolphe (trans. Mrs. George Sturge), *The Niger and the Benueh: Travels in Central Africa* (London, 1880).
Burton, Richard Francis, *First Footsteps in East Africa, or an Exploration of Harar* (London, 1856).
———, *The Lake Regions of Central Africa* (London, 1860), 2v.
———, *Abeokuta and the Cameroons Mountains* (London, 1863), 2v.
———, *Wanderings in West Africa from Liverpool to Fernando Po* (London, (1863).
———, *A Mission to Gelele, King of Dahome* (London, 1864), 2v.
———, *Zanzibar: City, Island and Coast* (London, 1872), 2v.
——— (trans. and ed.), *The Lands of Cazembe* (London, 1873).
———, and Verney Lovett Cameron, *To the Gold Coast for Gold* (London, 1883).
Caillaud, Frédéric, *Voyage à Méroë, au fleuve Blanc, au-delà de Fâzoql dans le midi du royaume de Sennàr, à Syouah et dans cinq autres oasis, fait dans les années 1819–1820* (Paris, 1826–1827), 4v.
Caillié, René, *Travels Through Central Africa to Timbuctoo, and Across the Great Desert to Morocco, Performed in the Years 1824–1828* (London, 1830), 2v.
Cameron, Verney Lovett, *Across Africa* (London, 1877).
Capello, Hermenegildo, and Roberto Ivens (trans. Alfred Elwes), *From Benguella to the Territory of Yacca* (London, 1882), 2v.
Clapperton, Hugh, *Journal of a Second Expedition into the Interior of Africa from the Bight of Benin to Soccatoo* (London, 1829).
Compiègne, Victor Dupont le Marquis de, *L'Afrique équatoriale: Gabonais, Pahouins, Gallois* (Paris, 1875).
———, *L'Afrique équatoriale: Okanda, Bangouens, Osyéba* (Paris, 1875).
Decken, Carl Claus von der, *Reisen in Ost-Afrika in den Jahren 1859 bis 1865* (Leipzig, 1869–1879) 4v.
Delany, Martin Robinson, *Official Report of the Niger Valley Exploring Party* (London, 1861).
† Denham, Dixon, Hugh Clapperton, and Walter Oudney, *Narrative of Travels and Discoveries in Northern and Central Africa in the Years 1822, 1823 and 1824* (London, 1826).
Du Chaillu, Paul Belloni, *Explorations and Adventures in Equatorial Africa* (New York, 1862).
———, *A Journey to Ashango-Land and Further Penetration into Equatorial Africa* (London, 1867).
Dupuis, Joseph, *Journal of a Residence in Ashantee* (London, 1824).
Faidherbe, Louis Leon César, *Le Sénégal: la France dans l'Afrique occidentale* (Paris, 1889).
French-Sheldon, Mary, *Sultan to Sultan: Adventures Among the Masai and Other Tribes of East Africa* (London, 1892).
Gallwey, H. L., "Journeys in Benin Country, West Africa," *The Geographical Journal*, I (1893), pp. 122–130.
Gamitto, António C. Pedroso (trans. Ian Cunnison), *King Kazembe and the Marave, Cheva, Bisa, Bemba, Lunda, and Other Peoples of Southern Africa* (Lisboa, 1960 [orig. ed., Lisboa, 1854]), 2v.
Grant, James Augustus, *A Walk Across Africa, or Domestic Scenes from My Nile Journal* (Edinburgh, 1864).
Gray, William, *Travels in Western Africa* (London, 1825).
Hastings, Archibald Charles Gardner (ed.), *The Voyage of the Dayspring: Being the Journal of the Late Sir John Hawley Glover* (London, 1926).
Höhnel, Ludwig (trans. Nancy Bell), *Discovery of Lakes Rudolf and Stefanie* (London, 1894).
Hore, Edward Coode, *Tanganyika: Eleven Years in Central Africa* (London, 1892).
Hornemann, Friedrich (ed. William Young), *The Journal of Frederick Hornemann's Travels, from Cairo to Mourzouk, Capital of the Kingdom of Fezzan, in Africa, in the Years 1797–8* (London, 1802).
Hozier, Henry Montaque, *The British Expedition to Abyssinia* (London, 1869).
Hulbert, Charles (ed.), *African Fragments: Comprising Mr. William Lee's Narrative of Two Expeditions into the Interior of Africa, Etc.* (Shrewsbury, 1826).
Hutchinson, Thomas Joseph, *Narrative of the Niger, Tshadda and Binue Explora-*

tion . . . with Remarks on the Malaria and Fevers of Western Africa (London, 1855).

Hutton, William, *A Voyage to Africa: Including a Narrative of an Embassy to One of the Interior Kingdoms, in the Year 1820, with Remarks on the Course and the Termination of the Niger* (London, 1821).

Johnston, James, *Reality Versus Romance in South Central Africa* (London, 1893).

Junker, Wilhelm (trans. A. H. Keane), *Travels in Africa During the Years 1875–1886* (London, 1890–1892), 3v.

Kingsley, Mary H., *Travels in West Africa* (London, 1897).

———, *West African Studies* (London, 1899).

Krapf, Ludwig, *Travels, Researches, and Missionary Labors During an Eighteen Years' Residence in Eastern Africa* (Boston, 1860).

———, *Travels, Researches, and Missionary Labors in Eastern Africa and Abyssinia* (London, 1867).

Laffitte, J., *Le Dahomé: souvenirs de voyage et de mission* (Tours, 1873).

Laing, Alexander Gordon, *Travels in the Timannee, Looranko, and Soolima Countries, in Western Africa* (London, 1825).

Laird, Macgregor, and Richard A. K. Oldfield, *Narrative of an Expedition into the Interior of Africa by the River Niger in the Steam Vessels Quorra and Alburkah in 1832, 1833, and 1834* (London, 1837), 2v.

Lander, Richard (ed.), *Records of Captain Clapperton's Last Expedition to Africa* (London, 1830), 2v.

——— and John, *Journal of an Expedition to Explore the Course and Termination of the Niger* (London, 1832), 3v.

Lenz, Oskar, *Skizzen aus Westafrika: Selbsterlebnisse* (Berlin, 1879).

Livingstone, David, *Missionary Travels and Researches in South Africa* (London, 1857).

——— and Charles, *Narrative of an Expedition to the Zambesi and Its Tributaries, and of the Discovery of the Lakes Shirwa and Nyassa, 1858–1864* (London, 1865).

——— (ed. Horace Waller), *The Last Journals of David Livingstone in Central Africa* (London, 1874), 2v.

Lyon, George Francis, *A Narrative of Travels in Northern Africa, in the Years 1818, 1819 and 1820* (London, 1821).

M'Leod, John, *A Voyage to Africa, with Some Account of the Manners and Customs of the Dahomian People* (London, 1820).

Mage, Eugène, *Voyage dans le Soudan occidental* (Paris, 1868).

Mauch, Karl, *Reisen im Inneren von Süd-Afrika, 1865–1872* (Paris, 1874).

Mollien, Gaspard Théodore (trans. and ed. Thomas Edward Bowdich), *Travels in the Interior of Africa to the Sources of the Senegal and Gambia* (London, 1820).

Monteiro, Joachim John, *Angola and the River Congo* (London, 1875), 2v.

Nachtigal, Gustav, *Sahara und Sudan: Ergebnisse sechsjähriger Reisen in Afrika* (Berlin, 1879–1889), 3v.

New, Charles, *Life, Wanderings and Labours in Eastern Africa* (London, 1873).

Owen, William Fitzwilliam (ed. H. B. Robinson), *Narrative of Voyages to Explore the Shores of Africa, Arabia, and Madagascar* (New York, 1833), 2v.

Parkyns, Mansfield, *Life in Abyssinia: Being Notes Collected During Three Years' Residence and Travels in That Country* (London, 1853), 2v.

Pearce, Nathaniel (ed. J. W. Halls), *Life and Adventures During a Residence in Abyssinia, from 1810 to 1819* (London, 1831).

Plowden, Trevor Chicele (ed.), *Travels in Abyssinia and the Galla Country, with an Account of a Mission to Ras Ali in 1848* (London, 1868).

Pogge, Paul, *Im Reiche des Muata Jamvo* (Berlin, 1880).

Prior, James, *Voyage Along the Eastern Coast of Africa, to Mosambique, Johanna and Quiloa; to St. Helena . . . in the Nisus Frigate* (London, 1819).

Rankin, Daniel J., *The Zambesi Basin and Nyasaland* (Edinburgh, 1893).

Rankin, F. Harrison, *The White Man's Grave: A Visit to Sierra Leone in 1834* (London, 1836), 2v.

Rassam, Hormuzd, *Narrative of the British Mission to Theodore, King of Abyssinia* (London, 1869).

Rochet de Haricourt, Charles E. Xavier, *Voyage sur la côte orientale de la Mer rouge dans le pays d'Adel et le royaume de Choa* (Paris, 1841–1846), 2v.

Rohlfs, Friedrich Gerhard, *Reise durch Nord-Afrika vom mittelländischen Meere bis zum Busen von Guinea, 1865 bis 1867* (Gotha, 1868–1872).

———, *Quer durch Afrika: Reise vom Mittelmeer nach dem Tschad-See und zum Golf von Guinea* (Leipzig, 1874–1875), 2v.

———, *Meine Mission nach Abessinien* (Leipzig, 1883).
Salt, Henry, *A Voyage to Abyssinia and Travels into the Interior of That Country* (London, 1814).
Savorgnan de Brazza, Pierre Paul (ed. Jules Napoleon Ney), *Conférences et lettres de Pierre Savorgnan de Brazza sur ses trois explorations dans l'Ouest africain* (Paris, 1887).
Schön, James Frederick, and Samuel Crowther, *Journals of . . . the Expedition up the Niger in 1841, in Behalf of the Church Missionary Society* (London, 1842).
Schweinfurth, Georg (trans. E. E. Frewer), *The Heart of Africa: Three Years' Travels and Adventures in the Unexplored Regions of Central Africa* (London, 1873).
Serpa Pinto, Alexandre Alberto da Rocha de (trans. Alfred Elwes), *How I Crossed Africa from the Atlantic to the Indian Ocean Through Unknown Countries* (Philadelphia, 1881).
Silva Pôrto, António Francisco Ferreira da (ed. I. Sousa Dias), *Silva Pôrto e a travessia do continente africano* (Lisboa, 1938).
———, *Viagens e apontaméntos de um portuense em África* (Lisboa, 1942).
Smith, John, *Trade and Travels in the Gulph of Guinea* (London, 1851).
Speke, John Hanning, *Journal of the Discovery of the Source of the Nile* (London, 1863).
———, *What Led to the Discovery of the Source of the Nile* (Edinburgh, 1864).
Stanley, Henry Morton, *The Captive Missionary: Being an Account of the Country and People of Abyssinia* (London, 1868).
———, *Through the Dark Continent, or the Sources of the Nile Around the Great Lakes of Equatorial Africa* (London, 1878), 2v.
———, *The Congo and the Founding of Its Free State: A Story of Work and Exploration* (New York, 1885), 2v.
———, *How I Found Livingstone: Travels, Adventures and Discoveries in Central Africa, Including an Account of Four Months' Residence with Dr. Livingstone* (London, 1895).
——— (ed. Dorothy Stanley), *The Autobiography of Henry Morton Stanley* (Boston, 1909).
Stern, Henry Aaron, *Wanderings Among the Falashas in Abyssinia* (London, 1862).
Thomas, Thomas Morgan, *Eleven Years in Central South Africa: A Journey into the Interior* (London, 1872).
Thompson, Joseph, *Through Masai Land: A Journey of Exploration Among the Snowclad Volcanic Mountains and Strange Tribes of Eastern Equatorial Africa* (London, 1883).
———, "To Lake Bangweolo and the Unexplored Region of British Central Africa," *The Geographical Journal*, I (1893), pp. 97–121.
Tibbu Tib (trans. Wilfred H. Whiteley), *Maisha ya Hamed bin Muhammed el Murjebi yaani Tippu Tib* (Arusha, 1959).
Tucker, Charlotte Maria, *Abbeokuta, or Sunrise Within the Tropics: An Outline of the Origin and Progress of the Yoruba Mission* (London, 1853).
Tuckey, James Kingston (ed. anonymously, but probably by Sir John Barrow), *Narrative of an Expedition to Explore the River Zaïre, Usually Called the Congo, in South Africa* (London, 1818).
Whitford, John, *Trading Life in Western and Central Africa* (Liverpool, 1877).
Wissmann, Hermann von, *Unter deutscher Flagge quer durch Afrika von West nach Ost* (Berlin, 1889).

C. Slavery and the Slave Trade

Bandinel, James, *Some Account of the Trade in Slaves from Africa as Connected with Europe and America* (London, 1842).
Benezet, Anthony, *Some Historical Account of Guinea, Its Situation, Produce, and the General Disposition of Its Inhabitants, with an Inquiry into the Rise and Progress of the Slave Trade* (Philadelphia, 1771).
† Berbain, Simone, *Études sur la traite des noirs au golfe de Guinée: le comptoir français de Juda (Ouidah) au XVIIIe siècle* (Paris, 1942).
Buxton, Charles, *Memoirs of Sir Thomas Fowell Buxton, Baronet* (London, 1849).
Buxton, Thomas Fowell, *The African Slave Trade* (London, 1839).
Canot, Theodore (ed. Brantz Mayer), *Memoirs of a Slave Trader* (New York, 1854).
Clarkson, Thomas, *An Essay on the Comparative Efficiency of Regulation or Abolition as Applied to the Slave Trade* (London, 1789).
———, *The Substance of the Evidence of Sundry Persons on the Slave-Trade Collected in the Course of a Tour Made in*

the Autumn of the Year 1788 (London, 1789).

———, *The History of the Rise, Progress and Accomplishment of the Abolition of the African Slave-Trade by the British Parliament* (Philadelphia, 1808), 2v.

Colomb, Philip Howard, *Slave-catching in the Indian Ocean* (London, 1873).

Cooper, J., *Lost Continent, or Slavery and the Slave Trade in Africa* (London, 1875).

* Coupland, Reginald, *The British Anti-Slavery Movement* (London, 1933).

Crane, Verner, *A Rhode Island Slaver* (Providence, 1922).

Crow, Hugh, *Memoirs* (London, 1830).

Curtin, Philip D., and Jan Vansina, "Sources of the Nineteenth-Century Atlantic Slave Trade," *The Journal of African History*, V (1964), pp. 185–208.

D'Auvergne, Edmond Basil Francis, *Human Livestock* (London, 1933).

Davis, David B., "James Cropper and the British Anti-Slavery Movement, 1823–1833," *The Journal of Negro History*, XLVI (1961), pp. 154–173.

Delcourt, André, "La Finance parisienne et le commerce négrier au milieu du XVIIIe siècle," *Bulletin de la Société d'Études Historiques, Géographiques et Scientifiques de la Région Parisienne*, XXII (1948), pp. 21–28.

Donnan, Elizabeth (ed.), *Documents Illustrative of the History of the Slave Trade to America* (Washington, 1930–1939), 4v.

* Dow, George Francis (ed.), *Slave Ships and Slaving* (Salem, 1927).

Dowd, Jerome, "The African Slave Trade," *The Journal of Negro History*, II (1917), pp. 1–20.

Drake, Richard, *Revelations of a Slave Smuggler: Being the Autobiography of Richard Drake* (New York, 1860).

Du Bois, W. E. Burghardt, *The Suppression of the African Slave Trade to the United States of America, 1638–1870* (Cambridge, Mass., 1896).

Duignan, Peter, and Clarence Clendenen, *The United States and the African Slave Trade, 1619–1862* (Stanford, 1963).

Dumont, Pierre Joseph (ed. R. Phillips), *Narrative of Thirty-Four Years' Slavery and Travels in Africa* (London, 1819).

Edwards, Bryan, *The History, Civil and Commercial, of the British Colonies in the West Indies* (London, 1794), 2v.

Falconbridge, Alexander, *An Account of the Slave Trade on the Coast of Africa* (London, 1788).

Forde, Daryll (ed.), *Efik Traders of Old Calabar* (London, 1956).

Jenkinson, Hilary, "The Records of the English African Companies," *Transactions of the Royal Historical Society*, VI (1912), pp. 185–220.

Johnson, Thomas Louis, *Africa for Christ: Twenty-Eight Years a Slave* (London, 1882).

Kersaint-Gilly, Felix de, "Essai sur l'évolution de l'esclavage en A.O.F.: son dernier stade au Soudan français," *Bulletin du Comité d'Études Historiques et Scientifiques de l'Afrique Occidentale Française*, VII (1924), pp. 469–478.

Laffitte, J., *Le Pays des nègres et la Côte des Esclaves* (Tours, 1876).

Liverpool and Slavery: An Historical Account of the Liverpool African Slave Trade (Liverpool, 1884).

* Mannix, Daniel P., and Malcolm Cowley, *Black Cargoes: A History of the Atlantic Slave Trade, 1518–1865* (New York, 1962).

Martin, Gaston, *Nantes au XVIIIe siècle: l'ère des négriers, 1714–1774* (Paris, 1931).

———, *Histoire de l'esclavage dans les colonies françaises* (Paris, 1948).

Mason, George C., "The African Slave Trade in Colonial Times," *The American Historical Record*, I (1872), pp. 311–319.

Newbury, Colin W., "An Early Enquiry into Slavery and Captivity in Dahomey," *Zaïre*, XIV (1960), pp. 53–67.

Newton, John (eds. Bernard Martin and Mark Spurrell), *The Journal of a Slave Trader, 1750–1754* (London, 1962).

Norris, Robert, *Memoirs of the Reign of Bossa Ahádee, King of Dahomey . . . and a Short Account of the African Slave Trade* (London, 1789).

Owen, Nicholas (ed. Eveline Christiana Martin), *Journal of a Slave-Dealer* (London, 1930).

Plimpton, George Arthur (ed.), *The Journal of an African Slaver, 1789–1792* (Worcester, Mass., 1930).

Polanyi, Karl, "Sortings and the 'Ounce Trade' in the West African Slave Trade," *The Journal of African History*, V (1964), pp. 381–393.

† Robert, Henri, "Les trafics coloniaux du port de La Rochelle au XVIIIe siècle, 1713–1789," *Bulletin de la Société des Antiquaires de l'Ouest*, 1 (1949), pp. 135–177.

Scelle, Georges, *La Traité négrière aux Indes de Castile: contrats et traités d'Asiento* (Paris, 1906), 2v.

Snelgrave, William, *A New Account of Some Parts of Guinea and the Slave Trade* (London, 1734).
Stanfield, James Field, *The Guinea Voyage* (Edinburgh, 1807).
Vidalenc, Jean, "La Traite des nègres en France au début de la Révolution française, 1789–1793," *Annales Historiques de la Révolution Française,* XXIX (1957), pp. 56–69.
Williams, Eric, *Capitalism and Slavery* (Chapel Hill, N.C., 1944).
* Wyndham, Hugh Archibald, *The Atlantic and Slavery* (London, 1935).
* ———, *The Atlantic and Emancipation* (London, 1937).

D. Secondary Sources

Ajayi, J. F. Ade, "The British Occupation of Lagos, 1851–1861," *Nigeria Magazine,* 69 (1961), pp. 96–105.
———, "Nineteenth-Century Origins of Nigerian Nationalism," *Journal of the Historical Society of Nigeria,* II (1961), pp. 196–210.
Albuquerque Felner, Alfredo de, *Angola: apontamentos sôbre a ocupoção e início do estabelcimento dos Portugueses no Congo, Angola e Benguela* (Coimbra, 1933).
Anstey, Roger T., "British Trade and Policy in West Central Africa Between 1816 and the Early 1880's," *Transactions of the Historical Society of Ghana,* III (1957), pp. 47–71.
Ashe, Robert Pickering, *Two Kings of Uganda, or, Life by the Shores of Victoria Nyanza* (London, 1889).
Atger, Paul, "Les Comptoirs fortifiés de la Côte d'Ivoire (1843–1871)," *Revue Française d'Histoire d'Outre-Mer,* XLVII (1960), pp. 427–474.
———, *La France en Côte d'Ivoire de 1843 à 1893: cinquante ans d'hésitations politiques et commerciales* (Dakar, 1962).
Axelson, Eric Victor, *South-East Africa, 1488–1530* (London, 1940).
———, *Portuguese in South-East Africa, 1600–1700* (Johannesburg, 1960).
Baker, J. N. L., "Burton and the Nile Sources," *The English Historical Review,* LIX (1944), pp. 49–60.
Bartels, F. L., "Jacobus Eliza Johannes Capitein, 1717–1747," *Transactions of the Historical Society of Ghana,* IV (1959), pp. 3–13.
Bascom, William, "Lander's Routes Through Yoruba Country," *Nigerian Field,* XXV (1960), pp. 12–22.
Bastos, Augusto, *Monographis de Catumbella* (Lisboa, 1912).
Beckingham, Charles F., "Notes on an Unpublished Manuscript of Francisco Alvares: *Verdadera informacum das terras do Preste Joam das Indias,*" *Annales d'Éthiopie,* III (1961), pp. 139–154.
Bennett, Norman R., *Studies in East African History* (Boston, 1963).
Berlioux, Étienne-Félix, *André Brue, ou l'origine de la colonie française du Sénégal* (Paris, 1874).
Bevin, H. J., "The Gold Coast Economy about 1880," *Transactions of the Gold Coast and Togoland Historical Society,* II (1956), pp. 73–86.
Blake, John William, *European Beginnings in West Africa, 1454–1578* (London, 1937).
——— (trans. and ed.), *Europeans in West Africa, 1450–1560* (London, 1942), 2v.
Boahen, A. Adu, "The African Association, 1788–1805," *Transactions of the Historical Society of Ghana,* V (1961), pp. 43–64.
† ———, *Britain, the Sahara, and the Western Sudan, 1788–1861* (Oxford, 1964).
Bonnel de Mézières, Albert, *Le Major A. Gordon Laing, Tombouctou, 1826* (Paris, 1912).
Bowdich, Thomas Edward, *An Account of the Discoveries of the Portuguese in the Interior of Angola and Moçambique* (London, 1824).
† Boxer, Charles R., *Salvador de Sá and the Struggle for Brazil and Angola, 1602–1686* (London, 1952).
———, *Race Relations in the Portuguese Colonial Empire, 1415–1825* (Oxford, 1963).
———, and Carlos de Azevedo, *Fort Jesus and the Portuguese in Mombasa, 1593–1729* (London, 1960).
Boyd, Willis D., "The American Colonisation Society and the Slave Recaptives of 1860–1861: An Early Example of United States–African Relations," *The Journal of Negro History,* XLVII (1962), pp. 108–126.
Brackenbury, Henry, *The Ashanti War: A Narrative . . .* (Edinburgh, 1874), 2v.
Bridges, R. C., "Sir John Speke and the Royal Geographical Society," *The Uganda Journal,* XXVI (1962), pp. 23–43.
Brunschwig, Henri, "Colonisation fran-

çaise," *Revue Historique,* CCXXII (1959), pp. 113–156.
———, "Expéditions punitives au Gabon (1875–1877)," *Cahiers d'Études Africaines,* 2 (1962), pp. 347–361.
Carrère, Frédéric, and Paul Holle, *De la Sénégambie française* (Paris, 1855).
Casely Hayford, Joseph Ephraim, *Gold Coast Native Institutions* (London, 1903).
Catala, René, "La Question de l'échange de la Gambie britannique contre les comptoirs français du Golfe de Guinée de 1866 à 1876," *Revue d'Histoire des Colonies,* XXXV (1948), pp. 114–137.
Ceulemans, R. P. P., "Le Séjour de Stanley à Zanzibar (18 mars–fin mai, 1879)," *Zaïre,* XI (1957), pp. 675–685.
Charliat, P. J., "L'Économie maritime de la France sous le règne de Louis XV," *Revue d'Histoire Économique et Sociale,* XXXIV (1956), pp. 171–194.
Charpy, Jacques, *La Fondation de Dakar, 1845–1857–1869* (Paris, 1958).
Chevalier, August, *Michel Adanson: voyageur, naturaliste et philosophe* (Paris, 1934).
Claridge, W. Walton, *A History of the Gold Coast and Ashanti* (London, 1915), 2v.
Collins, Edmund, "The Panic Element in Nineteenth-Century British Relations with Ashanti," *Transactions of the Historical Society of Ghana,* V (1962), pp. 79–144.
Coombs, Douglas, *The Gold Coast, Britain and the Netherlands, 1850–1874* (London, 1963).
Cornevin, Robert, *L'Histoire du Togo* (Paris, 1959).
Cortesão, Armando, and Avelino Teixeira da Mota, *Portugaliae monumenta cartographica* (Lisboa, 1960), 6v.
* Coupland, Reginald, *East Africa and Its Invaders from the Earliest Times to the Death of Seyyid Said in 1856* (Oxford, 1938).
* ———, *The Exploitation of East Africa, 1856–1890: The Slave Trade and the Scramble* (London, 1939).
Crawford, Osbert Guy Stanhope, "Some Medieval Theories About the Nile," *The Geographical Journal,* CXIV (1949), pp. 6–29.
Crooks, John Joseph, *A History of the Colony of Sierra Leone, Western Africa* (Dublin, 1903).
———, *Records Relating to the Gold Coast Settlements from 1750–1874* (Dublin, 1923).
Cultru, Prosper, *Les Origines de l'Afrique occidentale: histoire du Sénégal du XVe siècle à 1870* (Paris, 1910).
† Curtin, Philip D., *The Image of Africa: British Ideas and Action, 1780–1850* (Madison, Wisc., 1964).
Cuvelier, J., *L'Ancien Royaume de Congo* (Bruges, 1946).
———, *Documents sur une Mission française au Kakongo, 1766–1776* (Bruxelles, 1953).
———, and Louis Jadin, *L'Ancien Congo d'après les archives romaines (1518–1640)* (Bruxelles, 1954).
Danquah, Joseph B., "The Historical Significance of the Bond of 1844," *Transactions of the Historical Society of Ghana,* III (1957), pp. 1–29.
Dardel, Pierre, *Navires et marchandises dans les ports de Rouen et du Havre au XVIIIe siècle* (Paris, 1963).
Davies, K. G., *The Royal African Company* (London, 1957).
Dean, David, "Joseph Wall of Gorée Island," *African Affairs,* LVII (1958), pp. 295–301.
De Kun, N., "Le Voyage de Ladislas Magyar dans l'interieur du Congo en 1850–1852," *Bulletin des Séances de l'Académie Royale des Sciences l'Outre-Mer,* VI (1960), pp. 605–636.
Delavignette, Robert Louis, and Charles-André Julien (eds.), *Les Constructeurs de la France d'outre-mer* (Paris, 1946).
† Delcourt, André, *La France et les établissements français au Sénégal entre 1713 et 1763* (Dakar, 1952).
Denoix, L., "La Compagnie des Indes au XVIIIe siècle: ses activités diverses," *Revue d'Histoire Économique et Sociale,* XXXIX (1956), pp. 141–152.
Denucé, Jean, *L'Afrique au XVIe siècle et le commerce anversois* (Anvers, 1937).
Diffie, Bailey W., *Prelude to Empire: Portugal Overseas Before Henry the Navigator* (Lincoln, Neb., 1960).
† Dike, K. Onwuka, *Trade and Politics in the Niger Delta, 1830–1885* (Oxford, 1956).
———, "John Beecroft, 1790–1854: Her Brittanic Majesty's Consul to the Bights of Benin and Biafra, 1849–1854," *Journal of the Historical Society of Nigeria,* I (1956), pp. 5–14.
* Duffy, James, *Portuguese Africa* (Cambridge, Mass., 1959).
Dunbar, A. R., "European Travellers in Bunyoro-Kitara, 1862 to 1877," *The*

Uganda Journal, XXIII (1959), pp. 101–117.

† Dunglas, Édouard, "Contribution à l'histoire du Moyen-Dahomey: royaumes d'Abomey, de Ketou et de Ouidah," *Études Dahoméennes*, XIX–XXI (1958), *passim*.

Earp, Charles A., "The Role of Education in the Maryland Colonization Movement," *The Journal of Negro History*, XXVI (1941), pp. 365–388.

Ellis, Alfred Burdon, *A History of the Gold Coast of West Africa* (London, 1893).

Ellison, R. E., "Three Forgotten Explorers of the Latter Half of the Nineteenth Century, with Special Reference to Their Journeys to Bornu," *Journal of the Historical Society of Nigeria*, I (1959), pp. 322–330.

Fage, John D., "The Administration of George Maclean on the Gold Coast, 1830–1844," *Transactions of the Gold Coast and Togoland Historical Society*, I (1955), pp. 104–120.

* ———, *Ghana: A Historical Interpretation* (Madison, Wisc., 1959).

Faure, Claude, *Histoire de la presqu'île du Cap-Vert et des origines de Dakar* (Paris, 1914).

Flint, John E., "Mary Kingsley: A Reassessment," *The Journal of African History*, IV (1963), pp. 95–104.

Foà, Édouard, *Le Dahomey* (Paris, 1895).

Fonseca, Quirino da, "João Baptista: pioneiro da dupla travessia de África em princípios do sécula XIX," *Boletim da Sociedade de Geographia de Lisboa*, LIII (1935), pp. 141–157.

Fosbrooke, Henry A., "Richard Thornton in East Africa," *Tanganyika Notes and Records*, 58/59 (1962), pp. 43–63.

Fox, A. J. (ed.), *Uzuakoli: A Short History* (London, 1964).

Freeman-Grenville, G. S. P., *The French at Kilwa Island: An Episode in Eighteenth-Century East African History* (Oxford, 1965).

Fyfe, Christopher H., "Thomas Peters: History and Legend," *Sierra Leone Studies*, 1 (1953), pp. 4–13.

———, "Four Sierra Leone Recaptives," *The Journal of African History*, II (1961), pp. 77–85.

† ———, *A History of Sierra Leone* (London, 1962).

Gaffarel, Paul, *La Politique coloniale en France de 1789 à 1830* (Paris, 1908).

Gailey, Harry A., *A History of the Gambia* (London, 1964).

Gallagher, John, "Fowell Buxton and the New African Policy, 1838–1842," *The Cambridge Historical Journal*, X (1950), pp. 36–58.

Galliéni, Joseph Simon, *Mission d'exploration du Haut-Niger: voyage au Soudan français, 1879–1881* (Paris, 1885).

Gertzel, Cherry J., "The Early Years of an African Trader: John Holt, 1862–1874," *Ibadan*, 10 (1960), pp. 12–16.

Glover, Elizabeth, *Life of Sir John Hawley Glover, R.N., C.M.G.* (London, 1897).

† Godlonton, W. A., "The Journeys of Antonio Fernandes: The First Known European to Find the Monomotapa and to Enter Southern Rhodesia," *Rhodesia Scientific Association: Proceedings and Transactions*, XL (1945), pp. 71–103.

Gray, John Milner, *A History of the Gambia* (Cambridge, Eng., 1940).

———, "Rezende's Description of East Africa in 1634," *Tanganyika Notes and Records*, 23 (1947), pp. 2–28.

———, "A Journey by Land from Tete to Kilwa in 1616," *ibid.*, 25 (1948), pp. 37–47.

———, "The French at Kilwa, 1776–1784," *ibid.*, 44 (1956), pp. 28–49.

———, *The British in Mombasa, 1824–1826: The Story of Captain Owen's Protectorate* (London, 1957).

———, "Early Portuguese Visitors to Kilwa," *Tanganyika Notes and Records*, 52 (1959), pp. 117–128.

———, "Fort Santiago at Kilwa," *ibid.*, 58/59 (1962), pp. 175–178.

———, "Ernest Linant de Bellefonds," *The Uganda Journal*, XXVIII (1964), pp. 31–54.

Hair, P. E. H., "An Account of the Liberian Hinterland, c. 1780," *Sierra Leone Studies*, 16 (1962), pp. 218–226.

Haliburton, G., "The Nova Scotia Settlers of 1792," *Sierra Leone Studies*, 9 (1957), pp. 16–25.

† Hallett, Robin, "The European Approach to the Interior of Africa in the Eighteenth Century," *The Journal of African History*, IV (1963), pp. 191–206.

Hamilton, R. A., "The Route of Gaspar Bocarro from Tete to Kilwa in 1616," *The Nyasaland Journal*, VII (1954), pp. 7–14.

Hardy, Georges, *L'Enseignement au Sénégal de 1817 à 1854* (Paris, 1920).

———, *La Mise en valeur du Sénégal de 1817 à 1854* (Paris, 1921).

Hardy, Jules, *Les Dieppois en Guinée en 1364* (Dieppe, 1864).

† Hargreaves, John Desmond, *Prelude to the Partition of West Africa* (London, 1963).

———, "African Colonization in the Nineteenth Century: Liberia and Sierra Leone," *Boston University Papers in African History*, I (1964), pp. 55–76.

Hevesi, Ludwig, *Wilhelm Junker: Lebensbild eines Afrikaforschers* (Berlin, 1896).

† Hill, Richard Leslie, *Egypt in the Sudan, 1820–1881* (London, 1959).

Hillelson, S., "David Reubeni: An Early Visitor to Sennar," *Sudan Notes and Records*, XVI (1933), pp. 55–66.

Hinaway, Mbarak Ali, *Al Akida and Fort Jesus, Mombasa* (London, 1950).

Hoare, Prince (ed.), *Memoirs of Granville Sharp, Esq.* (London, 1820).

Hooker, James R., "The Foreign Office and the 'Abyssinian Captives,'" *The Journal of African History*, II (1961), pp. 245–258.

Horton, James Africanus Beale, *West African Countries and Peoples, British and Native, with the Requirements Necessary for Establishing That Self Government Recommended by the Committee of the House of Commons, 1865, and a Vindication of the African Race* (London, 1868).

Hoyt, William D., Jr., "John McDonogh and Maryland Colonization in Liberia, 1834–35," *The Journal of Negro History*, XXIV (1939), pp. 440–453.

Huberich, Charles Henry, *The Political and Legislative History of Liberia* (New York, 1947), 2v.

Ifemesia, C. C., "The 'Civilizing' Mission of 1841: Aspects of an Episode in Anglo-Nigerian Relations," *Journal of the Historical Society of Nigeria*, II (1962), pp. 291–310.

Jamieson, Robert, *An Appeal to the Government and People of Great Britain Against the Proposed Niger Expedition* (London, 1840).

Johnston, Henry Hamilton [Harry], *Liberia* (London, 1906), 2v.

Kamal, Youssouf, *Quelques éclaircissements épars sur mes Monumenta Cartographica Africae et Aegypti* (Leiden, 1935).

Kirk-Greene, Anthony H. M., "David George: The Nova Scotian Experience," *Sierra Leone Studies*, 14 (1960), pp. 93–120.

Kup, A. P., "Early Portuguese Trade in the Sierra Leone and Great Scarcies Rivers," *Boletim Cultural da Guiné Portuguesa*, XVIII (1963), pp. 107–124.

Latrobe, John Hazelhurst Boneval, *Maryland in Liberia* (Baltimore, 1885).

Laughon, Samuel W., "Administrative Problems in Maryland in Liberia, 1836–1851," *The Journal of Negro History*, XXVI (1941), pp. 325–364.

Lawrence, Arnold Walter, *Trade Castles and Forts of West Africa* (London, 1963).

Le Febre de Vivy, Léon, *Documents d'histoire précoloniale belge (1861–1865)* (Bruxelles, 1955).

Lefebvre, Gabriel, *L'Angola: son histoire, son économie* (Liège, 1947).

Lehmann, Joseph H., *All Sir Garnet: A Life of Field-Marshal Lord Wolseley* (London, 1964).

Lobato, Alexandre, *Historia do presido de Lourenço Marques* (Lisboa, 1949), 2v.

———, *A expansão portuguesa em Moçambique de 1498 a 1530* (Lisboa, 1954–1960), 3v.

———, *Evolucão administrativa e económica de Moçambique, 1752–1763* (Lisboa, 1957).

Ludolf, Hiob [Job Ludolphus] (trans. John Phillips), *A New History of Ethiopia: Being a Full and Accurate Description of the Kingdom of Abessinia, Vulgarly, Though Erroneously, Called the Empire of Prester John* (London, 1682).

Lupton, K., "The Death of Mungo Park at Bussa," *Nigeria Magazine*, 72 (March, 1962), pp. 58–70.

Lyne, Robert Nunez, *Zanzibar in Contemporary Times* (London, 1905).

———, *An Apostle of Empire: Being the Life of Sir Lloyd William Mathews, K.C.M.G.* (London, 1936).

Machat, Jules, *Documents sur les établissements français de l'Afrique occidentale au XVIIIe siècle* (Paris, 1906).

McIntyre, W. D., "British Policy in West Africa: The Ashanti Expedition of 1873–4," *The Historical Journal*, V (1962), pp. 19–46.

———, "Commander Glover and the Colony of Lagos, 1861–1873," *The Journal of African History*, IV (1963), pp. 57–80.

MacQueen, James, *A Geographical and Commercial View of Northern Central Africa: Containing a Particular Account of the Course and Termination of the Great River Niger in the Atlantic Ocean* (Edinburgh, 1821).

Magalhães, Godinho Vitorino, *Documentos sôbre a expansão portuguesa* (Lisboa, 1943–1956), 3v.

———, *A economia dos descobrimentas henriquinos* (Lisboa, 1962).

Marinescu, Constantin, "Le Prêtre Jean: son pays; explication de son nom," *Académie Roumaine: Bulletin de la Section Historique*, X (1923), pp. 93–112.

Markham, Clements Robert, *History of the Abyssinian Expedition, with a Chapter Containing an Account of the Mission and Captivity of Mr. Rassam and His Companions, by Lieutenant W. F. Prideaux* (London, 1869).

Marston, Thomas E., *Britain's Imperial Role in the Red Sea Area, 1800–1878* (Hamden, Conn., 1961).

Martin, Eveline Christiana, *The British West African Settlements, 1750–1821* (London, 1927).

Martin, Gaston, *Nantes et la Compagnie des Indes, 1664–1769* (Paris, 1927).

Masson, Paul, *Marseille et la colonisation française* (Marseille, 1906).

† Mauny, Raymond, "Les Prétendues Navigations dieppoises à la côte occidentale d'Afrique au XIVe siècle," *Bulletin de l'Institut Français d'Afrique Noire*, XII (1950), pp. 122–134.

† ———, "Note sur les 'grands voyages' de Léon l'Africain," *Hespéris*, XLI (1954), pp. 379–394.

———, *Les Navigations médiévales sur les côtes sahariennes antérieures à la découverte portugaise (1434)* (Lisboa, 1960).

Metcalfe, G. E., *Maclean of the Gold Coast: The Life and Times of George Maclean, 1801–1847* (London, 1962).

Mower, J. H., "The Republic of Liberia," *The Journal of Negro History*, XXXII (1947), pp. 265–306.

Mustafa bin Kisi bin Hamadi Mutafi (trans. B. D. Copland), "The Bombardment of Zanzibar," *Journal of the East African Swahili Committee*, 27 (1957), pp. 66–76.

Nathan, Mathew, "The Gold Coast at the End of the Seventeenth Century Under the Danes and the Dutch," *Journal of the African Society*, IV (1904), pp. 1–32.

Newitt, M. D. D., "Ignacio Caetano Xavier's Account of Portuguese East Africa, 1758," *Conference of the History of the Central African Peoples* (Lusaka, 1963), no pagination.

Nobrega, Moita I. de, *Os Portugueses no Congo (1482–1520)* (Lisboa, 1959).

Nowell, Charles E., "The Historical Prester John," *Speculum*, XXVIII (1953), pp. 435–445.

Pageard, Robert, "Un Mystérieux Voyage au pays de Bambouc (1789)," *Notes Africaines*, 89 (1961), pp. 23–27.

Paiva Manso, Visconde de Levy Maria Jordão, *Historia do Congo* (Lisboa, 1877).

Pearce, Francis Barrow, *Zanzibar: The Island Metropolis of Eastern Africa* (London, 1920).

Pope-Hennessy, James, *Verandah: Some Episodes in the Crown Colonies, 1867–1889* (London, 1964).

Porter, Arthur T., "Family Histories and West African Social Development: The Role of the Creole in Nineteenth-Century Sierra Leone," *Historians in Tropical Africa* (Salisbury, S.R., 1962), pp. 305–316.

Postlethwayt, Malachy, *The Importance of the African Expedition Considered* (London, 1758).

* Prestage, Edgar, *The Portuguese Pioneers* (London, 1933).

——— (ed.), *Chapters in Anglo-Portuguese Relations* (Watford, Eng., 1935).

Priestley, Herbert Ingram, *France Overseas Through the Old Regime: A Study of European Expansion* (New York, 1939).

Priestley, Margaret A., "Richard Brew: An Eighteenth-Century Trader at Anomabu," *Transactions of the Historical Society of Ghana*, IV (1959), pp. 29–46.

† ———, "The Ashanti Question and the British: Eighteenth-Century Origins," *The Journal of African History*, II (1961), pp. 35–60.

———, "Trade and Politics on the Gold Coast in the Eighteenth Century: A Survey of Contemporary Evidence," *Historians in Tropical Africa* (Salisbury, S.R., 1962), pp. 283–288.

Prothero, R. Mansell, "Heinrich Barth and the Western Sudan," *The Geographical Journal*, CXXIV (1958), pp. 326–339.

Randles, W. G. L., *L'Image du sud-est africain dans la littérature européenne au XVIe siècle* (Lisboa, 1959).

Ravenstein, Ernst Georg, "The Voyages of Diogo Cão and Bartholomeu Dias, 1482–88," *The Geographical Journal*, XVI (1900), pp. 625–655.

Ricketts, H., *Narrative of the Ashantee War with a view . . . of Sierra Leone* (London, 1831).

Robinson, Charles Henry, *Hausaland, or Fifteen Hundred Miles Through the Central Soudan* (London, 1896).

Rogers, Francis M., *The Travels of the Infante Dom Pedro of Portugal* (Cambridge, Mass., 1961).

———, *The Quest for Eastern Christians: Travels and Rumor in the Age of Discovery* (Minneapolis, 1962).

Roussier, Paul (ed.), *L'Établissement d'Issiny, 1687–1702* (Paris, 1935).
Russell, Lillian M. (ed.), *General Rigby, Zanzibar and the Slave Trade* (London, 1935).
Ryder, A. F. C., "The Re-Establishment of Portuguese Factories on the Costa Da Mina to the Mid-Eighteenth Century," *Journal of the Historical Society of Nigeria*, I (1958), pp. 157–183.
———, "An Early Portuguese Trading Voyage to the Forcados River," *ibid.*, I (1959), pp. 294–321.
† ———, "Missionary Activity in the Kingdom of Warri to the Early Nineteenth Century," *ibid.*, II (1960), pp. 2–27.
Sabatie, Alexandre Camille, *Le Sénégal: sa conquête et son organisation, 1364–1925* (Saint-Louis, Sénégal, 1926).
Saintoyant, Jules François, *La Colonisation française sous l'ancien régime, XVe siècle—1789* (Paris, 1929), 2v.
Sampson, Magnus J., "George Ekem Ferguson of Anomabu," *Transactions of the Gold Coast and Togoland Historical Society*, II (1956), pp. 30–45.
Saulnier, Eugène, *La Compagnie de Galam au Sénégal* (Paris, 1921).
† Schnapper, Bernard, *La Politique et le commerce français dans le Golfe de Guinée de 1838 à 1871* (Paris, 1961).
Seaver, George, *David Livingstone: His Life and Letters* (London, 1957).
Serpa Pinto, Carlota de, *A vida breve e ardente de Serpa Pinto* (Lisboa, 1937).
Sherwood, Henry Noble, "Early Negro Deportation Projects," *The Mississippi Valley Historical Review*, II (1916), pp. 484–508.
† ———, "The Formation of the American Colonization Society," *The Journal of Negro History*, II (1917), pp. 209–228.
———, "Paul Cuffe," *ibid.*, VIII (1923), pp. 153–232.
Silva Rego, António da, *Portuguese Colonization in the Sixteenth Century: A Study of the Royal Ordinances* (Johannesburg, 1959).
Slessarev, Vsevolod, *Prester John: The Letter and the Legend* (Minneapolis, 1959).
Sparks, Jared, *Life of John Ledyard: The American Traveller* (Boston, 1847).
Staudenraus, P. J., *The African Colonization Movement, 1816–1865* (New York, 1961).
Stone, Thora G., "The Journey of Cornelius Hodges in Senegambia, 1689–90," *The English Historical Review*, XXXIX (1924), pp. 89–95.
Strandes, Justus, *Die Portugiesenzeit von Deutsch- und Englisch-Ostafrika* (Berlin, 1899).
——— (trans. Jean F. Wallwork), *The Portuguese Period in East Africa* (Nairobi, 1961 [an abridgement]).
Sutherland, William, *Alexandrine Tinne: Een Haagsch Meisje als dappere Ontdekkings-reizigster en Dochter der Liefde (Bint mtacke) in Noord-Afrika* (Amsterdam, 1935).
Swanzy, Henry, "A Trading Family in the Nineteenth-Century Gold Coast," *Transactions of the Gold Coast and Togoland Historical Society*, II (1956), pp. 87–120.
Tracey, Hugh (trans. Gaetano Montez), *António Fernandes: Descobridor do Monomotapa, 1514–15* (Lourenço Marques, 1940).
Varley, W. J., "The Castles and Forts of the Gold Coast," *Transactions of the Gold Coast and Togoland Historical Society*, I (1952), pp. 1–17.
Verbeken, Auguste, and M. Walraet (trans. and eds.), *La Première Traversée du Katanga en 1806* (Bruxelles, 1953).
Villard, André, *Histoire du Sénégal* (Dakar, 1943).
* Ward, William E. F., *A History of Ghana* (London, 1958).
Washburn, Wilcomb E., "The Meaning of 'Discovery' in the Fifteenth and Sixteenth Centuries," *The American Historical Review*, LXVIII (1962), pp. 1–21.
Welch, Sidney R., *Some Unpublished Manuscripts Relating to the History of South and East Africa* (Pretoria, 1930).
Wesley, Charles H. "The Struggle for the Recognition of Haiti and Liberia as Independent Republics," *The Journal of Negro History*, II (1917), pp. 369–383.
Zook, George Frederick, *The Company of Royal Adventurers Trading into Africa* (Lancaster, Pa., 1919).

IV. The Period of Partition

Adams, Margaret, "The British Attitude to German Colonization, 1880–5," *Bulletin of the Institute of Historical Research*, XV (1937), pp. 190–193.
Aderibigbe, A. B., "The Ijebu Expedition, 1892: An Episode in the British Penetration of Nigeria Reconsidered," *Historians in Tropical Africa* (Salisbury, S.R., 1962), pp. 267–282.
Alagoa, Ebiegberi Joe, *The Small Brave City-State: A History of Nembe-Brass in the Niger Delta* (Madison, Wisc., 1964).

Albéca, Alexandre L. d', *Côte occidentale d'Afrique: les établissements français du Golfe de Bénin* (Paris, 1889).

Alberto, Manuel Simoẽs, and Francisco A. Toscano, *O Oriente Africano Português: síntese cronológica da Historia Moçambique* (Lourenço Marques, 1942).

Alderson, Edwin Alfred Hervey, *With the Mounted Infantry and the Mashonaland Field Force, 1896* (London, 1898).

Alldridge,Thomas Joshua, *The Sherbro and Its Hinterland* (London, 1901).

* Allen, Bernard Meredith, *Gordon and the Sudan* (London, 1931).

Almeida de Eca, Filipe Gastao, *História das guerras no Zambeze: Chicoa e Massangano (1807–1888)* (Lisboa, 1953–1954).

Anene, J. C., "The Foundations of British Rule in 'Southern Nigeria' (1885–1891)," *Journal of the Historical Society of Nigeria,* I (1959), pp. 253–262.

Anstey, Roger T., *Britain and the Congo in the Nineteenth Century* (Oxford, 1962).

Arcin, André, *Histoire de la Guinée française* (Paris, 1911).

Armitage, Cecil Hamilton, and Arthur Forbes Montanaro, *The Ashanti Campaign of 1900* (London, 1901).

* Ascherson, Neal, *The King Incorporated: Leopold II in the Age of Trusts* (London, 1963).

Ashe, Robert Pickering, *Two Kings of Uganda, or, Life by the Shores of Victoria Nyanza* (London, 1889).

———, *Chronicles of Uganda* (London, 1894).

Austin, Herbert Henry, *With Macdonald in Uganda: A Narrative Account of the Uganda Mutiny and Macdonald Expedition . . .* (London, 1903).

Aydelotte, William Osgood, *Bismarck and British Colonial Policy: The Problem of Southwest Africa, 1883–1885* (Philadelphia, 1937).

———, "The First German Colony and Its Diplomatic Consequences," *The Cambridge Historical Journal,* V (1937), pp. 291–313.

———, "Wollte Bismarck Kolonien?" W. Conze (ed.), *Deutschland und Europa* (Düsseldorf, 1951), pp. 41–68.

Baden-Powell, Robert Stephenson Smyth, *The Downfall of Prempeh: A Diary of Life with the Native Levy in Ashanti, 1895–96* (London, 1896).

———, *The Matabele Campaign, 1896* (London, 1897).

Banning, Émile, *Le Partage politique de l'Afrique d'après les transactions internationales les plus récentes (1885 à 1888)* (Bruxelles, 1888).

Batalha-Reis, Jayme, "The Portuguese in Nyasaland," *The Scottish Geographical Magazine,* V (1889), pp. 256–268.

Battaglia, Roberto, *La Prima Guerra d'Africa* (Torino, 1958).

Bayol, Jean M., "La France au Fouta-Djalon," *Revue des Deux Mondes,* LIV (1882), pp. 903–932.

———, *Voyage en Sénégambie, Haut Niger, Bambouck, Foutadjallon et Grand-Beledougou, 1880–1885* (Paris, 1888).

Becker, A., *Aus Deutsch Ost Afrikas Sturm- und Drangperiode* (Berlin, 1892).

Behr, S. F. von, *Kriegsbilder aus dem Araberaufstand in Deutsch-Ostafrika* (Leipzig, 1891).

Bentley, William Holman, *Pioneering on the Congo* (New York, 1900), 2v.

Berkeley, George F.-H., *The Campaign of Adowa and the Rise of Menelik* (London, 1902).

Bindloss, Harold, *In the Niger Country* (Edinburgh, 1898).

Binger, Louis Gustave, *Du Niger au Golfe de Guinée, par le pays de Kong et le Mossi* (Paris, 1892), 2v.

Biss, Harold C. J., *The Relief of Kumasi* (London, 1901).

Bissy, R. de Lannoy de, "Recent French Explorations in the Ogowe-Congo Region," *Proceedings of the Royal Geographical Society,* VIII (1886), pp. 770–778.

Bixler, Raymond W., "Anglo-Portuguese Rivalry for Delagoa Bay," *The Journal of Modern History,* VI (1934), pp. 425–440.

Blackwell, H. F., *The Occupation of Hausaland, 1900–1904* (Lagos, 1927).

Bodelsen, Carl Adolph Gottlieb, *Studies in Mid-Victorian Imperialism* (Copenhagen, 1924).

Bohner, Theodor, *Der eroberte Erdteil* [Nachtigal] (Berlin, 1934).

Bois, Alexis, *Sénégal et Soudan: de Dakar au Niger* (Paris, 1887).

Bonnefont de Varinay, P. de, *La Compagnie de Moçambique: sa concession, son administration, ses résultats, 1898* (Lisboa, 1899).

Bouchard, T., *La Côte du Cameroun dans l'histoire et la cartographie: ses origines à l'annexion allemande* (Paris, 1952).

Bovill, Mai, and G. R. Askwith, *Roddy Owen: A Memoir* (London, 1897).

Bretignere, Amédée, *Aux temps héroïques de la Côte d'Ivoire* (Paris, 1931).

Brode, Heinrich (trans. H. Havelock), *Tippoo Tib: The Story of His Career in Central Africa* (London, 1907).

Brown, Richard, "The Scramble and African Politics in Matabeleland," *Conference of the History of the Central African Peoples* (Lusaka, 1963), no pagination.

Brunet, Louis, and Louis Giethlen, *Dahomey et dépendances* (Paris, 1900).

Brunschwig, Henri, *L'Expansion allemande outre-mer du XVe siècle à nos jours* (Paris, 1957).

† ———, *Mythes et réalités de l'impérialisme colonial français, 1871–1914* (Paris, 1960).

† ———, *L'Avènement de l'Afrique noire du XIXe siècle à nos jours* (Paris, 1963).

Buchanan, John, *The Shire Highlands . . . as Colony and Mission* (London, 1885).

Buck, Jean Marie de, *Jacques de Dixmude* (Paris, 1933).

† el-Buhry, Hemedi Abdallah bin Said (trans. and ed. J. W. T. Allen), *Utenzi wa Vita vya Wadachi kutamalaki Mrima, 1307* A.H. (Dar es Salaam, 1960).

Bullock, Fred, *La Fondation de la colonie française de la Côte d'Ivoire* (London, 1912).

Burdo, Adolphe, *Les Arabes dans l'Afrique centrale* (Paris, 1885).

———, *Les Belges dans l'Afrique centrale: de Zanzibar au Lac Tanganyika* (Bruxelles, 1886).

Burns, Alan M., *History of Nigeria* (London, 1955).

Cambier, René, "L'Affaire Stokes," *Revue Belge de Philologie et d'Histoire*, XXX (1952), pp. 109–134.

Caprivi, Léopold von, *Die ostafrikanische Frage und der Helgoland-Sansibar-Vertrag* (Berlin, 1934).

Carnegie, David Wynbord, *Letters from Nigeria, 1899–1900* (Brechin, 1902).

Carton de Wiart, Edmond, *Les Grandes Compagnies coloniales anglaises du XIXe siècle* (Louvain, 1899).

Cattier, Félicien, *Droit et administration de l'État indépendant du Congo* (Bruxelles, 1898).

———, *Étude sur la situation de l'État indépendant du Congo* (Bruxelles, 1906).

Ceulemans, R. P. P., *La Question arabe et le Congo (1883–1892)* (Bruxelles, 1959).

Chaput, J., "Treich-Laplène et la naissance de la Côte d'Ivoire française," *Revue d'Histoire des Colonies*, XXXVI (1949), pp. 87–153.

Chavannes, Charles de, *Avec Brazza: souvenirs de la mission de l'Ouest africain* (Paris, 1935).

Chéradame, André, *La Colonisation et les colonies allemandes* (Paris, 1905).

Coillard, François (trans. and ed. Catherine W. Mackintosh), *On the Threshold of Central Africa: A Record of Twenty Years' Pioneering Among the Barotsi of the Upper Zambesi* (London, 1897).

Collins, Robert O., *The Southern Sudan, 1883–1898: A Struggle for Control* (New Haven, 1962).

Colvile, Henry E., *The Land of the Nile Springs: Being Chiefly an Account of How We Fought Kabarega* (London, 1895).

Coquery-Vidrovitch, Catherin, "L'Intervention d'une société privée à propos du conteste franco-espagnol dans le Rio Muni: la Société d'Explorations Coloniales (1899–1924)," *Cahiers d'Études Africaines*, 4 (1963), pp. 22–68.

Cornet, René J., *Katanga* (Bruxelles, 1946).

———, *La Bataille du rail* (Bruxelles, 1947).

Cornevin, Robert, "Les Divers Épisodes de la lutte contre le royaume d'Abomey (1877–1894)," *Revue Française d'Histoire d'Outre-Mer*, XLVII (1960), pp. 161–212.

Crawford, Daniel, *Thinking Black: Twenty-Two Years Without a Break in the Long Grass of Central Africa* (London, 1912).

* Crowe, Sybil Eyre, *The Berlin West African Conference, 1884–1885* (London, 1942).

Darcy, Jean, *France et Angleterre: cent années de rivalité coloniale, l'Afrique* (Paris, 1904).

Decle, Lionel, *Three Years in Savage Africa* (London, 1900).

Delcommune, Alexandre, *Vingt années de vie africaine . . . au Congo belge, 1874–1893* (Bruxelles, 1922), 2v.

Duboc, Albert Alfred, *L'Épopée coloniale en Afrique occidentale française* (Paris, 1938).

Dunbar, A. R., "The British and Bunyoro-Kitara, 1891 to 1899," *The Uganda Journal*, XXIV (1960), pp. 229–241.

Dupré, Édouard Paul François (ed. Alfred Martineau), *La Campagne du Cayor en 1883* (Paris, 1934).

Ennes, António, *A guerra d'Africa em 1895* (Lisboa, 1898).

Étienne, Eugène, *Les Compagnies de colonisation* (Paris, 1897).

* Flint, John E., *Sir George Goldie and the Making of Nigeria* (London, 1960).

Gaffarel, Paul, *Le Sénégal et le Soudan français* (Paris, 1890).

———, *Notre expansion coloniale en Afrique de 1870 à nos jours* (Paris, 1918).

Gailey, Harry A., Jr., "European Rivalry and Diplomacy in the Mellacourie, 1879–1882," *Sierra Leone Studies,* 15 (1961), pp. 135–147.

Gallagher, John, and Ronald Robinson, "The Imperialism of Free Trade," *The Economic History Review,* VI (1953), pp. 1–15.

Galliéni, Joseph Simon, *Deux campagnes au Soudan français, 1886–1888* (Paris, 1891).

Galway, Henry, "The Rising of the Brassmen," *Journal of the African Society,* XXXIV (1935), pp. 144–162.

Gelfand, Michael, *Lakeside Pioneers: Socio-medical Study of Nyasaland (1875–1920)* (Oxford, 1964).

Gentil, Émile, *La Chute de l'empire de Rabah* (Paris, 1902).

Gertzel, Cherry J., "Commercial Organization on the Niger Coast, 1852–1891," *Historians in Tropical Africa* (Salisbury, S.R., 1962), pp. 289–304.

Giglio, Carlo, *L'impresa di Massaua, 1884–85* (Roma, 1955).

———, *Ethiopia: Mar Rosso* (Roma, 1958–1960), 3v.

† Gillard, D. R., "Salisbury's African Policy and the Heligoland Offer of 1890," *The English Historical Review,* LXXV (1960), pp. 631–653.

Gillier, L., *La Pénétration en Mauritanie* (Paris, 1926).

Gray, John Milner, "Mutesa of Buganda," *The Uganda Journal,* I (1934), pp. 22–49.

———, "Stanley *Versus* Tippoo Tib," *Tanganyika Notes and Records,* 18 (1944), pp. 11–27.

———, "The Year of the Three Kings of Buganda: Mwanga-Kiwewa-Kalema, 1888–1889," *The Uganda Journal,* XIV (1950), pp. 15–52.

———, "Acholi History, 1860–1901," *ibid.,* XV (1951), pp. 121–143; XVI (1952), pp. 32–50, 132–144.

———, "Kakunguru in Bukedi," *ibid.,* XXVII (1963), pp. 31–60.

Gregory, John Walter, *The Foundation of British East Africa* (London, 1901).

Grenville, John Ashley Soames, *Lord Salisbury and Foreign Policy: The Close of the Nineteenth Century* (London, 1964).

Grumbach, Salomon, *Das annexionistische Deutschland* (Lausanne, 1917).

Hanna, Alexander John, *The Beginnings of Nyasaland and North-Eastern Rhodesia, 1859–1895* (Oxford, 1956).

† Hargreaves, John Desmond, "The Establishment of the Sierra Leone Protectorate and the Insurrection of 1898," *The Cambridge Historical Journal,* XII (1956), pp. 56–80.

———, "The French Occupation of the Mellacourie, 1865–67," *Sierra Leone Studies,* 9 (1957), pp. 2–15.

Heyse, Theodore, *Les Origines diplomatiques du Congo belge* (Bruxelles, 1934).

Hill, Richard Leslie, *Slatin Pasha* (London, 1964).

Hinde, Sidney Langford, *The Fall of the Congo Arabs* (New York, 1897).

Hole, Hugh Marshall, *The Making of Rhodesia* (London, 1926).

† Holt, Peter Malcolm, *The Mahdist State in the Sudan, 1881–1898* (Oxford, 1958).

Jackson, Frederick John, *Early Days in East Africa* (London, 1930).

Jackson, Henry Cecil, *Osman Digna* (London, 1926).

Jantzen, Günther, *Ostafrika in der deutsch-englischen Politik, 1884–1890* (Hamburg, 1934).

Johnston, Henry Hamilton [Harry], *The Kilimanjaro Expedition* (London, 1886).

———, *British Central Africa: An Attempt to Give Some Account of a Portion of the Territories Under British Influence North of the Zambesi* (London, 1897).

———, *The Uganda Protectorate* (London, 1902), 2v.

———, *George Grenfell and the Congo* (London, 1908).

———, *The Story of My Life* (Indianapolis, 1923).

Justin, Sameni ole Kivasis (trans. by Henry A. Fosbrooke), "The Life of Justin," *Tanganyika Notes and Records,* 41 (1955), pp. 31–57.

Keith, Arthur Berriedale, *The Belgian Congo and the Berlin Act* (Oxford, 1919).

Kirk-Greene, Anthony H. M., *Adamawa: Past and Present* (London, 1958).

Kitching, Arthur Leonard, *On the Backwaters of the Nile* (London, 1912).

Klose, Heinrich, *Togo unter deutscher Flagge: Reisebilder und Betrachtungen* (Berlin, 1899).

Königk, Georg, *Die Berliner Kongo-Konferenz, 1884–1885* (Berlin, 1938).

Krätschell, Herman, *Carl Peters, 1856–1918* (Berlin, 1959).

Lane Poole, Edward Humphrey, "Mpeseni and the Exploration Companies, 1885–1898," *The Northern Rhodesia Journal,* V (1963), pp. 221–232.

Lippert, Julius, "Rabah," *Mitteilungen des*

seminars für orientalische sprachen, II (1899), pp. 242–256.

* Lloyd, Alan, *The Drums of Kumasi: The Story of the Ashanti Wars* (London, 1964).

Long, Norman, "Bandawe Mission Station and Local Politics, 1878–86," *The Rhodes-Livingstone Journal,* XXXII (1962), pp. 1–22.

Louis, William Roger, "The Anglo-German Hinterland Settlement of 1890 and Uganda," *The Uganda Journal,* XXVII (1963), pp. 71–84.

———, *Ruanda-Urundi, 1884–1919* (Oxford, 1963).

Low, D. Anthony, "British Public Opinion and the Uganda Question, October–December, 1892," *The Uganda Journal,* XVIII (1954), pp. 81–100.

———, *Religion and Society in Buganda, 1875–1900* (Kampala, 1956).

† ———, "Lion Rampant," *Journal of Commonwealth Political Studies,* II (1964), pp. 235–252.

Lugard, Frederick D., *The Rise of Our East African Empire* (London, 1893), 2v.

———, *The Story of the Uganda Protectorate* (London, 1901).

Lyne, Robert Nunez, *Mozambique: Its Agricultural Development* (London, 1913).

McDermott, P. L., *British East Africa, or Ibea* (London, 1893).

Machat, Jules, *Les Rivières du Sud et le Fouta-Diallon* (Paris, 1905).

McKay, Donald Vernon, "Colonialism in the French Geographical Movement, 1871–1881," *The Geographical Review,* XXXIII (1943), pp. 214–232.

Masoin, Fritz, *Histoire de l'État indépendant du Congo* (Namur, 1912–1913), 2v.

Maugham, R. C. F., *Africa as I Have Known It* (London, 1929).

Maxwell, John, "Ashanti," *Journal of the African Society,* XXVII (1928), pp. 219–233.

Ménioud, Jacques, *Les Pioneers du Soudan avant, avec et après Archinard, 1879–1894* (Paris, 1931), 2v.

Mévil, André, *Samory* (Paris, n.d., but 1899).

Michel, Charles, *Mission de Bonchamps: vers Fachoda à la rencontre de la mission Marchand à travers l'Éthiopie* (Paris, 1900).

Moloney, Joseph Augustus, *With Captain Stairs to Katanga* (London, 1893).

Monçoda, Cabral, *A Companda do Bailundo* (Luanda, 1903).

Monteil, Parfait Louis, *De Saint-Louis à Tripoli par le Lac Tchad* (Paris, 1895).

Mouteney-Jephson, A. J., *Emin Pasha and the Rebellion at the Equator* (London, 1890).

† Müller, Fritz Ferdinand, *Deutschland-Zanzibar-Ostafrika* (Berlin, 1959).

Muffett, David J. M., *Concerning Brave Captains: Being a History of the British Occupation of Kano and Sokoto and of the Last Stand of the Fulani Forces* (London, 1964).

Murphy, Agnes, *The Ideology of French Imperialism, 1871–1881* (Washington, 1948).

Musgrave, George Clark, *To Kumassi with Scott: A Description of a Journey from Liverpool to Kumassi with the Ashanti Expedition, 1895–6* (London, 1896).

Newbury, Colin W., "The Development of French Policy on the Lower and Upper Niger, 1880–98," *The Journal of Modern History,* XXXI (1959), pp. 16–26.

———, "A Note on the Abomey Protectorate," *Africa,* XXIX (1959), pp. 146–155.

Nigmann, Ernst, *Geschichte der kaiserlichen Schutztruppe für Deutsch-Ostafrika* (Berlin, 1911).

Noirot, Ernest, *À travers le Fouta-Diallon et le Bambouc* (Paris, 1885).

Nowell, Charles E., "Portugal and the Partition of Africa," *The Journal of Modern History,* XIX (1947), pp. 1–17.

Oliveira Martins, Joaquim Pedro, *Portugal em Africa: a questão colonial, o conflito anglo-português* (Lisboa, 1891).

Oliver, Roland, "Some Factors in the British Occupation of East Africa, 1884–1894," *The Uganda Journal,* XV (1951), pp. 49–64.

———, *Sir Harry Johnston and the Scramble for Africa* (London, 1957).

Oppenheim, Max G. von, *Rabeh und das Tschadseegebiet* (Berlin, 1902).

Pankhurst, Richard, "Italian Settlement Policy in Eritrea and Its Repercussions, 1889–1896," *Boston University Papers in African History,* I (Boston, 1964), pp. 119–156.

Parreira, C., *O Sertanejo do Bié, Silva Pôrto* (Lisboa, 1945).

Pélissier, René, *Les Territoires espagnols d'Afrique* (Paris, 1963).

Penson, Lillian M., "The Principles and Methods of Lord Salisbury's Foreign Policy," *The Cambridge Historical Journal,* V (1935), pp. 87–106.

Perham, Margery Freda, *Lugard: The Years of Adventure* (London, 1956).

———, *Histoire politique du Congo belge* (Bruxelles, 1911).

Werner, J. R., *A Visit to Stanley's Rear Guard, with an Account of River Life on the Congo* (Edinburgh, 1889).

Wichterich, Richard, *Dr. Carl Peters: Der Weg eines Patrioten* (Berlin, 1934).

Wingate, Francis Reginald, *Mahdiism and the Egyptian Sudan* (London, 1891).

Woolbert, Robert Gale, "The Purchase of Assab by Italy," Donald C. McKay (ed.), *Essays in the History of Modern Europe* (New York, 1936), pp. 114–129.

Wrigley, Christopher C., "The Christian Revolution in Buganda," *Comparative Studies in Society and History*, II (1959–1960), pp. 33–48.

Yarnal, Howard E., *The Great Powers and the Congo Conference . . . 1884–1885* (Gottingen, 1934).

Zaghi, Carlo, *Le origini della colonia Eritrea* (Bologna, 1934).

——— (ed.), *Crispi e Menelich: nel diario inedito del conte Salimbeni* (Torino, 1956).

Zusmanovich, A. Z., *Imperialisticheskiy Razdel Basseyna Kongo* [*The Imperial Partition of the Congo Basin*], *1876–1894* (Moskva, 1962).

V. The Colonial Interlude

Abadie, Maurice Jean Joseph, *La Colonie du Niger* (Paris, 1927).

Abbas, Mekki, *The Sudan Question: The Dispute over the Anglo-Egyptian Condominium, 1884–1951* (London, 1952).

Adimola, A. B., "The Lamogi Rebellion, 1911–1912," *The Uganda Journal*, XVIII (1954), pp. 166–177.

Alldridge, Thomas Joshua, *A Transformed Colony: Sierra Leone as It Was and as It Is . . .* (London, 1910).

Allen, G. Keith, "Gold Mining in Ghana," *African Affairs*, LVII (1958), pp. 221–240.

Altrincham, Edward Grigg Baron, *Kenya's Opportunity: Memories, Hopes and Ideas* (London, 1955).

Aluko, Samuel Adepoju, *The Problems of Self-Government for Nigeria: A Critical Analysis* (Ilfracombe, 1955).

Amon d'Aby, F. J., *La Côte d'Ivoire dans la cité africaine* (Paris, 1951).

Anderson, Robert Earle, *Liberia: America's African Friend* (Chapel Hill, N.C., 1952).

† Andersson, Efraim, *Messianic Popular Movements in the Lower Congo* (Uppsala, 1958).

Apter, David E., *The Political Kingdom in Uganda: A Study in Bureaucratic Nationalism* (Princeton, 1961).

Aubert de la Rue, Edgar, *La Somalie française* (Paris, 1939).

Avice, Emmanuel, *La Côte d'Ivoire* (Paris, 1951).

Azikiwe, Benjamin Nnamdi, *Liberia in World Politics* (London, 1934).

Baddour, Abdfel-Fatta Ibrahimmel-Sayed, *Sudanese-Egyptian Relations: A Chronological and an Analytical Study* (The Hague, 1960).

Badoglio, Piètro, *La Guerra d'Etiopia* (Milano, 1936).

Balandier, Georges, *Sociologie actuelle de l'Afrique noire: dynamique des changements sociaux en Afrique centrale* (Paris, 1955).

Banton, Michael, "The Origins of Tribal Administration in Freetown," *Sierra Leone Studies*, 2 (1954), pp. 109–119.

———, "African Prophets," *Race*, V (1963), pp. 42–55.

Barber, J. P., "The Karamoja District of Uganda: A Pastoral People Under Colonial Rule," *The Journal of African History*, III (1962), pp. 111–124.

Barns, Thomas Alexander, *Angolan Sketches* (London, 1928).

———, "Through Portuguese West Africa," *Journal of the African Society*, XXVIII (1929), pp. 224–234.

Bascom, William, "Urbanization Among the Yoruba," *American Journal of Sociology*, LX (1954–1955), pp. 446–454.

Basden, George Thomas, *Among the Ibos of Nigeria* (London, 1921).

Battersby, Henry Francis Prevost, *Richard Corfield of Somaliland* (London, 1914).

Beattie, John, "Democratization in Bunyoro: The Impact of Democratic Institutions and Values on a Traditional African Kingdom," *Civilisations*, XI (1961), pp. 8–18.

Beech, Mervyn W. H., "Kikuyu System of Land Tenure," *Journal of the African Society*, XVII (1917), pp. 46–59.

Beer, George Louis (ed. Louis Herbert Gray), *African Questions at the Paris Peace Conference* (New York, 1923).

Bell, Hesketh Joudou, *Glimpses of a Governor's Life* (London, 1946).

Bell, R. M., "The Maji-Maji Rebellion in the Liwale District," *Tanganyika Notes and Records*, 28 (1950), pp. 38–57.

Bennett, George, "The Development of Political Organizations in Kenya," *Political Studies*, V (1957), pp. 113–130.

———, "Paramountcy to Partnership: J. H. Oldham and Africa," *Africa,* XXX (1960), pp. 356–361.

* ———, *Kenya, A Political History: The Colonial Period* (London, 1963).

Betts, Raymond D., *Assimilation and Association in French Colonial Theory, 1890–1914* (New York, 1961).

bin Jamaliddini, Abdul Karim (trans. Wilfred H. Whiteley), *Utenzi wa Vita vya Maji-Maji* (Arusha, 1957).

Bixler, Raymond W., *The Foreign Policy of the United States in Liberia* (New York, 1957).

Boateng, J. A., *Problems of Local Government in Ghana* (Obuasi, Ghana, 1957).

Bohannan, Paul, "The Impact of Money on an African Subsistence Economy," *The Journal of Economic History,* XIX (1959), pp. 491–503.

———, and George Dalton (eds.), *Markets in Africa* (Evanston, Ill., 1962).

* Bourret, F. M., *Ghana: The Road to Independence, 1919–1957* (London, 1960).

Bradley, Kenneth, *Copper Venture: The Discovery and Development of Roan, Antelope and Mufulira* (London, 1952).

Brausch, Georges, *Belgian Administration in the Congo* (London, 1961).

Brown, George W., *The Economic History of Liberia* (Washington, 1941).

Brown, Godfrey N., "British Educational Policy in West and Central Africa," *The Journal of Modern African Studies,* II (1964), pp. 365–377.

Brown, R. E., "Local Government in the Western Provinces of Nigeria," *The Journal of African Administration,* II (1950), pp. 15–21.

* Bruel, Georges, *L'Afrique équatoriale française* (Paris, 1918).

Brunschwig, Henri, *La Colonisation française du pacte colonial à l'Union française* (Paris, 1949).

———, "Colonisation, Décolonisation: essai sur le vocabulaire usuel de la politique coloniale," *Cahiers d'Études Africaines,* 1 (1961), pp. 44–54.

† Buell, Raymond Leslie, *The Native Problem in Africa* (New York, 1928), 2v.

———, *Liberia: A Century of Survival, 1847–1947* (Philadelphia, 1947).

Bunche, Ralph J., "The Land Equation in Kenya Colony," *The Journal of Negro History,* XXIV (1939), pp. 33–43.

———, "The Irua Ceremony Among the Kikuyu of Kiambu District, Kenya," *The Journal of Negro History,* XXVI (1941), pp. 46–65.

Burke, Fred G., *Local Government and Politics in Uganda* (Syracuse, 1964).

Burns, Alan M., *Colonial Civil Servant* (London, 1949).

Burrows, Guy, *The Curse of Central Africa* (London, 1903).

Butt-Thompson, Frederick William, *Sierra Leone in History and Tradition* (London, 1926).

———, *The First Generation of Sierra Leoneans* (Freetown, 1952).

Byatt, Horace, "Tanganyika," *Journal of the African Society,* XXIV (1924), pp. 1–9.

Cadbury, William, *Labour in Portuguese West Africa* (London, 1910).

Calvert, Albert Frederick, *Nigeria and Its Tin Fields* (London, 1910).

———, *The German African Empire* (London, 1916).

Cameron, Sir Donald, *My Tanganyika Service and Some Nigeria* (London, 1939).

Cardinall, A. W., "Our Mandate in Togoland," *Journal of the African Society,* XXI (1922), pp. 302–308, XXII (1922), pp. 43–49.

Casely Hayford, Joseph Ephraim, *Ethiopia Unborn: Studies in Race Emancipation* (London, 1911).

Challaye, Félicien, *Le Congo français: la question internationale du Congo* (Paris, 1909).

Charlewood, C. J., "Naval Actions on the Tanganyika Coast, 1914–1917," *Tanganyika Notes and Records,* 54 (1960), pp. 120–138, 55 (1960), pp. 153–180.

Chéron, G., *La Société noire de l'Afrique occidentale française* (Paris, 1908).

Chidzero, Bernard T. G., *Tanganyika and International Trusteeship* (London, 1961).

Chomé, Jules, *La Passion de Simon Kimbangu, 1921–1951* (Bruxelles, 1959).

Chukwuemeka, Nwanko, *Industrialization of Nigeria* (New York, 1952).

Clegg, Edward, *Race and Politics: Partnership in the Federation of Rhodesia and Nyasaland* (London, 1960).

Clifford, Elizabeth Bonham de la Pasture (ed.), *Our Days on the Gold Coast, in Ashanti, in the Northern Territories and the British Sphere of Occupation in Togoland* (Accra, 1918).

Clifford, Hugh, "Recent Developments on the Gold Coast," *Journal of the African Society,* XVIII (1919), pp. 241–253.

———, "United Nigeria," *ibid.,* XXI (1921), pp. 1–14.

Clozel, François Joseph, *Dix ans à la Côte d'Ivoire* (Paris, 1906).

Cocks, Frederick Seymour, *E. D. Morel: The Man and His Work* (London, 1920).
Cole, J. S. R., "A History of the Tanganyika Legislature," *Tanganyika Notes and Records*, 58/59 (1962), pp. 179–186.
Coleman, James, *Nigeria: Background to Nationalism* (Berkeley, 1960).
Cook, Albert, "Further Memories of Uganda," *The Uganda Journal*, II (1934), pp. 97–115.
Cook, Arthur Norton, *British Enterprise in Nigeria* (Philadelphia, 1943).
Corni, Guido, *Somalia italiana* (Milano, 1937), 2v.
Coryndon, Robert T., "Problems of Eastern Africa," *Journal of the African Society*, XXI (1922), pp. 177–186.
Cowan, Laing Gray, *Local Government in West Africa* (New York, 1958).
Cox-George, N. A., *Finance and Development in West Africa: The Sierra Leone Experience* (London, 1961).
Cranworth, Bertram Francis Baron, *Kenya Chronicles* (London, 1939).
Cripps, Arthur Shearley, *An Africa for Africans* (London, 1927).
Crocker, Walter Russell, *Nigeria: A Critique of British Colonial Administration* (London, 1936).
Crofton, Richard Hayes, *Zanzibar Affairs, 1914–1933* (London, 1953).
Crowder, Michael, *Senegal: A Study in French Assimilation Policy* (London, 1962).
———, "Indirect Rule, French and British Style," *Africa*, XXXIV (1964), pp. 197–205.
Cunha, Joaquim Moreira da Silva, *O trabalho indígena: estudo de direito colonial* (Lisboa, 1949).
Cuvilleir-Fleury, Henri, *La Mise en valeur du Congo français* (Paris, 1904).
Dalton, John H., "Colony and Metropolis: Some Aspects of British Rule in Gold Coast and Their Implications for an Understanding of Ghana Today," *Journal of Economic History*, XXI (1961), pp. 552–565.
Dareste, Pierre, *Traité de droit colonial* (Paris, 1931–1932), 2v.
Darmstaedter, Paul, *Geschichte der Aufteilung und Kolonisation Afrikas* (Berlin, 1913–1920), 2v.
Davidson, Basil, *The African Awakening* (London, 1955).
Davidson, J. W., *The Northern Rhodesian Legislative Council* (London, 1948).
Davis, J. Merle (ed.), *Modern Industry and the African* (London, 1933).
Delavignette, Robert Louis, *Freedom and Authority in French West Africa* (London, 1950).
Delcommune, Alexandre, *L'Avenir du Congo belge menacé* (Bruxelles, 1920), 2v.
Deppe, Ludwig, *Mit Lettow-Vorbeck durch Afrika* (Berlin, 1919).
Deschamps, Hubert Jules, *Les Methodes et les doctrines coloniales de la France, du XVIe siècle à nos jours* (Paris, 1953).
Dilley, Marjorie Ruth, *British Policy in Kenya Colony* (New York, 1937).
Disney, A. W. M., "English Law in the Sudan, 1899–1958," *Sudan Notes and Records*, XL (1959), pp. 121–123.
DuBois, William E. Burghardt, "Liberia, the League and the United States," *Africa Seen by American Negroes* (Paris, 1958), pp. 329–344.
Duff, Hector Livingston, *Nyasaland Under the Foreign Office* (London, 1903).
Dundas, Charles Cecil Farquharson, *African Crossroads* (London, 1955).
Duprey, A. Gingold, *De l'invasion à la libération de l'Éthiopie* (Paris, 1955).
Eberlie, R. F., "The German Achievement in East Africa," *Tanganyika Notes and Records*, 55 (1960), pp. 181–214.
Edwards, Adrian C., *The Ovimbundu Under Two Sovereignties: A Study of Social Control and Social Change Among a People of Angola* (London, 1962).
Ehrlich, Cyril, *The Uganda Company, Limited: The First Fifty Years* (Kampala, 1953).
Elias, Taslim Olawale, *British Colonial Law: A Comparative Study of the Interaction Between English and Local Laws in British Dependencies* (London, 1962).
Eliot, Charles Norton, *The East Africa Protectorate* (London, 1905).
Elkan, Walter, *Migrants and Proletarians: Urban Labor in the Economic Development of Uganda* (London, 1960).
———, *The Economic Development of Uganda* (London, 1961).
Enke, Stephen, "Western Development of a Sparsely Populated Country: The Rhodesias," *The American Economic Review*, L (1960), pp. 387–400.
Fabunmi, L. A., *The Sudan in Anglo-Egyptian Relations: A Case Study in Power Politics, 1800–1956* (London, 1960).
Fallers, Lloyd, *Bantu Bureaucracy: A Study of Integration and Conflict in the Political Institutions of an East African People* (Cambridge, Eng., 1959).

Farson, Negley, *Behind God's Back* (London, 1940).
* Fehderau, Harold W., "Kimbanguism: Prophetic Christianity in the Congo," *Practical Anthropology*, 9 (1962), pp. 157–178.
Fendall, Charles Pears, *The East African Force, 1915–1919* (London, 1921).
Floyd, Barry Neil, *Changing Patterns of African Land Use in Southern Rhodesia* (Lusaka, 1961), 3v.
Folarin, Abebesin, *The Demise of the Independence of Egbaland: The Ijemo Trouble* (Lagos, 1916).
Forgeron, Jean-Baptiste, *Le Protectorat en Afrique occidentale française et les chefs indigènes* (Bordeaux, 1920).
Fox-Bourne, Henry Richard, *Civilisation in Congoland: A Story of International Wrongdoing* (London, 1903).
Full, August, *Kamerun* (Berlin, 1932).
———, *Fünfzig Jahre Togo* (Berlin, 1935).
Gaitskell, Arthur, *Gezira: A Story of the Development in the Sudan* (London, 1959).
Gann, Lewis H., "The End of the Slave Trade in British Central Africa, 1889–1912," *The Rhodes-Livingstone Journal*, XVI (1954), pp. 27–51.
———, "The Southern Rhodesia Land Apportionment Act, 1930: An Essay in Trusteeship," *Occasional Papers of the National Archives of Rhodesia and Nyasaland*, I (1963), pp. 71–91.
———, *A History of Northern Rhodesia: Early Days to 1953* (London, 1964).
———, and Michael Gelfand, *Huggins of Rhodesia: The Man and His Country* (London, 1964).
Garigue, Philip, "The West African Students' Union," *Africa*, XXIII (1953), pp. 55–69.
Geary, William Nevill Montgomerie, *Nigeria Under British Rule* (London, 1927),
Gee, Thomas W., "Uganda's Legislative Council Between the Wars," *The Uganda Journal*, XXV (1961), pp. 54–64.
Gelfand, Michael, *Northern Rhodesia in the Days of the Charter: A Medical and Social Study, 1878–1924* (Oxford, 1961).
Gide, André, *Voyage au Congo* (Paris, 1927).
———, *Le Retour du Tchad* (Paris, 1928).
Gillman, Clement, "A History of the Tanganyika Railways," *Tanganyika Notes and Records*, 13 (1942), pp. 14–56.
———, "Dar-es-Salaam, 1860–1940," *ibid.*, 20 (1945), pp. 1–23.
Girault, Arthur, *Principes de colonisation et de législation coloniale* (Paris, 1913).
——— (ed. Charles Gide), *The Colonial Tariff Policy of France* (Oxford, 1916).
Glennie, A. F. B., "The Barotse System of Government," *The Journal of African Administration*, IV (1952), pp. 9–13.
Gorges, Edmund Howard, *The Great War in West Africa* (London, 1930).
Gouldsbury, Cullen, and Hubert Sheane, *The Great Plateau of Northern Rhodesia* (London, 1911).
* Gray, Richard, *The Two Nations: Aspects of the Development of Race Relations in the Rhodesias and Nyasaland* (London, 1960).
Gregory, Robert G., *Sidney Webb and East Africa: Labour's Experiment with the Doctrine of Native Paramountcy* (Berkeley, 1962).
Guèbré-Séllassie (trans. Tèsfa Séllassie), *Chronique du règne de Ménélik* II (Paris, 1930–1932), 2v.
* Guernier, Eugène Leonard (ed.), *Afrique équatoriale française* (Paris, 1950).
Guèye, Lamine, *De la situation politique des Sénégalais* (Paris, 1922).
Guggisberg, F. Gordon, "The Goal of the Gold Coast," *Journal of the African Society*, XXI (1922), pp. 81–91.
———, and Decima Moore Guggisberg, *We Two in West Africa* (London, 1909).
Gutkind, Peter C. W., "The African Urban Milieu: A Force in Rapid Change," *Civilisations*, XII (1962), pp. 167–191.
Hailey, William Malcolm Baron, *Native Administration in British African Territories* (London, 1950–1953), 5v.
† Hancock, W. Keith, *Survey of British Commonwealth Affairs;* II: Problems of Economic Policy, 1918–1939 (London, 1942), 2.
Hanotaux, Gabriel, and Alfred Martineau (eds.), *Histoire des colonies françaises et de l'expansion de la France dans le monde* (Paris, 1931), IV.
Hardinge, Arthur Henry, *A Diplomatist in the East* (London, 1928).
Hardy, Georges, *Histoire sociale de la colonisation française* (Paris, 1953).
Hargreaves, John Desmond, "The Evolution of the Native Affairs Department," *Sierra Leone Studies*, 3 (1954), pp. 168–184.
———, *A Life of Sir Samuel Lewis* (London, 1958).
Harmand, Jules, *Domination et colonisation* (Paris, 1919).
Harris, John Hobbis, *Portuguese Slavery: Britain's Dilemma* (London, 1913).

———, *Germany's Lost Colonial Empire and the Essentials of Reconstruction* (London, 1917).
———, *The Chartered Millions: Rhodesia and the Challenge to the British Commonwealth* (London, 1920).
Harris, Marvin, "Portugal's African 'Wards,'" *Africa Today*, V (November–December, 1958), pp. 3–36.
Harris, Philip J., *Local Government in Southern Nigeria* (Cambridge, Eng., 1957).
Hayman, Arthur I., and Harold Preece, *Lighting up Liberia* (New York, 1943).
Henderson, Kenneth David Druitt, *The Making of Modern Sudan: The Life and Letters of Sir Douglas Newbold* (London, 1953).
Henderson, William Otto, *Studies in German Colonial History* (Chicago, 1962).
Hendry, W., "Some Aspects of Education in Zanzibar," *Journal of the African Society*, XXVII (1928), pp. 342–352.
Hess, Robert L., "The 'Mad Mullah' and Northern Somalia," *The Journal of African History*, V (1964), pp. 415–433.
Hill, Mervyn F., *Planters' Progress: The Story of Coffee in Kenya* (Nairobi, 1956).
———, *Permanent Way: The Story of the Tanganyika and Kenya and Uganda Railways* (Nairobi, 1957, 1960), 2v.
Hill, Polly, *The Gold Coast Cocoa Farmer: A Preliminary Survey* (London, 1956).
* Hilliard, F. H., *A Short History of Education in British West Africa* (London, 1957).
Hobley, Charles William, *Kenya: From Chartered Company to Crown Colony* (London, 1929).
Hole, Hugh Marshall, *Old Rhodesian Days* (London, 1928).
* Hollingsworth, L. W., *The Asians of East Africa* (London, 1960).
Homet, Marcel, *Congo: terre de souffrances* (Paris, 1934).
———, *Afrique noire, terre inquiète: garderons-nous nos colonies d'Afrique?* (Paris, 1939).
Hone, Percy F., *Southern Rhodesia* (London, 1909).
Huxley, Elspeth, *White Man's Country: Lord Delamere and the Making of Kenya* (London, 1935), 2v.
Ingham, Kenneth, "British Administration in Lango District, 1907–1935," *The Uganda Journal*, XIX (1955), pp. 156–168.
———, *The Making of Modern Uganda* (London, 1958).
* ———, *A History of East Africa* (London, 1962).
Jackson, Henry Cecil, *Sudan Days and Ways* (London, 1954).
Jardine, Douglas, *The Mad Mullah of Somaliland* (London, 1923).
Jones, Herbert Gresford, *Uganda in Transformation, 1876–1926* (London, 1926).
Jones-Quartey, K. A. B., "A Note on J. M. Sarbah and J. E. Casely Hayford: Ghanaian Leaders, Politicians and Journalists, 1864–1930," *Sierra Leone Studies*, 14 (1960), pp. 57–62.
Jonghe, Édouard de, "Formations récentes de sociétés secrètes au Congo belge," *Africa*, IX (1936), pp. 56–63.
Judd, A. S., "Native Education in the Northern Provinces of Nigeria," *Journal of the African Society*, XVII (1917), pp. 1–10.
July, Robert W., "Nineteenth-Century Negritude: Edward W. Blyden," *The Journal of African History*, V (1964), pp. 87–98.
Kenyatta, Jomo, *Facing Mount Kenya: The Tribal Life of the Gikuyu* (London, 1938).
† Kimble, David, *A Political History of Ghana: The Rise of Gold Coast Nationalism, 1850–1928* (Oxford, 1963).
Knight, M. M., "French Colonial Policy: The Decline of 'Association,'" *The Journal of Modern History*, V (1933), pp. 208–224.
Landor, Arthur Henry Savage, *Across Widest Africa* (London, 1907).
Le Cornec, Jacques, *Histoire politique du Tchad de 1900 à 1962* (Paris, 1963).
Lefébure, Jules, *Le Régime des concessions au Congo* (Paris, 1904).
Lettow-Vorbeck, Paul Emil von, *My Reminiscences of East Africa* (London, 1920).
Leubuscher, Charlotte, *Tanganyika Territory: A Study of Economic Policy Under the Mandate* (London, 1944).
† Lewis, Martin Deming, "One Hundred Million Frenchmen: The 'Assimilation' Theory in French Colonial Policy," *Comparative Studies in Society and History*, IV (1962), pp. 129–153.
Leys, Colin, *European Politics in Southern Rhodesia* (Oxford, 1959).
Leys, Norman, *Kenya* (London, 1924).
———, *A Last Chance in Kenya* (London, 1931).
Little, Kenneth, "West African Urbanization as a Social Process," *Cahiers d'Études Africaines*, 3 (1961), pp. 90–102.

Logan, Rayford Whittingham, *The African Mandates in World Politics* (Washington, 1948).

———, "Education in Former French West and Equatorial Africa and Madagascar," *The Journal of Negro Education*, XXX (1961), pp. 277–285.

Londres, Albert (trans. Sylvia Stuart), *A Very Naked People* (New York, 1929).

Louis, William Roger, "Roger Casement and the Congo," *The Journal of African History*, V (1964), pp. 99–107.

Low, D. Anthony, and R. Cranford Pratt, *Buganda and British Overrule, 1900–1955* (London, 1960).

Lugard, Frederick D., *The Dual Mandate in British Tropical Africa* (London, 1922).

McLoughlin, Peter F. B., "The Sudan's Gezira Scheme: An Economic Profile," *Social and Economic Studies*, XII (1963), pp. 179–199.

MacMichael, Harold Alfred, *The Sudan* (London, 1954).

McPhee, Allan, *The Economic Revolution in British West Africa* (London, 1926).

Mair, Lucy Phillips, *Native Policies in Africa* (London, 1936).

———, *Native Administration in Central Nyasaland* (London, 1952).

Malengreau, Guy, *Vers un paysannat indigène: les lotissements agricoles au Congo belge* (Bruxelles, 1949).

Mangin, Charles, *La Force noire* (Paris, 1910).

———, *La Mission des troupes noires* (Paris, 1911).

———, *Regards sur la France d'Afrique* (Paris, 1924).

* Mason, Philip, *The Birth of a Dilemma: The Conquest and Settlement of Rhodesia* (London, 1958).

Massiou, Jacques, *Les Grandes Concessions au Congo français* (Paris, 1920).

Maugham, R. C. F., *The Republic of Liberia* (London, 1920).

Maurice, Albert, *Félix Éboué: sa vie et son oeuvre* (Bruxelles, 1954).

Meek, Charles Kingsley, W. M. Macmillan, and E. R. J. Hussey, *Europe and West Africa: Some Problems and Adjustments* (London, 1940).

Meinertzhagen, Richard, *Kenya Diary, 1902–1906* (Edinburgh, 1957).

Mendiaux, E., "Pour une revision de la Charte coloniale," *Zaïre*, XI (1957), pp. 1031–1052.

Migeod, Frederick William Hugh, *A View of Sierra Leone* (London, 1926).

Mille, Pierre, "The 'Black Vote' in Senegal," *Journal of the African Society*, I (1901), pp. 64–79.

Mitchell, Philip, *African Afterthoughts* (London, 1954).

Moffett, J. P., "A History of the Development of Native Courts from German Times," *The Journal of African Administration*, IV (1952), pp. 17–21.

Montague, F. A., and F. H. Page-Jones, "Some Difficulties in the Democratisation of Native Authorities in Tanganyika," *The Journal of African Administration*, II (1951), pp. 21–27.

Moreira, Eduardo, *Portuguese East Africa* (London, 1936).

Morel, Edmund Dere, *The British Case in the French Congo* (London, 1903).

———, *King Leopold's Rule in Africa* (London, 1904).

———, *Red Rubber: The Story of the Rubber Slave Trade* (London, 1906).

———, *The Stannard Case* (Liverpool, 1906).

———, *The Future of the Congo* (London, 1909).

———, *Nigeria, Its Peoples and Its Problems* (London, 1911).

Murray, A. Victor, *The School in the Bush* (London, 1929).

Nevinson, Henry Woodd, *A Modern Slavery* (London, 1906).

Newbury, Colin W., "The Formation of the Government General of French West Africa," *The Journal of African History*, I (1960), pp. 111–128.

———, "The Government General and Political Change in French West Africa," *St. Antony's Papers*, X (1961), pp. 41–59.

Newman, E. W. Polson, *Italy's Conquest of Abyssinia* (London, 1937).

Nketia, J. H., "Progress in Gold Coast Education," *Transactions of the Gold Coast and Togoland Historical Society*, I (1953), pp. 1–9.

Nussbaum, Manfred, "Togo unter deutscher Kolonialherrschaft und der west-deutsche Neokolonialismus," *Jahrbuch für Wirtschaftsgeschichte*, I (1961), pp. 9–28.

———, "Zwei Dokumente zur Geschichte des deutschen Kolonialismus," *ibid.*, II pp. 303–317.

Ogot, Bethwell A., "British Administration in the Central Nyanza District of Kenya, 1900–1960," *The Journal of African History*, IV (1963), pp. 249–274.

Orizu, A. A. Nwafor, *Without Bitterness: Western Nations in Post-War Africa* (New York, 1944).

Orr, Charles William Jones, *The Making of Northern Nigeria* (London, 1911).
Pankhurst, Estelle Sylvia, *Ethiopia and Eritrea: Last Phase of the Reunion Struggle, 1941–1952* (Woodford Green, 1953).
Pankhurst Richard, "Transport and Communications in Ethiopia, 1835–1935," *The Journal of Transport History*, V (1961), pp. 69–88, VI (1962), pp. 166–181, 233–254.
Pasquier, Georges, *L'Organisation des troupes indigènes en Afrique occidentale française* (Paris, 1912).
Perham, Margery Freda, "The System of Native Administration in Tanganyika," *Africa*, II (1931), pp. 302–312.
———, *Native Administration in Nigeria* (London, 1937).
* ———, *The Government of Ethiopia* (London, 1948).
——— (ed.), *Mining, Commerce, and Finance in Nigeria* (London, 1948).
———, *The Colonial Reckoning* (London, 1961).
———, and Elspeth Huxley, *Race and Politics in Kenya* (London, 1944).
Perrot, Émile Constant, *Où en est l'Afrique occidentale française?* (Paris, 1939).
Picard, Edmond, *L'Enseignement technique en Afrique équatoriale française* (Lyon, 1927).
Pick, Frederick Walter, *Searchlight on German Africa: The Diaries and Papers of Dr. W. Charles Regendanz; a Study in Colonial Ambitions* (London, 1939).
Porter, Arthur T., *Creoledom: A Study of the Development of Freetown Society* (London, 1963).
Postlethwaite, John Rutherfoord Parkin, *I Look Back* (London, 1947).
Purvis, John Bremner, *Through Uganda to Mount Elgon* (London, 1909).
Puttkamer, Jesko von, *Gouverneursjahre in Kamerun* (Berlin, 1912).
Ranger, Terence O., "Revolt in Portuguese East Africa: The Makombe Rising of 1917," *St. Antony's Papers*, XV (1963), pp. 54–80.
———, "The Last Days of the Empire of Mwenemutapa," *Conference of the History of the Central African Peoples* (Lusaka, 1963), no pagination.
———, "Traditional Authorities and the Rise of Modern Politics in Southern Rhodesia, 1898–1930," *ibid.*
Reeve, Henry Fenwick, *The Gambia* (London, 1912).
———, *The Black Republic: Liberia* (London, 1923).
Richardson, Nathaniel R., *Liberia's Past and Present* (London, 1959).
Roberts, Stephen Henry, *History of French Colonial Policy (1870–1925)* (London, 1929), 2v.
Robinson, Kenneth E., "The *Sociétés de Prévoyance* in French West Africa," *The Journal of African Administration*, II (1950), pp. 29–34.
———, "French West Africa," *African Affairs*, I (1951), pp. 123–132.
* ———, "French Africa and the French Union," C. Grove Haines (ed.), *Africa Today* (Baltimore, 1955), pp. 311–331.
———, "Senegal: The Elections to the Territorial Assembly, March 1957," W. J. M. Mackenzie and Kenneth Robinson (eds.), *Five Elections in Africa* (Oxford, 1960), pp. 281–390.
———, *The Dilemmas of Trusteeship: Aspects of British Colonial Policy Between the Wars* (London, 1965).
Rolin, Henri, *Les Lois et l'administration de la Rhodésie* (Bruxelles, 1913).
Ross, Edward Alsworth, *Report on Employment of Native Labor in Portuguese Africa* (New York, 1925).
Ross, W. McGregor, *Kenya from Within: A Short Political History* (London, 1927).
Rotberg, Robert I., "The Federation Movement in British East and Central Africa, 1889–1953," *Journal of Commonwealth Political Studies*, II (1964), pp. 141–160.
Rowan-Robinson, H., *England, Italy, Abyssinia* (London, 1935).
Rudin, Harry R., *Germans in the Cameroons, 1884–1914: A Case Study in Modern Imperialism* (London, 1938).
Russell, A. Major, "The Landing at Tanga in 1914," *Tanganyika Notes and Records*, 58/59 (1962), pp. 103–107.
Ryckmans, Pierre, "Belgian 'Colonialism,'" *Foreign Affairs*, XXXIV (1955), pp. 89–101.
Sampson, Magnus John, *Gold Coast Men of Affairs: Past and Present* (London, 1937).
Sandford, G. R., *An Administrative and Political History of the Masai Reserve* (Nairobi, 1919).
Sarraut, Albert, *La Mise en valeur des colonies françaises* (Paris, 1923).
Saxe, Jo W., "Dilemmas of Empire," Robert Strausz-Hupe and Henry W. Hazard (eds.), *The Idea of Colonialism* (New York, 1958), pp. 46–69.
Schmokel, Wolfe W., "Reform and Rubber: The United States and the Crisis of Liberian Independence, 1929–1934,"

Boston University Papers in African History (Boston, 1965), II.
Schnee, Heinrich, *Deutsch-Ostafrika im Weltkriege* (Leipzig, 1919).
———, *German Colonization: Past and Future* (New York, 1926).
Schwarzenberg, Adolph, *A Kenya Farmer Looks at His Colony* (New York, 1946).
Seitz, Theodor, *Vom Aufstieg und Niederbruch deutscher Kolonialmacht* (Karlsruhe, 1927–1929), 3v.
Sembritzki, Emil, *Kamerun* (Berlin, 1909).
Shepperson, George A., "Ethiopianism and African Nationalism," *Phylon,* XIV (1953), pp. 9–18.
———, "The Politics of African Church Separatist Movements in British Central Africa, 1892–1916," *Africa,* XXIV (1954), pp. 233–245.
———, "The Literature of British Central Africa," *The Rhodes-Livingstone Journal,* XXIII (1958), pp. 12–46.
———, "External Factors in the Development of African Nationalism, with Particular Reference to British Central Africa," *Historians in Tropical Africa* (Salisbury, S.R., 1962), pp. 144–159.
———, "Nyasaland and the Millennium," Sylvia L. Thrupp (ed.), *Millennial Dreams in Action* (The Hague, 1962), pp. 144–159.
† ———, and Thomas Price, *Independent African: John Chilembwe and the Origins, Setting and Significance of the Nyasaland Native Rising of 1915* (Edinburgh, 1958).
Shibeika, Mekki, *The Independent Sudan* (New York, 1959).
Simpson, Clarence Lorenzo, *The Memoirs of . . . the Symbol of Liberia* (London, 1961).
Skinner, Elliott P., "Traditional and Modern Patterns of Succession to Political Office Among the Mossi of the Voltaic Republic," *Journal of Human Relations,* VIII (1960), pp. 394–406.
———, *The Mossi of the Upper Volta: The Political Development of a Sudanese People* (Stanford, 1964).
Smith, Edwin Williams, *Aggrey of Africa: A Study in Black and White* (London, 1929).
Sophie, Ulrich, *Le Gouverneur général Félix Éboué* (Paris, 1950).
Southall, Aidan W. (ed.), *Social Change in Modern Africa* (London, 1961).
Spence, C. F., *The Portuguese Colony of Moçambique: An Economic Survey* (Cape Town, 1951).
* Steer, George L., *Caesar in Abyssinia* (London, 1936).
Stengers, Jean, "La Rôle de la Commission d'Enquête de 1904–1905 au Congo," *Annuaire de l'Institut de Philologie et d'Histoire Orientales et Slaves,* X (1950), pp. 701–726.
———, *Belgique et Congo: l'élaboration de la Charte coloniale* (Bruxelles, 1963).
Stenmans, Alain, *La Reprise du Congo par la Belgique: essai d'histoire parlementaire et diplomatique* (Bruxelles, 1949).
Stoeker, Helmuth (ed.), *Kamerun unter deutscher Kolonialherrschaft* (Berlin, 1960).
Strange, Nora Kathleen, *Kenya Today* (London, 1934).
Suret-Canale, Jean, *Afrique noire, occidentale et centrale: l'ère coloniale, 1900–1945* (Paris, 1958).
———, "La Guinée dans le système colonial," *Présence Africaine,* XXIX (1959), pp. 21–62.
Symes, G. Stewart, *Tour of Duty* (London, 1946).
Temple, Charles Lindsay, *Native Races and Their Rulers: Sketches and Studies of Official Life and Administrative Problems in Nigeria* (Cape Town, 1918).
Theobald, A. B., "Darfur and Its Neighbours under Sultan 'Ali Dinar, 1898–1916," *Sudan Notes and Records,* XL (1959), pp. 113–120.
Thomas, H. B., "Capax Imperii: The Story of Semei Kakunguru," *The Uganda Journal,* VI (1939), pp. 125–136.
Togue, Georges, *Les Massacres du Congo* (Paris, 1907).
Tothill, John Douglass (ed.), *Agriculture in Uganda* (London, 1940).
———, *Agriculture in the Sudan* (London, 1954).
Toynbee, Arnold J., *Survey of International Affairs, 1935: Abyssinia and Italy* (London, 1936), II.
Tucker, Alfred Robert, *Eighteen Years in Uganda and East Africa* (London, 1908).
Tucker, John Taylor, *Drums in the Darkness* (New York, 1927).
———, *Angola: The Land of the Blacksmith Prince* (London, 1933).
Van Der Kerken, George S., *La Crise économique en Afrique Belge* (Bruxelles, 1931).
* ———, *La Politique coloniale Belge* (Anvers, 1943).
Vandervelde, Émile, *La Belgique et le Congo* (Paris, 1911).
Vandevalle, F. A., "Mutineries au Congo belge," *Zaïre,* I (1947), pp. 487–514.

Vassal, Gabrielle M., *Life in French Congo* (London, 1925).
Vietor, Johann Karl, *Geschichtliche und kulturelle Entwicklung unserer Schutzgebiete* (Berlin, 1913).
Wallace, Lawrence A., "The Beginnings of Native Administration in Northern Rhodesia," *Journal of the African Society,* XXI (1922), pp. 165–176.
Webster, James Bertin, *The African Churches Among the Yoruba, 1888–1922* (London, 1964).
Welbourn, Frederick B., *East African Rebels: A Study of Some Independent Churches* (London, 1961).
Wheare, Joan, *The Nigerian Legislative Council* (London, 1950).
Wigglesworth, Alfred, "Kenya's Tribulations," *Journal of the African Society,* XXI (1921), pp. 217–221.
Wight, Martin, *The Gold Coast Legislative Council* (London, 1947).
Wigny, Pierre, "Methods of Government in the Belgian Congo," *African Affairs,* I (1951), pp. 310–317.
Williams, C. Kingsley, *Achimota: The Early Years* (London, 1962).
* Wilson, Charles Morrow, *Liberia* (New York, 1947).
Wingate, Ronald, *Wingate of the Sudan: The Life and Times of General Sir Reginald Wingate* (London, 1955).
Wood, Alan, *The Groundnut Affair* (London, 1950).
Wrigley, Christopher C., *Crops and Wealth in Uganda: A Short Agrarian History* (Kampala, 1959).
Ydewalle, Charles d', *L'Union minière du Haut Katanga à l'âge colonial à l'indépendance* (Paris, 1960).
Yudelman, Montague, *Africans on the Land: Economic Problems of African Agricultural Development in Southern, Central and East Africa* (Cambridge, Mass., 1964).
* Ziéglé, Henri, *Afrique équatoriale française* (Paris, 1952).

VI. The Period of Nationalism

Aaronovitch, S. and K., *Crisis in Kenya* (London, 1947).
Albinski, Henry S., "The Concept of Partnership in the Central African Federation," *Review of Politics,* XIX (1957), pp. 186–204.
Apter, David E., *The Gold Coast in Transition* (Princeton, 1955).
———, "The Role of Traditionalism in the Political Modernization of Ghana and Uganda," *World Politics,* XIII (1960), pp. 45–68.
Arden-Clarke, Charles, "Eight Years of Transition in Ghana," *African Affairs,* LVII (1958), pp. 29–37.
———, "Gold Coast into Ghana: Some Problems of Transition," *International Affairs,* XXXIV (1958), pp. 49–56.
Austen, Ralph, "Notes on the Pre-History of Tanu," *Makerere Journal,* 9 (1963), pp. 1–6.
Austin, Dennis, *Politics in Ghana, 1946–1960* (London, 1964).
Awa, Eme O., *Federal Government in Nigeria* (Berkeley, 1964).
Awolowo, Obafemi, *Path to Nigerian Freedom* (London, 1957).
———, *Awo: The Autobiography of Chief Obafemi Awolowo* (Cambridge, Eng., 1960).
Azikiwe, Benjamin Nnamdi, *The Evolution of Federal Government in Nigeria* (Orlu, 1956).
———, *The Development of Political Parties in Nigeria* (London, 1957).
———, *Zik: A Selection from the Speeches of Dr. Nnamdi Azikiwe* (Cambridge, Eng., 1961).
Balandier, Georges, "Messianismes et Nationalismes en Afrique noire," *Cahiers Internationaux de Sociologie,* XIV (1953), pp. 41–65.
Banda, Hastings Kamuzu, and Harry Mwaanga Nkumbula, *Federation in Central Africa* (London, 1951).
Bello, Ahmadu, *My Life* (Cambridge, Eng., 1962).
Bennett, George, "The Gold Coast General Election of 1954," *Parliamentary Affairs,* VII (1954), pp. 430–439.
———, "Kenya's Frustrated Election," *World Today,* XVII (1961), pp. 254–261.
———, "An Outline History of Tanu," *Makerere Journal,* 7 (1962), pp. 15–32.
———, and Carl G. Rosberg, Jr., *The Kenyatta Election: Kenya, 1960–1961* (London, 1961).
Berg, Elliott J., "The Economic Basis of Political Choice in French West Africa," *The American Political Science Review,* LIV (1960), pp. 391–405.
Biebuyck, Daniel, and Mary Douglas, *Congo: Tribes and Parties* (London, 1961).
* Blanchet, André, *L'Itinéraire des partis africains depuis Bamako* (Paris, 1958).
Blondel, J., "Constitutional Changes in

Former French Black Africa," *Parliamentary Affairs*, XIV (1961), pp. 507–517.
Blundell, Michael, *So Rough a Wind: The Kenya Memoirs of Michael Blundell* (London, 1964).
Bonardi, Pierre, *La République du Niger: naissance d'un État* (Paris, 1960).
Bosoppem, J. E. Y., *The Legislative Assembly of the Gold Coast* (Accra, 1955).
Bourcart, Robert, *Le Grand Conseil de l'Afrique occidentale française* (Paris, 1956).
Carter, Gwendolen M. (ed.), *African One-Party States* (Ithaca, 1962).
———, *Five African States: Responses to Diversity* (Ithaca, 1963).
Chidzero, Bernard T. G., "Central Africa: The Race Question and the Franchise," *Race*, I (1959), pp. 53–60.
———, "African Nationalism in East and Central Africa," *International Affairs*. XXXVI (1960), pp. 464–475.
Chisiza, Dunduzu K., *Africa: What Lies Ahead* (New Delhi, 1961).
Coleman, James S., and Carl G. Rosberg, Jr. (eds.), *Political Parties and National Integration in Tropical Africa* (Berkeley. 1964).
Corfield, F. D., *Historical Survey of the Origins and Growth of Mau Mau*, Cmnd. 1030 (London, 1960).
Cox, Richard, *Pan-Africanism in Practice: An East African Study; Pafmecsa, 1958–1964* (London, 1964).
Creighton, Thomas R. M., *Anatomy of Partnership: Southern Rhodesia and the Central African Federation* (London, 1960).
Crowley, Daniel J., "Politics and Tribalism in the Katanga," *The Western Political Quarterly*, XVI (1963), pp. 68–78.
Danquah, Joseph B., *Self-Help and Expansion* (Accra, 1943).
De Andrade, Mario, "Le Nationalisme angolais," *Présence Africaine*, XLII (1962), pp. 5–24.
Delf, George, *Jomo Kenyatta: Towards Truth About 'The Light of Kenya'* (London, 1961).
Duncan, John S. R., *The Sudan's Path to Independence* (Edinburgh, 1957).
Elias, T. Olawale, *Ghana and Sierra Leone* (London, 1962).
Epstein, A. L., *Politics in an Urban African Community* (Manchester, 1958).
Ezera, Kalu, *Constitutional Developments in Nigeria* (Cambridge, Eng., 1960).
Fallers, Lloyd A., "Ideology and Culture in Uganda Nationalism," *American Anthropologist*, LXIII (1961), pp. 677–686.
——— (ed.), *The King's Men: Leadership and Status in Buganda on the Eve of Independence* (London, 1964).
Farson, Negley, *Last Chance in Africa* (London, 1949).
Fortes, Meyer, "The Impact of the War on British West Africa," *International Affairs*, XXI (1945), pp. 206–219.
Franck, Thomas C., *Race and Nationalism* (New York, 1960).
Franklin, Harry, *Unholy Wedlock: The Failure of the Central African Federation* (London, 1963).
Ganshof van der Meersch, W. J., *Fin de la souveraineté belge au Congo: documents et réflexions* (Bruxelles, 1963).
Ghai, Y. P., "The Kenya Council of State and the African Affairs Board of the Central African Federation: An Experiment in the Protection of Minorities," *The International and Comparative Law Quarterly*, XII (1963), pp. 1089–1132.
Gillis, Charles-André, *Kasa-Vubu au coeur du drame congolais* (Bruxelles, 1965).
Gutteridge, W. F., "The Nature of Nationalism in British West Africa," *The Western Political Quarterly*, XI (1958), pp. 574–582.
* Hodgkin, Thomas, *Nationalism in Colonial Africa* (London, 1956).
Ibbotson, Percy, "Federation of Native Welfare Societies in Southern Rhodesia," *The Rhodes-Livingstone Journal*, II (1944), pp. 35–39.
Ikeotuonye, Vincent C., *Zik of New Africa* (London, 1961).
Jones, Creech A., "Africa and the British Political Parties: A Labour View," *African Affairs*, XLIV (1945), pp. 111–115.
* Jones, Griff, *Britain and Nyasaland* (London, 1964).
Kariuki, Josiah Mwangi, *"Mau Mau" Detainee* (London, 1963).
Kaunda, Kenneth David, *Zambia Shall Be Free* (London, 1962).
Kilner, Peter, "A Year of Army Rule in the Sudan," *The World Today*, XV (1959), pp. 430–441.
———, "Military Government in Sudan: The Past Three Years," *ibid.*, XVIII (1962), pp. 259–268.
Kilson, Martin L., "Land and Politics in Kenya: An Analysis of African Politics in a Plural Society," *The Western Political Quarterly*, X (1957), pp. 559–581.
———, "The Rise of Nationalist Organizations and Parties in British West Africa," *Africa Seen by American Negroes* (Paris, 1958), pp. 35–69.

———, "Social Forces in West African Political Development," *Journal of Human Relations,* VIII (1960), pp. 576–598.

———, "Grass-Roots Politics in Africa: Local Government in Sierra Leone," *Political Studies,* XII (1964), pp. 47–66.

Koinange, Mbiyu, *The People of Kenya Speak for Themselves* (Detroit, 1955).

Labrique, Jean, *Congo politique* (Léopoldville, 1957).

Leakey, Louis S. B., *Mau Mau and the Kikuyu* (London, 1952).

———, *Defeating the Mau Mau* (London, 1954).

* Legum, Colin, *Congo Disaster* (Harmondsworth, 1961).

* ———, *Pan-Africanism: A Short Political Guide* (London, 1962).

Leigh, Ione, *In the Shadow of Mau Mau* (London, 1954).

Lemarchand, René, *Political Awakening in the Belgian Congo* (Berkeley, 1964).

LeVine, Victor T., *The Cameroons from Mandate to Independence* (Berkeley, 1964).

Leys, Colin, "Tanganyika: The Realities of Independence," *International Journal,* XVII (1962), pp. 251–268.

Little, Kenneth, "The Role of Voluntary Associations in West African Urbanization," *American Anthropologist,* LIX (1957), pp. 579–596.

Lloyd, Peter C., "Some Comments on the Elections in Nigeria," *The Journal of African Administration,* IV (1952), pp. 82–92.

Lofchie, Michael, "Party Conflict in Zanzibar," *The Journal of Modern African Studies,* I (1963), pp. 185–207.

Low, D. Anthony, *Political Parties in Uganda, 1949–1962* (London, 1962).

† ———, "The Advent of Populism in Buganda," *Comparative Studies in Society and History,* VI (1964), pp. 424–444.

Lowenkopf, Martin, "Tanganyika Achieves Responsible Government," *Parliamentary Affairs,* XIV (1960–1961), pp. 244–257.

———, "Uganda: Prelude to Independence," *ibid.,* XV (1961–1962), pp. 74–86.

Mackenzie, W. J. M., and Kenneth Robinson (eds.), *Five Elections in Africa* (Oxford, 1960).

Mair, Lucy Phillips, *The Nyasaland Elections of 1961* (London, 1962).

Majdalany, Fred, *State of Emergency: The Full Story of Mau Mau* (London, 1962).

Malengreau, Guy, "Recent Developments in Belgian Africa," C. Grove Haines (ed.), *Africa Today* (Baltimore, 1955), pp. 337–357.

Mason, Philip, *Year of Decision: Rhodesia and Nyasaland in 1960* (London, 1960).

Middleton, John, "Society and Politics in Zanzibar," *Civilisations,* XII (1962), pp. 375–383.

Morgenthau, Ruth Schacter, "Single-Party Systems in West Africa," *The American Political Science Review,* LV (1961), pp. 294–307.

———, *Political Parties in French-speaking West Africa* (Oxford, 1964).

Mulira, E. M. K., *Troubled Uganda* (London, 1950).

Mustafa, Sophia, *The Tanganyika Way* (Dar es Salaam, 1961).

Nii, Kwabena Bonne, *Milestones in the History of the Gold Coast* (London, 1953).

Nkrumah, Kwame, *Ghana: The Autobiography of Kwame Nkrumah* (Edinburgh, 1957).

———, *I Speak of Freedom* (New York, 1961).

Nye, Joseph S., "East African Economic Integration," *The Journal of Modern African Studies,* I (1963), pp. 475–502.

Nyerere, Julius, "Tanganyika Today: The Nationalist View," *International Affairs,* XXXVI (1960), pp. 43–47.

Padmore, George, *Africa: Britain's Third Empire* (London, 1949).

———, *The Gold Coast Revolution: The Struggle of an African People from Slavery to Freedom* (London, 1953).

——— (ed.), *History of the Pan-African Congress* (London, 1963).

Phillips, John, *Kwame Nkrumah and the Future of Africa* (London, 1960).

Post, Kenneth W. J., *The Nigerian Federal Election of 1959* (London, 1963).

Pratt, R. Cranford, " 'Multi-Racialism' and Local Government in Tanganyika," *Race,* II (1960), pp. 33–49.

———, "Nationalism in Uganda," *Political Studies,* IX (1961), pp. 157–178.

Rawcliffe, Donovan Hilton, *The Struggle for Kenya* (London, 1954).

* Robinson, Kenneth, "Political Development in French West Africa," Calvin Stillman (ed.), *Africa in the Modern World* (Chicago, 1955), pp. 140–181.

Rotberg, Robert I., "The Rise of African Nationalism: The Case of East and Central Africa," *World Politics,* XV (1962), pp. 75–90.

———, *The Rise of Nationalism in Central*

Africa: The Making of Malawi and Zambia, 1873–1964 (Cambridge, Mass., 1965).

Rubin, Leslie, and Paul Murray, *The Constitution and Government of Ghana* (London, 1961).

Ryckmans, Pierre, "Belgian 'Colonialism,'" *Foreign Affairs,* XXXIV (1955), pp. 89–101.

Sanger, Clyde, *Central African Emergency* (London, 1960).

———, and John Nottingham, "The Kenya General Election of 1963," *The Journal of Modern African Studies,* II (1964), pp. 1–40.

Senghor, Léopold Sédar, "West Africa in Evolution," *Foreign Affairs,* XXXIX (1960–1961), pp. 240–246.

Shepherd, George, *They Wait in Darkness* (New York, 1955).

Sithole, Ndabaningi, *African Nationalism* (Cape Town, 1959).

Sklar, Richard L., "The Contribution of Tribalism to Nationalism in Western Nigeria," *Journal of Human Relations,* VIII (1960), pp. 407–418.

———, *Nigerian Political Parties: Power in an Emergent African Nation* (Princeton, 1963).

Slater, Montagu, *The Trial of Jomo Kenyatta* (London, 1955).

Stahl, Kathleen M., *Tanganyika: Sail in the Wilderness* (London, 1961).

Stoneham, Charles Thurley, *Mau Mau* (London, 1953).

Taylor, John V., and Dorothea A. Lehmann, *Christians of the Copperbelt: The Growth of Church in Northern Rhodesia* (London, 1961).

Thompson, Virginia, and Richard Adloff, *French West Africa* (Stanford, 1958).

* ———, *The Emerging States of French Equatorial Africa* (Stanford, 1960).

Timothy, Bankole, *Kwame Nkrumah: His Rise to Power* (London, 1955).

Trachtman, Lester N., "The Labor Movement of Ghana: A Study in Political Unionism," *Economic Development and Cultural Change,* X (1962), pp. 183–200.

† Van Bilsen, Antoine A. A. J., "Un Plan de trente ans pour l'émancipation de l'Afrique belge," *Les Dossiers de l'Action Sociale Catholique,* XXXIII (1956), pp. 83–111.

———, *Vers l'indépendance du Congo et du Ruanda-Urundi* (Bruxelles, 1958).

———, *L'Indépendance du Congo* (Bruxelles, 1962).

———, "Some Aspects of the Congo Problem," *International Affairs,* XXXVIII (1962), pp. 41–51.

Van den Berghe, Pierre L., "Apartheid, Fascism and the Golden Age," *Cahiers d'Études Africaines,* 2 (1962), pp. 598–608.

Wallerstein, Immanuel, "Ethnicity and National Integration in West Africa," *Cahiers d'Études Africaines,* 3 (1960), pp. 129–139.

Welensky, Sir Roy, *Welensky's Four Thousand Days: The Life and Death of the Central African Federation* (London, 1964).

Wood, Anthony St. John, *Northern Rhodesia: The Human Background* (London, 1961).

Zolberg, Aristide R., "Effets de la structure d'un parti politique sur l'intégration nationale," *Cahiers d'Études Africaines,* 1 (1961), pp. 140–149.

———, *One-Party Government in the Ivory Coast* (Princeton, 1964).

INDEX

This index does not include reference entries in the footnotes, names in the preface, or entries in the bibliography. Omnipresent general categories, i.e., "western Sudan," "East Africa," have not been indexed separately.

C D E F G H I J 9 0 1 2 3 4